POLITICAL ECONOMY IN NINETEENTH-CENTURY AMERICA

Selected and Introduced by
Morgen Witzel

Volume 1

History of American Thought

Political Economy in Nineteenth-Century America

Selected and Introduced by **Morgen Witzel**

Volume 1
Mathew Carey
Essays on Political Economy, 1822

Volume 2
Francis Wayland
The Elements of Political Economy, 1837

Volume 3
George Tucker
Political Economy for the People, 1859

Volume 4
Amasa Walker
The Science of Wealth: A Manual of Political Economy, 1866

Volume 5
William Graham Sumner
Problems in Political Economy, 1884 and
Essays on Political Economy, 1885

Volume 6
Francis A. Walker
Political Economy, 1892

Printed in England by Antony Rowe Ltd, Chippenham

ESSAYS ON POLITICAL ECONOMY

Mathew Carey

With an Introduction by
Morgen Witzel

THOEMMES PRESS

Published by Thoemmes Press, 2003

Thoemmes Press
11 Great George Street
Bristol BS1 5RR, England

http://www.thoemmes.com

Political Economy in Nineteenth-Century America
6 Volumes : ISBN 1 84371 048 X

British Library Cataloguing-in-Publication Data
A CIP record of this title is available from the British Library

This book is printed on acid-free paper, sewn, and
cased in a durable buckram.

INTRODUCTION

At the beginning of the nineteenth century, the study of political economy in the United States was based almost entirely on foreign texts, mostly of the British followers of Adam Smith though with some influence from the physiocrats. A hundred years later, that picture had greatly changed. Foreign influences were now primarily the French and German historical schools, and there was a thriving domestic school – indeed, several schools – of political economy. The study of the subject had gone from a marginal position to being integrated into the curriculum of virtually every major university in the land.

Along the way there was also a change in the profile of those who engaged in the study and teaching of political economy. The first American political economists, men like Mathew Carey and Francis Wayland, were self-professed amateurs. But by the middle of the century, men such as Amasa Walker, George Tucker and Mathew Carey's son Henry C. Carey could confidently be described as political economists – primarily, if perhaps not solely. And by the end of the century Walker's son Francis A. Walker had taken economics to the status of profession, complete with its own professional organization, its own journal, its own corpus of study and thought – and its own dissidents and radicals, keen to change the status quo and reshape the discipline to their own ideas.

Like so much in American thought, economics went from nil status to full development in a remarkably short period of time. The works chosen for this set represent that development and chart the course of the growth in American economic thinking during the nineteenth century. They show not only how American thinking about economics developed, but also how the status of the discipline changed and grew. The works we have chosen here represent the main stream of that development, from Carey's first essays and Wayland's initial, enormously influential textbook to the younger Walker's confident assertion of the place of economics in society.

This introduction is not intended to describe the works in the collection, as these are easily comprehensible and speak for themselves. Instead, the intention is to describe briefly the men who wrote them and their backgrounds and motives for doing so. Briefly, they fall into three groups. Mathew Carey and Francis Wayland, the pioneers, are men whose primary interests lay outside of economics but who saw the necessity for the study of economics in a broader context. For Amasa Walker and George Tucker, economics was seen as more important in its own right and both were concerned to define the field as broadly as possible, though still concerned to link economics to other fields. Finally, William Graham Sumner and Francis Walker represent the full flowering of economics as an independent discipline in America.

Mathew Carey (1760–1839)

Mathew[1] Carey was better known in his own time as a radical journalist and publisher than as a writer and thinker on economics. Born in Dublin in 1760 into an educated Catholic family, Carey was apprenticed to a bookseller and publisher. By the time he was in his late teens he was producing essays and pamphlets on social and political issues. In 1781 one of Carey's pamphlets was suppressed and he himself was threatened with arrest. He fled to Paris, where as a writer against the British establishment he was quickly taken up by the American community in Paris (the War of Independence was of course still ongoing). He met Benjamin Franklin, who gave him a job as a printer which allowed Carey the means to support himself, and was introduced to Lafayette. Returning to Dublin in 1783 as a fully paid-up member of the anti-British radical movement, Carey founded his own newspaper, the *Volunteer's Journal*, which espoused nationalist causes and quickly became the second best-selling newspaper in Dublin. But the authorities were now watching Carey closely, and when a cartoon deemed to be seditious appeared in the journal Carey was arrested and imprisoned. Charges of sedition were dropped and he was released, but other charges including libel were brought forward and Carey realized his days in Dublin were numbered. In September 1784 he took passage on a ship for Philadelphia in the newly independent United States of America. Virtually destitute, he required a loan from Lafayette to get himself established and begin to make a living as a writer and publisher.

Carey's activities over the following decade were widely spread, and are chronicled in an amusing serial autobiography patterned on that of his early mentor, Benjamin Franklin. He founded and edited several newspapers, initially strongly endorsing the Federalists but later switching his support to Jefferson. He first imported books from Britain but then, believing that a strong country should have a strong economy and should produce its own books, he began reprinting European works and commissioning new work. In 1819 he founded the Philadelphia Society for the Promotion of National Industry, and later the Pennsylvania Society for the Promotion of Internal Improvements, both dedicated to promoting indus-

[1] His surname is sometimes spelled Matthew, and both forms of his name can be found. He appears as Mathew Carey on the flyleaf of *Essays on Political Economy* and so we have chosen to use that form here.

trial growth and economic reform. Although his early radicalism dimmed, the passion with which he supported various causes did not. He fought a duel with a rival newspaper editor, and was wounded in the leg by a pistol shot. He incurred considerable enmity for his positions on tariffs and slavery, both of which he abhorred; he was an early believer in the idea that slave labour in the Southern cotton plantations was actually harming national competitiveness, and argued that free markets and free black labour were the best way for America to defend itself against imports (his son Henry C. Carey was to take up this position in much greater detail). He supported many philanthropic causes both in Philadelphia and elsewhere, and despite his hot temper and often cranky disposition, seems to have been much loved; when he died (of injuries sustained in a road accident) in 1839, the city went into mourning and local newspapers recorded that his funeral procession was one of the largest ever seen in the city.

Carey believed that to be strong a nation needed not only to have a strong economy; it also needed to be able to think for itself. He argued that America should not base its policies and its ideals on models borrowed from Europe, but should create its own future. His activities as a publisher, journalist and writer on economics were all devoted to this end.

Francis Wayland (1796–1865)

At first sight, the Irish Catholic radical Carey and the American Baptist minister Wayland do not seem to have much in common. But their visions of knowledge generally and of the role of economics in society more particularly have much in common. In both Carey and Wayland, we see a concern that knowledge about economics should be more widely taught and diffused, and that it ought to have a specifically American feel to it rather than being imported from Europe.

Nor was Wayland any stranger to controversial situations. Born in New York in 1796, he was educated at Union College and then at Andover Theological Seminary. In 1821 he was appointed pastor of the First Baptist Church of Boston, where he made a name for himself as a preacher and theologian. In 1826 he took up a teaching position at Union College, and then in 1827 was called upon to take over as president of Brown University. Brown, the leading Baptist educational institute in the country, had been wracked by internal power struggles for the previous three years, as conservative Baptists on faculty and outside the university sought to remove the incumbent president, Asa Messer, who had publicly espoused liberal and unitarian doctrines. Messer's resignation was finally compelled in 1827 and Wayland, a rising star in the American Baptist community who was at once intelligent, well-educated and theologically sound, was appointed in his stead. Wayland would remain president of Brown for the next twenty-eight years.

Like Carey, Wayland's interests spread across many fields. He promoted public free libraries, and is sometimes credited with instigating national legislation authorizing towns and cities to fund libraries out of tax revenues. He supported prison reform and, again like Carey, campaigned against slavery. The portrait painted of him in the voluminous biography by his son Francis (who went on to become a notable teacher and academic in his own right) sometimes makes him out to be a sort of renaissance man. This may be overstating the case. Wayland never professed to excellence in any particular field; his concern was first of all to diffuse learning as widely as possible, and second to broaden the scope of learning so that more people were affected by it. He not only reorganized the system of teaching and degrees at Brown, but wrote more widely on educational reform in general, travelling to Europe to study the older university systems there and encouraging the US federal government to adopt a more systematic approach to tertiary education.

As well as his reforms at Brown, Wayland left a lasting legacy in two books: *The Elements of Moral Science* (1835) and *The Elements of Political Economy* (1837). The reader may be reminded, in this juxtaposition of political economy and moral theory, of Adam Smith, and this is probably a comparison of which Wayland would have approved; but it is a superficial one. Wayland was not a deep thinker in either field, and his efforts are ones of synthesis, bringing together existing theory in easily accessible texts that can be used for teaching in a broad range of settings.

In this he was notably successful. Both books became standard teaching texts for several decades. Famously, the Japanese reformer Fukuzawa Yukichi brought a copy of *The Elements of Political Economy* back to Japan after his first journey to the USA, translated it and made it a standard textbook in Japan as well. In their desire to see education reformed and made stronger and their sure conviction that education was the key to a nation's well-being and prosperity, Wayland and Fukuzawa had much in common.

George Tucker (1775–1861)

A generation older than Wayland, George Tucker nevertheless represents a new and more progressive approach to political economy in America. Carey and Wayland had urged that American economists should think for themselves; Tucker showed how they were beginning to do so.

Although born in Bermuda, Tucker was essentially part of the Virginia gentry class that also produced the likes of George Washington and Thomas Jefferson. After attending William and Mary College, Tucker was admitted to the Virginia bar in 1801 and practised as a lawyer for the next decade or so, with mixed fortunes. He served two terms as a representative in the Virginia Assembly and then three terms in Congress; he seems to have been a conscientious congressman though not an overly distinguished one. He tried his hand at novel-writing, with *The Valley of the Shenandoah* (1824) being well received, and at writing pamphlets. His most important work, however, was a volume of essays on morals and tastes, which was read by both Jefferson and James Madison, then engaged in establishing the University of Virginia. So impressed were they that they invited Tucker to become professor of moral philosophy; and in a conscious imitation of British practice, Tucker asked that political economy be made part of his remit as well. He continued to lecture and write on both fields for the next twenty years until his retirement, and even then remained active, writing *Political Economy for the People* among other works and travelling throughout the southern states. His death at age 85 was the result of an accident suffered while travelling by steamboat in Alabama.

We must not overstate Tucker's importance. He created no new theories of his own, but he did critique, sometimes from an original angle, the theories of others, notably Ricardo and Malthus. One overriding theme in Tucker's work, however, not only his earlier essays but also *Political Economy for the People*, based on his lectures at Virginia, is the need to interpret economic thinking in the light of American experience. He believed that economics had not yet reached the state of being a science, but that it was proceeding in that direction, and that there were fundamental economic truths waiting to be discovered. He is important for two reasons: he represents an essentially southern point of view, whereas many other writers on political economy from this time came from New England or elsewhere in the north; and more importantly, he represents a growing confidence in America's own voice and mind on economic matters.

Political Economy for the People was written as a teaching textbook, probably with the idea of replacing the now creaking volume by Wayland. In this as in so much in his life, Tucker was only partly successful. *Political Economy for the People* did well, but it had nothing like the impact of the work of another, younger writer, Amasa Walker.

Amasa Walker (1799–1875)

Like Mathew Carey, Amasa Walker came from a humble background, the son of a blacksmith in Woodstock, Connecticut. As a young men he went into commerce rather than to college, and by the time he was forty was a highly successful businessman and director of a bank. He learned his economics by practice, so to speak, and although he was much more theoretically accomplished than any of his three predecessors in this collection, he too retained a pragmatic outlook in much of his work. In many of his books he uses real-life examples, often from his own experience, to illustrate economic points, and he wrote for practitioner-based journals like *Hunt's Merchant Magazine* as well as educational texts.

A Democrat, Walker was a reformer rather than a radical. He served in the Massachusetts state House of Representatives and then the Senate; during the Civil War he served briefly as a Congressman in Washington, but did not seek re-election. His strong campaigning for the abolition of slavery led to an offer to join the board of Oberlin College, a strongly abolitionist institution. In 1845 he retired from business and took up the post of professor of political economy at Oberlin, later teaching at Amherst College. He helped reform the Massachusetts banking sector after the crash of 1857, and served on various public committees.

His most important book, *The Science of Wealth*, appeared in 1866. The timing was good: the Civil War had just ended, economic reconstruction was beginning, and more, the United States was about to begin the prolonged, railway-enabled boom that would see its economy grow many times over during the next few decades. As was to be expected in a boom, questions of money and credit were becoming burning issues in economic thinking, and again Walker helped to put an American 'spin' on older ideas. He has been compared to Bastiat, and more distantly to Say, but there are British liberal influences as well; Walker had corresponded with John Stuart Mill, among others, and sent a copy of *The Science of Wealth* to him (Mill donated it to a library, so his reaction may not have been entirely favourable). He was a metallist, and distrusted paper money and credit; he was also a strong advocate of free markets and opposed tariffs.

The most notable thing about *The Science of Wealth*, however, is its attention to evidence. Statistics, including time-series data, are deployed along with case studies to show how economic phenomena can be observed in real life. This, we may infer, is Walker the businessman triumphing over Walker the economist. Not for him the abstract speculations of his predecessors and peers: Walker believed that economics could be observed in action, and those actions could be described and set down almost as natural laws. Though he himself was not a professional economist, Walker took a long step forward in helping to make economics in America more professional.

William Graham Sumner (1840–1910)

Like Francis Wayland, William Graham Sumner was a clergyman, but there most resemblances in their careers end. Born in New Jersey, the son of a poor emigrant family from Lancashire, Sumner grew up in an austere and frugal family environment, an influence that later appears in some of his work. The frugality had its compensations, however, as the family's savings proved sufficient to send its most talented member to Yale, from which he graduated in 1863. Further education at Oxford and on the Continent was followed by a stint as a tutor in classics at Yale. In 1869 Sumner was ordained as an Episcopalian clergyman. Although he was clearly a firm believer, the religious side of Sumner struggled with the rational side. He took up a living at a church in New Jersey, but was never able to reconcile his rational outlook with the needs of his parishioners. In 1872 he abandoned the ministry and returned to Yale, where he was appointed professor of political economy.

It seems fair to say that Sumner was a good economist but a better sociologist. He was a disciple of Spencer, and adopted the latter's *Study of Sociology* as a textbook; this provoked a scandal in the university, as Spencer's views were considered to be atheistic. The resulting struggle between Sumner and his critics became a battle for free expression, and had ramifications not just for Sumner and Yale but for American universities as a whole. He went on to teach some of America's most important early sociologists, and exercised a huge influence over this growing discipline. Although he was in poor health in later years, he continued to write and generate new ideas. In late 1909 he was elected president of the American Sociological Society and travelled to New York to deliver his inaugural address. Caught in a snowstorm, he became ill (most probably with pneumonia) and never recovered; he died in the spring of 1810 at his home in New Haven.

A radical in terms of sociology, Sumner was a conservative in economics, though his position did change over the course of his life. In the 1870s he advocated free markets and attacked trade unions as creating monopolies of labour and therefore interfering with *laissez-faire* capitalism as it should be. But by the 1880s he was becoming uneasy with the excesses of unfettered capitalism. He was one of the first to attack the trusts, the giant monopolies that were coming to dominate the American landscape. This position is not necessarily inconsistent, but many free market advocates defended trusts as a natural outcome of that free market, while Sumner's attacks on them put him in the same camp as more left-wing writers and academics such as Henry Demarest Lloyd, Jeremiah Jenks and William Zebina Ripley. In the end, Sumner did call for state intervention in the economy to regulate and legislate against excesses and to alleviate poverty.

One of the curious things about Sumner is that although he wrote prolifically on both economics and sociology and often considered the same problem from both perspectives, he never married the two disciplines into one in the same way as, for example, Thorstein Veblen. There is always just a little hint in Sumner's work that economics is economics while sociology is sociology. An eminent Spencerian, he rarely refers to Spencer when writing about economics. This does not make Sumner in any way unique. Since the time of Amasa Walker, the trend had been to consider economics as a discipline in its own right, not as a relative of any other; and under Amasa Walker's son Francis, that trend became more fully developed.

Francis Amasa Walker (1840–1897)
While the other five authors represented in this set came to the study of economics through various and diverse routes, Francis Walker could be fairly said to have been born to it. He was, as noted, the son of Amasa Walker, and graduated from Amherst College in 1860; he is said to have assisted his father in the preparation of some of his lectures on economics at Amherst, and almost certainly collaborated with him later on *The Science of Wealth*. In August 1861 Walker was commissioned into the Union Army and fought in the opening battles of the Civil War. At the disastrous action of Chancellorsville in 1863, Walker was wounded and captured, and spent several months in a Confederate prisoner-of-war camp. He was repatriated as part of a prisoner exchange in 1864 and returned to active duty. Like many young men of his generation in both armies, Walker was quickly promoted, and was a brigadier-general by the age of 24. But his wound and the rigours of the prison camp acted on his health, and he was finally forced to retire from the army in January 1865, a few months before the end of the war.

Retirement found Walker at something of a loose end. He taught mathematics for a time and also worked as a journalist, as well as continuing his work with his father. The turning point came in 1870 when the Grant administration appointed him to the post of director of the US Treasury's Bureau of Statistics. Statistical work became Walker's metier, and he became one of the best-known statisticians of his day, known internationally as well as in the USA. He produced the first statistical atlas of the United States, and statistical work informed nearly all his writings on economics. Even after leaving government service he continued private research and work in this field.

In 1871 Walker took on a second post, that of Commissioner of Indian Affairs with responsibility for government policy towards Native Americans. He succeeded the famous Ely Parker, a Seneca from New York state who had joined the Union Army and, like Walker, had risen to the rank of brigadier-general; it is even possible they knew each other, for Parker had served on Grant's staff and had actually written out the surrender terms dictated to the Confederates at Appamattox (Robert E. Lee, the Confederate commander, had entered the courthouse where the surrender took place and greeted Parker by saying he was glad to see at least one 'real American' present). Parker had done much to ameliorate conditions for Native Americans on reservations, but he was impeached on corruption charges in 1871 and Walker quickly took over from him. Walker continued Parker's policies until his own resignation in 1872; sadly, future commissioners proved rather less enlightened.

In 1873 Walker moved into academia, becoming professor of political economy at the Sheffield Scientific School in New Haven; he also taught occasionally at Yale where, it will be remembered, Sumner was the professor of political economy. He turned down a post at Johns Hopkins University in 1874 – his father's ill health and death the following year may have been a factor – but in 1882 moved to Boston to become president of the Massachusetts Institute of Technology, a post which he held until his early death in 1897.

During his time in New Haven, Walker produced a series of books on economics which were landmarks in the thinking of the time. These culminated in *Political Economy*, which replaced his father's work as the standard economics textbook of the day. Like earlier writers, Walker's work is informed by European ideas, but now it is the German historical school that dominates, not the classical economists. Economics was moving on and Walker was helping to move it. When the American Economic Association was established in 1885, Walker was chosen by a large majority as its first president, serving in that role until 1892 and helping to cement in place a moderate, liberal approach to economics as the dominant paradigm in American economic thinking.

Moderation is one of the keys to Walker's economics. He is in favour of free markets but recognizes a role for government and regulation; opposed to trade unions but prepared to recognize a role for organized labour. He also establishes, probably for the first time in America, a value-neutral role for economics. As he states at the outset of *Political Economy*:

> Political Economy, or Economics, is the name of that body of knowledge which relates to wealth. Political Economy has to do with no other subject, whatsoever, than wealth. Especially should the student of economics take care not to allow any purely political, ethical or social considerations to influence him in his investigations.

In other words, it is the role of the economist to study wealth; it is up the politicians and the moral thinkers to decide to what purpose wealth should be put. This angered both right-wing and left-wing economists, but particularly the latter: Henry George would attack Walker vigorously, and the attacks would be renewed by the younger generation of socialists influenced by George. But the main stream was solidly behind him.

The impression of Walker often conveyed today is that he was a rather plodding economist, neoclassical in outlook and unduly influenced by statistics. But he could be unorthodox, as his work at the Bureau of Indian Affairs had already shown. Before Schumpeter, Walker identified the pivotal role of the entrepreneur and suggested this latter might form a fourth factor of production. His views on bimetallism were not always in line with those of his contemporaries. He could be an original thinker when he chose to be. But the overriding purpose of Walker's work, or so it seems today, was to put economics on a sound and unassailable footing as an important and widely taught discipline. And he succeeded. Even his critics had to acknowledge that the platforms on which they stood to attack him had largely been built by him.

The journey of American economic thinking from Mathew Carey to Francis Walker is not a long one in terms of time. But as with so much else in American intellectual life, time is compressed. Developments which took centuries in Europe happened in America in a few decades. The works in this set are a fascinating parade of ideas and influences, from the radical to the mainstream in just sixty years. It is to be hoped that re-reading them will shed some light on the currents that American economic thought took at the time, and has taken since.

Morgen Witzel
2003

ESSAYS

ON

POLITICAL ECONOMY;

OR,

THE MOST CERTAIN MEANS

OF

PROMOTING THE WEALTH, POWER, RESOURCES,

AND

HAPPINESS OF NATIONS:

Applied particularly to the United States.

BY M. CAREY,

MEMBER OF THE AMERICAN PHILOSOPHICAL SOCIETY, AND OF THE AMERICAN ANTIQUARIAN SOCIETY—AUTHOR OF THE POLITICAL OLIVE BRANCH, VINDICIÆ HIBERNICÆ, &c.

"I have neglected nothing to procure correct information. I do not, however, pretend to publish a perfect work. All that I can pledge myself for, is, that it emanates from honest intentions."—*Chaptal, sur L'industrie Françoise.*

"To be independent for the comforts of life, we must fabricate them ourselves. We must now place the manufacturer by the side of the agriculturist." *Jefferson.*

"*Manufactures are now as necessary to our independence as to our comfort.*"—Idem.

"While the necessities of nations exclusively devoted to agriculture for the, fabrics of manufacturing states, are constant and regular; *the wants of the latter, for the products of the former, are liable to very considerable fluctuations and interruptions.*"—A. Hamilton.

"Not only the *wealth* but the *independence* and *security* of a country, appear to be *materially connected with the prosperity of manufactures.* Every nation, with a view to these great objects, ought to endeavour to possess within itself all the essentials of national supply. These comprise the means of subsistence, habitation, clothing, and defence."—*Idem.*

"If Europe will not take from us the products of our soil, on terms consistent with our interest, *the natural remedy is to contract as fast as possible our wants of her.*"—Idem.

PHILADELPHIA:

H. C. CAREY & I. LEA—CHESNUT STREET.

....

1822.

SUBSCRIBERS' NAMES.

A.

Andrew Anderson, Philadelphia.
Thomas Amies, Lower Merion.
Armsby, Tucker, & Co. Boston.

B.

Lydia R. Bailey, Philadelphia.
Richard Barnard, jun. Wilmington.
William Brobson.
Abner Bourne, Brunswick.
J. B. Brown, Boston.
James Bradley.
Joseph P. Bradlee.
Samuel Billings & Co.
William Barret.
J. Smith Boice.
A. Binney.
Kirk Boot.
Silas Bullard.
Benjamin Butler, New York.

C.

J. Cushing, jun. Salem.
Joshua Clapp, Boston.
Joel Carter.
R. Crowninshield, Danvers.
——— Coppinger, Havanna.
De Witt Clinton, Albany.

D.

T. W. Dyott, Philadelphia.
E. I. Dupont, Wilmington.
Victor Dupont.
Samuel Davis & Co. Boston.
Alfred Dutch & Co.
Benjamin Dearborn.

E.

George P. Ellis, Walpole.

F.

Henry Fiske & Co. Boston.
William Few, New York.

G.

John Greiner, Philadelphia.
Levi Garrett.
Richard Graves, Boston.
Robert Graves.
Orra Goodell, Milbury.

H.

Gavin Hamilton, Philadelphia.
Thomas Hopkins & Co.
Benjamin Hawks, Salem.
William Hovey, Boston.
Jonathan Hunnewell.
D. Hale.
Holbrook & Dexter.
Hall J. How & Co.
S. P. Haywood.
Josiah J. Hastings.
Samuel Harris.
Eliphalet Hale.
Holmes & Rogers.
Thomas Hand, Chelmsford.
Edward Howard, Oxford.

J.

Isaac Jones & Son, Philadelphia.
P. T. Jackson, Boston.

K.

C. Keen, Philadelphia.
Caleb Kirk, Wilmington.
Sewall Kenny, Weathersfield.

L.

J. G. Langstroth, Philadelphia.
Thomas Leiper.
William Laird.
T. J. Lobdell, Boston.
Thomas Lord.
William Lawrence.
Jonathan Lock, Swansey.
Ezekiel Lord, New York.
H. & J. Lovering.

M.

M'Carty & Davis, Philadelphia, 25 copies.
Samuel Mansfield, Salem.
Townsend M'Coun, New York.
Wm. F. Mott.
Samuel Mott.

N.

J. P. Norris, Philadelphia.
William Nassau.
J. & J. Newhall, Salem.
Francis H. Nicoll, New York.

O.

Otis & Holbrook, Boston.
John Osborne.
John Oliff, New York.

P.

Richard Povall, Philadelphia.
Charles Parker, Salem.
George Prichard & Co. Boston.
William Phillips.
Isaac Pierson, New York.
Jeremiah H. Pierson.

R.

James Ronaldson, Philadelphia, 6 copies.
Mark Richards.
James Rundlett, Portsmouth.
Robert Rogerson & Co. Boston.
Henry Robinson, New York.

S.

Abraham Small, Philadelphia, 10 copies.
Joseph R. A. Skerrett, 2 copies.
John Siddall, Brandywine.
Henry Southard, New Jersey.
George H. Smith, Salem.
Richard Stickney.
Jonathan Stitson, Marshfield.
Horace Seaver, Portland.
Peter H. Schenck, New York.
Peter A. Schenck, Fishkill.
A. H. Schenck.
J. W. Stephens, Poughkeepsie.
Richard Savery, Salem,
J. Shepard & Co. Boston.
John Spring.
N. Somes & Co.

T.

John Torbert, Wilmington.
William Tileston, Boston.
Dexter Tiffany & Co.
Rev. Wm. Taylor.

V.

James Vila & Co. Boston.

W.

James Way, Philadelphia.
Robert Wilson.
Wells & Lilly, Boston, 12 copies.
N. G. Williamson, Wilmington, 2 copies.
George Whitelock.
Pierce L. Wiggins, Salem.
Isaac Wendell, Dover, 2 copies.
James Wolcott, jun. Boston.
Williams & Wendell, do.
Francis J. Williams.
Thomas G. Whittemore.
Wing & Sumner.
Whitwell, Bond & Co.
Jonathan Winship, Brighton.
Enoch Wiswall, Watertown.
Oliver M. Whipple, Chelmsford.
T. B. Wakeman, New York.
Jacob T. Walden.
Wm. W. Watkinson.
White & Bliss, 54 copies.
J. Wolcott, Southbridge.

Y.

William Young, Philadelphia, 10 copies.

PREFACE.

THIS collection of Essays is liable to one very strong objection, which I state in the foreground, as a sort of *caveat emptor*, that the purchaser may be early aware of what he has to expect, and form his determination accordingly.

Many of the facts and arguments are repeated twice and thrice, and some few even four times. This circumstance, which arises out of the nature of the case, can be easily accounted for. The arguments opposed to the doctrines herein advocated, are few in number; but have been, for above thirty years, unceasingly repeated by almost every writer who has discussed the subject, and often in the same words. It is evident, that an objection once fully answered, if twenty or fifty times repeated, must be twenty or fifty times refuted by nearly the same arguments. The reasonings against, and the dissuasives from, vice and guilt, as well as the arguments in favour of virtue, used by the earliest moralists, have been repeated from age to age ever since, with mere variations of style and manner, by their successors in the same useful and honourable career.

The principal objections alleged in 1789 against interposing the powerful ægis of governmental protection in favour of that important portion of the national industry devoted to convert the rude produce of the earth into such shapes and forms as are demanded by the necessities, the comfort, or the luxury of mankind, were—that we had not capital to spare for manufactures on an extensive scale—that it would divert capital from more to less useful objects—that our labour was too dear to allow us to compete with European or Asiatic industry—that while we had so much vacant lands, it was our duty to direct our industry to the cultivation of the soil—that manufacturing establishments tended to demoralize those occupied in them—that agriculture was the most useful and most innocent employment of mankind—that protecting or prohibitory duties would destroy commerce, afford a monopoly to one class of our own citizens, and thus tax the many for the benefit of the few, &c. To these objections was added, after the late war, the danger of a repetition of the extortion, confidently asserted to have been perpetrated by the manufacturers during its continuance.

Now, every one of these objections, except the last, which of course did not exist in his time, was discussed and triumphantly refuted by Alexander Hamilton in 1791. They have been, nevertheless, throughout the whole period that has since intervened, as flippantly advanced, and as pertinaciously insisted on, not only as if they had never been refuted, but as if they were so thoroughly and completely established as to bid defiance to argument. What can be done in such a case, but repeat the refutation as often as the objection is repeated?

The various essays contained in this work were written at different periods, during the last three years, to meet and refute some of the great number of essays and memorials against the protection of manufactures, in which the old arguments were repeated—and of course it was indispensable to pursue the course above traced out. And as truth travels slowly, it is probable, that whoever takes up the subject ten or twenty years hence, may have to adduce many of the same arguments as I have done.

I will exemplify this reasoning by the case of the accusation of extortion, of which such use was made in 1816, to defeat the hopes of the manufacturers, and consign so many of them to destruction. This accusation has been times without number in newspaper essays, paragraphs, petitions and memorials, and was advanced in conversation almost hourly in 1816 in every company. The proper answer to it is, that the cotton planter who raised the price of his cotton from thirteen cents per pound to twenty-seven, between 1814 and 1816—the tobacco planter, who in 1816 raised the price of tobacco from $96 to $185—the farmer who raised that of wheat from one dollar per bushel to three dollars during the wars of the French revolution—and the merchants, who availed themselves of every opportunity of scarcity, to lay enormous advances on their goods, often ten, twenty, and thirty per cent. in a month—could not, without the most manifest disregard of justice and propriety, charge their fellow-citizens with extortion, for an increase of prices, which arose chiefly out of the increase of the price of raw materials, labour, and sites for establishments. This answer was repeatedly and fully made in 1816, and ought to foreclose the objection for ever. But it is still adduced with undiminished confidence, and by men, against whom the accusation would lie with infinitely more propriety. So little attention is paid to the scriptural admonition: "*First take the beam out of thine own eye,* "*and then thou shalt see clearly to cast out the mote out of* "*thy brother's eye.*"

It may be said, that in the republication, the repetitions might have been avoided, and the matter condensed. This arrangement I contemplated, and had determined on—but on trial, I found it would so totally derange the different essays, that the whole work would require to be moulded anew, which would consume nearly as much time as the original composition. I could not reconcile myself to encounter this labour —and was therefore under the necessity of either abandoning the whole, or republishing in the present form.

To the former alternative I had strong objections. Many of the facts, (of these, I presume, I may speak freely,) collected with considerable research, are immensely important, and shed great light on the subject. They deserve to be put into permanent form, for the use of those who may hereafter devote themselves to this most important study—otherwise many of them, derived from scarce works, not easily procured, might be sought for in vain, or require trouble in the research, which few persons would be willing to undertake.

But let it be observed, that the whole amount of the repeated matter would not probably extend to fifty pages—and the volume contains about that quantity beyond the size I proposed to give.

To conclude this point, I wish it distinctly understood, that this volume is presented to the public merely as a collection of pamphlets, written at different times on one subject, and of course containing many repetitions—and not by any means as one continued work, in which the topics are discussed in regular order, and then dismissed. Should the latter estimate be formed of it, it would be found greatly deficient. It is to be regarded merely as a work of occasional reference, in which I hope it will be found useful.

Throughout these essays, there are various assumptions made, two of which I have already discovered to be erroneous—and others may probably be in the same situation. I therefore wish the reader to subject them universally to a severe scrutiny—and to admit none until they have undergone that ordeal. The proper data, on which to predicate assumptions in political economy, are difficult of attainment, even in countries where much greater facilities are afforded than are accessible by writers here. This circumstance pleads powerfully in extenuation of errors.

The recent census proves, that in pages 331 and 479 I have greatly erred in fixing the proportions of the different classes of society—having rated the agricultural class too low, and the other classes too high. I have, moreover, elsewhere, in two instances, estimated very differently the consumption of food and drink by each member of society. I regret this discrepancy, and other errors, "*quos incuria fudit*"—and throw myself on the indulgence of a public, a sincere desire to promote whose welfare and happiness has given birth to this work, which is published with a full conviction of its manifold imperfections. Let me be permitted to add, in the words of the great Chaptal—"I have neglected nothing to "procure correct information. I do not, however, pretend "to publish a perfect work. All that I can pledge myself "for, is, that it emanates from honest intentions."* Such is the language of the Minister of the Interior of France, respecting his admirable work on "French Industry." If, with the immense advantages he possessed through his official station, and his unlimited command of the national statistics—he found it necessary to propitiate public opinion for the indulgence of his errors—how incomparably more necessary is such propitiation for this work, labouring as I have done, under almost every kind of disadvantage to which a writer is liable.† Let me observe, as an additional reason for critical indulgence, that before I began to write the Addresses of the Philadelphia Society for the Promotion of National Industry in 1819, I had never devoted three days to the study of political economy.

As some of the articles contained in this volume, viz. the Addresses of the Philadelphia Society for the promotion of National Industry—the Memorial to Congress—the Report of a Committee of the Citizens of Philadelphia—and the Circular Letter of the same committee, were issued in the names of public bodies, it may be proper to state how far the authorship has been correctly appropriated. They were all written by the same hand as the rest of the contents of the volume—put into type—carefully corrected—and then read to the bodies respectively, in whose name they were published. Emendations were occasionally suggested by the members, and were generally adopted by the writer. No. 12 and 13 of the first-mentioned set of papers, were written by Dr. Samuel Jackson.

* "Je crois n'avoir rien négligé pour obtenir des renseignemens exacts; "cependant je ne prétends pas publier un ouvrage parfait. *Tout ce dont je "puis répondre, c'est que c'est un ouvrage de bonne foi.*"

† The pains I have taken to procure correct information are scarcely credible—as are the difficulties I have experienced, where none were to have been expected. Numbers of persons, deeply interested in the result of these discussions, have not condescended to reply to civil letters requesting information fully within their power.

It is an extraordinary fact, that there were 4750 copies of the circular letter, page 229, distributed throughout the United States, one to every post-office, of which the number was about 3600—the remainder in different directions—and that not more than ten or a dozen answers were received.

Philadelphia, April 6, 1822.

ADDRESSES

OF

THE PHILADELPHIA SOCIETY

FOR

THE PROMOTION

OF

NATIONAL INDUSTRY.

"A trade is disadvantageous to a nation which *brings in things of mere luxury or pleasure*, which are entirely or for the most part consumed among us.

"Much worse is that trade which brings in a commodity that is not only consumed among us, but *hinders the consumption of the like quantity of ours.*

"That trade is eminently bad, which *supplies the same articles as we manufacture ourselves, especially if we can make enough for our consumption.*"—British Merchant, vol. i. p. 4.

"Foreign luxuries, and needless manufactures, imported and used in a nation, *increase the people of the nation that furnishes them, and diminish the people of the nation that uses them.*

"Laws, therefore, that prevent such importations, and, on the contrary, promote the exportation of manufactures, to be consumed in foreign countries, may be called, (with respect to the people that make them,) *generative laws; as, by increasing subsistence, they encourage marriage.*

"Such laws, likewise, *strengthen a nation doubly*, by increasing its own people, and diminishing its neighbours."—*Franklin's Works*, vol. iv. pp. 188, 189.

SIXTH EDITION.

PHILADELPHIA.

....

1822.

ERRATA.

The reader is requested to correct with his pen the following and some minor errors which have escaped attention.

Page 9, line 22, dele *Holland.*
26, line 19, for *conferences* read *consequences.*
225, line 36, dele *and the Netherlands.*
294, line 25, for *four* read *three.*
470, line 29, for 130,107, read 80,107.
471, line 4, for *fifty-seven* read *sixty.*
540, line 3, for *only* read *duty.*

PREFACE TO THE ADDRESSES.

IN presenting our fellow citizens with these addresses, collected together, we cannot refrain from expressing our high sense of the very favourable reception they have experienced. The various defects of style and arrangement which pervade them, have been overlooked, in consideration of the magnitude of the subject they embrace.

We feel persuaded that the cause we advocate yields to none in importance. It is a great error to suppose, as unhappily is too frequently done, that it is the cause of the manufacturers alone. Nothing can be more foreign from the real fact. It is the cause of the nation. It is the mighty question, whether we shall be really or nominally independent—whether we shall persevere in a policy, which, in four or five years, has done more to prostrate our strength and resources, than a fierce war of equal duration could have done—a policy similar to that which has sunk and degraded Spain for centuries, notwithstanding her immense internal and colonial resources—a policy which has never failed, and never can fail, to debilitate and impoverish every country where it has prevailed or may prevail—a policy discarded by every wise nation in Europe—a policy in direct hostility with that of England, Russia, Austria, France, Holland, and Denmark—a policy, in a word, that fosters and promotes the wealth, power, resources, industry, and manufactures of foreign nations, and represses and paralizes those of our own country.

If there be any one truth in political economy more sacred and irrefragable than another, it is, that the prosperity of nations bears an exact proportion to the encouragement of their domestic industry—and that their decay and decrepitude commence and proceed *pari passu* with their neglect of it. The wonderful resources of England, so far beyond her intrinsic advantages, and the prostrate state of Spain and Portugal, notwithstanding the numberless blessings bestowed on them by nature, place these great truths on the most impregnable ground.

The United States pursue a wayward and short-sighted policy, of which the world affords few examples, and which evinces how little we have profited by the experience of other nations—and how much we neglect the maxims of the wise statesmen of Europe, as well as of our own country.

With a capacity to raise cotton to supply the whole world, our treasures are lavished in Hindostan to purchase cotton of inferior quality, which is now manufactured in the United States,* to the injury of our cotton planters. And with skill, talents, water-power, capital, and machinery to supply our utmost demand for cambrics and muslins, millions of money are in a similar manner lavished in Hindostan and England, to procure those articles; while tens of thousands of our own citizens, capable of furnishing them, are pining in indigence; their employers ruined; and machinery, which cost millions of dollars, rusting and rotting; and while hundreds of manufacturers, invited to our shores by the excellence of our form of government, are unable to earn a subsistence at their usual trades, and are forced to go to Canada or Nova Scotia, or to return to Europe.† About fifty sailed from hence in one vessel, a few days since.

Under the influence of such a mistaken system, is it wonderful, that distress and embarrassment pervade the nation—that the enlivening sound of the spindle, the loom, and the hammer, has in many places almost ceased to be heard—that our merchants and traders are daily swept away by bankruptcy, one after another—that our banks are drained of their specie—that our cities exhibit an unvarying scene of gloom and despair—that confidence between man and man is almost extinct—that debts cannot in general be collected—that property cannot be sold but at enormous sacrifices—that capitalists have thus an opportunity of aggrandizing themselves at the expense of the middle class of society, to an incalculable extent—that money cannot be borrowed, but at an extravagant interest—in a word, that with advantages equal to any that Heaven has ever bestowed on any nation, we exhibit a state of things at which our enemies must rejoice—and our friends put on sackcloth and ashes?‡

We trust the day is not far distant, when we shall cast a retrospective eye on this lamentable folly, with as much as-

* [At the time this was written, there were large quantities of East India Cotton used by the manufacturers of the U. S.]

† [It is probable, that above one thousand emigrants returned from the U. S. to their native countries in 1819.]

‡ [For a statement of the distress of this period, see the New Olive Branch, Chapter VII.]

tonishment, as we now do at the folly and wickedness of our ancestors in hanging and burning witches. The folly in both cases is about equal. Theirs, however, was limited to a narrow sphere, out of which it was perfectly innocuous. But ours extends its baneful influence to the remotest extremities of the nation.

We are gravely told, by writers on whom, unfortunately, great reliance is placed, that our circumstances as a nation being materially different from those of other nations, we require a totally different policy—and that, however proper or necessary it may be for England or France, to encourage manufactures, sound policy dictates a different course for the United States.

These maxims are the reverse of truth; and having had great influence on the operations of our government, have proved highly pernicious. We are, on the contrary, more imperiously called on to encourage manufactures than most other nations, unless we be disposed wantonly to sacrifice the interests of a most important and numerous portion of our population, those farmers and planters who are remote from the seaboard. We request a patient hearing while we offer our reasons.

In a compact country, like England, where inland navigation is carried to such a wonderful extent, there are few parts of the kingdom that are not within one or two days' carriage of the seaboard—and consequently their productions can be transported to foreign markets at a moderate expense. Whereas a large portion of our agricultural citizens are from three hundred to a thousand miles distant from any seaport, and therefore almost wholly debarred from all foreign markets, especially at the present and all probable future prices.

Flour has been forwarded to the Philadelphia market from Pittsburg, at a freight of four dollars per barrel. Some of it was probably brought to Pittsburg, from fifty to a hundred and fifty miles, at considerable expense. Deduct the expenses and profits of the Pittsburg merchants, from six or seven dollars, and in what a lamentable situation it places the farmer—how miserable a remuneration he has for his labour—and how "*dear he pays for the whistle*," in buying his goods cheap in Hindostan, and depending on European markets for the sale of his productions!

The consequences of this system are so pernicious, that it requires a little further notice. A farmer in the neighbourhood of Pittsburg, sends his produce to that city, whence it is conveyed to Philadelphia, three hundred miles by land—or to New Orleans, two thousand by water. It is thence conveyed four thousand to Liverpool, from whence he receives his china, his delftware, and his pottery. From the amount of his flour as sold in England, all the expenses of transportation are to be deducted—and to the price of his china and other articles, the expenses of the return voyage are to be added. What a frightful view of the situation of a large portion of the people of the western country does this sketch exhibit? Is it difficult to account for the prostrate state of affairs in that part of the union, and under a government, which, emanating more completely from the mass of the people than any other that ever existed, might have been expected to have extended a more paternal care over its citizens than the world ever witnessed!

It is therefore indubitable, that to the reasons for encouraging manufactures, existing in England and France, all of which apply here, is to be added a powerful one peculiar to the United States, arising from the distance between so large a portion of our territory and any seaport towns, as well as the immense distance from those towns to the countries from whence we draw our supplies.

Let us suppose for a moment, that the western farmer, instead of purchasing his pottery and delftware in England, had, in his own neighbourhood, manufactories of those articles, whence he could procure them free of the enormous expenses of sea and land carriages, amounting in many instances to treble the first cost—and that in return, he supplied the manufacturer, of whom he purchased them, with his wheat and corn and other articles! —What a different face that country would wear!—What rapid strides it would then make in the career of prosperity!—What additional allurements it would hold out to immigrants!

We offer for reflection, fellow-citizens, an important fact, that sheds the strongest light on this theory. The settlement of Harmony in the western country, was conducted on this plan. This little commonwealth depended wholly on itself for supplies. It had, to use the cogent language of Mr. Jefferson, "*placed the manufacturer beside the agriculturist.*" What was the consequence? The settlement made more rapid advances in wealth and prosperity, than any equal body of men in the world at any period of time—more, in one year, than other parts of the United States, which depend on foreign markets for the sale of their produce and the supply of their wants, have done in ten.

It is frequently stated, that as some of the cotton manufacturers in the eastern states have prospered, the protection to the manufacture is abundantly adequate. If this argument warranted the inference drawn from it, it would prove that the policy of Spain is sound, and fraught with wisdom; for notwithstanding the decay of that nation, there are in it many prosperous manufactures, which, from particular circumstances, are, like some of those in the eastern states, enabled to struggle against foreign competition.—But the decay of so large a portion of the manufacturing establishments in the middle and eastern states, notwithstanding the enterprise, large capital, and industry of the proprietors, is a full proof that there is not sufficient protection to this important branch.

Public attention has unfortunately been diverted from the real sources of our prostrate state, by certain trite common places, re-echoed throughout the union,—that it is a time of general suffering—that distress and embarrassment pervade the whole civilized world—that we are no worse than other nations—and that we cannot hope for an exemption from the common lot of mankind.

This appears plausible—but will not stand the test of examination. It is not wonderful, that the nations of Europe, exhausted by a twenty years war—pillaged and plundered by hostile armies—with expensive governments and immense armies to support in time of peace—and groaning under the weight of enormous debts, and grinding tithes and taxes, should be in a state of suffering But there is no parallel between their situation and ours. Our short war, far from exhausting our resources, developed them. We retired from it, prosperous and glorious. Our fields are as fertile—our citizens as industrious and ingenious—our capacity for manufacturing as great as ever—and our taxes are comparatively insignificant. Our distresses cannot therefore be traced to the same source as theirs. They flow wholly from our own mistaken policy, which leads us to purchase abroad what we could produce at home—and, like thoughtless prodigals and spendthrifts, to incur debts beyond our utmost means of payment.

The restoration of peace, however, as might have been naturally expected, greatly affected our commerce, particularly the carrying trade, of which the war had given us an inordinate share. An immense capital, invested in commerce, was thus rendered wholly unproductive; and, had manufactures been encouraged, as sound policy dictated, hundreds of our merchants, whose property has since wasted away, and who have been swallowed up in the vortex of bankruptcy, would, as was the case during the war, have transferred their talents, their industry, and their capital to that department, to the advancement of their own interest and the general welfare; instead of a vain struggle in a branch which was so overstocked, that it could not afford support to more than half the persons engaged in it.—Those that remained in the mercantile profession, after such a transfer of a portion of its members to profitable employment of another description, might and probably would have prospered. And thus it is as clear as the noon-day sun, that an efficient protection of manufactures would have been highly advantageous to the merchants; although many of them, from taking a superficial view of the subject, have been under an opposite impression, and have, unfortunately, been hostile to such protection.

The advocates of the system of Adam Smith ought to be satisfied with the fatal experiment we have made of it. It is true, the demands of the treasury have not allowed us to proceed its full length, and to discard import duties altogether. But as our manufactures are paralized, so large a portion of our manufacturers ruined, and our country almost wholly drained of its metallic medium, to pay for foreign merchandize, notwithstanding the duties imposed *for the purpose of revenue*, it is perfectly reasonable to conclude, that the destruction would have been more rapid and complete, had those duties not existed. This, we hope will be regarded as decisive; for, if our woolen manufacture, for instance, protected, as it is termed, by a duty of 27 1-2 per cent., has been more than one half destroyed, so that it was no longer an object to preserve the invaluable breed of Merino sheep, in which millions of dollars were invested, and of which the greater part have been consigned to the shambles, to the great and manifest injury of the proprietors, it cannot be doubted, that, without such duty, it would have been at once wholly annihilated, as our citizens would, in that event, have been utterly unable to maintain a struggle against foreign rivals. If argument were of avail against the dazzling authority of great names, and against ingrained, inveterate prejudice, this case would settle this question forever. Where are now, we ask, the "*collateral branches*," to which the thousands of our artists, mechanics, and manufacturers, "*thrown out of their ordinary employment, and common method of subsistence*," can "*easily transfer their industry*,"* as Dr. Smith asserts?

Another part of Dr. Smith's theory, is, that when a particular branch of industry is destroyed by "*the home market being suddenly laid open to the competition of foreigners*," "*the stock will still remain in the country, to employ an equal number of people in some other way*." And, therefore, "*the capital of the country remaining the same, the demand for labour will still be the same, though it may be exerted in different places, and for different occupations*."† These maxims are now fairly tested in the United States, as they have been for centuries in Spain. The cotton, woollen, pottery, glass, and various other manufactures, have been in a great measure suspended in the middle states, by "*the home market being suddenly laid open to the competition of foreigners*" at the close of the war. Is there a man who will venture to assert, that "*the demand for labour is the same?*" that "*the stock remains the same?*" or that it "*employs an equal number of people in some other way?*" We flatter ourselves that the

* Wealth of Nations, Hartford Edition, I. 329—30. † Ibid.

most decided advocate of the doctor's system will admit, on calm reflection, that these maxims are utterly destitute of even the shadow of foundation.

We urge this point on the most sober and serious reflection of our fellow citizens. It is a vital one, on which the destinies of this nation depend. The freedom of commerce, wholly unrestrained by protecting duties and prohibitions, is the keystone of the so-much-extolled system of the doctor, which, though discarded, as we have stated, in almost every country in Europe, has, among our most enlightened citizens, numbers of ardent, zealous, and enthusiastic admirers. We have made an experiment of it as far as our debt and the support of our government would permit. We have discarded prohibitions; and, on the most important manufactured articles, wholly prohibited in some countries, and burdened with heavy prohibitory duties in others, our duties are comparatively low, so as to afford no effectual protection to the domestic manufacturer. *The fatal result is before the world*—and, in almost every part of the union, is strikingly perceptible. In addition to the example of Spain and Portugal, it holds out an awful beacon against the adoption of theories, which, however splendid and captivating on paper, are fraught with ruin when carried into practice.

There is one point of view, in which, if this subject be considered, the egregious errors of our system will be manifest beyond contradiction. The policy we have pursued renders us dependent for our prosperity on the miseries and misfortunes of our fellow-creatures! Wars and famines in Europe are the keystone on which we erect the edifice of our good fortune!—The greater the extent of war, and the more dreadful the famine in that quarter, the more prosperous we become! Peace and abundant crops there undermine our welfare! The misery of Europe ensures our prosperity! its happiness promotes our decay and prostration!! What an appalling idea! Who can reflect without regret on a system built upon such a wretched foundation!

What a contrast between this system and that developed with such ability by Alexander Hamilton, which we advocate! Light and darkness are not more opposite to each other. His admirable system would render our prosperity and happiness dependent wholly on ourselves. We should have no cause to wish for the misery of our fellow men, in order to save us from the distress and embarrassment which at present pervade the nation. Our wants from Europe would, by the adoption of it, be circumscribed within narrower limits, and our surplus raw materials be amply adequate to procure the necessary supplies.

Submitting these important subjects to an enlightened community, and hoping they will experience a calm and unbiassed consideration, we ardently pray for such a result as may tend to promote and perpetuate the honour, the happiness, and the real independence of our common country.

To the legislature of the United States, on whose decision depends the perpetuation of existing distress, or the restoration of the country, to that high grade of prosperity from which a false policy has precipitated her, we present the following luminous maxims; viz.

" *The uniform appearance of an abundance of specie, as the* " *concomitant of a flourishing state of manufactures, and of the* " *reverse where they do not prevail, afford a strong presumption* " *of their favourable operation on the wealth of a country.**

" *Considering a monopoly of the domestic market to its own* " *manufactures, as the reigning policy of manufacturing nations,* " *a similar policy, on the part of the United States, in every pro-* " *per instance, is dictated, it might almost be said, by the princi-* " *ples of distributive justice; certainly, by the duty of endeavour-* " *ing to secure their own citizens a reciprocity of advantages.*"†

" *The United States cannot exchange with Europe on equal* " *terms.*"‡

" *That trade is eminently bad which supplies the same goods* " *as we manufacture ourselves; especially, if we can make enough* " *for our own consumption.*"§

* Hamilton's Works, vol. I. p. 217. † Idem, p. 225.
‡ Idem, 186. § British Merchant, vol. I. p. 4.

ADDRESSES

OF THE

PHILADELPHIA SOCIETY,

TO THE CITIZENS OF THE U. STATES.

NO. I.

Philadelphia, March 27, 1819.

Definition of political economy. Its importance. Influence of great names. Leading feature of Adam Smith's theory. Pernicious consequences of its adoption.

FRIENDS AND FELLOW CITIZENS,

THE Philadelphia Society for the Promotion of National Industry, respectfully solicit your attention to a few brief essays on topics of vital importance to your country, yourselves, and your posterity. They shall be addressed to your reason and understanding, without any attempt to bias your feelings by declamation.

Political economy shall be the subject of these essays. In its broad and liberal sense, it may be correctly styled the 'science of promoting human happiness;' than which a more noble subject cannot occupy the attention of men endowed with enlarged minds, or inspired by public spirit.

It is to be regretted that this sublime science has not had adequate attention bestowed on it in this country. And unfortunately, so many contradictory systems are in existence, that statesmen and legislators, disposed to discharge their duty conscientiously, and for that purpose to study the subject, are liable to be confused and distracted by the unceasing discordance in the views of the writers.

It is happily true, nevertheless, that its leading principles, calculated to conduct nations safely to the important and beneficent results, which are its ultimate object, are plain and clear; and, to be distinctly comprehended, and faithfully carried into effect, require no higher endowments than good sound sense and rectitude of intentions.

It is a melancholy feature in human affairs, that imprudence and error often produce as copious a harvest of wretchedness as absolute wickedness. Hence arises the imperious necessity, in a country where so many of our citizens may aspire to the character of legislators and statesmen, of a more general study of this science, a thorough knowledge of which is so essential a requisite, among the qualifications for those important stations.

To remove all doubt on this point, numberless instances are to be found in history, in which single errors of negotiators and legislators have entailed full as much, and in many cases more misery on nations, than the wild and destructive ambition of conquerors. Unless in some extraordinary instances, a sound policy, on the restoration of peace, heals the wounds inflicted by war, and restores a nation to its pristine state of ease and comfort. But it has frequently occurred, that an article of a treaty, of ten or a dozen lines, or an impolitic or unjust law, has produced the most ruinous consequences for a century.

It is our intention,

1. To review the policy of those nations which have enjoyed a high degree of prosperity, with or without any extraordinary advantages from nature; and likewise of those whose prosperity has been blasted by fatuitous counsels, notwithstanding great natural blessings:

2. To examine the actual situation of our country, in order to ascertain whether we enjoy the manifold blessings to which our happy form of government and numerous local advantages entitle us; and, if we do not, to investigate the causes to which the failure is owing:

3. To develop the true principles of political economy, suited to our situation and circumstances, and calculated to produce the greatest sum of happiness throughout the wide expanse of our territory.

In this arduous undertaking, we request a patient and candid hearing from our fellow-citizens. We fondly hope for success; but, if disappointed, we shall have the consolation of having endeavoured to discharge a duty every good citizen owes to the country which protects him; the duty of contributing his efforts to advance its interest and happiness.

As a preliminary step, we propose to establish the utter fallacy of some maxims, supported by the authority of the name of Adam Smith, author of The Wealth of Nations, but pregnant with certain ruin to any nation by which they may be carried into operation. This course is prescribed to us by the circumstance, that the influence of these maxims has been most sensibly and perniciously felt in our councils; has deeply affected our prosperity; and been the main source whence the prevailing distress of the nation has flowed.

This writer stands so pre-eminent in the estimation of a large portion of Christendom, as the Delphic Oracle of political economy, and there is such a magic in his name, that it requires great hardihood to encounter him, and a high degree of good fortune to obtain a fair and patient hearing for the discussion.

But at this enlightened period, we trust our citizens will scorn to surrender their reason into the guidance of any authority whatever. When a position is presented to the mind, the question ought to be, not who delivered it, but what is its nature? and, how is it supported by reason and common sense, and especially by fact? A theory, how plausible soever, and however propped up by a bead-roll of great names, ought to be regarded with suspicion, if unsupported by fact—and, *a fortiori*, if contrary to established fact, ought to be unhesitatingly rejected. This course of procedure is strongly recommended by the decisive circumstance, that, in the long catalogue of wild, ridiculous, and absurd theories on morals, religion, politics, or science, which have domineered over mankind, there is hardly one that has not reckoned among its partisans, men of the highest celebrity.* And in the present instance, the most cogent and conclusive facts bear testimony against the political economist, how great soever his reputation.

We hope, therefore, that our readers will bring to this discussion, minds wholly liberated from the fascination of the name of the writer whose opinions we undertake to combat, and a determination to weigh the evidence in the scales of reason, not those of prejudice.

In order to render Dr. Smith full justice, and to remove all ground for cavil, we state his propositions at length, and in his own language:

1. "To give the monopoly of the home market to the produce of domestic industry, in any particular art or manufacture, is in some measure to direct private people in what manner they ought to employ their capitals; and must, in almost all cases, be either a useless or a hurtful regulation. If the domestic produce can be brought there as cheap as that of foreign industry, the regulation is evidently useless. If it cannot, it must generally be hurtful.

2. "It is the maxim of every prudent master of a family, never to attempt to make at home what it will cost him more to make than to buy. The tailor does not attempt to make

* Montesquieu, whose reputation was as great as that of Dr. Smith, and whose Spirit of Laws has had as extensive a currency as the Wealth of Nations, held the absurd idea, which remained uncontroverted for half a century, that the habits, manners and customs, and even the virtues and vices of nations, were in a great measure governed by climate; whence it would result that a tolerable idea might be formed of those important features of national character, by consulting maps, and ascertaining latitudes and longitudes! Bacon studied judicial astrology! All the great men of his day believed in magic and witchcraft! Johnson had full faith in the story of the Cocklane-Ghost! So much for great names.

"his own shoes, but buys them of the shoemaker. The shoe-
"maker does not attempt to make his own clothes, but employs
"a taylor. The farmer neither attempts to make one nor the
"other, but employs those different artificers. All of them find
"it for their interest to employ their whole industry in a way in
"which they have some advantage over their neighbours; and
"to purchase, with a part of its produce, or, what is the same
"thing, with the price of a part of it, whatever else they have
"occasion for.

3. "That which is prudence in the conduct of every private
"family, can scarcely be folly in that of a great kingdom. If
"a foreign country can supply us with a commodity cheaper
"than we ourselves can make it, better buy it from them, with
"some part of the produce of our country, employed in a way
"in which we have some advantage.

4. "The general industry of the country being in propor-
"tion to the capital which employs it, will not thereby be dimi-
"nished, any more than that of the above-mentioned artificers;
"but only left to find out the way in which it can be employed
"with the greatest advantage. It is not so employed, when di-
"rected to an object which it can buy cheaper than it can make.
"The value of its annual produce is certainly more or less di-
"minished, when it is thus turned away from producing com-
"modities evidently of more value than the commodity which
"it is directed to produce. According to the supposition, that
"commodity could be purchased from foreign countries cheaper
"than it can be made at home. It could, therefore, have been
"purchased with part only of the commodities, or, what is the
"same thing, with a part only of the price of the commodities,
"which the industry employed by an equal capital would have
"produced at home, had it been left to pursue its natural
"course."*

There is in the subordinate parts of this passage much sophistry and unsound reasoning, which we may examine on a future occasion; and there is likewise, as in all the rest of the doctor's work, a large proportion of verbiage, which is admirably calculated to embarrass and confound common understandings, and prevent their forming a correct decision. But, stripped of this verbiage, and brought naked and unsophisticated to the eye of reason, the main proposition which we at present combat, and to which we here confine ourselves, is, that,

"If a foreign country can supply us with a commodity
"cheaper than we ourselves can make it, better buy of them,
"with some part of the produce of our own industry, employed
"in a way in which we have some advantage."

* Wealth of Nations, Hartford, 1818, vol. i. p. 319.

The most rational mode of testing the correctness of any maxim or principle is, to examine what have been its effects where it has been carried into operation, and what they would be in any given case where it might be applied. This is the plan we shall pursue in this investigation.

Great Britain affords a felicitous instance for our purpose. Let us examine what effect the adoption of this maxim would produce on her happiness and prosperity.

There are above a million of people, of both sexes and of all ages, employed in that country, in the woollen and cotton manufactures.* By their industry in these branches, they make for themselves and families a comfortable subsistence. They afford a large and steady market for the productions of the earth, giving support to, probably, at least two millions of persons engaged in agriculture, who furnish the one set of manufacturers with the raw materials, and both with food. They moreover, enrich the nation by bringing into it wealth from nearly all parts of the earth. The immense sums of money they thus introduce into their native country afford means of employment, and ensure happiness to other millions of subjects—and thus, like the circles made on the surface of the stream by the central pebble thrown in, the range of happiness is extended so wide as to embrace the whole community.

From this cheering prospect, let us turn the startled eye to the masses of misery, which Dr. Smith's system would produce; and we shall then behold a hideous contrast, which, we trust, escaped the doctor's attention; for the acknowledged goodness and benevolence of his character, will not allow us to believe that he would have been the apostle of such a pernicious doctrine, had he attended to its results. We fondly hope, that, like many other visionary men, he was so deeply engaged in the fabrication of a refined theory, that he did not arrest his progress to weigh its awful consequences.

The East Indies could at all times, until the recent improvements in machinery, have furnished cotton goods at a lower rate than they could be manufactured in England, which had no other means of protecting its domestic industry, but by a prohibition of the rival fabrics. Let us suppose that France, where provisions and labour are much lower than in England, has possessed herself of machinery, and is thus enabled to sell woollen goods at half, or three-fourths, or seven-eighths of the price of the English rival commodities. Suppose, further, that articles manufactured of leather are procurable in Germany, and

* Dr. Seybert states, that in 1809, there were 800,000 persons in Great Britain engaged in the cotton manufacture alone. It has since increased considerably. It is, therefore, probable that the two branches employ at least 1,300,000 persons.—*Statistics*, p. 92.

iron wares in Sweden, below the rates in England. Then, if the statesmen of the last nation were disciples of Adam Smith, as "foreign countries could supply them with those commodities "cheaper than they themselves can make them," they must, according to the doctor, "buy from them with some part of the "produce of their own country," and accordingly open their ports freely to those various articles, from these four particular nations. Who can contemplate the result without horror? What a wide spread scene of ruin and desolation would take place? The wealth of the country would be swept away, to enrich foreign, and probably hostile nations, which might, at no distant period, make use of the riches and strength thus fatuitously placed in their hands, to enslave the people who had destroyed themselves by following such baneful counsels. The labouring and industrious classes would be at once bereft of employment; reduced to a degrading state of dependence and mendicity; and, through the force of misery and distress, driven to prey upon each other, and upon the rest of the community. The middle classes of society would partake of the distress of the lower, and the sources of the revenues of the higher orders be dried up.* And all this terrific scene of wo, and wretchedness, and depravity, is to be produced for the grand purpose of procuring broadcloth, and muslins, and shoes, and iron ware, in distant parts of the earth, a few shillings per yard, or piece, or pound, cheaper than at home! The manufacturers of Bombay, and Calcutta, and Paris, and Lyons, and Frankfort, and Stockholm, are to be fed, and clothed, and fostered by English wealth, while those of England, whom it ought to nourish and protect, are expelled from their workshops, and driven to seek support from the overseers of the poor. We trust this will not be thought a fancy sketch! Such a view of it would be an extravagant error. It is sober, serious reality; and puts down forever this plausible, but ruinous theory. Ponder well on it, fellow citizens.

Let us suppose another strong case. The cotton produced in this country, amounts, probably, to thirty millions of dollars annually at present prices—but to forty at least, at the prices of 1815 and 1816. We will suppose the minimum of the price, at which it can be sold, to pay for the labour and interest on the capital employed in its culture, to be twelve cents per pound. We will further suppose, that the southern provinces of Spanish America have established their independence, and are able to supply us with this valuable raw material at the rate of ten cents. Ought we, for the sake of saving a few cents per pound, to destroy the prospects, and ruin the estates of nearly 800,000 inhabitants of the southern states—to paralize a culture so immense-

* No small portion of this picture is [1819] rapidly realizing in this country.

ly advantageous, and producing so large a fund of wealth, and strength and happiness? Should we, for such a paltry consideration, run the risk of consequences which cannot be regarded without awe, and which could not fail eventually to involve in ruin, even those who might appear in the first instance to profit by the adoption of the system?

It may be well worth while to proceed a step further, and take the case of a nation able to supply us fully and completely, with wheat and other grain at a lower rate than our farmers can furnish them. Thus then we should find ourselves pursuing Adam Smith's sublime system; buying cheap bargains of wheat or flour from one nation; cotton from another; hardware from a third; and, to pursue the system throughout, woollen, and cotton, and linen goods from others; while our country was rapidly impoverishing of its wealth, its industry paralized, the labouring part of our citizens reduced to beggary, and the farmers, planters, and manufacturers, involved in one common mass of ruin. The picture demands the most sober, serious attention of the farmers and planters of the United States.

It may be asserted, that the supposition of our country being fully supplied with cotton and grain, by foreign nations, is so improbable, as not to be admissible even by way of argument. This is a most egregious error; our supposition, so far as it respects cotton, is in "the full tide of successful experiment." That article, we repeat, to a great amount, is even at present* imported from Bengal, and sold at a price so far below our own, (difference of quality considered) that our manufacturers find the purchase eligible. Let it be considered, that in 1789, doubts were entertained whether cotton could be cultivated in the United States;† that in the year 1794, there were exported from this country, of foreign and domestic cotton, only seven thousand bags;‡ and yet, that in 1818, the amount exported was above ninety-two millions of pounds. No man can be so far misled as to suppose that Heaven has given us any exclusive monopoly of the soil and climate calculated for such extraordinary and almost incredible advances. The rapid strides we have made, may be also made by other nations. Cotton is said to be shipped at Bombay for three pence sterling per lb.; and therefore, setting South America wholly out of the question, it can hardly be doubted, from the spirit with which the culture of that plant is prosecuted in the East Indies, and the certainty that the seeds of our best species have been carried there, that in a few years that country will be able, provided Adam Smith's theory continues to be acted upon here, to expel our planters from their own markets, after having driven them from those of Europe.

[* 1819.] † Seybert's Statistics, page 84. ‡ Idem, p. 94.

It is not, therefore, hazarding much to assert, that the time cannot be very remote, when southern cotton industry will be compelled to supplicate congress for that legislative protection, for which the manufacturing industry of the rest of the union has so earnestly implored that body in vain; and which, had it been adequately afforded, would have saved from ruin numerous manufacturing establishments, and invaluable machinery, which cost millions of dollars—now a dead and irreparable loss to the enterprising proprietors. Had these establishments been preserved, and duly protected, they would have greatly lessened our ruinously unfavourable balance of trade, and of course prevented that pernicious drain of specie, which has overspread the face of our country with distress, and clouded (we trust only temporarily) as fair prospects as ever dawned on any nation.*

We have given a slight sketch of the effects the adoption of this system would produce in England and the United States, if carried into complete operation; and also glanced at the consequences its partial operation has already produced here. We now proceed to cast a very cursory glance (reserving details for a future occasion) at its lamentable results in Spain and Portugal, where the statesmen are disciples of Adam Smith, and where the theory, which now goes under the sanction of his name, has been in operation for centuries. As "foreign coun-" tries can supply them with commodities cheaper than they them-" selves can make them," they therefore consider it "better to " buy from them, with some part of the produce of their own " country."

* This view may appear too gloomy. Would to heaven it were! A cursory glance at some of the great interests of the United States, will settle the question. Cotton, the chief staple of the country, is falling, and not likely to rise:† as the immense quantities from the East Indies have glutted the English market, which regulates the price in ours. Affairs in the western country, on which so many of our importers depend, are to the last degree unpromising.—The importers, of course, have the most dreary and sickening prospects before them. They are deeply in debt, their resources almost altogether suspended, and a large proportion ultimately precarious. Our commerce and navigation languish every where, except to the East Indies, the most ruinous branch we carry on. Further, notwithstanding nearly eight millions of specie were imported by the Bank of the U. States at a heavy expense, in about one year; so great has been the drain, that the banks are generally so slenderly provided, as to excite serious uneasiness. We are heavily indebted to England, after having remitted immense quantities of government and bank stock, whereby we shall be laid under a heavy and perpetual annual tax for interest. Our manufactures are in general drooping, and some of them are one-half or two-thirds suspended. Our cities present the distressing view of immense numbers of useful artizans, mechanics, and manufacturers, willing to work, but unable to procure employment. We might proceed with the picture to a great extent; but presume enough has been stated to satisfy the most incredulous, that the positions in the text are by no means exaggerated.

[†At the time this was written, the price in Liverpool was for Uplands, about 16d. sterling—for Sea Islands, 34d. It is now for the former, 10d.—for the latter, 18d.]

These countries are in a forlorn and desperate state, notwithstanding the choicest blessings of nature have been bestowed on them with lavish hand; industry is paralized, and the enormous floods of wealth, drawn from their colonies, answer no other purpose but to foster and encourage the industry, and promote the happiness of rival nations; and all obviously and undeniably the result of the system of "*buying goods where they are to be had cheapest*," to the neglect and destruction of their domestic industry. With such awful beacons before your eyes, can you contemplate the desolating effects of the system in those two countries, without deep regret, that so many of our citizens, and some of them in high and elevated stations, advocate its universal adoption here, and are so far enamoured of Dr. Smith's theory, that they regard as a species of heresy the idea of appealing to any other authority, on the all-important and vital point of the political economy of nations!

To avoid prolixity, we are obliged to postpone the consideration of other positions of Dr. Smith on this subject; and shall conclude with a statement of those maxims of political economy which we shall endeavour to inculcate, the soundness of which is established by the experience of the wisest as well as of the most fatuitous nations of the earth.

1. Industry is the only sure foundation of national virtue, happiness, and greatness; and, in all its useful shapes and forms, has an imperious claim on governmental protection.

2. No nation ever prospered to the extent of which it was capable, without due protection of domestic industry.

3. Throughout the world, in all ages, wherever industry has been duly encouraged, mankind have been uniformly industrious.

4. Nations, like individuals, are in a career of ruin when their expenditures exceed their income.

5. Whenever nations are in this situation, it is the imperious duty of their rulers to apply such remedies, to correct the evil, as the nature of the case may require.

6. There are few, if any, political evils, to which a wise legislature, untrammelled in its deliberations and decisions, cannot apply an adequate remedy.

7. The decay and distress, for a long series of years, of Spain, Portugal, and Italy, prove, beyond controversy, that no natural advantages, how great or abundant soever, will counteract the baleful effects of unsound systems of policy; and the cotemporaneous prosperity enjoyed by Switzerland, Holland, and Scotland, equally prove, that no natural disadvantages are insuperable by sound policy.

8. Free government is not prosperity. It is only the means,

but, wisely employed, is the certain means of insuring prosperity.

9. The interests of agriculture, manufactures, and commerce, are so inseparably connected, that any serious injury suffered by one of them must materially affect the others.

10. The home market for the productions of the earth and manufactures, is of more importance than all the foreign ones, even in countries which carry on an immense foreign commerce.

11. It is impossible for a nation, possessed of immense natural advantages, in endless diversity of soil and climate—in productions of inestimable value—in the energy and enterprize of its inhabitants—and unshackled by an oppressive debt—to suffer any great or general distress, in its agriculture, commerce, or manufactures, (war, famines, pestilence and calamities of seasons excepted) unless there be vital and radical errors in its system of political economy.

NO. II.

Philadelphia, April 7, 1819.

Further review of Adam Smith's maxims. Their pernicious conferences admitted by himself. Proposed remedy in collateral manufactures and country labour. Futility of the proposition. Ignorance of the nobility, country gentlemen and merchants, asserted by Dr. Smith. Position utterly unfounded.

Dr. Smith's maxim, discussed in our first number, inevitably involves in its consequences, as we have proved, the destruction of those manufacturing establishments, which produce articles that can be purchased "cheaper abroad than they can be made at home;" and its necessary result is, to deprive those engaged in them of employment. The doctor, after having inflicted a deadly wound by this maxim, undertakes to provide a sovereign and infallible remedy for the evil, which, to do him and his system justice, we shall exhibit in his own words:—It remains to examine how far the prescription applies a remedy to the evil.

I. "Though a number of people should, *by restoring the freedom of trade, be thrown all at once out of their ordinary employment, and common method of subsistence*, it would by no "means follow, that they would thereby be deprived either of "employment or subsistence."*

II. "To the *greater part* of manufactures, there are other

* Wealth of Nations, I. 329.

"*collateral manufactures* of so familiar a nature, that a work-
"man can easily *transfer his industry* from one to the other.

III. "The greater part of such workmen, too, are occasion-
"ally employed in *country labour*.

IV. "The stock, which employed them in a particular manu-
"facture before, will still remain in the country, to employ an
"equal number of people in some other way.

V. "*The capital of the country remaining the same, the de-*
"*mand for labour will still be the same*, though it may be exerted
"in different places, and for different occupations.*"

Here are five distinct propositions, more clear and plain than Dr. Smith's usually are; but, as we hope to make appear, all highly erroneous, calculated to lead those statesmen astray, who square their systems by them, and pregnant with ruin to those nations which may be impolitic enough to carry them into operation.

The main point is the facility of "*transferring industry*" from one branch to a "*collateral manufacture*." All the rest are but subsidiary to, or explanatory of this fallacious assumption.

Two questions arise here, both important, and both demanding affirmative answers, in order to support the doctor's hypothesis.

I. Are there such "*collateral manufactures*," as he assumes, in which men, bereft of employment in those departments of manufacture, which are to be destroyed by the doctor's grand and captivating idea of "*restoring the freedom of commerce*," may "*transfer their industry?*"

It may be conceded, that there is a species of affinity between the weaving of cotton and woollen, and a few other manufactures. But this cannot by any means answer the doctor's purpose. Where will he, or any of his disciples, find "*collateral manufactures*," to employ printers, coach-makers, watch-makers, shoemakers, hatters, paper-makers, book-binders, engravers, letter-founders, chandlers, saddlers, silver-platers, jewellers, smiths, cabinet-makers, stone-cutters, glass-makers, brewers, tobacconists, potters, wire-drawers, tanners, curriers, dyers, rope-makers, brick-makers, plumbers, chair-makers, glovers, umbrella-makers, embroiderers, calico-printers, paper-stainers, engine-makers, turners, wheelwrights, and the great variety of other artists and manufacturers? There are no such collateral manufactures as he has presumed. And it may be asserted, without scruple, that if, by what the doctor speciously styles "*restoring the freedom of trade*," five hundred, or a thousand, or ten thousand hatters, shoemakers, printers, or chandlers, are "thrown out of their ordinary employment," there is no "*collateral manufacture of so familiar a nature*," that they "*can easi-*

* Wealth of Nations, I. 330.

ly transfer their industry from one to another." For the truth of this assertion we freely appeal to the common sense of an enlightened public.

We state a case, plain and clear. We will suppose five hundred workmen, and a capital of five hundred thousand dollars, employed in the manufacture of watches, coaches, and silver-plate; and that Switzerland, or Paris, or London, fills our markets at such rates as to overwhelm at once all competition, and suppress the home manufactories, as has often been the case in various branches, in this and other countries. Where are the "*collateral manufactures*," to receive and employ those oppressed and forlorn workmen, whose prospects, and those of their families are thus blasted? Are they to become hatters, or shoemakers, or tailors, or saddlers, or weavers, or smiths, or carpenters? Is there a man who can persuade himself into the belief of such an order of things? Is there a man fatuitous enough to suppose, that "*the general industry of the country will not thereby be diminished?*" No: and it is a matter of inexpressible astonishment, that such an idea could have ever been hazarded, in a sober and serious book, which has been so long regarded as a guide to statesmen and legislators, and as the infallible oracle of political economy. It will not stand the test of a moment's investigation. As well might we suppose, that, on shutting up the courts of justice, and expelling the whole corps of lawyers, they might at once commence the medical or clerical profession, without any previous study, as that hatters, or tailors, or shoemakers, or weavers, or watch-makers, or printers, whom the grand system of "*purchasing commodities cheap*," and the equally grand system of "*restoring the freedom of commerce*," might bereave of employment, should find those "*collateral manufactures*," which Dr. Smith has so kindly provided for them.

We explicitly declare, that we are far from charging the doctor with an intention to mislead or deceive. We believe him, like many other theorists, to have been deluded by his own system. But be this as it may, we trust it will appear that a more deceptious ground never was assumed. We use strong and unequivocal language; as the political heresy we combat is of the most pernicious tendency; is supported by the most imposing and formidable name in the whole range of political science; and, as has been observed, embraces among its disciples a large portion of those of our citizens whose situations as legislators of the Union and of the several states, render their errors on this vital point pregnant with the most destructive and ruinous consequences.

II. Suppose every branch of manufactures, without exception, to have some "*collateral manufacture*," can those who are devested of employment by what is speciously and captivatingly styled "*restoring the freedom of trade*," "*transfer their industry*" so "*easily*" as Dr. Smith assumes?

We answer distinctly, No: or, at all events, on so very small and insignificant a scale, as to be unworthy of notice, in discussions involving the best interests and the happiness of nations. To test the correctness of this opinion, let it be observed, that, in manufacturing countries, all the departments are generally full, and not only full, but there are almost always supernumeraries in abundance: and therefore, even did these "*collateral manufactures*" really exist, to the full extent the doctor's theory would require, and not been "fancy sketches," derived from his fertile imagination, there would be no vacancy, to which the objects of the doctor's care could "*transfer their industry*."

Although this appears so plain and palpable, as not to admit contradiction or dispute, yet, on a point of such magnitude, it cannot be time ill-spent, to illustrate it by example.

There are scarcely any branches between which there is so much affinity as the cotton and woollen. And if the doctor's theory would ever stand the ordeal of examination, it would be in the case of these two "*collateral manufactures*." Suppose, then, that, by the introduction of East India muslins, four or five hundred thousand persons, (about one-half of the whole number engaged in the cotton manufacture) in England, are at once thrown out of employment:—can any man be led to believe, that they could find a vacuum in the "*collateral*" woollen "*manufacture*" to which "*they could easily transfer their industry?*" Fatuity alone could harbour the supposition. They would find all the situations in that branch full and overflowing.

But the strongest argument against the doctor's "*collateral manufactures*," and "*transfers of industry*," remains. He obviously did not calculate the results of his own system, nor take into consideration, that, to give it free operation, its pernicious effect would not be confined to one or two branches of industry. It would extend to the whole mass. The flood of importation on the "*restoration*" of the Doctor's "*freedom of trade*," would bear down in one common ruin, all those manufactures, of which the articles fell within his description of being "purchased cheaper elsewhere." What then becomes of his "*collateral manufactures?*" and "*transfers of industry*," and "*employment of capital*," and all those elegant, sounding phrases, with which he rounds off his paragraphs? Are they not swept away, "like the baseless fabric of a vision," not leaving "a trace behind?"

The doctor with great gravity informs us, that "*the greater part of such workmen are occasionally employed in country labour*." This is most extravagantly erroneous; for of all the manufacturers of England or any other country, there is not probably one in five, who has ever been in his life twelve months at "*country labour.*" Their habits and manners wholly incapacitate them for that kind of employment. A jeweller, a watchmaker, a hatter, a shoemaker, or a weaver, would be almost as unfit for "*country labour,*" as a ploughman, or a gardener, or a shepherd, to make hats or coats.

But suppose, for a moment, through courtesy, that we admit with Dr. Smith, that all these different manufacturers are so much accustomed to "*country labour,*" as to be adepts at it, what inference is to be drawn from the admission? Did the doctor believe, did he intend the world to believe, or does there live a man who can believe, that when, by the grand project of "*restoring the freedom of trade,*" and "*buying commodities from foreign countries,*" which can supply us with them "*cheaper than we ourselves can make them,*" thousands and tens of thousands of people are "*all at once thrown out of their ordinary employment, and common means of subsistence,*" they can find employment at "*country labour?*" However extravagant and childish the idea is, the doctor must have meant this, or the words were introduced without any meaning whatever.

But it is well known, that except in harvest time, there is in the country no want of auxiliaries. The persons attached to farms are generally, at all other seasons, amply adequate to execute all the necessary "*country labour*" without "transferring" to that department the industry of those "manufacturers" who are "*all at once thrown out of their ordinary employment, and common means of subsistence.*"

Dr. Smith, in order to prove the impropriety of those laws, whereby rival manufactures are wholly excluded, observes,

"*If the domestic produce can be brought there as cheap, the regulation is evidently useless. If it cannot, it is evidently hurtful.*"*

This passage is written in a style very different from that usual with Dr. Smith, who is as lavish of words as any writer in the English language, and equally lavish of explanations and amplifications. But here he falls into the contrary extreme, and his brevity renders his positions ambiguous; as he does not condescend to give us the reason for those assertions. He leaves the reader to divine why "*the regulation is useless?*" why "*hurtful?*" We must, therefore, endeavour to explore the meaning. It appears to be, if we understand the first sentence, that "all restrictions or regulations," in favour of domestic industry, to the exclusion of rival manufactures, are "*useless,*" if "*the articles can be made at home as cheap,*" as the imported ones; be-

* Wealth of Nations, I. 319.

cause, in that case, the domestic manufacturer is secure from injury by the competition.

This is extravagantly erroneous. Suppose our woollen manufacturers sell their best broadcloth at eight dollars per yard, and that foreign broadcloth to an immense amount, is imported "*as cheap.*" Is it not obvious, that the glut in the market, and the ardent competition between the two parties, would produce the effect which such a state of things has never failed to produce, that is, a reduction of the price below the minimum at which the manufacturer could support himself by his labours, and that he would therefore be ruined?

We now proceed to consider the last proposition:—

"*The capital of the country remaining the same, the demand "for labour will still be the same, though it be exerted in different "places and in different occupations.*"*

To prove the extreme fallacy of this position, we will take the case of any particular branch, in which there are one hundred master manufacturers, each worth ten thousand dollars, forming together, "*a capital,*" of one million, whose business is destroyed by the "*restoration of the freedom of commerce,*" and "*the purchase of articles from abroad cheaper than we ourselves can make them.*"

It is well known that the property of manufacturers generally consists in buildings for their works, machinery, raw materials, manufactured goods, and outstanding debts. The result of "*the restoration of the freedom of commerce*" on Dr. Smith's plan, would be to reduce the value of the four first items, from twenty to fifty per cent, and to bankrupt a large proportion of the proprietors.

As this is a point of considerable importance, we shall take a single instance, which is always more easily comprehended than a number, and yet affords as clear an illustration.

We will suppose the case of a tanner, worth thirty thousand dollars, of which his various vats, buildings, and tools amount to ten thousand; his hides and leather, ten thousand; and his outstanding debts, an equal sum. By the inundation of foreign leather, sold, we will suppose, far below the price which affords him a reasonable profit, or even a reimbursement of his expenses, he is unable to carry on his business, which sinks the value of his vats and buildings three fourths, and of his stock one-half. At once, his fortune is reduced above twelve thousand dollars: and thus, with a diminished capital and broken heart, perhaps in his old age, he has to go in quest of, but will not find, a "*collateral manufacture,*" to employ that diminished capital.—Analogous cases without number would occur, by the doctor's

* Wealth of Nations, I. 330.

system of "*restoring the freedom of trade:*" and let us add, as we can with perfect truth, and we hope it will sink deep into the minds of the citizens of the United States, that throughout this country there are numberless cases equally strong, which no man of sound mind and heart can regard without the deepest sympathy for the ill-fated sufferers, and regret at the mistaken policy which produced such a state of things.

It therefore irresistibly follows, that Dr. Smith's idea, that "*the capital of the country will be the same,*" after the destruction of any branch of manufacture, is to the last degree unsound: and, of course, that the superstructure built on it partakes of its fallacy.

The doctor gravely informs us, "*The tailor does not make his* "*own shoes, but buys them of the shoemaker. The shoemaker* "*does not attempt to make his own clothes, but employs a tailor.*"* And he adds farther:

"By means of glasses, hot-beds, and hot-walls, very good "grapes can be raised in Scotland, and very good wine too "can be made of them, at about thirty times the expense for "which at least equally good can be brought from foreign coun- "tries. Would it be a reasonable law to prohibit the importa- "tion of all foreign wines, merely to encourage the making of "Claret and Burgundy in Scotland?"†

From these positions, to which no man can refuse assent, he deduces the specious, but delusory maxim of "*restoring the freedom of trade,*" which, in fact and in truth, is nothing more or less than opening the door to the admission of foreign goods to an unbounded extent, to the ruin of the citizens or subjects engaged in the manufacture of articles of a similar description—and thereby impoverishing the nation, and sacrificing its domestic industry at the shrine of avarice, in order to purchase goods "*cheaper than they can be made at home.*"

But by what process of sound reasoning does it follow, because the shoemaker will not become a tailor, or the tailor a shoemaker; or because it would be extravagant folly to exclude foreign wines, in order to introduce the culture of the vine into Scotland, a country wholly unfit for that object; that therefore thousands of men employed in useful branches of business, diffusing happiness among tens of thousands of workmen and their numerous families, and enriching their country, are to have their usefulness destroyed, their prospects blasted, their workmen with their families reduced to distress, and the country exposed to a ruinous drain of specie?

These maxims are the basis on which a large portion, indeed the most important part of Dr. Smith's work, depends. If the

* Wealth of Nations, I. 320. † Idem, 320.

basis be solid and impregnable, the fabric will stand firm: but if the foundation be sandy, the superstructure will crumble into ruins. We trust we have fully proved that the foundation is sandy; and that the necessary and inevitable consequence follows, that the theory itself is wholly untenable and pernicious.

With one more extract, we shall conclude this review:

"That foreign trade enriched the country, experience demon-" "strated to the nobles and country gentlemen, as well as to the" "merchants; but, *how, or in what manner, none of them knew!*" "The merchants knew perfectly in what manner it enriched" "themselves. It was their business to know it. But *to know*" "*in what manner it enriched the country, was no part of their*" "*business!* The subject never came into their consideration," "but when they had occasion to apply to their country for some" "change in the laws respecting foreign trade."*

It is hardly possible to conceive a passage more absurd or erroneous than this. That "*the nobles, and country gentlemen, and merchants,*" were ignorant "*how foreign trade enriched their country,*" is almost too ludicrous to be assailed by argument, and is a strong instance of the delirium, in which enthusiastic theorists are liable to be involved, by the ignis fatuus of their visionary views. Can there be found a man, in the wide extent of the United States, to believe that sir Joshua Gee, Josiah Child, Theodore Janssen, Charles King, Thomas Willing, Robert Morris, George Clymer, Thomas Fitzsimons, Governeur and Kemble, and the thousands of other merchants, of equal mind, who have flourished in Great Britain and this country, could be ignorant "*in what manner foreign commerce enriched a country,*" without the aid of the Wealth of Nations? It is impossible. Take any man of sound mind, who has followed the plough, or driven the shuttle, or made shoes all his life, and clearly state the operations of trade to him, and he will rationally account for the "*manner in which foreign trade enriches a country.*" Indeed a merchant's apprentice of six months standing, could not mistake "*the manner.*" Any one of them would at once pronounce, that foreign trade enriches a country, exactly as farmers, planters, or manufacturers are enriched; that is, by the very simple process of *selling more than they buy.* No nation ever was, none will ever be enriched in any other way. And it is unaccountable that Dr. Smith should have supposed that it was reserved for him to make the grand discovery. The principle was well understood by the merchants of Tyre 3000 years before Adam Smith was born. And if Spain be one of the most forlorn and wretched countries in Europe, it has not arisen from ignorance of the true principles of political econo-

* Wealth of Nations, I. 303.

my, but from neglecting them, as well as the counsels of her wisest statesmen. Ustariz, who flourished about a hundred years ago, in that ill-fated and impoverished country, has ably developed the grand principles of that noble science, in a system as far superior to Dr. Smith's as the constitution of the United States is superior to the form of government of Spain.

Postscript, October 23, 1821.

[The grand point, on which the political economists of the new and old school are at issue, is the unlimited freedom, or the qualified restriction of Commerce: the disciples of the new school contending for the former, as the best means of promoting national prosperity and happiness, and the adverse party contending for such restrictions as raised England to that height of power which she now possesses, and to that prosperity which she enjoyed till her wild and wasteful wars crippled her resources, impaired her prosperity, and entailed on her an enormous debt, with a most burdensome and oppressive taxation—such restrictions, in fine, as retrieved the desperate circumstances in which France was sunk, when subjugated by the Holy Alliance. In corroboration of the doctrines advanced on this vital topic in the preceding pages [written in March, 1819] I am happy to be able to adduce the powerful testimony and unanswerable arguments, of the Quarterly Review for January 1821, which are respectfully submitted to the consideration of the statesmen of the United States.]

[" Questions of commercial policy have been lately treated in " so abstract a manner that their connection with common life " and practice seems to be entirely forgotten. Speculative wri- " ters send forth from their closets general propositions and " paradoxical dogmas upon matters relative to the common in- " ercourse of the world, with the most confident affirmation of " their universal applicability. They find supporters in persons " of rank and influence, pleased with this sort of 'royal road to " geometry;' while practical men, too much occupied to weigh " theoretical notions of this difficult nature, or to examine their " operation in the varied and conflicting movements of traffic " and national interests, add their conclusive assent. The adopt- " ed opinions thus acquire general reception, and are promul- " gated as undisputed and unconditional truth, and the sole " panacea for existing evils.

[" Our forefathers could not maintain with greater zeal, that a " favourable balance of trade and an abundant circulation of the " precious metals were essential to prosperity, than has recently " been manifested for the necessity of universal freedom of " trade, with a view to the attainment of the same object."*

* Quarterly Review, No. 48, page 281.

[" In the conversion of unwrought into wrought commodities " lies the great field in which legislators have endeavoured to " appropriate by regulations—understood to operate as encou- " ragements—the largest portion of skilful industry and pro- " duction.

[" It has been by means of complete prohibition, or the conve- " nient expedient of taxes on importation, that governments have " aimed to effect this appropriation of wealth. The duties im- " posed upon commodities which we cannot produce, as cotton, " rice, coffee, are to be considered as merely financial: such as " are laid upon productions common to the growth of this coun- " try, as flax, wool, deals, are protective as well as financial. " The prohibition and duties laid upon some raw, and all " wrought articles, are designed to advance the home produc- " tion and manufacture; as in the instance of grain, wrought " wool, linen, cotton, silk, refined sugar."*

[" With regard to wrought goods, the manufacture of which " requires small space and occupies a numerous and usually " wealthy population, giving much value in a little bulk, it has " been held the soundest policy to engross the largest possible " portion of such productions. Either all foreign fabrics have " been prohibited, or duties have been placed upon their intro- " duction so heavy as to exclude the chance of an equal compe- " tition with the home manufacture.

[" *These principles of restriction, exclusion, and encouragement,* " *occurred at periods of the earliest application of the mind to the* " *means of advancing the public wealth, and have been the rule of* " *conduct for governments for centuries past.* They appear in " the oldest enactments of the statute book, commencing with " our first Edwards and Henrys; were long inculcated as in- " controvertible, and at this day prevail in every stage of so- " ciety:—in China and Turkey, in England, France, and the " United States, the most ancient and the last instituted;—un- " der every form, the freest and the most arbitrary governments " alike act upon the system.

[" This has been tenaciously adhered to in practice, though " for more than half a century all writers upon commercial po- " licy have held an opposite argument; every one, from the time " of Quesnay and Smith, however differing on other points, " agreeing in this one principle, that general freedom of trade " is the surest and most rapid way to wealth. It is maintained " that to force the consumer to pay dearer for home productions " than he can purchase from abroad, is not to promote the na- " tional advantage, but the interest of the producer at the ex- " pense of that of the consumer. It is asserted, that the freest

* Quarterly Review, No. 48, page 282.

"admission of foreign products and manufactures will best as-"sist, in the early stages of society, the progress of agriculture, "till the accumulation of capital necessarily raises manufac-"tures, foreign commerce, and navigation. In the advanced "state, every individual, intent on the increase of his own ad-"vantage and fortunes, and left to the unrestrained pursuit of "his interest, will follow it with most zeal and effect: and from "prevalent private success results the general prosperity.

["A main principle insisted upon by the advocates of freedom "of commerce, is, that no industry or source of wealth is lost by "the declension or disappearance of a home manufacture, in con-"sequence of the opening of the country to the admission of a "like foreign fabric possessing a superiority; because some-"thing must be given in payment for the new importation, and "the labourers in the declining manufacture will transfer them-"selves to the production of this other object required to effect "the exchange.

["The truth of this position rests upon the power of the home "manufacturer to find occupation in some other labour, which "will afford the value wanted to give in exchange for the new "foreign imports. We must retain yet in our possession a suf-"ficient diversity of departments of industry, or some of so much "magnitude as to receive the labourers dislodged from their usu-"al employment by the introduction of foreign commodities. It "can hardly be expected that any material new opening for la-"bour can at this day be discovered; those remaining depart-"ments of industry, therefore, must be productive of objects, "which will be received in other countries to an extent to pay "for our new importations; and those increased in proportion "to our transferred labour."]*

["The transition from one description of labour to another "would not be easy. *A man accustomed for a number of years* "*to a particular kind of work, cannot readily pass over to another* "*altogether different.* Persons, especially of the class of life of "artizans and labourers, are slow to form and slow to change "their habits; the skill which they tardily acquire, they tena-"ciously adhere to, and come with difficulty to learn any other. "A farmer's labourer will not readily become a mechanic; a "silk-weaver be made a cutler; a lace-maker or glover be con-"verted into a maker of woollens."

["*Not only would a change of occupation be requisite, but also* "*of the seat of industry.* The Norfolk farming labourer might "have to make hose in Leicester or Nottingham; the East Lo-"thian cottager to weave muslins at Glasgow or checks at Car-"lisle; and the Spitalfields weaver to become a japanner at Bir-

* Quarterly Review, No. 48, page 283.

" mingham or a cotton spinner at Manchester. Whole districts " of Ireland might have to interchange residence with those of " England and Scotland, the north with the south, and the east " with the west, with the rapidity of a horde of Tartars. *There " must be a transference of the disengaged people to the seats of " retained manufacture, or the retained manufacture must extend " to their residence.* The latter is scarcely practicable, when the " convenience or necessity is considered of concentration, in " manufacturing industry, of the several connected processes and " branches.

[" The advocates of freedom of trade meet this objection by " inculcating a gradual change, according to the nature of the " industry which they see must be lost. If the silk and kersey- " mere weavers cannot convert their skill to a beneficial use in " other employments, they are willing to allow a period equal " to the probable lives of the silk and kerseymere weavers. " Even then the opening of a foreign import of silk and kersey- " mere must overtake numbers of those exercising these trades; " and it will be incumbent, first, to inquire whether this positive " loss is likely to be accompanied with any commensurate bene- " fit.

[" While the peculiar skill of many trades cannot be turned " to any other manufacture, the capital to a considerable extent, " which employs that skill, and which is, in a great degree, fixed " in machinery, buildings, implements, &c. *is applicable to no " other object, and must be lost.* In the uncertainty, with all quar- " ters of the world open, how far a manufacture may be affected, " *the capital in many branches will be retained in a delusive hope " till it decays within the hand.* The knowledge of a particular " business which is frequently conjoined with capital, and leaves " a double advantage in the remuneration of the skill and the " interest of the money, causes an unwillingness to remove to " other departments of industry, in ignorance of their nature " and with but a chance of improvement. In such transitions, " especially in the smaller, which, in the aggregate, form the " most considerable portion of capital, more is wasted than " transferred; and all is commonly wrecked in the gulf of " bankruptcy."*]

[" Freedom of trade seems more peculiarly to favour the in- " terests of merchants trading with foreign states, and most to " prejudice certain branches of manufacture and agriculture; " but of the labour constituting wealth,—*the commercial, which " interchanges commodities, however useful and important,—is " still subordinate to the manufacturing and agricultural, which " produce those commodities:* and the greater the produce of agri-

* Quarterly Review, No. 48, page 285.

"culture and manufacture, which is raised and interchanged in "a given country, the greater must be its affluence "*

[" The slightest examination of the history of commerce "shews *how many manufactures*, *and also natural productions of "homogeneous climates*, *have owed their introduction amongst a "people to special encouragement*, and have risen by protection "till they flourished in self-supported excellence and extension. "Because interference and encouragements may be carried to an "extreme, are they, therefore, in all cases, impolitic and inju- "rious? Are governments to be considered as having done "every thing, when, in fact, they have done nothing whatever?"†

"A superiority in a manufacture arises from skill, the result "of manual dexterity, of chemical or mechanical ability, indi- "vidual or co operative. This, at times, will proceed from ac- "cident, or, when numbers are engaged in an employment, it "will occur to the observing and reflecting: it becomes mani- "fest in the qualities of finer texture, in brighter or more per- "manent colours, and in method of finishing. These are nice- "ties and refinements, the effect of long labour and attention "applied in a particular direction. *It may be the interest of a nation "to preserve within itself*, *when at a moderate cost of restriction*, "*the rudiments of all manufactures. Practice will confer skill*, "*opportunity give rise to invention*, *and perseverance and the "growth of wealth bestow importance and stability*."‡

[" Florence owed her splendour to the woollen manufacture, "with which she supplied the world."] ***** [" The spirit of "the woollen manufacture, by a kind of Pythagorean transmi- "gration, now resides in France, Flanders, and England. How "has it escaped from Florence? *Can any reason be assigned "but the absence of a sufficient safeguard from external intrusion "and subversion?*"§

[" The favourite idea of our political economists is to banish "regulations, and to leave every species of industry to its own di- "rection. They dwell on the course which wealth naturally takes "in its free progress to its greatest height, through the various sta- "ges of society, from the hunter, through the pastoral, agricul- "tural, manufacturing, and commercial state. They hold every "interruption to perfect freedom to be prejudicial to the speediest "advance. *They beg the question of a never-failing activity and "love of accumulation;* they count not on the disposition to in- "dolence, the contentment with little, taught and actually prac- "tised by so many; the calls of religion; the love of pleasure; "the passion for honour overcoming that for wealth: all which "may arrest the advance of public opulence in its free course

* Quarterly Review, No. 48, page 292. † Idem, page 293.
‡ Idem, page 295. § Idem, page 296.

"through the early and middle stages. We would call into ac-"tion more motives than one. Individual exertion, on our adop-"tion of liberty of trade, may not be allowed free play: if home "regulations do not cramp it, external arts and rivalry will.

"If we endeavour to ascertain the result of freedom of trade "in the commercial history of the world, it will, we believe, be "found that *its effects have not been to create any material "branches of manufactures, nor yet to retain those previously pos-"sessed.* It has, in fact, proved rather favourable to commerce "than to manufactures. *Italy, once the seat of numerous manu-"factures, which admits all foreign goods upon moderate duties, "has nothing remaining but some small fabrics of silk goods.* "Switzerland receives foreign manufactures, and possesses a few "herself; but these have probably arisen from the forced situa-"tion of the war—she had none previously. Hume remarks "'that agriculture may flourish even where manufactures and "other arts are unknown and neglected. Switzerland is, at "present, a remarkable instance; where we find at once the most "skilful husbandmen and the most bungling tradesmen that are "to be met with in Europe.'* *Many small territories and is-"lands are to be observed in different parts of the globe enjoying "absolute liberty of commerce, Humburgh, Lisbon, Malta, Guern-"sey, St. Thomas, &c. yet no manufactures have been found to "mix amongst them;* and though possessed of certain portions "of commerce, this may be ascribed more to favourable position, "or vicinity to countries under restriction, than to any inherent "virtue of an open commerce.

["The doctrine of free trade has something very generous in "its professions. It aims to remove all impediments and ob-"structions on the intercourse of nations; to withdraw much "complication in government with regard to legal enactments, "to customs, and custom-house officers; to prevent the callous "commission of vice in a profusion of oaths, of smuggling, "and other encroachments on revenue; with endless jealousies "and contentions of trade. In these feelings we participate: "and *could the dreams of the theorists be verified, we would wil-"lingly enter into the adoption of that entire liberty of trade "which was to lead to the realization of them.* But many of "the evils enumerated are inseparable from the constitution of "society; *laws are possibly as necessary to the protection of na-"tional industry as they are to that of individual property;* the "safeguards and resources of the revenue must be maintained. "If wealth be an essential part of power and a security of inde-"pendence, we must admit and establish the system best fitted "for its preservation. Narrow, malignant, or hostile feelings

* Essay XI. On the populousness of Ancient Nations.

" spring from the mind, and not from the existence of restric-
" tions of self-defence or patriotic encouragement. If ill pas-
" sions are bred by prohibitive regulations, their removal might
" lead to others of a nature not more benevolent—abjectness,
" sense of inferiority, and of inability to protect ourselves."*]

[" *It is a strong reason to doubt the practicability of these*
" *schemes, that statesmen have no where ventured upon them;*
" *not from ignorance, as has been petulantly pretended, but from*
" *extended knowledge.* Neither in old nor new states, do legis-
" latures find the Utopian ideas of these philosophers to be fea-
" sible: yet Adam Smith, the great advocate for the most unre-
" stricted trade, is read in all countries and languages, and his
" doctrines have been moulded into all shapes, *whether to in-*
" *form youth or puzzle the learned!!!* Reflection and practice
" seem to show, that this valuable writer, in the zeal of his ar-
" gument, *carried too far his views of freedom of trade, as he as-*
" *suredly did those of unlimited production and unrestrained par-*
" *simony.*"†]

It is impossible attentively to read this reasoning, without a thorough conviction of the futility of the remedy proposed for the destruction of particular branches of industry by free importation, in Adam Smith's "*collateral branches*" and "*country labour.*"

NO. III.

Philadelphia, April 12, 1819.

Policy of Great Britain. Extracts from British tariff of 1818. *Wonderful profits of the British nation by manufactures. American system compared with that of Great Britain.*

We proceed to take a view *of that portion of the system of political economy pursued in England, which regards the protection of her manufacturing industry*, and which has elevated that country to a degree of wealth, power, and influence, far beyond that to which her population or natural resources would entitle her. This part of her system displays profound policy and wisdom, and may with safety be taken as a pattern by other nations, with such variations as particular circumstances may require. We do not pretend that it is altogether perfect; nothing human ever deserved this character. But that it has more excellence than, and as little imperfection as, that of any other na-

* Quarterly Review, No. 48, page 300. † Idem page 301.

tion in ancient or modern times, can hardly be questioned. The nearer any nation approximates to its leading principles, the more certain its career to prosperity. Indeed, it is not hazarding much to aver, that no nation ever did or ever will arrive at the degree of power, or influence, or happiness, of which it is susceptible, without adopting a large portion of her plan of protecting the industry of her subjects. There are parts of her system, however, which are "more honoured in the breach than the observance:" we mean those, particularly, which restrain personal liberty, in preventing the emigration of artists and mechanics.

The grand and leading object of this system, into which all its subordinate regulations resolve themselves, is to encourage domestic industry, and to check and restrain whatever may injure it. This pervades the whole political economy of the nation ; and as industry has ever been, and, according to the fixed laws of nature, must eternally be, a great security to virtue and happiness, this is among the primary duties of every legislative body : and their neglect of, or attention to, this duty, affords an unerring criterion of their merits or demerits. To enable her to effect this object, Great Britain is unwearied in her efforts—

I. To facilitate the importation of raw materials, for the employment of her artisans and manufacturers ;

II. To discourage, or wholly prohibit, the exportation of raw materials ;

III. To export her manufactures in the most finished form possible ;

IV. To secure her own manufacturers from the ruinous effects of foreign rivalship ;

V. To prohibit the emigration of artists and mechanics, and the exportation of machinery.

To accomplish these purposes, she has steadily employed the powerful means of—

1. Bounties on, or encouragement to, the establishment of new manufactures ;

2. Absolute prohibitions, or such heavy duties as nearly amount to prohibition on the importation of such articles as interfere with her own manufactures :

3. Drawbacks, on exportation, of the whole or chief part of the excise paid on the various articles, or on the raw materials of which they are composed.

All great undertakings, such as the establishment of extensive manufactures, require heavy disbursements previous to their commencing operations ; and in their incipient state are attended with great difficulty, in consequence of which they too frequently fail of success in all countries, and involve the undertakers in ruin. While they are in this perilous situation, the aid of government is necessary, and wisdom commands to afford it.

Small temporary sacrifices are abundantly compensated, by immense permanent national advantages. We shall furnish noble instances of this kind, on a large and liberal scale, worthy of a great nation, when we enter on the discussion of the policy of Prussia.

It was by these means that the woollen manufacture was first established in England. Edward III. a most sagacious prince, held out great inducements to the manufacturers in that branch to remove from Flanders to England. "*Very great privileges* "*were granted, and pensions were allowed to them from the* "*crown, till they should be able to gain a comfortable livelihood* "*by their ingenuity and industry.*"*

Further to favour and foster this infant manufacture, the exportation of wool, and the importation of foreign cloth were prohibited.†

Such was the degree of care and attention undeviatingly bestowed on it, that "in the short and turbulent reign of Henry IV." who reigned but fourteen years, and was almost constantly at war, "there were no fewer than twelve acts of parliament "made for the regulation and encouragement of that manufac- "ture; for preventing the exportation of wool and importation of "cloth; and for guarding against frauds in the fabrication of it "at home."*

It is obvious that the continuance of bounties beyond the infancy of manufactures, would be oppressive to a nation, and waste its treasures. And therefore as soon as they are fully established, the English government usually adopts a cheaper and equally effectual mode of fostering them, by the prohibition of the rival articles, or by the imposition of such heavy duties as nearly to amount to prohibition, and thus securing to its own subjects the whole or principal part of the domestic market.

In the year 1463, under Edward IV. the wisdom and policy of fostering domestic industry, having become generally understood, the prohibition of importation, which had previously been confined chiefly to woollens, was extended to a very great variety of articles, viz:

Woollen caps	Andirons	Buskins
Woollen cloths	Gridirons	Shoes
Laces	Locks	Galoches
Rings of copper, or latten gilt	Dice	Combs
	Tennice balls	Pattens
Chaffing dishes	Points	Pack-needles
Crosses	Purses	Painted ware
Ribands	Globes	Forcers

* Henry's History of Great Britain, X. 187.
* Mortimer's Elements of Commerce, p. 16.
† Anderson's History of Commerce, I. 401.

Fringes of Silk
Ditto of thread
Laces of thread
Silk-twined
Silk in anywise embroidered
Laces of gold
Ditto of Silk and gold
Saddles
Stirrups
All harness pertaining to saddles
Spurs
Bosses for bridles
Hammers
Pincers
Fire tongs
Girdles
Harness for girdles, of iron, latten, steel, tin, or alkemine
Any thing wrought of tanned leather
Any tanned furs
Corks
Knives
Daggers
Sword blades
Bodkins
Shears
Scissors
Razors
Chessmen
Playing cards
Caskets
Chaffing balls
Hanging candlesticks
Rings for curtains
Ladles
Scummers
Sacring-bells
Counterfeit basins
Ewers
Hat brushes
Wool-cards
White wire

If detected in the importation, they were to be forfeited, one half to the king and the other to the informer.*

Under Charles II. the prohibition was extended to

Wool-cards
Card-wire
Iron-wire
Dripping-pans
Bone-lace
Cut-work
Embroidery
Fringe
Buttons
Button or needle work†

The list of articles at present prohibited to be imported into Great Britain, is not quite so extensive as that of Edward IV. They are as follows:—

Brocades
Calicoes
Chocolate and Cocoa paste
Cocoa nut shells or husks
Embroidery
Silk
Silk stockings
Thread
Fringe
Girdles
Silk or leather mits and gloves
Manufactures of gold, silver, or metal
Tobacco stalks and snuff work
Velvet
Laces
Needle work
Plate
Ribands
Laces
Shapes for gloves or mits
Wire‡

The penalties for the importation of some of those articles are very severe. For example, besides the confiscation of the goods, there is a forfeiture of two hundred pounds sterling for every offence in the case of leather gloves.

The most general mode, however, of encouraging domestic industry in Great Britain, at present, is by the imposition of such heavy duties as in most cases amount to prohibition; or if the rival articles will still admit of importation, they cannot, from the necessary advance of price, materially affect the native manufacturer. We annex a list of some of the articles, thus protected, with the amount of the duties imposed on them.

Extracts from the British Tariff of 1818.

Articles subject to duty of 59*l*. 7*s*. 6*d*. per 100*l*. value.

Baskets
Musical instruments
Nuts
Oil of pine
Oils not particularly enumerated
Almond paste
Dressing-boxes
Snuff-boxes
Manufactures of brass
Pens
Pomatum
Telescopes
Thread, not otherwise enumerated
Turnery, not otherwise enumerated

* Anderson's History of Commerce, I. 636.
† Postlethwaite's Dictionary of Commerce, I. 975.
‡ Pope's Practical Abridgment of the Laws of Customs and Excise. Title 284.

Paintings on glass
Pencils
Pieces of skins and furs
Spouts of wood
Statues, except of marble or stone
Steel not otherwise enumerated
Ticking
Ticks
Tin-foil
Tooth-powder
Toys
Tubes for smoaking
Tubs
Watches
Stone pots
Coloured paper and prints
Sago powder
Scratch brushes
Seeds not particularly enumerated
Silk-worm guts
Skates
Skins and furs
Walking sticks
Thread or worsted stockings
Filtering stones
Open tapes
Worsted tapes
Tapestry, not of silk
Vases, except of stone or marble
Wicker-ware
Silver, gilt, or plated wire
Worsted yarn
Goods of all kinds, in part or wholly manufactured.
Bronze figures
Worsted caps
Carpets
Carriages
Clocks
Manufactures of copper
Copperplates engraved, &c. &c.

To 31*l.* 13*s.* 4*d.* per 100*l.*

Chalk
Copper in pigs
Hoofs of cattle
Horns
Silk laces
Pig lead
Cast iron
Minerals not otherwise enumerated
Polishing rushes
Ships with their tackle
Lime-stone
Polishing stones
Rag stones
Tanners' waste
Tare
Touchstone

To 79*l.* 3*s.* 4*d.* per 100*l.*

China ware
Earthen ware
Shawls
Tobacco pipes

To 63*l.* 6*s.* 8*d.* per 100*l.*

Linen, not being chequered or striped
Gause of thread

To 85*l.* 10*s.* per 100*l.*

Cotton stockings
Cotton caps
Cotton thread
Linen sails.

To 114*l.* per 100*l.*

Glass bottles, Rough plate glass, German sheet glass, Glass manufactures.

To 142*l.* 10*s.* per 100*l.*

Leather fan mounts
Linens chequered or striped, painted, or stained
Skins or furs, tanned, tawed, curried, or any way dressed.
Articles made of leather
Articles whereof leather is the most valuable part.
Hides, or pieces of hides, tanned tawed, or in any way dressed.

An idea has been long entertained, by many well meaning people, that to secure the home market to our own manufacturers, operates merely to enable them to prey on and oppress their fellow-citizens, by extorting extravagant and exorbitant prices for their productions. And hence many of our planters and farmers in congress have uniformly opposed duties for the mere purpose of protecting manufactures. There are some who have openly avowed, that their sole view in laying impost duties, is to provide a revenue for the expenses of the government. And a writer of considerable celebrity, John Taylor, esq. of Caroline county, Virginia, has devoted a number of chapters of his Arator, to prove that every dollar given by a nation as bounty, or imposed as duty, to protect domestic manufactures, is a dollar robbed from the pockets of the farmers and planters!

It is a trite but indisputable truth, that one solid, well-established fact, bearing upon any particular point, will countervail a long train of arguments, however plausible, which militate against that fact. Behold a case, which must operate to open the eyes of every man accessible to conviction. There is probably no country in the world, where the system of heavy prohibitory duties is carried farther than in England : and yet, notwithstanding this circumstance, and the enormous burden of taxation which she sustains, as well as the boundless extent of her paper money, which must enhance the expenses of living, she is able to meet in their own markets, and undersell, a large portion of the manufacturers of all the other nations of Christendom. This fact sets the question at rest forever; and establishes, on the firmest basis, the luminous maxim of Alexander Hamilton, a maxim that ought to be written in letters of gold, and affixed in a conspicuous place in the hall of congress, that powerful body, on whose wisdom or errors depends the prosperity or decay of a mighty empire:—

"*Though it were true, that the immediate and certain effect* "*of regulations controlling the competition of foreign with do*-"*mestic fabrics was an increase of price, it is universally true,* "*that* THE CONTRARY IS THE ULTIMATE EFFECT WITH EVERY "SUCCESSFUL MANUFACTURE. *When a domestic manufacture* "*has attained to perfection, and has engaged in the prosecution of* "*it a competent number of persons,* IT INVARIABLY BECOMES "CHEAPER. *Being free from the heavy charges which attend* "*the importation of foreign commodities, it can be afforded cheap*-"*er, and accordingly seldom or never fails to be sold cheaper, in* "*process of time, than was the foreign article for which it is a* "*substitute. The internal competition which takes place, soon* "*does away every thing like monopoly; and by degress* REDUCES "THE PRICE OF THE ARTICLE TO THE MINIMUM OF A REASONA-"BLE PROFIT ON THE CAPITAL EMPLOYED. *This accords with* "*the reason of the thing, and with experience.*"*

The true tests of the excellence or folly of any system, are its results, when carried fully into operation. These confirm sound theories, however unpopular they may appear on a superficial view; and set the seal of reprobation on pernicious ones, how plausible soever an aspect they wear on paper.

By this touchstone, let us judge the political economy of England, respecting her manufactures; and, on a fair examination, we shall unhesitatingly bestow the most unqualified plaudits on her parliament, for the admirable and incomparable system it has devised. We may fairly assert, without the least danger of contradiction, that there never existed a legislative body which bestowed more attention on the solid, substantial, and vital interests of its constituents, *so far as respects national industry in all its various forms.*

* Hamilton's works, I. 212.

We might extend the consideration of the wonderful excellence, and immense advantages of the policy of Great Britain respecting manufactures, trade, and commerce, to volumes. The subject appears inexhaustible. But our limits forbid much detail, and constrain us to confine ourselves to two points:—

I. The immense wealth she acquires by this system ; and

II. The astonishing increase of power it has secured her.

I. We shall, on the first point, confine ourselves to the four great manufactures, linen, cotton, woollen, and leather, and make no doubt, the statement will astonish our fellow-citizens, and remove all doubt of the correctness of the eulogiums we have hazarded on the British political economy.

According to Colquhoun*, the annual proceeds of the cotton manufacture are		£ 29,000,000
The woollen		26,000,000
The linen		15,000,000
The leather		15,000,000
Total		£ 85,000,000
Whereas the raw materials of the cotton cost	£ 6,000,000	
The woollen	8,000,000	
The linen	5,000,000	
The leather	3,000,000	
		£ 22,000,000
Balance		£ 63,000,000

Thus a gain is secured to the nation of 63,000,000 of pounds sterling, or above 270,000,000 of dollars annually. This at once solves the mystery of the wonderful "*power and resources*" of Great Britain, and establishes beyond controversy the wisdom of its policy, which is, in every respect, let us observe, the antipodes of the doctrines of Adam Smith in the Wealth of Nations.

What stupendous facts! What a lesson to the legislators of other countries, particularly the United States! We possess the capacity of raising the raw materials of the cotton manufacture, the chief of the four kinds above stated, to an extent commensurate with the demand of the whole world ; and we could, with ease, if proper encouragement were offered, produce the materials of the other three, in sufficient quantity for all our purposes.

* Treatise on the wealth, power, and resources of the British Empire, p. 91

II. The second point, to which we wish to turn the attention of our fellow-citizens, in order to establish the soundness of the system of political economy, *respecting her manufactures*, pursued in England, is the wonderful increase of power it has secured her.

For twenty years she was the main support of a war of unexampled expenditure, against the most gigantic combination of power, and the most formidable monarch, that Europe has beheld for a thousand years. Her resources alone prevented him from arriving at universal empire. She not only preserved herself from the loss of her possessions, but conquered colonies and dependencies of her enemies, of great extent and immense value. Her revenue for the year 1812, was about 63 500,000*l.** and in the same year her expenditure was above 112,000,000*l.*†

During the whole of this war, she was not obliged to borrow money from any other nation; but made large loans to several. She has subsidized some of the first-rate monarchs in Europe.

Her enormous debt, which, according to Colquhoun, amounted at the close of 1813, to above 900,000,000 .‡ is wholly owned by her own subjects, except about 17,000,000*l.* purchased and owned by foreigners.

It is no impeachment to the merits of her system, that her paupers amount to above 1,500,000, and her poor tax to 6,000,000*l.* sterling, equal to 26,000,000 of dollars.§ This lamentable feature in her affairs, arises partly from the labour of the working class being superseded by machinery, and partly from the wasteful and ruinous wars she has maintained, which alone have prevented the country from being an earthly paradise.

Since our recent war, she has been enabled to lay this country under heavy contribution, so that there is an enormous debt due her, notwithstanding she has possessed herself of a very large portion of our bank and other public stocks, in payment for her manufactures, which will yield her a great and permanent income, at the expense of the United States.

To her suppport of domestic industry alone, she chiefly owes these capacities and advantages, and the inordinate power she possesses. Were she to abandon her system, and adopt that of Adam Smith, she could not fail, in a few years, to be reduced to a level with Spain and Portugal. All her treasures would be drawn away to the East-Indies, France, Germany, &c.

We shall close with a comparison between her policy and that of the United States, on a few plain and simple points:

* Colquhoun on the wealth, power, and resources of the British Empire, p. 258.

† Idem, 261.

‡ Page 273. He states, however, in this page, that 236,000,000*l.* of this debt have been redeemed.

§ Idem, 125.

GREAT BRITAIN	THE UNITED STATES
Prohibits the importation of calicoes, silks, threads, ribands, velvets, &c. even from her own dependencies. (See page 43.)	Prohibit no manufactured articles whatev :r, however great the capacity of our citizens to supply them.
She imposes a duty of 85 per cent. ad valorem on various articles of cotton, the production of those dependencies.	They admit all cotton fabrics, of every denomination, from Great Britian *and her dependencies,* and any other part of the globe, at 27 1-2 per cent. (except those below 25 cents per square yard, which are dutied as at 25 cents.)
She imposes a duty of 79 per cent. ad valorem on earthenware.	Although they could supply themselves superabundantly with earthenware, *they admit it at 22 per cent!*
She imposes a duty of 142 1-2 per cent, on leather manufactures.	They admit leather manufactures at 33 per cent.

COMPARISON CONTINUED.

BRITISH DUTIES.	UNITED STATES' DUTIES.
Woollen cloths, per yard, 34*s*. sterling, equal to about 7 dolls. 50 cts.	27 1-2 per cent. ad valorem.
Hats, per piece, 34*s*. or 7dolls. 50cts.	33 per cent.
Glass bottles, 114 per cent.	22 per cent.
Linens, not chequered or striped, 63 per cent.	16 1-2 per cent.
Linens, chequered or striped 142 per cent.	16 1-2 per cent.

The annals of legislation and revenue cannot produce a stronger constrast between the most profound policy and its direct opposite.

Thus we see that Great Britain, possessing machinery which increases her powers of manufacturing at the rate of two hundred for one, does not rely on it for the protection of her domestic manufactures, but interposes the powerful shield of prohibition and enormous duties, to preserve them from danger; while the United States, which had, at the close of the war, a great number of important and extensive manufacturing establishments, and invaluable machinery, erected and advantageously employed during its continuance, and although blessed by a bounteous heaven with a boundless capacity for such establishments, have, for want of adequate protection, suffered a large portion of them to go to decay, and their proprietors to be involved in ruin, the helpless victims of a misplaced reliance on that protection!

The comparison might be pursued to a very great extent: but we trust there is enough stated to enable our fellow-citizens to account for the prostrate situation of our affairs. No two nations ever carried on intercourse on terms more entirely destitute of reciprocity: and hence our citizens on the banks of the Missouri are clothed with fabrics manufactured in England and Hindostan, while thousands of useful men, women, and children, capable of furnishing superior goods, at equal prices, are literally pining in wretchedness, in our towns and cities, for want of employment, and many of them driven to mendicity, to support a miserable existence! and while our country is impoverished, to support the manufacturers of the East Indies and various parts of Europe. And why (let us solemnly ask) does this lamentable state of things exist? Because, in the language of Adam Smith, "*foreign countries can furnish us with commodities* "*cheaper than we ourselves can make them;*" and we have thought it "*better to buy from them, with some part of the produce of our* "*own industry!*"

Every prudent merchant, farmer, or planter, commencing his career of business, will naturally inquire into the plans acted on by those engaged in similar pursuits, before he determines on his own. Those dictated by wisdom, tested by long experience, and attended with success, he will study as guides by which to regulate his conduct. Those emanating from folly, sinister views, or empiricism, he will regard as beacons to warn him to beware.

This conduct, indisputably wise in private life, is imperiously the duty of those on whom rests the high responsibility of regulating the career of nations, particularly in their infancy or youth. This is a duty which no enlightened or honest legislature will ever neglect.

We trust, therefore, that a calm and candid observation of the fatal consequences of adopting the doctrines of Adam Smith, as well as of the transcendent benefits, public and private, resulting from the English system, which is in undeviating hostility with that of the doctor, will serve to display the true policy which this country ought to pursue, in order to fill the high destiny which appears allotted to her in the course of human events; and induce the legislature of the union, to devote that attention to the protection of domestic manufactures, without which the united states can never hope to be really independent, or to enjoy that degree of prosperity and happiness which God and nature have placed within their grasp; and which cannot be neglected without a most culpable dereliction of our duty to ourselves, and to our posterity, on whom the folly or wisdom of our councils will operate when we are consigned to the peaceful grave.

NO. IV.

Philadelphia, April 26, 1819.

Policy of Russia. Extracts from her tariff. State of cotton manufactures in Rhode Island. Prussian policy. Bounties and premiums for manufactures.

We have presented to your view, fellow-citizens, a cursory sketch of the admirable and beneficent policy of Great Britain* on the all-important and vital point of fostering and protecting domestic industry—a policy, we repeat, and wish steadily borne in mind, in direct hostility with the doctrines of Adam Smith, which rank among their supporters so large a portion of our citizens.

We now request your attention to the policy of a mighty empire, whose situation bears considerable analogy to that of this country.

Russia, like the united states, possesses territories of most immoderate extent, which are very slenderly peopled. The cultivation of her vacant lands, according to the captivating and plausible theories of many of our citizens, might find employment for all her inhabitants. And as other nations, if "*the freedom of trade were restored, could furnish her with commodities cheaper than she could manufacture them*," she ought, according to Adam Smith, to open her ports to the merchandize of all the world.

But, low as we fastidiously and unjustly rate her policy, she has too much good sense to adopt a maxim so pernicious in its results, although so plausible in its appearance. And let us add, its plausibility is only in appearance. It vanishes on even a cursory examination.

Russia fulfils the indispensible duty of fostering and protecting domestic industry, and guarding it against the destructive consequences of overwhelming foreign competition. This is the great platform of her political system, as it ought to be of all political systems; and it is painful to state, that so far as respects this cardinal point, she is at least a century in advance of

* Objections have been made to our statement of the prosperity of England resulting from her protection of domestic industry, grounded on the oppression she exercises on, and the abject state of, some of her dependencies. This does not in the least militate with our view, which went to prove, from indisputable facts, that the protection of domestic industry in the island of Great Britain, had there produced as great a mass of wealth and prosperity as ever existed. Her wars, which greatly impair that prosperity, and her treatment of her dependencies, which is unjust and oppressive in the extreme, have not the most remote connection with our theory.

the united states. She is not satisfied with the imposition of heavy duties for the purpose of raising a revenue, which, with too many statesmen, appears to be the chief, if not the only object worthy of consideration in the formation of a tariff. No. She prohibits, under penalty of confiscation, nearly all the articles with which her own subjects can supply her, unaffected by the terrors, so powerfully felt in this country, of giving a monopoly of the home market to her own people—terrors which have probably cost the United States one hundred millions of dollars since the war—terrors which the profound and sage maxim of Alexander Hamilton, quoted in our last number,* ought to have laid in the grave of oblivion nearly thirty years ago, never to rise again to impair the prosperity of the nation, or the happiness of its citizens.

The annexed list deserves the most pointed attention, and cannot fail to surprise the citizens of a country, where unfortunately nothing is prohibited, how great soever the domestic supply, and where there are hardly any duties deserving the name of prohibitory, and few affording adequate protection.

List of goods the importation of which is prohibited into the Russian empire, according to the tariff of 1816.†

Alabaster.
Ale.
Bronze, gilt or ungilt, statues, busts, vases, urns, girandoles, lustres, candelabras, &c.
Beads of all kinds.
Blacking for boots and shoes.
Brandy, distilled from grain of every kind.
Brandy, poured on cherries, pears, or other fruits.
Brooms, of twigs or rushes for cleaning clothes.
Bolts of metal, of every kind for fastening doors, &c.
Books, counting house books in blank.
Buttons of all kinds.
Baskets of straw or twigs.
Butter of cows or sheep.
Besoms, brushes of all kinds.
Bellows, for fire-places.
Blankets, or bed-covers, of cotton, linen, or wool, with embroidery, or woven with silver or gold; also of silk or half silk, without exception.
Boxes, sand and spitting boxes.
Bedding of all kinds, excepting those of passengers.
Balls of lead.
Beer of all kinds, except English porter.
Boots of all kinds.
Baizes of all sorts.
Cotton goods, wrought of cotton intermixed with gold and silver; also dyed, printed or chintz.
Candles.
Chess-boards, and other boards for games, with their appendages.
Carpets interwoven with gold or silver.
Cranes of all kinds.
Confectionary of all kinds.
Cringles.
Coffee-mills.
Coin, base coin, or being of a less value than its denomination. Russian bank notes.
Combs of Horn.
Copper utensils of every kind
Copper articles, whether hammered or cast, &c. ornamented with designs, gilt or ungilt, of every kind; also handles, plates, and suchlike articles; the same applies to brass.
Clothes of all kinds, except those of passengers.
Canary seed.
Crystal or cut-glass ware of all kinds.

* *See supra, page 45.*

† *Rordansz, on European Commerce, page 54.*

Cases of all kinds.
Cords of silk, cotton, camel's hair, or worsted.
Cloth, fine black cloth, and all coarse cloths and baizes.
Cicory, ground in imitation of coffee.
Crystal drops, for lustres and girandoles.
Chocolate.
Clocks, for tables or walls, with metal or glass ornaments of any kind.
Clocks or watches in enamel with striped edges.
Caps of all kinds.
Carriages of all kinds, except those belonging to travellers.
Doors for stoves of all kinds.
Down of all kinds, except those specified as admitted.
Dried fruits
Embroidery of gold of every description of material.
Earthenware, vessels, or utensils of common clay, delft, fayance or china, Porcelain and the like, with gold silver or painted borders.
Fringes of all kinds.
Fans.
Feathers.
Flesh of all kinds, dried, salted or smoked.
Fruits, preserved, wet or dried in sugar.
Garden fruits of all sorts, salted in vinegar, fresh or dried.
Fumigating powder.
Frames for windows.
Frames for pictures, except belonging to pictures or engravings imported.
Flax for wicks.
Fishing tackle.
Gallantry ware, including all sorts of high priced trifles, ornamented or unornamented, with high priced stones and pearls, except those otherwise specified.
Galloon.
Gold and silver, or gilt plate, or vessels of all kinds.
Glue, made of fish or leather.
Gold and silver lace, edgings, tassels, cords, nets, gauze, &c.
Gloves, of woollen, cotton, or linen.
Garters.
Gun-powder.
Glass drops, for lustres, girandoles, all glass-ware, and utensils of every kind, glass girandoles, lustres, &c. Window glass in circles.
Gaiters, of leather.
Gingerbread.
Gin or Geneva.
Gricus, (a kind of common mushroom or fungus.)
Hair, human hair.
Hair powder.
Horn combs, horns of elk, reindeer and other sorts unwrought, except such as are imported in Russian ships having been taken by Russian huntsmen.
Hilts, for swords, sabres, daggers, &c.
Harpsichords or piano fortes, with bronze ornaments on the bodies, except such as are applied to strengthen them, or upon the legs, or as locks.
Hides, prepared, and every article made of leather, except those specified as admitted.
Hats of all kinds.
Harness and such like for horses.
Honey, in the comb and prepared.
Handkerchiefs printed on linen, cloth, silk of every kind, with a border woven or printed.
Hangings of tapestry, or paper, or cloth, paper and wool together, woven, painted linen, or woollen, and all other kinds.
Iron, cast, in guns, shot, plates thick or thin, kettles, and other cast iron work.
Iron wrought into bars, double, or single for plates.
Iron, pig iron unwrought or wrought in pieces, wire utensils of every kind, blacksmith's work small ware, every sort of locksmith's and whitesmith's work, except those specified elsewhere as permitted.
Iron anchors.
Ink, of all sorts in bottles or powders, also Indian ink (printer's ink, duty free.)
Inkstands of all kinds.
Jewelry.
Isinglass, of fish (glue.)
Kingees, or fur shoes and boots of every kind.
Linen, as shirts, &c. of all kinds, except passengers' baggage.
Linen manufactures of all kinds except cambric.
Locks of all kinds.
Lime, slaked or unslaked.
Lace.
Liqueurs, of brandy.
Lustres of all sorts.
Lanterns.

Lines, coarse, twisted, such as are used in fishing nets and the like.
Leather, see hides.
Ladies' ornaments of all kinds.
Looking glasses, see mirrors.
Mustard, dry or prepared in glasses, or jars.
Mead.
Mirrors, or glasses intended for them.
Macaroni.
Muslin, or muslin handkerchiefs embroidered.
Mills, for grinding coffee.
Muffs, of all kinds.
Marble and Alabaster clocks, table slabs, pillars, utensils, and all other (ornaments) not specified as admitted.
Mats, made of straw to put on tables under dishes.
Mats, straw and rush.
Mittens, and leather for warm mittens.
Marienglass, or talc.
Night caps of all kinds, except those specified as admitted.
Nails, of copper and brass, or with copper and brass heads, or washed, plated, gilt, tinned, or of iron and tin.
Nets of all kinds, and netting.
Oil, rape oil.
Ornaments for ladies.
Pins and skewers of all kinds.
Paper of all kinds, not specified as admitted.
Plate, gold and silver vessels of every description, also gilt plate.
Parchment.
Playing cards.
Pocket books of all kinds.
Pens, quills, and feathers.
Powder, hairpowder, pomatum, fumigating powders, gunpowder for guns or cannon.
Porcelain.
Pipes for fire engines.
Pipes for smoking of all kinds, except of plain meerschaun.
Pickles, see fruit or vegetables.
Ribands of orders of knighthood.
Rum.
Sausages of all kinds.
Spirits, extracted from grain, double, or spirit of wine sweetened.
Shoes of all kinds.
Shot of lead and balls.
Sashes of all kinds.
Soap of all kinds, except Venice, Spanish, Turkish and Greek.
Sticks of all kinds.
Suspenders for gentlemen, except those specified as admitted.
Saltpetre, rough, or refined, except for the use of apothecaries.
Silver plate and utensils of every kind.
Silver ware or thread flattened, spangles and foil.
Slippers of all kinds, except those specified as admitted.
Sugar, fruits in sugar, dry or wet.
Sealing wax.
Spices of all kinds.
Saddle cloths.
Snuff boxes.
Sword belts.
Silk of all kinds, silk or half silk goods, except those specified for admittance.
Toys of all sorts.
Tapes of all kinds.
Tiles for stoves.
Tapestry, see hangings.
Tin, grain tin, or tin ware of any kind.
Tea of every sort.*
Tinsel, or foil, flat, woven, red, white in lace, lace in liveries, galloons, ribands, edgings, or bindings, &c.
Vermicelli, or macaroni.
Vinegar of all sorts, except wine vinegar.
Wash basins, tea pots, coffee pots, candlesticks, waiters, stands, or such like goods, whether of copper, red or green, say copper or brass, iron, tinned, or untinned, varnished, plated, gilt or silvered, argent, hache, or with silver edges separately applied.
Whips for coachmen.
Waddings.
Wafers.
Wigs.
Ware, white, yellow, or coloured.
Wood, manufactured, except in such articles as are required by passengers for their baggage.
Window frames.
Wicks for candles of flax or thread.
Window glass, in circles.
Watches.
Woollen goods, baizes of all sorts; see cloth.

* *Tea is admitted over land from China.*

An appalling reflection arises from the view here given of the policy of Russia; a reflection which we would willingly suppress, but which, fellow citizens, justice to the subject forces us to present to your minds. We are imperiously led to offer it from a conviction, that to induce a patient to submit to medicine or regimen, it is necessary he should be convinced of the existence of his disease. And in the present disordered state of our manufactures, trade, and commerce, it is absolutely necessary to "hold the mirror up to nature," and "nought extenuate, nor aught set down in malice."

The united states, as is admitted by writers of various nations, enjoy the best form of government in the world. It would therefore be natural to presume, that with such a government, and with a representation probably as freely and fairly chosen, as any legislative body in any age or country, the interests of its various descriptions of citizens would be more scrupulously guarded than those of any other nation. Yet we have here us the most cogent proof of the extreme fallacy of such a presumption, so far as regards the large and important class of citizens engaged in manufactures, on whose success and prosperity so much of the strength and resources of nations depends. This description of citizens* must look with envy at

* It is too common, we apprehend, for many of the farmers and planters of the southern states, to regard with disesteem, or, in common parlance, "to look down" on manufacturers as beneath them in point of respectability. To this source may probably be ascribed the inflexible refusal of that protection which was so earnestly solicited for the manufacturing interest throughout the union. It is hardly possible to conceive of a greater absurdity. We touch this delicate subject freely. We, however, mean no offence, and hope none will be taken. Our object, we trust, will be regarded by liberal-minded men as not only innocent, but laudable. It is to correct a deep-rooted and pernicious prejudice, which tends to produce jealousy and alienation between the different members of one family, who ought to cherish for each other kindly sentiments of regard and good will, and who are so closely connected in point of interest, that it is impossible for one to suffer heavily, without the others being deeply affected. We freely ask, and request a candid reply, can there, in the eye of reason and common sense, be found, on the most impartial scrutiny, any superiority in a South Carolina or Virginia planter, surrounded by three or four hundred slaves, over a proprietor of one of the extensive factories in Rhode Island, in which an equal number of free, independent, and happy workmen, with their wives and children, are employed? As our object is conciliation, we forbear to assert any superiority on the other side. But in order to afford a fair opportunity of deciding this important question, of the merits, demerits, and usefulness of the different descriptions of citizens, we state some important facts, which bear forcibly on this subject. In the year 1816, there were, as stated in a memorial to Congress of the cotton manufacturers of the town of Providence, within thirty miles of that town,*

Cotton manufactories		140
Containing in actual operation,	spindles	130,000
Using annually,	bales of cotton	29,000
Producing yards of the kinds of cotton goods usually made		27,840,000
The weaving of which at eight cents per yard amounts to		$ 2,227,200
Total value of the cloth		$ 6,000,000
Persons steadily employed		26,000

We may demand, whether throughout the world, there is to be found any equal space devoted wholly to agriculture, which furnishes employment to one-fourth

* Weekly Register, vol. ix. page 44.

the paternal and fostering care bestowed on persons of the same class by the emperor of Russia, one of the most despotic monarchs of Christendom. The contrast is decisive. It reflects honour on the profound wisdom and sound policy of that prince —and, fellow citizens, cannot fail to excite painful sensations in your minds, to reflect how the united states lose on the comparison.

It could never have entered into the mind of Hancock, Adams, Franklin, Washington, or any other of those illustrious men, who, in the field or cabinet, achieved the independence of this country, that before the lapse of half a century, American citizens should be forced to make invidious comparisons between their own situation and that of the subjects of a despotic empire; and that the protection denied to their industry is liberally afforded to that of the subjects of Russia.

In order to render this extraordinary fact more striking, we shall, fellow citizens, compare the situation of a subject of Russia and a citizen of the united states, engaged, for instance, in the cotton manufacture.

The former, we will suppose, embarks $50,000 in that business. He has no competition to dread but that of his fellow subjects. His paternal government closes the door against his destruction, by shutting out the interference of any other nation. He has a large and beneficial market, and, in consequence, enriches himself, and adds to the wealth, strength, power, and resources of his country.

What a chilling and appalling contrast when we regard the situation of the American engaged in the same useful line of business! When he has expended his capital, established his works, and entertains what he has ground to deem a reasonable hope of success, and of that reward to which honest industry has so fair a claim, the market, on the supply of which he formed all his calculations, is deluged with rival articles, manufactured at a distance of thousands of miles, which can be afforded at lower prices than his, and which accordingly destroy his chances of sale. He casts an imploring eye to his representatives for the

part of the number of individuals, or produces one-fourth of the amount of wealth or happiness?

We trust this brief view will serve to remove the film from the eyes of those citizens who, for want of due consideration, have cherished opinions on the subject of manufactures, and manufacturers, so diametrically opposite to fact, and so pregnant with ruinous consequences.

> "Honour or shame from no condition rise:
> "Act well your part: there all the honour lies."

And the manufacturer of cottons, woollens, watches, paper, books, hats or shoes, who "acts well his part" has no reason to shrink, and we trust will never shrink, from a comparison with any of his fellow men, whether merchants, farmers, planters, or men of overgrown wealth.

same kind of relief which England, France, Russia, Prussia, Denmark, and Austria, afford their subjects, and the refusal of which is a manifest dereliction of duty. His representatives, acting on the maxims of Adam Smith, and disregarding the admonitory lessons of those mighty nations, meet him with a positive refusal; and he sinks a victim of a policy long scouted out of all the wise nations of Europe, and which now only lingers in, and blights and blasts the happiness of, Spain and Portugal. Hundreds of useful citizens in every part of the union, with large families, mourn the ruinous consequences of our mistaken policy.

The subject is too important not to warrant us in casting another slight glance at it.

The united states are peculiarly fitted for the cotton manufacture, being, as we have already stated, capable of raising the raw material, in quantities commensurate with the demand of the whole world. And yet cotton goods of every description (except those below twenty-five cents per yard, which are dutied as at twenty-five cents) are freely admitted at the very inefficient duty of twenty-seven and a half per cent. in consequence of which, great numbers of the most promising establishments have been destroyed. The raw material is transported across the Atlantic, 3000 miles, at sixteen to fifty cents per pound, and returned to us at the rate of from one dollar to five dollars —thus fostering the industry and the manufactures of Europe, and consigning our workmen to poverty and often to mendicity— their employers to the long lists of bankrupts which are daily increasing in our towns and cities—and impoverishing the nation. On this system and its consequences we shall descant more at large on a future occasion. For the present we shall barely state that the policy of England during the dark ages of Edward III. and Henry IV. as sketched in our last number, was far superior to ours, with all our boasted illumination.

At the close of the war, powerful and eloquent memorials were presented to Congress from the cotton manufacturers of Rhode Island, New London, New York, Baltimore, Philadelphia, Pittsburg, and various other parts of the United States, in which they besought the aid of government, in the most respectful terms. To narrow the range of objection, they bounded their requests generally to a prohibition of cotton manufactures, from the East Indies, except nankeens, and to such an increase of duties on those from other quarters, as would save the revenue from injury by the prohibition. The memorials were filled with predictions of the ruinous consequences that would result from the contrary policy. Their simple request, enforced by a most luminous train of reasoning, was unhappily rejected: and it is almost demonstrable, that to this rejection a large portion of the difficulties and embarrassments which at present overspread the face of the country may be ascribed. All the gloomy predictions of the memorials have unfortunately become history.

A consideration of the rejection of the first prayer of the memorials, which respects the prohibition of East India cottons, is calculated to excite an equal degree of regret and astonishment. The East India trade, during the continuance of the wars in Europe, when we had markets there, and in some of the colonies of the belligerents, for the surplus of our importations from beyond the Cape of Good Hope, was possibly advantageous, or at least not injurious. But as at present carried on, it is highly pernicious, by the exhausting drain of specie it creates. On this strong ground, and moreover as the coarse fabrics from that quarter, as stated in the memorials, are made of inferior materials : and as we possess a boundless capacity of supply, every principle of sound policy, regard for the vital interests of their country, as well as the paramount claim on congress from so useful a body of citizens, for protection, ought to have insured compliance with the request. To all these considerations fatally no attention was paid.

Policy of Frederic II. of Prussia.

From the view given of the policy of Russia, we invite attention to that of Frederic II. His integrity and regard for the rights of his neighbours, no upright man will assert. But on his profound wisdom and sagacity as a statesman, the world is agreed. A dissenting voice is no where heard. On these points he would stand comparison with any monarch of ancient or modern times, and rise paramount over ninety-nine out of a hundred. His system of political economy is therefore worthy of the most serious consideration, and cannot fail to shed strong light on the important subject we are discussing.

To the promotion of the industry of his subjects, he bestowed the most unremitting attention, well knowing that it was the most certain means of increasing the population of his dominions, and of course the wealth and happiness of his subjects, as well as his own power. From this grand and paramount object he was never for a moment diverted by his ambitious wars ; and notwithstanding the desolation they caused, he doubled the population of his paternal estates during his reign. To foster and protect arts and manufactures, he spared neither pains nor expense ; " *The king protects and encourages manufactures in every* " *possible manner, especially by advancing large sums of money*

"*to assist them in carrying on their manufactures, animating*
"*them by rewards, and establishing magazines of wool in all the*
"*little towns, for the benefit of the small woollen manufactures.*"*
He was so completely successful, that he not only doubled and trebled the number of artists and manufacturers in those branches already established, but introduced a great variety, formerly not practised by his subjects; "*Before the commencement of this*
"*reign, Prussia had but few silk manufactures, and those of little*
"*importance. But the present king has established and given*
"*liberal encouragement to so great a number*, that they employ
"more than five thousand workmen; and the annual value of
"the goods manufactured by them is two millions of crowns.–
"In the course of the last year 1,200,250 ells of silk stuffs have
"been manufactured at Berlin, and 400,000 of gauze.

"The cotton manufacture alone employs nearly five thousand
"workmen."* And thus, instead of being as formerly tributary to other nations, Prussia was enabled to export her manufactures to an immense extent to distant countries.

"We are in possession of almost every possible kind of manu-
"factures; and we can not only exclusively supply the Prus-
"sian dominions, but *also furnish the remote countries of Spain*
"*and Italy with linen and woollen cloths; and our manufactures*
"*go even to China, where some of our Silesia cloths are conveyed*
"*by the way of Russia.* We export every year linen cloth, to
"the amount of SIX MILLIONS OF CROWNS, and woollen cloths
"and wool to the amount of FOUR MILLIONS."†

The measures he adopted for attaining these great ends, were worthy of the high character he enjoys as a statesman. He made large loans to needy artists and manufacturers, to enable them to establish their various branches of business. "If the king
"has greatly increased population by his encouragement of agri-
"culture, *he has advanced it as much, and perhaps more, by the*
"*great numbers of manufactures and trades of all kinds, which he*
"*has caused to be established, or to which he has given encourage-*
"*ment at Berlin, at Potsdam, and in almost every city and town*
"*in his dominions.*"‡ He purchased large quantities of raw materials, and provided magazines, where they were sold at reasonable rates. He bestowed liberal rewards on artists and manufacturers, for excellence in their various branches, and moreover exempted them in various places from military service. In a word, he devoted all the powers of his great mind, and made most liberal drafts on his treasury, for the accomplishment of this mighty object, which has attracted so small a share of attention in this country, from those whose peculiar duty it was to promote its success.

* Hertzberg's Discourses delivered at Berlin, 1786, p. 25.
* Idem 26. † Idem 23. ‡ Ibid.

"It is with a view to encourage trade that the inhabitants of "Berlin and Potsdam *are exempted from military service;* and "his majesty grants nearly the same indulgence to the inhabit-"ants of the circles of the mountains of Silesia, where the poor "but industrious and sober weavers, who are settled in a narrow "and barren district, *carry on those flourishing linen manufac-"tures which produce us an exportation of so many millions; and "to the little city of Hirchberg only, a trade of two millions of "crowns annually.* The king has in this district a canton for "his foot-guards; but from his unwillingness to disturb the "population of the district, he seldom draws from hence any re-"cruits."*

The calm and candid observer, who casts his eye on the system of Frederic, and contrasts it with that of the united states, cannot fail to feel the same degree of mortification and deep regret, which the contrast with that of Russia produced. He will behold, on one side, a grand, liberal, and magnanimous policy, disregarding expense in sowing prolific seed, which sprouted forth abundantly and repaid the cultivator ten-fold, nay, a hundred fold.† Loans, bounties, premiums, and important immunities, as we have stated, were freely and liberally awarded.

In the united states the seed was sown by individual exertion and enterprise. It required little care to foster and make it strike deep root. There was no demand of loans—bounties premiums—or immunities. All that was asked—all that was necessary—was mere protection from foreign interference—a protection which would have cost the government nothing, and would have enriched the nation. It was fatally withheld: and a large portion of the seed so plentifully sown and so promising

* Idem, 25.

† "As *national industry* forms the second basis of the felicity and power of a "state, I shall endeavour to prove here in a summary manner, that the Prussian "monarchy possesses it in an eminent degree; and, perhaps, immediately after "France, England, and Holland; those powers which, for two centuries, have had "the almost exclusive monopoly of manufactures, of commerce, and of navigation; "of which the Prussians have had no part, but since the close of the last century, "and the beginning of the present. This is not the place to make an exact and "general table of the Prussian manufactures; I shall therefore confine myself to "giving a general idea, and some particular examples. We have almost all the "trades and manufactures that can be conceived, as well for things of absolute "necessity, as for the conveniences and luxuries of life. Some of them have at-"tained to a great degree of perfection, as those of woollen cloth, linen, porcelain, "and others. The greater part are in a state of mediocrity, and may be brought "by degrees to perfection, if there is continued to be given to them the same at-"tention, assistance and support, which the Prussian government has hitherto "most liberally bestowed; and especially when to these are added the motives "and inducements of emulation, which are absolutely necessary for bringing ma-"nufactures and works of art to perfection. *Our manufactures exclusively supply "all the Prussian dominions; and, with a very favourable rivalship, especially for "cloths, linens, and woollens, Poland, Russia, Germany, Italy, and especially Spain and "America.* In order to afford a more strong and clear conviction, I shall here add

of a fertile harvest, has perished; and those who withheld, as well as those who besought, the protection, are now in common, suffering the most serious injury from that mistaken policy.

—

DISBURSEMENTS OF FREDERIC II. FOR PROMOTION OF MANUFACTURES. ANNO 1785.*

In New March.

	Crowns.
For establishing a manufactory of leather, and for tanning at Landsberg	3,500
For a similar manufactory at Drisen - - - - - - - -	3,000
Ditto Ditto at Cottbus - - - - - - - -	1000
For erecting a fulling mill at Drambourg - - - - - - - -	200
For increasing the magazines of wool for the manufacturers of small towns	3,000

In Pomerania.

For enlarging the manufactory of leather at Anclam - - - -	3,000
For establishing a manufactory of leather at Treptow - - -	1,500
For establishing a manufactory at Griffenhagen - - - - -	1,500
For establishing a manufactory of fustians and cottons at Frederickshold	1,000
For increasing the magazines of wool in the small towns - - -	4,000
For establishing a manufactory of beaver stockings at Lawenberg -	2,000
For establishing a cotton manufactory at New Stettin - - -	2,400
For a magazine of cotton for the benefit of the manufacturers of Pomerania - - - - - - - - - - - - -	6,000

East and West Prussia.

For repairing the damage occasioned by the burning of woollen cloths near Preusch Eilau - - - - - - - - - - - -	3,500
carried over,	35,600

"a compendious table of the principal trades and manufactures, which exist in the "Prussian monarchy, of their produce, and of the number of traders and manufac- "turers who are employed in them:"—

"The Prussian dominions had in the course of the year 1784,†

	Looms.	Manufacturers.	Produce of the Manufactures in Rix dollars.
In linens - - - - - - - -	51,000	80,000	9,000,000
In cloths and woollens - - - -	18,000	58,000	8,000,000
In silk - - - - - - - -	4,200	6,000	3,000,000
In cotton - - - - - - -	2,600	7,000	1,200,000
In leather - - - - - - - - - - -		4,000	2,000,000
In iron, steel, copper, &c. - - - - - - -		3,000	2,000,000
In tobacco, of which 140,000 quintals are the growth of the country - - - - - - -		2,000	1,000,000
Sugar - - - - - - - - - - - -		1,000	2,000,000
Porcelain and earthenware - - - - - - -		700	200,000
Paper - - - - - - - - - - -		800	200,000
Tallow and soap - - - - - - - - -		300	400,000
Glass, looking-glasses - - - - - - -		—	200,000
Manufactures in gold, silver, lace, embroidery, &c. -		1,000	400,000
Silesia madder - - - - - - - - -		—	300,000
Oil - - - - - - - - - - - -		600	300,000
Yellow amber, - - - - - - - -		600	50,000
		165,000	30,250,000

* *Hertzberg's Discourses*, p. 44. † Idem, p. 101, 103.

carried over,	35,600
For establishing a manufactory of muslin at Konigsberg	1,000
For a manufactory of leather at Preusch Eilau	5,000
For a dye-house at Gastrow	2,600
For magazines of wool in the little towns of West Prussia	6,000
For a manufactory of press-boards	6,000

Silesia.

For the establishment of forty weavers at Striegaw and in the neighbourhood	17,368
For premiums relative to manufactures	2,000

Brandenburgh.

For establishing work shops for carding of wool	1,360
For rewards, intended for the encouragement of spinning in the country	2,000
For the erection of silk mills at Berlin	24,000
For purchasing the cods of silk worms, and causing them to be well spun	10,000
For machines for carrying on the Manchester manufacture	10,000

ANNO 1786.

In Brandenburgh.

For procuring Spanish sheep	22,000
For increasing the magazines of wool	17,000
For improvements relative to the spinning of wool	4,000
For a manufactory of woollen cloths at Zinna	3,000
For a plantation of Mulberry trees at Nowawest	2,000
For the purchase of cods of silk worms and establishing a magazine of them	20,000

In the New March.

For several small manufactures of wool and leather, and for fulling mills in Custrin, Newedel, Falckenburgh, and Somerfeldt, towns of the New March	4,020

In Pomerania.

For increasing the magazines of wool	6,000
For a manufactory of cotton stockings at Gartz	4,000
For a manufactory of leather at Anclam	8,000
For a manufactory of leather at Treptow	1,500
For a manufactory of sail cloth at Rugenwalde	5,000
For a manufactory of cables in the same city	4,000
For a manufactory of cloth for flags at Stettin	3,000

In East Prussia.

For a manufactory of morocco leather at Konigsberg	3,000
For a manufactory of English earthenware in the same city	4,000
For a manufactory of leather	1,000
For a manufactory of ribands and bags	600
For a cotton manufactory at Gumbinnen	1,000

In West Prussia.

For a dye-house at Darkhenen	2,600
For a dye-house at Bromberg	2,600
For a manufactory of fine Cloth at Culm	7,200

In Silesia.

Premiums for manufactures and for encouraging and supporting weavers	17,000
Total expended in two years,	265,448

NO. V.

Philadelphia, May 3, 1819.

Fallacy of the objections to the protection of manufactures—Demoralization—Injury to commerce—High wages—Vacant lands—Extortion—Loss of revenue—Smuggling.

The friends of domestic manufactures in this country have had to combat a host of objections, maintained with great zeal and plausibility, many of which, though utterly destitute of foundation, have had universal currency. We shall devote the present number to obviate some of them.

I. The demoralizing and debasing effects of manufacturing establishments.

II. Their injurious interference with commerce.

III. The high rate of wages in the united states.

IV. The great extent of our vacant lands, which ought to be settled previously to the erection of manufacturing establishments on a large scale.

V. The extortions practised, and the extravagant prices charged by manufacturers during the war.

VI. The loss of revenue that would arise from protecting or prohibitory duties.

VII. The danger of encouraging smuggling by high duties.

I. *Demoralization.*

The most specious and generally prevalent argument against manufacturing establishments, is grounded on their debasing and demoralizing effects. The honest feelings and the sympathy of the humane and enlightened part of the community, and the passions and prejudices of the remainder, have, in consequence, been enlisted and excited to activity against them. The changes have been rung, times without number, on the depravity, corruption, and pauperism inseparable from large assemblages of men, women, and children, collected in a small compass, inhaling a pestiferous atmosphere, both moral and physical. The most captivating pictures have been drawn, by way of contrast, of the purity, the innocence, the healthiness, and the independence of agricultural employments—and the whole has been wound up by deprecating the folly and insanity of seducing the Arcadian cultivators of the soil into the business of manufacturing, so destructive to their health, their morals, and their happiness.

This objection, like a thousand other common places, has been almost universally assumed, and freely admitted without demur or scruple. Even the friends of manufactures have hardly dared to doubt its correctness, barely lamenting it as one of the many serious evils inseparable from society in its present state. And had it not been for the investigations of a recent writer, [Colquhoun], it might have continued for another century to lead mankind astray.

But even if these views were correct as regarded the overgrown manufacturing establishments in England, and some other parts of Europe, they would be inapplicable here; as the best friends of manufactures in this country have confined their views to the home market generally; and in so wide a country as this, if the manufacturers were degraded and oppressed by men of great wealth in one district, they would be able to resort to establishments in another, of which, were manufactures duly protected, there would be numbers in every quarter of the union, and, at all events, the western lands would afford an asylum for the oppressed, and a safeguard against oppression.

The most eminent statistical writer in Europe at present is probably Colquhoun, author of the "Police of London," and various other important works, bearing the strongest marks of profound research, deep penetration, and philosophical inquiry. This writer has published a curious and important table of *the population*, *offenders*, *and paupers* of every county in England, which settles this important point forever, and which we annex. The character of the author and the authenticity of the work, forbid all appeal from its authority, and cannot fail to remove the doubts of the most sceptical.

*Comparative view of nearly an equal population in one part of the kingdom with the same in another.**

Counties.	Population.	Offenders.	Paupers.	Counties.	Population.	Offenders.	Paupers.
Middlesex - - -	818,129	1217	63,173	Yorkshire - - -	858,892	245	77,661
Kent - - - -	307.624	210	41,632	Lancashire - -	672,731	371	46,200
Surry - - - -	269,043	199	36.138	Stafford - - -	239.153	91	22,510
Essex - - - -	226,437	144	38,337	Devon - - -	343,001	96	43,674
Gloucester, including Bristol } -	250,809	141	36,904	Lincoln - - -	208,557	58	18,845
Warwick - - -	208,190	160	30,200	Somerset - - -	273.750	106	33,979
Norfolk - - -	273.371	163	42,707	Chester - - -	191,751	30	22.152
Suffolk - - -	210,431	109	36,110	Durham - - -	160,361	27	15,307
Sussex - - -	159,311	105	37,076	Cornwall - - -	188.269	45	12,853
Wilts - - - -	185,107	75	42,128	Salop - - - -	167,639	79	17.306
Hampshire - -	219.656	147	32.581	Worcester - -	139,330	51	18 896
Nottingham - -	140,350	74	9,805	Northampton -	131,757	42	20,534
Leicester - - -	130,081	47	19,154	Northumberland -	157,101	38	14,304
Derby - - -	161,142	39	13.167	Cumberland - -	117,230	18	8,445
Dorset - - -	115,319	38	15.785	Bucks - - - -	107,444	33	19,650
Berks - - -	109,215	62	22,088	Cambridge - -	89,346	40	11.294
Oxford - - -	109.650	38	21,025	Hereford - - -	89,191	31	11,779
Herts - - - -	97,577	43	13 349	Monmouth - -	45.582	20	4.479
Bedford - - -	63,393	20	7,276	Westmoreland -	41.617	6	4.615
Huntingdon - -	37,568	15	4,746	Rutland - - -	16,356	4	1,338
South Wales, 6 Counties -	288,761	50	23,384	North Wales - 6 counties. - -	252,785	28	28,131
	4.381,134	309	586,764		4,491,846	1509	453,952

This writer furnishes another table, of the state of pauperism throughout England, which we also annex—

Counties.		Per cent. on the population.
5.	In Cumberland, Cornwall, Lancaster, Nottingham, and East Riding of Yorkshire, the number of paupers in each 100 of the population - - - - - -	7 (less than $\frac{1}{15}$)
3.	In Derby, Middlesex, and Rutland -	8 (less than $\frac{1}{13}$)
4.	In Lincoln, Northumberland, Stafford, and North Riding of Yorkshire - - -	9 (above $\frac{1}{11}$)
4	West Riding of York, Durham, Monmouth, and Salop, - - - - - - - - - - -	10 - ($\frac{1}{10}$)
4	Bedford, Chester, Somerset and Westmoreland, - - - - - - - - - - - - -	12 (under $\frac{1}{8}$)
9	Cambridge, Devon, Hereford, Huntingdon, Surry and Worcester, - - - - - - -	13 (above $\frac{1}{8}$)
3	Herts, Dorset and Kent, - - - - - -	14 (under $\frac{1}{7}$)
4	Gloucester, Leicester, Southampton, and Warwick - - - - - - - - - - - -	15 (above $\frac{1}{7}$)
2	Norfolk and Northampton, - - - - - -	16 (under $\frac{1}{6}$)
2	Essex and Suffolk, - - - - - - - -	17 (above $\frac{1}{6}$)

* Colquhoun on Indigence, p. 272.

1	Buckinghamshire, - - - - - - - - -	18 (above $\frac{1}{6}$)
1	Oxfordshire, - - - - - - - - - - - -	20 - ($\frac{1}{5}$)
1	Berkshire, - - - - - - - - - - - - -	21 (above $\frac{1}{5}$)
2	Sussex and Wiltshire, - - - - - - - - -	23 (nearly $\frac{1}{4}$)
12	Counties in Wales, averaging, - - - -	9 (above $\frac{1}{11}$)*

On the first of these tables he makes the following pointed and decisive remarks:

"From this comparative statement," it appears, "*that contrary* "*to the generally received opinion, the numbers of paupers in the* "*counties which are chiefly agricultural, greatly exceed those* "*where manufactures prevail!!!* Thus in Kent and Surry, "where the aggregate population is 576,687, there appear to be "77,770 paupers; while in Lancashire, where the population "is 672,731, the paupers relieved are only 46,200.†"

He has not compared the two descriptions of the population on the subject of crimes. But the contrast in this respect, it appears, is equally unfavourable to the agricultural districts.—However, as manufactures are spread throughout the kingdom, and as all the counties partake to a certain degree of the double character of agriculture and manufactures, it is impossible to institute a general comparison. But it will answer every valuable purpose of testing the truth or falsehood of the prevailing opinions, to take a view of six counties, three decidedly agricultural, and three as decidedly manufacturing.

Manufacturing counties.	Population.	Offenders.	Paupers.	Agricult. counties.	Population.	Offenders.	Paupers.
Lancashire	672,731	371	46,000	Norfolk	273,371	163	42,707
Yorkshire	858,892	245	77,661	Kent	307,624	210	41'632
Stafford	239,153	91	22,510	Surry	269,043	199	36,138
	1,770,776	707	146,171		850,038	572	120,477‡

In the three manufacturing counties, there is only one offender for every 2500 people; whereas, in the agricultural, there is one for 1600; whereby it appears that the latter districts have above fifty per cent. more criminals than the manufacturing, in proportion to their population. This is a strong and decisive fact.

In the three manufacturing counties, the paupers are only eight per cent. of the population; whereas, in the agricultural, they are about fourteen.

We are tempted to cast a further glance on this table, and to call the attention to a more striking comparison. Yorkshire contains a greater population than the three specified agricultural counties, and yet has far below half the number of offenders, and not two-thirds of the number of paupers.

* Colquhoun on Indigence, p. 265. † Idem, 273. ‡ Idem, 272.

	Population.	Offenders.	Paupers.
Yorkshire, - - -	858,892	245	77,661
Norfolk, Kent, and Surry, -	850,038	572	120,477

This result may appear extraordinary and paradoxical. But a very slight reflection on the subject will remove the paradox, and enable us to account satisfactorily for the existing state of things. Idleness is as much the parent of poverty and guilt, as industry is of independence and virtue. In agricultural districts there is a very large proportion of the labour of the women, and a still greater proportion of that of the young people wholly lost. The latter waste a great part of their early years in total idleness and in the contraction of bad habits. Hence arises a fruitful source of pauperism and guilt.

These statements, independent of their overwhelming bearing on the present question, may have another very important advantage. They serve to display, in strong colours, the danger of trusting to mere assertions, unsupported by facts. There is not in the whole range of political economy, a dogma that has been more universally received, or appeared more plausible than the one here combated, now unequivocally proved by the best authority in Europe, to be not only not true, but the very reverse of truth.

II. *Interference with Commerce.*

Among the opponents of the manufacturing system, were formerly great numbers of those citizens, engaged in commerce, who appeared impressed with an idea that in proportion as manufactures are patronized and extended, in the same proportion commerce must be impaired. Hence a degree of jealousy has been fostered among the commercial, of the manufacturing class of our population, as if there were a great hostility between their respective interests. The most enlightened merchants at present are convinced of the errors of these views. It is not difficult to prove, that they rest on as sandy a foundation as the superior purity and freedom from pauperism of the agricultural districts.

It will not, we trust, be denied, that in every community, in proportion to the variety of pursuits and employments, the field for exertion is extended, and the danger of rivalship, or of any of them being too much crowded, is diminished. Hence an obvious consequence of the destruction of so many manufacturing establishments, as, during the war, were in 'the full tide of successful experiment,' has been to divert much of the capital and industry engaged in them to commercial pursuits, whereby the latter are so overstocked as to narrow or almost destroy all chance of success. The forlorn state of our wharves, our coffee houses, and the numberless assignments in our newspapers, as well as the almost daily sheriffs' sales of property, fully prove that commerce is overdone, and that it has unfortunately become a most precarious profession. Whereas, had manufactures been properly protected, commerce would be relieved from the superfluous portion of citizens who pursue it, and who, by the eagerness of their competition in the markets, domestic and foreign, destroy each others' chances of success.

Another source of indemnification to commerce for any disadvantage it might suffer from the patronage of manufactures, would be the trade in various kinds of raw materials imported from foreign countries, for the use of the manufacturers.*

An important consideration remains. The diminution of our foreign trade, which is at all times precarious, and often ruinous, would be further compensated by the vast increase of the coasting trade, in the transportation of raw materials from the southern to the middle and eastern states, and of manufactured articles from the latter to the former.

We do not deem it necessary to enter into further detail, or to exhaust the subject. We trust enough has been said, to prove, that a liberal patronage extended to manufactures would be eminently beneficial even to the mercantile part of our citizens, not merely by reducing within reasonable bounds the extravagant number of competitors in that department, whereby so many engaged in it have been ruined; but by affording profitable employment to a portion of that capital which has escaped the destruction arising from the ruinous state of our commerce since the war, and also by the general prosperity it would produce. This system, moreover, would afford commercial men opportunities of providing for a part of their children in a less hazardous line of business than commerce.

III. *High Wages.*

The high wages said to be given in this country have been used as a powerful argument against encouraging manufactures, and have led many of our citizens to believe that we would not be capable of manufacturing extensively for perhaps a century to come. This idea has maintained its ground against the strong and palpable fact, that many of our manufactures have thriven very considerably, notwithstanding the rivalship of foreign competitors. The difference, however, between the wages here and in England, in many branches of business, is far less than is

* An intelligent citizen, who has carefully examined the entries into the port of Philadelphia, assures us, that the tonnage employed even now in the importation of raw materials, leather, dye-wood, iron, lead, &c. &c. is equal to that employed in the importation of bale goods.

generally supposed. But the argument falls to the ground, when we reflect that in most of those branches depending wholly on manual labour, our manufacturers have met the rival articles from Europe with great success. Our hatters, shoemakers, saddlers, coachmakers, printers, cabinet makers, type founders, curriers, glovers, smiths, and various other classes, wholly debarred of the advantage of machinery, have maintained their ground far better than those citizens concerned in branches in which machinery is employed, of whom a large portion have been ruined!

This is a very extraordinary fact, and could not have entered into any previous calculation. The endless variety of mill-seats throughout the United States, and the acknowledged talents of our citizens in mechanical pursuits, would have led to form conclusions wholly different. It would have been believed that whatever we might suffer in cases in which manual labour alone was employed, we should be triumphant wherever water power and machinery could be called into operation.

IV. *Vacant Lands.*

Among the formidable objections against the protection of national industry in the form of manufactures, the extent of our vacant lands holds no mean place. Many members of congress, and others, when they hear of the decline of manufactures —the bankruptcy of the manufacturers—and the sufferings of the workmen, with great gravity advise the sufferers "*to go back*," and cultivate the soil in the wilderness, where there is an ample field for their industry. This is prescribed as a sovereign and infallible remedy for their evils, and has been a sort of shibboleth from the establishment of the government to the present hour.

So much importance is attached to this idea, and its use is so general, we had almost said, so universal, that it requires to be dilated on at some length. We shall consider it under two points of view—

I. Are manufacturers in general capable of cultivating vacant lands?

It requires but a moment's reflection to be satisfied, that the mass of persons engaged in manufactures are wholly unfit for agricultural employments; more particularly for clearing and cultivating those vacant lands to which they are directed to resort, as a terrestrial paradise. A man who has spent the prime of his life in making watches, cabinet ware, hats, or shoes, or weaving cloth, would be nearly as much out of his element at agricultural labour as a farmer would be in a shoemaker's or hatter's workshop.

Moreover, a large portion, in many cases three fourths of the persons engaged in the cotton, woollen and other branches, are women and children, wholly unfit for farming.

II. Suppose the thousands of manufacturers now out of employment, and those who are likely, from the present stagnation of manufactures, trade, and commerce, to be discharged, were to apply themselves to agriculture, is there any chance of a market for the surplus of their productions?

This is a vital question, and demands the most serious and sober consideration. Its decision must affect the character of the past political economy of our government, and clearly demonstrate the future course pointed out to this rising empire by sound political wisdom.

It is palpable, that, so far from an increase of agriculturists being necessary in the interior of this state, and in the whole of the western states, they are too numerous for their own prosperity; and hence agricultural productions are almost constantly a drug, and afford a very slender remuneration for the labours of the field. Increase the number, and you increase the evil. Increase the number of manufacturers, you diminish it.

In consequence of having an over proportion of our population engaged in agricultural pursuits, the foreign markets are almost constantly glutted with our staple articles, which are quently sold in the West Indies and Europe at a lower rate than in our seaport towns. And hence the most ruinous losses are sustained by our merchants, of whom a large proportion are almost every year blotted from the map of the commercial world.

When the cause, not of the manufacturers alone, as was erroneously supposed, but of the whole nation, which was deeply involved in the question, was powerfully pleaded before congress, the southern planters were admonished to secure themselves a grand domestic market, independent on the caprice of foreign nations. They were prophetically warned of the ruinous consequences that must inevitably follow from the adoption of the contrary system. Trusting to a continuance of the very favourable markets they then enjoyed, in which they could anticipate no change, the petitions and memorials were rejected. But the delusion is past and gone. The age of sober reflection has arrived. And we trust it is impossible for those whose votes prevented such adequate protection to the cotton manufactures as would have secured an unfailing and increasing home market, to reflect on those votes without the most heartfelt regret at the course they pursued, not merely as it has affected their own interests, but for the deleterious effects it has produced, and is likely to continue to produce on the welfare of the nation.

At the time those votes were given, which signed and sealed the destruction of a large portion of the cotton manufactures in the middle states, cotton was thirty cents per pound. It was not necessary for congress to have adopted the policy of Russia or France, which nations prohibit the importation of all cotton manufactures—nor that of Great Britain which imposes a duty of 85 per cent. on them. Had they barely prohibited the low priced articles, and laid an adequate protecting duty on all other descriptions, the price of cotton would probably have never been reduced. So large and so constantly increasing a portion of it would be consumed in this country, that it could not be materially affected by the fluctuation of foreign markets. It now sells at sixteen or eighteen cents: and it is not easy to calculate how long it will remain at that rate. The value of the estates of the southern planters is thus reduced above one-third. Dearly, therefore, do they expiate their rejection of the earnest prayers of their fellow citizens, who, as we have stated, were actually, as is now in full proof, pleading the cause of the whole nation, and at least as much that of the cotton planters as of any other portion of our citizens.

The depreciation of the price of the two other great staples of the country, tobacco and flour, is at least as ruinous as that of cotton.

The reduction of the value of estates is not confined to those of cotton planters. Real estate generally throughout the union, has suffered a vast depreciation. In many places it has fallen one-fourth—in others one-third, and in some even one-half.

We do not pretend that the low tariff proceeded solely from the southern planters. This would be contrary to the historical fact. Members from every state in the union, except three, voted for the existing rates. But of all the members from the five southern states, Maryland, Virginia, North Carolina, South Carolina, and Georgia, only five voted against the reduction of the duty on cotton goods to twenty-five per cent.*

To test more fully the correctness of the prevailing idea we here combat, we will suppose it carried generally into operation, and that a large portion of the persons at present employed in manufactures, had "*gone back*," and were "*cultivating our vacant lands*." The obvious consequence would be, that the quantity of the agricultural productions of the country, and our demands for manufactured goods from abroad, would both have been greatly increased. Of course the prices of the former would have been still more ruinously reduced, and the nation

* In order to present a correct view of this interesting subject, we annex the yeas and nays on a motion made by Mr. Forsyth, on the 2d of April, 1816, to amend the report of the committee on the bill to regulate the duties on imports,

still more drained of its circulating medium. It does not require much skill to calculate what ruinous consequences such a system of policy would have produced.

Before we dismiss this part of our subject, we wish, fellow-citizens, to present it in another point of view. Suppose 10,000 agricultural citizens settled in the interior of any of the western states, and acting on the maxim of Adam Smith, that is, "buying where they can purchase cheapest"—of course in Europe and in the East Indies, at a distance of from three to ten thousand miles,

by striking out *thirty per cent.* on cotton goods proposed by that committee, and substituting *twenty-five*

YEAS.—(For twenty-five per cent.)

New-Hampshire.
Atherton
Cilley
Hale
Webster
Wilcox
Voss
Massachusetts.
Bradbury
Nelson
Pickering
Reed
Ruggles
Taggart
Ward
Vermont.
Langdon
Connecticut.
Champion
Law
Mosely
Stearns
Sturgis
New York.
Grosvenor
Kent
Lovett
Root
Pennsylvania.
Burnside
Hiester
Hopkinson
Ross
Whiteside
Delaware.
Clayton
Maryland.
Archer
Baer
Goldsborough
Hanson
Herbert
Moore
Pinkney
Smith
Stuart
Wright
Virginia.
Barbour
Basset
Breckenridge
Goodwyn
Hawes
Hungerford
Jewett
Johnson
Kerr
Lewis
Lyon
M'Coy
Nelson
Noyes
Pleasants
Randolph
Roane
Sheffey
Smith
Tait
North Carolina.
Clarke
Culpepper
Edwards
Forney
Gaston
King
Love
Pickens
Yancey
South Carolina.
Chapel
Huger
Lowndes
Middleton
Taylor
Woodward
Georgia.
Cuthbert
Forsyth
Hall
Lumpkin
Telfair
Wilde
Kentucky.
Hardin
M'Kee
Tennessee.
Henderson
Thomas.—81.

NAYS.

Massachusetts.
Baylies
Connor
Hulbert
Paris
Strong
Wheaton
Connecticut.
Davenport
Pitkin
Rhode Island.
Boss
Mason
Vermont.
Chipman
New York.
Adgate
Betts
Birdsall
Brooks
Comstock
Crocheron
Gold
Savage
Schenck
Throop
Townsend
Wendover
Ward
Wilkin
Willoughby
Yates
New Jersey.
Baker
Bateman
Bennet
Southard
Pennsylvania.
Crawford
Darlington
Glasgow
Griffin
Hahn
Ingham
Irwin
Lyle
Maclay
Milnor
Piper
Sergeant
Wallace
Wilson
Virginia.
Jackson
Marsh
Newton
South Carolina.
Calhoun
Mayrant
Ohio.
Alexander
Clendenin
Creighton
Kentucky.
Desha
Johnson
M'Lean
Sharpe
Taul
Tennessee.
Powell
Reynolds.—60.

subject to all the variety of charges incident to such a commerce, and then transmitting their surplus productions three thousand miles, subject to similar charges! what a state of dependence and poverty this policy is calculated to produce! Yet it is to a certain extent the situation of a large portion of the interior of the united states. And hence the general depression, the stagnation of business, the drain of the circulating medium, and the consequent depreciation of their bank paper.

Of this policy the state of Ohio has long been, and all the other western states are gradually becoming, melancholy victims. It can never be sufficiently regretted, that with a boundless capacity of supplying themselves with nearly every thing they require, a very large proportion of their clothing and other articles should be drawn from Europe, and that the produce of their industry should depend for its value on the state of the markets in that quarter of the globe!

Let us exhibit a brighter picture, on which the mind can dwell with delight; a picture, which a correct tariff could not have failed to produce, and which, we trust, the wisdom of congress will ere long produce. Let us suppose that these 10,000 citizens had linen, cotton, woollen, and leather manufactures adequate to their wants, in their immediate vicinity, and that instead of sending their flour and tobacco to New-Orleans and thence to Liverpool, the former at four or five dollars per barrel, and of course purchasing a coat with six or eight barrels, they had a market for it at home, and could purchase a coat for three or four barrels, and in the same proportion for other articles. The difference between the two situations is exactly the same as between affluence and penury—happiness and wretchedness.—What a contrast! what a lesson does this superficial view furnish the legislature of the united states—and what a strong sentence of condemnation it pronounces on Adam Smith's theory!

V. *Extortion during the War.*

This stands on nearly the same ground of error as the preceding objections. During that period, the wages of labour were high—the expenses of transportation of the raw materials, as well as the manufactured articles, very exorbitant—and those raw materials were sold at high rates. All these circumstances combined to enhance the price of goods of every description. Moreover, the heavy disbursements for the purchase of mill-seats and erecting machinery, required extraordinary profits—And finally the disorders and irregularities of a state of warfare, forbid men of sound minds from grounding any general inferences on the occurrences of such a period.

But suppose all the charges of this class were judicially proved; with what propriety, we boldly, but respectfully ask, could a planter who raised cotton for 10 *a* 12 cents, and for years sold it at 20 and 30, and who would without scruple have sold it at 75 or 100—or a merchant who buys flour at six dollars, carries it to the West Indies, when the people are in a state of starvation, and there, taking advantage of their distress, sells at 20, 30, or 40 dollars—with what propriety, we say, can they reproach the manufacturer for having sold cloth which cost him 9 or 10 dollars, at 12 or 14? The application of the parable of the beam and the mote, was not confined to the commencement of the Christian era. Its lessons are as necessary now as they were 1800 years ago.

On this point we once more refer to the luminous maxim of Alexander Hamilton, contained in our third number,† which is beyond the power of refutation, and which points out the proper course to be pursued, with the hand of a master.

This maxim has received the strongest corroboration from the practical experience of the united states, which is within the knowledge of almost every individual in it. There is probably not a single article manufactured here which is not sold at a fair price. This can never fail to be the case, in a country where there is so much enterprize, so much capital, and so much industry, at all times ready to be employed in any pursuit which affords a reasonable prospect of remuneration, and likewise such a spirit of competition. In fact the rivalship is, in many cases, carried so far, that prices are reduced too low, and in consequence many of the competitors ruined.

But facts speak louder than words. For years the nation has been led astray by groundless accusations of the extortions of manufacturers, which have been an unceasing source of declamation, and been regarded as an unanswerable argument against complying with the requests of this class of citizens. During this whole time the farmers and planters have been realizing the most exorbitant profits; amassing large and independent fortunes, and exhibiting a degree of prosperity rarely exceeded.* On the contrary nearly one-half of the "*extortionate*" manufacturers of cotton and woollen fabrics, victims of a pernicious policy, have been ruined, and a large portion of the remainder are barely able to struggle along in hopes of a change in the policy of the country!

† See supra page 45.

* The losses resulting from the excessive quantities of our produce, with which foreign markets are so frequently overstocked, have hitherto scarcely touched the farmers or planters, who have almost universally sold their produce at high rates. The injury, as already stated, has fallen on the merchants. The farmers and planters, however, now begin to participate largely in the pernicious effects of this system.

VI. *Loss of Revenue.*

The solicitude to avoid impairing the revenue, by prohibiting the importation of any merchandize, or by such high protecting duties as might operate to diminish importation, has been openly avowed in congress among the reasons for rejecting the prayers of the manufacturers for protection!

It is lamentable to think that in the enlightened nineteenth century, it should be necessary to combat such a prejudice.

Let us calmly examine this objection, and see on what ground it rests. Let us suppose the annual amount of our importations of cotton fabrics, to be 15,000,000 of dollars; and that by adequate protection, they could be manufactured among ourselves, and this large sum retained in the country; can it be admitted for a moment, that the question of manufacturing or importing should be decided by the operation on the fiscal concerns of the country? or that a government, whose paramount duty it is to protect the interests and to promote the prosperity of a nation, should for a moment prefer to have its wealth, to such an extent, drained away for the benefit of a foreign country, merely because it could by such a wasting policy draw a portion of the amount to the coffers of the state? That is to say, in order to simplify the business, can it be reconcilable to sound policy, to send 15,000,000 of dollars to India and China, or elsewhere, to support the industry, the manufactures, and the agriculture of those countries, instead of retaining it at home for the advantage of our own citizens, merely because the treasury could raise three or four millions from the articles thus purchased! Whatever plea there might be for this system in countries whose immoderate debts, and enormous expenses require paramount attention to raising a large revenue, it is wholly inapplicable in the united states, whose debts and expenses are comparatively light, and whose means of discharging them are so abundant.

Any diminution of revenue, resulting from the imposition of the duties necessary to protect national industry would only affect the question of the duration of the debt itself; that is, whether it should be paid off in a greater or less period of time! It is, in a word, a question whether the nation shall pay off the debt, for instance, in ten, twelve, or fifteen years, and during that period feel the distress, embarrassment, and poverty which have never failed and never can fail to result from the neglect of protecting national industry—or take twenty or twenty-five years to pay it off, and in the mean time enjoy the bounties, the blessings, the happiness which heaven has placed within its reach. We trust there never will be, certainly there never ought to be, any hesitation in future on the choice.

But we feel persuaded, that even confining our views to the mere secondary object of revenue, and utterly disregarding all higher concerns, the low tariff has been highly impolitic, as will appear manifest from the following consideration:

It has encouraged extravagant importations, for a few years, whereby the revenue has, it is true, gained in proportion as the country has been impoverished. *But that impoverishment, and the ruin that spreads far and wide, must necessarily produce a diminution of future importations proportioned to the past excess, and has further produced the lamentable consequence of a diminution of the power of paying taxes!!*

The utter impolicy of depending almost wholly on the impost for a revenue, was so striking during the last war, and reduced the country to such a deplorable state in point of resources and finances, that sound wisdom enters a most solemn protest against the continuance of such a system. It brought the united states to the verge of destruction. On the commencement of the war, when our utmost energies ought to have been called into immediate operation, the grand source of revenue was at once cut off, and invaluable time was wasted in preparing a substitute. This must be the case in all future wars, from which the experience of all mankind forbids us to hope for an exemption. Whereas, if manufactures were duly protected, they would bear, and the manufacturers would cheerfully pay, moderate duties; which, in the time of war, might be enlarged as circumstances would require. England, the most commercial nation in the world, derives only one-fifth part of her revenues from customs. In 1793, her revenue was above sixty-three millions of pounds sterling, of which the customs yielded not quite twelve.*

The customs of the united states for the years 1807 and 1808, were above thirty-two millions, or an average of sixteen; whereas, in 1814, *they were not six millions!* thus this source of revenue, like a deceitful friend, deserted the nation completely in the hour of need; and, like a deceitful friend, whose falsehood is fully proved, *ought never to be implicitly relied on again.*

VII. *Encouragement of Smuggling.*

The refusal of adequate duties for the protection of the manufactures of the united states has been too generally defended, among other reasons, by the apprehension of affording encouragement to smuggling. This plea will not stand scrutiny. It is a remarkable fact, that the duties are beyond comparison higher on a variety of articles, not at present, nor likely to be, raised or manufactured in this country, than on those which in-

* Colquhoun on the Power and Resources of Great Britain, p. 258.

terfere with or destroy our national industry—So that this plea falls to the ground.

In order to enable you, fellow citizens, to form a correct idea on this subject, and to appreciate the incorrectness of the plea, we annex a table of duties on sundry articles of both descriptions.

ARTICLES.	Prices at the places of export.	Specific duty.	Rate of duty per cent.
	cents.	cents.	
Imperial tea, per lb. - - -	65 *a* 67	50	80
Hyson do. do. - -	38 1-2 *a* 40	28	70 *a* 80
Souchong do. do. - - -	20 *a* 35	25	70 *a* 125
Madeira wine, per gallon - -	260	100	40
Sherry do. do. - -	100 *a* 112	60	55 *a* 60
Cinnamon, per lb. - - - -	40	25	60
Cloves do. - - -	55 *a* 50	25	50 *a* 52
Cotton fabrics, (except those below 25 cents the square yard)			27 1-2
Woollen manufactures - - -			27 1-2
On all articles manufactured of brass, steel, pewter, lead, or tin, brass wire, cutlery, pins, needles, buttons, earthenware, pottery, porcelain, china, &c. -			22

It is painful to us to state, but regard to truth, and to the dearest interests of our country, oblige us to state that we doubt whether the tariff of any country has ever exhibited more impolitic features than are to be seen in the above abstract. If the apprehension of encouraging smuggling by high duties had any influence in regulating the tariff, ought it not to have prevented the imposition of 80 per cent. on teas, 50 per cent. on wines, 60 per cent. on cinnamon, and 50 per cent. on cloves? Is it not as easy to smuggle boxes of tea, as bales of cottons or woollens? Would it not have been as safe to impose a duty of 80 per cent. on the latter as on the former? The want of sufficient protection of the national industry, which is so conspicuous throughout the tariff, *cannot therefore for a moment be defended on the ground of the apprehension of promoting smuggling, a plea which must be abandoned forever.* The utterly inadequate duty on woollen goods sealed the condemnation and destruction of more than half the merino sheep in the country, which cost above one million of dollars to our citizens; were beyond price; and ought to have been cherished as '*the apple of the eye.*'

Had the cotton and woollen manufactures been protected by the lowest rate of duties on the seven first articles, in the above list, the united states would probably have saved 60,000,000 of dollars since the war, and would now exhibit a most enviable spectacle of prosperity. It rends the heart of every citizen possessed of public spirit to behold the melancholy and appalling contrast that pervades the nation.

The united states possess a capacity of raising, and water power and mechanical skill to manufacture, cotton to an extent commensurate with the demand probably of the whole world, and our means of securing a constant supply of wool are amply adequate. It will not, therefore, admit of a doubt, that by proper encouragement, in a few years, this nation might have fully supplied itself with cotton and woollen manufactures to the utmost extent of its wants; and yet, wonderful to tell, two-thirds of our cotton fabrics are brought from countries, from three to ten thousand miles distant—and one third of our woollens, three thousand.

We wish it to be clearly and distinctly understood, that though these addresses appear to advocate exclusively the interests of the manufacturers, yet it is in appearance only. Our object is to promote the interests of the whole nation, on the most extended scale. We scorn all partial views; and are convinced, that were every manufacturer in the United States in a prosperous situation, still sound policy would require a radical revision of the tariff, in order to arrest the impoverishing drain of specie, resulting from an unfavourable balance of trade, and from the pernicious intercourse with India. The motive to our addresses is a clear and decided conviction, that this nation can never be great, happy, or respectable, while '*it buys more than it sells*,' as it has done ever since the war; while its treasures are lavished at a distance of ten thousand miles, to purchase fabrics, with which it could abundantly supply itself; while it exports raw materials at thirty cents a pound* and receives the articles, manu-

* Two pieces of cambric, each containing twelve yards, weighed, the one two pounds one-eighth—the other, two pounds one-fourth. The first is sold in this city at one dollar, and the other at sixty-two and a half cents per yard. And there are much finer and higher priced cambrics than either—some at a dollar and a quarter, and some at two dollars. Thus the cotton, which we sell raw from eighteen to fifty cents per pound, is returned to us, manufactured, at the rate of from two dollars to seven or eight—an advance of from six hundred to about eighteen hundred per cent!

We submit to the calm consideration of the reader, a calculation which cannot fail to astonish him. In 1816 we exported to Great Britain about fifty millions of pounds of cotton, which, at thirty cents, amounted to $15,000,000

Suppose that we received only 7,500,000 of pounds manufactured into cambrics and muslins, at the low average of 33 cents per yard, equal to two dollars per lb. it would amount to - -	15,000,000
Being for 7,500,000 lbs. the full value of the whole raw material exported, exclusive of the surplus 42,500,000 of pounds of raw cotton, which at prime cost is - - - - - - - -	12,750,000
	27,750,000
Thus leaving to Great Britain by this single transaction, a gain of	12,750,000

What an appalling view of the policy of a nation, which has had the experi-

factured of them at from one dollar to six or eight; and while we suffer our machinery to go to ruin, consign our manufacturers to poverty, and furnish employment for the machinery and manufacturers of other countries.

We shall conclude this address with a new view of this subject which will appear paradoxical, but which, nevertheless, we hope will not be rejected without due consideration.

We are strongly inclined to believe, that such additional protection to the national industry, as would have considerably diminished our importations, would not only have rescued this country from its present distress and embarrassment, and ensured it a high degree of happiness and prosperity, but, extraordinary as it may appear, would have proved advantageous even to Great Britain.

The value of a market depends not on the quantity of goods sold, but on the quantity paid for. And as the present paralysis of the national industry, and the impoverishment of the country, have chiefly arisen from our excessive importations and the want of adequate protection to our manufactures, by which many of them have received a severe, and some a deadly stroke; and, moreover, as this impoverishment has reduced many of our importers to bankruptcy, and incapacitated a considerable proportion of the remainder from discharging their engagements at present; whereby the merchants of Great Britain experience not only very great temporary disappointments and difficulties, but will ultimately suffer immense losses; it conclusively follows, that our impolitic tariff has injured Great Britain as well as the united states.

Its injurious operation has been moreover greatly aided by a system pursued in Great Britain, which deserves reprobation.

That her policy, on the subject of manufactures, trade, and commerce, is generally very profound, is too obvious to require enforcement. Yet we are persuaded, that she has, in the case of this country, very much mistaken her true interest.

That the united states were her best customer, is beyond doubt—and had the trade with us been conducted with care and caution, she would have derived vastly more benefit from it than she has done, or is ever likely to do.

Our importers order as many goods as suit the consumption of the country, and in general rather a superabundance. Had the supplies for this market been confined to goods thus ordered, the importers might have prospered, and the debts to Great Bri-

ence of all the world to guide its career! Is it wonderful, after reflecting on this and so many analogous features of our intercourse with foreign countries, that with advantages superior to those of any nation of ancient or modern times, we should be surrounded by embarrassments and difficulties, and that bankruptcy should stare us in the face!

tain been paid with tolerable punctuality. But it very frequently happens, that after an order is received from the united states, and filled, one, two, or three similar assortments are made up, shipped, consigned to an agent here, and sacrificed at vendue, at very reduced prices, on account of the exporter.—The market is thus immoderately glutted, the prices of goods greatly reduced, the fair trader deeply injured, and sometimes absolutely ruined, by those who receive his orders.

Thus, independent of the heavy loss sustained by the sacrifice of the goods sent on consignment, immense losses arise from the failure of those whose prospects in business are destroyed by this overtrading.

It is, therefore, not improbable, that the British merchants would receive nearly as large returns for two-thirds, perhaps for one half, of the goods they export to this country, as they do for the whole. By the policy at present pursued, they absolutely ruin their most valuable customers, and destroy their best market: and the recent accounts from England prove that many of them ruin themselves. The numerous bankruptcies in that country, it appears, are greatly owing to the failure of remittances from hence.

NO. VI.

Philadelphia, May 15, 1819.

Memorial to the President of the U. S. urging an early call of Congress. View of the state of the nation.

THE Society for the Promotion of National Industry, impressed with a belief that the calamitous situation of our agriculture, manufactures, trade and commerce—the unfavourable balance of trade—the exhausting drain of specie—and the reduction of the prices of real estate, and of the grand staples of our country, require the exercise of the wisdom of the legislature of the united states to apply an early and efficient remedy, hope it will not be regarded as an undue interference, that they venture to submit to the consideration of their fellow citizens throughout the union, the following form of a respectful applicatiou to the president, for an early call of congress. Should the measure be found necessary, it is of little consequence with whom it originates: should the contrary opinion prevail, the motive cannot fail with all good men, to apologize for the suggestion.

To the President of the united states.

Sir,—The subscribers, with all due respect, submit to your most serious consideration, the following reasons on which they venture to suggest the propriety of convening an extra session of congress.

Our agricultural productions, the great staples of our country, on which we relied to pay for our enormous importations, and which, even at their highest rates, would have been inadequate for that purpose, are either excluded from foreign markets, or reduced in price from twenty-five to forty per cent. without any probability of a favourable change.

Our markets are deluged with merchandize from foreign nations; while thousands of our citizens, able and willing to work, and capable of furnishing similar articles, are unable to procure employment; our manufacturing establishments are generally in a languishing condition, and many of them, in which immense sums have been invested, wholly abandoned, whereby their proprietors, who placed reliance on the protection of government, are ruined.

Our commerce is almost equally prostrate, and the capital of the country, engaged in that useful branch, reduced, since the war, at least one-third, probably one-half.

The balance of trade, in consequence of excessive importations, has been, and continues, most ruinously against us, whereby, after having remitted an immense amount of our government and bank stock in payment, which subjects the nation to a heavy, permanent annual tax—we have been and are alarmingly drained of our circulating medium, in consequence of which our monied institutions are impoverished and crippled in their operations; agriculture, manufactures, trade, and commerce paralized: and all classes of our citizens more or less injuriously affected in their pursuits.

Real estate has depreciated throughout the union from fifteen to thirty-five per cent.; and in many cases fifty or sixty.

The subscribers are impressed with a conviction, that for all these alarming evils there is no adequate remedy but a reduction of the amount of our imports within that of our exports; it being undeniably true, that nations, like individuals, which *buy more than they sell*, or, in other words, expend beyond their income, must be reduced to bankruptcy.

To depend on this salutary effect being produced by the restoration of the spirit of economy which is to result from general distress, or from the forbearance of our merchants to import, is to allow a violent fever to rage in the body politic, and exhaust itself, or the national strength, without the application of any remedy to arrest its destructive career.

Even if our own merchants were to reduce their importations

within those bounds which our means of payment would require, this would afford no security: as our markets would probably continue to be, as they have been, inundated with goods consigned by foreign merchants, which would perpetuate the calamitous situation into which our country is plunged.

A radical remedy to the evil can only be applied by the legislature of the united states, in such a revision and regulation of the tariff, as shall reduce our importations, and effectually protect national industry.

In England, France, Germany, Russia and Prussia, and most other countries in Europe, national industry is adequately protected by prohibitions and heavy duties; whereas, while many of our agricultural productions, and almost all our manufactures, are excluded from nearly all the markets of the world; ours are open to those of all other nations, under duties by no means affording sufficient protection; a case probably without example in the annals of mankind.

We therefore respectfully pray that you will be pleased to convene congress as early as circumstances may permit.*

NO. VII.

Philadelphia, May 20, 1819.

Fallacy of the maxim that trade will regulate itself. Strong case supposed of France and Spain. Prosperous state of woollen manufactures in Portugal. Methuen treaty. Fatal consequences. Impoverishment of Portugal, by the drain of her specie—its influx into Great Britain.

On almost every subject of discussion, fellow-citizens, there are certain hacknied phrases, which pass current as oracular, and, though extremely fallacious, are received with scarcely any investigation. There is probably no science that has been more distorted in this respect than that of political economy, on which so much of human happiness depends.

We propose, in the present number, to consider a maxim of this description, fraught with destruction to any nation by which it is adopted; but which is implicitly believed in by a large portion of our citizens, and has had considerable influence on the legislature of the union.

This specious maxim is, that

* [To this memorial no attention whatever was paid, except by a few printers of newspapers, who united in a clamour against it.]

"TRADE WILL REGULATE ITSELF,"

which, in all probability, led to that refusal of adequate protection to the national industry, which has overspread the nation with distress—lowered the price of some of our chief staples, by depriving them of a domestic market—bankrupted so many of our merchants and traders—deprived so many thousands of our citizens of employment—and, in a word, reduced us from the most towering prospects to a most calamitous reverse.

It will be perceived that this is a vital part of Adam Smith's doctrine—indeed, the basis on which he has raised his great superstructure; and that we have already animadverted on it incidentally. But its immense influence on the fate of nations, and its most destructive tendency, demand a more minute investigation, to which we now solicit your attention.

How far its advocates deem it proper to have it carried, we are not quite certain. In its strict acceptation, it means a total exclusion of all regulations of commerce, so that the intercourse between nations should be as free as between different provinces of the same empire. In fact, if it does not mean this, it is difficult to define what it can mean; for if a government enacts any regulation whatever, it cannot with truth or justice be said, that "*trade regulates itself.*" We shall, therefore, consider it in its utmost latitude, as excluding all regulations. The result, however, would not be materially affected by any modification, or restriction of its provisions, short of effectual protection of national industry. These would, as the case might be, only accelerate or procrastinate the final catastrophe, to which it infallibly leads.

This maxim ought to have been consigned to oblivion centuries since, by the considerations, that no trading or commercial nation has ever prospered without "*regulation of trade;*" that those nations which have devoted the most scrupulous attention to its regulation, have been the most prosperous; and that in proportion as it has been neglected, exactly in the same proportion have nations gone to decay. The cases of England, France, Spain, and Portugal, offer powerful illustrations of these positions. But we shall not rest satisfied with this mode of defence. We shall trace the operation of the maxim in its full extent.

As it would be nugatory to suppose that the existing regulations of commerce could, by any convention, be annulled, and its entire freedom be universally established, we shall merely suppose it adopted only by a portion of the commercial world, and see what would be its effects on those nations wherein it was carried into operation?

To form an accurate idea on this or any other subject, the safest and best mode is to state the case on a small scale, which the mind can readily embrace without distraction, and thence to argue on the widest range to which the subject extends.

We will, therefore, here confine our view to two nations, France and Spain, and suppose that in the latter country the maxim we combat is carried into full operation, and that trade is allowed "*to regulate itself*"—but that in the former, it is "regulated" by the government, for the protection and encouragement of national industry, after the example of Great Britain, and indeed almost every other country in Christendom.

In order to do the maxim justice, we will assume, that both nations are on a perfect equality in every other respect than the "*regulation of trade*." We will further assume that at the commencement of the rivalry between them, each nation possesses a circulating medium of 20,000,000 of dollars, and has 200,000 people employed in the cotton, and as many in the woollen manufacture, who produce annually four millions of yards of each kind of goods, which are exactly adequate to their consumption. To simplify the discussion, we confine ourselves to those two branches. But the reasoning will equally apply to every other species of manufactures.

4,000,000 yards of cotton goods, say *a* 50 cents	$2,000,000
4,000,000 ditto of woollen, *a* 6 dollars - -	24,000,000
	26,000,000
On which they realize a profit of twelve and a half per cent. - - - - - - -	$3,250,000

To the French manufacturers, according to our hypothesis, the home market is secured. All foreign competition is effectually cut off. They have, therefore, every encouragement to extend and improve their fabrics; and in the first year of rivalship, having a surplus on hand, they export, we will suppose, 400,000 yards of each kind to Spain, and increase the exportation annually an equal amount. This operation produces the treble effect of lowering the price of the Spanish goods by the competition; circumscribing their sale; and depriving, during the first year, about 40,000 people of employment.

It being our determination to afford as little room for objection, as possible, we will suppose the reduction of price to be only seven and a half per cent. which is far less than is usual in such cases.* Let us see the situation of the parties at the end of the

* Instances have recently occurred of domestic goods being reduced at once, ten, fifteen, and twenty per cent. in our markets, in consequence of great quantities of similar articles suddenly introduced from Europe.

First year:

	$
The French manufacturers gain in their domestic market, as before - - -	3,250,000
And on 400,000 yards of each kind, sold in Spain, amounting to 2,600,000, at 5 per cent. - - - -	130,000
Dollars	3,380,000

Whereas, the Spanish manufacturers, whose sales are reduced to 3,600,000 yards of each kind, amounting to 23,400,000 dollars, gain at 5 per cent. only - - - - Dollars 1,170,000*

This is the operation in the very first year, producing a difference at once of about 2,210,000 dollars of actual profit against the infatuated nation, which allows "*trade to regulate itself*," and, according to Adam Smith, buys where "*goods can be had the cheapest*." The second year commences with increased energy on the part of the French, and dismay and discouragement on that of the Spanish manufacturers. The former double their exportations, and send 800,000 yards into the rival markets amounting to $5,200,000, of which we trace the operation.

Second year.

French profit, as before, on the home market - -	3,250,000
And on 800,000 yards of each kind sold in Spain, amounting to 5,200,000 dollars, at 5 per cent. - - - - -	260,000
	$3,510,000

Whereas the sales of the Spaniards are reduced to 3,200,000 yards of each kind, amounting to 20,800,000 dollars, on which they gain at 5 per cent. - - - - - - - $1,040,000

Third year.

French profit, as before, on the home market - -	3,250,000
They increase their exportation to 1,200,000 yards of each kind, amounting to 7,800,000 dollars, at 5 per cent. - - - - - -	390,000
	$3,640,000

The Spaniards find their sales diminished to 2,800,000 yards of each kind amounting to 18,200,000 dollars, whereon they realize a profit of 5 per cent. $910,000

Fourth year.

French profit at home, as before - - - - - -	3,250,000
They increase their exportation to 1,600,000 yards of each kind, amounting to 10,400,000 dollars, which, at 5 per cent, afford a gain of - - -	520,000
	$3,770,000

The Spanish manufacturers are reduced to 2,400,000 yards of each kind, amounting to 15,600,000 dollars, on which, at 5 per cent, they gain - - - - - $780,000

* This view of the effect of the rivalry has, we apprehend, almost wholly escaped the notice of our political economists. When the prices of our manufactures are reduced in the home market by foreign competition, the reduction is *on the whole we offer for sale.* Whereas the reduction to the rival nation is only on such part of her's as she exports to us. The contest is therefore carried on at an immense inequality.

It is, we trust, needless to pursue the calculation any further. You can readily, fellow citizens, perceive that the contest must soon terminate. The Spanish manufacturers, oppressed, impoverished, and dispirited, would be soon driven from the market, which would be monopolized by the more sagacious nation which, we repeat, had the good sense to "*regulate trade.*" Their immense gains would be at the expense, and to the destruction, of the nation, which was deluded by the specious maxim to "*let trade regulate itself.*" The successful rivals would soon indemnify themselves for the temporary reduction of price, by a proportionate advance in future.

Let us compare the result of the four years operations on the two nations :—

France		*Spain.*	
First year's profit	3,380,000	First Year's profit	1,170,000
Second Year	3,510,000	Second Year	1,040,000
Third year	3,640,000	Third Year	910,000
Fourth year	3,770,000	Fourth Year	780,000
	$14,300,000		$3,900,000

Effect on the working people..

France.	*Spain.*
Six hundred thousand people industriously employed, supporting themselves in comfort and happiness, and adding to the wealth and strength of the nation.*	Four hundred thousand people gradually thrown idle ;—dragging on a wretched existence in mendicity; or looking in vain for those "*collateral branches*" which sound so harmoniously in Adam Smith, but which are not elsewhere to be found; or emigrating to France, to strengthen that nation at the expense of their own.

We have hitherto confined our calculations of the effects of this plausible but destructive system, to the manufacturers alone. Its pernicious consequences, if they extended no farther than to this class of citizens, would be sufficient to induce liberal minded men—those worthy to legislate for this rising empire, to abandon the maxim. But those consequences, how deplorable soever, are but as "*mere dust in the balance*" compared with its general effects on the wealth, strength, resources, power, and happiness of any devoted nation which enlists itself under the banners of Adam Smith.

* It is obvious that by the transfer of the manufactures from Spain to France, for every workman reduced to idleness in the former country, there would be one additional employed in the latter. We have, therefore, in the text assumed 600,000, as the average number in France.

In the first year France sells to Spain to the amount of - - - - - - -	$2,600,000
In the second - - - - - - -	5,200,000
In the third - - - - - - -	7,800,000
In the fourth - - - - - - -	10,400,000
	26,000,000

This is a debt which, in the first place, drains all the metallic medium, as far as the merchants can collect it; and next all the evidences of public debt, or whatever valuable articles can be had. And still a heavy and oppressive debt is accruing from year to year afterwards!

The result is easily seen. A prosperous nation, with a specie capital of $20,000,000, is by this simple process in four years reduced to a most abject, impoverished, and dependent state. Its wealth is drained away to support a foreign rival. Every species of industry is paralized. Ships rot at the wharves. Trade languishes. Merchants and traders, as well as manufacturers, become bankrupts. Artisans, mechanics, and labouring people, who had largely contributed to the welfare of the state, are transformed into mendicants, or driven to desperate courses to prolong their existence; and desolation extends itself over the face of the land.

This, fellow citizens, is very nearly our present case. It is true, we have not absolutely let '*trade regulate itself*,' by a total absence of all duties. The necessities of the treasury, which, by many members of congress, are freely admitted to be the leading, and by some to be the only object of a tariff,* forbade the adoption of the maxim in its fullest extent: and therefore our imported merchandize pays duty. But it is obvious that where the tariff of one nation is so wholly inefficient, that she can be completely undersold in her own markets by another, as the people of the united states are at present, the ultimate effect is actually the same, as if '*trade were allowed to regulate itself*.' The duties imposed by our tariff have merely delayed, not averted, the work of destruction. But that it is as sure in its operation, is placed beyond the reach of doubt by the desolation and ruin that pervade so many invaluable manufacturing establishments throughout the union, on which millions of dollars have been expended, and whose fall, as we have so often repeated, and must re-echo in the ears of those who alone have the

* We have already stated that col. John Taylor, a popular writer in Virginia, has taken the broad ground, that every dollar imposed as duty on foreign merchandize, is a dollar robbed out of the pockets of the agriculturists! This maxim, admirably calculated to excite the selfish passions of one class of citizens against another, has unfortunately had too many proselytes in and out of congress.

power of applying a remedy, involved the ruin of the citizens engaged in them.

The most cursory reader must perceive, and no one possessed of candour can deny, that we have given the advocates of the maxim, '*let trade regulate itself*,' far more advantage in the argument than was necessary, or proper. When we stated the reduction of price at seven and a half per cent. and a gradual increase of exportation from France to Spain, of only ten per cent. of the amount originally manufactured in each country, we did our cause manifest injustice. We might have assumed at once a reduction of price not of seven and a half per cent.—but of ten or more—and an exportation of double the amount, which, combined, would produce the immediate ruin of the Spanish manufacturers, of whose fabrics a large proportion would remain on hand, and the residue be sold at or below cost.—This is and has ever been the uniform operation of the system of letting '*trade regulate itself*.'

A physician who found his patient in a raging fever, and let the disorder take its course, or '*regulate itself*,' would be deservedly reprobated as unworthy of his profession. But his conduct would not be more irrational than that of a statesman, who saw the agriculture, manufactures, trade, and commerce of his country going to decay, and let them '*regulate themselves*.' Government is instituted to guard the interests of the nation confided to its care: and, by whatever name it may be called, is no longer estimable than as it fulfils this sacred duty. It was painful to us to state in a former address—it is equally painful to us to repeat—but we must repeat—the appalling truth, that our manufacturers, a large and important class, embracing some of the most valuable members of the community, must, with mixed sensations of regret and envy, regard the situation of the manufacturers of England, Denmark, France, Russia, Austria, and most other countries in Europe, who enjoy that protection from their governments, which the former sought in vain from their fellow citizens and representatives, who are now themselves involved in the general distress resulting from the want of that protection.

We refer you, fellow citizens, to the plain, but impressive lesson afforded by the fable of the belly and the members. The latter starved the former to death—and perished victims of their own folly. We need not pursue it in detail. It is on the mind of almost every individual in the country, young and old. We cannot refrain from expressing our fears, that posterity will pronounce our policy to be a full exemplification of the soundness of its moral, and of our destitution of those broad and liberal views, that regard with '*equal eye*' all descriptions of society.

It will probably be objected by those whose interests or prejudices enlist them in hostility to our views, that all we have here submitted to you, fellow citizens, is merely theory; that however plausible, it cannot be relied on in the regulation of the political economy of a great nation; that Adam Smith being the oracle of that science, no theory opposed to his should be received, at least without the support of strong and well-established facts.

Well, we meet them, and are fairly at issue, on this ground—and are willing to stand or fall as we furnish this support to our theory. We offer an historical case which exemplifies the baleful consequences of a system exactly similar to ours in its features and operation—which blighted and blasted the happiness of a prosperous nation—and which pronounces a strong sentence of condemnation on the theory of Adam Smith.

In the year 1681, Portugal established the woollen manufacture on an extensive scale; and, by absolute prohibitions, excluded the woollen cloths of all other nations.—In consequence she enjoyed a high degree of prosperity for above twenty years, and had the balance of trade in her favour universally. Fatally for her, in 1703, the British minister, Mr. Methuen, induced her to enter into a treaty, called by his name, which stipulated that she should never prohibit British woollen manufactures, provided Port wines were admitted into Great Britain at two-thirds of the duty paid on those of France. The agriculturists of Portugal deluded themselves into the opinion, that they should derive a double benefit from this regulation; that is, secure a market for their wines, and likewise buy their cloths at reduced prices; in other words, according to the maxim of Adam Smith, buy them where *they could be had the cheapest.*' But they were soon awakened out of this '*day dream.*' The flourishing manufacture was destroyed—the circulating medium of the country drained away—and the nation precipitated from the most flourishing state of prosperity to that pitiable situation of poverty and debasement which holds her up to other nations as a beacon to shun the rocks whereon she shipwrecked her resources and her happiness, and on which our political bark is at present striking with violence.*

* These admonitory facts evince the unsoundness of the theory of Col. Taylor, as well as of many of the members of congress, his disciples and zealous partizans of his doctrines. Regardless of the ruinous consequences to their fellow citizens who had embarked millions in manufacturing establishments, they fondly persuaded themselves that by reducing the duties as low as possible, consistently with the necessity of providing a revenue, which we repeat, was their paramount object, they were consulting the interests of the agriculturists, who would thereby be enabled to purchase foreign merchandize at low prices, and whose produce they believed always so certain of finding an advantageous market and high prices in Europe, that they might disregard the home market! Fatal de-

The important lesson held out by this case of Portugal—its close affinity to our situation—and the hope of its eradicating prejudices destructive to the strength, happiness, and independence of our country, induce us to give our authorities at full length. They are derived from two works of high character, "the British Merchant," written by a society of the most eminent merchants in England, in the reign of queen Anne; and "Anderson on the means of exciting a spirit of National Industry."

"In the year 1681, one *Courteen*, an Irishman, a servant in "the family of the then queen of England, afterwards queen "dowager, carried over several clothiers and bay-makers "into Portugal, where they presently set up the manufactures, "both of cloth and bays, particularly at Port *Alegre* and *Covil-"han.*

"It was soon found that the staple of their wool was too short "for bays; therefore their bay-makers were dismissed.

"But they proceeded in their manufacture of cloth; and soon "brought it to such perfection, that in 1684, either in June or "July upon the Conde *d'Ereicera's* project to encrease their "exportations, and lessen the consumption of foreign manufac-"tures, as well as to encourage their own, the king of Portugal "made a sumptuary law to restrain several excesses in the "kingdom; and, among the rest, *the importation of all foreign "woollen cloths was prohibited.*

"Upon this the foreign merchants in that country made "several remonstrances; but could by no means obtain that the "prohibition should be set aside: yet they gained a year's time "to bring in those that were on the way; but were obliged to "reship whatever should arrive after the time limited.

"The Portuguese soon became so expert in the manufacture "of woollen cloths, that they sent home our English clothiers in "a distressed condition; and the renegadoes were forced for "some time to beg their bread."*

"The *Portuguese* went on successfully: their manufacture of "woollen cloths increased to that degree, that *both Portugal and "Brazil were wholly supplied from their own fabrics: and the "materials of this manufacture were of their own and Spanish "wool, and no other.*

lusion! Utter disregard of the sound systems and experience of all wise nations, and of the warning example of all unwise ones! They are now broad awake from those deceptious 'day dreams.' Their flour, excluded from the European markets, has fallen from thirty to forty per cent; their cotton has suffered an equal depreciation; and their tobacco is reduced 50 per cent. If liberality insures its own reward, illiberal policy never fails to carry its own punishment.

* British Merchant, vol. III. p. 69.

"To make ourselves some amends, and to evade the ill con-"sequences of this prohibition of our woollen cloths, we intro-"duced into Portugal in their stead cloth-serges and cloth drug-"gets; *against which their fabric of cloth, which was then but in* "*its infancy, would have been as unable to contend, as against a* "*free importation of our woollen cloths. Therefore, that their* "*own cloth might have no such thing as a rival in their own coun-*"*try, they proceeded to prohibit foreign cloth-serges and cloth* "*druggets*."*

"Mr. Methuen's treaty, (1703,) by taking off the prohibition "of British cloths, and by providing, that neither these, nor any "of the *British* woollen manufactures in Portugal, should here-"after be prohibited, was *the immediate ruin of all the fabrics in* "*that country*."†

"Our gain by the treaty, and so vast an enlargement of our "exportations to Portugal, is, that we have saved vast sums of "money, which otherwise might have gone out of the nation to "pay our armies in Portugal and other countries; and *have* "*greatly added to the treasure of the kingdom; that the balance* "*annually due from Portugal has subsisted great numbers of our* "*people, employed in making manufactures to the value of the* "*balance*.

"*The product of the lands is a considerable part of every manu-*"*facture; the balance therefore due from Portugal has paid great* "*sums for the product of our lands: and our rents are nothing* "*else but the value paid for the product of the lands; and conse-*"*quently all that part of the Portugal balance which has been paid* "*for the product of the lands, is so much added to the rents of the* "*kingdom. Yet this is not the whole profit the landed interest* "*has received from this balance*. The people that have been sub-"sisted by that great overbalance of manufactures might other-"wise have come very great numbers of them upon the parish; "it is a gain to the landed interest to be saved from this charge. "*Our gain then by our Portugal treaty, and our excess of ex-*"*portations on that account, is a vast increase of the nation's* "*treasure, the employment and subsistence of great numbers of* "*manufacturing people, an augmentation of our rents, and the* "*saving the landed interest from the charge of maintaining such* "*numbers of poor, as have subsisted themselves by the excess of* "*exportations*.‡

"The stipulation of the king of Portugal in this treaty, has "helped us to so *prodigious a vent for our woollen manufactures* "*in that country*, as has abundantly made up the loss of that "balance we heretofore received from Spain."§

* British Merchant, vol. iii. p. 71.
† Idem, p. 76.
‡ Idem, p. 254.
§ Idem, p. 38.

Previous to the Methuen treaty, Portugal coins were so rare in England, that they were almost regarded as medals. Whereas, after the treaty had gone into operation, there was an annual balance in favour of England, *of one million sterling*, or 4,444,000 dollars, equal to three millions at present. Portugal was drained, as the United States are now, first of her silver, and then of her gold, so that she had "*very little left for her necessary occasions*." This balance fully accounts for her impoverishment; and at that period was an immense sum, as will appear from the circumstance that the whole of the balance of trade in favour of England with all the world was then only 2,000,000*l*.—and her whole exports scarcely 7,000,000*l* * In consequence, the coins of Portugal flowed into Great Britain so abundantly, that she was not only enabled to pay her armies abroad with them—but they formed a considerable portion of the circulating medium of the nation—and the chief part of the bullion melted and coined in her mint.

"During the twenty years prohibition, the Portuguese succeed- "ed so well in their woollen manufactures, that *we brought* "*thence no gold or silver; but after the taking off that prohibition* "*we brought away so much of their silver, as to leave them very* "*little for their necessary occasions; and then we began to bring* "*away their gold*."†

"From that treaty's taking place, the balance of trade began "to take place: and the year 1703, was the first year *we began* "*to bring off the silver of that nation*."‡

"The intent of the treaty was, to increase the consumption of "our woollen cloths in Portugal; and has it not been increased "by means of this treaty? *had we any balance before from Por-* "*tugal, and do we not now gain every year a million by that* "*treaty?*"§

"We never before the treaty, had any armies to pay in Portu- "gal; yet *we brought none of their coin to our mint; not such a* "*thing as a Portugal piece was seen in England; or if it was, it* "*was almost as great a curiosity as our medals*."‖

"Our exports to Portugal since that treaty have amounted to "1,300,000*l*. per annum, and perhaps to a much greater sum."¶

"*The payment of our armies, the coinage in the mint, the quan-* "*tities of Portugal coin still current in the country*, are so many "demonstrations that we have exported vast quantities of wool- "len manufactures, and other goods and merchandize to that "kingdom."**

* British Merchant, vol. ii. p. 110.
† Idem. vol. iii. p. 15.
‡ Idem, vol. ii. p. 35.
§ Idem, vol. iii. p. 33.
‖ Idem, vol. iii. p. 253.
¶ Idem, 20.
** Idem, p. 257.

The analogy between the case of Portugal and that of the united states is strong and striking. The important woollen manufacture was established and brought to such perfection in four years in the former country, as not only to supply its own consumption but that of its colonies. In the course of three or four years it was completely destroyed.

"Thus did Portugal, by the spirited exertion of one able min- "ister, (the Conde *d'Ereicera*,) gain in a few years a perfect "knowledge in a principal branch of the woollen manufacture; "which they might have possessed, to the infinite emolument of "the poor subjects of his Faithful Majesty till this hour, *had not "the nation, by the death of that patriotic nobleman, lost her best "counsellor, and been overreached by the more able British minis- "ter, Mr. Methuen.*"*

"*Thus in four years did their woollen manufactures attain to "such perfection, as to enable them to dispense with foreign cloths "entirely.*"†

It may perhaps, be supposed that the total destruction of this flourishing manufacture, could not have taken place so rapidly unless the English woollen fabrics were admitted duty free.— This would be an egregious error. The stipulation of the Methuen treaty was, that they should not be prohibited, nor be subject to a higher duty than before the prohibition had taken place; that is, twenty-three per cent. which, *like so many of the duties in the united states, was found utterly inadequate to preserve the manufacture from destruction.*

"The duties of importation, before the prohibitions, had the "name of twenty-three per cent. But *the goods were undervalu- "ed; those duties of twenty-three per cent, were not above twelve "per cent. of their real value.* To such low duties has the king "of Portugal obliged himself with respect to the several sorts "of woollen manufactures, which stood before prohibited in "that country."‡

We invite your attention, fellow-citizens, to the striking similarity between the case of Portugal, as stated above, and that of the united states. In this country, the woollen manufacture and that of cotton rose to maturity during the two years and a half of warfare: and had the war continued two or three years more, or had those manufactures received adequate protection after the peace, they would probably have attained to such maturity, and taken such deep root, as to defy foreign competition. But the four years of peace have crushed a large portion of both descriptions. One of the most eminent merchants in Baltimore writes us—"I am sorry to say, that our cotton manufactures are "likely to fall through, unless more effectually protected—*En-*

* Anderson on National Industry, page 267. † British Merchant.
‡ Idem, vol. iii. page 37.

"*glish cotton goods have been selling at about half the cost and* "*charges*. Under such circumstances it is impossible for home "manufactures to stand the competition." A merchant in New York likewise writes—"The manufacturers (of cotton particu- "larly) will require all the aid they can get from congress next "session to sustain themselves. The enormous imports of for- "eign goods have so affected the price, that the cost cannot be "obtained."

The preceding view of the enviable state of prosperity, and the rapid and lamentable downfall of Portugal, demands the most pointed attention of every friend of the prosperity of this country. It is like the hand-writing on the wall—the "*mene tekel upharsin*,"—the warning to flee the road that is leading us to a similar state. Let these facts be carefully compared with the theory laid down in the commencement of this address, and they will afford the most irresistible proof of its soundness, as well as of the utter impolicy that has prevailed in the regulation of our tariff, which has done this country more injury in four years of peace, than she suffered in both her wars. At the close of the last, she commenced her career under as favourable auspices as any nation in the world—A high character at home and abroad—her merchants wealthy and prosperous—her manufactures flourishing—her people all employed—her staples of immense value. What a deplorable contrast she exhibits at present! Who can reflect on it without agony! Her character impaired by the impracticability of her citizens paying their debts abroad—her merchants, one after another, daily swallowed up in bankruptcy—her manufactures prostrate—thousands and tens of thousands of her people unemployed—her staples sunk in value, probably more than 20,000,000 dollars per annum—and no prospect of relief at hand. If Adam Smith's work consisted of twenty volumes instead of two—and if the commentaries on it had extended to two hundred, were the whole thrown into one scale, and the single case of Portugal thrown into the other, the former would kick the beam.

We conjure you, fellow citizens, by your regard for our common country—by the duty you owe yourselves, your wives and your children—by the memory of your Washington, Franklin, Hancock, and Adams—by the desire you must feel to arrest the progress of the depreciation of the grand staples of your agriculture, as well as the destruction of your manufactures, trade and commerce—all victims of a pernicious policy—by the claim posterity has on you to make a good use of the immense advantages you possess—by that liberty on which you justly pride yourselves, but which loses its value, if accompanied by beggary and ruin—in a word, by all you hold near or dear on earth—weigh well the subject of this address. Examine it in all its bearings and aspects. And should it satisfactorily establish, as we trust it will, the danger of the course you are pursuing, arouse from the lethargy in which you are enthralled—and, as congress alone has the power of applying a remedy, memorialize your representatives to change their system—to follow the maxims of all the wise nations of ancient and modern times—to remove, as far as possible, the distresses of the nation---and to save from the vortex of bankruptcy those who have escaped the ravages of the storm which threatens to blast all our hopes of happiness, and to reduce us to the same state of prostration and decrepitude as Spain and Portugal, who, it is unfortunately true, have not made a worse use of the bounties of heaven than the united states!

The immense importance of the case of Portugal, induces us to place before the eyes of our fellow citizens two comparisons of her conduct with ours---in the one, the soundness of her policy places us in the back ground an entire century in point of political wisdom---in the other, her impolicy and her consequent sufferings and distress are the counterpart of the system we have pursued, and the calamities under which we writhe.

Striking contrast.

PORTUGAL

"The Portuguese set up a fabric of "their own, and proceeded in it with "very good success, *after the prohibi-* "*tion of ours and all foreign coloured* "*cloth.* We had then nothing left "against their cloths, but to introduce "our cloth serges and cloth druggets "into that country. They quickly "found that these gave some interrup- "tion to their manufactures, and there- "fore *they proceeded also to prohibit* "*foreign serges and druggets.*"*

THE UNITED STATES

Prohibit nothing whatever—and afford utterly inadequate protection to the great and leading manufactures of cottons, woollens, and iron, lest '*the many should be taxed for the benefit of the few!!!*' and in order to '*buy where goods can be had cheapest!!!*'

Striking likeness.

PORTUGAL.

"Before the treaty, our woollen "cloths, cloth serges, and cloth drug- "gets were prohibited in Portugal. "They had set up fabrics there for "making cloth, and proceeded with "very good success: and we might "justly apprehend they would have "gone on to erect other fabrics, till at "last they had served themselves with "every species of woollen manufac- "tures. The treaty takes off all pro- "hibitions, and obliges Portugal to ad- "mit forever all our woollen manufac-

THE UNITED STATES.

During the war, cotton, woollen, and other kinds of goods, were not, it is true, prohibited. There were, however, very few imported. The citizens of the United States set up fabrics for making cloth, both woollen and cotton; and, had the war continued, or had they received protection after it was concluded, they would have gone on to erect other fabrics, till they had served themselves with every species of manufacture. The treaty of peace opened our ports to foreign merchandize, under

* British Merchant, vol. iii. p. 35.

"tures. *Their own fabrics by this were* "*presently ruined.* And we exported "100,000*l.* value in the single article of "cloths, the very year after the trea- "ty."*

"*The court was pestered with remon-* "*strances from their manufacturers when* "*the prohibition was taken off, pursuant* "*to Mr. Methuen's treaty.* But the "thing was past. *The treaty was rati-* "*fied: and THEIR LOOMS WERE* "*ALL RUINED.* And yet there was "no tendency to a revolt, although so "many people were deprived of their "employment in that country by ta- "king off the prohibition."†

"The balance was so very great, that "notwithstanding we paid subsidies to "the king of Portugal, and paid for "troops, (there were also vast sums for "supplies of our armies in Valencia and "Catalonia,) yet still the overbalance "lay so much against them, that there "was ten, twelve, and fifteen per cent. "difference between the exchange and "the intrinsic value of the money."‡

duties utterly inadequate for protection, whereby *a large portion of our fabrics were wholly ruined*—and, probably within a year after the war $30,000,000 of cottons and woollens were imported into this country.

Congress was most respectfully entreated for adequate protection, by the manufacturers, when the war was closed. It was refused: and the distress and ruin of the manufacturers and the impoverishment of the nation followed.

The balance of trade is so great, that notwithstanding we have shipped immense quantities of produce at high prices—and remitted probably from $15,000,000 to 20,000,000 of government and bank stock, we are still heavily in debt, and unable to pay.

The following picture of the state of the western country, taken from the Frankfort Argus, evinces the insanity of not making some prompt and decisive effort to relieve the nation from its disastrous situation.

"Never within the recollection of our oldest citizens has the aspect of times, as respects property and money, been so alarming. Already has property been sacrificed in considerable quantities, in this and the neighbouring counties, for less than half its value. We have but little money in circulation, and that little is daily diminishing by the universal calls of the banks. Neither lands, negroes, nor any other article can be sold for half their value in cash; while executions, to the amount of many hundred thousand dollars, are hanging over the heads of our citizens. WHAT CAN BE DONE? In a few months no debt can be paid, no money will be in circulation to answer the ordinary purposes of human life. Warrants, writs, and executions will be more abundant than bank notes: and the country will present a scene of scuffling for the poor remnants of individual fortunes, which the world has not witnessed."

* British merchant, vol. iii. p. 253. † Idem, p. 75. ‡ Idem, p. 91.

NO. VIII.

Philadelphia, May 27, 1819.

Synopsis. Grand Jury Presentment.

When we first ventured, fellow citizens, to call your attention to the subject of political economy, we were influenced to adopt that measure, by the calamitous situation of our affairs, public and private. Agriculture had received a deep wound by the reduction of the prices of its staple articles from twenty to forty per cent.—real estate was reduced in the same proportion—navigation and commerce were languishing—manufactures were prostrated by an inordinate influx of foreign commodities, calculated to excite a spirit of luxury and extravagance in our citizens—the narrow, illiberal, and selfish maxims, '*to buy where goods could be had the cheapest*,' and '*not to tax the many for the benefit of the few*,' had produced a system whereby the wealth of our nation was converted into a means of fostering and encouraging the industry of a distant hemisphere, and supporting foreign governments, while our own citizens were turned adrift for want of employment, and many of them reduced to mendicity, and our country impoverished—we were involved in far heavier debts than ever before, with greatly diminished means of payment—and the character of our country, from the inability of our merchants to pay their debts, and their frequent bankruptcy, was greatly impaired in the eyes of the world. In a word, under whatever aspect our affairs were viewed, they presented the most serious cause for uneasiness and apprehension.

We looked around for the causes which, in the short space of four years, without war, famine, pestilence, or failure of any of the bounties of heaven, have reduced to this state, from the pinnacle of reputation and happiness—a people justly celebrated for their enterprise, their industry, their mechanical skill, their wealth, and enjoying in the highest degree, every gift of heaven in soil, climate, and extent of territory.

Several causes, we found, had combined to produce this calamitous result. The prosperity of the country had engendered a spirit of extravagance—and the inordinate spirit of banking, carried in many cases to a most culpable excess, had done much mischief. But the great paramount evil, in comparison with which all the rest sink into insignificance, is the immoderate extent of our importations, whereby we are involved in debts, for which our produce, at the highest prices, would have been inadequate to pay; and their great recent reduction of course increases our disabilities. The evils arising from other sources would have gradually cured themselves—or involved in ruin only the deluded parties. Whereas the loss of our industry, the drain of our specie, and the consequent impoverishment of our country, affect all classes of citizens, the economical and the extravagant—the labourer, the artisan, the cultivator of the soil, as well as the landholder, the manufacturer, the trader and the merchant.

On the most mature consideration of the subject, we are persuaded that the only radical remedy for those evils is to limit the importation of such articles as we can manufacture ourselves and thus foster our domestic industry. Other measures may be adopted to co-operate and aid in this great work. But without the grand restorative of "*buying less than we sell*," which a proper tariff alone can effect, they will operate as mere palliatives of an evil whose immense extent and magnitude require prompt and decisive remedies. All our efforts have been directed to convince our fellow citizens of this truth, so important to their virtue, their happiness, their independence.

We are, like other men, liable to error, and may have viewed the subject through an incorrect medium. But we declare, as we can with truth, that should we be mistaken—should any man or body of men devise a better plan, we shall rejoice in the discovery, abandon our present views, and support theirs with all our ardour. We contend not for victory, which is no object in the discussion of such a momentous question, involving the happiness or misery of millions. We contend for the happiness of our citizens—and for the honour and prosperity of our beloved country.

A document has just reached us, which does honour to the head and heart of the writer, as well as to the respectable body of citizens by whom it was adopted, and which deserves the serious attention of our citizens throughout the union. It is the presentment of a late grand jury of Newcastle county, which points out with infallible certainty the road to prosperity. We warmly recommend associations throughout the country to carry its salutary objects into operation, and thus arrest the impoverishment of our citizens. Should they be general—should the plan proposed be faithfully adhered to, and the tariff be properly modified—the thick clouds that environ our horizon will disappear—the sun of prosperity will again shine on us—we shall recover from our disastrous situation—and only remember our sufferings, to warn us to avoid the fatal source, a false and mistaken policy, from whence they burst forth on us with destructive violence.

Delaware claims the high honour of having first adopted the federal constitution. It will be another just cause of pride, that she has taken the lead on this occasion, more particularly should the sound views she has given of the causes of our distresses, and the excellent remedies she has prescribed, lead to their radical cure.

Grand Inquest of Newcastle county, state of Delaware.

The grand jury of Newcastle county beg leave to represent—That they are deeply impressed with the distressed and calamitous situation of the agricultural, commercial, and manufacturing interests of the state; that in their opinion these evils have arisen from—

I. A failure of crops.*

II. An unfavourable balance of trade, *the result of excessive importations of foreign goods, exceeding, to an immense amount, the value of our exports;*

III. Thus draining the state of its specie, and circulating medium;

IV. Depressing the value of real estate; and,

V. Increasing poverty and distress.

The only practicable remedies for those evils, in the opinion of the grand jury, are—

I. A regular and strict economy in the expenses of the people.

II. A retrenchment in the use of imported goods, and foreign luxuries.

III. A steady attention to the improvement of our agricultural products.

IV. ☞ *And the encouragement of a market at home, by fostering and protecting domestic manufactures.*

To a serious consideration of this important subject, the Grand Jury would most earnestly invite the attention of the citizens, more especially of this county.

Unanimously agreed to, and ordered to be printed.

ARCHD. ALEXANDER, *Foreman.*

Attest, S. H. BLACK, *Clerk of G. J.*

19*th May*, 1819.

NO. IX.

Philadelphia, June 3, 1819.

In our preceding Addresses, fellow-citizens, we have presented you with sketches of the policy of England, Russia, Prussia and Portugal—and displayed the wisdom and beneficial results of the system of the three first nations, and even of the last at one period of her history. We have shown, from authentic doc-

* The failure of crops has not prevailed in other parts of the united states—but the distress from the other causes, is equally felt elsewhere.

uments, the rapid destruction of the prosperity and happiness of Portugal, when she relaxed the system of protecting her national industry—whereby she was precipitated from a most flourishing situation, in two or three years, exactly as the united states have been, and in about the same space of time. We feel a confident hope, that those who have brought to the discussion the spirit of candour and impartiality, requisite to a correct decision, and which the importance of the subject demanded, have been convinced of the vital and radical errors in our system of policy.

We now present to your view the essence of the Report of Alexander Hamilton, on the encouragement of National Manufactures, one of the most luminous and instructive public documents ever produced in this, or perhaps in any other country. It is a complete body of political economy on the subject of national industry, and sheds a glare of light on this all-important subject which points out with unerring certainty, the course this nation should pursue. Happy would it have been, had the legislature of the union been guided by its dictates. We should then have made rapid advances in the career of prosperity which was open to us, and in which we were invited to proceed. But unfortunately our whole system of political economy has been in hostility with the profound views developed in this valuable report—and the united states now pay a heavy forfeit for the error of neglecting its sage counsels.

There are circumstances attending it, which entitle it to most peculiar attention. Mr. Hamilton's habits and associations lay among the commercial part of the community, of which the great mass accorded with him in politics, and regarded him as their grand leader. The politics of the majority of the manufacturing interest were hostile to his. There was strong jealousy between them. Had he, therefore, been unfriendly to manufactures, in order to foster and protect commerce, (according to the narrow views entertained by many of our citizens of the fancied hostility between their interests) his politics might be suspected of producing an undue bias on his mind, and warping him to support an erroneous system.

But when, in opposition to the dictates of his politics, he appeared the strenuous advocate of manufactures, as the grand means of promoting the happiness, the power, the greatness, and independence of his country, it behoves those, who, in point of mind, are no more to compare with him, than a dwarf with "*the man of Gath*," to weigh well the grounds of their opinions, and, once for all, consider, whether they will continue the disciples of Adam Smith, to the utter rejection of whose theory in all its parts, his own country owes her colossal power—or of Alexander Hamilton advocating that system which has never failed to insure the prosperity and happiness of every nation, ancient or modern, that has pursued it—that is, *the protection of national industry ;* in other words, whether they will continue to lead their country on "the road to ruin," under the banners of Adam Smith, or take the road to true independence under those of Alexander Hamilton. Light and darkness are not more opposite to each other, than Adam Smith and Alexander Hamilton on this point of political economy, so essential to insure "*the wealth of nations.*"

On the decision of this great question, depend the future destinies, not only of this country, but of a large portion of mankind, whose fortunes cannot fail to be deeply affected by the result of our experiment of free government. We, therefore, solemnly invoke the aid and co-operation of the wise and the good of every section of the union in the discussion of this all-important topic.

Extracts from the Report of Alexander Hamilton, Esquire, Secretary of the Treasury, Dec. 5, 1791.

"The expediency of encouraging manufactures in the united "states, which was, not long since, deemed very questionable, "appears at this time to be pretty generally admitted. The "embarrassments, which have obstructed the progress of our "external trade, have led to serious reflections on the necessity "of enlarging the sphere of our domestic commerce: *the restric-* "*tive regulations, which in foreign markets abridge the vent of* "*the increasing surplus of our agricultural produce, serve to beget* "*an earnest desire, that a more extensive demand for that surplus* "*may be created at home.* And the complete success which has "rewarded manufacturing enterprise, in some valuable branches, "conspiring with the promising symptoms which attend some "less mature essays in others, justify a hope, that the obstacles "to the growth of this species of industry, are less formidable "than they were apprehended to be; and that it is not difficult to "find in its further extension, a full indemnification for any ex-"ternal disadvantages, which are, or may be experienced, as "well as an accession of resources favourable to national inde-"pendence and safety.

"There still are, nevertheless respectable patrons of opinions, "unfriendly to the encouragement of manufactures. The fol-"lowing are, substantially, the arguments by which these opinions "are defended:

"In every country," say those who entertain them, "agricul-"ture is the most beneficial and productive object of human "industry. This position, generally, if not universally true, "applies with peculiar emphasis to the united states, on account

" of their immense tracts of fertile territory, uninhabited and " unimproved. Nothing can afford so advantageous an employ- " ment for capital and labour, as the conversion of this exten- " sive wilderness into cultivated farms. Nothing equally with " this, can contribute to the population, strength, and real riches " of the country.

" To endeavour, by the extraordinary patronage of govern- " ment, to accelerate the growth of manufactures, is, in fact, to " endeavour, by force and art, to transfer the natural current of " industry, from a more to a less beneficial channel. Whatever " has such a tendency must necessarily be unwise: indeed it " can hardly ever be wise in a government, to attempt to give a " direction to the industry of its citizens. This, under the " quick-sighted guidance of private interest, will, if left to itself, " infallibly find its own way to the most profitable employment; " and it is by such employment, that the public prosperity will " be most effectually promoted. To leave industry to itself, " therefore, is in almost every case, the soundest as well as the " simplest policy.

" This policy is not only recommended to the united states, " by considerations which affect all nations; it is, in a manner, " dictated to them by the imperious force of a very peculiar " situation. The smallness of their population, compared with " their territory—the constant allurements to emigration from " the settled to the unsettled parts of the country—the facility " with which the less independent condition of an artisan can be " exchanged for the more independent condition of a farmer— " these, and similar causes, conspire to produce, and, for a length " of time, must continue to occasion, a scarcity of hands for " manufacturing occupation, and dearness of labour, generally. " To these disadvantages for the prosecution of manufactures, a " deficiency of pecuniary capital being added, the prospect of a " successful competition with the manufacturers of Europe, " must be regarded as little less than desperate. Extensive " manufactures can only be the offspring of a redundant, at least " of a full population. Till the latter shall characterize the " situation of this country, 'tis vain to hope for the former.

" If, contrary to the natural course of things, an unseasonable " and premature spring can be given to certain fabrics, by heavy " duties, prohibitions, bounties, or by other forced expedients; " this will be only to sacrifice the interests of the community to " those of particular classes. Besides the misdirection of labour, " a virtual monopoly will be given to the persons employed on " such fabrics; and an enhancement of price, the inevitable con- " sequence of every monopoly, must be defrayed at the expense " of the other parts of the society. It is far preferable, that " those persons should be engaged in the cultivation of the "earth; and that we should procure, in exchange for its productions, the commodities, with which foreigners are able to supply us in greater perfection, and upon better terms."

"This mode of reasoning is founded upon facts and principles, which have certainly respectable pretensions. If it had governed the conduct of nations, more generally than it has done, there is room to suppose that it might have carried them faster to prosperity and greatness, than they have attained by the pursuit of maxims too widely opposite. Most general theories, however, admit of numerous exceptions; and there are few, if any, of the political kind, which do not blend a considerable portion of error with the truths they inculcate.

"In order to an accurate judgment, how far that, which has has been just stated, ought to be deemed liable to a similar imputation, it is necessary to advert carefully to the considerations which plead in favour of manufactures, and which appear to recommend the special and positive encouragement of them, in certain cases, and under certain reasonable limitations.

"It ought readily to be conceded, that the cultivation of the earth, as the primary and most certain source of national supply—as the immediate and chief source of subsistence to man—as the principal source of those materials which constitute the nutriment of other kinds of labour—as including a state most favourable to the freedom and independence of the human mind—one, perhaps, most conducive to the multiplication of the human species—has intrinsically a strong claim to pre-eminence over every other kind of industry.

"But, that it has a title to any thing like an exclusive predilection, in any country, ought to be admitted with great caution. That it is even more productive than every other branch of industry, requires more evidence than has yet been given in support of the position. That its real interests, precious and important as, without the help of exaggeration, they truly are, will be *advanced, rather than injured by the due encouragement of manufactures, may, it is believed, be satisfactorily demonstrated.* And it is also believed, that the expediency of such encouragement, in a general view, may be shown to be recommended by the most cogent and persuasive motives of national policy.

"It has been maintained, that agriculture is not only the most productive, but the only productive species of industry. The reality of this suggestion, in either respect, has, however, not been verified by any accurate detail of facts and calculations; and the general arguments, which are adduced to prove it, are rather subtile and paradoxical, than solid or convincing.

"Those, which maintain its exclusive productiveness, are to this effect:

"Labour, bestowed upon the cultivation of land, produces "enough, not only to replace all the necessary expenses incurred "in the business, and to maintain the persons who are employed "in it, but to afford, together with the ordinary profit on the "stock or capital of the farmer, a net surplus, or rent for the "landlord or proprietor of the soil. But the labour of artificers "does nothing more than replace the stock which employs them, "or which furnishes materials, tools, and wages, and yield the "ordinary profit upon that stock. It yields nothing equivalent "to the rent of land. Neither does it add any thing to the total "value of the whole annual produce of the land and labour of "the country. The additional value given to those parts of the "produce of land, which are wrought into manufactures, is "counterbalanced by the value of those other parts of that pro-"duce, which are consumed by the manufacturers. It can "therefore only be by saving or parsimony, not by the positive "productiveness of their labour, that the classes of artificers can "in any degree augment the revenue of the society."

"To this it has been answered,

1. "That inasmuch as it is acknowledged, that manufacturing "labour reproduces a value equal to that which is expended or "consumed in carrying it on, and continues in existence the ori-"ginal stock or capital employed, it ought, on that account alone, "to escape being considered as wholly unproductive; that "though it should be admitted, as alleged, that the consumption "of the produce of the soil, by the classes of artificers or manu-"facturers, is exactly equal to the value added by their labour "to the materials upon which it is exerted; yet it would not "thence follow, that it added nothing to the revenue of the so-"ciety, or to the aggregate value of the annual produce of its "land and labour. If the consumption, for any given period, "amounted to a given sum, and the increased value of the pro-"duce manufactured, in the same period, to a like sum, the total "amount of the consumption and production during that period, "would be equal to the two sums, and consequently double the "value of the agricultural produce consumed. And though the "increment of value, produced by the classes of artificers, should "at no time exceed the value of the produce of the land consu-"med by them, yet there would be at every moment, in conse-"quence of their labour, a greater value of goods in the market, "than would exist independent of it.

2. "That the position, that artificers can augment the reve-"nue of a society, only by parsimony, is true in no other sense, "than in one which is equally applicable to husbandmen or cul-"tivators. It may be alike affirmed of all these classes, that "the fund acquired by their labour, and destined for their sup-"port, is not, in an ordinary way, more than equal to it. And

" hence it will follow, that augmentations of the wealth or capi-
" tal of the community (except in the instances of some extra-
" ordinary dexterity or skill,) can only proceed, with respect to
" any of them, from the savings of the more thrifty and parsimo-
" nious.

3. " That the annual produce of the land and labour of a
" country can only be increased, in two ways, by some improve-
" ment in the productive powers of the useful labour, which ac-
" tually exists within it, or by some increase in the quantity of
" such labour; that with regard to the first, the labour of arti-
" ficers being capable of greater subdivision and simplicity of
" operation, than that of cultivators, it is susceptible, in a pro-
" portionably greater degree, of improvement in its productive
" powers, whether to be derived from an accession of skill, or
" from the application of ingenious machinery; in which parti-
" cular, therefore, the labour employed in the culture of land
" can pretend to no advantage over that engaged in manufactures:
" that with regard to an augmentation of the quantity of useful
" labour, this, excluding adventitious circumstances, must de-
" pend essentially upon an increase of capital, which again must de-
" pend upon the savings made out of the revenues of those who
" furnish or manage that, which is at any time employed, whether
" in agriculture, or in manufactures, or in any other way."

" It is now proper to enumerate the principal circumstances,
" from which it may be inferred—that *manufacturing establish-
" ments not only occasion a positive augmentation of the produce
" and revenue of the society, but that they contribute essentially
" to rendering them greater than they could possibly be, without
" such establishments.* These circumstances are,

1. " The division of labour.
2. " An extension of the use of machinery.
3. " Additional employment to classes of the community not
" ordinarily engaged in the business.
4. " The promoting of emigration from foreign countries.
5. " The furnishing greater scope for the diversity of talents
" and dispositions which discriminate men from each other.
6. " The affording a more ample and various field for enter-
" prise.
7. " The creating, in some instances, a new, and securing, in
" all, a more certain and steady demand for the surplus produce
" of the soil.

" Each of these circumstances has a considerable influence
" upon the total mass of industrious effort in a community: to-
" gether, they add to it a degree of energy and effect, which are
" not easily conceived. Some comments upon each of them, in
" the order in which they have been stated, may serve to explain
" their importance.

I. " As to the division of labour.

" It has been justly observed, that there is scarcely any thing " of greater moment in the economy of a nation, than the pro- " per division of labour. The separation of occupations causes " each to be carried to a much greater perfection than it could " possibly acquire, if they were blended. This arises principal- " ly from three circumstances:—

1st. " The greater skill and dexterity naturally resulting from " a constant and undivided application to a single object. It is " evident, that these properties must increase, in proportion to " the separation and simplification of objects and the steadiness " of the attention devoted to each; and must be less, in propor- " tion to the complication of objects, and the number among " which the attention is distracted.

2d. " The economy of time, by avoiding the loss of it, inci- " dent to a frequent transition from one operation to another, of " a different nature. This depends on various circumstances; " the transition itself—the orderly disposition of the implements, " machines, and materials employed in the operation to be relin- " quished—the preparatory steps to the commencement of a new " one—the interruption of the impulse, which the mind of the " workman acquires, from being engaged in a particular opera- " tion—the distractions, hesitations, and reluctances, which at- " tend the passage from one kind of business to another.

3d. " An extension of the use of machinery. A man occupi- " ed on a single object, will have it more in his power, and will " be more naturally led to exert his imagination in devising " methods to facilitate and abridge labour, than if he were per- " plexed by a variety of independent and dissimilar operations. " Besides this, the fabrication of machines, in numerous instan- " ces, becoming itself a distinct trade, the artist, who follows it, " has all the advantages which have been enumerated, for im- " provement in this particular art; and in both ways the inven- " tion and application of machinery are extended.

" And from these causes united, the mere separation of the " occupation of the cultivator, from that of the artificer, has the " effect of augmenting the productive powers of labour, and with " them, the total mass of the produce of revenue in a country.— " In this view of the subject, therefore, the utility of artificers " or manufacturers, towards promoting an increase of productive " industry, is apparent.

II. " As to an extension of the use of machinery, a point " which, though partly anticipated, requires to be placed in one " or two additional lights.

" The employment of machinery forms an item of great im- " portance in the general mass of national industry. 'Tis an ar- " tificial force brought in aid of the natural force of man; and to "all the purposes of labour, is an increase of hands; an accession of strength, unincumbered too by the expense of maintaining the labourer. May it not therefore be fairly inferred that those occupations which give greater scope to the use of this auxiliary, contribute most to the general stock of industrious effort, and, in consequence, to the general product of industry?

"It shall be taken for granted, and the truth of the position referred to observation, that manufacturing pursuits are susceptible in a greater degree of the application of machinery, than those of agriculture. If so, all the difference is lost to a community, which, instead of manufacturing for itself, procures the fabrics requisite to its supply from other countries. *The substitution of foreign for domestic manufactures is a transfer to foreign nations of the advantages accruing from the employment of machinery in the modes in which it is capable of being employed, with most utility and to the greatest extent.*

"The cotton-mill invented in England, within the last twenty years, is a signal illustration of the general proposition, which has been just advanced. In consequence of it, all the different processes for spinning cotton are performed by means of machines, which are put in motion by water, and *attended chiefly by women and children;* and by a smaller number of persons in the whole, than are requisite in the ordinary mode of spinning. And it is an advantage of great moment, that the operations of the mill continue with convenience, during the night, as well as through the day. The prodigious effect of such a machine is easily conceived. To this invention is to be attributed essentially the immense progress, which has been so suddenly made in Great Britain, in the various fabrics of cotton.

III. "As to the additional employment of classes of the community, not originally engaged in the particular business.

"This is not among the least valuable of the means by which manufacturing institutions contribute to augment the general stock of industry and production. In places where those institutions prevail, besides the persons regularly engaged in them, they afford occasional and extra employment to industrious individuals and families, who are willing to devote the leisure resulting from the intermissions of their ordinary pursuits to collateral labours, as a resource for multiplying their acquisitions or their enjoyments. *The husbandman himself experiences a new source of profit and support from the increased industry of his wife and daughters; invited and stimulated by the demands of the neighbouring manufactories.*

"Besides this advantage of occasional employment to classes having different occupations there is another of a nature allied to it, and of a similar tendency. This is, the employment of

" persons who would otherwise be idle, (and, in many cases, a " burden on the community) either from the bias of temper, hab- " it, infirmity of body, or some other cause, indisposing or dis- " qualifying them for the toils of the country. It is worthy of " particular remark, that, in general, women and children are " rendered more useful, and the latter more early useful, by " manufacturing establishments, than they would otherwise be. " Of the number of persons employed in the cotton manufacto- " ries of Great Britain, it is computed that *four-sevenths nearly " are women and children; of whom the greatest proportion are " children, and many of them of a tender age.*

" And thus it appears to be one of the attributes of manufac- " tures, and one of no small consequence, to give occasion to the " exertion of a greater quantity of industry, even by the same " number of persons, where they happen to prevail, than would " exist, if there were no such establishments.

IV. " As to the promoting of emigration from foreign coun- " tries.

" Men reluctantly quit one course of occupation and liveli- " hood for another, unless invited to it by very apparent and " proximate advantages. Many who would go from one coun- " try to another, if they had a prospect of continuing with more " benefit, the callings to which they have been educated, will not " often be tempted to change their situation by the hope of doing " better in some other way. Manufacturers, who (listening to " the powerful invitation of a better price for their fabrics, or " for their labour; of greater cheapness of provisions and raw " materials; of an exemption from the chief part of the taxes, " burdens and restraints, which they endure in the old world; " of greater personal independence and consequence, under the " operation of a more equal government; and of, what is far more " precious than mere religious toleration, a perfect equality of " religious privileges) would probably flock from Europe to the " united states to pursue their trades, or professions, if they " were once made sensible of the advantages they would enjoy, " and were inspired with an assurance of encouragement and " employment; will with difficulty, be induced to transplant " themselves, with a view of becoming cultivators of land.

" If it be true, then, that it is the interest of the united states " to open every possible avenue to emigration from abroad, it " affords a weighty argument for the encouragement of manu- " factures; which, for the reason just assigned, will have the " strongest tendency to multiply the inducements to it.

" Here is perceived an important resource, not only for ex- " tending the population, and with it the useful and productive " labour of the country, but likewise for the prosecution of manu- " factures, without deducting from the number of hands which "might otherwise be drawn to tillage; and even for the in-"demnification of agriculture for such as might happen to be "diverted from it. Many, whom manufacturing views would "induce to emigrate, would afterwards yield to the temptations, "which the particular situation of this country holds out to ag-"ricultural pursuits. And while agriculture would in other "respects derive many signal and unmingled advantages, from "the growth of manufactures, it is a problem, whether it would "gain or lose, as to the article of the number of persons em-"ployed in carrying it on.

V. "As to the furnishing greater scope for the diversity of "talents and dispositions, which discriminate men from each "other.

"This is a much more powerful mean of augmenting the fund "of national industry than may at first sight appear. It is a just "observation, that minds, of the strongest and most active pow-"ers for their proper objects, fall below mediocrity, and labour "without effect, if confined to uncongenial pursuits. And it is "thence to be inferred, that the result of human exertion may "be immensely increased by diversifying its objects. When "all the different kinds of industry obtain in a community, each "individual can find his proper element, and call into activity "the whole vigour of his nature. And the community is bene-"fited by the services of its respective members, in the manner, "in which each can serve it with most effect.

"If there be any thing in a remark often to be met with, "namely, that there is, in the genius of the people of this coun-"try, a peculiar aptitude for mechanical improvements, it would "operate as a forcible reason for giving opportunities to the "exercise of that species of talent, by the propagation of manu-"factures.

VI. "As to the affording a more ample and various field for "enterprise.

"This also is of greater consequence in the general scale of "national exertion, than might perhaps on a superficial view be "supposed, and has effects not altogether dissimilar from those "of the circumstance last noticed. To cherish and stimulate "the activity of the human mind by multiplying the objects of "enterprise, is not among the least considerable of the expedi-"ents, by which the wealth of a nation may be promoted. Even "things, in themselves not positively advantageous, sometimes "become so, by their tendency to provoke exertion. Every "new scene which is opened to the busy nature of man to rouse "and exert itself, is the addition of a new energy to the general "stock of effort.

"The spirit of enterprise, useful and prolific as it is, must "necessarily be contracted or expanded in proportion to the sim-

" plicity or variety of the occupations and productions which
" are to be found in a society. It must be less in a nation of
" mere cultivators, than in a nation of cultivators and merchants;
" less in a nation of cultivators and merchants, than in a nation
" of cultivators, artificers and merchants.

VII. " As to the creating, in some instances, a new, and se-
" curing in all a more certain and steady demand for the surplus
" produce of the soil.

" This is among the most important of the circumstances which
" have been indicated. It is a principal mean, by which the es-
" tablishment of manufactures contributes to an augmentation
" of the produce or revenue of a country, and has an immediate
" and direct relation to the prosperity of agriculture.

" It is evident, that the exertions of the husbandman will be
" steady or fluctuating, vigorous or feeble, in proportion to the
" steadiness or fluctuation, adequateness, or inadequateness of
" the markets on which he must depend, for the vent of the sur-
" plus, which may be produced by his labour ; and that such sur-
" plus, in the ordinary course of things, will be greater or less
" in the same proportion.

" For the purpose of this vent, *a domestic market is greatly to
" be preferred to a foreign one;* because it is, in the nature of
" things, far more to be relied on.

" It is a primary object of the policy of nations, to be able to
" supply themselves with subsistence from their own soils ; and
" manufacturing nations, as far as circumstances permit, endea-
" vour to procure from the same source, the raw materials ne-
" cessary for their own fabrics. This disposition, urged by the
" spirit of monopoly, is sometimes even carried to an injudi-
" cious extreme. It seems not always to be recollected, that
" nations which have neither mines nor manufactures, can only
" obtain the manufactured articles of which they stand in need,
" by an exchange of the products of their soils ; and that if
" those who can best furnish them with such articles, are unwil-
" ling to give a due course to this exchange, they must of neces-
" sity make every possible effort to manufacture for themselves ;
" the effect of which is, that *the manufacturing nations abridge
" the natural advantages of their situation through an unwilling-
" ness to permit the agricultural countries to enjoy the advantages
" of theirs ;* and sacrifice the interest of a mutually beneficial in-
" tercourse to the vain project of selling every thing and buy-
" ing nothing.

" But it is also a consequence of the policy, which has been
" noted, that the foreign demand for the products of agricultural
" countries, *is in a great degree rather casual and occasional, than
" certain or constant.* To what extent injurious interruptions of
" the demand for some of the staple commodities of the united

" states, may have been experienced, from that cause, must be " referred to the judgment of those who are engaged in carry- " ing on the commerce of the country: but it may be safely af- " firmed, that such interruptions are at times very inconvenient- " ly felt; and that cases not unfrequently occur, in which mar- " kets are so confined and restricted, as to render the demand " very unequal to the supply.

" Independently likewise of the artificial impediments, which " are created by the policy in question, *there are natural cau- " ses tending to render the external demand for the surplus of " agricultural nation a precarious reliance.* The differences of " seasons in the countries which are the consumers, make im- " mense differences in the produce of their own soils, in differ- " ent years, and consequently in the degrees of their necessity " for foreign supply. Plentiful harvests with them, especially " if similar ones occur at the same time in the countries which " are the furnishers, occasion of course a glut in the markets of " the latter.

" Considering how fast and how much the progress of new " settlements in the united states must increase the surplus pro- " duce of the soil. and weighing seriously the tendency of the " system, which prevails among most of the commercial nations " of Europe, whatever dependence may be placed on the force " of natural circumstances to counteract the effects of an artifi- " cial policy; *there appear strong reasons to regard the foreign " demand for that surplus, as too uncertain a reliance, and to de- " sire a substitute for it in an extensive domestic market.*

" To secure such a market, *there is no other expedient, than to " promote manufacturing establishments.* Manufacturers, who con- " stitute the most numerous class, after the cultivators of land, " are for that reason the principal consumers of the surplus of " their labour.

" This idea of an extensive domestic market for the surplus pro- " duce of the soil, is of the first consequence. It is, of all things, " that which most effectually conduces to a flourishing state of " agriculture. If the effect of manufactories should be to de- " tach a portion of the hands, which would otherwise be engag- " ed in tillage, it might possibly cause a smaller quantity of " lands to be under cultivation; but by their tendency to pro- " cure a more certain demand for the surplus produce of the " soil, they would, at the same time, cause the lands, which were " in cultivation, to be better improved and more productive. " And while, by their influence, the condition of each individual " farmer would be meliorated, the total mass of agricultural " production would probably be increased. For this must evi- " dently depend as much, if not more, upon the degree of im- " provement, than upon the number of acres under culture.

" It merits particular observation, that *the multiplication of " manufactories not only furnishes a market for those articles " which have been accustomed to be produced in abundance, in a " country; but it likewise creates a demand for such as were either " unknown or produced in inconsiderable quantities.* The bow- " els, as well the surface of the earth, are ransacked for articles " which were before neglected. Animals, plants, and minerals " acquire a utility and value, which were before unexplored.

" The foregoing considerations seem sufficient to establish, as " general propositions, that it is the interest of nations to diver- " sify the industrious pursuits of the individuals who compose " them—that *the establishment of manufactures is calculated not " only to increase the general stock of useful and productive la- " bour, but even to improve the state of agriculture in particular,* " certainly to advance the interests of those who are engaged in " it. There are other views, that will be hereafter taken of the " subject, which, it is conceived, will serve to confirm these in- " ferences.

1. " If the system of perfect liberty to industry and commerce " were the prevailing system of nations, the arguments which " dissuade a country in the predicament of the united states, " from the zealous pursuit of manufactures, would doubtless " have great force. It will not be affirmed, that they might not " be permitted, with few exceptions, to serve as a rule of na- " tional conduct. In such a state of things, each country would " have the full benefit of its peculiar advantages to compensate " for its deficiencies or disadvantages. If one nation were in a " condition to supply manufactured articles on better terms than " another, that other might find an abundant indemnification in " a superior capacity to furnish the produce of the soil. And " a free exchange, mutually beneficial, of the commodities which " each was able to supply, on the best terms, might be carried " on between them, supporting in full vigour the industry of each. " And though the circumstances which have been mentioned, " and others which will be unfolded hereafter, render it proba- " ble, that nations merely agricultural, would not enjoy the same " degree of opulence, in proportion to their numbers, as those " which united manufactures with agriculture; yet the progres- " sive improvement of the lands of the former, might, in the " end, atone for an inferior degree of opulence in the meantime; " and in a case in which opposite considerations are pretty " equally balanced, the option ought perhaps always to be in fa- " vour of leaving industry to its own direction. But the sys- " tem, which has been mentioned, is far from characterising the " general policy of nations. The prevalent one has been re- " gulated by an opposite spirit. The consequence of it is, that " *the united states are to a certain extent, in the situation of a*

" *country precluded from foreign commerce.* They can, indeed, " without difficulty, obtain from abroad the manufactured sup-" plies, of which they are in want; but *they experience nume-" rous and very injurious impediments to the emission and vent " of their own commodities.* Nor is this the case in reference " to a single foreign nation only. The regulations of several " countries, with which we have the most extensive intercourse, " throw serious obstructions in the way of the principal staples " of the united states. *In such a position of things, the united " states cannot exchange with Europe on equal terms; and the " want of reciprocity would render them the victim of a system, " which should induce them to confine their views to agriculture, " and refrain from manufactures.* A constant and increasing " necessity, on their part, for the commodities of Europe, and " only a partial and occasional demand for their own, in return, " could not but expose them to a state of impoverishment, com-" pared with the opulence to which their political and natural " advantages authorize them to aspire. Remarks of this kind " are not made in the spirit of complaint. It is for the nations, " whose regulations are alluded to, to judge for themselves, " whether, by aiming at too much, they do not lose more than " they gain. It is for the united states to consider by what " means they can render themselves least dependent, on the com-" binations, right or wrong, of foreign policy. It is no small " consolation that already the measures which have embarrass-" ed our trade, have accelerated internal improvements, which " upon the whole have bettered our affairs.

" To diversify and extend these improvements, is the surest " and safest method of indemnifying ourselves for any inconve-" niences, which those or similar measures have a tendency to " beget. *If Europe will not take from us the products of our soil, " upon terms consistent with our interest, the natural remedy is " to contract as fast as possible, our wants of her.*

2. " The conversion of their waste into cultivated lands, is " certainly a point of great moment in the political calculations " of the united states. But the degree in which this may pos-" sibly be retarded by the encouragement of manufactories, does " not appear to countervail the powerful inducements to afford-" ing that encouragement.

" An observation made in another place, is of a nature to " have great influence upon this question—If it cannot be de-" nied, that the interests even of agriculture may be advanced, " more by having such of the lands of a state as are occupied, " under good cultivation, than by having a greater quantity oc-" cupied under a much inferior cultivation; and if manufacto-" ries, for the reasons assigned, must be admitted to have a ten-" dency to promote a more steady and vigorous cultivation of

" the lands occupied, than would happen without them, it will " follow, that they are capable of indemnifying a country for a " diminution of the progress of new settlements; and may serve " to increase both the capital value and the income of its lands, " even though they should abridge the number of acres under " tillage. But it does by no means follow, that the progress of " new settlements would be retarded by the extension of manu- " factures. The desire of being an independent proprietor of " land, is founded on such strong principles in the human breast, " that where the opportunity of becoming so is as great as it is " in the united states, the proportion will be small of those, " whose situations would otherwise lead to it who would be di- " verted from it towards manufactures. And it is highly proba- " ble, as already intimated, that the accession of foreigners, who, " originally drawn over by manufacturing views, would after- " wards abandon them for agricultural, would be more than an " equivalent for those of our citizens, who might happen to be " detached from them.

" The remaining objections to a particular encouragement of " manufactures in the united states, now require to be examined.

" One of these turns on the proposition, that industry, if left " to itself, will naturally find its way to the most useful and " profitable employment. Whence it is inferred, that manufac- " tures, without the aid of government, will grow up as soon, " and as fast, as the natural state of things, and the interest of " the community, may require.

" Against the solidity of this hypothesis, in the full latitude " of the terms, very cogent reasoning may be offered. These " have relation to the strong influence of habit, and the spirit of " imitation; the fear of want of success in untried enterprises; " the intrinsic difficulties incident to first essays towards a com- " petition with those who have previously attained to perfection " in the business to be attempted; the bounties, premiums, and " other artificial encouragements, with which foreign nations " second the exertions of their citizens, in the branches in which " they are to be rivalled.

" Experience teaches, that men are often so much governed " by what they are accustomed to see and practise, that the sim- " plest and most obvious improvements, in the most ordinary " occupations, are adopted with hesitation, reluctance, and by " slow gradations. The superiority antecedently enjoyed by " nations, who have pre-occupied and perfected a branch of in- " dustry, constitutes a more formidable obstacle, than either of " those which have been mentioned, to the introduction of the " same branch into a country, in which it did not before exist. " *To maintain between the recent establishments of one country,* " *and the long-matured establishments of another country, a com-*

"*petition upon equal terms, both as to quality and price, is in*
"*most cases impracticable.* The disparity in the one, or in the other, or in both, must necessarily be so considerable as to forbid a successful rivalship, *without the extraordinary aid and protection of government.*

"But the greatest obstacle of all to the successful prosecution of a new branch of industry in a country in which it was before unknown, consists, as far as the instances apply, in the bounties premiums, and other aids, which are granted in a variety of cases, by the nations in which the establishments to be imitated are previously introduced. It is well known, that certain nations grant bounties on the exportation of particular commodities, to enable their own workmen to undersell and supplant all competitors, in the countries to which those commodities are sent. *Hence the undertakers of a new manufacture have to contend, not only with the natural disadvantages of a new undertaking; but with the gratuities and remunerations which other governments bestow. To be enabled to contend with success, it is evident, that the interference and aid of their government are indispensable.* Combinations by those engaged in a particular branch of business in one country, to frustrate the first efforts to introduce it in another by temporary sacrifices, recompensed perhaps by extraordinary indemnifications of the government of such country, are believed to have existed, and are not to be regarded as destitute of probability. The existence or assurance of aid from the government of the country in which the business is to be introduced, may be essential to fortify adventurers against the dread of such combinations—to defeat their effects, if formed—and to prevent their being formed, by demonstrating that they must in the end prove fruitless. Whatever room there may be for an expectation that the industry of a people, under the direction of private interest, will, upon equal terms, find out the most beneficial employment for itself; there is none for a reliance, that it will struggle against the force of unequal terms, or will of itself surmount all the adventitious barriers to a successful competition, which may have been erected either by the advantages naturally acquired from practice and previous possession of the ground, or by those which may have sprung from positive regulations, and an artificial policy. This general reflection might alone suffice as an answer to the objection under examination; exclusively of the weighty considerations which have been particularly urged."

"To all the arguments which are brought to evince the impracticability of success in manufacturing establishments in the "united states, it might have been a sufficient answer to have "referred to the experience of what has been already done: it "is certain that several important branches have grown up and "flourished with a rapidity which surprises; affording an en-"couraging assurance of success in future attempts; of these it "may not be improper to enumerate the most considerable—

"I. *Of Skins.* Tanned and tawed leather; dressed skins, "shoes, boots and slippers, harness and saddlery of all kinds, "portmanteaus and trunks, leather breeches, gloves, muffs and "tippets, parchment and glue.

"II. *Of Iron.* Bar and sheet iron, steel, nail rods and nails, "implements of husbandry, stoves, pots and other household "utensils, the steel and iron work of carriages, and for ship "building; anchors, scale beams, and weights, and various "tools of artificers; arms of different kinds; though the manu-"facture of these last has of late diminished for want of demand.

"III. *Of Wood.* Ships, cabinet wares and turnery, wool and "cotton cards, and other machinery for manufactures and hus-"bandry, mathematical instruments, coopers' wares of every "kind.

"IV. *Of Flax and Hemp.* Cables, sail-cloth, cordage, twine "and packthread.

"V. Bricks and coarse tiles, and potters' wares.

"VI. Ardent spirits, and malt liquors.

"VII. Writing and printing paper, sheathing and wrapping "paper, pasteboards, fullers' or press papers, paper hangings.

"VIII. Hats of fur and wool, and of mixtures of both. "Women's stuff and silk shoes.

"IX. Refined sugars.

"X. Oils of animals and seeds, soap, spermaceti and tallow "candles.

"XI. Copper and brass wares, particularly utensils for dis-"tillers, sugar refiners, and brewers; andirons and other articles "for household use—philosophical apparatus.

"XII. Tin wares for most purposes of ordinary use.

"XIII. Carriages of all kinds.

"XIV. Snuff, chewing and smoaking tobacco.

"XV. Starch and hair powder.

"XVI Lampblack and other painters' colours.

"XVII. Gunpowder.

"Besides manufactories of these articles which are carried on "as regular trades, and have attained to a considerable degree "of maturity, there is a vast scene of household manufacturing, "which contributes more largely to the supply of the communi-"ty, than could be imagined, without having made it an object "of particular inquiry. This observation is the pleasing result "of the investigation, to which the subject of this report has "led; and is applicable as well to the southern as to the middle "and northern states. Great quantities of coarse cloths, coat-"ings, serges and flannels, linsey woolseys, hosiery of wool, "cotton, and thread, coarse fustians, jeans and muslins, checked "and striped cotton and linen goods, bedticks, coverlets and "counterpanes, tow linens, coarse shirtings, sheetings, towelling "and table linen, and various mixtures of wool and cotton, and "of cotton and flax, are made in the household way; and in "many instances to an extent not only sufficient for the supply "of the families in which they are made, but for sale; and even "in some cases for exportation. It is computed in a number of "districts, that two thirds, three fourths, and even four-fifths of "all the clothing of the inhabitants are made by themselves. "The importance of so great a progress, as appears to have "been made in family manufactures, within a few years, both "in a moral and political view, renders the fact highly interest-"ing.

"Neither does the above enumeration comprehend all the ar-"ticles that are manufactured as regular trades. Many others "occur, which are equally well established, but which, not being "of equal importance, have been omitted. And there are many "attempts still in their infancy, which, though attended with ve-"ry favourable appearances, could not have been properly com-"prised in an enumeration of manufactories already established. "There are other articles, also, of great importance, which, "though, strictly speaking, manufactures, are omitted, as being "immediately connected with husbandry; such are flour, pot and "pearl ash, pitch, tar, turpentine, and the like.

"There remains to be noticed an objection to the encourage-"ment of manufactures, of a nature different from those which "question the probability of success—this is derived from *its* "*supposed tendency to give a monopoly of advantages to particu-*"*lar classes, at the expense of the rest of the community, who, it* "*is affirmed, would be able to procure the requisite supplies of* "*manufactured articles, on better terms from foreigners, than from* "*our own citizens;* and who, it is alleged, are reduced to the ne-"cessity of paying an enhanced price for whatever they want, by "every measure, which obstructs the free competition of foreign "commodities.

"It is not an unreasonable supposition, that measures which "serve to abridge the free competition of foreign articles, have "a tendency to occasion an enhancement of prices: and it is not "to be denied, that such is the effect in a number of cases; but "the fact does not uniformly correspond with the theory.—"*A reduction of prices has, in several instances, immediately suc-*"*ceeded to the establishment of a domestic manufacture.* Whether "it be that foreign manufacturers endeavour to supplant by un-

"dersełling our own, or whatever else be the cause, the effect has "been such as is stated, and the reverse of what might have been "expected.

"But though it were true, that the immediate and certain ef- "fect of regulations controlling the competition of foreign with "domestic fabrics, was an increase of price, it is universally "true, that the contrary is the ultimate effect with every suc- "cessful manufacture. *When a domestic manufacture has attain- "ed to perfection, and has engaged in the prosecation of it a com- "petent number of persons, it invariably becomes cheaper.* Being "free from the heavy charges which attend the importation of "foreign commodities, *it can be afforded, and accordingly sel- "dom or never fails to be sold cheaper, in process of time, than "was the foreign article for which it is a substitute. The inter- "nal competition which takes place, soon does away every thing "like monopoly;* and by degrees reduces the price of the article "to the minimum of a reasonable profit on the capital em- "ployed. This accords with the reason of the thing, and with "experience.

"Whence it follows, that *it is the interest of the community, with "a view to eventual and permanent economy, to encourage the "growth of manufactures.* In a national view, a temporary en- "hancement of price must always be well compensated by a per- "manent reduction of it.

"It is a reflection, which may with propriety be indulged here, "that this eventual diminution of the prices of manufactured ar- "ticles, which is the result of internal manufacturing establish- "ments, has a direct and very important tendency to benefit ag- "riculture. It enables the farmer to procure, with a smaller "quantity of his labour, the manufactured produce of which he "stands in need, and consequently increases the value of his in- "come and property.

"The objections which are commonly made to the expedien- "cy of encouraging, and to the probability of succeeding in "manufacturing pursuits, in the United States, having now "been discussed, the considerations, which have appeared in "the course of the discussion, recommending that species of in- "dustry to the patronage of the government, will be materially "strengthened by a few general and some particular topics, "which have been naturally reserved for subsequent notice.

1. "There seems to be a moral certainty that *the trade of a "country, which is both manufacturing and agricultural, will be "more lucrative and prosperous, than that of a country which is "merely agricultural.*

"One reason for this is found in that general effort of nations, "(which has been already mentioned) to procure from their "own soils, the articles of prime necessity requisite to their own

"consumption and use; and which serves to render their de-
"mand for a foreign supply of such articles in a great degree oc-
"casional and contingent. Hence, *while the necessities of na-*
"*tions exclusively devoted to agriculture, for the fabrics of manu-*
"*facturing states are constant and regular, the wants of the lat-*
"*ter for the products of the former, are liable to very considerable*
"*fluctuations and interruptions.* The great inequalities result-
"ing from difference of seasons have been elsewhere remarked;
"this uniformity of demand, on one side, and unsteadiness of it
"on the other must necessarily have a tendency to cause the
"general course of the exchange of commodities between the
"parties, to turn to the disadvantage of the merely agricultural
"states. Peculiarity of situation, a climate and soil adapted to
"the production of peculiar commodities, may, sometimes, con-
"tradict the rule; but there is every reason to believe, that it
"will be found, in the main, a just one.

"Another circumstance which gives a superiority of commer-
"cial advantages to states that manufacture, as well as cultivate,
"consists in the more numerous attractions, which a more di-
"versified market offers to foreign customers, and in the greater
"scope which it affords to mercantile enterprise. It is a posi-
"tion of indisputable truth in commerce depending too on very
"obvious reasons, that the greatest resort will ever be to those
"marts, where commodities, while equally abundant, are most
"various. Each difference of kind holds out an inducement;
"and it is a position not less clear, that the field of enterprise
"must be enlarged to the merchants of a country, in proportion
"to the variety as well as the abundance of commodities, which
"they find at home for exportation to foreign markets.

"A third circumstance, perhaps not inferior to either of the
"other two, conferring the superiority which has been stated,
"has relation to the stagnations of demand for certain commo-
"dities, which, at some time or other, interfere more or less
"with the sale of all. The nation which can bring to market
"but few articles, is likely to be more quickly and sensibly af-
"fected by such stagnation; than one which is always possessed
"of a great variety of commodities; the former frequently finds
"too great a portion of its stock of materials, for sale or exchange,
"lying on hand—or is obliged to make injurious sacrifices to
"supply its wants of foreign articles, which are numerous and
"urgent, in proportion to the smallness and the number of its
"own. The latter commonly finds itself indemnified, by the
"high prices of some articles, for the low prices of others: and
"the prompt and advantageous sale of those articles which are
"in demand, enables its merchants the better to wait for a fa-
"vourable change, in respect to those which are not. There is
"ground to believe, that a difference of situation, in this particu-

"lar, has immensely different effects upon the wealth and pros-
"perity of nations.

"From these circumstances, collectively, two important in-"ferences are to be drawn; one, that there is always a higher "probability of a favourable balance of trade, in regard to "countries, in which manufactures founded on the basis of a "thriving agriculture, flourish, than in regard to those, which "are confined wholly or almost wholly to agriculture; the other "(which is also a consequence of the first) that countries of the "former description are likely to possess more pecuniary wealth "or money, than those of the latter.

"But *the uniform appearance of an abundance of specie, as the "concomitant of a flourishing state of manufactures, and of the "reverse, where they do not prevail, afford a strong presumption "of their favourable operation upon the wealth of a country.*

"*Not only the wealth, but the independence and security of a "country appear to be materially connected with the prosperity "of manufactures.* Every nation, with a view to these great "objects, ought to endeavour to possess within itself all the "essentials of national supply. These comprise the means of "subsistence, habitation, clothing and defence.

"The possession of these is necessary to the perfection of the "body politic, to the safety as well as to the welfare of the soci-"ety; the want of either is the want of an important organ of po-"litical life and motion; and in the various crises which await a "state, it must severely feel the effects of such deficiency. *The "extreme embarrassments of the united states, during the late "war, from an incapacity of supplying themselves, are still mat-"ter of keen recollection: a future war might be expected again "to exemplify the mischiefs and dangers of a situation, to which "that incapacity is still in too great a degree applicable,* unless "changed by timely and vigorous exertions. To effect this "change, as fast as shall be prudent, merits all the attention, and "all the zeal of our public councils; it is the next great work to "be accomplished.

"The want of a navy to protect our external commerce, as "long as it shall continue, must render it a peculiarly precari-"ous reliance, for the supply of essential articles; and must "serve to *strengthen prodigiously the arguments in favour of "manufactures.*

"To these general considerations are added some of a more "particular nature.

"Our distance from Europe, the great fountain of manufac-"tured supply, subjects us, in the existing state of things, to "inconvenience and loss in two ways.

"The bulkiness of those commodities which are the chief "productions of the soil, necessarily imposes very heavy charges

" on their transportation, to distant markets. These charges, in " the cases, in which the nations, to whom our products are " sent, maintain a competition in the supply of their own mar- " kets, principally fall upon us, and form material deductions, " from the primitive value of the articles furnished. The charges " on manufactured supplies brought from Europe, are greatly " enhanced by the same circumstance of distance. These " charges, again, in the cases in which our own industry main- " tains no competition in our own markets, also principally fall " upon us; and are an additional cause of extraordinary deduc- " tion from the primitive value of our own products ; these be- " ing the materials of exchange for the foreign fabrics which we " consume.

" The equality and moderation of individual property, and " the growing settlements of new districts, occasion, in this " country an unusual demand for coarse manufactures; the " charges of which being greater in proportion to their greater " bulk, augment the disadvantage, which has just been des- " cribed.

" As in most countries domestic supplies maintain a very " considerable competition with such foreign productions of the " soil, as are imported for sale; if the extensive establishment " of manufactories in the united states does not create a similar " competition in respect to manufactured articles, it appears to " be clearly deducible, from the considerations which have been " mentioned, that they must sustain a double loss in their ex- " changes with foreign nations; strongly conducive to an un- " favourable balance of trade, and very prejudicial to their in- " terests.

" These disadvantages press with no small weight, on the " landed interest of the country. *In seasons of peace, they cause " a serious deduction from the intrinsic value of the products of " the soil.* In the time of a war. which should either involve " ourselves, or another nation. possessing a considerable share " of our carrying trade, the charges on the transportation of our " commodities, bulky as most of them are. could hardly fail to " prove a grievous burden to the farmer, while obliged to depend " in so great a degree as he now does, upon foreign markets for " the vent of the surplus of his labour."

" It is not uncommon to meet with an opinion. that though " the promoting of manufactures may be the interest of a part " of the union, it is contrary to that of another part. The north- " ern and southern regions are sometimes represented as having " adverse interests in this respect. Those are called manufac-

" turing, these agricultural states ; and a species of opposition is " imagined to subsist between the manufacturing and agricultu-" ral interest.

" *This idea of an opposition between those two interests is the " common error of the early periods of every country ; but experi-" ence gradually dissipates it.* Indeed they are perceived so " often to succour and to befriend each other, that they come at " length to be considered as one ; a supposition which has been " frequently abused, and is not universally true. Particular en-" couragements of particular manufactures may be of a nature to " sacrifice the interests of land-holders to those of manufacturers ; " but it is nevertheless a maxim well established by experience, " and generally acknowledged where there has been sufficient " experience, that *the aggregate prosperity of manufactures, and " the aggregate prosperity of agriculture are intimately connected.* " In the course of the discussion which has had place, various " weighty considerations have been adduced operating in support " of this maxim. Perhaps the superior steadiness of the demand " of a domestic market for the surplus produce of the soil, is " alone a convincing argument of its truth.

" Ideas of a contrariety of interests between the northern " and southern regions of the union, are in the main as unfound-" ed as they are mischievous. The diversity of circumstances, " on which such contrariety is usually predicated, authorizes a " directly contrary conclusion. Mutual wants constitute one of " the strongest links of political connexion ; and the extent of " these bears a natural proportion to the diversity in the means " of mutual supply.

" Suggestions of an opposite complexion are ever to be de-" plored, as unfriendly to the steady pursuit of one great common " cause, and to the perfect harmony of all the parts.

" In proportion as the mind is accustomed to trace the inti-" mate connexion of interests, which subsists between all the " parts of society, united under the same government—the in-" finite variety of channels which serve to circulate the prosperity " of each to and through the rest—in that proportion it will be " little apt to be disturbed by solicitudes and apprehensions, " which originate in local discriminations. It is a truth as im-" portant as it is agreeable, and one to which it is not easy to " imagine exceptions, that every thing tending to establish sub-" stantial and permanent order, in the affairs of a country, to " increase the total mass of industry and opulence, is ultimately " beneficial to every part of it. On the credit of this great truth, " an acquiescence may safely be accorded, from every quarter, " to all institutions, and arrangements, which promise a confir-" mation of public order, and an augmentation of national re-" source.

" But there are more particular considerations which serve to "fortify the idea, that the encouragement of manufactures is the "interest of all parts of the union. If the northern and middle "states should be the principal scenes of such establishments, "they would immediately benefit the more southern, by creating "a demand for productions, some of which they have in com- "mon with the other states and others which are either pecu- "liar to them, or more abundant, or of better quality than else- "where. These productions, principally, are timber flax, hemp, "cotton, wool, raw silk, indigo, iron, lead, furs, hides, skins and "coals; of these articles, cotton and indigo are peculiar to the "southern states: as are hitherto, lead and coals; flax and hemp "are or may be raised in greater abundance there, than in the "more northern states; and the wool of Virginia is said to be of "better quality than that of any other state; a circumstance "rendered the more probable by the reflection, that Virginia "embraces the same latitudes with the finest wool countries of "Europe. The climate of the south is also better adapted to "the production of silk.

" The extensive cultivation of cotton can perhaps hardly be "expected, but from the previous establishment of domestic "manufactories of the article; and the surest encouragement "and vent, for the others, would result from similar establish- "ments in respect to them.

" A full view having now been taken of the inducements to "the promotion of manufactures in the united states, accompa- "nied with an examination of the principal objections which are "commonly urged in opposition, it is proper, in the next place, "to consider the means by which it may be effected as intro- "ductory to a specification of the objects which, in the present "state of things, appear the most fit to be encouraged, and of "the particular measures which it may be advisable to adopt, "in respect to each.

" In order to a better judgment of the means proper to be "resorted to by the united states, it will be of use to advert to "those which have been employed with success in other coun- "tries. The principal of these are—

I. " Protecting duties—or duties on those foreign articles "which are the rivals of the domestic ones intended to be en- "couraged.

" Duties of this nature evidently amount to a virtual bounty "on the domestic fabrics, since, by enhancing the charges on "foreign articles, they enable the national manufacturers to un- "dersell all their foreign competitors. The propriety of this "species of encouragemect need not be dwelt upon; as it is not "only a clear result from the numerous topics which have been "suggested, but is sanctioned by the laws of the united states,

"in a variety of instances; it has the additional recommenda-
"tion of being a resource of revenue. Indeed all the duties im-
"posed on imported articles, though with an exclusive view to
"revenue, have the effect in contemplation, and, except where
"they fall on raw materials, wear a beneficent aspect towards
"the manufactures of the country.

II. "Prohibitions of rival articles, or duties equivalent to
"prohibitions.

"This is another and an efficacious means of encouraging
"national manufactures; but in general it is only fit to be em-
"ployed when a manufacture has made such a progress, and is
"in so many hands, as to insure a due competition, and an ade-
"quate supply, on reasonable terms. Of duties equivalent to
"prohibitions, there are examples in the laws of the united
"states, and there are other cases, to which the principle may
"be advantageously extended; but they are not numerous.

"*Considering a monopoly of the domestic market to its own
"manufacturers as the reigning policy of manufacturing nations,
"a similar policy on the part of the united states, in every proper
"instance, is dictated, it might almost be said, by the principles of
"distributive justice; certainly by the duty of endeavouring to
"secure to their own citizens a reciprocity of advantages.*

III. "Prohibitions of the exportation of the materials of man-
"ufactures.

"The desire of securing a cheap and plentiful supply for the
"national workmen, and, where the article is either peculiar to
"the country, or of peculiar quality there, the jealousy of ena-
"bling foreign workmen to rival those of the nation, with its
"own materials, are the leading motives to this species of regu-
"lation. It ought not to be affirmed, that it is in no instance
"proper; but it is certainly one which ought to be adopted with
"great circumspection and only in very plain cases. It is seen
"at once, that its immediate operation is to abridge the demand,
"and keep down the produce of some other branch of industry,
"generally speaking, of agriculture, to the prejudice of those
"who carry it on; and though, if it be really essential to the
"prosperity of any very important national manufacture, it may
"happen that those who are injured, in the first instance, may
"be eventually indemnified, by the superior steadiness of an
"extensive domestic market depending on that prosperity: yet
"in a matter, in which there is so much room for nice and diffi-
"cult combinations, in which such opposite considerations com-
"bat each other, prudence seems to dictate, that the expedient
"in question ought to be indulged with a sparing hand.

IV. "Pecuniary bounties.

"This has been found one of the most efficacious means of
"encouraging manufactures, and it is, in some views, the best.

" Though it has not yet been practised upon by the government " of the united states, (unless the allowance on the exportation " of dried and pickled fish and salted meat could be considered " as a bounty) and though it is less favoured by public opinion " than some other modes—its advantages are these—

1. " It is a species of encouragement more positive and direct " than any other, and for that very reason, has a more immedi- " ate tendency to stimulate and uphold new enterprises. increas- " ing the chances of profit, and diminishing the risks of loss, in " the first attempts.

2. It avoids the inconvenience of a temporary argumentation " of price, which is incident to some other modes, or it produces " it to a less degree; either by making no addition to the char- " ges on the rival foreign article, as in the case of protecting du- " ties, or by making a smaller addition. The first happens when " the fund for the bounty is derived from a different object " (which may or may not increase the price of some other arti- " cle, according to the nature of that object;) the second, when " the fund is derived from the same or a similar object of foreign " manufacture. One per cent. duty on the foreign article, con- " verted into a bounty on the domestic, will have an equal effect " with a duty of two per cent. exclusive of such bounty; and " the price of the foreign commodity is liable to be raised, " in the one case, in the proportion of one per cent. in the other, " in that of two per cent. Indeed the bounty, when drawn from " another source, is calculated to promote a reduction of price; " because, without laying any new charge on the foreign article, " it serves to introduce a competition with it, and to increase " the total quantity of the article in the market.

3. " Bounties have not, like high protecting duties, a tendency " to produce scarcity. An increase of price is not always the " immediate, though, where the progress of a domestic manufac- " ture does not counteract a rise, it is commonly the ultimate " effect of an additional duty. In the interval, between the laying " of the duty and a proportionable increase of price, it may dis- " courage importation, by interfering with the profits to be ex- " pected from the sale of the article.

4. " Bounties are sometimes not only the best, but the only " proper expedient, for uniting the encouragement of a new ob- " ject of agriculture, with that of a new object of manufacture. " It is the interest of the farmer to have the production of the " raw material promoted, by counteracting the interference of the " foreign material of the same kind—It is the interest of the man- " ufacturer to have the material abundant or cheap. If, prior to " the domestic production of the material, in sufficient quantity, to " supply the manufacturer on ood terms, a duty be laid upon " the importation of it from abroad, with a view to promote the

" raising of it at home, the interest both of the farmer and man- " ufacturer will be disserved. By either destroying the requisite " supply, or raising the price of the article, beyond what can be " afforded to be given for it, by the conductor of an infant man- " ufacture, it is abandoned or fails; and there being no domes- " tic manufactories, to create a demand for the raw material, " which is raised by the farmer, it is in vain, that the competition " of the like foreign articles may have been destroyed.

" It cannot escape notice, that a duty upon the importation of " an article, can no otherwise aid the domestic production of it, " than by giving the latter greater advantages in the home mar- " ket. It can have no influence upon the advantageous sale of " the article produced in foreign markets; no tendency, there- " fore, to promote its exportation.

" The true way to conciliate those two interests, is to lay a " duty on foreign manufactures of the material, the growth of " which is desired to be encouraged, and to apply the produce of " that duty by way of bounty, either upon the production of the " material itself, or upon its manufacture at home, or upon both. " In this disposition of the thing, the manufacturer commences " his enterprise, under every advantage, which is attainable as to " quantity or price of the raw material; and the farmer, if the " bounty be immediately given to him, is enabled by it to enter " into a successful competition with the foreign material: if the " bounty be to the manufacturer on so much of the domestic " material as he consumes, the operation is nearly the same; he " has a motive of interest to prefer the domestic commodity, if " of equal quality, even at a higher price than the foreign, so " long as the difference of price is any thing short of the bounty, " which is allowed upon the article.

" Except the simple and ordinary kinds of household manu- " facture, or those for which there are very commanding local " advantages, pecuniary bounties are in most cases indispensa- " ble to the introduction of a new branch. *A stimulus and a " support not less powerful and direct is, generally speaking, es- " sential to the overcoming of the obstacles which arise from the " competitions of superior skill and maturity elsewhere. Bounties " are especially essential, in regard to articles, upon which those " foreigners who have been accustomed to supply a country, are in " the practice of granting them.*

" The continuance of bounties on manufactures long estab- " lished, must almost always be of questionable policy: because " a presumption would arise in every such case, that there were " natural and inherent impediments to success. But *in new un- " dertakings, they are as justifiable as they are oftentimes neces- " sary.*

" There is a degree of prejudice against bounties, from an

"appearance of giving away the public money, without an immediate consideration, and from a supposition, that they serve to enrich particular classes, at the expense of the community.

"But neither of these sources of dislike will bear a serious examination. *There is no purpose to which public money can be more beneficially applied, than to the acquisition of a new and useful branch of industry; no consideration more valuable than a permanent addition to the general stock of productive labour.*

"As to the second source of objection, it equally lies against other modes of encouragement which are admitted to be eligible. As often as a duty upon a foreign article makes an addition to its price, it causes an extra expense to the community, for the benefit of the domestic manufacturer. A bounty does no more. *But it is the interest of the society, in each case, to submit to a temporary expense, which is more than compensated, by an increase of industry and wealth—by an augmentation of resources and independence—and by the circumstance of eventual cheapness, which has been noticed in another place.*

V. "Premiums.

"These are of a nature allied to bounties, though distinguishable from them in some important features.

"Bounties are applicable to the whole quantity of an article produced, or manufactured, or exported, and involve a correspondent expense: premiums serve to reward some particular excellence or superiority, some extraordinary exertion or skill, and are dispensed only in a small number of cases. But their effect is to stimulate general effort; contrived so as to be both honorary and lucrative, they address themselves to different passions; touching the chords as well of emulation as of interest. They are accordingly a very economical mean of exciting the enterprise of a whole community.

"There are various societies in different countries, whose object is the dispensation of premiums for the encouragement of agriculture arts, manufactures, and commerce; and though they are, for the most part, voluntary associations, with comparatively slender funds, their utility has been immense. Much has been done by this means in Great Britain; Scotland in particular, owes materially to it a prodigious amelioration of condition. From a similar establishment in the united states, supplied and supported by the government of the union, vast benefits might reasonably be expected.

VI. "The exemption of the materials of manufactures from duty.

"The policy of that exemption, as a general rule, particularly in reference to new establishments, is obvious. It can hardly ever be advisable to add the obstructions of fiscal burdens to

" the difficulties which naturally embarrass a new manufacture; " and where it is matured and in condition to become an object " of revenue, it is, generally speaking, better that the fabric, " than the material, should be the subject of taxation. Ideas " of proportion between the quantum of the tax and the value " of the article, can be more easily adjusted in the former than " in the latter case. An argument for exemptions of this kind " in the united states, is to be derived from the practice, as far " as their necessities have permitted, of those nations whom " we are to meet as competitors in our own and in foreign " markets.

VII. " Drawbacks of the duties which are imposed on the " materials of manufactures.

" It has already been observed, as a general rule, that duties " on those materials ought, with certain exceptions, to be for- " borne. Of these exceptions, three cases occur, which may " serve as examples—one, where the material is itself an object " of general or extensive consumption, and a fit and productive " source of revenue; another, where a manufacture of a simpler " kind, the competition of which with a like domestic article is " desired to be restrained, partakes of the nature of a raw ma- " terial, from being capable by a further process, to be converted " into a manufacture of a different kind, the introduction or " growth of which is desired to be encouraged: a third, where " the material itself is a production of the country, and in suffi- " cient abundance to furnish a cheap and plentiful supply to the " national manufacturers.

" Under the first description comes the article of molasses. " It is not only a fair object of revenue, but being a sweet, it is " just that the consumers of it should pay a duty as well as the " consumers of sugar.

" Cottons and linen in their white state, fall under the second " description—a duty upon such as are imported is proper to " promote the domestic manufacture of similar articles in the " same state—a drawback of that duty is proper to encourage " the printing and staining at home, of those which are brought " from abroad. When the first of these manufactures has at- " tained sufficient maturity in a country, to furnish a full supply " for the second, the utility of the drawback ceases.

" The article of hemp either now does or may be expected " soon to exemplify the third case, in the united states.

" Where duties on the materials of manufactures are not laid " for the purpose of preventing a competition with some domes- " tic production, the same reasons which recommend, as a " general rule, the exemption of those materials from duties, " would recommend, as a like general rule, the allowance of " drawbacks in favour of the manufacturer; accordingly, such

" drawbacks are familiar in countries which systematically pur-" sue the business of manufactures; which furnishes an argu-" ment for the observance of a similar policy in the united states; " and the idea has been adopted by the laws of the union, in the " instances of salt and molasses. It is believed that it will be " found advantageous to extend it to some other articles.

VIII. " The encouragement of new inventions and discove-" ries, at home, and of the introduction into the united states of " such as may have been made in other countries; particularly " those which relate to machinery.

" It is customary with manufacturing nations to prohibit, un-" der severe penalties, the exportation of implements and ma-" chines, they have either invented or improved. There are " already objects for a similar regulation in the united states; " and others may be expected to occur from time to time. The " adoption of it seems to be dictated by the principle of recipro-" city. Greater liberality, in such respects, might better com-" port with the general spirit of the country; but a selfish and " exclusive policy in other quarters, will not always permit the " free indulgence of a spirit which would place us upon an un-" equal footing. As far as prohibitions tend to prevent " foreign competitors from deriving the benefit of the improve-" ments made at home, they tend to increase the advantages of " those by whom they may have been introduced; and operate " as an encouragement to exertion.

IX. " Judicious regulations for the inspection of manufactured " commodities.

" This is not among the least important of the means by which " the prosperity of manufactures may be promoted. It is indeed in " many cases one of the most essential. Contributing to prevent " frauds upon consumers at home, and exporters to foreign " countries—to improve the quality and preserve the character " of the national manufactures, it cannot fail to aid the expediti-" ous and advantageous sale of them, and to serve as a guard " against successful competition from other quarters. The rep-" utation of the flour and lumber of some states, and of the pot-" ash of others, has been established by an attention to this point. " And the like good name might be procured for those articles, " wheresoever produced, by a judicious and uniform system of " inspection throughout the ports of the united states. A like " system might also be extended with advantage to other com-" modities.

" X. The facilitating of pecuniary remittances from place to " place.

" XI. The facilitating of the transportation of commodities.

" The foregoing are the principal of the means, by which the " growth of manufactures is ordinarily promoted. It is, how-

"ever not merely necessary that measures of government, "which have a direct view to manufactures, should be calculat-"ed to assist and protect them; but that those which only collat-"erally affect them, in the general course of the administration, "should be guarded from any peculiar tendency to injure "them.

"The possibility of a diminution of the revenue may pre-"sent itself, as an objection to the arrangements which have been submitted.

"*But there is no truth which may be more firmly relied upon,* "*than that the interests of the revenue are promoted by whatever* "*promotes an increase of national industry and wealth.*

In proportion to the degree of these, is the capacity of eve-"ry country to contribute to the public treasury; and when the "capacity to pay is increased, or even is not decreased, the only "consequence of measures which diminish any particular re-"source, is a change of the object. If, by encouraging the "manufacture of an article at home, the revenue, which has "been wont to accrue from its importation, should be lessened, "an indemnification can easily be found, either out of the manu-"facture itself, or from some other object which may be deemed "more convenient."

NO. X.

Philadelphia, June 18, 1819.

Report of the Committee of Commerce and Manufactures on the cotton branch. Its slow progress till 1805. *Rapid progress afterwards. Consumption of cotton in the united states. People employed in the manufacture. Amount of their wages, and of the goods produced. Predictions of the consequences of the neglect of manufactures. Their fulfilment. Report on woollen manufacture. Affecting memorial from Oneida county. Calamitous state of affairs unheeded. Ruin of manufacturers.*

An idea appears to be entertained by many persons that our views lead to great innovations, and to advocate visionary and new formed projects, of which the results may be pernicious. The extracts from the report of Alexander Hamilton, on manufactures, contained in our last address, ought to remove these unfounded impressions. That most excellent document presented to the united states a plan of policy which embraced, on the most liberal scale, that protection of the manufacturing industry of the united states, of which we are endeavouring, with our feeble efforts, to prove the necessity.

We now submit to the public two reports of the committee of commerce and manufactures of the congress of 1816—that congress by which was enacted the tariff that has produced the present calamitous state of affairs. These documents fully prove, that the subject had been duly considered, and was fully understood by that committee, whose wise counsels, unfortunately, were over-ruled by the disciples of Adam Smith, those gentlemen, whose maxim is '*to buy where articles can be had cheapest*'—a maxim, we repeat, to the utter rejection of which Great Britain owes the great mass of her wealth, power, and resources—a maxim which has never failed to ruin any nation by which it has been adopted.

A cursory view of these reports will evince the sagacity of the gentlemen by whom they were drawn up. Their predictions have unhappily become history. The present impoverishment of the country, obviously resulting from the neglect of protecting domestic manufactures, was as clearly foretold by them, in 1816, as it can now be described by the most accurate pencil. In an ill hour, the admonitions of the committee were disregarded—and heavily the nation at present pays the forfeit.

We annex to these reports the petition of the cotton manufacturers of Oneida county, in the state of New York, presented to congress in the year 1818, a pathetic appeal to their fellow citizens for protection—an appeal to which no attention whatever was paid. They were consigned to ruin, without the least attempt to interpose in their favour.

Report of the committee of commerce and manufactures, to which were referred the memorials and petitions of manufacturers of cotton wool.—February 13, 1816.

"The committee of commerce and manufactures, to which were "referred the memorials and petitions of the manufacturers "of cotton wool, respectfully submit the following RE-"PORT—

"The committee were conscious, that they had no ordinary "duty to perform, when the house of representatives referred to "their consideration, the memorials and petitions of the manu-"facturers of cotton wool. In obedience to the instructions of "the house, they have given great attention to the subject, and "beg leave to present the result of their deliberations.

"They are not a little apprehensive, that they have not suc-"ceeded in doing justice to a subject so intimately connected "with the advancement and prosperity of agriculture and com-

" merce—a subject which enlightened statesmen and philoso- " phers have deemed not unworthy of their attention and con- " sideration.

" It is not the intention of the committee to offer any theo- " retical opinions of their own, or of others. They are persuaded " that a display of speculative opinions would not meet with " approbation. From these views, the committee are disposed " to state facts, and make such observations only as shall be " intimately connected with, and warranted by them.

" Prior to the years 1806 and 1807, establishments for manu- " facturing cotton wool had not been attempted, but in a few " instances, and on a limited scale. Their rise and progress are " attributable to embarrassments to which commerce was sub- " jected; which embarrassments originated in causes not within " the control of human prudence.

" While commerce flourished, the trade which had been car- " ried on with the continent of Europe, with the East-Indies, " and with the colonies of Spain and France, enriched our enter- " prising merchants, the benefits of which were sensibly felt by " the agriculturists, whose wealth and industry were increased " and extended. When external commerce was suspended, the " capitalists throughout the union became solicitous to give ac- " tivity to their capital. A portion of it, it is believed, was " directed to the improvement of agriculture, and not an incon- " siderable portion of it, as it appears, was likewise employed in " erecting establishments, for manufacturing cotton wool. To " make the statement as satisfactory as possible—to give it all " the certainty that it is susceptible of attaining, the following " facts are respectfully submitted to the consideration of the " house. They show the rapid progress which has been made " in a few years, and evidence the ability to carry them on with " certainty of success, should a just and liberal policy regard " them as objects deserving encouragement.

" In the year	1800	500	Bales of cotton manufactured in manufacturing establishments.
	1805	1,000	
	1810	10,000	
	1815	90,000	

" This statement the committee have no reason to doubt; nor " have they any to question the truth of the following succinct " statement of the capital which is employed, of the labour " which it commands, and of the products of that labour.

" Capital - - - - - - -	$40,000,000
" Males employed, from the age of seventeen and upwards - - - - - - - -	10,000
" Women and female children - - - - -	66,000

" Boys, under seventeen years of age - -	24,000
" Wages of one hundred thousand persons, averaging $150 each - - - - -	$15,000,000
" Cotton wool manufactured, ninety thousand bales, amounting to - - - - - *lbs.*	27,000,000
" Number of yards of cotton, of various kinds,	81,000,000
" Cost, per yard, averaging 30 cents - -	$24,300,000

" The rise and progress of such establishments can excite no " wonder The inducements to industry in a free government " are numerous and inviting. Effects are always in unison with " their causes. The inducements consist in the certainty and " security which every citizen enjoys, of exercising exclusive " dominion over the creations of his genius, and the products " of his labour ; in procuring from his native soil, at all times, " with facility, the raw materials that are required ; and in the " liberal encouragement that will be accorded by agriculturists " to those who, by their labour, keep up a constant and increas- " ing demand for the produce of agriculture.

" Every state will participate in those advantages. The re- " sources of each will be explored, opened, and enlarged. Dif- " ferent sections of the union will, according to their position, " the climate, the population, the habits of the people, and the " nature of the soil, strike into that line of industry, which is " best adapted to their interest and the good of the whole ; an " active and free intercourse, promoted and facilitated by roads " and canals, will ensue ; prejudices which are generated by dis- " tance, and the want of inducements to approach each other, " and reciprocate benefits, will be removed ; information will be " extended ; the union will acquire strength and solidity ; and " the constitution of the united states, and that of each state, " will be regarded as fountains from which flow numerous " streams of public and private prosperity.

" Each government, moving in its appropriate orbit, perform- " ing with ability, its separate functions, will be endeared to the " hearts of a good and grateful people.

" The states that are most disposed to manufactures, as regular " occupations, will draw from the agricultural states all the raw " materials which they want, and not an inconsiderable portion " also of the necessaries of life ; while the latter will, in addition " to the benefits which they at present enjoy, always command, " in peace or in war, at moderate prices, every species of manu- " facture, that their wants may require. Should they be incli- " ned to manufacture for themselves, they can do so with suc- " cess ; because they have all the means in their power to erect " and extend at pleasure manufacturing establishments. Our " wants being supplied by our own ingenuity and industry, "exportation of specie to pay for foreign manufactures, will "cease.

" *The value of American produce at this time exported, will not " enable the importers to pay for the foreign manuufctures import-* "ed. Whenever the two accounts shall be fairly stated, the bal- "ance against the united states will be found to be many mil- "lions of dollars. Such is the state of things, that the change " must be to the advantage of the united states. The precious " metals will be attracted to them, the diffusion of which, in a " regular and uniform current through the great arteries and " veins of the body politic, will give to each member health and " vigour.

" In proportion as the commerce of the united states depends " on agriculture and manufactures, as a common basis, will it " increase and become independent of those revolutions and fluc- " tuations, which the ambition and jealousy of foreign govern- " ments are too apt to produce. Our navigation will be quick- " ened; and, supported as it will be by internal resources never " before at the command of any nation, will advance to the extent " of those resources.

" New channels of trade, to enterprise no less important than " productive, are opening, which can be secured only by a wise " and prudent policy appreciating their advantage.

" If want of foresight should neglect the cultivation and im- " provement of them, the opportune moment may be lost, per- " haps for centuries, and the energies of this nation be thereby " prevented from developing themselves, and from making the " boon which is proffered, our own.

" By trading on our own capital, collisions with other nations, " if they be not entirely done away, will be greatly diminished.

" This natural order of things exhibits the commencement of " a new epoch, which promises peace, security and repose by a " firm and steady reliance on the produce of agriculture, on the " treasures that are embosomed in the earth, on the genius and " ingenuity of our manufacturers and mechanics, and on the in- " telligence and enterprise of our merchants.

"The government possessing the intelligence and the art of " improving the resources of the nation, will increase its efficient " powers; and, enjoying the confidence of those whom it has " made happy, will oppose to the assailants of the nation's rights, " the true, the only invincible Ægis, the unity of will and strength. " Causes producing war will be few. Should war take place, " its calamitous consequences will be mitigated, and the expen- " ses and burdens of such a state of things will fall with a weight " much less oppressive and injurious on the nation. The ex- " penditures of the last war were greatly increassd by a depend-

"ence on foreign supplies. The prices incident to such a de-"pendence will always be high.

"Had not our nascent manufacturing establishments increased "the quantity of commodities, at that time in demand, the ex-"penditures would have been much greater, and consequences "the most fatal and disastrous, alarming even in contemplation, "would have been the fate of this nation. The experience of "the past teaches a lesson never to be forgotten, and points em-"phatically to the remedy. A wise government should heed "its admonitions, or the independence of this nation will be ex-"posed to 'the shafts of fortune.'

"The committee, keeping in view the interests of the nation, "cannot refrain from stating that cotton fabrics imported from "India, interfere not less with that encouragement to which ag-"riculture is justly entitled, than they do with that which ought "reasonably to be accorded to the manufacturers of cotton wool. "The raw material of which they are made is the growth of In-"dia, and of a quality inferior to our own.

"The fabrics themselves, in point of duration and use, are "likewise inferior to the substantial fabrics of American manu-"facture. Although the India cotton fabrics can be sold for a "lower price than the American, yet the difference in texture is "so much in favour of the American, that the latter may be "safely considered as the cheapest.

"The distance of most of the western states from the ocean, "the exuberant richness of the soil, and the variety of its pro-"ducts, forcibly impress the mind of the committee with a belief "that all these causes conspire to encourage manufactures, and to "give an impetus and direction to such a disposition. Although "the western states may be said to be in the gristle, in contem-"plation of that destiny, to which they are hastening, yet the "products of manufactures in those states are beyond every cal-"culation that could reasonably be made; contrary to the opin-"ion of many enlightened and virtuous men, who have suppos-"ed that the inducements to agriculture and the superior advan-"tages of that life, would suppress any disposition to that sort "of industry. But theories, how ingeniously soever they may "be constructed, how much soever they may be made to conform "to the laws of symmetry and beauty, are no sooner brought in-"to conflict with facts, than they fall into ruins. In viewing "their fragments, the mind is irresistibly led to render the hom-"age due to the genius and taste of the architects; but cannot "refrain from regretting the waste, to no purpose, of superior "intellects. The western states prove the fallacy of such theo-"ries; they appear in their growth and expansion to be in ad-"vance of thought, while the political economist is drawing "their portraits, their features change and enlarge, with such "rapidity, that his pencil in vain endeavours to catch their ex-"pression, and to fix their physiognomy.

"It is to their advantage to manufacture, because, by decreas-"ing the bulk of the articles, they at the same time increase "their value by labour, bring them to market with less expense, "and with the certainty of obtaining the best prices.

"Those states, understanding their interest, will not be di-"verted from its pursuit. In the encouragement of manufactures "they find a stimulus for agriculture.

"The manufacturers of cotton, in making application to the "national governments for encouragement, have been induced "to do so for many reasons.—They know that *their establish-"ments are new and in their infancy, and that they have to en-"counter a competition with foreign establishments, that have ar-"rived at maturity, that are supported by a large capital, and "have from the government every protection that can be re-"quired.*

"The American manufacturers expect to meet with all the "embarrassments which a jealous and monopolizing policy can "suggest. The committee are sensible of the force of such "considerations. They are convinced that old practices and "maxims will not be abandoned to favour the united states.—"The foreign manufacturers and merchants will put in requisi-"tion all the powers of ingenuity; will practice whatever art can "devise and capital can accomplish, to prevent American manu-"facturing establishments from striking root and flourishing in "their rich and native soil. By the allowance of bounties and "drawbacks, the foreign manufacturers and merchants will be "furnished with additional means of carrying on the conflict, "and of ensuring success.

"The American manufacturers have good reason for their ap-"prehensions; they have much at stake. They have a large ca-"pital employed, and are feelingly alive for its fate. Should "the national government not afford them protection, the dan-"gers which invest and threaten them, will destroy all their hopes "and will close their prospects of utility to their country. A "reasonable encouragement will sustain and keep them erect; "but if they fall, they fall never to rise again.

"*The foreign manufacturers and merchants know this, and "will redouble with renovated zeal, the stroke to prostrate them. "They also know, that should the American manufacturing es-"tablishments fall, their mouldering piles, the visible ruins of a "legislative breath, will warn all who shall tread in the same "footsteps, of the doom, the inevitable destiny of their establish-"ments.*

"The national government, in viewing the disastrous effects "of a short sighted policy, may relent; but what can relenting "avail? Can it raise the dead to life? Can it give for injuries "inflicted, the reparation that is due? Industry, in every rami-"fication of society, will feel the shock, and generations will, as "they succeed each other, feel the effects of its undulations.—"Dissatisfaction will be visible every where, and the lost confi-"dence and affection of the citizen, will not be the least of the "evils the government will have to deplore. But should the na-"tional government, pursuing an enlightened and liberal policy, "sustain and foster the manufacturing establishments, a few "years would place them in a condition to bid defiance to foreign "competition, and would enable them to increase the industry, "wealth, and prosperity of the nation; and to afford to the gov-"ernment, in times of difficulty and distress, whatever it may "require to support public credit, while maintaining the rights "of the nation.

"Providence, in bountifully placing within our reach, what-"ever can minister to happiness and comfort, indicates plainly "to us our duty—and what we owe to ourselves. Our resour-"ces are abundant and inexhaustible.

"The stand that Archimedes wanted, is given to the national "and state governments—and labour-saving machinery tenders "the lever—the power of bringing those resources into use.

"This power imparts incalculable advantages to a nation "whose population is not full. The united states require the "use of this power, because they do not abound in population. "The diminution of manual labour, by means of machinery, in "the cotton manufacture of Great Britain, was, in the year 1810, "as two hundred to one.

"Our manufacturers have already availed themselves of this "power, and have profited by it. A little more experience in "making machines, and in managing them with skill, will enable "our manufacturers to supply more fabrics than are necessary "for the home demand.

"Competition will make the prices of articles low, and the "extension of the cotton manufactories will produce that com-"petition.

"One striking and important advantage, which labour-saving "machines bestow, is this, that in all their operations they re-"quire few men; as a reference to another part of this report "will show. No apprehensions can then be seriously entertain-"ed, that agriculture will be in danger of having its efficient "labourers withdrawn from its service.

"On the contrary, *the manufacturing establishments, increasing "the demand for raw materials, will give to agriculture new life "and expansion.*

"The committee, after having with great deference and re-"spect, presented to the house this important subject in various

" points of view, feel themselves constrained, before concluding " this report, to offer a few more observations, which they con- " sider as being immediately connected with it, and not less so " with the present and future prosperity of this nation.

" The prospects of an enlarged commerce are not flattering.

" Every nation in time of peace will supply its own wants " from its own resources, or from those of other nations.

" When supplies are drawn from foreign countries, the inter- " course which will ensue, will furnish employ to the naviga- " tion only of the countries connected, by their reciprocal wants.

" Our concern does not arise from, nor can it be increased " by, the limitation which our navigation and trade will have " prescribed to them, by the peace and apparent repose of Eu- " rope.

" Our apprehensions arise from causes that cannot animate " by their effects. Look wheresoever the eye can glance, and " what are the objects that strike the vision? On the continent " of Europe, industry, deprived of its motive and incitement, is " paralized; the accumulated wealth of ages, seized by the hand " of military despotism, is appropriated to and squandered on " objects of ambition; the order of things unsettled, and confi- " dence between man and man annihilated. Every moment is " looked for, with tremulous, anxious, and increased solicitude; " hope languishes; and commercial enterprize stiffens with fear. " The political horizon appears to be calm: but many of no or- " dinary sagacity think they behold signs portentous of a change, " the indications of a violent tempest which will again rage, and " desolate that devoted region.

" Should this prediction fail, no change for the better, under " existing circumstances, can take place. Where despotism— " military despotism reigns—silence and fearful stillness must " prevail.

" Such is the prospect which continental Europe exhibits, to " the enterprize of American merchants.

" Can it be possible for them to find in that region, sources " which will supply them with more than seventeen millions of " dollars, the balance due for British manufactures imported? " this balance being over and above the value of all the exports " to foreign countries from the united states. The view which " is given of the dreary prospect of commercial advantages ac- " cruing to the united states by an intercourse with continental " Europe, is believed to be just. The statement made of the " great balance in favour of Great Britain due from the united " states, is founded on matter of fact.

" In the hands of Great Britain are gathered together and held " many powers, which they have not been accustomed hitherto " to feel and to exercise.

"No improper motives are intended to be imputed to that "government. But does not experience teach a lesson that "should never be forgotten, that governments, like individuals, "are apt "to feel power and forget right?" It is not inconsis- "tent with national decorum to become circumspect and pru- "dent. May not the government of Great Britain be inclined, "in analizing the basis of her political power, to consider and "regard the united states as her rival, and to indulge an improper "jealousy, the enemy of peace and repose?

"*Can it be politic, in any point of view, to make the united states* "*dependent on any nation for supplies, absolutely necessary for* "*defence, for comfort, and for accommodation?*

"Will not the strength, the political energies of this nation, be "materially impaired at any time, but fatally so in those of diffi- "culty and distress, by such dependence?

"*Do not the suggestions of wisdom plainly show, that the se-* "*curity, the peace, and the happiness of this nation depend on* "*opening and enlarging all our resources, and drawing from* "*them whatever shall be required for public use or private accom-* "*modation?*

"The committee, from the views which they have taken, con- "sider the situation of the manufacturing establishments to be "perilous. Some have decreased, and others have suspended "business. *A liberal encouragement will put them again into* "*operation with increased powers; but should it be withheld, they* "*will be prostrated. Thousands will be reduced to want and* "*wretchedness. A capital of near sixty millions of dollars will* "*become inactive, the greater part of which will be a dead loss to* "*the manufacturers.* Our improvidence may lead to fatal con- "sequences: the powers, jealous of our growth and prosperity, "will acquire the resources and strength which this government "neglects to improve. It requires no prophet to foretel the use "that foreign powers will make of them. The committee, from "all the considerations which they have given to this subject, "are deeply impressed with a conviction that the manufacturing "establishments of cotton wool are of real utility to the agricul- "tural interest, and that they contribute much to the prosperity "of the union. Under the influence of this conviction, the com- "mittee beg leave to tender, respectfully, with this report, the "following resolution:

"*Resolved*, That from and after the 30th day of June next in "lieu of the duties now authorised by law, there be laid, levied, "and collected on cotton goods, imported into the united states, "and territories thereof, from any foreign country whatever, " per centum ad valorem, being not less cents per "square yard.

" *Report of the committee of commerce and manufactures on the " memorials and petitions of the manufacturers of wool—* " March 6, 1816.

" The committee of commerce and manufactures, to which " were referred the memorials and petitions of the manu- " facturers of wool, respectfully submit the following RE- " PORT—

" The committee having given this subject all the considera- " tion that its importance merits, beg leave to present, with due " respect, to the house, the result of their investigation.

" The correctness of the following estimate the committee are " no wise disposed to question :

" Amount of capital supposed to be invested in buildings, machinery, &c.		$12,000,000
" Value of raw material consumed annually	7,000,000	
" Increase of value by manufacturing,	12,000,000	
" Value of woollen goods manufactured annually,		$19,000,000

" Number of persons employed, { Constantly, 50,000; Occasionally, 50,000 } ——100,000

" The committee having, in a report presented to the house " on the 13th of February last, on the memorials and petitions " of the manufacturers of cotton, expressed their opinion on the " policy of fostering manufacturing establishments, consider " themselves relieved from the necessity of repeating the same " arguments. Every reason then urged for sustaining the cotton " manufacturing establishments, applies with equal force in fa- " vour of the woollen. The committee, influenced by the same " reasons, feel themselves bound to accord the same justice to " the manufacturers of wool.

" The following resolution is, therefore, with due respect, " submitted to the house.

" *Resolved*, That from and after the 30th day of June next, in " lieu of the duties now authorised by law, there be laid, levied, " and collected on woollen goods imported into the united states " and territories thereof, from any foreign country whatever, " per centum ad valorem.

" *A memorial presented to the Senate of the United States, January* 7, 1818.

" To the honourable the Senate and House of Representatives " of the united states, in congress assembled, the petition of "the inhabitants of the county of Oneida, in the State of New "York, as well manufacturers as others, RESPECTFULLY "SHEWETH:

"That the above county contains a greater number of manu- "facturing establishments, of cotton and woollen, than any coun- "ty in the state, there being invested in said establishments at "least 600,000 dollars.

"That although the utmost efforts have been made by the pro- "prietors to sustain those establishments, their efforts have prov- "ed fruitless: and more than three-fourths of the factories re- "main necessarily closed, some of the proprietors being whol- "ly ruined, and others struggling under the greatest embarrass- "ment.

"In this alarming situation, we beg leave to make a last ap- "peal to the congress of the united states. While we make this ap- "peal, at the present crisis, the extensive embarrassments in most "of the great departments of industry, as well as the peculiar "difficulty in affording immediate relief to manufacturers, are "fully seen and appreciated. Yet your petitioners cannot be- "lieve that *the legislature of the union will remain an indifferent "spectator of the wide-spread ruin of their fellow citizens, and "look on, and see a great branch of industry, of the utmost impor- "tance in every community, prostrated under circumstances fatal "to all future attempts at revival, without a further effort for re- "relief.* We would not magnify the subject, which we now pre- "sent to congress beyond its just merits, when we state it to be "one of the utmost importance to the future interests and wel- "fare of the united states.

"Before we proceed farther, and at the very threshold, we "disclaim all legislative patronage or favour to any particular "class or branch of industry at the expense of the other classes "of the community. We ask of congress the adoption of no "measure for the relief of manufacturers, which is not deemed "consistent with sound national policy, and the best interests of "the united states at large. But if a compliance with our pray- "ers be the dictate of wisdom, and for the public good; if our "application be justified by the examples of all wise and pa- "trio ic states; *if no government of modern Europe is so short- "sighted, or regardless of its duties, as not to constantly watch "over, and yield a steady and protecting support to the manufac- "turers of the state*, we humbly hope this appeal in behalf of "American manufactures will not be made in vain.

"That clothing for our citizens in peace, and our army and "navy in war, are indispensable, and that the necessary supply "should be independent of foreign nations, are positions that "will be controverted by none. The last war afforded most "lamentable proof: your soldiers, exposed to the inclemencies "of a northern climate, were at times found fighting in the "ranks almost naked. It will not escape observation, that na-"tional collision and hostility are most likely to arise with "that nation from which our supplies are principally derived, "and that the operations of war must be prosecuted on the "ocean; hence, regular supplies being cut off, smuggling, viola-"tions of law, with all the concomitant evils *experienced in the* "*late war, are the certain consequences*. The same disgraceful "scenes are to be acted over and over again, to the deep re-"proach of the country. *If the present manufactories are suffer-* "*ed to fall, the government will look in vain for means to avert* "*those calamities.* Surrounded with many embarrassments, "government, during the war, saw fit to encourage manufactur-"ing establishments; and those who embarked their capital, it "is humbly conceived, were warranted in the expectation of "such continuing support of government as should protect their "interest against that foreign rivalship and hostility which is "now operating to their ruin. They had a right, as they con-"ceive, to expect this from what the government owed to itself, "and to the independence and best interests of the country, as "well as from the example of other nations in like circumstan-"ces.

"In reviewing the discussions on this great question, your "petitioners feel themselves justified in saying, that the question "has not been at all times fairly met on its true merits. We "have been constrained to witness alarm sounded, as though a "new principle was to be introduced, and the country now for "the first time, taxed for the mere benefit of manufacturers.— "What can be more untrue and unjust? We need not remind the "honourable the congress of the united states of what is known "to all, that from the first establishment of the government, spe-"cial regard has been had, in laying imposts and taxes, to *the* "*protection of domestic manufactures*, by increasing the duties on "imported articles coming in competition. Again, the tariff, "in protecting manufactures, has been represented as taxing the "farmer and planter for the benefit of the manufacturer; and "hence, attempts have been made to excite popular prejudice "against the latter. We need not dwell on this topic, in show-"ing how unjust to individuals, and injurious to the country the "charge is. As it respects the manufacturing districts of the "united states, there is no distinct class of manufacturers, no "separation of the manufacturer and farmer; it is the farmer "himself who is the manufacturer; he invests his money in man-"ufacturing stock. With the exception of a few factories, in "or near the great towns, by far the greater part of manufactur-"ing stock will be found in the hands of the farmers.

"Between different districts or states, one manufacturing and

" the other not, a different question arises, which resolves itself " into a mere equality or apportionment of taxes on the different parts of the union : and here it will be seen, on a view of " the whole system of imposts and taxes, that no injustice is " done, as *the manufacturing districts have, and still do, contribute their full proportion to the public treasury.* Of the internal taxes, it will appear, that they have paid an amount " greatly beyond the numerical standard or rule of apportionment " prescribed by the constitution. The fact is not here mentioned " for the purpose of complaint; but to show how fallacious " it is to select the duty on a particular article, to settle the " question of equality in the general apportionment of taxes.— " We might again confidently appeal to the tariff of impost, and " ask if the duty is not greater on many articles than on imported cloths (with the exception of certain coarse and almost useless cottons of the East Indies.) This is believed to be the " the case with most of the specific duties, and eminently so in " some instances. Were the government to proceed much farther than is now contemplated, and bestow premiums for the " encouragement of particular branches of industry, examples to " justify the measure would be found in the wisest and best administered governments. While the provision in the constitution *prohibiting any duty on exports*, favours the great staple " productions of the south, it injures the domestic manufacturer, " and is subversive of the great principle adopted by most nations, to *restrain the exports of the raw material necessary in manufactures.* But neither of this provision do your petitioners complain.

" We hope to find excuse in the importance of the subject, for " submitting to the consideration of congress the following " principles of political economy, which have been adopted by " the most enlightened governments, and are deemed not altogether inapplicable to the united states.

" *That the public good requires of government to restrain by duties, the importation of articles which may be produced at home, and to manufacture as much as possible of the raw materials of the country.*

" *That the branches of industry, particularly necessary or useful to the independence of the community, ought to be encouraged by government.*

" *That the most disadvantageous commerce, is that which exchanges the raw material for manufactured goods.*

" *That any nation which should open its ports to all foreign importations, without a reciprocal privilege, would soon be ruined by the balance of trade.*

" The policy of Great Britain, in support of which, no wars " however bloody, no expense, however enormous, are too great

" a sacrifice, ought never to be lost sight of by the united states. " That nation assumes to *manufacture for all nations, but will re-" ceive the manufactures of none.* So tenacious, so jealous is " she of the first dawnings of manufactures elsewhere, that she " binds even the hands of her own colonists. The jealousy of " parliament was excited, nearly a century ago, by the petty hat " manufactory of Massachusetts ; and an act of parliament actu-" ally passed in the reign of George the Second, prohibiting the " erection of furnaces, in British America for slitting iron.

" The great Chatham, the least hostile to British America, of " British ministers, in his speech in the house of Lords, on the " address to the throne, in 1770, expressed his utmost alarm at " the first efforts at manufactures in America.

" Mr. Brougham, a distinguished member of the British par-" liament, recently declared in his place, that it was well worth " while, at the close of the late war, to incur a loss on the expor-" tation to the united states, in order to stifle in the cradle our " rising manufactures. It is in vain for any man to shut his " eyes against the active rivalship and persevering hostility of " British manufacturers : and when the capital, the deep-rooted " establishments, the improved machinery, and the skill of the " British manufacturer, protected as he always is by the govern-" ment, are considered, it ought not to excite surprise, that the " American manufacturer, without the support of his government, " is found unequal to the contest. But yielding to manufacto-" ries reasonable support in their infancy, the government will, " at no distant period, find them able to defend themselves " against foreign competition and hostility, and at the same " time, make ample returns to the nation for its protecting kind-" ness.

" It was the opinion of Mr. Hamilton, former secretary of the " treasury of the united states, as well as of sir James Steuart, " that *no new manufactory can be established, in the present state " of the world, without encouragement from government.*

" *It cost the English parliament a struggle of forty years, com-" mencing in the reign of Edward III. to get the better of the estab-" lished manufactures of Flanders.* It is believed that much less " encouragement from government would place the manufactures " of the united states on a secure foundation. While the writers " of that nation are seen to highly commend the principle of " Adam Smith, that industry ought to be left to pursue its own " course, without the interference of the legislature, *the govern-" ment has, at all times, and under every vicissitude, turned a deaf " ear to the lesson, as though it were intended for other nations ; " and carried legislative regulations into every department and " avenue of industry.* The British statute book groans under " these regulations. The policy of the government has proved

" triumphant; immeasurable wealth flowed in upon the nation, " giving it a power and control over other nations never before " attained, nor so long enjoyed, by any people so inconsiderable " in numbers.

" But let no one imagine that a general system of manufac- " tures is now proposed to be introduced into the united states. " We would be understood as limiting our views to the manu- " factories already established; *to save those which have not al-* " *ready fallen, from the ruin which threatens them.*

" *After all that the present manufactories can supply, there will* " *remain to foreign importation an amount, it is believed, equal, if* " *not exceeding the means of the country to pay for.* That im- " portation, let it be remembered, will be mostly from a country " which shuts her ports against the productions of the united " states, and keep them so unless the necessities of her manufac- " tories, or hunger and sedition open them; and then the *fatal* " *suspension* often proves, as the experience of the ill-fated ship- " pers of bread stuffs, the present year, will attest, a mere decoy " to ruin. Lord Sheffield, in the year 1783, declared, that ex- " cept in time of war, there never was a market for American " wheat in Great Britain, exceeding three or four years in the " whole.

" There was a time when a balance of trade, believed in both " countries to be generally against the united states, was, in " some degree, satisfied or counter-balanced by a favourable " trade with the West Indies: but a recent change of policy in " the British councils has cut off that resource, and the parent " state prefers exposing her colonies to starving, rather than " open her ports to American commerce.

" It is obvious how much that government presumes on its " advantages over us, on the predilection of our citizens for " British manufactures, and the influence of the liberal pur- " chases in the south, of the material for her cotton manufac- " tures.

" We hope to be excused in repelling the unwarrantable im- " putation bestowed on manufactories of woollen and cotton as " being *injurious to the health and morals of the community.* On " this point we may content ourselves with referring to the " healthful sites of our factories, the spacious work-rooms, (re- " quired by the necessary machinery,) and appeal to every man " who has visited a factory, for testimony against the imputa- " tion. What is the experience on the subject? Scotland " manufactures not only what is required for its inhabitants, but " about five millions of dollars annually in the article of cotton " alone, for exportation; and yet, in both its physical and moral " character, that nation sustains a high elevation. We look in " vain for evidence that the arms of Scotchmen have been with-

" ered by their manufactories, nor do we recollect the field of " battle in Europe, where the arms of any nation were found " stronger in conflict.

" To swell the tide of prejudice against manufactures, it is " said that *unreasonable prices for goods were demanded at the* " *period of the late war. To reason with such objections would* " *be a mere waste of time. We might ask, what merchant, me-* " *chanic, or farmer, in any age or country, ever forbore to raise* " *his prices according to the demand in the market?* It enters " into first principles. Did the importer treble his first cost on " his cloths, even on smuggled goods, and does he make the " charge of extortion against manufacturers? The war unhinged " every thing, and changed the whole order of society and " course of business.

" *It might have been expected that the present fallen condition* " *of manufacturers would have soothed prejudice and disarmed* " *hostility. With all their alleged war profits, there are now none* " *so poor.* Is it not seen, that the destruction of the present " manufactories must inevitably produce the same evils of ex- " travagant prices, in the event of a future war, as were experi- " enced in the last?

" As to the imputed effect of the tariff, in enhancing the prices " of imported goods, it is believed that goods were never so low " as under the operation of the present duties; and so far as " competition between domestic and foreign goods has contri- " buted to this, credit is justly due to our mauufacturers.

" It is objected, that the entire industry of the country may " be most profitably exerted in clearing and cultivating our ex- " tended vacant lands. But *what does it avail the farmer, when* " *neither in the nation from which he purchases his goods, nor* " *elsewhere, can he find a market for his abundant crops?* Be- " sides, the diversion of labour from agriculture to manufactures, " is scarcely perceptible. Five or six adults, with the aid of " children, will manage a cotton manufactory of two thousand " spindles.

" From the gloomy condition of the manufacturers, the mind, " turning to another quarter, is cheered with the brightest " prospects of others. In the more southern states, it is be- " lieved, that the amount received, during the last year, from " the export of two or three articles of agricultural produce " only, exceeds forty millions of dollars.

" *An appeal is made to the equity, to the patriotism of the* " *southern statesman: his aid and co-operation are invoked for the* " *relief of the suffering manufacturers of the northern and middle* " *states.*

" In conclusion, your petitioners humbly pray, that provision " may be made by law, for *making the present duties on import-*

"*ed woollens and cottons* PERMANENT; *for prohibiting the im-*
"*portation of cotton goods from beyond the Cape of Good Hope,*
"*for consumption or use in the united states*, (according to the
"example of several European governments;) for restraining
"auction sales of goods; and for the more general introduction
"and use of domestic goods in the army and navy in the uni-
"ted states." *October* 1, 1817.

NO. XI.

Philadelphia, June 17, 1819.

Our policy not only injurious to the manufacturers but to the merchants and farmers, and even ultimately to Great Britain—Protection of agriculture—Of commerce—Wonderful progress of American navigation—Exports and population of the united states—Estimate of the profits on the culture and manufacture of cotton—Importation of cotton into England—Manufactures of the united states.

MISTAKEN opinions having been long entertained of an hostility between the interest of manufacturers, and those of merchants and agriculturists, it is supposed that the system we advocate is calculated to sacrifice those of the two last to the first. Nothing can be more foreign from the truth. Our views are decidedly favourable to commerce and the mercantile interest: because the commerce to or from a ruined country, such as ours will be under its present policy, affords little advantage to its merchants; and our plans tending to restore the prosperity, must of course improve the commerce of the united states, whose industry has been sacrificed to that of nations distant from us thousands of miles. We are equally and as decidedly the friends of agriculture; because our object is to secure to the farmer and planter for their productions a domestic market, which cannot fail them, instead of the precarious dependence on foreign ones, subject to unceasing fluctuations, and blasting the fairest hopes of the cultivator and merchant.

It will doubtless appear extraordinary, but it is nevertheless true, that the system we advocate is calculated to promote as well the advantage of the merchants of Great Britain and of those other foreign nations with which we trade, as that of the united states.

The commerce of a country impoverished as ours is, can be of little advantage to a trading nation, which loses all its profits, and part of its principal by bankruptcy. The deficiency of remittances, which is daily increasing, cannot fail to produce destructive consequences in Great Britain. Thousands in that country with shattered fortunes, will have to lament the infatuation that led them to inundate the united states with their merchandize, whereby they calculated on making splendid fortunes, which disappeared "like the baseless fabric of a vision," and left "not a trace behind," but disappointment and ruin.

The British merchants disregarded the valuable lesson of Esop's fable of the goose that laid the golden eggs. They killed the goose by their determination to enjoy all the benefits of our trade at once.

Having no mines of gold or silver, no pearl fisheries, we have no means of paying for our foreign importations but by the fruits of our industry. And the combined operation of the fatal impolicy of our tariff, the cupidity of our importers, and the infatuation of the British merchants, has so completely paralized our industry and impoverished the country, as to render us utterly unable to pay. The destruction of Spanish industry did not produce the same effect on her commerce with other nations. Her mines furnished ample means of payment. But having, we repeat, no mines, the destruction of our industry is almost as pernicious to Great Britain, or any other nation with which we trade on credit, as to ourselves.

This plain view of our affairs, demands the most serious attention from the public. We are so thoroughly satisfied of its correctness, that were we agents for the promotion of the English interest, and had supreme power over the tariff, we would have it so modified as to protect national industry; for even if that industry were carried to double or treble its present extent, there would be, as stated in the Oneida memorial, ample room for the importation of as much goods as we can pay for—more especially in the present prostrate state of the prices of our staples.

This theory receives the most ample corroboration from the present state of our commerce, which is nearly as calamitous as that of our manufactures. Our vessels are either rotting at our wharves, or dispatched on voyages, which, even at the commencement, afford hardly any hope of profit, and which too generally close with heavy and ruinous losses. It has been computed by intelligent merchants, that the mercantile capital of this country has been diminished seventy millions of dollars, since the peace. Agriculture has begun to partake of the general calamity.

It is painful to reflect, fellow citizens, how numerous and how ruinous are the errors prevalent on that important portion of political economy, which regards the protection of national industry employed in manufactures. In the discussions that arose in congress on the subject of the tariff, there were few, even of the best informed members of that body, who appeared to regard the protection afforded to manufacturers in a national point of view. They considered the duties imposed for this purpose, according to the doctrine of colonel Taylor, of Caroline County, Va. as taxes levied on the agricultural part of the community, solely for the benefit of the manufacturers—and as proofs of the munificence of the former. One ardent member of the house of representatives, on the rejection of a motion for reducing the duties on imported cottons, made an attempt to have the decision re-considered, in order to set aside the votes of some members of the majority, said to be concerned in cotton establishments.* The inadmissibility of this procedure is as obvious as the attempt was novel. Were his plan adopted, the merchants ought to retire on all questions in which commerce is involved—the farmers and planters on those connected with agriculture—and the gentlemen of the bar on all that respect the judiciary. In the vehemence of the gentleman's zeal against manufactories and manufacturers, he wholly overlooked the incongruity of the measure he recommended.

Under a well-organized government, administered with due regard to duty, the legislature ought to "*look with equal eye*," on all classes and descriptions of the nation—and therefore, the interests of the manufacturing part of the community deserve as much and as pointed attention as those of any equal number of other citizens.—But how important soever the subject may be in this point of light, it presents itself, under another aspect, transcendently higher. And an enlightened statesman or legislator will take a far more comprehensive view of it, as it regards the general interests of the nation, which are deeply interwoven with it.

It is frequently asked, why do not the agriculturists and the merchants demand protection? And if they do not demand it, why is it to be given to the manufacturers?

We reply, that both agriculture and commerce are protected, more particularly commerce, as will appear in the sequel.

The agriculture of the united states has not required much protection. The fertility of our soil, the immense extent of our country, and the great proportion of our citizens engaged in agricultural pursuits, render our crops so abundant, and our distance from other nations so great, that there is little temptation for foreigners to seek our markets with the produce of the earth. Our farmers have hitherto generally had ready markets and high prices. There has not been any serious interference with them, nor, until the importation of Bengal cotton, with our planters. Congress has, however, extended its watchful care over their interests. Every article, without an exception, raised by the agriculturist, is subject to a duty which is sufficient for its protection: We annex a list of the most prominent.

* "Mr. Wright," ex-governor of Maryland, "after declaring his belief that many members had voted on the question, who, from being interested in its decision, were of right excluded by a rule of the house, submitted a resolution to reject the votes of those members interested in any manufactory of cotton.†" An adjournment took place, which prevented a decision on the resolution—which does not appear to have been resumed.

† Weekly Register, vol. x. page 95.

Protecting Duties on agricultural productions.

Wheat,	Peas,	Hams,	15 per cent. ad valorem, and one tenth.
Barley,	Boards,	Apples,	
Oats,	Hay,	Pears,	
Rye,	Pitch,	Nuts,	
Rice,	Rosin,	Apricots,	
Flour,	Tar,	Plums,	
Indian corn,	Turpentine,	Peaches,	
Tobacco,	Pork,	Onions,	
Beans,	Beef,	Butter,	
		&c. &c.	

Cheese, 9 cents }
Cotton, 3 cents } per lb.
Hemp, 150 cents. per 112 lbs.

We trust it will be admitted, that the fruits of the earth, raised by hard labour, to which machinery cannot afford any aid, are better protected by a duty of fifteen per cent. than cotton fabrics, in which the rival manufacturers have such immense advantages by machinery, would be at forty—and more particularly than linen and silk are protected by a duty of sixteen and a half, and pottery by twenty two per cent.

The duties on cheese, cotton, and hemp, deserve particular attention. They are fair examples of the system of protection, which the manufacturers have sought in vain.

	Cents.
Gloucester cheese is sold in England at about 10*d*. equal to - - - - - - - -	18 1-2
Cheese in Holland averages about 25 guilders per 100 lbs. equal per lb. to - - - - - - -	10
In France it is about 76 cts. per killogram, or 112 lbs. English, equal to - - - - - - - -	13

Thus English cheese pays a duty of about 50 per cent.—Dutch 90—and French 70—averaging on the whole 70 per cent. This is very nearly equivalent to an absolute prohibition.

In the East Indies, cotton is sold at from three pence to seven pence sterling per lb. or an average of about 10 cents. The duty is three cents, which is thirty per cent.

Nothing but the great distance from Hindostan, and the consequent heavy expense of transportation, could prevent the cotton planter from sharing the lamentable fate of the cotton manufacturer, and being driven out of his own market, even with a duty of 30 per cent. on the cost of the article. Attention to the culture in the East Indies, with the advantage of having gained possession of the seeds of our best species, render it almost certain that the cotton planters will at no distant day, be under the same necessity of soliciting prohibitions or prohibitory duties, as the cotton and woollen manufacturers were in 1816. We hope when they do thus apply, they will be treated with more attention, and their application be more favourably received than those of the manufacturers were. We hope for this result not merely for their sake, but for the general prosperity of the nation.

Hemp is sold in Russia at about 110 dollars per ton. The duty is, therefore, about 26 per cent.

We flatter ourselves, therefore, that it will be readily conceded, that agriculture is protected. Except on the three articles last enumerated, the duties are, it is true, moderate. But they are very far higher in proportion to the chance of competition, than most of the duties on manufactured articles. Should an increase of duties, however, be necessary, we trust it will be adopted, and without opposition.

That the merchants have enjoyed a large portion of the fostering care and protection of congress cannot be doubted. The statute book is full of laws enacted for their benefit. They have always had powerful advocates on the floor of that body, who never failed to urge their grievances with eloquence, and to propose the proper remedies. They were ever heard with attention, and their requests generally accorded. We annex a list of some of the laws passed in their favour.

I. 1789. An act passed at the outset of the government for regulating tonnage which imposed 30 cents on American built vessels, owned in whole or in part by foreigners; and 50 cents on foreign vessels; while vessels belonging to the united states were subject only to six cents.*

II. 1789. In order to secure to our merchants the whole of the China trade to and from this country, a decisive advantage was given them as may be seen by the following contrast—

Duties on teas Imported from China.†		In American vessels. *Cents.*	In foreign vessels. *Cents.*
Bohea tea - - - - -	Per lb.	6	15
Souchong and other black teas - -		10	22
Hyson - - - - - - -		20	45
All other green trees - - - -		12	27

This immense difference of duty, however, does not at present exist—but there still remains sufficient to shut out foreign rivals, viz.

Existing duties on teas imported from China.		In American vessels. *Cents.*	In foreign vessels. *Cents*
Bohea - - - - -	Per lb.	12	14
Souchong and other black - -		25	34
Hyson and Young Hyson - - -		40	56
Hyson skin and other green - -		28	38
Imperial, Gunpowder, and Gomee -		50	68

* Laws United States, vol. ii. p. 6. † Ib. 3, 4.

III. 1789. A discount of ten per cent. allowed on all import duties upon goods imported in vessels built in and owned by citizens of the united states, or in foreign vessels owned by them.*

IV. 1789. Five cents bounty on every quintal of dried, or barrel of salted fish, and on every barrel of salted provisions.†

V. 1789. Fifty cents per ton on each entry, laid on all vessels not built within the united states, or owned by a citizen or citizens, employed in the transportation of the produce or manufactures of the united states coastwise; whereas American vessels paid but once a year.‡

VI. 1792. One dollar and a half per ton bounty allowed on vessels engaged in the fishery, if of twenty tons and below thirty—and two dollars and a half, if above thirty tons. One dollar per ton on all fishing boats above five and below twenty tons.§

VII. 1794. Ten per cent. additional on the duties upon goods imported in vessels not of the united states.‖

VIII. 1802. An act for the protection of the seamen and commerce of the united states against the Tripolitan cruisers.¶

IX. 1804. An act further to protect the commerce and seamen of the united states against the Barbary powers.** By this act an additional duty of two and a half per cent. ad valorem was imposed on goods imported in American vessels—and ten per cent. additional on the duties upon importations in foreign ones. One million of dollars were appropriated for the purpose of carrying on the war against the Barbary powers.

X. 1812. An act for imposing ten per cent. extra on the duties upon goods, wares, and merchandize imported in vessels not belonging to the united states; and likewise laying an additional duty of one dollar and a half per ton on all such vessels.††

XI. 1813. An act for paying a bounty on the exportation of pickled fish, and on all vessels employed in the fishery.‖‖

XII. 1817. An act subjecting to a tonnage duty of two dollars per ton, all foreign vessels arriving from ports to which vessels of the united states are not allowed to trade.‡‡

XIII. 1817. An act prohibiting the importation of all goods, wares, and merchandize in foreign vessels, except those of the nation in which they are produced; prohibiting, under penalty of forfeiture, all vessels, belonging in whole or in part to foreign powers, from carrying on the coasting trade, and limiting the bounties on the fisheries to vessels of which the officers and three fourths of the crews are citizens of the united states.§§

XIV. 1817. An act prohibiting the importation of plaster of Paris from any country, or its dependencies, from which the

* Laws of the united states, vol. ii. p. 5. † Ibid. ‡ Idem p. 6.
§ Idem, p. 242. ‖ Idem, p. 437. ¶ Idem, iii. p. 447. ** Idem, p. 613.
†† Idem, vol. iv. p. 460. ‖‖ Idem, p. 584. ‡‡ Idem, vol. vi. p. 200.
§§ Idem, p. 213.

vessels of the united states are not permitted to bring that article.*

XV. 1818. An act prohibiting the entry into our ports of any vessels belonging to subjects of his Britannic majesty from any port or place in his colonies that is closed against vessels of the united states.†

XVI. American vessels entering from any foreign port or place, pay - - - - - - - *per ton, cents* 6

All foreign vessels from ports where the American flag is not interdicted - - - - - - *per ton, cents* 100

Dutch vessels from places where the American flag is interdicted‡ - - - - - - - - *per ton, cents* 225

The narrow limits we are obliged to prescribe to ourselves prevent us from enlarging on the above list. A cursory view of it will satisfy the reader how undeviating an attention has been paid to the subject—and that no opportunity has ever been lost of counteracting the hostile policy of foreign nations, when directed against the mercantile interest.

The coasting and China trade were fully and completely secured to our merchants, the first by absolute prohibition, and the second by duties undeniably equivalent to a prohibition.—And whatever measures were necessary to secure them their full proportion of every other trade, have been adopted. The specious complaint of "*sacrificing the interests of the many for the benefit of the few*," with which the papers have been filled, and which has furnished such a fertile theme to orators in congress and newspaper writers, was never heard, even in a whisper, in the case of the liberal protection afforded to the merchants. No.—It was reserved to defeat the just demands and expectations of the manufacturers.

In those laws, and others of similar character to be found in our statute books, we behold a spirit worthy of the representatives of a great nation, determined to guard the interests of a respectable portion of their constituents—and affording an ample and adequate protection, which completely guaranteed the promise it held out. The miserable idea of sacrificing native wealth, industry, and talent—of hiring or purchasing vessels, according to Adam Smith's destructive theory, "*where they could be had the cheapest*," was spurned with the contempt it deserved. Those wise laws, which do honour to the legislature of the united states, saved the navigation of this country from destruction. But for them, our shipbuilders would have been ruined, as so large a portion of the cotton and woollen and other manufacturers have been—and our shipping would have rotted in

* Laws of the united states, vol. vi. p. 227. † Idem, ‡ Tariff, p. 25.

our ports, while our navigation was carried on by foreigners, as so large a portion of our clothing is now manufactured by them.

A statement of the results of this wise policy, cannot fail to be satisfactory—

In 1789 the British vessels which entered inwards in Great Britain, engaged in the trade of the united states, were - - - - - - -	253
Those cleared for the united states - - - - - - - - -	358
In 1799 those that entered inwards were only - - - - -	42
Outwards - - - - - - - - - - - -	57
In 1790 the American vessels engaged in the British trade were only -	464
In 1800 there were - - - - - - - - - -	1057*

"In 1806, 561 vessels engaged in the trade of the united "states, entered inwards in Great Britain; of these only 56 were "British.

"In the same year, of 575 entered outwards, only 39 were "British."†

Under this fostering system, the tonnage of the united states made a more rapid progress than ever was made by that of any other nation in the world.

	Tons.
In 1789 it was - - - - - - -	201,562
1790 - - - - - - - -	478,377
1792 - - - - - - - -	564,437
1794 - - - - - - - -	628,816
1796 - - - - - - -	831,700
1798 - - - - - - - -	898,328
1801 - - - - - - - -	1,033,218‡

The contrast between the magnanimous spirit that presided over those laws—and the miserable and blighting spirit that dictated, in 1790, five per cent. on all manufactures of flax, hemp, silk, cotton, wool, brass, cutlery, iron, steel, tin, lead, wood, china, pottery, and stone, in order to enable us to "*buy goods where they could be had cheapest*," is as astonishing as it is lamentable. On the one side we see a dignified policy, honourable to the nation—and on the other a policy unworthy of a rising empire, which has produced the most disastrous consequences.

A few lines more on the subject of the protection of commerce. The navy of the united states, which has been created chiefly for that purpose, has cost in 20 years above 56,000,000 of dollars.‖ The last war with Great Britain, which arose wholly

* Seybert's Statistics, p. 295 † Ibid. ‡ Idem p. 317.

‖ Idem 713, and Weekly Register.

from the duty of protecting commerce, cost, exclusive of the naval department, $52,000,000.*

The expense of foreign intercourse, that is, for ambassadors, charges des affaires, consuls, agents, bearers of despatches, &c. &c. for twenty-four years, have been 10,872,424 dollars, or above 450,000 dollars per annum,† and for the Barbary powers, in twenty years, 2,457,278 dollars, or above 120,000 dollars per annum.‡ Thus, in these two items, there is *a positive disbursement*, for the protection of commerce, of 570,000 dollars annually: whereas, the government has never paid one dollar, as bounty or premium, to foster, protect, or promote the productive industry employed in manufactures; and has rarely imposed any duties beyond what was called for by the exigencies of the treasury.

It is painful to state, but candour calls on us to state, that a portion of the merchants, who have thus enjoyed such a high degree of care and protection, bestowed at such enormous expense, have too generally been averse to affording adequate protection to their fellow citizens, engaged in manufactures; for which impolicy they now suffer in common with the manufacturers, by the consequent universal calamity of the times and impoverishment of the country.

Let us now turn from the fostering care bestowed on commerce—the various statutes enacted in its favour—the expense incurred for that purpose—and the complete protection it has experienced, to the situation of the manufacturer. Has he had his equal share of the care and attention of government? No. The paternal guardianship of their own manufacturers, generally exercised by other governments, shuts him out of nearly all the foreign markets of the world. And the impolicy of our system leaves him at home at the mercy of rivals from every quarter of the globe, who, availing themselves of the advantage of superior capital, and their own governmental protection, vanquish him in his own market, and reduce him to bankruptcy.

That the manufacturers, particularly those of cotton and woollen fabrics, have not been protected from foreign rivalship—that they have been victims of an inadequate tariff, is palpable from the immense quantities of rival foreign articles with which our markets have been inundated; from the ruin of so many respectable citizens who invested large capitals in manufacturing establishments; and from the great proportion of those establishments, which are wholly suspended in their operations; many of which have been sold for 20, 30, or 40 per cent. of the first cost.

Of these facts the proofs are within the knowledge of the great mass of our citizens. They admit neither doubt nor denial.

* Seybert's Statistics, p. 716. † Idem 713. ‡ Ibid.

Thus, while the manufacturer appears to enjoy the advantages of a free government, he is, we repeat, incontestibly in a worse situation, so far as respects the acquisition of property, and protection of industry, two principal objects of good government, than the subjects of the monarchs of Europe, whose situation he must regard with envy. The English, the French, the Russian, the Austrian, and the Danish manufacturers are generally secured in the home market.

There is but one way to account for the care bestowed on the commercial, and the neglect of the manufacturing interest. The former has been at all times well represented in congress, and the latter never. It is, as we have observed on a former occasion, nearly as much unrepresented in that body as this country in its colonial state was in the British parliament.

A CONTRAST.

The Agriculturist.	*The Manufacturer.*	*The Merchant.*
With hardly an exception, secured in the home market. Nearly all the foreign markets in the world open to him.	Shut out of nearly all the foreign markets in the world, and beaten out of his own for want of adequate protection.	The coasting trade secured to him by absolute and unqualified prohibition. Every possible advantage that the government can give, afforded to his shipping in the foreign trade.

We appeal, fellow citizens, to your candour, to your justice, whether there can be a reason why the farmer should be protected by duties, which, in most cases,* are nearly equal to prohibitions—and the merchant have the coasting and China trade secured to him, the former by absolute prohibition, and the latter by duties equivalent to prohibitions; while there is *no one manufactured article whatever prohibited*, and while the cotton and woollen manufacturers (to pass over others) are sacrificed to foreign rivals, by the utterly inadequate duty of twenty-seven and a half per cent?† This is a vital point—and demands the most serious reflection. The whole question at issue may be said to turn on it. We put it to the understanding of our fellow citizens throughout the union—and to the consciences of the members of congress. If any adequate reason can be assigned for this very unequal distribution of protection, let it be proclaimed, in order to silence complaint.

That several extensive establishments have survived the ge-

* Hemp, as already stated, pays about 26 per cent.—cheese 70— cotton 30—and all other agricultural productions 16½. It is obvious that the latter duty is far more effectual than 50 per cent. would be on pottery, glass bottles, or linen—the two first of which are subject to only 22, and the last to 16½ per cent. We might go on with the enumeration and comparison to a great extent, but deem it unnecessary.

† Cottons, below 25 cents per square yard, are effectually protected.

neral wreck—that they are still in profitable operation—is no disproof of our allegations. Their proprietors have generally had some peculiar advantages in point of capital or long establishment, that saved them from the fate of the others. But supposing that the prohibition of the coasting trade had not been enacted—that it had generally fallen into the hands of foreigners; but that twenty or thirty of our merchants were able to support themselves by that portion of it which foreign rivalship left them, would that be admitted for a moment to disprove the ruin of the hundreds of others who had fallen sacrifices?

—

We are persuaded that very few of our citizens attach an adequate degree of importance to the industry of the manufacturing class of the community, and that it is prodigiously underrated. To form a correct estimate of it, requires to enter into minute calculations, which have rarely been made. It never could have been supposed, without such calculations, that the cotton fabrics, produced by 100,000 manufacturers in 1815, amounted to more than one half of the whole value of the domestic exports, of every description, of that year; which is nevertheless the fact, as will appear in the course of this address.

—

In order to aid you, fellow citizens, in comparing the products of manufacturing and agricultural industry, we submit a table of the exports of the united states for the year 1815, extracted from the returns of the Secretary of the Treasury. We have annexed in the second column, a statement of the population of the several states according to the census of 1810; and in the third column, an estimate of what was the probable population in 1815, assuming, an increase of only 15 per cent. for the whole period.

Domestic exports and population of the united states for 1815.

STATES AND TERRITORIES.	Domestic Exports, 1815. Dollars.	Population by Census of 1810.	Supposed Population 1815.
Massachusetts - - -	3,547,463	700,745	805,856
New-Hampshire - - -	101,203	214,460	246,629
Vermont - - - - -	161,002	217,895	250,479
Rhode-Island - - -	357,684	76,931	88,470
Connecticut - - - -	383,135	261,942	301,233
New-York - - - -	8,230,278	959,049	1,102,909
New-Jersey - - - -	5,279	245,562	282,396
Pennsylvania - - -	3,569,551	810,091	931,604
Delaware - - - -	105,102	72,674	83,575
Maryland - - - -	4,086,274	380,546	437,627
Virginia - - - - -	6,632,579	974,622	1,120,815
Ohio - - - - - -		230,760	265,371
Kentucky - - - -		406,511	467,487
North-Carolina - - -	1,012,967	555,500	638,825
Tennessee - - - -		261,727	300,986
South-Carolina - - -	6,574,783	415,115	477,382
Georgia - - - - - -	4,146,057	252,433	290,297
Orleans - - - - -		76,556	88,039
Mississippi - - -	2,573	40,352	46,404
Louisiana - - - - -	5,055,858	20,845	23,972
Indiana - - - - - -		24,520	28,198
Illinois - - - - -		12,282	14,125
Michigan - - - - -	36,909	4,762	5,476
District of Columbia - -	1,965,626	24,023	27,662
	45,974,323	7,239,903	8,326,281

Same table differently arranged.

STATES.	Assumed Population 1815.	Domestic Exports. 1815.	Exports per head.
Massachusetts - - - -	805,856	$3,547,463	$4,40
Connecticut - - - - -	301,233	383,135	1,27
New-Hampshire - - - -	246,629	101,203	41
Vermont - - - - -	250,479	161,002	64
Rhode-Island - - - -	88,470	356,784	4,03
New-Jersey - - - - -	282,396	5,279	02
	1,975,163	4,554,866	2,30

New-York - - - - -	1,102,909	8,230,278	7,46
Pennsylvania - - - -	931,604	3,569,551	3,83
	2,034,513	11,799,829	5,95

STATES.	Assumed population 1815.	Exports 1815.	Exports per head.
Delaware - - - - -	83,575	$105,102	$1.2[illegible]
Maryland - - - - -	437,627	4,086,274	9.3[illegible]
Virginia - - - - -	1,120,815	6,632,579	5.91
North Carolina - - -	638,825	1,[illegible]12,967	1.58
District of Columbia - -	27,626	1,965,626	71.15
	2,308,468	13,802,548	5.95
South Carolina - - -	447,382	6.574,783	13.77
Georgia - - - - -	290,297	4,146,[illegible]5	14.28
	767,679	10,720,84	13.95
Ohio - - - - - -	265,371	6055858	4.78
Kentucky - - - - -	467,48[illegible]		
Tennessee - - - - -	300,98[illegible]		
Louisiana - - - - -	23,972		
	1,057,816	1,057,858	4 78

It appears, on an examination of the preceding tables, that, The average exports of the whole union, per head, were about - - - - - - - $5.62

Of New Hampshire, Vermont, Massachusetts, Rhode Island, and New Jersey - - - - $2.30
Of New York - - - - - 7.46
Of Pennsylvania - - - - - 3.83
Of Delaware, Maryland, Virginia, District of Columbia and North Carolina - - - - - 5.95
Of South Carolina, and Georgia - - 13.95
Of Ohio, Kentucky, Tennessee, and Louisiana - 4.78

Whereas the surplus of the labour of 100,000 cotton manufacturers in that year beyond the price of the raw material and the wages, was $1,200,000 or $12 per head. This appears by a report submitted to congress by the committee of commerce and manufactures, Feb. 13, 1816, which states that there were in the preceding year, about 100,000 persons employed in the united states in the cotton manufacture, viz.—10,000 men, 66,000 women and female children, and 24,000 boys.*

Who used - - - -	bales of cotton 90,000
Containing - - - - -	pounds 27,000,000
Amounting, at 30 cents, to - -	$ 8,100,000
And producing of cotton fabrics -	yards 81,000,000
Averaging 30 cents per yard - -	24,300,000
Estimating the wages at $150 per annum -	$15,000,000

* See supra, pp. 131, 132.

Result.

Gross amount of articles manufactured -	$24,300,000
Cost of Cotton - - - - -	8,100,000
Net annual gain to the nation on the labour of 100,000 manufacturers - - -	$ 16,200,000

This leaves a gain of one hundred and sixty two dollars per head, on the labour employed, let it be observed, on articles of low price.

It is impossible to reflect on this statement, without being struck most forcibly with the extent of the advantages of this important branch.

Analysis.

I. The difference between the price of the raw materials, if exported, that is $8,100,000—and that of the manufactured articles,—$24,300,000,—viz. $16,200,000, was clearly saved to the country.

II. The amount of the goods manufactured, $24,300,000, was more than half—and the amount thus saved to the country, $16,200,000, was more than one-third, of the value of the entire domestic exports of the united states for that year, which were only $45,974,403.

III. A certain market was provided for the great staple of the southern states, the cultivation of which, were the manufacture duly protected, might be extended to double or treble its present amount.

IV. The value of lands and the interest of the agriculturists in the vicinity of those establishments, were greatly advanced, by the supplies of provisions required for the support of the manufacturers.

—

The amount of the goods produced by the labour of these 100,000 manufacturers, viz. $24,300,000 was

I. Nearly equal to the whole of the domestic exports of Delaware, Maryland, Virginia, North Carolina, South Carolina, Georgia, and the district of Columbia, containing above 3,000,000 inhabitants.

II. Considerably more than the whole of the domestic exports of New Hampshire, Vermont, Massachusetts, Connecticut, Rhode-Island, New-York, Pennsylvania, New Jersey, Ohio, Kentucky, Tennessee, and Louisiana, containing above 5,000,000 inhabitants.

The money retained in the country by the labour of these 100,000 manufacturers, viz. $16,200,000, was

I. Nearly equal to the domestic exports of New York Pennsylvania, Ohio, Kentucky, Tennessee, and Louisiana, containing above 3,000,000 inhabitants; and

II. About equal to the domestic exports of New Hampshire, Vermont, Massachusetts, Connecticut, Rhode Island, New Jersey, South Carolina and Georgia, containing above 2,700,000 inhabitants.

—

It may on a cursory view appear that we have gone into too much detail with these statements. But we trust that the magnitude of the errors prevalent on those topics, and more particularly the deleterious consequences these errors have produced on the prosperity of our country, as well as the probability of their continuing to produce a copious harvest, will fully justify us.

Those immense advantages, produced by 10,000 men, 66,000 women and female children, and 24,000 boys, if duly appreciated by congress, would have led to a system widely different from the one pursued in the tariff. Such a source of wealth deserved to have been cherished with the utmost care and attention, which would have been amply repaid by the most beneficial results.

It may, and probably will, be demanded, if the advantages of this manufacture be so great, why have so many of those engaged in it been ruined? The answer is obvious. The inundation of foreign articles, a large portion of which were sold at vendue, far below first cost, has so far glutted our markets, as greatly to limit the sale of the domestic fabrics, indeed almost wholly to debar them from a market, and produce ruinous sacrifices on those that are sold.

Our manufacturers, moreover, in the event of an overstocked domestic market, have no foreign one in which to dispose of their superfluous goods. Whereas our markets are open for the superfluous goods of all the manufacturers in the world!! Never was there such disparity of advantage.

We do not avail ourselves of the obvious advantage we might derive from the circumstance that a portion of the exports were manufactured and in a highly finished state, and were of course at prices far beyond what they bore, when they came from the hands of the agriculturalist. In some cases the value was doubled or trebled. All this advance of price ought to be deducted from the total amount as reported by the custom house, in order to carry on the comparison fairly, and do the argument justice. But we waive this advantage, great as it is, and admit the whole as if it had been in its rude state.

The situation of the four western states claims particular attention. Unfortunately there are no data on which to form an estimate of their exports individually; such an estimate would be valuable, as it would more thoroughly evince the ruinous policy this country has pursued, by its pernicious effects on Ohio, Kentucky, and Tennessee. But in the deficiency of correct data, we must rely on the best estimate that the case admits.

From the extraordinary fertility of the soil of Louisiana, and the great value of its staples, we believe it will not be extravagant to suppose, that of the sum of 5,055,868 dollars exported from Ohio, Kentucky, Tennessee and Louisiana, there was above a million and a half raised in the last state. This reduces the surplus of the other three, devoted chiefly to agriculture, and containing above a million of people, to three dollars and a half per head! And from the immense distance from which a large portion of it is drawn, and the consequent heavy expenses, it is not extravagant to suppose, that it did not produce to the cultivator above 75 per cent. of this value—probably in many cases not above 60 per cent.

We submit, fellow citizens, a fair comparison of the proceeds of the labour of 50 000 persons employed in the culture of cotton, with that of the same number employed in its manufacture, in order more fully to establish the importance of the latter.

Cotton is now about 16 cents per lb. at the manufactories;—about 14 in the seaports of the states where it is raised, and cannot net the planter more than 13, deducting the merchant's profits. That cotton will rise beyond this price is possible—but not probable. The prices in England, which must always regulate our markets, are more likely to fall than to rise, from the improvement of the culture in the East Indies—the ardour with which it is pursued,—and the low price of labour there; and in fact it would not be extraordinary, if, from the abundance of the East India supplies, the British market were, at no distant day, virtually closed to our cotton, as it has actually been by order of council to our flour.

Culture of Cotton.

Ten slaves, five of them capable of working in the field, the other five women and children, will produce of cotton annually about - - - - - - - - -	*lbs.* 8,500
At this rate 50,000 would produce - -	*lbs.* 42,500,000
Which, at 13 cents per *lb.* amount to - -	$5,525,000

Manufacture of Cotton.

We now proceed to state the situation and results of the Waltham cotton manufactory in the neighbourhood of Boston.

It contains men - - - - - - - -	14
Women and children - - - - - - - -	286
	300

And produces, with power looms and other machinery, at the rate per annum of square yards of cloth - - - - -	1,500,000
Which at 25 cents per yard amount to* - -	$312,500
Deduct 1500 bales, or 450,000 lbs. of cotton, at 16 cents per lb. - - - - - - - -	72,000
Annual saving to the nation by the labour of 14 men and 286 women and children,	$240,500

For the correctness of this statement, fellow citizens, we pledge ourselves to the world. We defy contradiction.

Let us now calculate the result of the labours of 50,000 men, women, and children, in the same proportions, and at the same kind of employment:

As 300 : $240,500 : : 50,000 : $40,083,333.†

That is to say, the clear saving to the nation by the labour of 50,000 persons, 2500 men, and 47,500 women and children, em-

* [This was about the price of cottons, in 1819, the time when the present address was written.]

† [Criticism and cavilling have exhausted themselves on this statement: but it is beyond their united exertions. The number of yards manufactured, and the number of persons who produced them, are both open to investigation and enquiry, and will be found correctly stated. To test the calculations of the result is therefore within the capacity of a schoolboy.

At the present prices of cotton goods, the result would be different. I submit a new calculation, assuming the same number of people, and yards of goods —but admit the average price to be 15 cents, instead of 25:

Square yards of cloth - - - - - - - - - - -	1,500,000
Amount at 15 cents per yard - - - - - - - - -	$225,000
Deduct 1500 bales of cotton, at 50 dollars per bale - - - - -	75,000
Annual saving to the nation - - - - - - - - -	$150,000

As 300 : $150,000 : : 50,000 : $25,000,000

It thus clearly appears, that at the rate at which the Waltham factory has pro-

ployed in the cotton manufacture, would amount to above 40.000,000 of dollars annually, after paying for the raw material.

The reason why the result of this calculation so far exceeds the proceeds of the labour of the 100,000 manufacturers, in 1815, as stated in page 158, is, that the machinery of the establishment near Boston, has been brought to the last degree of perfection—and that the power looms, which afford immense facilities to the operations, were very rare in 1815.

It cannot escape the attention of even a cursory observer, that all our calculations of the results of the cotton manufacture are predicated on low-priced fabrics—and that the profits on the high priced are far greater. A large proportion of those imported from Great Britain are of the latter description. This greatly enhances the profits of the manufacture. It results from hence that the work of 50,000 Manchester cotton manufacturers, principally women and children, would be able to pay for half of the exports of a nation, containing above 9,000,000 of people!

There are probably at this hour from 30 to 40,000 persons skilled in this branch, idle in the united states, who could produce, according to the preceding calculations, cotton fabrics to the amount of 15 to 20,000,000 of dollars annually, at the present reduced prices. What a lamentable waste of industry!

Who can ponder on these facts without astonishment at the impolicy of our system, which, under the auspices of Adam Smith, has sacrificed the labour of ten, twenty, thirty, forty, fifty, or sixty of our citizens for that of one foreign manufacturer? If the absurdity were capable of being heightened, it would be by the circumstance, that the dearness of labour is so frequently assigned as an argument against our fostering manufactures.—But surely if our labour be so dear and valuable, we ought not to squander it away thus prodigally.

Can it, therefore, be a subject of wonder, that we are an impoverished nation—that we are drained of our specie—that our water power has been, by a bounteous heaven, lavished upon us in vain—that so many of our manufacturers are beggared and bankrupted—that our workmen are wasting their time in idleness—and that those artists and manufacturers, who, unfortunately for themselves, have been allured to our coasts, by our

ceeded, 50,000 persons, if fully employed in the cotton manufacture, would actually produce a clear saving to the united states of 25,000,000 dollars annually. And let it be distinctly observed that this production, however extraordinary it may appear, is in a less ratio by far, than the ratio of increase in England. The raw material in the above calculation, is allowed to cost one third of the value of the cloth: whereas, according to Colquhoun, the increase of the value of the manufacture is nearly five fold. See Colquhoun on the wealth, power and resources of the British Empire, page 91.]

excellent form of government, have either returned to Europe, gone to Nova Scotia or Canada, or are obliged to resort to servile employments to support existence?

—

We now submit to your consideration, fellow-citizens, an important table of the imports of cotton into the British dominions, for seventeen years. The first fifteen are taken from Dr. Seybert's Statistics,* and the remaining two from the Journal of Trade and Commerce.†

Table of the Importation of Cotton into Great Britain.

	1802.	1803.	1804.	1805.	1806.	1807.	1808.	1809	1810.
American	107,40[illegible]	105,831	104,103	124,279	124,939	171,267	37,672	301,107	389,605
Brazil	74,720	76,297	48 588	51,242	51,034	18,981	50,442		
East India	8,535	10,296	2,561	1,983	7,787	11,409	12,512	35,764	79,382
Other Sorts	90,634	45,474	86,385	75,116	77,978	81,010	67,512	103,511	92,186
No. of bags.	281,383	[illegible]38,898	241,637	252,620	261,738	282,667	168,138	440,382	561,173

	1811.	1812.	1813.	1814.	1815.	1816.	1817.	1818.
American	128,102	95,331	37,7[illegible]0	48,853	103,037	166,077	198,917	205,881
Brazil	118,514	98 704	137,168	150,930	91,955	123,450	114,816	161,087
East Indies	14,646	2,607	1,4[illegible]	13,048	22,357	30,670	117,454	247,604
Other sorts	64,789	64,563	73,21[illegible]	74,800	52,840	49,235	47,208	50,878
No. of bags	326,141	261,205	249,536	287,631	270,189	369,432	478,305	665,450

To the intelligent cotton planter, this table furnishes matter for most serious and sober reflection. It seals the death warrant of the hopes which he lately cherished, of an increasing market and continued high prices in England—and, independent of all care and concern for his fellow citizens, engaged in the cotton manufacture, establishes the necessity of securing a steady market for his raw material at home. The following analysis deserves peculiar attention.

I. The importation of American cotton has not quite doubled in sixteen years.

II. East India cotton has in the same space of time increased 3000 per cent.

III. United States cotton has increased but *three per cent. in the last year.*

IV. East India cotton has increased *in the same time* 110 *per cent.*; and the total increase of importation in that year has been 55 per cent.

V. Brazil cotton has more than trebled since the year 1808.

* Page 92. † Feb. 1819, page 113.

According to the report of the committee of commerce and manufactures, already quoted, the consumption of cotton in the united states in 1805, was only - - *bags* 1,000
But in 1815, it rose to - - - - 90,000
Containing - - - - - *lbs.* 27,000,000

Such was the rapid increase of this manufacture, with no other protection than that afforded by the war, in excluding foreign rivalship.

Dr. Seybert states that the greatest amount of cotton ever exported from this country was 93,000,000 pounds in 1808.* The whole quantity exported in 1815, to all parts of Europe, was about 81,000,000 pounds.†

It thus appears that the quantity actually consumed by our manufacturers in 1815, viz. 27,000,000 lbs. was equal to one third part of all we exported in that year—and what is still more extraordinary, it was actually *one-third part of the whole quantity imported in the same year into England, the most manufacturing country in Europe!*‡ And it will not, we trust, be doubted, that a moderate degree of protection would have increased the home demand to such an extent as to consume nearly the whole. What inexhaustible mines of wealth, far beyond those of Golconda or Potosi, have we in our power! How lamentable a sacrifice have we made of them! and how prosperous and happy should we now be, had we made a proper use of them!

In order to enable you, fellow citizens, duly to appreciate the advantages that would have accrued from the manufacture of one half of the quantity of cotton exported in 1808, we submit a sketch of its results.

Deducting one-sixth for waste, and supposing each net pound to make four yards, 45,000,000 lb. gross weight would produce 150,000,000 yards; which, at an average of 20 cents per yard, would amount to - - - - 30,000,000
From which deduct the price of the cotton,
45,000,000 lb. at 30 - - 13,500,000

It would leave a clear saving to the nation, of $16,500,000

* Statistics, p. 92. † Idem, p. 152.

‡ To these facts particular attention is requested. The imports of cotton into Great Britain in 1815, were 270,000 bags: in 1816, 369,000; in 1817, 377,000; of which considerable quantities were exported to the continent of Europe.—Whereas the actual consumption in the united states in 1815 was, as before stated, 90,000 bags; a striking proof of the laudable enterprize and industry of our citizens.

The raw cotton exported from this country, in 1818, amounted to 6,457,335 lbs. of Sea Islands, and 86,013,843 lbs. uplands; the former estimated by the treasury, at 60 cents, and the latter at 31 cents per lb. The total value, as stated in the treasury returns, was $31,334,258. We offer a calculation of its results in favour of Great Britain, supposing she had imported the whole. The reasoning will apply to France or any other country, so far as a portion went there.

Cost of 92,471,178 lbs. of cotton	-	$31,384,258
Deduct 15,411,863 for waste.		
Net lbs. 77,059,315		
Yards, 308,237,260 at 25 cents	-	$77,059,315
	National gain,	$45,725,057

On this interesting result a long chapter might be written, every page of which would evince the great impropriety of our system, in the most glaring colours—and carry condemnation to the theory of Adam Smith and his followers. And the most extraordinary part of the affair is, that however enormous the national benefits appear, they are far below the reality—as the gain is only 150 per cent.; whereas, by the indisputable authority of Colquhoun, the national profit of the cotton manufacture in England, is about 380 per cent. He states, that the cotton used in that country, in 1812, cost but - *£6,000,000
Whereas the manufactured goods amounted to 29,000,000

Of course the national gain was	£23,000,000
Equal to above	$100,000,000

And this all-important manufacture, for which the united states are peculiarly adapted from the possession of the raw material, and capacity of producing it, to a boundless extent, has been half strangled by our tariff! What agonizing reflections this view of the subject forces on the mind!

* Colquhoun on the Power and Resources of Great Britain, p. 91.

Having discussed the subject of the cotton manufacture, we proceed to take a view of the woollen, which is equally deserving of the most serious consideration.

By a report of the committee of commerce and manufactures, submitted to the house of representatives, March, 1816,* it appears that in the year preceding there was invested in the woollen branch a capital of - - - -		$12,000,000
The raw material amounted to -	$7,000,000	
The value was increased by the manufacture - - -	$12,000,000	
Value of goods manufactured annually		19,000,000
Persons constantly employed -	50,000	
Occasionally - - -	50,000	
		100,000

Analysis.

I. By this manufacture, articles were produced in the united states, which would otherwise have been imported, to the amount of - -	$19,000,000
Deduct price of wool, which, but for this branch, would have been exported - -	7,000,000
Clear saving to the country - -	12,000,000

II. Seven millions of dollars expended among the farmers, for the wool of about 5,000,000 sheep.

III. A clear gain to the nation, by the labour of each person thus employed, of 120 dollars.

The following table of the value of the national manufactures for the year 1810, will enable you, fellow citizens, to form a correct idea of the importance of the subject. It is an estimate deduced by Tench Coxe, Esq. from the marshals' returns, taken with the census of that year. It is probable that during the progress of the war, they were increased to above $250,000,000.

Maine - - - - - - - -	$3,741,116
Massachusetts - - - - - - -	21,895,528
New Hampshire - - - - - - -	5,225,045
Vermont - - - - - - -	5,407,280
Rhode Island - - - - - - -	4,106,074
Amount carried over.	$40,375,043

* Supra, page 139.

Amount brought over	$40,375,048
Connecticut	7,771,928
New York	25,370,289
New Jersey	7,054 594
Pennsylvania	33.691,111
Delaware	1.733 744
Maryland	11 468,794
Virginia	15,263.473
Ohio	2,894,290
Kentucky	6,181,024
North Carolina	6.653 152
Tennessee	3,611,029
South Carolina	3 623,595
Georgia	3,658,481
Orleans Territory	1,222,357
Mississippi Territory	419,073
Louisiana Territory	200,000
Indiana Territory	300,000
Illinois Territory	120,000
Michigan Territory	50,000
Columbia (District)	1,100,000
Total,	$172,761,977

The repetition of objections to which we have already fully replied, obliges us, fellow citizens, to resume topics which we had supposed exhausted.

Among these, the most prevalent and popular is the extortion said to have been practised by the manufacturers during the war. This theme is hacknied from New-Hampshire to Georgia, not merely by men of little minds, and narrow views, with whom such an objection would be perfectly in character: but men of higher spheres of life, and superior order of mind and endowments, allow themselves to give it countenance.

Even admitting it to have existed to the extent assumed, the inference drawn from it, to prevent adequate protection to manufactures, would not apply at present; as, according to the irrefragable maxim of Alexander Hamilton, already quoted at full length, founded on fact and reason, '*the internal competition which takes place soon does away every thing like monopoly, and reduces by degrees the price to the minimum of a reasonable profit on the capital employed.*'

But we will suppose for a moment that the allegations are all just—and that the manufacturers of broad cloth sold, as we have already stated, at 13 or 14 dollars per yard, what cost them only 9 or 10. With what propriety, we repeat, can the importer, who, at the same period, sold his goods at 50 or 100 per cent. beyond the old prices—the planter who raised cotton at 10 or 12 cents per lb. and sold at 30, and would at 40, 50, or 100—the merchant who bought flour at 10 dollars and sold at 20 to 40—reproach the manufacturer for an advance far less than that of which they availed themselves?

We pass over the inconsistency of such conduct, which is too palpable and gross to require comment: and we trust that the miserable spirit which would prefer the consumption of fabrics manufactured in Hindostan, because sold a few cents cheaper per yard, (and thus exhaust the wealth of the country to support a distant nation, while our fellow citizens, who invested millions of money in manufacturing establishments, are bankrupted and beggared, and their workmen thrown for support on the overseers of the poor) will never influence the councils of a great nation.

But the enormous expenses of those establishments, in which investments were made, to the amount of 20, 30, 40, 50 or 60,000 dollars, for buildings and machinery, would require and fully justify extraordinary prices in the commencement.—To bring this home to the cotton planters—and to enable them to conceive the force of the argument, we will suppose for a moment, that, during the war, they for the first time commenced their plantations—and purchased slaves at 8 or 900 dollars each —and plantations for 5 to 10,000 dollars. Could they, in the incipient state of their operations, afford to sell their cotton for 16 to 20 cents per *lb?* Certainly not. This is a case perfectly analogous, and ought to set this miserable objection at rest for ever.

NO. XII.*

Philadelphia, June 24, 1819.

General view of the subject of political economy. Eulogium of Hamilton's report. State of this country previous to the Revolution, and after the adoption of the federal constitution. Effects of the war in Europe. Calamitous consequences of the return of peace.

We have presented for your consideration, the essence of the able and luminous report of Alexander Hamilton, then secretary of the treasury, on manufactures. The principles contained in

* This address was written by Dr. Samuel Jackson, and is here inserted merely to preserve unbroken the whole series.

that admirable state paper, are the principles of political economy, that have been practised by those statesmen, whom the concurrent testimony of ages, has pronounced the most wise; and have constituted the policy of every nation, that has advanced in civilization; in which the principles of free government have been developed; or which has grown in wealth and power.

Did it comport with the design of these essays, it would be no difficult task to establish, by historical references, the facts, that the amelioration of society, the evolution of those just rights, which are the inheritance of every individual, and the weight and influence of the people in their government, had their origin in the establishment of manufacturing industry. With its progression, have they progressed; and by the diffusion of wealth through every class of the community, which is its necessary concomitant, have been diffused civilization and knowledge. The principles by which these important results have been effected, we shall shortly elucidate. But other considerations first invite attention.

The arguments by which Mr. Hamilton has sustained the principles he advocated, are lucid and conclusive. We believe them to be irrefutable. At least, we have not as yet met with any opposing writers, who have shaken one of the positions he advanced. Those diversified combinations, which grow out of, and affect all human transactions, did not escape his penetration. They are too commonly overlooked by theorists, who, intent on general principles, disregard the minuter circumstances, that arise out of their very action, and frequently render them impracticable in operation, however just they may appear in themselves.

In no science, are the general maxims of mere theorists more delusive, and more to be distrusted, than in political economy. This branch of knowledge is yet in its infancy. It is composed of relations so commingled and commixed together, that like a skein of tangled thread, they require to be traced out with great patience, perseverance, and close attention. Its principles are not yet established. Those which have been considered as the most fixed, have been overthrown; those which have been taught as self-evident, are questioned; and the whole are the subject of ardent discussion. In this state of the science, general maxims can serve no other purpose, than to give flippancy on an abstruse subject, and to overleap difficulties, that cannot be removed.

While the elements of political economy are thus undetermined, we are called upon to set at nought the harmonising examples of the most prosperous states—the accumulated experience of centuries; and to confide the character, the resources, the power of this nation—the wealth and happiness of this people—the safety perhaps of the government itself, to the operation of abstract principles, which have not yet been confirmed by practice, nor even settled by authority.

In human affairs, abstract principles, though they may captivate the fancy by their simplicity, are often defeated by those subordinate accidents, which they must necessarily exclude. The principles of 'Political Justice,' of the English, and the 'perfectibility of human nature' of the French Philosophers, as well as unlimited freedom of moral action in the abstract, may be true. But overlooking the very constitution of human nature, the discordancy of its sentiments, the complexedness of its affinities, the variety of its affections, the perverseness of the human heart, and obliquity of human intellect, they can only be regarded as the visions of benevolent enthusiasts.

The abstract principles of political eeonomy, are of similar character. Resulting from general reasoning, which seldom descends to minute particulars, they bear all the evidences of correct deductions, until brought into practice. Their inefficiency is then disclosed, and their partial nature made manifest. The involutions and compound nature of human interest, we are convinced, set distinctive limitations at defiance. They often open suddenly into new channels that have not been traced, or flow through others, so obscure, that they have escaped our notice. Our generalities are defeated by unanticipated combinations, which give results never calculated; and re-actions are produced, that work effects never suspected.

In a science thus uncertain, and in things thus complicated and indistinct, it is the part of prudence to tread the paths of sober experience; to trust those guides, whose long practice has imparted substantial knowledge, and whose knowledge is verified by their success. To reject the long-acquired wisdom of ages, and the well-earned experience of mankind, from confidence in superior wisdom, may justly subject us to the imputation of self-sufficiency, and hazard the dearest interests of our country.

It is against such visionary projects, that we have raised our hands; it is to warn you from the closet speculations of theorists, to invite you to common sense practice, founded on the nature of things, that we have intruded with the best intentions on your notice. We have presented to you in succession, the systems of various powers in Europe, for the advancement of their welfare; and have shown some errors of policy, bearing a strong similarity to principles generally entertained in the united states, which proved fatal to those by whom they were adopted. We have, finally, presented you with a system, that has been proposed by one of our most enlightened statesmen, as best adapted to promote the wealth and power, by exciting and fostering the industry of this country, *in the circumstances of a general and continued peace in Europe.* This system was prepared with an experience of the operation of the peace policy of Europe on our affairs, subsequent to the peace of 1783, and after mature reflection on the commercial relations between this country and foreign powers. Its principles, founded on well-substantiated facts, are drawn from the examples of the most prosperous and most powerful nations; and its materials derived from the abundant sources of European commercial legislation. These are circumstances which entitle it to great weight, and to be received with the most marked and serious attention.

Let it not be presumed, that we are influenced by any feelings of political partiality, in favour of Mr. Hamilton. Most of those, who thus tender the tribute of their applause to his merits as a statesman, and thus highly appreciate this particular fruit of his labours, were, and continue to be, the decided opponents of his political principles. It is bigotry alone, that denies or would obscure merit in those, beyond the pale of its own belief, in church or state. To this feeling, we wish to have no claim; and while we confess a contrariety of sentiment on some essential points, we would not withhold our acknowledgment of the brilliancy of the genius, the extent and solid nature of the acquirements, and the strength of intellect, that distinguished Alexander Hamilton.

In the present situation of the country, when it cannot be concealed, that its progress has received a sudden check, and society labours under the shock of a rapid recoil, the discussions of political parties sink into minor importance, in comparison with the great principles of the prosperity and happiness of the people and of the nation. These are the principles that should rise paramount in the view, occupy the thoughts, and animate the feelings of every citizen of the great American republic. Divesting yourselves, therefore, of party feelings, prejudices, and partialities; casting aside, as derogatory to the character of American citizens, the petty jealousies of sectional interests, take into candid consideration that system of policy, which, in the early establishment of our government, was deemed best to comport with our interests as an independent people. If its principles should appear to you just and the reasoning by which it is sustained, consonant to truth; if you should be satisfied, it is the best adapted to our present and probable future circumstances, you will not hesitate to trust to it, for the advancement of individual and national prosperity.

An inquiry naturally arises into the causes, which led the government, after having matured this system, and contemplated its adoption, to lay it aside. They are developed in our commercial history, and will be found to strengthen the principles and views on which it was erected, and for which we contend.

The peace concluded in 1783, continued undisturbed; Europe offered but partial markets to our productions while it closed its commerce to our marine. The annual value of exports of our domestic productions was less in amount than the annual value of our consumption of foreign commodities: and we possessed no collateral sources of wealth to compensate the deficiency. The government had assumed a large debt which subjected it to a heavy annual interest; other expenses were accumulating, the increase of which might be confidently anticipated; and the prospects of revenue from foreign commerce, or an impoverished people, were but gloomy. In these circumstances, the attention of our statesmen must have been directed to internal resources. Yet from this quarter could be derived little to inspire their hopes. Commerce brought no money into the country; circulation was limited and slow; the industry or labour-power of the country was but partially exerted; and consequently much wealth lost, that might have been created. Without a circulating medium, and full employment for industry, revenue must have been oppressive to the people, of difficult collection to the government, and uncertain in its proceeds.

The difficulties of the colonial governments, and the evils endured by the colonists, were then fresh in remembrance: and their causes were well understood. The commerce, to which they had been limited, was that which at this time is recommended to our adoption. Confined almost exclusively to the tillage of the soil, they exchanged their raw productions for the manufactured articles of the mother country. This kind of barter or "mutual exchange," to which the colonies were *forced* by the colonial system of England, kept them poor, to favour industry at home. This commerce, to which the jealous policy of Great Britain limited her colonial possessions in America, it was acknowledged both in and out of parliament, in the colonies and in England, and cannot now be denied, was intended solely to render them subservient to her interests, to which theirs were unhesitatingly sacrificed. Their progress in wealth and power, was looked upon with a distrustful eye. In order to its retardation, to keep them poor and dependent, they were forbidden to manufacture and compelled to supply their wants from England.—Even the earl of Chatham, who is considered to have been the friend of America, as he was the advocate of her rights, was still so much an Englishman in this respect, that he was unwilling that a single hob-nail should be manufactured in America.

The cultivation of the soil to its greatest extent, excited no apprehensions that it would enable the colonies to become independent. England well knew, that in the mutual exchange of raw products for manufactured goods, all the advantage was on her side, the loss on that of the colonies. She therefore, restricted them to the cultivation of the soil, except permitting a few handicrafts of first necessity, and the fisheries to the New England colonies, which raised no production she required.

This system kept the colonies in a wretched condition. They were totally destitute of the precious metals, either to constitute or regulate a currency. Every hard dollar that found its way into them, was immediately exported to England in payment of debts. "Those that are acquainted with America, know, as I do," said capt. Luttrel in a debate in parliament, "that from Rhode Island northwards, they have no money; that their trade is generally carried on by barter, from the most opulent merchant to the most necessitous husbandman. Sir, before your fleet and armies visited their coasts, you might almost as soon have raised the dead, as one hundred pounds in specie from any individual, in those provinces."*

In order to procure some kind of currency to make those mutual exchanges, which the wants of civilized life render indispensable, and which cannot with convenience be effected by barter, the colonists were forced into various expedients. They altered the standard of money; they issued paper money of different kinds; they constituted it a legal tender. But all was ineffectual. While they had to hire workmen in England to perform their labour, they could not retain their gold and silver, which was sent to pay wages abroad. Altering the standard did not affect the value of gold and silver, which could not be restrained by an arbitrary limitation; and their paper money, having no guarantee for its safety, constantly depreciated.

Such, it was known to our government, were the results that had been produced by a commerce, engaged in the exchange of the productions of the soil, for manufactured goods. They could not, therefore, anticipate, that a similar commerce would have other effects; and consequently, that by such a commerce, a metallic currency could be given to the people, or even a metallic basis acquired, for an adequate paper currency. There was then no other course left them to pursue, but to adopt the manufacturing policy of Europe. By supplying a portion of those wants with our own industry, for which the colonies had been compelled by the parent country to hire and pay for labour in England, we would diminish the amount of our imports, without diminishing the amount of our exports; because England took from us no more of our productions, than she really wanted, and those she would take under any circumstances, while the other nations to which we

* Parliamentary Register.

traded, were never influenced by other views than the mere supply of their wants. Thus the balance of our trade with the West Indies, which had always been paid in specie, but immediately remitted to England, would have been retained in circulation; while a portion of the balance with France and the Mediterranean, would also have found its way back to this country, instead of always being transferred to England. In this manner, and in this manner only, in a state of general peace in Europe, could a circulating medium have been procured, that could be kept pure, free from depreciation, and fluctuations.

But the rapid occurrence of events wholly unexpected, unfolded new prospects, and enabled the united states to acquire with ease and rapidity, the wealth and power necessary to give stability to their recently formed institutions. In the midst of the agitations of the French revolution, the crops failed in France and other parts of Europe. At once a market was opened to our agricultural production, stimulated to its greatest energy. The labour-power of the country, was instantly employed to the full extent of its capacity. The war that soon ensued, and involved almost every power in Europe, constituted us at once the carriers of an immense commerce. Our sails swelled on every ocean, and our flag streamed on every shore. Every dollar of capital we possessed or could borrow, and every hand in the nation, before idle, found employment. A road was thus opened to a rapid acquirement of wealth, and it was a natural policy to pursue it. The capital and industry of the country, before stagnant and depressed, rushed into the new formed channel. Manufactures, under these circumstances, were neglected, and the project was dropped. All the benefits that were expected to arise from them, were to be obtained with certainty and expedition, by prosecuting our newly-disclosed and widely-extended commerce. Wealth rolled in apace: and the metallic capital, in the space of ten or twelve years, was increased to twenty or twenty-five millions of dollars. But the whole of this prosperity depended upon contingencies. A general peace in Europe would bring it to a close. As it was, we could not enjoy it undisturbed. The celerity of our progress awakened the jealousy of a rival. It was sought to destroy, by new principles of national law, the advantages we derived from our neutral character. The difficulties that were thus generated, terminated finally in the war, which arose, let it be remarked, not from a spirit of manufactures, but from a spirit of commerce. The expenses and sacrifices necessary to its prosecution, were, in fact, a tax upon the country, in favour of commerce; yet it was cheerfully borne, by the agricultural and manufacturing interests.

Out of this contest, the nation came with an accession of character; whilst the rapidity of circulation, the full employment of capital, and its retention in the country, caused individuals to feel but little comparative distress, notwithstanding its burdens. The attack directed against the physical strength of the country, only served to develop its power and resources. The war now waging against its moral strength, has paralized its energies, and laid it prostrate in the dust. It is no exaggeration to assert, that the two last years of peace have produced more commercial embarrassment and distress, a greater destruction of capital and increase of individual misery, than was caused by the whole war.

This apparent anomaly deserves to be examined. We believe its solution will be attained in the following considerations. The general pacification of Europe had preceded the treaty of Ghent: and most of the powers of the eastern hemisphere had re-assumed their usual peace policy. The object of this policy is to foster their own marine, agriculture, and manufactures, to the exclusion of those of other nations. We consequently lost the commercial relations, that had existed in a state of European warfare. In fact, we reverted back to our old commercial position, prior to the French revolution, or when colonies. Had this circumstance been understood, it would have been foreseen, that the same effects would have grown out of the same causes now as formerly. The principles, views, and reasonings, adapted to the then situation of the country, it would have been perceived, were again applicable. But the habits and modes of thinking, which had been formed during twenty years of a lucrative commerce; the complete mutations which had taken place in the commercial world, during that time leaving few individuals possessed of a practical knowledge of the effects of a general peace, on the interests of the country, occasioned the revolution our commerce had undergone to be overlooked or disregarded.

Most of those engaged in commerce, who also, it will be recollected, preside over the monied institutions which regulate our currency, had little other experience of commerce, than such as existed during the wars of the French revolution. They naturally supposed, that it would continue to work the same effects, as during that period, except in smaller amount. The failure of two successive crops in Europe, in 1815, and 1816, which stayed for a time the operation of the new state of affairs, served to continue this delusion. The time, however, is not remote, when we shall be awakened to the true situation of our commercial relations with Europe, and its consequences. The evils, which now press on us, many vainly flatter themselves, are mere temporary effects, similar to those which have before arisen from slight derangements of commerce. We are firmly persuaded, they are of a very different character, and of a more formidable nature. We have no doubt, that they are the same, as the evils under which this country suffered when colonies, and during the peace subsequent to the revolution. The sooner we satisfy ourselves that such is the case, the earlier we shall extricate ourselves from the embarrassments, that must grow out of the position, in which we are placed. We propose to enter into the examination of this subject in a future number; and trust we shall exhibit by a comparison of the commerce of the colonies, and the effects it produced on them, extracted from authentic documents, with the present commerce of this country, and the effects now begun to be felt, that they are of similar character. We fear, that from this view of the subject, though little flattering to our pride, it will be apparent, that after having expended the best blood of the nation, and millions of treasure to shake off the yoke of colonization, we have voluntarily adopted the colonial policy of England, and placed ourselves with respect to her, and in truth to most of the world, in the situation of colonies. From this state of humiliating and injurious dependency, the united states are bound to vindicate the sovereignty of a free people. For in vain will they make pretensions to a perfect independence, while they incur through the medium of their wants, all the consequences of subjection.

NO. XIII.*

Philadelphia, July 5, 1819.

Proportion of persons who raise the necessaries of life. Crafty policy of Henry IV. *Crusades. Progress of freedom in England, France and Germany. Labour power in England.*

VARIOUS causes concur to produce the present unhappy state of affairs. It is our belief, however, that the main root, whence branch all the evils we suffer, is the neglect of furnishing full employment, to the productive labour of the country.

National wealth does not consist in land, people, or the precious metals, but in the possession of products or values, created by labour.

A country with an extended territory, and a scattered population, must be poor and feeble. Such is Spain at this moment, and such was this country when in the state of colonies.

There is a paper in the Spectator, No. 200, that contains some excellent reflections on this subject, which, as they cannot be better expressed, we shall extract in full.

"If the same omnipotent Power, which made the world,

* This No. like the former, was written by Dr. S. Jackson.

"should at this time raise out of the ocean and join to Great Britain, an equal extent of land, with equal buildings, corn, cattle, "and other conveniences and necessaries of life, but no men, "women nor children, I should hardly believe this would add, "either to the riches of the people, or revenue of the prince."— And again—

"That paradox, therefore, in old Hesiod, πλεονημισυ παντος, or "half is more than the whole, is very applicable to the present "case; since nothing is more true, in political arithmetic, than "that the same people with half a country, is more valuable "than with the whole. I begin to think there was nothing absurd in Sir W. Petty, when he fancied if all the Highlands of "Scotland, and the whole kingdom of Ireland, were sunk in the "ocean, so that the people were all saved, and brought into the "lowlands of Great Britain; nay, though they were to be reimbursed the value of their estates by the body of the people, yet "both the sovereign and the subjects in general would be enriched by the very loss."

The same sentiment is contained, and placed in a striking point of view with relation to this country, in a petition to parliament, in the year 1767. General Phineas Lyman, it appears, contemplated the establishment of a settlement on the Ohio, in the present state of Illinois; and for this purpose applied to parliament for a tract of land. He enforced the propriety of the measure by the argument, that there could be little danger of the colonies becoming independent, if confined to agricultural pursuits, and the inhabitants were diffused over the country. The position is perfectly correct; and is a very suitable and forcible reply to those who are incessantly advising the same policy to these free and independent states, instead of promoting manufacturing industry on the seaboard, and the already thickly settled parts of the country. This is purely an English doctrine, and one which the English government unquestionably warmly approves.

"A period," observes the petition we allude to, "will doubtless come, when North America will no longer acknowledge a "dependence on any part of Europe. But that period seems to "be so remote, as not to be at present an object of rational policy "or human prevention [and] it will be made still more remote, "by opening new scenes of agriculture, and widening the "space, which the colonies must first completely occupy."*

While it is thus demonstrated, that territory thinly peopled confers neither riches nor power, we have examples in Egypt, modern Greece and other provinces of the Turkish empire, and in Persia, that people, deficient in industry, contribute as little to national wealth or strength; while Spain and Portugal are fami-

* Macpherson's Annals of Commerce, 1767.

liar instances, that they are not necessarily concomitant with the possession of the precious metals.

When we reflect on the distribution of labour in society, which is necessary to give value to production, we shall be more sensible of the truth and operation of the principles laid down.

It has been judged from experience, and admitted by the best authorities, that the labour of twenty-five persons, will procure all the common necessaries of life, as food, drink, apparel, housing, furniture, &c. for one hundred. This supposition takes the above articles as coarse, though plentiful and good. One half, it is supposed, from being too old, or too young, sick or infirm, will produce nothing. There will then remain about twenty-five individuals of every hundred, capable of working, who are necessarily idle or non-productive. Now, on the quantity and quality of the employment, with which these twenty-five individuals are occupied, depend the wealth, power, intelligence, and degrees of civilization of a nation.

The objects which can alone occupy this class, which, for the sake of distinction, we shall call non-necessary producers, as there is sufficient of sustenance and raiment, &c. for necessary wants, produced without them, must be, in part, to give to those products greater refinement, and consequent value: that is, to give to food a higher relish and more diversity; and to apparel, furniture, &c. more of ornament and beauty. These operations are the chief constituents of manufacturing industry, and absorb a considerable part of the labour, which would otherwise be idle. The cultivation of letters, of the fine arts, of the physical and abstract sciences, the offices of state, and its protection in the army or navy, in civilized society, give occupation to the remainder.

When that portion, which is employed in creating material products or values, finds full occupation, and is predominant, then national wealth is on the increase; circulation is kept full, brisk and steady; contentment and ease, comfort and happiness, are in the power of each individual to obtain; the government is invigorated, and its finances in a flourishing state. This is the situation of a prosperous people, and to attain and preserve it, should be the constant aim of an enlightened government.

The reverse of this state of productive industry, brings on a lamentable change in the affairs of a nation. In proportion as the employment of this class diminishes, national production or wealth declines; circulation becomes dull, languid, and stagnant; embarrassments and difficulties surround traders; poverty and misery assail labourers; being idle, they become vicious; and, oppressed by pauperism, they become criminal. The materials for riots, and civil commotions; the ready instruments of designing demagogues, are formed and accumulated, to the hazard of all good citizens, and the safety of civil government.

It is not improbable, that it was this state of things, which was one of the principal causes of the violences of the French revolution. The derangement of the finances; the immense and unequal exactions of the government, which fell chiefly on the industrious poor; the vacillation of its measures, which overthrew all confidence; and the operation of the impolitic treaty of commerce with England in 1786, all tended to ruin the productive industry of France. Large fragments of its population were thus disjointed from their usual situation, and floated, loose and unemployed, endangering the existence of organized society, with the first agitations that should arise.

The commencement of the revolution seems a demonstration of the fact. A starving multitude surrounded the Hotel de Ville, vociferating for bread; and, whenever the king appeared in public, his ears were stunned with the same incessant clamour from the crowd, that thronged around his coach.

The same principle explains satisfactorily the cause of the extraordinary military energy of France, at that period. Her commerce ruined; her manufactures languid; her trades sinking from diminished consumption; her agriculture oppressed and declining; and the total destruction of her finances, threw an immense mass of physical and labour-power out of employment. The army offered the only mode of occupation, by which it could be absorbed. Hence, more than a moiety of the non-necessary producers, whose labour had been appropriated on a thousand different objects, was suddenly devoted to arms. In the armies of the republic were found every rank and grade of society, and every variety of trade and profession.

Europe, which had confederated against that devoted country, and anticipated an easy conquest, was surprized alarmed, and confounded, at the spectacle presented by this nation, which had seemed prostrated with calamity, sending forth at one time "eleven distinct armies"* to the field, and her extended frontier bristling with bayonets.

This principle was so well understood in England, before the establishment of manufacturing industry secured permanent employment, that it became a maxim with her kings to engage in wars, whenever this portion of her population accumulating, became idle, restless, and discontented.

"It was the dying injunction of the late king, (Henry IV.) to his son, not to allow the English to remain long in peace, which was apt to breed intestine commotions; but to employ them in foreign expeditions, by which the prince might acquire

* Stevens's Wars of the French Revolution, vol. i. p. 266.

honour; the nobility, by sharing his dangers, might attach themselves to his person; and all the restless spirits find occupation for their inquietude."*

By this means employment was found for her superabundant labour, which had become oppressive and troublesome to the government, because it could not find any other occupation.

On the disposition which is made by the government, of this class of non-necessary producers, depends the character of a nation. If the greater portion be occupied in agricultural and manufacturing industry, the nation will be wealthy and prosperous, but not enlightened. This is the case with China and Hindostan.

If engaged in arts, letters, and sciences, it will be distinguished for its writers, poets, philosophers, historians, orators, statesmen, sculptors, and painters. Greece in its maturity, Rome in the Augustan age, and Italy at the time of the revival of letters, illustrate our doctrine.

If arms be made their trade, the people become warlike, make extensive conquests, and are renowned for heroes, commanders, and warriors. This was the character of Greece in its early history, of Macedon, and of Rome. It is also the condition of most semibarbarous states; like the Scythian tribes, which destroyed the western empire; and the Arabs, who carried the crescent over more than half the world, and have thundered at the gates of most of the capitals of Europe. In the vigour of its feudal institutions, Europe presented the same aspect. Arms and a rude agriculture constituted the chief employment of its inhabitants, who, poor and oppressed, were the dependant vassals of their lords.

Unoccupied by trades or manufactures, they were ever ready to follow their chieftains to the field, reckless of the cause which summoned them to the work of destruction. Under the banners of the cross, were arrayed such multitudes, that Europe, remarks Anna Comnena, loosened from its foundations, and impelled by its moving principle, seemed in one united body to precipitate itself on Asia.† The plains of Palestine and the borders of the Nile, for near two centuries, were deluged with the blood of millions of human beings, vainly shed in the fruitless battles of the crusades.

When the exertions of a population of this character, are not directed on some one object, and combined by the control of an efficient government, or by some ruling motive of religion or interest, society is in complete disorganization. Civil wars, the contests of petty chieftains, plundering and robbing by armed

* Hume's History of England, vol. 2. chap. xix. p. 59.
† Alexias, lib. 10.

bands, ranging over the country, are then the predominant features. The dominions of the Grand Signior, Africa, and many Asiatic states, are instances of this constitution of things; and there are strong indications of its commencement in Spain.

This was the condition of feudal Europe. The crown possessed little constraint over its great feudatories; each of which avenged his own wrong with his sword; and most of them supported their petty dignity, and their retainers, by predatory incursions on the domains of their neighbours.

From the disorders incident to, and the degradation consequent on feudalism, man was rescued by the establishment of manufactures. They drew him into towns and villages; and association sharpening his intellectual faculties, he began to understand his rights. By his labour, wealth was created; and with his wealth, and by his combination, he acquired power to enforce his rights, or the means to purchase their enjoyment.

Tracing the causes, whence have proceeded the abrogation of feudal institutions, and the emancipation of society from the debasing and depraving influence of feudal obligations, it will be seen, that they have disappeared, like darkness yielding to the day dawn, before the genial and invigorating influence of manufacturing industry.

The people of Italy, acquiring wealth and power, arts, letters and science, by their industry, first cast aside the shackles of feudal bondage. Flanders and the Netherlands, treading in their steps, next succeeded in the list of free states. As manufactures progressed in England, the people gradually rose into consequence and independence. Yet, from the many obstructions they met with, by the impolicy of the different kings, vassalage was not completely annulled until 1574. In that year, Elizabeth, in order to raise money, directed a charter to her lord treasurer Burleigh, and Sir William Mildmay, chancellor of the exchequer, "to inquire into the lands, tenements, and other goods of all her bond-men and bond-women in the counties of Cornwall, Devon, Somerset, and Gloucester, viz.: such as were by blood, (*i. e.* birth) in a slavish condition, by being born in any of her manors; and to compound with all or any such bond-men or bond-women in these four counties, for their manumission or freedom; and for enjoying their said lands, tenements and goods as freemen."* Thus terminated feudalism in England, from the commonalty being enabled by the wealth acquired by manufacturing industry, to purchase their emancipation.

In France, the progress of commerce and manufactures was slower than in England, and a consequent slower progress is observable in escaping from feudal oppression. Those, who

* Anderson on the origin of Commerce.

had engaged in commerce and manufactures, were, however, the first who became exempt; and the agriculturist, at the period of the revolution, which brought it to a close, alone was subject to its hardships.

The peasantry of nearly all the Germanic states, of Hungary, and of Russia, are at this time trammelled with its fetters. But the period of their liberation rapidly hastens on. The immense sums, disbursed by the contending powers in the late contests, have diffused much property among the commonalty, and excited their industry. The continental system of Bonaparte excited a spirit of manufacturing, which is still maintained. The sovereigns in the last grand confederacy against Napoleon, could not rely, as formerly, solely on mercenary troops, but were thrown on the people for support. A military spirit, and the sentiments it gives birth to, have thus been infused among their subjects, who have learnt the dangerous secret of their power and its extent. The consequences have been, that Bavaria and Baden now enjoy the best constituted and freest governments in Europe, while almost all the people of the states of Germany, are perseveringly and anxiously demanding from their rulers, an acknowledgment and guarantee of their rights in written constitutions, and a participation, by their representatives, in the government.

The more close and attentive the examination of this interesting subject, the more conclusively will be established the position, that the modern principles and practice of free governments; the amelioration and refinement of society; the advancement of civilization and the cultivation of the higher intellectual pursuits, have grown out of the diffusion and division of productive labour, and the multiplication of the objects of its exercise.

When the labour or producing power of a nation, is not too much concentrated, in any one or two particular occupations, but is diffused in due and regular proportion, among those professions that constitute civilization, such a nation is, then, in its most prosperous, happy, powerful, and intelligent condition. It will be equally famed for its wealth, its power, its laws, its arms, its letters, its sciences, and its arts. This constitutes the most improved state of society, which it is the duty of government to establish and cherish. In different degrees, this is the case with different nations of Europe. There are various causes, into the detail of which, we have not leisure, and which would lead us too far from our object to enter, that cast over each of them, different complexions and tints, but which do not, however, destroy their similitude.

We shall barely confine ourselves to remark, that in England, her political policy, and her labour-saving machinery, produce modifications of the general result on her population, which at first view, seem to militate against our proposition. But a little inspection will dissipate the incongruity.

The population of Great Britain is estimated at 17,000,000.— Let us allow three-fourths to be productive of material values, which will make 12,750,000, as the physical labour population. But according to Mr. Owen of Lanark, the machinery of Great Britain creates a production equivalent to the labour of 180,000,-000 individuals. The physical population, therefore, of Great Britain, is, to what may be called her moral population, as 1 is to 14. Now, it is chiefly the labour population, and that generally which is devoted to the coarsest and lowest labour, that is subject to pauperism. They are made paupers, by whatever interferes with their industry, or competes with their labour. But as a moral or a machinery labour-power is similar, and equivalent in its production, to a physical labour-power, the physical labour-power of Great Britain, that is rendered paupers, ought in strictness, to be compared not to its physical productive power alone, but to its whole productive power; that is, not to twelve or seventeen millions, but to 192 or 197,000,000. Let us suppose Mr. Owen's calculation to be erroneous, and let us strike off eighty millions, and take the productive power of machinery in England as equal to 100,000,000 of people, still, viewing it in the light we have presented, the discrepancy that is often pointed out, disappears.

The aristocratic provisions of the English constitution, and operation of the vast funding system now established, also disturb that equable and regular diffusion of labour, production, and the burdens for the support of government throughout the community, which is essential to the highest state of political prosperity and happiness.

Its order of nobility is supported in the magnificence and splendor of an illustrious rank, by inordinate salaries, attached to petty and mostly useless offices of state; and by enormous pensions and extravagant sinecures. These are taxes, levied on the industrious and productive members of society, to pamper the luxury, and glut the pride, of the idle and non-productive.

The laws of primogenitureship and of entailments, abstract and withhold from the general circulation, a large portion of the landed property, in favour of this privileged rank, to the manifest detriment and oppression of the industrious class; and as Lord Coke observes, "what contentions and mischiefs have crept into the quiet of the law, by these fettered inheritances, daily experience teacheth."

The limits of these essays forbid us to develop, through all their ramifications, the operation of circumstances peculiar to European society, and of the political policy of its governments which counteract and frequently destroy the beneficial results of its principles of economical policy. The two are not necessarily connected. The one can be embraced with ease, without adopting the other. We have confined ourselves exclusively to the consideration of the political economy of England and other European powers, without reference to their politics. Whatever prosperity they are found to possess, can be attributed solely to its operation. We have, therefore, recommended it to the imitation of this country. But we have to lament, that some of those who have opposed our views, have refused to draw the distinction, and have seized on the vices of their politics, as objections to the principles of their economy.

Applying the above principles to the united states, we shall discover, that during the prosperity which they enjoyed in the first twelve or fifteen years subsequent to the French revolution, the labour power of the country was fully exerted. The wars in Europe creating a constant market for their agricultural products; the carrying trade, and the various branches of business connected with it, gave employment to the greater portion of their labour. Agriculture and commerce were then the characteristic pursuits of the nation. Literature, science, and the arts, were but little cultivated; and few original works of importance were produced. Those liberal professions, however, which are connected with the ordinary transactions of society, and are made the business of individuals, flourished with a vigour unsurpassed in any other country. Of this character are politics, medicine, and law. The improvements those sciences have undergone, and the ability of our citizens devoted to them, place the united states in a very favourable light as respects the intellectual powers of its citizens, and excite auspicious hopes for the future.

Turning our attention to the situation of the nation, at the present time, with reference to the principles laid down, it is obvious, that the sources, which formerly absorbed the superabounding labour power of our country, have ceased to exist, and consequently that a portion of the population which was occupied by them, is daily thrown out of employment. Hence we notice the effects, we have described, as characteristic of such a state of things. Consumption is less in amount, and consequently the value of almost every species of property is on the decline; bankruptcies are numerous; credit nearly extinct; the circulation stagnant; labour fallen in price; workmen discharged by their employers; and the number of the poor augmenting.

As this is the most unfavourable state in which a nation can find itself placed, it is the duty of the statesmen, to whose hands is confided its direction, to inquire into the causes which have created those unfavourable circumstances. If they find them to be merely transient, temporary remedies, adapted to alleviate present distress, or to enable the community to sustain the shock of passing events, should be sought for and applied. But if found to originate in causes, which cannot be confidently anticipated to disappear of themselves, it is also their duty to devise a new system of policy, adapted to the new situation of the nation. If the class of industrious poor be found unemployed, and their production at a stand, the state should devise some mode to procure them employment, and give a fresh impetus or a new direction to their production. If the consumption of the productions of the industrious poor, on which they depend to obtain the comforts and necessaries of life, and to pay the taxes that are required for the support of society, be diminishing, remedies should be speedily applied to counteract this injurious operation. The neglect of these important points in legislation, may overwhelm a large portion of society, hitherto happy, prosperous, and contented, with suffering and calamity; and a consequent feeling of discontent and inflammatory excitement be occasioned, which is greatly to be deprecated.

We apprehend the situation of our country is of the above character. Agriculture, commerce, the retailing of the fabrics of foreign countries, and the branches of business subordinate thereto, formerly gave full occupation to the greater part of our people; but the foreign markets which were heretofore opened, being now closed to our agriculture; our commerce much contracted; the capacity of the people to consume diminished; those occupations have become overstocked, and no longer give full or profitable employment to those who are engaged in them.

In the present posture of affairs, there are no rational indications, which can lead us to expect, that those pursuits, while it continues, will give full employment to our industry: and it surely cannot be urged, that this or any nation, should trust its prosperity to the possible occurrence of favourable accidents.—Yet, while we continue to direct our industry chiefly to those employments, we must depend on the contingent circumstances of a war, or deficient harvests in Europe, for its maintenance, and to procure adequate markets for our productions, when carried to the extent of our productive power. In the meantime, the non-necessary class of producers, must constantly increase; its capacity to pursue the vocations, in which it was engaged, must lessen; its means of sustenance daily decline; and the whole retrograde from the higher species of labour to the lower. The inferior labourers thus pressed upon, while employment is decreased, must be thrust into pauperism, and come on the public for support.

If these revolutions take place quietly, from operating on a sluggish population, the only effect will be, to place society back in the position it had previously occupied, before it had known its days of prosperity; or had acquired a taste for, with a knowledge of, the indulgences and refinements of advanced civilization, growing out of its increased wealth and the cultivation of intellectual enjoyments, in the fine arts, letters, and science. But should this retrocession be resisted, and a struggle once commence against this state of things, inevitable if left to themselves, it is utterly impossible to calculate the course it might pursue, or the aspect it might assume. All the ills, that universal experience has shown to be the concomitants of want of employment, are incurred, and can only be avoided, by opening new means of occupation as the old disappear. Every nation in Europe, that is esteemed wise, has directed its attention to manufactures, not only as the chief source of wealth and power, but as the most salutary mode of absorbing the accumulating class of non-necessary producers. It now rests with us to imitate in this respect the examples, by adopting the experience, of the most illustrious people of ancient and modern times; or, by determining to procure experience for ourselves, to run through a course of suffering and distress. But, when exhausted by the process we have undergone, who can answer for the recovery of our past state of prosperity; whether we shall rise to that greatness, to which we have been looking forward with pride and exultation, or sink into the feebleness and debility that have always attended those nations, which have neglected the sound policy of distributing employment of every kind, throughout their population?

NEW SERIES.

NO. I.

Exports of flour, cotton and tobacco. Alarming depression of the price of cotton. East India and South American cotton. Immense loss by the reduction of the price of cotton. Total importation into Great Britain.

"Is commerce of importance to national wealth? Ours is *at the lowest point of* "*declension.* Is a violent and unnatural decrease in the value of land, a symptom of "national distress? The price of improved land, in most parts of the country, is "much lower than can be accounted for by the quantity of waste lands at market; "and can only be fully explained *by that want of public and private confidence, which* "*are so alarmingly prevalent among all ranks,* and which have a direct tendency to "*depreciate property of every kind.* Is private credit the friend and patron of indus-"try? That most useful kind, which relates to borrowing and lending, is reduced "within the narrowest limits, and this still more from an opinion of insecurity than "from a want of money.

"This is the melancholy situation to which we have been brought by these "very councils" [of purchasing cheap goods abroad, and thereby destroying the industry of our own citizens] *** "which, not content with having conducted us "to the brink of a precipice, seem resolved *to plunge us into the abyss that awaits "us below* Here, my countrymen, impelled by every motive that ought to influ-"ence an enlightened people, *let us make a firm stand for our safety, our tranquili-"ty, our dignity, our reputation.* Let us at last *break the fatal charm which has too "long seduced us from the paths of felicity and prosperity.*" FEDERALIST, No. XV.

Philadelphia, November 15, 1819.

THE reasoning, in our former addresses, in favour of affording adequate protection to that portion of the national industry engaged in manufactures, might have appeared intended solely for the benefit of the manufacturers, distinct from the rest of the community. This would be a great misapprehension of our views, which are directed to the promotion of the permanent prosperity of the nation, on a grand and liberal scale. So close and intimate, in fact, is the connexion between the different interests of the same country, that each must participate in the advancement or decay of any of the others. It is therefore as impossible for either agriculture, manufactures, or commerce, to suffer severely, without the others partaking of the evils, as for one of the members of the human body to be maimed without the whole frame being affected. This theory, always advocated by the wisest political economists, has been completely corroborated by the recent experience of the united states, in which the decay of so large a portion of the manufacturing establishments has spread distress and embarrassment over the whole country.

In the present addresses, we shall attempt to prove, by facts, founded on indisputable authority, quoted at full length, and by fair and logical deduction,—

I. That there is no prospect of a favourable change in the European markets for our staples.

II. That the promotion of manufactures is in the most eminent degree beneficial to agriculture. And

III. That the markets for our agricultural productions, throughout the world, being generally glutted, it would be unwise to divert to farming or planting any of the persons usually devoted to manufactures, even if they were all capable of those employments.

The three grand staples of our country are cotton, flour, and tobacco, which form nearly three-fourths of the total of our exports, as may be seen from the subjoined table. Their great extent and high prices have enabled us to pay for the extravagant amount of our importations, and greatly enriched our farmers and planters. We enjoyed the blessing, and never anticipated a change. We sailed gaily along, with wind and tide in our favour, and without a dark speck in the horizon. No louring storm was anticipated. But the sky at length became overcast. A hurricane arose; and, in its course, not only prostrated some of our most wealthy citizens, who had invested their entire fortunes in those staples, but greatly impaired and impoverished the resources of the entire nation.

Exports.	1815.	1816.	1817.	1818.
	Dolls.	*Dolls.*	*Dolls.*	*Dolls.*
Flour - - - - - - - -	6,202,000	6,712,000	17,751,376	11,576,970
Cotton - - - - - - -	17,529,000	24,106,000	22,627,614	31,334,258
Tobacco - - - - - - -	8,253,000	12,809,000	9,230.020	9,867,429
	31,984,000	43,627,000	49,609,010	52,778,657
Total Domestic Exports.	45,974.000	64,782.000	68,313,500	73,854,437

It is impossible for any man of enlarged and liberal views, to examine this table even superficially—to consider the recent reduction in the prices of those articles—and the limitation of the market for them, without feeling dismay at the prospects that present themselves to our country, and an unalterable conviction that if we wish to secure its prosperity, happiness, resources, and real independence, a radical change in our system is imperiously necessary.

Cotton.

The alarming depression in the prices of our great staples, came on our farmers and planters unawares. There were, nevertheless, unerring symptoms of the change, more particularly so far as regards cotton. Intelligence had been received in this country of large orders sent to the East Indies for that article, and it was almost prophetically announced, in 1817,* that the price of ours would necessarily be greatly reduced.

A considerable time previous to the close of the last session of congress, the most explicit accounts had been received from England of the great progress making in the consumption of East India cotton, and its alarming interference with that of the united states. Most of the circulars of the eminent merchants of Liverpool of that period conveyed this view distinctly. Out of a great number now in our possession, all of the same tenor, we submit an extract from one written by John Richardson, of Liverpool, and dated the 11th of November, 1818.

* Memoir on the culture and manufacture of cotton, by Tench Coxe, passim.

"It was confidently expected by many, that prices would have "rallied before the close of the year: but the immense quantity "of East India cotton which is weekly forced on the market by "auction, renders this speculation extremely uncertain; particu-"larly as *by a recent discovery in the preparation of Bengals and "Surats, the spinners are enabled to make better yarn and spin "finer numbers; this has very materially interfered with the con-"sumption of American cotton, and will prevent it from ever reach-"ing such prices as it has of late years done.*"

This letter arrived in Philadelphia in December. There was then ample time to profit by the important information it contained. But its salutary warnings, like those of 1817, were totally disregarded. The parties immediately interested, and the country at large, reposed in a dangerous security. There were no preparations made to parry the stroke, by the infallible means of providing a home market, a measure dictated by every principle of regard for self-interest, as well as for the welfare of the nation. The duty of twenty-seven and a half per cent. on cotton goods, (except on those below twenty-five cents per square yard, which are dutied as at twenty-five cents) remained unaltered, notwithstanding the earnest and reiterated applications of the manufacturers—the ruin of hundreds of our best citizens—the suspension of establishments, on which millions had been expended—and notwithstanding so large a portion of those who had been employed in them, were driven to idleness and want, many of them with large families. A prohibition of low-priced muslins at that period, and an advance of duty on high-priced to 35 per cent. would have produced such a great increase of consumption in the united states, and of course such a reduction of the quantity in the British market, as to prevent any material depression in the price, and would have saved the planters and the nation millions of dollars, as will appear in the sequel.

Great Britain derives nine-tenths of her supplies of cotton from the East Indies, South America, and the united states. Of each in order.

East India Cotton.

The importation of cotton from the East Indies into the British dominions, to any considerable extent, is of recent date.—The whole amount in twelve years, from 1802 to 1813 inclusive, was only 188,911 bags,* or an average of about 15,700 per annum.

There have been two objections to the general use of this species of cotton, the shortness of the staple, and the great want of care in cleaning and packing it. The latter has been in a great

* Seybert, 92.

degree obviated, so far as regards a large portion of what is received in England. But in some cases it still exists; hence the great difference of price between the extremes, which is frequently three or four pence per lb.

The staple has likewise been considerably improved. We have now before us printed circular letters which shed strong light on this subject, and cannot fail to be duly appreciated by every enlightened planter. One is from the house of Humberston, Graham, & Co. of Liverpool, and dated as early as June 28, 1817. "With the chief part of the uplands now brought for-"ward, *East India cotton begins materially to interfere:* and if "the quality of the crop yet to be received should not improve, "this will occur, to a more considerable extent; for in the late "imports of Bengal cotton, *there is a decided improvement in the "staple;* and, by reference to the annexed list of sales, it is evi-"dent *they are coming into more general use.*"

There is likewise an item in the London price current for August 31, 1819, which confirms the preceding statement. Surat cotton is therein quoted at 7*d.* to 9½*d.*: but *Surat extra fine* is 9*d.* to 11½*d.* This implies a great improvement, either in the quality of the seed, or the mode of preparation, or both: and when the strong incentive to further improvement is considered, it may be presumed that every effort will be made, and no doubt successfully, to remove any existing objections. It is to be observed, that in no other price current that we have seen, is this item of *Surat extra fine cotton* to be found.

One other remark is called for. The best Surat cotton in the Liverpool market generally comes very near in price to the Tennessee.

	January 2, 1819.			*June* 2, 1819.		
	d.		*d.*	*d.*		*d.*
Surat, fair to good	11	to	14½	9	to	1[illegible]½
Tennessee - -	14½	to	15½	10½	to	11½

The improvements made in the culture and preparation of the East India cotton, have been greatly promoted by the very high prices of ours and those of the Brazils, Bourbon, &c. It is only wonderful, that they did not take place much earlier.

We annex a table of the importation of East India cotton into Great Britain, for two successive periods, each of four years.

	Bags.		Bags.
Imported in 1811	14,646	Imported in 1815	23,357
1812	2,607	1816	30,670
1813	1,429	1817	117,454
1814	13,048	1818	247,604
	31,730		419,085*

This table affords matter for serious reflection, not merely to the cotton planters, but to the people and government of this country. It speaks volumes on the rapid strides making in the British markets by the East India cotton. The increase is probably without example. It was nearly four-fold in 1817 of the amount in 1816 ; and in 1818, more than two-fold that of the preceding year The capacity of the East Indies to produce this article is without limits. By a Calcutta paper of Jan. 20, 1819, it appears that

	Bags.
The export of cotton from Calcutta in the year 1818 was	336,848
from Bombay - - - - - - -	323,807
	660,655

equal to about 190,000,000 lbs.

It is supposed by many of our citizens, that there is a radical and insuperable inferiority in the East India cotton. This is an egregious error. The finest muslins in the world are manufactured in Hindostan, of the cotton of that country. It therefore follows, that the great superiority assumed for ours cannot be regarded as any security against the East India competition. We are informed by a writer of high authority, that " *a fine sort of* " *cotton is still grown in the eastern districts of Bengal, fit for the* " *most delicate manufactures*."†

The rise in the price of our cotton in the British market, as stated from the price current of September 30, may lead our planters and merchants to hope that they will regain the ground they have lost, and thus lead to extensive speculations. This would probably prove a fatal error‡ to hundreds of those who

* Seybert, 92, and Journal of Trade and Commerce, vol. ii. page 113.

† Colebrook's Remarks on the husbandry and internal commerce of Bengal, page 138.

‡ [The predictions here hazarded, have been fully verified. The price of cotton in the Liverpool market has not only not risen since the above period, but has fallen considerably ; sea island above 33 and upland 8 per cent. This address was written, as may be seen by its date, in Nov. 1819 ; at which time

Upland cotton was sold in Liverpool at - - - - - -	12*d.* to 12½
Sea island fine - - - - - - - - - - -	34*d.* to 36*d*
Whereas, on the 21st August, 1821,	
The former was - - - - - - - - - - -	11*d* to 11½
Sea island fine - - - - - - - - - - -	17½ to 23*d*

might be led astray by it, and exhibit another decisive proof of the insanity of a nation depending on contingent and fluctuating foreign markets, when it can create and secure an unfailing domestic one, subject to but slight variations.

To the sober reflection of the cotton planters we submit these important facts. They cannot be too deeply or seriously weighed. Their dearest interests are vitally involved in them. Abstracted from all considerations of the general prosperity of their country, which has fallen a sacrifice to the policy hitherto pursued—as well as of the wide-spread scene of ruin that has swallowed up the fortunes and the happiness of so large a portion of their fellow citizens, engaged in manufactures, their own interest most explicitly points out the necessity of pursuing a different policy, and securing to themselves a home market, beyond the control of foreign nations. Had this market been thus secured, it can hardly be doubted that so large a portion of the cotton at present raised in this country would, we repeat, have been consumed at home, that the quantity exported would have experienced little reduction of price.

The contrast between the situation of the British and American manufacturers is extremely striking, and must mortify the pride and excite the sympathy of every citizen who feels an interest in the credit of our government and the welfare of the nation. The British manufacturers, completely secured in the home market by prohibitions, and prohibitory duties, are struggling, with all their energies, to monopolize not only our markets, but those of half the world. In this contest, they are aided in every way that can be devised, by a government which many of our citizens affect to despise. Whereas, our manufacturers only contend for the humble boon of security in the domestic market; and with whom do they contend? not with foreign nations—but with their fellow citizens in congress, whom they merely request to afford them a portion of that protection, which, as we have often repeated, England, France, Russia, Austria, and nearly all the other governments of Europe, afford their subjects engaged in manufactures!!!

This paragraph would require a volume of explanations—but we must be brief; and, referring to our former addresses, shall barely observe,

I. That Austria prohibits the importation, throughout her whole dominions, of all kinds of silk, cotton and woollen manufactures.

II. That England prohibits silks, laces, calicoes, and manufactures of gold, with various other articles; and subjects cotton generally to 85 per cent—glass to 114—and chequered linens, manufactures of leather, tanned hides, &c. &c. to 142 per cent.

III. That Russia prohibits above two hundred articles, among which are all manufactures of wool, printed cottons, glass, pottery, silk, iron, leather, &c. &c. &c.

IV. That France prohibits cotton twist, manufactures of wool, silk, leather, steel, iron, brass, tin, &c. &c. &c.

It is therefore obvious, as already often stated, that the manufacturers of those countries enjoy a degree of fostering care and protection from their respective governments, which our citizens of that class have never experienced—and the want of which has not only ruined hundreds of them—but inflicted more lasting injury on this country in five years, than it could have suffered in a war of twice the duration.

We will suppose for a moment a majority in congress to be composed of manufacturers; and such immense quantities of wheat and flour to be imported from Odessa, and of cotton from Brazil and the East Indies, as to reduce the price of those articles below the fair rate of affording a profit to the cultivator. Suppose that the farmers and planters, at every stage of their progress to ruin, were to supplicate congress either to prohibit, or discourage by high duties, the importation of wheat, flour, and cotton. Suppose, further, that the majority in congress, resolutely determined to buy those articles, "*where they could be had cheapest*," steadily rejected their petition. What opinion, fellow citizens, would you form on such conduct? would it not meet with your most marked disapprobation? But is it not precisely the conduct that has been pursued towards the manufacturers? Have they not, in their career to ruin, earnestly and respectfully solicited protection from Congress? Have not their entreaties been rejected?* Has not a large proportion of them been sacrificed by the ruinous policy of purchasing cheap goods abroad? And has not the nation at large shared in the sufferings inflicted on them?

* Of above forty petitions presented to the house of representatives of the united states, in 1816–17, by different bodies of manufacturers, in various parts of the united states, praying for relief, *there was not one read in the House! and very few of them were ever reported on by the Committee of Commerce and Manufactures!* There was not one of them successful, although the ruin suffered by some, and impending over others, of the petitioners, had every possible claim to prompt and effectual redress. On this treatment of constituents, no comment is necessary.

We exported last year [1818] to Great Britain, bales of cotton - - - - - - - -	205,881
Equal to - - - - - - - - - lbs.	61,764,300
Deduct for waste, 50 lbs. per bale, - - -	10,294,050
Pounds net, - - - - - - - -	51,470,250
Producing, at 4 yards to the pound, - yards	205,881 000
Which, at 20 cents per yard, amount to -	$41,176,200
Supposing we sold the whole of the raw cotton at 30 cents, it produced the united states -	18,529,290
Leaving a clear gain to Great Britain of -	$22,646 910
If the exports of cotton to that country this year are equal to the last, and average only 20 cents per pound, it makes an addition to the British profit of - - - - - - -	6,167,430
Total - - - - - - -	$28,823,340

Nearly the whole of this sum might be saved to this country by a proper tariff.

NEW SERIES.

NO. II.

Philadelphia, December 24, 1819.

State of the country at the close of the war—Present state, [1819] *—Taxing the many for the benefit of the few—Smuggling—Rates of duties on imports—Protection of Commerce—American tonnage.*

It is painful to us, to be obliged again to combat objections which we regarded as fully disproved in our former addresses, beyond the probability of a revival. In this opinion we were completely supported by hundreds of intelligent citizens, whose views of the subject had on a fair examination undergone a total change, and who at present as strenuously advocate the policy of retaining our wealth at home to support the industry of our own citizens, as they formerly did that of squandering it in Europe and the East Indies, to support the industry of foreign nations, under the idea of "letting trade regulate itself," which it has never done in any age or country.

But however painful this procedure may be, it is a duty. The persons opposed to our views, without replying to our arguments, far less refuting any of them, repeat the hacknied common places of free trade, taxing the many for the benefit of the few, impairing the revenue, smuggling, extortion, &c. Free trade with them means, in strict propriety, to remove the restrictions that protect our own citizens, while all other nations maintain rigorous restrictions in favour of their subjects.

We therefore crave indulgence for any repetitions that may appear in this essay, as the inevitable consequence of the course pursued by the opposers of the system which we advocate.—Whenever they advance new arguments, we shall meet them with new replies. To old arguments ten times repeated, and as often refuted, we can only advance repetitions.

When we first began to address our fellow citizens, about nine months ago, on the distress and embarrassment so generally prevalent throughout the union, the existence of that distress and embarrassment was denied; endeavours were used to convince the public, that our statements on the subject were erroneous; that the country at large enjoyed a high degree of prosperity; and that whatever pressure existed was confined to a few towns and cities where banks and over-trading had produced some ruin. It was unhesitatingly asserted, that the farmers and planters, the great body of the nation, had no reason to complain—and accordingly made no complaint; and that all the clamour arose from a few manufacturers, who were, to the whole nation, as a few stray sheep to an immense flock.

These assertions, although radically wrong, were made with such confidence, as to gain credence with those who looked not beyond the mere surface of things. Unfortunately for the country, as well as for the credit of those who made them, their want of foundation is now so obvious and so palpable, as to admit of no denial. Calamity has advanced upon us with such rapid strides, that whatever doubts may have been entertained heretofore, have now vanished. There is but one sentiment on the subject. That the distress is more intense in some parts of the union, than in others, favoured by local circumstances, is admitted—but that it is felt every where, is equally clear.

Would to heaven our descriptions had been unreal, and that we had been deceived. To none of our readers would the discovery of the error have been more agreeable than to ourselves. We present an outline of the leading features of our situation at the close of the war, and at present, which affords a most melancholy contrast, appaling to every friend not merely of this country, but of human happiness generally.

Our situation at the close of the war.

1. Every man, woman or child in the nation, able and willing to work, could procure employment.

2. We had an extensive and profitable cotton manufacture, spread throughout the union, and producing above 24,000,000 of dollars annnally, which might, by proper encouragement, have been extended to 50,000,000 in a few years.

3. This manufacture consumed above one-fourth part of our whole crop of cotton.

4. We had a capital vested in merino sheep to the amount of one million of dollars.

5. We possessed a valuable woollen manufacture which produced us annually clothing to the amount of nineteen millions of dollars—and which might have been extended before now to double the amount.

6. Almost all our manufacturing establishments were fully and advantageously employed.

7. Confidence between our citizens was general.

8. Our debts to Europe were fairly and honourably discharged.

9. Little, if any of our public stock was held in that quarter of the globe.

10. Money could be easily borrowed at legal interest.

11. Debts were collected without difficulty.

12. Our character, as a mercantile people, stood fair with the world.

13. Every man who had capital, could find advantageous employment for it in regular business.

14. The country was generally prosperous, except a few places which had suffered desolation during the war.

Our present situation.

1. Our profitable commerce nearly annihilated.

2. Our shipping reduced in value one half.

3. Of our merchants a considerable portion bankrupt, and many tottering on the verge of bankruptcy. The commercial capital of the country reduced, it is believed, seventy millions of dollars.

4. Our manufacturing establishments in a great measure suspended, and many of them falling to decay.

5. Many of their proprietors ruined.

6. Thousands of citizens unemployed throughout the united states. [About 11,000 in the city of Philadelphia have been deprived of employment.]

7. Our circulating medium drawn away to the East Indies and to Europe, to pay for articles which we could ourselves furnish, or which we do not want.

8. A heavy annual tax incurred to Europe in the interest payable on probably 15 or 20,000,000 of dollars of government and bank stock, likewise remitted in payment.

9. Real estate every where fallen thirty, forty or fifty per cent.

10. Our great staples, cotton, flour, tobacco, &c. reduced in price from thirty to forty per cent.

11. Our merino sheep, for want of protecting the woollen manufacture, in a great measure destroyed, and those that remain not worth ten per cent. of their cost.

12. Large families of children become a burden to their parents, who are unable to devise suitable means of employment for them.

13. Numbers of our citizens possessed of valuable talents, and disposed to be useful, but unable to find employment, are migrating to Cuba, where, under a despotic government, among a population principally of slaves, and subject to the horrors of the inquisition, they seek an asylum from the distress they suffer here!*

14. Hundreds of useful artisans and mechanics, who, allured by our form of government, migrated to our shores, have returned to their native countries, or gone to Nova Scotia or Canada, broken hearted and with exhausted funds.*

15. Men of capital are unable to find profitable employment for it in regular business.

16. Citizens who own real estate to a great amount—have large debts due them—and immense stocks of goods, cannot mortgage their real estate, dispose of their stocks but at extravagant sacrifices, nor collect their debts.

17. Citizens possessed of great wealth, have it in their power to increase it immoderately, by purchasing the property of the distressed, sold at ruinous sacrifices by sheriffs, marshals, and otherwise—thus destroying the equality of our citizens, and

* *Emigration to Cuba.*—"The schooner Three Sally's, captain Warner, sailed from this port on Sunday last, for Fernandina de Yuaga, a new port and settlement on the south side of Cuba, with 101 passengers, principally respectable mechanics, and their families, and late residents of this city."—*Philadelphia Daily Advertiser, Dec.* 2, 1819.

"In the schooner John Howe, lately sailed upwards of one hundred passengers for the new settlement of Fernandina, in Cuba."—*Philadelphia Gazette.*

* "*Liverpool, Nov*, 2, 1819.—The Ann, Captain Crocker, from New York, is now off this port, with upwards of one hundred returned emigrants."

aggrandizing the rich at the expense of the middle class of society. The extent of this serious evil is difficult to be ascertained with precision.

18. The interest of money extravagantly usurious.

19. Distress and suffering, to an extent not to be conceived but by those who have an opportunity of beholding them, spreading among the labouring classes, in our towns and cities.

20. Bankruptcy and poverty producing an alarming increase of demoralization and crime.

21. The attachment to our government impaired in the minds of those who are ruined by the policy it has pursued.

22. After having prostrated our national manufactures, lest we should injure the revenue, the revenue itself fails, and we are likely to be obliged to recur to loans,* or direct taxes to meet the exigencies of the government.

23. Numbers of banks in different parts of the union, deprived of their specie by the extravagant drains for Europe and the East Indies, and obliged to stop payment.

24. Legislatures driven, by the prevalence of distress, to the frightful measure of suspending the collection of debts.

That this is an unexaggerated picture of the actual situation of our country, is, alas! too true. It affords a proof that our system has been radically unsound—and that a change is imperiously called for. Any change can scarcely fail to be beneficial.

These ruinous consequences were prophetically depicted with 'a pencil of light,' and also distinctly presented to the view of congress in their progress. Happy, thrice happy would it have been, had the warnings and heartrending statements which that body received, been duly attended to—What shoals and quicksands would our prosperity have escaped!

The committee of commerce and manufactures in 1816 declared, that—

" The situation of the manufacturing establishments is peri-
" lous. Some have decreased—and some have suspended busi-
" ness. *A liberal encouragement will put them again into opera-*
" *tion.* But should it be withheld, they will be prostrated.
" *Thousands will be reduced to want and wretchedness. A capi-*
" *tal of nearly sixty millions of dollars will become inactive, the*
" *greater part of which will be a dead loss to the manufacturers.*"

Again—

" Can it be politic in any point of view, to make the united
" states *dependent on any nation for supplies, absolutely neces-*
" *sary for ease, for comfort, or accommodation?*

" Will not *the strength, the political energies of this nation be*
" *materially impaired* at any time, but fatally so in time of diffi-
" culty and distress, by such dependence?

* This anticipation has unhappily been verified.

"Do not the suggestions of wisdom plainly show, that *the* "*security, the peace, and the happiness of this nation, depend on* "*opening and enlarging all our resources, and drawing from* "*them whatever shall be required for public use or private con-* "*venience?*"

The suffering citizens laid their calamitous situation before congress in the most eloquent appeals, but in vain. No part of the union suffered more than Pittsburg. From the address of that city we quote a single paragraph—

"The tide of importation has inundated the country with fo- "reign goods. *Some of the most valuable and enterprizing citi-* "*zens have been subjected to enormous losses*, and others over- "whelmed with bankruptcy and ruin. *The pressure of war was* "*less fatal to the hopes of enterprise and industry, than a gene-* "*ral peace, with the calamities arising from the present state of* "*our foreign trade.*"

Part of the long catalogue of ills, it was out of our power to prevent; among the rest, the reduction of our commerce, and the consequent depreciation in the value of our shipping. The nations of Europe could not be expected to allow us to continue the commerce that naturally belonged to them, longer than suited their convenience. Nor could we by any means have prevented the reduction of the price of our wheat, flour, &c. &c. when a cessation of the destruction caused by war, and the return of so many of the soldiery to the labours of the field, not only increased the capacity of supply, but diminished the consumption of Europe. But a sound policy would have averted three-fourths of our sufferings, and mitigated the residue. It would have afforded other employment for our superfluous commerical capital; made a domestic market for our cotton; and fostered our woollen and various other manufactures to an extent almost commensurate with our wants.

We enjoyed for twenty years a very great proportion of the trade of the world, far beyond our due share—and, to use the words of an English statesman, were "hardly scratched by our war" of two years and a half. We closed it in a most prosperous situation, calculated to excite the envy of our enemies, and the gratulations of our friends. All that was necessary to insure the permanence of our happiness and prosperity, was to protect our national industry, after the example of all the wise nations of Europe. We fatally abandoned it to a hopeless struggle with foreign rivalship. It sunk a victim in the unequal contest. And our melancholy example is added to those of Spain and Portugal to warn other nations against the rocks on which we have shipwrecked our happiness. By our system of buying goods where they could be had cheapest, supporting foreign manufacturers, and consigning our own to ruin, we have, during a period of profound peace of nearly five years, not only lost all the advantages acquired by our long-continued neutrality, but find ourselves in as unprosperous a situation as when the wars of the French revolution began.

The transition is immense and lamentable: and we are persuaded that, except in the case of Portugal at the commencement of the last century, there is no instance to be found in the annals of Europe for two hundred years, of so precipitous a fall in so short a space of time, without war, famine, or pestilence. Spain, which exhibits the mouldering ruins of a mighty empire, fell, it is true, from a higher pinnacle to a lower abyss; but the descent required centuries of misrule, with bloody wars, and remorseless persecutions.

The source of the change is by some of our citizens sought for in the transition of the world from a state of war to a state of peace, which has produced distress, it is said, in most parts of Europe. This idea is erroneous. The distress is far from general. It prevails extensively, it is true, in Great Britain, where machinery, superseding so large a portion of the manual labour of the country, has driven a tenth part of the population to a dependence on the poor rates, and where the nation is borne down by an enormous debt, an expensive government, and grinding tythes and taxes. It would be lost labour to prove, what is obvious to the world, that between her case and ours there is no analogy.

We have given a faithful picture of the disastrous situation in which this great nation is placed by a mistaken policy. It now remains to trace the outlines of a policy by which the evils we suffer might have been averted—and the course to be pursued, in order to extricate ourselves from our embarrassments.

We have bought and consumed more than we have sold. Our imports for five years have been above one hundred millions of dollars more than our exports. This solves the mystery. The distress and embarrassment arising from all the other sources, would have been but temporary. Bankruptcy and ruin tread on the heels of individuals whose expenses exceed their income. No law, human or divine, exempts nations from the same fate. Spain and Portugal, to which we have so often referred, are standing monuments of the soundness of the maxim, that even inexhaustible mines and rich colonies will not secure the prosperity or happiness of nations that are so misguided as to expose the productive industry of their people to destruction, by the overwhelming competition of foreigners. How much stronger and more irresistibly does the argument apply to the united states, possessing neither mines nor colonies, and whose resources solely depend on the fruits of their industry! How carefully therefore should that industry be cherished!

The imports of the united states for the last five years, exclusive of what has been re-exported, have been about 420,000,000 dollars, viz.

1815	$118,914.000
1816	60,569,000
1817	73,516,000
1818	94,477,000
1819 (*per estimate*)	74,000,000
	$421,476,000

Our exports have fallen one hundred millions short of our imports. As this was a result that might easily have been, and indeed was foreseen, it ought to have been guarded against as far as legislation could afford a remedy. The remedy was to exclude, or reduce our consumption of, the fabrics of the old world, so as to bear a proper proportion to its demand for our staples. This was fatally neglected.

It required but little penetration to see that our means of payment were wholly inadequate to meet such enormous imports; that the country must be greatly impoverished by them; that its productive industry would be paralized; and that much misery must be the necessary consequence. All the sagacity of our statesmen ought to have been put into requisition, to avert the impending evils, and to steer our bark safe through the shoals and quicksands, by which she was menaced. Every month made appearances more and more portentous, and more strongly indicated the necessity of adopting bold and decisive measures. Unhappily the views of most of our statesmen were almost wholly bounded by the security of the revenue! and many were only anxious to avoid "*taxing the many for the benefit of the few!*" These were the grand objects of solicitude, and outweighed all other considerations. They viewed with unconcern the inundation of foreign merchandize, which drained our country of its wealth—ruined our manufacturers—and doomed our working people to idleness, to want, and too often to crime! The more foreign goods came in, the cheaper they were sold, and the higher the revenue rose! And this appeared to atone for all the disastrous consequences it produced!

On this point, it might be sufficient to reply with Alexander Hamilton—

"There is no truth that can be more firmly relied upon, than "that *the interests of the revenue are promoted by whatever pro-* "*motes an increase of national industry and wealth.*"*

It requires but little reflection to perceive the cogency of this

* Hamilton's Report.

maxim. A prosperous people will naturally indulge in luxuries, which are generally brought from foreign nations—and will bear high duties. A revenue resting on such a basis would be far more likely to increase than to diminish. It cannot be doubted that the customs at present, considering the impoverishment of the country, and the low state of our credit abroad, afford but a slender dependence for the treasury. The united states, if industry were duly protected, would be far better able to yield a revenue of 40,000,000 of dollars per annum, than they can now raise 25,000,000. A prosperous nation does not feel the weight of taxation. A tax of half a dollar on each hearth, is more oppressive to a poor nation, than a window tax of an equal sum for each pane of glass, would be to a prosperous one.

The warning voice of the wise statesmen of this country as well as of Europe, which bore testimony against the policy we pursued, was totally disregarded.

" It would be extending the freedom of trade far beyond its " proper bounds, to admit all the productions of a nation which " prohibits ours, *or admits them under duties equivalent to a pro-* " *hibition.*"*

" The substitution of foreign for domestic manufactures *is a* " *transfer to foreign nations of the advantages accruing from* " *machinery in the modes in which it is capable of being employed* " *with most ability and to the greatest extent.*"†

" The establishment of manufactures is calculated not only to " *increase the general stock of useful and productive labour, but* " *even to improve the state of agriculture in particular.*"†

" Considering a monopoly of the domestic market to its own " manufactures as the reigning policy of manufacturing nations, " *a similar policy on the part of the united states*, in every proper " instance, is dictated, it might almost be said *by the principles* " *of distributive justice—certainly by the duty of securing to their* " *own citizens a reciprocity of advantages.*"†

What admirable lessons! What sublime views! How lamentable that they were entirely disregarded! Our misguided policy is a century at least behind them. The plans of our statesmen unhappily did not extend so far. We once more repeat, that the hope of buying cheap goods from Hindostan and Europe—the dread of impairing the revenue—and the desire of fostering a commerce, which was expiring beyond the power of resuscitation, produced a policy of which the fatal consequences will be long felt, not merely by the sufferers, but by the whole nation.

Had our government prohibited some leading articles, which we could ourselves have supplied, such as all kinds of coarse

* Chaptal. † Hamilton's Report.

cotton goods, some of the woollen, &c. &c. and laid high additional duties on those we were obliged to receive from foreign countries, our importations would probably have been diminished one-fourth, without impairing the revenue—and the following salutary consequences would have resulted.

1. There would have been probably 100,000,000 of dollars, less debt contracted to Europe.

2. That amount would have been added to the stock of national wealth.

3. Our whole population would have been maintained in profitable employment.

4. The revenue would have been indemnified by the increase o the duties upon those goods imported, for what it might have l st by the exclusion of the others.

5. As the reduction of the revenue would have been prevented, we should not have a direct tax suspended over our heads.

6. We should have paid for our importations by our exports, a d not been obliged to remit government and bank stock in payment.

7. Our commercial credit in Europe, which has received a deep stain, would have remained unimpaired.

8. We should have consumed so large a proportion of our cotton, as would have prevented the ruinous reduction of its price in Europe, and produced immense advantage to our planters.

9 Our woollen manufacture would have insured a market for the wool of our Merinos, and prevented the destruction of that valuable race of animals; to the great benefit of our farmers.

10. Our banks would not have been drained of their specie, and obliged to press on their debtors.

11. We should have escaped the state of impoverishment, embarrassment and distress in which we find ourselves placed.

12. The prosperity universally felt would have increased the attachment of our citizens to our form of government, and drawn the bands of union tighter.

13. Our citizens would not seek an asylum in Cuba.

14. State legislatures would not have had recourse to the desperate measure of suspending the collection of debts.

15. Thousands of useful artists and manufacturers would have migrated to our country; and an incalculable amount of "*the manufacturing skill and capital*" *of foreign nations would have been* "*promptly transferred to the united states, and incorporated into the domestic capital of the union.*"*

* This sound view is taken from the late report of the secretary of the treasury. It is deeply to be lamented that so obvious and important an idea does not appear to have ever heretofore influenced our councils.

Although the millions of capital lost by this policy, cannot be regained, nor the thousands whom it has vitally injured or ruined be indemnified for their sufferings—yet in the midst of the gloom that surrounds us, there is matter for consolation, that congress have a remedy completely within their power. All that is necessary is to afford our manufacturing citizens a portion of such protection as England, France, Russia and Austria afford theirs. We should then reduce our wants within our means of payment. The whole face of affairs would at once be changed. Millions of dormant capital would be put into circulation. Our industrious population would find immediate employment. Property of every kind would rise in value. Confidence would be restored. Prosperity and happiness would again visit us with "*healing on their wings*."

Although we have already repeatedly stated in detail the protection afforded by those great nations to their manufacturers, we deem it proper to present an outline of it here.

Great Britain prohibits, even from her own dependencies, calicoes, manufactures of gold, silver, or metal; laces, ribands, silk goods, &c. and her protecting duties in most cases, are equivalent to prohibition. Manufactures of brass, copper, carriages, thread stockings, clocks, &c. are subject to fifty-nine per cent.; china and earthenware, shawls, &c. pay seventy-nine; cottons, cotton stockings, caps, thread, and linen sails, pay eighty-five; glass manufactures generally one hundred and fourteen; skins or furs tanned, tawed or curried, and articles made of leather, or whereof leather is the article of chief value, one hundred and forty-two per cent.*

Linen, when chequered or striped, printed or stained, is subject to one hundred and forty-two per cent. duty; but only to sixty-three when not chequered or striped. She hereby secures to her own subjects the profits of the staining and printing.*

—

Against the policy we advocate of affording protection to those of our citizens engaged in manufactures, the leading objections are—

I. That it is unjust to tax the many for the benefit of the few.

II. That high duties encourage smuggling.

I.

So much has been written against the protection of manufactures, on the injustice of "taxing the many for the benefit of the few," that a large portion of our citizens are persuaded, that the manufacturers alone are protected,—that this protection is abso-

* See British tariff, passim.

lutely gratuitous—and that neither agriculture nor commerce has any reciprocal advantage.

It is hardly possible to conceive of a much greater error.—It is in fact the reverse of truth.

We hope to prove—

That the protection afforded to manufactures bears no proportion in its effect to that afforded to agriculture and commerce.

To arrive at a correct conclusion, it is necessary to define what is meant by the word *protection*, as here employed. Otherwise we might spend our time and that of our readers to no purpose.

By "*protection*," then, we mean such a governmental regulation, by duties or prohibitions, as saves any class of our citizens, whether farmers, manufacturers, or merchants, from being undermined or ruined by foreign rivals. As we do not pretend to critical exactness, which cannot be deemed necessary, we trust this definition will be admitted, as sufficiently precise to answer our purpose.

It is obvious, that in this view, the word has reference not to the amount, but to the effect of the duty: for example, 15 per cent. may exclude one rival article, while 35 would not another. The former, therefore, is far more complete protection than the latter, in such particular cases.

It may be necessary to exemplify this theory. Hemp is a very bulky article in proportion to its value. The freight is high, and amounts to about eighteen per cent. Fine cambrics and muslins occupy but small space, and are probably not subject to more than one per cent. freight. It is therefore obvious, that a duty of five per cent. on hemp and 22 per cent on cambrics, would place the American farmer and manufacturer on precisely the same ground, so far as respects freight and duties; that is, they would have twenty-three per cent. advantage over their foreign rivals.

But another very important consideration remains. Articles which foreign nations possess great capacity to produce, require stronger protection than those of which the production is more limited. Thus the machinery of Great Britain affording her a capacity to produce muslins or cambrics to an almost unlimited extent—and the production of hemp being incapable of that extension, a further increase of duty on muslins or cambrics appears necessary, to place the manufacturer on the same ground of security as the farmer. Hence the duty ought to be adjusted on a compound ratio of the amount of freight and the difficulty or facility of production.

We trust these premises are clear and irrefutable, and that they cannot fail to dispel the clouds that have been spread over this subject.

The great mass of manufactured articles imported into this country, are subject to duties ad valorem. There are five different classes of those duties, seven and a half, fifteen, twenty, twenty-five, and thirty per cent. The amount of the importations of all these descriptions for 1818, was 58,795,574 dollars. There are, however, some manufactured articles subject to specific duties. But the amount is trivial; as the duties of this description, in 1818, except those on teas, wines, melasses, spirits, sugar, coffee, and salt, were only 1,591,701 dollars; under which were included oils, cocoa, chocolate, almonds, currants, prunes, figs, raisins, cheese, tallow, mace, nutmegs, cloves, pepper, pimento, cassia, indigo, cotton, ochre, white and red lead, hemp, coal, fish, &c. &c. When the duties on these are deducted from the above sum of 1,591,701 dollars, the manufactured articles, on which the remainder is collected, will, as we said, appear quite trivial.

The articles paying ad valorem duties, were divided as follows:—

$		Per cent. of the whole.
2,387,693	*a* 7½* per cent. equal to about	4
19,445,525	*a* 15 ——— equal to ———	33
9,524,531	*a* 20 ——— equal to ———	16
24,804,188	*a* 25 ——— equal to ———	42
2,633,637	*a* 30 ——— equal to ———	4½
58,795,574		

We annex a statement of the chief articles subject to those several duties.

TABLE I.

Articles subject to 7½ per cent. ad valorem.†

Articles composed wholly or chiefly of gold, silver, pearl or precious stones,
Embroidery,
Epaulets,
Gold watches,
Gold lace,
Jewelry,
Lace veils,
Lace shawls,
Lace shades,
Pastework,
Pearls, and other stones, set,
Silver lace,
Watches, and parts of watches of all kinds.

* To all the ad valorem duties herein stated is to be added 10 per cent. Thus 15 per cent is actually 16½, &c. &c.

† Add ten per cent. as before.

TABLE II.

*Articles subject to 15 per cent. ad valorem.**

Agricultural.	Manufactured.
Apricots,	Bricks,
Apples,	Brass in sheets,
Beans,	Brazing copper,
Barley,	Bolting cloths,
Buckwheat,	Combs,
Butter,	Copper bottoms,
Beef,	Clocks, and parts thereof,
Cider,	Corks,
Feathers for beds,	Gold leaf,
Flour	Hair-powder,
Grapes,	Ink-powder,
Hams,	Linens,
Hay,	Lampblack,
Honey,	Maps and Charts,
Hair,	Manufactures of flax not enumerated,
Indian corn,	Paints,
Linseed,	Printed books,
Malt,	Pictures,
Nuts,	Prints,
Onions,	Paper toys,
Oats,	Paper snuff boxes,
Potatoes,	Paintings,
Perry,	Silks,
Pearl Ashes,	Slates,
Pitch,	Starch,
Peas,	Stuff shoes,
Pork,	Silk stockings,
Pears,	Sealing wax,
Peaches,	Thread stockings,
Potashes,	Tiles,
Quills,	Worsted shoes, &c.
Rosin,	
Rice,	
Rye,	
Tobacco in the leaf,	
Tar,	
Turpentine,	
Wheat, &c. &c.	

TABLE III.

Articles subject to 20 per cent. ad valorem, wholly manufactured.*

Buckles,	Japanned wares,
Buttons,	Lead manufactures,
Brass manufactures,	Muskets,
Brass wire,	Printing types,
Button moulds,	Pottery,
China ware,	Pewter manufactures,
Cannon,	Pins,
Cutlery,	Plated ware,
Cloth, hempen	Steel manufactures,
Cotton stockings,	Stone ware,
Earthen ware	Side arms,
Fire arms,	Sail cloth,
Gilt wares,	Tin manufactures,
Glass,	Wood manufactures,
Iron manufactures,	Woollen stockings,

* Add ten per cent. as before.

To a candid public, we submit these three tables for their most serious consideration. The deductions from them are of immense importance to the future prosperity and happiness of this country. We trust they will be found to prove that the prevailing opinions on the exclusive protection of manufactures are destitute of foundation—and that, so far as these tables extend, the balance is most unequivocally in favour of agriculture, although agriculture itself is not sufficiently protected. Lives there a man who will not admit that

Beef,
Pork,
Hams,
Butter,
Indian Corn,
Flour,
Wheat,
Tar,

are incomparably better protected at 15 per cent. than

Clocks,
Gold leaf,
Linens,
Manufactures of flax,
Printed books,
Silk and thread stockings,
Stuff or worsted shoes,

at the same rate ? or than

China ware,
Cotton and woollen stockings,
Manufactures of steel,
Pins,
Plated ware,
Printing types,
Sail cloth, &c.

at 20 ? We submit the question to the most decided opposer of manufactures in the country, and cannot for a moment doubt the issue. It cannot be denied that hams, boards, Indian corn, tar, and turpentine are better protected by 15 per cent. than buckles, buttons, or cotton stockings, would be by 40 or perhaps 50.

The manufactured articles subject to 25 and 30 per cent. remain. The former are confined to cotton and woollen goods, manufactures of copper, silver and plated sadlery, and coach and harness furniture.

Half of the articles subject to 30 per cent. duty, are unimportant; do not interfere with our manufactures ; and are not to be taken into view in the present discussion—as

Artificial flowers,
Balsams,
Bristol stones,
Cosmetics,
Comfits,
Crapes,
Canes,
Fans,
Feathers,
Mats of flags, or grass,
Millinery,
Mustard,
Olives,
Ornaments for head dresses,
Perfumes,
Pickles,
Sallad oil,
Sticks for umbrellas,
Sweetmeats of all kinds,
Walking sticks,
Washes, &c. &c.

There are, however, some important articles included in this class; among which are manufactures of leather, hats, clothing ready made, carriages, cabinet wares, &c. But the amount of the whole class is insignificant, being not four per cent. of the importations of the country for 1818, as may be seen above, p. 207.

We will now compare the highest duties on productions of the soil and on manufactures. We select from the former, four articles, cotton, coal, hemp, and cheese; and shall add manufactured tobacco and snuff, the duties on which are calculated solely to aid the planter;* also, spirits, the duties on which are imposed to aid the farmer directly in the production of peach brandy, apple whiskey, &c. and indirectly in the consumption of his grain.

	Cost. dols. cts.	Duty. dols. cts.	Per cent.
Liverpool coal, per bushel	13	5	38½
Bengal cotton, per lb.	10	3	30
Russia hemp, per ton,	114	30	26
Holland cheese, per lb.	10	9	90
French cheese	13	9	70
English cheese	18½	9	49
Manufactured tobacco	10	10	100
Snuff	20	12	60
Jamaica rum, per gallon	70	48	68
Geneva	55	45	80

Comparison.

	Per cent.		Per cent.
Cotton Manufactures†	25	Cotton, raw,	30
Woollen manufactures	25	Hemp	26
Plated saddlery	25	Tobacco	100
Manufactures of leather	30	Snuff	60
Hats	30	Coal	38½
Carriages	30	Cheese	49, 70, 90
Cabinet wares	30	Rum	68
		Geneva	80

Three of the agricultural articles, which are raw materials, claim particular attention, flax, cotton, and hemp, with the corresponding fabrics.

	Duty per cent.		Duty per cent.
Flax†	15	Linen†	15
Hemp	26	Hempen cloth	20
Cotton	30	Cotton goods, (above 25 cents per square yard)	25

Here we find raw materials subject to higher duties than the articles manufactured of them! A case probably without parallel in the annals of trade and commerce! The general practice of the wisest nations of the old world, is, to discourage the exportation of raw materials; to admit them duty free, or at least under very light duties; and to burden the manufactured articles

* See this point satisfactorily cleared up in the strictures on Mr. Cambreleng's Examination of the tariff, postea.

† Add ten per cent. as before.

as high as they will bear. The whole of these regulations have two grand objects in view, of which a wise government will never lose sight—the protection of domestic industry, and the promotion of the national wealth, power, and resources. Whereas, in the plenitude of our great wisdom, we burden the raw material with a heavier duty than the manufactures in which it is employed!*

Another view of the subject.

Cotton, we see, is subject to three cents per lb. duty. The freight is equal to the duty—amounting together to 60 per cent. Whereas the duty on cottons (above 25 cents per square yard) is 25 per cent.—and freight about one per cent.

Wonderful contrast!

	Freight and duty. Per cent.		*Freight and duty. Per cent.*
Raw cotton - - - -	60	Cotton manufactures -	26

We are fully persuaded, that the tariff of no country, in the darkest ages of the world. presents such a fact as this, so admirably calculated to tear up industry by the roots! It is a century at least behind the policy of Edward III. and six behind the light of this age. That prince bestowed bounties, immunities, privileges, and premiums for the encouragement of the woollen manufacture, and prohibited the export of the raw material, and the importation of the manufactured article!

We will contrast this portion of our tariff, with corresponding parts of the tariff of France, England, and Russia.

French Tariff.

	Duty per cent.	
Flax - - - - -	1	Linen prohibited.
Hemp - - - -	1	Hempen cloth prohibited.
Cotton - - - - -	1	Cotton goods prohibited.

Cotton is admitted in Russia, *duty free*—but *all kinds of printed, stained, or painted cotton goods are wholly prohibited.*

Cotton pays only six per cent. duty in Great Britain, according to the latest regulations; but calicoes are wholly prohibited, and all kinds of cotton goods, which are admitted, are subject to 85 per cent duty.

It is hardly possible to conceive of a greater contrast than is here exhibited between our policy and that of those great nations. Their policy is that of Colbert, Sully, the Great Frederick, and all the other celebrated statesmen, who rank so high in history—whereas ours is exactly similar to that of Spain, Portugal, and Italy. We are in a dilemma. Either we are wiser than all the practical statesmen of Europe, or our system is radically wrong. If we "judge of the tree by its fruits," we may easily decide. Its results have been of the most destructive character.

* Yet manufacturers are gravely reproached for their ingratitude for the protection they enjoy.

Here we close the subject as respects the comparative protection afforded to the productions of the earth, and to manufactures. We trust that every reader who has given it a fair consideration, will readily agree that the interests of agriculture have not been overlooked; that the prejudices that prevail on the subject of the extraordinary protection afforded to manufactures, are not only not true, but the very reverse of truth; and that a large portion of our manufacturing establishments, for want of adequate protection, are prostrate, and their proprietors ruined.

Protection of Commerce.

It now remains to ascertain whether the mercantile interest has experienced the fostering care of the government—and whether the merchants are justified in uniting in the everlasting clamour against the manufacturers for "taxing the many for the benefit of the few." We hope to make it appear, that the policy of our government towards the commercial part of our citizens has been magnanimous and liberal to the last degree, and that it has afforded them as complete protection as was in its power. Happy for this country would it have been, had the same liberal and national spirit presided over its councils so far as regards manufactures! Instead of the lamentable scene we now present to the world, we should exhibit as grand a picture of happiness and prosperity as has ever been witnessed.

The policy of England, the wisest nationin the old world, on the subject of trade and commerce, is not, we hope to make appear, superior to that of our government on this point.

In a former address, No. 11, (see ante page 151) we enumerated sixteen acts, or parts of acts, passed for the especial protection of commerce, out of a much larger number to be found in our statute books. Being limited for room, we shall refer to the above address, and shall here confine ourselves to four acts, which will be amply adequate to establish our position on this subject.

The attention of congress was early alive to the interests of the mercantile part of the community—and it has never ceased to watch over them with the most laudable solicitude. By the second act passed by the first congress, the China trade was at one stroke secured to our merchants, by a decisive difference in the duties on teas—viz.

	In American vessels.	In foreign vessels.
	Cents.	*Cents.*
Bohea - - - - - Per lb.	6	15
Souchong and other black teas -	10	22
On all Hyson teas - - - -	20	45
On all other green teas - - - -	12	27

There was, moreover, a discrimination of ten per cent. made by the same act in favour of American tonnage in the duties on imports.

The third act had the same marked and decided character. The tonnage on foreign vessels was fixed at 50 cents—and on American only 6. But even this discrimination was not deemed sufficient; for the former were obliged to pay tonnage for every coasting voyage; whereas the latter paid but once a year.

"Our discriminations operated powerfully in favour of our shipping. Vessels not of the united states, of two hundred tons burden, on entering our ports, paid twenty pounds sterling tonnage duty; and for a cargo of the value of two thousand pounds sterling, they paid fifteen pounds sterling, extra duty, more than did the vessels of the united states, of the same tonnage, and laden as aforesaid. These extra charges were sufficient to drive from our ports, the greatest proportion of the foreign tonnage. All foreign nations were affected by the system we had adopted. It seemed to operate like magic in favour of the ship owners of the united states. The diminution of the foreign tonnage employed in our trade, was, with very few exceptions, rapid, regular, and permanent. In 1793, our tonnage exceeded that of every other nation, except one."*

From these facts there is no appeal. They are conclusive, and set the question at rest for ever. The effect was to multiply the American shipping to an extent unparalleled in the history of commerce. The following table exhibits the results.

TABLE

Of the tonnage employed in the Commerce of this country for twenty-two years.†

	American vessels.		Foreign vessels.
	Coasting trade.	Foreign trade.	Foreign trade.
1796	195,423	675,046	49,960
1797	214,077	608,708	76,693
1798	227,343	522,045	88,568
1799	220,904	626,945	109,599
1800	245,295	682,871	122,403
1801	246,255	849,302	157,270
1802	260,543	798,805	145,519
1803	268,676	787,424	163,714
1804	286,840	821,962	122,141
1805	301,366	922,298	87,842
1806	309,977	1,044,005	90,984
1807	318,189	1,089,876	86,780
1808	387,684	525,130	47,674
1809	371,500	603,931	99,205
1810	371,114	906,434	80,316
1811	386,258	948,247	33,202
1812	443,180	667,999	47,098
1813	433,404	237,348	113,827
1814	425,713	59,626	48,301
1815	435,066	706,463	217,376
1816	479,979	877,031	259,017
1817	481,547	780,136	212,420
	7,310,333	15,741,632	2,459,909

* Seybert, 294. † Idem, 317—18

Total coasting trade, American tonnage	tons 7,310,336
Foreign trade do.	15,741,632
American tonnage	23,051,965
Foreign tonnage in Foreign trade	2,459,909
Grand total	25,511,874

Thus it appears that the merchants have, from the commencement of the government, enjoyed an entire monopoly of the coasting trade, which employs above 28 per cent. of the whole of the shipping of the country; and above 90 per cent. of all the foreign trade.

The above two acts were the first passed by our government in favour of commerce. We will, as stated above, pass over the long list to be found scattered through our statute books, and refer only to the two last passed with the same view.—We mean the act on the subject of plaster of Paris, and that magnanimous national measure of prohibiting the entry into our ports, of vessels from those colonies of Great Britain, into which our vessels are prohibited to enter—an act of the most decisive and energetic character.

Besides the preceding protection to commerce, which, by the exclusion of foreign competition, produces the effect so much inveighed against in the case of manufactures, of "*taxing the many for the benefit of the few*," that is, in plain English, of enhancing the price of freight, at the expense of the whole nation, for the benefit of the merchants, there is another species of protection extended to commerce, of a more costly character. It is comprised under four heads. Expenses incurred for—

1. Foreign intercourse—
2. Barbary powers—
3. The navy—
4. War.

That the first and second items are chargeable wholly to commerce, will not be denied. Some question may arise respecting the third—but it is obvious, that for every other purpose than the protection of commerce, 150,000 dollars per annum would be adequate for the navy of the united states. The expenses for four entire years, 1791, 1792, 1793, and 1794, were below 70,000 dollars.

On the subject of the fourth item, there will be still more diversity of sentiment. It requires, however, but a moderate portion of candour to admit, that nine-tenths of all the difficulties we have had with foreign powers, have arisen wholly from commerce. From the wholesale depredations of 1793, down to the orders in council and the Berlin and Milan decrees, every page of our history bears this solemn truth in legible characters, that we should have steered our bark in peace through all the tremendous convulsive struggles of the wars arising from the French revolution, but for the collisions caused by our commerce. We state two facts within the knowledge of every man acquainted with our affairs for the last twenty-five years. When about three hundred of our vessels, engaged in the trade with the French colonies, were seized in 1793, we were in the most imminent danger of war—various retaliatory measures were proposed in congress, among which the sequestration of British debts stood conspicuous. Nothing saved the country from a recourse to arms at that time, but the interference of the president, and the mission of Mr. Jay to London. In 1805—6, the depredations were renewed with additional violence, and the merchants from Newburyport to Baltimore were most importunate in their requisitions on congress, for protection and redress, whence arose that series of restrictive measures which a few years afterwards eventuated in war.

We will now state the expense incurred for the naval department. foreign intercourse, and Barbary powers, for 20 years—and for the military department for four, embracing the three years in which war raged and the succeeding one.

	Naval department.	Foreign intercourse	Barbary powers.
1796	274,784	109,739	75,120
1797	382,631	172,504	497,284
1798	1,381,347	242,711	214,717
1799	2,858,081	199,074	72,000
1800	3,448,716	185,145	210,142
1801	2,111,424	139,851	155,825
1802	915,561	416,253	134,672
1803	1,215,230	1,001,968	108,866
1804	1,189,832	1,129,591	57,063
1805	1,597,500	2,655,767	142,259
1806	1,649,641	1,613,922	146,499
1807	1,722,054	419,845	157,980
1808	1,884,067	214,233	90,759
1809	2,427,758	74,918	91,387
1810	1,654,244	48,795	32,571
1811	1,965,566	181,746	83,158
1812	3,969,365	297,327	50,376
1813	6,446,600	153,791	56,170
1814	7,311,290	163,879	13,300
1815	8,660,000	223,781	67,110
	$53,055,691*	$9,644,840*	$2,349,568*

Expenses of the military department during the years 1812, 1813, 1814, 1815.

1812	$12,022,798	
1813	19,747,013	
1814	20,507,906	
1815	15,208,794	
		67,486,511†

*Seybert, 713. † Idem 712.

Aggregate.

Expense incurred in twenty years for the naval department,	$53,055,691
Foreign intercourse	9,448,140
Barbary powers	2,349,568
Military department for four years	67,486,511
Total	$132,339,910

In order duly to appreciate the proportion these expenses bore to our commerce, we annex a statement of the exports from the united states for the same twenty years, from 1796 to 1815, inclusive.

	Domestic Exports.	Foreign Exports.
1796	40,764,097	26,300,000
1797	29,850,206	27,000,000
1798	28,527,097	33,000,000
1799	33,142,522	45,523,000
1800	31,840,903	39,130,877
1801	47,473,204	46,642,721
1802	36,708,189	35,774,971
1803	42,205,961	13,594,072
1804	41,467,477	36,231,597
1805	42,387,002	53,179,019
1806	41,253,727	60,283,236
1807	48,699,592	59,643,558
1808	9,438,546	52,997,414
1809	31,405,702	20,797,531
1810	42,366,675	24,391,295
1811	45,294,043	16,022,790
1812	30,032,109	8,495,127
1813	25,008,152	2,847,845
1814	6,782,272	145,169
1815	45,974,403	6,583,350
	701,606,879	608,583,572*

Domestic exports	701,606,879
Foreign	608,583,572
Total exports	1,309,190,451
Expended for protection of commerce, as above stated	$131,516,912

It therefore irresistibly follows, that the *actual disbursements* for the protection of commerce for twenty years, have been eleven per cent. of the whole amount of our exports, domestic and foreign—and nearly twenty per cent. of the domestic! And yet we repeat, the merchants unite in the cry against the expense incurred for the protection of manufactures! although the government from its first establishment has never paid one dollar,

* Seybert, 793.

as loan, premium, or bounty, to encourage, foster, or promote that portion of the national industry employed in manufactures!

Let it be observed that the manufacturers, while they have been so frequently the objects of jealousy with their fellow citizens, have had the magnanimity never to prefer a complaint against the protection afforded to either farmers or merchants, or the enormous expense incurred in defence of the latter. Nor would we wish it understood that we regard the fostering care bestowed on them as otherwise than the duty of the government. Our object is merely to bring the subject fairly before our fellow citizens, and to prove that both agriculture and commerce are far more adequately protected than manufactures.

It may be useful to compare our system of "*purchasing where goods can be had cheapest*," and not "*taxing the many for the benefit of the few*," with that pursued in France, and to cast a glance at their results.

Mons. Chaptal, minister of the Interior, during the reign of Bonaparte, published, a few months since, a detailed and most exhilarating view of the affairs of France, and of the policy that has led to her present prosperity. The product of the manufactures of that country, in 1818, was 1,820,000,000 francs, composed of the following items:—

Domestic raw materials - - - - -	francs 416,000,000
Foreign do. - - - - - - - -	186,000,000
Labour - - - - - - - - -	844,000,000
Various expenses, as interest, firing, repairs, &c. - -	192,000,000
Profits of the manufacturer - - - - -	182,000,000
Total,	1,820,000,000
Equal to about - - - - - -	dollars, 360,000,000

France waged the most sanguinary wars for above twenty years. She was afterwards crushed by rapacious and depredating armies—and subject to a military contribution of above 100,000,000 of dollars. Yet she has already recovered from all her disasters, and is now the most prosperous nation in Europe. should the mighty secret be asked, by which this all-important change has been effected, it is reducible to a few words—she was not afraid of the ideal danger of "*taxing the many for the benefit of the few.*" She protected the industry of her subjects, making a small temporary sacrifice for an immense permanent benefit. While our statesmen were calculating about saving 8, 10, or 12 cents per yard, by buying goods in Europe and in the East Indies, she for a while bought at home at double price, in preference to purchasing cheap abroad. She trusted that competition would produce the effect it has ever produced, that is, to bring prices to a proper level. The magnanimous policy succeeded—and now affords a rich harvest of private happiness and public prosperity. We have bought cheap abroad—and distress overspreads our land! She bought dear for a while at home, and is repaid ten fold for the temporary sacrifice!

It is but just to state her policy in Chaptal's own words;—We hope they will sink deep into the minds of the statesmen and politicians of this country.

"Our casimers cost twenty-five francs per ell, *to the manu-*"*facturer*, at the commencement of our operations. The English "offered them at half price, *to the consumer.* Our cambrics and "calicoes, ill manufactured, cost us seven to eight francs. The "English delivered theirs at three.

"Ought we, therefore, to have renounced this project of ma-"nufacturing conquest? No. It was our duty to persist and im-"prove. This therefore is the course we pursued. And we "have arrived at such a degree of perfection, that our industry "excites the jealousy of those from whom we have borrowed it.

"If, during twelve or fifteen years, in which we pursued our "essays, our researches, our experiments, we had not *excluded* "*the competition of foreign rival articles by prohibitions*, I ask "of the partisans of fifteen per cent. duty, what would have be-"come of this admirable industry, which constitutes the orna-"ment, the glory, and the riches of France?"*

Smuggling.

While ruin was successively swallowing up various manufactories, and reducing to bankruptcy their owners, who were shut out of the markets of foreign nations by the wisdom of those nations—and deprived of their own by the want of protection, their prayers and supplications were met by a clamour against the danger of smuggling that would arise from high duties. On this real or supposed danger, the changes have been rung from New Hampshire to Georgia, and from the Atlantic to the Mississippi. Whatever might be the sufferings of the manufacturers, the assumed danger of smuggling was regarded as a conclusive

* "Nos casimirs coûtoient 25fr. l'aune au fabricant, dans le principe; et les "Anglois offroient les leurs au consommateur, á moitié prix; les percalles, les ca-"licots, mal fabriquès, nous revenoient á 7 á 8fr. l'aune; les Anglois les livroient "á 3fr.

"Falloit-il renoncer á ce projet de conquête manufacturière? Non, il falloit "persister et se perfectionner. C'est aussi la marche qu'on a suiviè: et nous "sommes arrivés à un tel degré de perfection, que notre industrie excite "aujourd'hui la jalousie de la nation qui nous l'a transmise.

"Si, pendant douze à quinze ans qu'ont duré nos essais, nos recherches, nos "tâtonnemens, on n'avoit pas èearté du concours, par la prohibition, les produits "étrangers, je demande aux partisans des 15 pour cent, ce que seroit devenue "cette belle industrie qui fait l'ornement, la gloire et la richesse de la France?" —*De l'Industrie Francoise, tom. II. p.* 431.

and unanswerable argument, and as forming an insuperable bar against making such a radical change in the tariff as would afford them protection.

An objection which is regarded as so powerful, and which closes the ears of the national legislature to the cries, and shuts their eyes against a view of the distresses, of so large a body of their fellow citizens, ought to be founded on an impregnable basis—and demands the most rigorous scrutiny before it be admitted as orthodox. An error on such a point is liable to produce deleterious consequences.

We shall therefore once more investigate the ground on which it rests, although we have already discussed the subject. Reduced to plain English, it is—

1. Smuggling is a dreadful and demoralizing evil that ought to be avoided.

2. High duties encourage smuggling.

3. Therefore high duties ought to be avoided.

To render this reasoning applicable to the case in hand, two things are necessary to be proved. If either fail, it falls to the ground:—

1. That the duties requested by, or necessary to afford adequate protection to, our manufacturers, would be so immoderately high as to encourage smuggling.

2. That our duties, in general, are calculated on a moderate scale, predicated on a dread of the danger of encouraging smuggling by high duties.

Neither of these positions is founded.

We will specify a few out of a great variety of manufactures, which have been either wholly ruined, or greatly impaired in their progress, since the peace, by the inundation of rival articles, and hope it will appear to our readers, that the duties might have been raised to double their present amount—so as to preserve the manufactories, without danger of smuggling—and without impairing the revenue.

Gold Leaf,
Linens,
Manufactures of flax,
Slates,
Sealing wax, &c. &c

are subject to fifteen per cent.—

Manufactures of Steel,
Brass,
Glass,
Iron,
Lead,
Earthen ware,
Japanned ware,
Pottery,
Stone ware,
Woollen stockings,

are subject to twenty per cent.—And

Fine cottons, and
Woollens,

are subject to twenty-five per cent.

Of these manufactures, several, which, in consequence of the exclusion of foreign rivalship, were in a flourishing state during the war, have since been laid prostrate. A duty of 30 per cent. on some, and 35 on others, would have effectually secured them.

Now, we freely appeal to men of candour and fairness, whether those duties would have been more likely to produce smuggling than the duties we have stated, on snuff. tobacco, rum or gin at sixty or eighty or one hundred per cent.? or those which we shall produce in the next table?

Will it be asserted, that if pottery, for instance, had been subject to a duty of 60 or 80 per cent. it would have been more likely to be smuggled than any of those articles? Surely not. The idea is inadmissible.

On the second head, the objection still more completely falls to the ground. Our tariff imposes duties on various articles extravagantly high.—We have already stated the cases of cheese, manufactured tobacco, snuff, rum, and Geneva. We proceed to wines, teas, and salt.

	Price.* cents.	Duty. cents.	Duty. per cent.
Sherry wine, per gallon,	100	60	68
Lisbon wine	125	60	48
Imperial tea, per lb.	65	50	78
Hyson	40	40	100
Young Hyson	40	40	100
Hyson Skin	24	28	116
Souchong	27	25	98
Bohea	13	12	90
Salt, per bushel,	16	20	125

Thus it appears that there are no terrors felt on the subject of smuggling, when those articles are in question which do not interfere with the national industry! On these 50, 60, 70, 80, 90 and 125 per cent. are unhesitatingly imposed. But when those manufactures are to be dutied, of which we have the raw material to the utmost extent of our wants (as, for instance, cottons, and, with some qualification as to present supply, we might add woollens) water power to manufacture them without limitation —and industry and enterprise never exceeded in the world— then the appalling spectre of smuggling arises, at the mention of 35, 40, 45, or 50 per cent. to blunt the feelings of our legislators —to ruin a large and valuable portion of our citizens—to make us tributaries to foreign nations, on whom our treasures are wantonly and prodigally lavished—and to tear up by the roots a large portion of the productive industry, the wealth, power and resources of our country!!

* Cost at the places of shipment respectively.

To these facts we most earnestly invite the attention of those who have any thing at stake on the welfare of their country. In five years, we repeat, without war, pestilence, or famine, we have fallen from a towering eminence into an abyss, where we find bankruptcy; character impaired at home and abroad; forced idleness, misery, and distress, among thousands able and willing to work; demoralization; emigration of our citizens in quest of an asylum which their own country does not afford them; and finally *legislative suspensions of payment.* We believe the great mass of those evils due to the policy we have pursued, the antipodes of that of all the wise nations of Europe—but the counterpart of that of Spain and Portugal. Nothing can save us but a full and complete protection of the domestic industry, which we fervently pray, may take place without delay, for the happiness of our citizens, and for the honour of our republican form of government.

AMERICAN MANUFACTURES.

An adjourned meeting of the citizens of the city and county of Philadelphia, friendly to American manufactures, was held in the county court house, on Saturday, the 2d of October, 1819.

MATTHEW LAWLER, Esq. Chairman.
C. RAGUET, Esq. Secretary.

The committee appointed for the purpose, presented the following

REPORT.

The committee appointed by a meeting of the citizens of the city and county of Philadelphia, held on the 21st August, at the county court house, to make enquiry into the situation of the manufactures of the city of Philadelphia and its vicinity, in 1814, 1816, and 1819, beg leave to report—

That they have performed the duty assigned them with as much attention as in their power; and regret that notwithstanding all their diligence, they have been able to procure the necessary information from only thirty branches of manufactures, of which they annex the result.

Although they made report in part, on the 4th ult. containing a statement of the situation of seventeen branches, they judge it proper to present their fellow-citizens with a connected view of the whole together; so as to enable them to form a correct estimate on a subject of immense importance not merely to the welfare of this community, but to the wealth, power, and resources of our common country; which never can be really independent, while it continues to buy more than it sells—paralizes the industry of its citizens, neglects its domestic manufactures, and supports those of foreign nations.

Branches of Manufactures.*	Number of hands employed.			Average value of their labour per week.			Value of goods manufactured per week.		
	1814.	1816.	1819.	1814.	1816.	1819.	1814.	1816.	1819.
Cotton	1761	2325	149	$3 75	$3 67	$4 65	$	$27380	
Hosiery	96	48	29	4 51	4 47		778	382	$ 145
Thread	444	191	20	4 24	3 50	3 6½	2690	1188	600
Silver Plating	114	210	30	9 00	8 00	6 00	3420	3200	1732
Smithery	852	750	149	9 00	8 00	6 00	15036	18500	1675
Coach making	220	185	67	9 00	9 00	8 00	5600	4625	629
Chemicals	71	52	16	6 63	7 55	6 44	5479	2755	
Hatting	134	172	60						
Carving and Gilding	62	121	24	7 50	8 50				
Pottery	132	132	27	5 48	5 48	5 83			
Tobacco Pipes	33	33	none	4 17	4 17				
Printing Ink	5	5	1	7 00	7 00	7 00			
Book Printing	198	241	170	7 70	7 21	5 83			
Type Foundery	74	90	42	4 35	4 32	4 46			800
Brass Foundery	300	240	80	6 33	6 00	5 00		2800	
Wire Factory	60	22	6	6 67	7 00	7 50			
Floor Cloth manufactory	50	30	25	6 00	6 00	4 50			
Woollen	1310	1226	260	3 12½	3 12½	3 12½			
Iron Castings	1093	1152	52	6 44	6 62½	11 54			
Paper making, 95 vats	950	950	175	5 00	5 00	5 00			
Copper smith and tin ware	77	77	35	5 75	5 75	2 00	2272	2272	381
Gunsmithery	154	124	93	7 23	3 75	8 67	2567	2145	1759
Cabinet making	180	250	70	7 00	7 00	7 00			
Brush making	65	112	50	6 00	7 50	5 00	1560	2688	1200
Plaster and Stucco	120	150	90	8 00	10 00	7 00			
Bricklaying	250	300	150	9 00	10 00	8 00			
Patent Lamp making	6	5	1	7 50	7 50	7 00			
Morocco Leather, &c.	62	111	84	8 26	7 66	8 52	2581	5358	2548
Rope making	110	200	100	6 48	7 50	5 52			
Paper hanging and playing cards	189	168	82	2 70	3 36	3 8			
	9188	9672	2137						

* These lists were collected, and this table compiled, by Dr. John Harrison.

The following is a list of the branches of business, on which the committee found it impracticable to procure the necessary information:

Shotmakers	Stone cutters
Plumbers	Glass manufacturers
Coopers	Brewers
Umbrella makers	Tanners
Bookbinders	Curriers
Sugar bakers	Dyers
Chocolate makers	Brick makers
Snuff and tobacco manufacturers	Chair makers
Carpenters	Glovers
Painters and glaziers	Embroiderers
Manufacturers of gunpowder	Calico printers
Shoemakers	Turners
Engravers	Wheelwrights, &c. &c.

It is obvious that these branches must have partaken of the general decay of business—but it is impossible to ascertain in what proportion.

We do not pretend that the above statements are critically exact. It is obvious, that it would be hardly possible to render them so, unless they were collected officially by public authority. But from the characters of the citizens who have furnished our data, we can confidently assert, that if there be any errors, they are neither numerous nor important; and that any slight excess in some is amply counterbalanced by deficiencies in others; of the latter description some have already fallen within our knowledge.

The preceding table demands the most serious reflection of our citizens. It is fraught with instruction.

The following is an analysis:

	Average of 1814, and 1816.	1819.	Diminution.
Persons employed,	9,425	2,137	7,288
Weekly Wages,	$58,340	$12,822	$45,518
Wages per annum,	$3,033,779	$666,844	$2,366,935

Thus in the articles of wages alone, there is in thirty branches of manufacture, an actual annual loss of $2,366,935 00

Supposing the materials only equal to the wages, they amount to - - - - - - - - 2,366,935, 00

Annual amount of productive industry smothered by our present system, - - - - - - 4,733,870 00

In this city and vicinity, there are, it appears, 7,288 persons thrown idle. And it is far from unreasonable to presume, that on every person thus deprived of employment, at least two other persons depend. Hence it follows that no less than 21,864 persons are bereft of maintenance in thirty branches of business, in one single district of no great extent, not forty miles in diameter.

The pecuniary loss arising from this state of things may be calculated with tolerable certainty. But who can calculate the injuries of another description that flow from it? The demoralization that necessarily results from want of employment, and its attendant, dissipation? the heart-rending pangs felt by parents, whose prospects of supporting their families are blighted and blasted? the numerous estimable females accustomed to earn a subsistence by spinning, and other employments adapted to their sex, and whose wants and distresses may force them to a life of guilt and wretchedness? the vice and immorality, to which children are exposed by a career of idleness? in a word, the flood of evils, moral and political, which are let loose on society, by the existing state of things?

It would far exceed the bounds of this report, to enter into details on those various branches of business. This must be left to the reflection of our citizens, and of the legislature of the united states, who alone are competent to apply a remedy to the existing evils. But we cannot forbear casting a glance at one particular branch, in order to establish the impolicy of our system.

The basis of the paper manufacture is a raw material, completely worthless for any other purpose. All the produce of it, therefore, is clear gain to the community, and a solid substantial addition to the wealth of the country. We exhibit a comparative view of the state of this branch in 1816, and 1819.

	1816.	1819.	Diminution.
Workmen employed	950	175	775
Annual wages,	$247,000	$45,000	$202,000
Annual production	$760,000	$136,000	$624,000
Tons of rags worked up	2,600	472	2.128

Thus in one single branch, of little comparative importance, an annual loss of 624,000 dollars is incurred in the vicinity of the city; and 775 persons are rendered destitute of employment, many of them men and women with large families. This is independent of the sacrifice of the capital of the employers, which in many cases is reduced to one half of its former value.

Our policy is in direct hostility with that of all the wise nations in the world for four or five hundred years past. They have always held out inducements to the migration of artists, mechanics, and manufacturers, whom they have received with open arms, and fostered and cherished, frequently by bounties and immunities. In some countries the emigration of such persons is made penal. But alas! with us the same ruinous policy that depresses the industry of our native citizens, discourages the migration to our shores of foreigners devoted to manufactures. Allured by the advantages of our excellent form of government, hundreds and thousands of them come to enrich us with their capital, their talents, and their industry; but on their arrival they find no room for the employment of either industry, talents, or capital. Many of those who seek support here in their respective trades and professions, are obliged to earn a maintenance by low and servile occupations, in which their skill and talents are literally thrown away; many, to our knowledge, have been reduced to mendicity; and hundreds are driven to Canada or Nova Scotia, or obliged to return to their native countries, where they hold out a beacon to others, not to try their fortunes in this new world. To England no less than one hundred lately returned in one vessel.

We beg leave to repeat, what we stated in our former report, that most of these manufactures are prostrated not for want of protecting duties, but in consequence of the general impoverishment of the country, arising principally from the want of protection to the great leading branches of cotton, wool, and iron. A large portion of our manufactures, including the chief of those depending on manual labour, have succeeded completely: and it is a singular and striking fact, notwithstanding the high price of labour is so often urged against the encouragement, and against the chance of success of manufactures here, that we yield the palm chiefly in those branches depending on machinery, in which from our numerous mill-seats, we have advantages beyond any nation in Europe.

A trite observation is used to palliate our sufferings, which, as it diverts public attention from their real sources, and thus may prevent the application of an adequate remedy, deserves to be met and refuted. We invite your attention.

It is asserted that the present is a season of general stagnation and embarrassment; that the commercial world is every where involved in distress, the necessary consequence of the transition from a state of war to a state of peace; and that we only participate in the general suffering, from which we have no right to claim an exemption.

These views, however plausible, are destitute of foundation, and are wholly unsupported by facts. That there is great distress in certain parts of Europe, we admit; but it is far from being as general as is asserted. Manufactures and trade are in a flourishing state in France, Russia, and the Netherlands, in consequence of the wise system of protecting national industry, pursued in those countries. The first, it is stated by travellers of undoubted veracity, was never in a more prosperous situation.

But admitting for a moment, that distress and embarrassment were not only general, but universal in Europe, it by no means follows that they should extend to this country. The nations of that quarter, with hardly any exception, were for twenty years wasted and consumed by a devouring war. Most of them were subjected to the often-repeated rapine and depredation of countless hordes of licentious and rapacious armies, which levied on them most exorbitant and ruinous contributions. Their people are generally subject to grinding taxes, rack-rents, and oppressive tythes. Their national debts are enormous, and their governments expensive—supported by numerous standing armies, a burden to the rest of the community.

We ask our fellow citizens, what analogy can be found between their situation and ours? None —As well might we compare the decay and decrepitude of seventy, to the vigour and alacrity of thirty, as compare some of the European nations with the united states.

For nineteen successive years we enjoyed as numerous and as important advantages as any nation ever did. We carried on a most extensive and lucrative commerce with all the world, and were the carriers for a large portion of the commercial nations. We were at war only about two years and a half, during which time our manufactures made a progress not often equalled, and perhaps never, under similar circumstances, exceeded. We closed the war with honour and glory, and in a state of high prosperity; our debt is moderate; our public contributions light; our government unexpensive; direct taxes are hardly known.—We pay no tythes; as the support of the clergy is wholly voluntary;—ninety-nine out of a hundred of our farmers and planters own the soil they cultivate; our people are ingenious, industrious, and persevering: yet notwithstanding all these, and various other advantages, in three years, without war, famine or pestilence, we have fallen from a high grade of prosperity. Distress in a greater or less degree pervades the nation; property of almost every description has fallen 10, 20, 30, 40, 50, or even 60 per cent. Industry is generally paralized, and every class of our citizens is embarrassed, except public officers, whose salaries remain unaltered, notwithstanding the rise in the value of money, and likewise great capitalists, who are enabled to possess themselves of the property of the distressed at one half or two-thirds of its value, and in some cases at one-third.

But with our system it could not be otherwise. It never has been otherwise with nations whose industry has not been protected. Had we, like the Spaniards, the mines of Potosi, we should, like them, be impoverished, under a system which opens our ports to the manufactures of all the world, while most of its markets are shut, not only against our manufactures, but in some cases against the most important produce of our soil; a system whereby we are deluged with immoderate quantities of luxuries, which we do not want, and of necessaries and conveniences, with which we could supply ourselves; a system which prodigally lavishes the wealth and resources of our country, to support the agriculture, manufactures, trade, and commerce, of foreign nations, and stints and starves our own—consigning our fellow citizens to distress and wretchedness: And thus, under the best form of government in the world, we wantonly inflict on ourselves many of the most serious and oppressive evils of the worst; for it is an awful truth, which we wish to be sounded in the ears of all the constituted authorities of the united and individual states, that *there is no country in the civilized world, in which the class of manufacturers, who have at all times been most zealously cherished by all wise governments, are in a more unprotected situation, than in the united states.* There is not a greater difference between light and darkness, virtue and vice, than between the fostering care bestowed on manufactures in England, France, Austria and Russia—and the cold and chilling neglect which the successive applications for relief, made to Congress, by our manufacturers in 1816, 1817, 1818, and 1819, have experienced. They produced no more effect, and were treated with no more respect, than the applications of the congress of 1774, to the ministers of his Britannic majesty. And in fact, it is a melancholy truth, that the manufacturers of the united states are almost as completely unrepresented in Congress, as this country, when in its colonial state, was in the British parliament: and history is replete with proofs that when the power of a country is exclusively vested in one portion of its people, the others rarely experience the beneficent consequences resulting from that "even-handed justice" which "does as it would be done by."

The committee believe that one of the chief ends of government is the protection of property acquired, and protection in the acquisition of property; that so far as respects the latter object, a large portion of the manufacturers are debarred of this right; that it is impossible for one large class of citizens to suffer without the others participating in the distress; and finally that although the manufacturers are the first and greatest sufferers by this baleful policy, which sacrifices their industry to that of foreign nations, yet, that the impoverishment of the country, arising from that sacrifice, has spread itself over the whole of the united states with the two exceptions already specified.

Although not exactly within the duty enjoined on your committee, they judged it not improper to exhibit a statement of the depreciation of the value and income of real estate in the city of Philadelphia, in order more fully to corroborate the view they have given of the existing distress.

Of 85 houses in six continuous squares in Market street, which were in 1818 rented for - - - - - - -	$88,260
There were, one month since, only 49 occupied, which rent for	35,205
Dimininution of annual income in part of a single street -	53,055

And there were no less than 36 houses wholly unoccupied.

In those squares, many of the houses are under lease, and therefore have undergone no change in the rent; and many are occupied by the owners, Of both descriptions no notice is taken. This view is wholly confined to houses of which the rent has been lowered, or which are unoccupied.

And on an examination of sundry streets, being about three-fourths of the whole city, there were found, a fortnight since, not less than about 400 houses unoccupied.

On a careful examination of the subject, your committee respectfully submit for consideration the following resolutions:

Resolved, That it is clearly established, on a careful examination, that the industry of a very large portion of the inhabitants of this city and its vicinity is completely destroyed, whereby thousands of useful citizens and their families are deprived of employment, and reduced to distress and difficulty.

Resolved, That the great difference between our situation, and that of those countries in Europe, which at present suffer distress and embarrassment, together with the solid advantages we possess, forbid the idea that our embarrassments are owing to the transition from a state of war to a state of peace.—(2 dissenting voices.)

Resolved, That the grand and primary cause of the prostrate state of our manufactures, is the extravagant inundation of foreign goods poured into our country, in consequence of the want of adequate protection for the national industry; which goods are sold at such reduced rates as to deprive our citizens of a chance of sale of their manufactures; whereby our country is plunged in debt, our wealth drained away to support the industry of foreign nations—and a heavy permanent annual tax imposed on us, to pay the interest of the government and bank stock, remitted in payment for those goods.—(1 dissenting voice.)

Resolved, That the intercourse between the united states and most of the countries of Europe, is carried on without adequate reciprocity; as our chief manufactures, and even some of our agricultural productions, are there excluded by positive prohibitions, or by extravagant duties, while our government prohibits no article whatever, and imposes on foreign manufactures duties comparatively light, and wholly inadequate for protection.

Resolved, That it be earnestly recommended to the friends of the welfare of their country, to unite their exertions to induce congress, at its next session, to remove the source of the evils under which the nation labours, by such a modification of the tariff, as will afford protection to the industry of the citizens of the united states, equal to what is afforded by the monarchies of Europe to the industry of their subjects.

Resolved, That the committee of correspondence appointed on the 4th ult. be a standing committee to correspond with such citizens of this and the other states, as may be disposed to co-operate in the support of the national industry.

Resolved, that it be earnestly recommended to the citizens of Boston, New-York, Baltimore, Wilmington, Pittsburg, and all other places, where industry is paralized, to appoint committees to make enquiry into the rise, progress and decline of their manufactures respectively, in order to lay the result before congress, at their next session, so as to enable that body fully to appreciate the ruinous consequences of the existing policy, and to apply an adequate remedy.

Resolved, That the memorial adopted at the meeting on the 4th ult. together with the proceedings of this meeting, be transmitted by the committee of correspondence to the members of the general and state governments, and to all the post-masters in the united states.

Resolved, That Thomas Leiper, M. Richards, James Ronaldson, Z. Phillips, and Thomas F. Gordon, be a committee of finance, for the purpose of raising subscriptions to defray the expenses of the publication of these documents.

A letter from the secretary of a society formed in Boston, for the purpose of encouraging domestic manufactures, to a citizen, was read—whereupon it was

Resolved, That the committee of correspondence open a communication with the said society upon the objects for which they have mutually been established.

The question being severally put on those resolutions, they were duly agreed to.

Adjourned to meet at this place on the last Monday in November next.

MATTHEW LAWLER, Chairman.

CONDY RAGUET, Secretary.

October 2, 1819.

Circular letter from the committee appointed at a meeting of the citizens of Philadelphia, held October 2, 1819.

CITIZENS,

HAVING been appointed, by a large and respectable meeting of the citizens of the city and county of Philadelphia, a committee to correspond with persons throughout the united states, friendly to the protection of national industry; and also to circulate the proceedings of that meeting, with their memorial to congress; we take the liberty to address you on those subjects.

That distress and embarrassment pervade our country, to an extent probably never before felt here, except during the period that elapsed between the close of the revolutionary war, and the adoption of the federal constitution, cannot be denied. A large proportion of our manufacturing establishments are suspended, and nine-tenths of those that are in operation have greatly curtailed their business. Of the proprietors, many are ruined, and those whom strength of capital, or other advantages, have enabled to maintain the struggle, are encouraged to persevere, merely by the hope of a favourable change in the policy of our government. The situation of a large portion of the workmen is truly deplorable. Numbers of them, with their families, are destitute of the means of subsistence; hundreds are working at laborious employments, for little more than their bare food; and many estimable men and women, with large families, are absolutely driven to beggary. Numerous emigrants, who, under many inconveniences, have come to this country, in the flattering expectation of having full employment in their various arts and trades, and enjoying the benefits of a free government, have been placed in the melancholy alternative of begging or starving. No small proportion of those who had the means, have returned to Europe, with disappointed hopes and broken spirits. Real estate has every where fallen one-third, one-half, and in many cases three-fifths; our bread-stuffs are greatly reduced in price, chiefly in consequence of their exclusion from the markets of that country which has maintained with us as lucrative a commerce as ever existed; a country which purchases our cotton at twenty, twenty-five, or thirty cents per pound, and returns it to us, improved by machinery, at two, three, and four dollars per pound. Our towns and cities, instead of being peopled with an active population, whose productive industry would add to the power and resources of their country, and promote their own happiness, are crowded with hucksters and retailers of the products of the industry of foreign nations, who are so numerous that the business affords them but a sorry subsistence. Of the merchants, who, a few years since, carried on an extensive commerce, some for twenty, thirty, and forty years, one-third, or one-half, are ruined. Our ships are a burden to their owners, whose utmost sagacity can hardly find out profitable employment for one-fourth of them; they are rotting at our wharves, and are often sold for thirty, twenty-five and even twenty per cent. of their cost. The farmers have not escaped the general distress; as thousands of farms, throughout the united states, are under execution; and, whenever brought to auction, are sacrificed, on an average, at half what they would have sold for two or three years since.

In this appalling state of affairs, indifference would be criminal. The sacred duty every citizen owes to his country, imperiously requires exertion. It behoves every man, who has acquired property by honest industry, and finds it, without any fault of his own, melting in his hands, like snow before the sun; who has goods which he cannot sell; real estate which he cannot mortgage or dispose of, to relieve himself; debts due, which his honest debtors are unable to pay, in consequence of the general stagnation; who has industry or talents of any kind, on which he relies for a decent support, but is unable to find employment for them; in a word, it behoves every man, who has a spark of public spirit, or any stake in the general welfare, to probe the festering ulcer of public distress to the bottom, in order to ascertain its real source, and whether a cure is hopeless. If not, to discover what is the remedy, and how, when, and by whom, it ought to be applied.

We are persuaded that it may be laid down as a general rule, which will scarcely admit an exception, that a nation like ours, whose citizens are ingenious, enterprising and industrious; which possesses almost every variety of soil and climate, as well as of vegetable, animal, and mineral productions; enjoys a free and unexpensive government; is unburdened by tithes or grinding taxes; and whose agriculturists generally own the fee simple of the lands they cultivate—cannot, unless by war, famine, or pestilence, suffer such general distress as we experience, without some enormous and radical error in its political economy.

Our vital error, to sum the whole in a few words, is, wasting our wealth and resources to foster and promote the agriculture, arts, manufactures, trade and commerce of other nations, and neglecting to protect those of our own country. Decay, decrepitude, and ruin, have uniformly attended such a system, in all past ages; and, by the eternal laws of the moral world, cannot fail to produce the same effect to the end of time. We have added our experience to that of Spain and Portugal, to prove this theory, and the deplorable state to which nations are reduced by a neglect to protect domestic industry.

Many of our citizens ascribe the whole of our distress to the misconduct of the banks, which, they assert, first by extravagant emissions, and then by pressing on their debtors, have produced the present stagnation.

We do not pretend to defend the banks. There are, in various parts of the country, three or four times more than are necessary. Many of them have been very ill-managed, and have done much mischief. But when the great mass of distress existing in this country, is charged to the account of those institutions, the effect is mistaken for the cause. The support and stay of banks is specie; and, being drained of this in immense quantities, to pay for foreign luxuries, they must, in their own defence, curtail their business, press on their debtors, and produce stagnation and distress. As well may we expect a human being to retain his elasticity and energy, when from a wide orifice in one of his arteries, his life's blood is gushing out, as that banks can accommodate the public, and by loans promote trade and commerce, when they are drained of what may be styled their life's blood, and themselves brought to the verge of ruin.

The first step requisite towards a cure, in every case of malady, physical or political, is to ascertain the nature and extent of the evil. The best mode to accomplish this object, in the present instance, is to appoint suitable committees to investigate the real state of the agriculture, manufactures, trade and commerce of the united states; how far they have advanced, maintained their ground, or declined; and if they have declined, to what cause it is owing.

We therefore earnestly request you will, as early as may be, convene the citizens of your district, in order to appoint committees for the above purpose, and to take their sense on the all-important question, whether we are to continue to lavish the treasures of our country on the manufacturers of Europe and Hindostan, while our own are consigned to ruin, and while the nation is, in consequence, impoverished, to procure articles abroad which we either do not want, or can produce ourselves.

When this nation was in its colonial state, it complained most grievously of the oppression it suffered by the restrictions and prohibitions of the mother country, whereby its industry was restrained and paralized, and its resources drained away. This was one of the most serious evils of its dependent situation. And it cannot be denied, that our present system, which equally paralizes our industry and impoverishes our country, entails on us some of the worst consequences of the colonial state.

The party distinctions that have heretofore so long divided our citizens, distracted our country, and, during the war, endangered its safety, have, in a great degree, subsided. We hope and trust, that henceforward they will assume a new form; and that the question will be between those who, by destroying the productive industry of the country, are disposed virtually to colonize us; and those who are for securing us a real independence. Unless our citizens be wanting to themselves, the friends of the colonial policy will in future, look in vain, on the day of election, for the support of an enlightened body of electors, and have leave to retire to the shades of private life.

The syren song of "*buying cheap goods abroad*," has been re-echoed in our ears with unceasing industry. We have fatally been seduced by it, and led to the brink of destruction. What are the facts of the case?

A few short years have elapsed, since the productions of our soil and our manufactures commanded high prices. Cotton was thirty cents per pound; wheat, two dollars and a half and three dollars per bushel; flour eleven and twelve dollars per barrel; prime beef, eighteen cents per pound; oak wood, seven dollars per cord; merino wool three dollars per pound; superfine cloth, ten or twelve dollars per yard; and all other articles in the same proportion. What was the result? Was the nation miserable or wretched, in consequence of paying these high prices? No: far from it. We enjoyed as high a degree of prosperity as any nation ever did. To this strong and important fact, we hope you will pay due attention. All our labouring people were fully employed. Our capitalists derived liberal profits from their wealth. Splendid manufacturing establishments arose, as it were by magic. The farmers and planters had high prices and ready markets for their produce. And, for a large portion of the time, commerce likewise throve, under those high prices. In a word, the face of the country exhibited an appearance cheering to our friends, and appalling to our enemies.

But now we have fallen on those "*cheap times*," which have been so much wished for, and so highly extolled, by those political economists, whose councils have unfortunately prevailed over the wise and profound system of Alexander Hamilton and Thomas Jefferson.* And what is the result? Has "cheapness" shed those blessings on the nation, that we were led to expect? Can those who have enabled us to buy cheap, congratulate themselves on the result of their plausible but destructive system of political economy? Can we find safety or happiness, in taking them for guides in our future career? No: it is fatally the reverse. Our country exhibits a scene which excites our friends to mourning, and affords matter of exultation and triumph to our enemies.

Wheat is one dollar and ten cents per bushel; flour is six dollars per barrel; cotton eighteen cents, and beef six to ten cents per pound; oak wood, five dollars per cord; merino wool, one dollar per pound; superfine cloth, six or eight dollars per yard. And has this state of things produced the millennium with which its patrons flattered us? Is the house owner, whose rents have fallen from two thousand dollars per annum to twelve hundred or a thousand, compensated by the saving of four dollars per barrel in eight or ten barrels of flour, and three dollars per yard in 2 or 3 suits of clothes, in the year? Where, we ask, and earnestly request a reply from those citizens who, with Adam Smith for their guide, advocate the purchase of goods abroad where they can be had cheap, is the advantage to the workman whose labour was worth five, six, or eight dollars per week,

* "We must place the manufacturer beside the agriculturist." *Jefferson.*
This single line embraces an abstract of political economy, of incalculable importance.

and who is totally bereft of employment, that the price of a barrel of flour is only six dollars, whereas he does not now earn six dollars per month, and has not wherewith to purchase, if it were reduced to three? Is it any consolation to the farmer, who expended a fortune on merino sheep, which the prostration of our woollen manufactures has condemned to the butcher's knife, and who sold his wool for three dollars per pound, of which the price is now one dollar, that he can buy broad cloth at six or eight dollars per yard, instead of ten or twelve? The loss on the fleeces of a dozen sheep, outweighs all the advantages he derives from the destruction of the capital, the prospects, and the happiness of his manufacturing fellow-citizens. What are the mighty benefits derived by the cotton planter, who saves from fifty to a hundred dollars per annum in his clothing and that of his slaves, when, in consequence of the want of a domestic market, he loses ten cents per pound, or a thousand dollars in the year, on his crop of cotton of ten thousand pounds? He saves by cents, and loses by dollars.

While all the energies of the human mind are called into activity, on the question who shall be president, governor, member of congress, representative in the state legislature, sheriff, and even county commissioner, so comparatively uninteresting to the major part of the community, it is lamentable to see what torpor and indifference prevail on this vital topic, which decides the important question, whether Washington, Greene, Montgomery, Warren, Mercer, Laurens, Clinton, Wayne, Stark, Pulaski, and Fayette, fought and bled—whether Franklin, Adams, Hancock, Jefferson, Otis, Randolph, Jay, Lee, Livingston, and Henry, pleaded—in vain. We have no hesitation in saying, this is the real state of the question: for the man whose capital is destroyed, whose talents are rendered useless, whose means of supporting himself are torn up by the roots by a false policy, looks in vain for the boasted blessings of the revolution. He compares his situation with that of the manufacturers of England, France, Austria, and Russia, and envies the fostering care bestowed on them by their monarchs, which forms such a contrast with the destruction to which he is consigned by his fellow-citizens. So far as property is concerned, there is little difference between the citizen of the united states, who is ruined for want of protection, as so many of our manufacturers have been, and the cringing slave, whom the despotism of the dey of Algiers, or the emperor of Morocco plunders of his substance. "Disguise it as we will," it is the same destruction, that robs existence of its charms, although differently administered: for, without property to render life comfortable, life itself is of little value. In one respect, the case of the American citizen appears worse than that of the Algerine slave. The former had every right to calculate on an exemption from the ruin that has blasted his prospects of happiness; whereas, the latter inherited from his ancestors the cruel destiny of holding not merely his property, but his life itself, on the precarious tenure of the mercy of a barbarous tyrant.

On the subject of "taxing the many for the benefit of the few," prolix essays and pamphlets without number have been written, and frothy speeches delivered. This has been adduced as an unanswerable argument against extending any protection to manufactures, further than what is afforded by the duties laid for the purpose of raising a revenue. It is a fertile subject, and would require much detail: but the limits of a letter are already transcended, and we must be brief. We will state a few cases, in which one part of the community is heavily taxed for the benefit of another, without murmur. The beneficial coasting trade has been secured to our merchants, by a total prohibition of foreign rivalship, under penalty of confiscation; whereas there is no manufactured article whatever prohibited. The protection of commerce has probably cost the nation one hundred millions of dollars, for foreign embassies,* fleets, and a wasting war, which commerce alone has rendered necessary. Of all this immense sum, not one cent has been levied for the benefit of manufactures. Foreign spirits are subject to duties from eighty-six to one hundred and twenty per cent., and cheese to about seventy per cent., for the protection of agriculture: while woollen and cotton goods pay only twenty-seven and a half per cent. (except the latter, when below twenty-five cents per yard) manufactures of brass, steel, tin, lead, glass, earthen-ware, pottery, sail-cloth, &c. pay only twenty-two; and linens only sixteen and a half. We do not censure, on the contrary we approve, the protection these duties afford to agriculture. We only deplore the lamentable difference between one hundred and twenty per cent. on gin, to protect domestic peach brandy and whiskey, and twenty-seven and a half per cent. on cottons and woollens!

Should you pursue the plan herein recommended, we respectfully advise that you communicate the result of your enquiries, in the form of a memorial, to the members of your state legisla-

* Some idea may be formed of the enormous expenses incurred for the protection of commerce, from a statement of two facts:—The expenses of foreign intercourse, that is, for ambassadors, chargès des affaires, consuls, agents, bearers of despatches, &c. &c. &c. for twenty four years, have been 10,872,494 dollars, or above 450,000 dollars per annum, (Seybert, 713;) and for the Barbary powers, in twenty years, 2,457,278 dollars, or above 120,000 dollars per annum. (Ibid.) Thus, in these two items, there is *a positive disbursement*, for the protection of commerce, of above half a million of dollars annually: whereas, the government has never paid one dollar, as bounty or premium, to foster, protect, or promote the productive industry employed in manufactures; and has rarely imposed any duties, beyond what were called for by the exigencies of the treasury.

ture, and to your members of congress. Should the former body be impressed with an idea of the correctness of the views we have taken on this mighty subject, they will doubtless use their constitutional right to request your representatives, and instruct your senators, in congress, to exert their influence to have the tariff so far modified, that it shall be no longer possible to say, as, alas! we can now say with perfect truth, that the manufacturers in the most arbitrary governments in Europe are fostered, cherished. and protected from foreign competition; while, under this free government, ours are exposed, by their fellow-citizens in congress, to the competition of the whole world! The appointment of a committee, to correspond with the different towns in your state, would be a highly beneficial measure; and is most earnestly recommended to your attention.

It is to be presumed. that our representatives in congress are disposed to do their duty, and only require to be well informed on the subject, to induce them to pursue a correct course. We therefore respectfully suggest to you. to take into serious consideration the propriety of an application to congress, from the manufacturers of the united states, to be heard by counsel at their bar. The most salutary consequences have resulted from this procedure in Great Britain; and it could not fail to produce consequences equally salutary here; as it must elicit such a mass of information as would destroy the deleterious prejudices, whose operation our country has so much reason to deplore.

There is one point to which we invite your serious attention, as of paramount importance. Notwithstanding the ruin that has overtaken so large a portion of our manufactures and manufacturers, there are some citizens, with immense capitals, engaged in the cotton branch particularly, who deprecate the idea of any further protection, and have impressed on the minds of the constituted authorities, that the present duties are amply adequate. This phenomenon in trade—a renunciation of further aid from government, of which the world has never hitherto had a parallel case—must arise from such a pure spirit of patriotism, as would reflect honour on Greece and Rome, in the most brilliant period of their history, or from some motive of a very opposite character. It has been successfully used by the friends of the existing system, as an irresistible argument against the host of petitioners, who have besought additional protection. As it has been thus employed, it becomes a duty to investigate it thoroughly, and ascertain, as far as may be practicable, the source from whence it springs. It is asserted, that the proprietors of those establishments prefer, as the least of two evils, encountering the desultory competition of foreigners, whose goods are often of inferior quality, to the steady and unceasing rivalship of a vast number of their fellow-citizens, who, in the event of a full protection to manufactures, would enter the lists, and divide the market with them. On this delicate point we cannot pretend to decide : we merely present it to view for public consideration.

We annex a few queries, which we request you will circulate, for the purpose of collecting the necessery information for forming your memorial.

To Farmers and Planters.

If manufacturing establishments have been erected in your neighbourhood, what consequences have they had upon agriculture?

What number of merino sheep were imported into your district—their first cost—the number killed—the causes of their being killed—their present value—the price of wool, before, during, and since the war?

To Manufacturers.

How many workmen did you employ in 1816? How many do you employ at present? What was and is the average of the wages at each period?

What number of manufacturing establishments were in operation in your neighbourhood in 1816? How many of them are wholly suspended? What have they cost? What is the loss sustained on them?

What is the cause of the decay of manufactures in your vicinity?

WILLIAM DUANE,
MATHEW CAREY,
SETH CRAIGE,
HENRY HORN,
JOSIAH RANDALL,
WILLIAM YOUNG.

Committee of Correspondence, appointed by a town meeting of the citizens of the City and County of Philad.—Oct. 4, 1819.

Philadelphia, Oct. 13, 1819.

MEMORIAL.

To the senate and house of representatives of the united states: the memorial of the Pennsylvania society for the encouragement of American manufactures,

RESPECTFULLY SHEWETH—

That your memorialists have read with the deepest regret, two remonstrances presented to your honourable houses, from agricultural societies in the state of Virginia, deprecating your interposition in favour of the manufacturing part of the community.

These documents, containing sundry allegations injurious to your memorialists, and resting, as shall be made to appear, on an unsound basis, require a detailed investigation, to which we respectfully request your attention.

We must premise, that we should have hoped that the ruin of so many of the manufacturers—the depressed state of those who have hitherto escaped the situation in which their brethren have been involved—and the distresses of that class whose sole dependence is on their labour—would have prevented this unkind interference, calculated to continue their sufferings ; that the generous sympathy which their situation ought to have excited in the breasts of their fellow-citizens—embarked in one common cause, would have averted this hostility, even had all the allegations of the remonstrances been irrefragable ; whereas, we hope to prove, that such as are of any importance, are easily susceptible of refutation. The disappointment fills us with surprize and regret—and is ill calculated to foster those kind regards and attachments which ought to subsist among members of the same community, and which we have always cherished towards our agricultural fellow citizens.

But our appeal and that of our brethren has not been made to the generosity or compassion of our fellow citizens. We appeal to their honour—to their justice. We ask, at length, after a lapse of thirty years, in which the government has existed, for a share of that protection so bountifully bestowed upon commerce, and which agriculture, as will appear, has abundantly enjoyed.

The allegations of the agricultural societies are principally confined to three points—

1. The extortions said to have been committed by manufacturers during the war.

2. The danger and oppression of monopolies, exclusive privileges, &c.

3. The injustice of affording protection to manufactures, when agriculture disclaims all protection.

There are sundry minor points, which we shall pass over, in order to avoid prolixity.

The charge of extortion is couched in these words :—

" We submit respectfully to your wisdom, the impolicy of " subjecting so large a portion of your fellow citizens to *such* " *unreasonable cupidity*—of laying them at the mercy of an as" sociation, who, competition being removed, *will no longer* " *consider the intrinsic value of an article, or what price would* " *afford a fair profit to the manufacturer, but how much the*

"*necessities of the consumer would enable them to extort. Of*
"*this spirit we had a sufficient specimen, during our late con-*
"*test with Great Britain.*"

This uncharitable accusation we hope to prove wholly destitute of foundation. The article on which it chiefly rests is superfine broad cloth, which was raised from eight or nine dollars, the price before the war, to twelve. thirteen, and fourteen, during the war. The reasoning applicable to this case, applies with equal force to all the others.

All doubt of the injustice of this allegation will be laid at rest forever by the simple fact, that merino wool, the raw material of that cloth, which, before and shortly after the commencement of the war, was sold at seventy-five cents per lb. was raised during the war to three dollars, an advance of three hundred per cent.; so that there was less profit per cent. on the capital employed by the manufacturer at the high prices of the cloth, so much the subject of complaint, than at the former moderate prices.

We trust that this strong fact, which can be judicially proved at the bar of your houses, will prevent any man of honour or candour, as he values his reputation, from ever again repeating so unfounded an accusation.

But if we have never retorted this charge against our accusers—if we have forborne recrimination—it has not been for want of materials, but from an unwillingness to cherish an unkind and unfriendly spirit towards our fellow citizens. And now, notwithstanding the repeated and wanton provocations we have received, we resort to the measure with pain. We should gladly have buried in oblivion all our causes of complaint, and cherished a kind and fraternal spirit, in the hope of exciting a suitable reciprocation. But the style and manner of the accusations against us, their unceasing repetition, the hostile disposition they display, and the ruinous consequences they are calculated to produce on the general welfare of the nation, render it a duty to ourselves, to our country, and to the cause of truth, to prove that our accusers are far from invulnerable in this point, and are under high obligations to us for past forbearance.

In the year 1788, flour was four dollars per barrel in our sea ports; which was regarded as a fair and liberal price. In the next year the demand for the supply of France took place, and this article was raised to five and six dollars; from year to year afterwards, it rose to ten. twelve, and fourteen dollars; and probably it averaged during the whole of the French revolution, above ten. We submit to a candid world, whether this fact does not more completely establish the charge of "*extortion*," than the rise of broad cloth from eight or nine to fourteen dollars, (or even to thirty, had it taken place,) when the raw material rose from seventy-five cents to three dollars per pound? And whether the rise on the wool itself is not incomparably more "*extortionate*" than that on the broad cloth? The latter was not only justifiable, but imperiously necessary, by the rise which we have stated on the raw material. But, for the rise on wool or flour, no such reason existed. It did not proceed from any advance "*in the intrinsic value of the article*," to borrow the words of the Petersburg remonstrance, "*nor from a consideration of what price would afford a fair profit to the*" farmers: "*but how much the necessities of the consumers enabled them to extort.*"

At the same period, 1788 butter was ten cents per lb.—beef and pork, five cents; tobacco, three or four; and all other agricultural articles in the same proportion. They have since been raised from one to two hundred per cent. above those prices.—Yet we have never alleged against the farmers or planters the odious charge of "*extortion*," at which they would have revolted. Have they, we ask, a right to raise their prices one or two hundred per cent. at pleasure, when the demand warrants it, without "*extortion*"—and yet to wound the feelings, and injure the characters of their fellow citizens, by the odious imputation of "*extortion*," when the advance of the raw material by themselves renders a rise of manufactures necessary? If this be a chartered privilege, we wish to know whence it is derived, and by what tenure it is held. Seriously, we presume this to be the strongest illustration of the parable of the beam and the mote that the variegated history of mankind presents.

Flour is now four dollars and seventy-five cents per barrel on the sea board. Should war or famine take place in Europe, the price would be immediately raised, one, two, three, four, or five dollars per barrel. And in proportion to the intensity of the distress would be the tax levied on the consumers in this country. There are about three millions of white people in the united states not engaged in agriculture, who consume on an average two barrels of flour per annum. A rise of three dollars, which might take place immediately, in case of a very extraordinary demand, would amount on this article to a gain of 18,000,000 of dollars, levied by the farmers on the rest of the community during the ensuing year, exclusive of probably an equal amount on all other agricultural productions, liable to a proportionate advance of price. And this is not a mere hypothesis of what may occur. It is the history of the last thirty years, and of the immense prices, again to borrow the vituperant language of the remonstrance, which "*the necessities of the consumers have enabled*" the farmers "*to extort.*"

Nothing but the endless, the irritating misrepresentations we have experienced, would induce us to retort this strong language upon our accusers.

The United Agricultural Societies of Virginia prefer a claim to a high degree of superiority over the other classes of the community, which calls for observation. They state that—

"In every nation with whose internal affairs we are familiarly acquainted, *the landed interest has been proverbial for their liberality in comparison with any other class.*"

It is unfortunate that this assumption of *liberality* appears in an instrument, the direct object of which is to bar the door to the relief of their fellow citizens, and to consign them and their families to that wretchedness and ruin which has befallen so many of their brethren! Before this claim to "*proverbial liberality*" can be admitted, proofs must be adduced different from the document in which it is asserted. The contrast between this strong assumption and the object of the remonstrance, though very striking, is not uncommon. Every day's experience so strongly proves the extreme discrepancy between profession and practice, that no illustration can be necessary.

The Societies distinctly hold forth to the world, that agriculture neither has been, nor is, secured by "*protecting duties.*"—They state—

"We solicit not the fostering care or patronage of the legislature to alleviate by bounties, *monopolies*, or *protecting duties*, calamities in their nature as inevitable, as they are incurable by legislative interposition."

The Fredericsburg Society also states—

"*We ask no tax upon manufacturers for our benefit.* Neither do we ask any thing of government to enable us to cultivate the soil as we could wish."

The high character of the members of those societies forbids the supposition, that this was an intentional misstatement. We are therefore inexpressibly astonished at the utter unacquaintance with the real state of the case, betrayed in these quotations, which evinces how superficially these gentlemen studied the subject on which they undertook to interpose to prevent the success of our applications for relief.

The view they present is so far from fact, that it is the reverse of fact. The average of duties on such agricultural productions as are usually imported into this country, has been, from the commencement of the government, far higher than those on manufactures.

We will state the case at two periods, remote from each other, viz. 1789 and 1820. The intermediate space exhibits the same features.

In the former period, cheese was subject to a duty equal to *fifty-seven per cent*; indigo, *sixteen*; snuff, *ninety*; manufactured tobacco, *one hundred*;* coals, *fifteen*; hemp and cotton, *twelve*; whereas seven-eighths of all the manufactures imported, including cottons, woollens, and iron, were subject to only *five per cent.* This, we presume, is full proof of the inequality of the system of legislation with which the government commenced, and of the care with which the agriculturists, who formed the great mass of the national legislature, guarded their own interests.

Hemp at present is subject to a duty equivalent to *twenty-six per cent.*; cotton, *thirty*‡; cheese, *ninety*; spirits, *eighty*; snuff, *seventy-five*; manufactured tobacco, *one hundred*; coals, *thirty-eight and a half*; sugar, *thirty-seven and a half*; and potatoes, *fifteen*; averaging *fifty-eight per cent.* Few other articles, the product of the earth are imported. But they are all, except three or four, subject to fifteen per cent.

Of the manufactures imported in the year 1818, one twenty-fifth part paid a duty of *seven and a half* per cent.; one-third *fifteen*; one-sixth, *twenty*; two-fifths, *twenty-five*; and one-twenty-fifth part, *thirty* per cent.†

On this striking contrast, which affords no proof of "the proverbial liberality" of the landed interest, we offer but a single comment. It adds one to the numerous melancholy instances with which history abounds, that where one particular interest predominates in a legislative body, the others rarely experience impartial justice. We will notice only one article, which places in a strong point of light the different degrees of protection experienced by agriculture and manufactures. Cotton, a raw material, is subject to a duty of thirty per cent ‡—and the freight is about the same. The cotton planter has therefore a protection of sixty per cent.; whereas fine muslins and cambrics pay but twenty-sev-

* The prohibitory duties on snuff and manufactured tobacco, were imposed in 1789, with a view to secure the exclusive market of the united states for our tobacco planters. This object was expressly avowed in Congress, and they completely answered this purpose. To suppose that a duty of one hundred per cent. was imposed on manufactured tobacco, and ninety per cent. on snuff, for the benefit of the manufacturers of these articles, while manufactures of cotton, wool, iron, lead, brass and tin were dutied at five per cent, without any regard to the manufacturers of those articles, is really too gross for the most Bœotian capacity.

† This is an error. Cotton, in the East Indies, has been sold for years at six cents per lb. and even lower. It therefore appears the cotton planters were secured by a protecting duty of fifty per cent.

‡ At 7½	$2,387,693
15	19,455,525
20	9,524,531
25	24,804,188
30	2,633,637
	$58,805,574

on and a half per cent. duty—and the freight is not more than one or two per cent. Thus the planter, who disclaims the idea of "protection," has an advantage over his manufacturing fellow-citizens, of above thirty per cent., independent of the immense difference between the protection necessary for articles produced by agriculture and those by machinery. It may be assumed without danger of contradiction, that cotton would be better protected by a duty of twenty per cent., than cambrics or muslins by sixty or seventy. We do not find that the tariff of any other country whatever presents such an extraordinary feature.

Great emphasis is laid by the agricultural societies on the danger of "monopolies granted to one class or order, at the expense of another."

This forms a fertile theme, on which they descant very freely —They remonstrate against

"Unequal and partial taxes—awarding *exclusive privileges* "—or sustaining the manufacturers in the enjoyment of *oppressive monopolies, which are ultimately to grind us and our* "*children after us to dust and ashes*."

"In this way alone, can the benefits of good government be "equalized among the various orders and classes of society, "the prosperity and happiness of which depend not upon *im*"*munities*, *privileges*, *and monopolies*, *granted to one* class or "order at the expense of another" &c.

We are constrained to state, that the want of due consideration which prevails throughout the remonstrances, is here very conspicuous. Monopoly, according to Johnson, means "the exclusive privilege of selling any thing." And a monopolist, according to the same authority, is "one who by engrossing or by patent, obtains the sole power or privilege of vending any commodity." There is not, therefore, such a thing or person, in this country, as a monopoly or monopolist: nor, while our present constitution exists, can there be a monopoly. For suppose manufactures of wool, cotton, iron, and leather were altogether prohibited, those branches would be open to the admission, and consequently to the competition, of any part of the community —to farmers, as well as others, and even to the capitalists from any and every part of Europe, if they judged proper to embark in them. Where then is the monopoly?

While the agricultural societies were thus denouncing what they thought proper to brand with the odious term, "*monopoly*," they did not reflect that they were themselves far more liable to the accusation, than those against whom they preferred it. The great mass of the manufactured articles purchased by the farmers and planters of the southern states, and probably one-half of what are purchased by those in the others, are imported.—Whereas, the manufacturers of the united states have not consumed of foreign articles of food and drink, since the organization of the general government, two per cent.

Thus while there has been an incessant clamour against "*the monopoly*" of the manufacturers, whose market is open to, and engrossed by, rivals from half the nations of Europe, it appears that the farmers and planters have what they term "*a monopoly;*" which, however, is only an exclusive supply of the home market.

It may be doubted whether a more extraordinary case is on record.

We shall conclude our observations on those memorials with one further extract—

"To guard," the Fredericsburg Society observes, "against "the possibility of misapprehension, we take this occasion to "say, that *we are incapable of feeling any thing like enmity* "*against manufacturers or any other useful description of citi-* "*zens:* but heartily wish them all the success to which their "skill and industry may entitle them, in whatever way ap- "plied."

This declaration would have been more acceptable, and claimed our gratitude, had it not accompanied an attempt on the part of those who make it, to do us all the injury in their power to inflict—to prevent a compliance with our just claims—and to perpetuate our present intolerable sufferings.

Your memorialists regret to find that the same adverse spirit towards them that prevails among these small bodies of their agricultural fellow-citizens, has been excited among a portion of the mercantile class. They request your favourable hearing of a few remarks on the memorial of the merchants of Salem on this subject. It

"Calls the attention of congress, to measures that have "been recently proposed and apparently approved, for the "purpose of *prohibiting the importation of foreign woollen and* "*cotton goods.*"

Your memorialists are constrained to state that this view is very uncandid. They never did contemplate "a prohibition of foreign cotton and woollen goods" generally. There is not a sane man in the country, who, if he had the power, would enact a total exclusion. A large portion of those goods is not, and, for a long time to come, cannot be, manufactured in this country, and therefore must be imported. Your memorialists deprecate and solemnly protest against the influence of a system which has been heretofore too successfully pursued, that is, defeating their fair and legitimate objects, by ascribing to them views, which they wholly disclaim. Of this unfair system, their dearest interests have been frequently the victims. Were it necessary, they could produce numerous instances, of early and recent date.

"If we are not willing to receive foreign manufactures, we "cannot reasonably suppose that foreign nations will receive "our raw materials."

"We cannot force them to become buyers, when *they are* "*not sellers*—or to consume our cottons, when they cannot "pay the price in their own fabrics."

"We cannot expect them to carry on a ruinous trade, when "*the profit is all on our side*."

These paragraphs are liable to the exceptions urged against the preceding one. They assume the extraordinary idea, which insanity alone could harbour, that importation is expected to be wholly prohibited. All that is necessary for the restoration of the country, and for the prosperity of the manufacturers, is such a modification of the tariff, as will reduce our imports within the limits of our exports—and prevent our manufactures and manufacturers from being overwhelmed by the inordinate inundation of foreign fabrics.

"While the manufacturers are left free to engage in their "own peculiar pursuits, enjoying, in common with others, a "reasonable protection from the government, the memorialists "trust it is no undue claim on their part to plead for the free"dom of commerce also, as the natural ally of agriculture and "naval greatness."

There is an assumption here, of "*freedom for the manufacturers*," which is not warranted by the fact. When their business is annihilated, and themselves ruined by the immoderate introduction of foreign merchandize, as has occurred to too many of them, can it be said that they "*are free to engage in their own peculiar pursuits?*" We will render this plain by applying it to the case of the merchants. The vessels employed in the coasting trade for thirty years, have averaged about 400,000 tons annually. Were foreign vessels allowed to engage in that trade, to the amount of 300,000 tons, would it not be a mockery, were the merchants informed, while their ships were rotting at the wharves, and themselves reduced to bankruptcy, that "*they were free to engage in their own peculiar pursuits?*" And is it not a perfectly analogous case, when the manufacturers are ruined, and their machinery rotting and rusting, through the extravagant influx of foreign articles, to be gravely told, that they are "free to engage in their own peculiar pursuits?"

"It is a sound political maxim, that *the more free trade is*, "and the more widely it circulates, the more sure will be its "prosperity. *Every restriction which is not indispensable* "*for the purposes of revenue, is a shoal, which will impede its* "*progress, and not unfrequently jeopard its security.*"

The doctrine here advanced, on the broad and unqualified scale on which it is predicated, is unsound, and contrary to the practice of the most prosperous states, and to the principles of the wisest statesmen. Can the prosperity of trade be promoted by the free introduction of foreign luxuries which destroy the industry of our own citizens? Has it been promoted by the immoderate quantities of goods imported into this country, whereby its circulating medium has been exhausted and an enormous debt contracted for articles which our own citizens could have supplied?

To test this plausible maxim, which has done infinite injury to this country, we will, as in the former case, apply it to the merchants themselves. The use of foreign vessels is almost virtually prohibited in this country, by "*restrictions not indispensable for the purposes of revenue.*" Suppose these "restrictions" were removed, and that foreign vessels were entitled to the same privileges as our own, what would be the consequence? They would be employed here in large numbers, to the ruin of the merchants and ship-builders. Would they not, in that case, as zealously contend against the maxim as they now uphold it? And can there be any just reason why the manufacturer, entitled to equal rights with the merchant, should be ruined by foreign rivals, and the merchant secured against this rivalship? In the scales of impartial justice, the rights of each ought to have equal weight.

Although the merchants of Salem invoke congress in such emphatical terms, to support that "freedom of trade" which impoverishes the nation, and, by exposing their manufacturing fellow citizens to the competition of rivals in every quarter of the world, has ruined so large a portion of them, there is scarcely a session in which the mercantile interest does not memorialize congress for protection against foreign competition. On this conduct, so partial to themselves, and so excessively unkind to us, we dare not trust ourselves to comment.

It would extend this memorial to an unreasonable length, if we particularized one-half of the "*restrictions*" of foreign commerce in favour of our merchants. We shall confine ourselves to a few prominent cases, to prove that this maxim, now so zealously urged, has had no weight when the interests of that class were at stake; and that the "restrictions" on foreign commerce which they succeeded in obtaining, were not only "not indispensable for the purposes of revenue," but in many cases pernicious to it.

When the competition of foreign merchants in the coasting

trade was wisely destroyed in the very outset of the government by a heavy prohibitory tonnage duty, and afterwards by positive prohibition. was this measure "*indispensable for the purposes of revenue?*" Was it not, according to the Salem memorial, "*a shoal to impede the progress of trade?*"

When, in the first session of congress, foreign merchants were excluded from the China trade, by extra duties on teas imported in foreign vessels, averaging one hundred and seven per cent., were they "*necessary for the purposes of revenue?*" Did they not rather impair the revenue?

When, more recently, an extra tonnage duty of two dollars per ton was imposed on foreign vessels arriving from ports which American vessels were not allowed to enter, was this "*necessary for the purposes of revenue?*" Where then was the alarm about "*shoals to impede the progress of trade?*"

Was the act prohibiting the introduction of plaster of Paris, in foreign vessels, "*necessary for the purposes of revenue?*" or was it not rather "*a shoal to impede the progress of trade?*"

Was the act passed in a late session of congress, of which the object was to coerce the British nation to abandon the chief feature of their navigation act, which they prize so highly "*necessary for the purposes of revenue?*" Has it not, on the contrary, injuriously affected revenue and agriculture?

And in fine, we ask, and hope for a fair and explicit answer, whether the strong "*restrictions*" now contemplated against both Great Britain and France, are "*necessary for the purposes of revenue?*" Whether they are not, like the former, "*shoals to jeopard*" agriculture and "*revenue?*"

The acts above alluded to, and a great variety of others which abound in our statute book, do not require much comment.—They speak a language not to be misunderstood. It appears, and cannot fail to astonish your honourable houses, that while the merchants have, from the commencement of the government, applied for, and been favoured with, "restrictions," not only "*not necessary for the purposes of revenue*" but in many cases pernicious to it, a portion of them now use all their energies to defeat the reasonable objects of your memorialists, and consign them to destruction, on the ground that the "restrictions" contemplated are "*not necessary for the purposes of revenue.*"

"One sacrifice is to be demanded after another—one prohi-"bition heaped upon another, until all the sources of foreign "commerce are dried up; and domestic manufactures, sus-"tained by *enormous bounties*, absorb the whole monied capi-"tal of the nation."

It ill becomes the advocates of a commerce, "sustained by *enormous bounties*" in the shape of tributes to Barbary powers; foreign intercourse; a most oppressive naval expenditure, amounting for the current year, to 3,500,000 dollars; a commerce which has entailed on the nation a war debt of nearly 80,000,000 of dollars; to hold this language, respecting manufactures, on which the *government has never expended a single cent* in thirty years. And what, we ask, has called forth this emphatical denunciation of manufactures? Merely a request, on the part of the manufacturers, of a duty of forty or fifty per cent.* on cottons, woollens, iron, and some other articles, in order to enable our citizens to compete with the half-starved and half-clothed workmen of foreign nations. This is the tremendous danger which is '*to dry up all the sources of foreign commerce*," and "*absorb all the monied capital of the nation!*"

We cannot forbear to state, that it is no proof of the intrinsic goodness of a cause, when its advocates are reduced to the necessity of drawing high-coloured and extravagant portraits of dangers, which have no existence but in their own heated imaginations.

"It is not a little remarkable, that these attempts are not "only repugnant to those maxims of free trade, which the uni-"ted states have hitherto so forcibly and perseveringly con-"tended for, as the sure foundation of national prosperity, but "they are pressed upon us at a moment, when *the statesmen* "*of the old world, in admiration of the success of our policy,* "*are relaxing the rigour of their own systems!* and yielding "themselves to the rational doctrine, that national wealth is "best promoted by *a free interchange of commodities, upon* "*principles of perfect reciprocity.*"

It is painful to us to state, that this entire paragraph rests on untenable ground. We look in vain for the evidences of "*the national prosperity*," on which the merchants predicate their reasonings. Where are those evidences to be found? Is it in the decay and destruction of so large a portion of the national industry? If this be a sign of "*national prosperity*," then is this nation prosperous to a degree unexampled in its annals, except in the interval between the close of the revolutionary war and the establishment of the present form of government. Is it in the decline of commerce and navigation? Is it in the bankruptcy of so large a portion of the merchants, traders, and manufacturers of the country? Is it in the violent measure which the legislatures of four or five of the states have adopted for arresting the course of justice, and suspending the collection of debts? Is it in the augmentation of poor rates—the increase of mendicants and soup houses? Is it in the failure of revenue to the enormous amount of five millions of dollars for the present year? Is it in the exclusion of one of our chief staples from

* This was a great error. The duty contemplated on woollens and fine cottons was only thirty-three per cent.

the British markets, and the very great depreciation of the price of the rest? Is it, in a word, in that state of affairs, justly characterised in a recent report, by the secretary of state, in these strong terms:—

"But few examples have occurred, of distress so general, "and so severe, as that which has been exhibited in the united "states."

These, alas! are no symptoms of "*national prosperity*"—and of "*the success of our policy*," which, we are told, and with a grave and sober air, as if the assertion were irrefragable, excites "*the admiration of the statesmen of the old world!!!*"

We look around in vain, we repeat, for this "*national prosperity*," which sounds so captivatingly. And we look equally in vain for "*the admiration of the statesmen of the old world*," of "*the success of our policy*," which is brought forward to tickle our national vanity. It would be in vain to seek for the "success of a policy," which, after twenty years of a most extensive commerce, in which we received exorbitant prices for all our staples, has, in five years of profound peace, with abundant harvests, and wholly free from any natural calamity, reduced an intelligent, industrious, active population, possessed of almost every possible advantage of soil and climate, with water power unequalled in the world, from a towering state of prosperity, to its present lamentable situation—a situation, which, notwithstanding "*the admiration of the statesmen of the old world*," emphatically warns us to change a policy, which built our prosperity not on the solid basis of national industry, but on the wretched foundation of foreign wars and famines, and which has rendered us dependent on foreign nations even for the chief part of the clothes we wear, although possessed of the most valuable raw material in the world, to an extent commensurate with the demand of nearly half the globe.

But if we look in vain for this "*national prosperity*," for "*the success of our policy*," and for "*the admiration of the statesmen of the old world*," we look equally in vain for "*the relaxation of the rigour of their systems.*" When this memorial was drafted, early in January last, and likewise when it was presented to congress, on the thirty-first of that month, there was not before the American nation a trace of such relaxation in any part of Europe whatever. The assumption, therefore, on which so much of the argument of the memorial is predicated, was unwarranted by fact.

The countries with which the chief part of our intercourse is carried on, are Great Britain and France. In the three last years, of our domestic exports, amounting to 192,000,000 of dollars, there were 141,000,000 exported to these two countries; whereas, to Russia, Sweden, Denmark, Norway, Prussia, the

Hanse towns, and all the ports of Germany, we only exported 11.000,000 of dollars. Of course, we are little interested in the commercial arrangements of those nations.

The signers of the Salem memorial are called upon to produce any symptom in Great Britain or France, of this very extraordinary "*admiration*" or its effects. Our policy is truly a subject of "*admiration*" for the desolation it has produced, as hurricanes and tornadoes are—but not of imitation to any wise nation. No symptoms of such imitation can be found. On the contrary, the cords are every day drawn tighter. So far as respects France, the Edinburgh Review, for July, 1819, informs us that—

> "The anti-commercial system of the ex-emperor, instead of "being modified or repealed, has, in fact, been adopted in all "its extent, by his legitimate successors; and *in their hands* "*has become doubly efficient*."

No alteration has taken place since that period. We are therefore warranted to state that the "*admiration*" and imitation of "*the success of our policy*" which form so capital an item in the Salem memorial, cannot be substantiated in France. And the rigorous acts recently passed, and now contemplated by this government, to counteract the British restrictive commercial policy, prove that that nation in like manner does not fall within the description of the Salem memorial, as excited to "*admiration*" or imitation of "*our policy*" by its wonderful "*success*."

When the Salem merchants laid down the maxim that "national wealth is best promoted by a *free interchange of commodities, upon principles of perfect reciprocrity*," did they mean to convey the idea, that the united states enjoy such a "*free interchange?*" It cannot be. There is no nation in the world which carries on commerce more completely destitute of "*perfect reciprocity*."

Our ports are open to the manufactures of all the world.—Whereas most of the ports of Europe, and all those of the colonies of that quarter of the globe, are shut against ours. This is a practical commentary on the "*perfect reciprocity*" which the Salem memorial insinuates we enjoy. Again:

We exchange necessaries of life and raw materials in the most rude state, for manufactures elaborated with the last finish of human industry and skill: thus in every case, we exchange the labour of two or three, and in many that of ten, twenty, and thirty persons for one. Our cotton is returned to us in a manufactured state, at an average of five fold its original cost.

It is this species of one-sided "perfect reciprocrity" which has, according to the secretary of the treasury, produced "*a distress so general and severe*" that "*few examples*" of equal intensity "*have occurred*," and which has rendered the situation of the united states an object of regret and sympathy for our friends, and of exultation for our enemies. It is full time for the guardians of the nation's rights to secure it something like "*reciprocity*" in its intercourse with the rest of the world.

We cannot close this memorial, without expressing our astonishment and regret, that an idea could ever have prevailed, of the existence of hostility between the interests of agriculture and manufactures; whereas, the great mass of the productions of the former derive their chief value from the market afforded by the latter. The hides, the skins, the furs, the wool, a large portion of the cotton, the timber, the coals, the lead, the iron, the pitch, the tar, the turpentine, the tallow, the indigo, the flax, of the farmer, find a ready sale among the manufacturers, who likewise consume of provisions one thousand per cent. more than the amount exported to all the world in the most flourishing period of our history.

Your memorialists are gratified to find that the opposition to their just requests has been confined to a small portion of the two great classes of their fellow citizens.

In submitting the premises to the most serious attention of your honourable houses, your memorialists hope that you will make such a modification of the tariff, as will secure to all persons interested in agriculture, manufactures, and commerce, a full and equal share of protection.

Philadelphia, April 3d, 1820.

THE

NEW OLIVE BRANCH:

OR,

AN ATTEMPT TO ESTABLISH AN IDENTITY OF INTEREST

BETWEEN

AGRICULTURE, MANUFACTURES, AND COMMERCE;

AND TO PROVE,

THAT A LARGE PORTION OF THE MANUFACTURING INDUSTRY OF THIS NATION HAS BEEN SACRIFICED TO COMMERCE; AND THAT COMMERCE HAS SUFFERED BY THIS POLICY NEARLY AS MUCH AS MANUFACTURES.

BY M. CAREY,

AUTHOR OF THE POLITICAL OLIVE BRANCH, VINDICIÆ HIBERNICÆ, &C. &C.

SECOND EDITION.

"*But few examples have occurred of distress so general and so severe as that "which has been exhibited in the united states.*"—Report of the Secretary of the Treasury.

"If any thing can prevent the consummation of public ruin, it can only be *new "councils; a sincere change, from a sincere conviction of past errors.*"—Chatham.

"*Men will sooner live prosperously under the worst government, than starve under "the best.*"—Postlethwait's Dictionary.

"A merchant may have a distinct interest from that of his country. He may "thrive by a trade that will prove her ruin."—*British Merchant.*

"Manufactures are now as necessary to our independence as to our comfort."
Jefferson.

"It is the interest of the community, with a view to eventual and permanent "economy, *to encourage the growth of manufactures.*"—Hamilton.

PHILADELPHIA:
M. CAREY & SONS.
1821.

TO THOSE

CITIZENS OF THE UNITED STATES,

WHOSE EXPANDED VIEWS

EMBRACE THE KINDRED INTERESTS

OF

AGRICULTURE, MANUFACTURES, AND COMMERCE;

WHO BELIEVE THAT

NATIONAL INDUSTRY

IS THE ONLY LEGITIMATE SOURCE OF

NATIONAL WEALTH AND PROSPERITY;

WITH DR. FRANKLIN,

"THAT INDUSTRY IN ALL SHAPES, IN ALL INSTANCES, AND BY ALL
"MEANS, SHOULD BE PROMOTED;"

WITH THOMAS JEFFERSON,

"THAT MANUFACTURES ARE NOW AS NECESSARY TO OUR INDEPENDENCE
"AS OUR COMFORT;"

WITH ALEXANDER HAMILTON,

"THAT THE INDEPENDENCE AND SECURITY OF A COUNTRY ARE
"MATERIALLY CONNECTED WITH THE PROSPERITY OF
ITS MANUFACTURES;"

WHO ARE OPPOSED TO THE POLICY OF

LAVISHING THE WEALTH OF THE NATION TO SUPPORT FOREIGN GOVERNMENTS AND FOREIGN MANUFACTURERS,

AND IMPOVERISHING

OUR OWN COUNTRY AND OUR FELLOW CITIZENS;

WHO HOLD THE SOUND DOCTRINE,

THAT NATIONS, LIKE INDIVIDUALS, MUST SUFFER DISTRESS AND MISERY WHEN THEIR EXPENSES EXCEED THEIR INCOME;

AND THAT A POLICY

WHICH CONVERTS A LARGE PORTION OF OUR CITIZENS INTO HUCKSTERS AND RETAILERS OF FOREIGN PRODUCTIONS,

INSTEAD OF

PRODUCERS FOR HOME CONSUMPTION

IS RADICALLY UNSOUND

AND FINALLY, THAT

THE RUINOUS EXPERIMENT WE HAVE MADE OF OUR PRESENT SYSTEM FOR FIVE YEARS,

POINTS OUT, "WITH A PENCIL OF LIGHT,"

THE IMPORTANT TRUTH, PUT ON RECORD BY LORD CHATHAM,

"THAT IF ANY THING CAN PREVENT THE CONSUMMATION OF
"PUBLIC RUIN, IT CAN ONLY BE NEW COUNCILS;
"A SINCERE CHANGE, FROM A SINCERE
"CONVICTION OF ERROR,"

THIS WORK

IS RESPECTFULLY DEDICATED,

BY THE AUTHOR.

March 17, 1820.

CONTENTS.

INTRODUCTION.

THIS work may be considered as a second edition, much enlarged and improved, of the Three Letters to Mr Garnett, recently published; as it contains nearly the whole of the matter of those letters.

It has been written with a thorough conviction, that there is a complete identity of interest between agriculture, manufactures, and commerce; that when any one of them suffers material injury, the others largely partake of it; and that a great proportion of the distress of this country has arisen from the erroneous views of our statesmen on the subject of manufactures, which have been cramped and stunted, and finally in part annihilated in the most important branches, for want of that fostering care bestowed on them in England for ages, and recently in France in the most exemplary manner, and with the most beneficial effect.

I have, therefore, endeavoured to prove—

1. That the policy pursued by this nation in its tariff, from the commencement of its career, has been radically wrong.

2. That this tariff has sacrificed a large portion of the national industry; to the incalculable injury of the united states, and to the immense advantage of the manufacturing nations of Europe.

3. That its tendency has been to render us tributary to those nations—converting a large portion of our population into hucksters and retailers of their productions, instead of producers for our own consumption; and rendering the great mass of the remainder consumers of those productions—thus prodigally lavishing our wealth to support foreign manufacturers and foreign governments—and impoverishing the nation to an alarming degree.

4. That this system has had the obvious and pernicious effect of narrowing the field for the exercise of native industry and talent—and consequently of crouding immoderately those professions that were open to the national enterprize. From this source has arisen the great number of merchants, so far beyond what was required by the commerce of the country.

5. I have hence deduced the ruin of so large a proportion of that class. It was a necessary consequence of the over-driven

spirit of competition. This may be exemplified in every department of human industry. In a town which would support two lawyers, doctors, or storekeepers genteely, three would barely make a living, and four be ruined. And finally—

6. I have endeavoured to shew, that a due degree of protection to manufactures would have been highly serviceable to agriculture and commerce.

These views of our affairs are presented to the public with a sincere belief of their soundness. But, like other theorists, I may have deluded myself. However, whether right or wrong, the discussion cannot fail to prove useful—as it will shed light on the most important subject that can occupy the public attention—the means of promoting individual happiness, and national "wealth, power, and resources"—of removing the present intolerable evils, of which the secretary of the treasury, in his report of the 21st ultimo, has justly declared, that "*few examples have occurred, of distress so general, and so severe, as that which has been exhibited in the united states.*" This important subject is worthy of the undivided attention of every man interested for the public welfare.

If my views be incorrect, I shall rejoice to have the errors pointed out, and shall cheerfully recant them. Any suggestions on the subject will be received with thankfulness, and attended to. But if the ground I have taken be correct, I hope and trust the investigation may lead to a different course of policy, calculated to enable us to realize the blessings promised to us by our constitution and our natural advantages, which at present so provokingly elude our grasp.

Philadelphia, March 17th, 1820.

THE

NEW OLIVE BRANCH.

CHAPTER I.

Preliminary observations. State of the nation. Whence it arises. Short-sighted policy. Decline of commerce inevitable. Substitutes ought to have been provided for the superfluous mercantile capital, talent and industry.

It is impossible for any one who can say with Terence—"I am a man—interested in whatever concerns my fellow men"—to take a calm and dispassionate view of the existing state of affairs, in this heaven-favoured land, without feeling deep distress, and a melancholy conviction, that we have made a most lamentable waste of the immense advantages, moral, physical, and political, we enjoy—advantages rarely equalled, scarcely ever exceeded; and that our erroneous policy has, in five years, produced more havoc of national wealth, power, and resources, and more individual distress, than, *in a period of profound peace*,* has taken place in the same space of time, within two hundred years, in any nation in Europe, except Portugal.

That governments are instituted for the protection, support, and benefit of the governed, is a maxim as old as the dawn of liberty in the world. The administrators are the mere agents of their constituents, hired to perform certain duties, for which they are here paid liberal salaries.

The grand objects of their care are—the security of person—security of property acquired, and in the acquisition of property—with the right of worshipping God as each man's conscience dictates. And government, by whatever name it may be called, is only estimable in proportion as it guards those sacred deposits. Our dear-bought experience proves, that the happiness of individuals and the prosperity of nations are by no means proportioned to the excellence of their forms of government. Did that excellence necessarily produce its natural results, we should rank among the happiest of nations, ancient or modern; whereas, unfortunately, at present we occupy a low grade in point of prosperity.

* Other nations usually and naturally recover in peace from the injuries inflicted by war. We rose in war—and alas! are sinking in peace!!! What an awful view!

It is a melancholy feature in human affairs, that no institutions, however perfect—no administration, however upright or wise, can guard the whole of a nation against distress and embarrassment. Accidents, not to be foreseen, or, if foreseen, not to be guarded against—imprudence, extravagance, and various other causes will frequently, in the most prosperous communities, produce a large portion of distress. This state of things is no impeachment to the goodness of the form of government, or the wisdom of its administrators.

But when, as is our case, considerable bodies of people, whole sections of a nation, are involved in distress and embarrassment—when a large portion of the productive industry of the country is laid prostrate—when most useful establishments, the pride, the glory, the main spring of the wealth, power, and resources of nations, are allowed to fall to ruins, without the slightest effort to save them on the part of the legislative power, whose paramount duty it is to interfere in their defence—when constituents, writhing in distress and misery, call in vain on their representatives for relief, which is within their power to afford—there must be something radically wrong in the people, or in the form of government, or radically vicious and pernicious in its legislation.

The policy of a free government, good or bad, emanates from the legislative body, which has the destinies of the nation in its hands. The executive officers in such nations, who are generally stiled the administration, have little power to avert the evils of a vicious, or to prevent the beneficent consequences of a wise legislation. This is peculiarly the case in our country.

That the decay of our prosperity—the sufferings of our citizens—could not exist in a time of profound peace, without some great natural calamity—some radical defects in the people—great vice in the form of government—or an unsound system of policy, will not be controverted.

Our distresses do not arise from any natural calamity. None has befallen us.

Nor from the people. They are shrewd, intelligent, industrious, active, and enterprizing to a high degree. A wise legislator or statesman could not desire sounder materials to form the structure of a happy and prosperous society, and render his name immortal.

Nor from the form of government. That, like every work of man, it has defects, must be conceded. But that it is the best the world ever witnessed, is susceptible of full proof on fair comparison with any that at present exist—or that ever existed.

Our sufferings, therefore, are chargeable to our policy, which, I repeat, emanates from our general legislature, to whom, if our evils are not irremediable, we must apply for relief.

This declaration, as to the source of our distresses, requires qualification, so far as regards the diminution of our commerce, and the depreciation of the prices of our staples generally, neither of which congress could have prevented.

Cotton is an exception. For the ruinous reduction that has taken place in that article, they are answerable to their country. They might have readily made a domestic market, which would have preserved the price from any material depreciation, and saved the cotton planters above 7,000,000 of dollars, and the merchants who purchased before the reduction, nearly 4,000,000.

It required but a slender view of the state of our affairs, and of our future prospects, to have enabled our statesmen to foresee that the new state of affairs throughout the world required a total change of policy. As we could no longer hope to be the carriers for Europe; and as the immense armies disbanded by the different belligerents, would be devoted partly to the labours of the field, and partly to work-shops and manufactories, whereby not only the markets for our staples, bread-stuffs particularly, would be diminished, but the quantity of manufactures there would be greatly increased; it required but little sagacity to see that a large portion of the talents, the capital, and the industry of our merchants, would be bereft of their usual employment: and therefore, every motive of policy, and regard for the public and private welfare, required that *some other channel should be opened to give them activity*. But these were views beyond the grasp of most of our statesmen; and, far from holding out any new inducements to enter on manufacturing pursuits, which would have absorbed the superfluous mercantile capital, they unwisely diminished those that existed, by repealing the double duties in June, 1816, whereby the revenue lost millions of dollars, and the manufacturing industry of the country received a severe wound.

The goal to which the policy we pursued after the late war, tended, was early foreseen and distinctly pointed out. The domestic exports of the country, the grand legitimate fund for the payment of our imports, for twenty years, from 1796 to 1815, inclusively, amounted to only 698,676,879 dollars, or an average of nearly 35,000,000. Whereas our imports in the year 1815, exclusive of re-exportations, amounted to above 118,000,000. Lives there a man who could for a moment doubt where such a course of proceeding would land us? Or, that our exports, which, under the immense advantages we enjoyed during the French revolution, only rose to the above average, would never, in a time of peace, enable us to pay for such extravagant importations? It was impossible to take the most superficial view of the subject, without being satisfied that we were as completely in the high road to destruction as a young man who has attained to the possession of a large estate, and who expends more than double his income.

A wonderful feature in the affair is, that the net impost which accrued in 1815, was 36,306,022 dollars, being one million more than the annual average of the whole of our exports for twenty years!!

Independent, therefore, of all concern for our manufacturers, some decisive efforts ought to have been made to diminish our imports, in order to arrest the career of national impoverishment. But the flourishing state of the revenue, which, with too many of our statesmen, absorbed all other considerations, appeared to promise a new fiscal millenium.* And hence the fatal repeal of the internal duties, which was carried by the overwhelming majority, in the house of representatives, of 161 to 5, in December, 1817—than which a more wild and injudicious measure could hardly have been devised. We have lived to see its folly, and to deplore its consequences.

What would be thought of the skill of a physician, who, while bleeding his patient to a state of inanition, was congratulating himself on the quantity and excellence of the blood pouring out of his veins!—such is the case precisely of those statesmen, who form their ideas of national prosperity from the great extent of the customs, more frequently, as it has proved with us, an unerring sign of decay. Ustariz, a celebrated Spanish political economist, gives an admirable lesson on this subject!—how deserving of attention! but how little attended to!

"It aggravates the calamity of our country that the customs "have improved and yielded more by the increase of imports; "since it is so unfortunate a circumstance for us, that *in order to* "*advance them a million of dollars, estimating one duty with ano-* "*ther at the rate of eight per cent., after an allowance for frauds* "*and indulgences, there must be drawn out of the kingdom twelve* "*millions of dollars.*"†

It cannot be too deeply lamented, that in placing before congress the calamitous situation of our manufactures and manufacturers, (which, by the way is, but very lightly touched on) both the president and the secretary of the treasury, the former in his message, and the latter in his annual report, in recommending attention to the relief of this suffering class of citizens, express some hesitation on the subject, and speak hypothetically, particularly the secretary.

* It is a fact, that some of our great statesmen, in 1817, were sanguine enough to believe that the treasury would continue to overflow so fast, that the national debt would be paid off in a very few years!

† Ustariz on the theory and practice of commerce and maritime affairs, vol. i. p. 6.

The president states :—

"It is deemed of importance to encourage our domestic "manufactures. In what manner the evils which have been ad- "verted to may be remedied, and how it may be practicable in "other respects, to afford them further encouragement, *paying* "*due regard to the other great interests of the nation*, is submit- "ted to the wisdom of congress."

The observation of the secretary is—

"*It is believed* that the present is a favourable moment for af- "fording efficient protection to that increasing and important in- "terest, *if* it can be done *consistently with the general interest* "*of the nation!*"

Good heavens ! what an appalling *if!* Was there ever such an unlucky word introduced into a public document ! "*If* it "can be done consistently with the general interest of the na- "tion !" As if a statesman could for an instant doubt whether protecting and fostering this all-important portion of the nation- al industry—reducing our imports or expenses, within our ex- ports or income—and arresting the progress of distress and de- cay, could, in any possible case, be otherwise than "*consistent* "*with the general interest of the nation!*" As if it could be a matter of doubt, whether the contingency of our citizens paying a few dollars more per annum, for American manufactures than for foreign ones, (supposing that to be the case, which I shall prove wholly destitute of foundation,) is to be put into compe- tition with the bankruptcy of our manufacturing capitalists— the beggary of our working people—and the impoverishment of the nation !

Some of my friends have endeavoured to dissuade me from using the freedom of style, which prevails in this work. They declare it imprudent, as likely to prevent attention to the ap- plications of the manufacturers. I have duly weighed this very prudent advice, and cannot persuade myself to adopt it. The manufacturers require no favours. They only seek justice—they only seek that protection which has been so liberally accorded to commerce. Believing the system pur- sued radically vicious and pernicious, it is the right and the duty of every man who suffers by it, to enter his protest against the ruinous course pursued—to trace it to its causes— and to display its consequences. I have used the language of a freeman. If the conduct I denounce, betray a manifest derelic- tion of duty, can there be any impropriety in marking the dere- liction? In countries less free than the united states, far great- er severity is used in discussing the conduct of government.

Why then should it be criminal or improper here? If any of my statements be incorrect, or my inductions illogical, I shall freely retract and apologize for them. But till then, I throw myself on the good sense of the community, and dare the consequences.

CHAPTER. II

Sketch of the state of the nation from the peace of Paris till the organization of the present federal government. Analogy with our present state. Unlimited freedom of commerce fairly tested

At the close of the revolutionary war, the trade of America was almost absolutely free and unrestrained in the fullest sense of the word, according to the theory of Adam Smith, Say, Ricardo, the Edinburgh Reviewers, and the authors of the Encyclopædia. Her ports were open, with scarcely any duties, to the vessels and merchandize of all other nations. In Pennsylvania, they were only about two and a half per cent. Even these were nugatory; because there was a free port established at Burlington, by the state of New Jersey, where a very large portion of the goods intended for Philadelphia were entered, and conveyed over to this city clandestinely. The same fraudulent scenes were acted in other states, and thus trade was, as I have stated, almost wholly free.

If enthusiasts did not too generally scorn to trammel themselves by attention to facts, this case would settle the question of unrestrained commerce for ever—and prove, that the system ought to be postponed till the millennium, when it is possible it may stand a chance of promoting the welfare of mankind. But till then, woe to the nation that adopts it. Her destruction is sealed.

But unfortunately theorists carefully avoid the facts that endanger their systems, how strong or convincing soever they may be. This saves an immensity of trouble. Hence in some of the grand systems of political economy, which have acquired great celebrity, you may travel through fifty or a hundred pages together, of most harmonious prose, all derived from a luxuriant imagination, without your career being arrested by a single fact. But on a little reflection or examination, you may as readily find a single fact, recorded elsewhere in ten lines, which demolishes the whole.

From almost every nation in Europe, large shipments were made to this country—many of them of the most ludicrous kind, which implied an utter ignorance of the wants, the situation and the resources of the united states. Among the rest, the recesses of Monmouth street, in London, and Plunket street, in Dublin, the receptacles of the cast-off clothes of these two capitals, were emptied of a portion of their contents; for it was supposed that the war had rendered the nation destitute of every thing, even of covering. Happy was the man who could send "*a venture*," as it was called, to this country, which the misguided Europeans supposed an El Dorado, where every thing was to be converted into gold with a cent per cent. profit at least. Goods often lay on the wharves for many days for want of store room. House rent rose to double and treble the former rates. The importers and consignees at first sold at great advances—and believed they were rapidly indemnifying themselves for the deprivations and sufferings of the war.

But these glorious times soon came to a close like those of 1815. From "day dreams" and delusive scenes of boundless wealth, the citizens awoke to pinching misery and distress. The nation had no mines to pay her debts. And industry, the only legitimate and permanent source of individual happiness, and national wealth, power, and resources, was destroyed, as it has recently been by the influx, and finally by the depreciation of the price, of the imported articles: for the quantity on hands being equal to the consumption of two or three years, of course the great mass of goods fell below cost—often to half and one-third. All our citizens were at once converted into disciples of Adam Smith. They purchased every species of goods "cheaper than they could be manufactured at home." Accordingly domestic manufactures were arrested in their career. The weaver, the shoemaker, the hatter, the saddler, the sugar baker, the brewer, the rope maker, the paper maker, &c. were reduced to bankruptcy. Their establishments were suspended. Their workmen were consigned to idleness and all its long train of evils. The payment for the foreign rubbish exhausted the country of nearly the whole of its specie, immense quantities of which had been introduced to pay the French and British armies, and likewise from the Spanish colonies. Two thirds probably of the specie then in the country were composed of French crowns.

However calamitous the present state of affairs, we have not yet sunk to so low an ebb, as at that period. I have in 1786 seen sixteen houses to let in two squares, of about 800 feet, in one of the best sites for business in Philadelphia. Real property could hardly find a market. The number of persons reduced to distress, and forced to sell their merchandize, was so great, and those who had money to invest, were so very few, that the sacrifices were immense. Debtors were ruined, without paying a fourth of the demands of their creditors. There were most unprecedented transfers of property. Men worth large estates, who had unfortunately entered into business with a view of increasing their fortunes, were in a year or two totally ruined—and those who had a command of ready money, quadrupled or quintupled their estates in an equally short space. Confidence was so wholly destroyed, that interest rose to two, two and a half, and three per cent. per month. And bonds, and judgments, and mortgages were sold at a discount of twenty, thirty, forty, and fifty per cent. In a word, few countries have experienced a more awful state of distress and wretchedness.

To corroborate these views, I annex historical statements of the situation of the country.

"In every part of these states, the scarcity of money has become a common subject of complaint. This does not seem to be an imaginary grievance, like that of hard times, of which men have complained in all ages of the world. The misfortune is general, and in many cases it is severely felt. The scarcity of money is so great, or the difficulty of paying debts has been so common, that *riots and combinations have been formed in many places, and the operations of civil government have been suspended.**"

"*Goods were imported to a much greater amount than could be consumed or paid for.*"†

"Thus was the usual means of remittance by articles the growth of the country, almost annihilated, and little else than specie remained, to answer the demands incurred by importations. *The money, of course, was drawn off; and this being inadequate to the purpose of discharging the whole amount of foreign contracts, the residue was chiefly sunk by the bankruptcies of the importers.* The scarcity of specie, arising principally from this cause, was attended with evident consequences; it checked commercial intercourse throughout the community, and furnished reluctant debtors with an apology for withholding their dues both from individuals and the public."‡

"On opening their ports, *an immense quantity of foreign merchandize was introduced into the country, and they were tempted by the sudden cheapness of imported goods*, and by their own wants, to purchase beyond their capacities for payment. Into this indiscretion they were in some measure beguiled by their own sanguine calculations of the value which a free trade would bestow on the produce of their soil, and by a reliance on those evidences of the public debt which were in the hands of most of them. So extravagantly too did many estimate the temptation which equal liberty and vacant lands would hold out to emigrants from the old world, as to entertain the opin-

* Dr. Hugh Williamson.
† Minot's history of the Insurrection in Massachusetts, p. 2.
‡ Idem, p. 13.

"ion that Europe was about to empty itself into America, and "that the united states would derive from that source such an "increase of population, as would enhance their lands to a price "heretofore not even conjectured."*

"The bonds of men, whose competency to pay their debts "was unquestionable, could not be negociated but at a discount "of *thirty, forty, and fifty per centum: real property was scarce-"ly vendible;* and sales of any articles for ready money could "be made only at a ruinous loss. The prospect of extricating "the country from those embarrassments was by no means flat-"tering. Whilst every thing else fluctuated, some of the causes "which produced this calamitous state of things were perma-"nent. The hope and fear still remained, that the debtor party "would obtain the victory at the elections; and instead of ma-"king the painful effort to obtain relief by industry and "economy, many rested all their hopes on legislative interfe-"rence. *The mass of national labour and national wealth was "consequently diminished.*"†

"*Property, when brought to sale under execution, sold at so low "a price as frequently ruined the debtor without paying the credi-"tor.* A disposition to resist the laws became common: assem-"blies were called oftener and earlier than the constitution or "laws required."‡

"Laws were passed by which *property of every kind was "made a legal tender in the payment of debts*, though payable "according to contract in gold or silver. Other laws installed "the debt. so that of sums already due, only a third, and after-"wards only a fifth, was annually recoverable in the courts of "law."§

"*Silver and gold, which had circulated largely in the latter "years of the war, were returning by the usual course of trade to "those countries, whence large quantities of necessary and un-"necessary commodities had been imported.* Had any general "system of impost been adopted, some part of this money might "have been retained, and some part of the public debt discharg-"ed; but the power of congress did not extend to this object; "and the states were not united in the expediency of delegating "new and sufficient powers to that body. The partial imposts, "laid by some of the states, were ineffectual, as long as others "found their interest in omitting them."||

"The people of New Hampshire petitioned; and to gratify "them the legislature enacted, that *when any debtor shall tender "to his creditor, in satisfaction of an execution for debt, either*

* Marshall's Life of Washington, V. p. 75. † Idem p. 88.
‡ Ramsay's S. Carolina. II. p. 428.
§ Belknap's History of New Hampshire, II. p. 352.
|| Idem, p. 356.

"*real or personal estate sufficient*, the body of the debtor shall "be exempt from imprisonment, and the debt shall carry an in-"terest of six per cent.; the creditor being at liberty either to "receive the estate, so tendered, at a value estimated by three "appraisers, or to keep alive the demand by making out an ali-"as, within one year after the return of any former execution, "and levying it on any estate of the debtor which he can find."*

While our citizens were writhing under these evils, destitute of a circulating medium, industry universally paralized, thousands every where deprived of the means of supporting their families, bankruptcy daily swallowing up in its vortex our merchants, tradesmen, manufacturers, and artisans—it is not wonderful that recourse was had to various indefensible means, to palliate the evils. The real source, that is, the want of an adequate tariff to protect national industry by high duties and prohibitions, was not explored—and even if it had been, there existed no authority competent to apply a remedy.

Among the expedients employed, emissions of paper money, legal tenders, appraisement acts, and suspensions of the operation of courts of justice in regard to the collection of debts, were the most prominent. These were but miserable palliatives of a disordor arising solely, I repeat, from the destruction of the national industry, and which nothing but its resuscitation could remove.

In Massachusetts, the suffering rose higher than in any other part of the united states. Riotous collections of people assembled in various parts at the periods for convening the courts of common pleas, to prevent their proceedings; and actually in every instance but one, according to judge Marshal, carried their purposes into execution. In fact, so severe was the distress, and so numerous were the debtors, that they more than once had a majority in the legislature. The evil under the existing form of government was incurable. It ended in an open insurrection, under Shays, a revolutionary officer, which was crushed by the energy of governor Bowdoin and his council—and the decisions of generals Lincoln and Sheppard.

Some idea may be entertained of the state of public affairs, quite as deplorable as those of individuals, from the circumstance that governor Bowdoin having raised four thousand militia against the insurgents, there was not money enough in the treasury to support that small army for one week; and they could not have been marched but for the patriotism of a number of public-spirited individuals, who subscribed the sum necessary for the purpose.

* Belknap's history of New Hampshire vol. II. p. 429.

"The public treasury did not afford the means of keeping this "force in the field a single week: and the legislature not being "in session, the constituted authorities were incapable of put-"ting the troops in motion. This difficulty was removed by in-"dividual patriotism!"*

The insurrection produced a salutary effect, by spreading a conviction of the utter inefficacy of the existing form of government, and of the imperious necessity of adopting a new one.—The difficulty under which the federal constitution laboured in its progress, notwithstanding the impetus it received from this alarming event, shews that it would have probably failed of success, had not the public distress arrived at its highest pitch.

Those of our citizens who ascribe the existing calamities to the baleful career of the banks, are advised to consider this parallel case, wherein banks had no agency. When the war closed, there was but one bank in the united states, that of North America, located in the city of Philadelphia, with a capital of 400,000 dollars. And in 1785, when embarrassment and distress pervaded the state, many of the citizens, in casting round to discover the source, believed, or affected to believe, that they sprang from the operation of this institution. Accordingly petitions were presented to the legislature to repeal its charter. Counsel were heard at the bar of the house for and against the bank—the late respected Judge Wilson in defence, and Jonathan Dickinson Sargeant, father of the present member of congress from Philadelphia, in opposition. The state, let it be observed, was then divided into two parties, very violently embittered against each other. The repeal was quite a party question, and decided by party views. The majority in the legislature were hostile to the institution, and repealed the charter, which measure they regarded as a sovereign remedy for all the existing evils. Had the repeal been effectual, it would have multiplied instead of diminishing them. But having a charter from congress, the bank set the legislature at defiance, and pursued "the even tenor of its way," unruffled by "the peltings of the pitiless storm."

It may gratify curiosity to see the view given of the tremendous influence which was conjured up for this institution, in order to alarm the citizens, and justify the repeal.

The committee to whom the petitions were referred, in their report stated—

"That foreigners will doubtless be more and more induced to "become stockholders, until the time may arrive when *this en-"ormous engine of power may become subject to foreign influ-"ence*. This country may be agitated with the politics of Euro-"pean courts; and *the good people of America reduced once more*

* Marshall's Life of Washington, vol. V. p. 121.

"*into a state of subordination and dependence upon some one or* "*other of the European powers!*"*

On the 17th of Feb. in the year 1784, the Massachusetts Bank was incorporated, with power to hold in real estate 50,000*l.* and to raise a capital stock of 500,000*l.* The subscription did not, I have reason to believe, exceed at that time 400,000 dollars.

In the same year the state of New York incorporated the bank of that name, with the extent of whose capital I am unacquainted.

These were the only banks in existence in the united states, previous to the adoption of the federal constitution. And as distress and embarrassment equally pervaded those states where there were none, it is absurd to ascribe the evil to those institutions where they existed.

In North Carolina there were two emissions of paper money, with a legal tender, from 1783, to 1787. They depreciated fifty per cent. in a short time.

The state of affairs described in the preceding pages accounts for a fact which has always excited deep regret, and which, I believe, has never been traced to its source. I mean the depreciation of the public securities, which the holders were obliged to part with at ten, twelve and fifteen cents in the dollar, whereby a large portion of the warmest friends of the revolution, who had risked their lives and embarked their entire property in its support, were wholly ruined, and many of its deadly enemies most immoderately enriched. Never was Virgil's celebrated line more applicable—

Sic vos—non vobis, mellificatis, apes.

The reader is requested to bear these pictures of distress in mind, during the perusal of the chapter in which I propose to investigate the causes assigned for the evils under which the community labours at present. They shed strong light on the subject.

Well as I am aware of the pertinacious adherence of mankind to theory, and the difficulty of breaking the intellectual chains by which it holds the mind, I cannot refrain from again urging the strong case of this country at that period on the most serious consideration of the disciples of Adam Smith, Say, Ricardo, and the other political economists of that school. It ought to dispel forever the mists, on the subject of unrestrained commerce, which that abstruse work, the Wealth of Nations, has spread abroad. Here the system had fair scope for operation.

* Journal of the house of representatives, March 28, 1785.

The ports of this country, I repeat, were open to the commerce of the whole world, with an impost so light as not even to meet the wants of the treasury. We had none of those "*restrictions*," "*prohibitions*" or "*prohibitory duties*," to which the new school of political economists ascribe the sufferings of England and of this country. We "*bought our merchandize where it could be had* "*cheapest*," and the consequences followed, which have never failed to follow such a state of things. Our markets were glutted. Prices fell. Competition on the part of our manufacturers was at an end. They were beggared and bankrupted. The merchants, whose importations had ruined them, were themselves involved in the calamity. And the farmers who had felicitated themselves on the grand advantage of "buying foreign "merchandize cheap," sunk likewise into the vortex of general destruction.

Would to heaven that the precious and invaluable lessons these facts afford may not in future be thrown away on our statesmen and the nation at large! Had they been duly attended to, at the close of the late war, the united states, instead of the afflicting scenes they now exhibit, would present a picture of prosperity, public and private, which would have realized the fondest anticipations of the philosophers of both hemispheres—anticipations which have been most lamentably disappointed—and "*like the baseless fabric of a vision*," scarcely "*left a trace* "*behind*."

CHAPTER III.

Adoption of the federal constitution. Its happy effects. Utter impolicy of the tariff. Manufactures and manufacturers not protected. Hamilton's celebrated report. Glaring inconsistency. Excise system. Its unproductiveness.

THE adoption of the federal constitution operated like magic; produced a total change in the state of affairs; and actually removed no small portion of the public suffering, by the confidence it inspired, even before the measures of the government could be carried into effect.

The united states began their career in 1789, with advantages never exceeded, rarely equalled. The early administrators of the government had a high degree of responsibility. They were laying the foundations of an empire which may be the most extensive and powerful the world ever knew, and whose destinies they held in their hands.

The tariff was fraught with errors of the most grievous kind. Disregarding the examples and the systems of the wisest nations of Europe, it was calculated to sacrifice the resources of the country for the benefit of foreign manufacturing nations. And indeed had it been framed by an agent of any of those nations, it could not have answered the purpose better. It afforded them nearly all the benefits usually derived from colonies, without the expense of their support. It deprived our manufacturing citizens of all the advantages of reciprocity in their intercourse with the rest of the world.

The era is not long passed over, when any man who dared to arraign the conduct of the early congresses under the federal constitution, and accuse them of having established tariffs which sacrificed the dearest interests of their country, and clipped its wings in its flight towards the high destinies to which its extent, its government, the energies of the people, and the great variety of other advantages which it possessed, bid it aspire, would be regarded with jealousy, and covered with obloquy. The voice of reason, of truth, and of history, would have been smothered amidst the loud clamours of prejudice and party. But I trust the fatal results of the system have prepared the public mind to hear with patience, and judge with candour, the facts on which I ground these opinions, and the inductions I draw from them.

To those who consider the mode in which the members of congress are elected—the various quarters from which they come—the different degrees of illumination that prevail in the districts they respectively represent—how many neglect to prepare themselves fully for the stations they occupy—it will not appear wonderful that the views of a portion of them are contracted, and do not embrace on a broad and comprehensive scale the interests of the nation as one grand whole.

The want of adequate protection to the productive industry of the manufacturers, conspicuous in the first and the succeeding tariffs, may be accounted for from the concurrence in one object of four descriptions of citizens, whose particular views, however, were entirely different.

I. The most influential members of the mercantile class have appeared at all times jealous of the manufacturers, and been disposed to regard adequate protection to them as injurious to the prosperity of commerce. Hence they have too generally and too successfully opposed prohibitions and prohibitory duties as limiting their importations of foreign goods. Although there are many gentlemen of this class whose views are expanded and liberal, there is a large proportion whose opposition remains unabated.

II. Many of the agriculturalists too have been equally jealous of the manufacturers—opposed the imposition of duties adequate to the protection of their fellow citizens—and not allowed a single article to be prohibited. They dreaded an extravagant rise of price as a necessary result of securing the home market to our own citizens. It does not appear to have ever entered into their calculations, that, in a country like the United States, where monopolies are excluded, and where industry and enterprize so generally prevail, and are so wholly uncontrolled, the competition would, to use the words of Alexander Hamilton, assuredly "*bring prices to their proper level.*"

III. The third description comprised the disciples of Adam Smith, who contended that trade ought to be allowed to regulate itself—that commerce should be left unrestrained—that all nations ought to buy wherever they could procure articles cheapest, &c. &c.

IV. The fourth class considered themselves, and were regarded by others, as of a higher order. The whole of their political economy was, however, confined within very narrow limits. It never travelled beyond the collection of revenue. The ways and means were their alpha and omega, their sine qua non. Provided the treasury was overflowing, they had neither eyes, nor ears, nor tongue for any other object. We have seen for years past seen that with statesmen of this description the spread of bankruptcy throughout our cities—the decay of splendid manufacturing establishments—the distress of thousands of useful men—the wailings of helpless women and children, never excited any alarm. The importation of foreign goods, to the amount of 60,000,000 dollars, which exhausted the country of its specie, produced almost universal distress, and devoted thousands of workmen to idleness, and part of them to beggary, was a subject of rejoicing—for it brought 15,000,000 of dollars into the treasury! This was the salve for every sore—the panacea, which, like the waters of the Jordan, cleansed off all the ulcers and foulnesses of the body politic.

This statement may appear too severe. But I beg the reader will not decide on the correctness or incorrectness of it, till he has read the chapter on the contumelious and unfeeling neglect of the pathetic applications of the manufacturers to congress for relief in 1816, 1817, and 1818.

The views of these four descriptions of citizens were aided by the extensive prevalence of a host of prejudices, which were sedulously inculcated by foreign agents, whose wealth and prosperity depended on keeping this market open to their fabrics, and repressing the growth of our manufactures.

1. The idea of the immense superiority of agricultural pursuits and agriculturists over manufactures and manufacturers, was almost universally prevalent. It had been fondly cherished by

Great Britain and her friends here during the colonial state of the country, and long afterwards: and no small portion of the citizens of the united states were unable to divest their minds of the colonial trammels, when the country assumed its independent rank among nations.

2. The same keen sensibility on the subject of smuggling was manifested, as we have so often witnessed more recently. This was assigned as a reason for admitting three-fourths of all the manufactured merchandize under a duty of five per cent.!!

3. The miserable outcry on the subject of "*taxing the many* "*for the benefit of the few*," which is still used as a sort of war whoop against the manufacturers, was then in full force.

4. The back lands, it was asserted, ought to be cultivated before the labour of our citizens was diverted off to manufactures.

5. The high price of labour in this country was by many regarded as an insuperable bar, and a proof that "we were not yet ripe for manufactures."

6. The demoralization asserted to be inseparable from manufacturing establishments, was among the prominent objections.

There is a magic in great names which renders their errors highly pernicious. That Mr. Jefferson is a truly great man, is now, I believe, universally admitted, since the baleful passions, excited by party, have subsided, and the atrocious calumnies with which, in the days of faction and delusion, he was overwhelmed, have sunk into deserved oblivion. But that he has had no small degree of instrumentality in giving currency to the system we have pursued, it would be vain to deny. He has drawn a contrast between manufactures and agriculture, so immensely advantageous to the latter, as to have fostered the old, and excited new prejudices against the former, many of which still maintain their influence. Mr. Jefferson was born, brought up, and lived in a slave-holding state, a large portion of the industry of which is devoted to the culture of tobacco, one of the most pernicious kinds of employment in the world. It more completely exhausts the soil, and debases and wears out the wretched labourer, than any other species of cultivation. How, under such circumstances, he could have drawn such a captivating picture of the labours of the field, it is difficult to say. His Arcadia must have been sought, not in Virginia or Maryland, but in Virgil's or Pope's pastorals, or Thomson's seasons.

This is not a place to enter into a comparison of these occupations, otherwise the boasted superiority might be found not to rest on so stable a basis as is generally supposed.

Mr. Jefferson lately retracted his opinions on those subjects. In a letter to B. Austin, Esq. of Boston, he distinctly states:—

"*To be independent for the comforts of life, we must fabricate* "*them ourselves. We must now place the manufacturer by the* "*side of the agriculturist.*"

"Experience has taught me, that *manufactures are now as necessary to our independence, as to our comfort.*"

In order to justify the character I have given of the tariff of 1789, I annex a description of two tariffs, one calculated to protect and promote individual industry and national prosperity, and the other to destroy both.

FEATURES.

A sound tariff

1. Renders revenue subservient to the promotion of individual industry and national prosperity.
2. Prohibits such articles as can be fully supplied at home on reasonable terms.
3. Imposes heavy duties on articles interfering with the rising manufactures of the country.
4. Admits on light duties articles that do not interfere with the industry of the nation.

A pernicious tariff

1. Regards revenue as the grand object of solicitude.
2. Prohibits no article whatever, however competent the country may be to supply itself.
3. Imposes such low duties on manufactures, as, while they serve the purposes of revenue, cannot promote national industry, or prevent or materially check importation.
4. Raises as large a portion of the revenue as possible on articles not interfering with the industry of the nation.

CONSEQUENCES.

A sound tariff

Secures employment to industry, capital, talent, and enterprize.

Preserves the circulating medium, and daily adds to the wealth, power, and resources of the nation.

Extends prosperity and happiness in every direction.

A pernicious tariff

Deprives a large portion of the industry, capital, talent, and enterprize of the citizens of employment.

Drains away the circulating medium, and exhausts the national resources.

Spreads misery and distress through the country, as we find by dear bought experience.

If the tariff in question be tried by this standard, which, I trust, will be found a correct one, and by its results, I shall be exonerated from censure. It was extremely simple. It enumerated about thirty manufactured articles, subject to seven and a half and ten per cent. duty—Coaches, chaises, &c. to fifteen—and about eight or ten to specific duties. All the remainder were thrown together, as non-enumerated, and *subject to five per cent.!!* Its protection of agriculture is reserved as the subject of another chapter.

At 7½ per cent.

Blank books,
Paper,
Paper hangings
Cabinet wares,
Buttons,
Saddles,
Tanned leather,
Anchors,
Wrought iron,
Gloves,
Millenery,
Tin and pewter ware,
Canes,
Whips,
Ready made clothing,
Brushes,
Gold, silver, and plated ware,
Jewelry,
Paste work,
Manufactures of leather,
Hats.

At 10 per cent.

Looking glasses,
Window and other glass,
Gunpowder,
China, stone, and earthen ware,
Buckles,
Gold and silver lace,
Gold and silver leaf,
Paints.

At 15 per cent.

Coaches, chariots, chaises, solos, &c.

Subject to specific duties.

	Cents.
Boots, per pair, - - - -	50
Leather shoes, - - - -	7
Silk shoes or slippers, - -	10
Cables, per cwt. - - - -	75
Tarred cordage, do. - -	75
Unwrought steel, per lb. -	56
Untarred cordage and yarn, per cwt. - - - - -	90
Twine or pack thread, per cwt. - - - - - -	200
Wool and cotton cards, per dozen, - - - -	50

Non-enumerated articles, subject to 5 per cent.

Bricks,
Brass in sheets,
Brazing copper,
Combs,
Clocks,
Copper bottoms,
Hair powder,
Inkpowder,
Linens and other manufactures of flax,
Maps and charts,
Paints,
Printed books,
Paintings,
Silks,
Slates,
Starch,
Sealing wax,
Worsted shoes,
Brass manufactures,
China ware,
Cannon,
Cutlery,
Cotton goods of all kinds,
Fire arms,
Gilt wares,
Hempen cloth,
Iron manufactures,
Japanned wares,
Lead manufactures,
Muskets,
Printing types,
Pottery,
Pins,
Steel manufactures,
Stone ware,
Side arms,
Sail cloth,
Tin wares,
Wood manufactures,
Woollen goods of every kind ! ! &c. &c

In order to form a correct estimate of the effect of those duties as protection, it is necessary to take a view of the situation of this country and of those with which our citizens were to compete—which were principally, Great Britain, France, Germany, and the East Indies.

The united states had recently emerged from a desolating war of seven years duration : and a peace of six years had been as destructive to their resources. Their manufacturers were possessed of slender capitals, and as slender credit. Workmen were inexperienced—and wages high. All the expenses, moreover, of incipient undertakings were to be encountered. The chief counterbalance for all these disadvantages, was the freight and commission on the rival articles.

Great Britain possessed every possible advantage in the conflict. Her manufacturers had the secure possession of their domestic market—and had only to send their surplus productions to this country—their machinery was excellent—they had drawbacks, in general equal to, and often greater than, the expenses of transportation—skilful workmen—and wages comparatively low—Her merchants were possessed of immense capitals, and gave most liberal credits.

The cheapness of living and labour in France, Germany, and more particularly in the East Indies, afforded the people of those countries advantages over our manufacturers, only inferior to those enjoyed by Great Britain.

Under these circumstances, I trust it will be admitted by every man of candour that it would be a mere mockery and insult to common sense, to pretend that five per cent., which, as appears above, was the duty on seven-eighths of all the manufactured articles imported into this country, was imposed with a view to protection. Revenue alone was the object.

Having to struggle with such a lamentably impolitic system, it is wonderful that our manufactures made any progress. It reflects great credit on our citizens, that they were able to emerge from such an overwhelming mass of difficulties, as they had to encounter.

While the grand leading manufactures of cotton, wool, iron, steel, lead, flax, and pottery, were thus subject to only five per cent. duty, lest smuggling should be encouraged, it may afford some gratification to curiosity to exhibit a statement of the very high duties on tea, coffee, rum, &c. which were wholly unrestrained by any fear of smuggling.

1789.	Price.	Duty.	Per cent.
Souchong, per lb. - - - - - - -	39	10	25
Hyson, do. - - - - - - - - -	49	20	40
Bohea, do. - - - - - - - - -	15	6	40
Madeira, per gallon, - - - - - - -	100	18	18
Jamaica rum, do. - - - - - - - -	40	10	25
Coffee, per lb. - - - - - - - - -	12½	2½	20
Sugar, do. - - - - - - - - - -	5	1½	30
Salt, per bushel, - - - - - - - -	12	6	50

Thus a yard of broad cloth or muslin, value four dollars, paid no more duty than a pound of hyson tea, value 49 cents!

The amount of goods subject to ad valorem duties, imported in 1789, 1790, and 1791, was as follows—

Per cent.	1789.	1790.	1791.
5	$7,136,578	$14,605,713	$11,036,477
7½	520,182	1,067,143	7,708,337
10	305,248	699,149	1,114,463
12½	5		314,206
15	2,700	4,876	5,654
	$7,969,731	$16,376,881	$19,179,137*

The duties on the above were about 2,600,000 dollars: and the whole amount of the impost for those three years, was 6,494,225 dollars.†

The residue, about 3,900,000 dollars, was collected principally from teas, wines, sugar, salt, spirits, spices, and coffee! This completely justifies the character of the tariff, that as large a portion as possible of the impost was levied on articles not interfering with national industry; and that the duties on manufactured merchandize were as light as the exigencies of the government would admit.

The manufacturers at this period, as they have done so often since, besought the protection and threw themselves on the liberality of congress. On the eleventh of April, 1789, Samuel Smith, Esq. of Maryland, presented to congress a memorial from the manufacturers of Baltimore, stating—

"That since the close of the late war, and the completion of "the revolution, they have observed with serious regret the man- "ufacturing and trading interest of the country rapidly declining, "and the attempts of the state legislatures to remedy the evil, "failing of their object; that in the present melancholy state of "our country, the number of poor increasing for want of em- "ployment, foreign debts accumulating, houses and lands depre- "ciating in value, and trade and manufactures languishing and

* Seybert, 158. † Idem, 395.

"expiring; they look up to the supreme legislature of the united "states, as the guardians of the whole empire. and from their "united wisdom and patriotism, and ardent love of their country, "expect to derive that aid and assistance, which alone can dissi- "pate their just apprehensions, and animate them with hopes of "success in future; by imposing *on all foreign articles which can "be made in America, such duties as will give a just and decided "preference to their labours;* discountenancing that trade which "tends so materially to injure them and impoverish their coun- "try: measures which in their consequences may contribute to "the discharge of the national debt, and the due support of gov- "ernment; that they have annexed a list of such articles as are, "or can be manufactured amongst them, and humbly trust in the "wisdom of the legislature to grant them, in common with oth- "er mechanics and manufacturers of the united states, that relief "that may appear proper."*

This application met with the same fate, as more recent ones have experienced from the successors of that congress.

It would require a long chapter to develope the utter impolicy of this tariff, and its inauspicious effects on the industry and happiness of a large portion of our citizens. and on the national prosperity. My limits forbid me to display the whole of its deformity. I annex one further view of it:

In 1793, the amount of merchandize imported at 7½ and 8 per cent. was about - -	$15,328,000†
On which the net duty was about - -	$1,200,000

This included all articles of clothing, whether cotton, woollen, or silk, (except India goods, subject to twelve and a half per cent.)

The net duty on coffee for the same year was -	$1,226,724‡

Being more than on the whole of the clothing of the nation.

Let us examine how this might have been arranged for the promotion of the prosperity of the country.

Suppose that the duty on coffee had been reduced so as to raise only - - - -	$700,000

* Debates of Congress, I. 29. † Seybert, 158. ‡ Idem, 438.

And that the duty on cotton and woollen goods had been raised to 20 per cent., which might have reduced the importation to $8,500,000, and produced - - - - - -	1,700,000
	$2,400,000

which is nearly the aggregate of the duties stated.

Or, suppose that the duty on coffee had remained unaltered, and on cottons and woollens been increased to 25 per cent.—and that the importations had been diminished to 5,000,000 of dollars, the revenue would have been unimpaired.

What an immense difference! In one case, nearly 7,000,000 and in the other 10,000,000 of dollars saved to the country!—Three or four hundred thousand people rendered happy! A market for the farmers for probably 6,000,000 lbs. of wool! and for the whole of the cotton then raised by our planters.

But it is a humiliating truth, that very few of our statesmen have ever predicated their measures on national views. They are almost all sectional. They do not fall within Rousseau's description:—

"*It belongs to the real statesman to elevate his views in the imposition of taxes, above the mere object of finance, and to transform them into useful regulations.*"

It is a melancholy operation for a real friend to the honour, power, resources, and happiness of the united states, to compare the tariff of 1789, and the principles on which it is predicated, with the preamble to a law of the state of Pennsylvania, passed anno 1785, four years before. The sound policy, the fostering care of its citizens, and of the resources of the state displayed in the latter, form a strong and decisive contrast with the utter impolicy of the tariff.

SECT. I. "Whereas divers useful and beneficial arts and manufactures have been gradually introduced into Pennsylvania, and the same have at length risen to a very considerable extent and perfection, insomuch that *during the late war between the united states of America and Great Britain, when the importation of European goods was much interrupted, and often very difficult and uncertain, the artisans and mechanics of this state, were able to supply in the hours of need, not only large quantities of weapons and other implements, but also ammunition and clothing, without which the war could not have been carried on, whereby their oppressed country was greatly assisted and relieved.*

SECT. II. "And whereas, *although the fabrics and manufactures of Europe and other foreign parts, imported into this country in times of peace, may be afforded at cheaper rates than they can be made here, yet good policy and a regard to the well being of divers*

"*useful and industrious citizens, who are employed in the making of*
"*like goods in this state, demand of us that moderate duties be laid on*
"*certain fabrics and manufactures imported, which do most interfere*
"*with, and which (if no relief be given) will undermine and destroy*
"*the useful manufactures of the like kind in this country:* For this
"purpose," &c. &c.

In December, 1791, Alexander Hamilton, who saw the errors of the tariff of the two preceding years, presented congress with his celebrated Report on Manufactures, the most perfect and luminous work ever published on the subject. It embraces all the great principles of the science of political economy, respecting that portion of the national industry, applied to manufactures, and is admirably calculated to advance the happiness of the people, and the wealth, power, and resources of nations. It more richly deserves the title of "The Wealth of Nations," than the celebrated work that bears the name.

The Report swept away, by the strongest arguments, all the plausible objections on which the paralizing influence of the tariff rested for support. The lucid reasoning, as level to the most common capacity, as to the most profound statesman, is not enveloped in those abstractions and metaphysical subtleties which abound in most of the books on this subject, and which, like the airy spectres of the dreamer, elude the grasp of the mind.

I annex a few of those grand and sublime truths, with which this work abounds, and which bear the strongest testimony against, and condemnation of, the course which this country has pursued.

"The substitution of foreign for domestic manufactures, *is a*
"*transfer to foreign nations of the advantages of machinery in*
"*the modes in which it is capable of being employed with most*
"*utility, and to the greatest extent.*"*

How many millions of the wealth of this country have been thus "transferred to foreign nations" during the thirty years of our career! How much of this wealth was used to scourge us at Washington, on the frontiers of Canada, and in the Chesapeake! What a lamentable use we have made of the advantages which heaven has lavished on us!

"The establishment of manufactures is calculated not only to
"increase the general stock of useful and productive labour, but
"even *to improve the state of agriculture in particular.*"*

What a lesson is here for the farmers and planters, who have been unhappily excited to view with jealousy and hostility those citizens who contribute so largely to their prosperity!

* Hamilton's Works, vol. I.

"It is the interest of the community, *with a view to eventual* " *and permanent economy*, to encourage the growth of manufac- " tures. In a national view, a temporary enhancement of price " must be always well compensated by a permanent reduction " of it."*

"The trade of a country, which is both manufacturing and " agricultural, will be *more lucrative and prosperous than that of* " *a country which is merely agricultural.*"*

"The *uniform appearance of an abundance of specie, as the* " *concomitant of a flourishing state of manufactures*, and of the " reverse where they do not prevail, afford a strong presumption " of their favourable operation upon the wealth of a country."*

" *Not only the wealth, but the independence and security of a* " *country, appear to be materially connected with the prosperity* " *of manufactures.* Every nation, with a view to these great " objects, ought to endeavour to possess within itself all the es- " sentials of national supply. These comprise the means of sub- " sistence, habitation, clothing, and defence."*

"Considering a monopoly of the domestic market to its own " manufactures as the reigning policy of manufacturing nations, " *a similar policy on the part of the united states*, in every proper " instance, is dictated, it might almost be said *by the principles* " *of distributive justice—certainly by the duty of securing to their* " *own citizens a reciprocity of advantages.*"*

Mr. Hamilton, however, displayed an extreme degree of inconsistency. Notwithstanding the conclusive and irresistible arguments of his report, in favour of a decided protection of manufactures, and notwithstanding the failure of many promising efforts at their establishment, in consequence of the deluge of goods poured into the market, instead of recommending an adequate enhancement of duties to supply some deficiency of revenue in 1790, he submitted a plan for an excise on spirituous liquors, which was one of the most universally odious and unpopular measures that could be devised. It excited the western insurrection; thereby tarnished the character of the country; and jeopardized the government in its infancy.

However strong the arguments may be in favour of an excise on spirits, in a moral point of view, it was, under existing circumstances, extremely impolitic. For the paltry amount raised from it for a considerable time after its adoption, it was not worth while to incur the disaffection of the citizens. The receipts for the first four years were—

* Hamilton's Works, Vol. I.

In 1792	$ 208,942
1793	337,705
1794	274,089
1795	337,755
Four years	$ 1,158,491*
Average	$289,622

What a miserable sum as a set-off against the oppression and vexation of an excise—and the insurrection it excited! How incalculably sounder policy it would have been, to have increased the duties on manufactured articles, which would not only have answered the purpose of meeting the additional demands of the treasury, and given a spring to the industry of our citizens; but made an important addition to the wealth, power and resources of the nation!

The importations subject to five and seven and a half per cent. duty—

In 1792 amounted to	$ 16,221,000†
1793, at 7½ and 8	14,966,000
1794, at 7½ and 10	17,700,000
1795, at 10	16,447,000
Four years,	$ 65,334,000
Two per cent. on this sum would have been	$ 1,306,620
Annual average	$ 326,655

which exceeds the net revenue arising from the excise, and with scarcely a dollar additional expense in the collection.

A variety of circumstances combined to rescue the united states from the ruinous consequences that would otherwise have naturally flowed from the impolicy of the tariffs of 1789, 1790, and 1804; of which, as I have already stated, the obvious tendency was to afford the manufacturing nations of Europe, nearly all the advantages they could have derived from this country in its colonial state.

The provision in 1790, for funding the debt of the united states, threw into circulation an immense capital, which gave life and activity to business. The establishment, about the same

* Seybert, 477. † Idem 159.

time, of the bank of the united states, afforded additional facilities to trade and commerce. And the wars of the French revolution opened a market for the productions of our agriculture, in many instances at most exorbitant prices; for instance, occasionally from fifteen to twenty dollars per barrel for flour in the West Indies, Spain and Portugal, and other articles in proportion. We were thus enabled to pay for the extravagant quantities of manufactures which we consumed, and with which we could and ought to have supplied ourselves.

The dreadful scenes in St. Domingo brought immense wealth into this country with the emigrants who purchased safety by flight from their paternal estates and their native land.

For a considerable time, moreover, we were almost the sole carriers of the colonial produce of the enemies of Great Britain, as her fleets were in full possession of the seas, and there was no safety for the vessels of those powers in hostility with her.

But it was obvious that this system rested the prosperity of the nation on the sandy foundation of the wars, desolation and misery of our fellow men. And as it was not probable that they would continue to cut each other's throats to promote our welfare, a close of this dazzling scene was to be expected, for which sound policy required provision to be made. But this duty was totally neglected. We proceeded as if this state of affairs were to last for ever. At length we were abruptly cut off from the markets of Europe, and then a new order of things arose, to dispel the lamentable delusion.

CHAPTER IV.

Memorials to congress. Deceptious report. List of Exports. Tariff of 1804. *Wonderful omission. Immense importations of cotton and woollen goods. Exportations of cotton.*

In the years 1802, 3, and 4, memorials were presented to congress from almost every description of manufacturers, praying for further protection. In the two first years they were treated with utter slight, and nothing was done whatever.

In 1804, the committee on commerce and manufactures made a very superficial report, from which I submit the following extract, as a specimen of the sagacity of its authors.

"There may be some danger in refusing to admit the manu-
"factures of foreign countries; for by the adoption of such a
"measure, we should have no market abroad, and industry
"would lose one of its chief incentives at home."

This paragraph is superlatively absurd, and indeed more than absurd: it is wicked. In order to defeat the object of the memorialists, it assumes for them requisitions which they did not contemplate, and which of course their memorials did not warrant. No sound man in the united states ever contemplated the total "*exclusion of foreign manufactures.*" It was merely requested that the memorialists should not themselves be "*excluded*" from the domestic market by foreign rivals—and that the industry of our citizens should be so far protected, that they might be enabled to supply a portion of the thirty millions of dollars, principally of clothing, imported that year.

But admitting for a moment, for the sake of argument, that foreign manufactures had been excluded, who could persuade himself, that we should therefore "have no market abroad for our produce?" War at that time raged in almost every part of Europe, and the West Indies: and those who purchased our produce, had at least as powerful reasons to purchase as we had to sell. The inhabitants of an island in danger of starvation would suffer more from being deprived of supplies, than the producers by the privation of a market.

To evince the futility of the ground assumed in the report, I annex a list of some of the great leading articles exported in that year:—

Flour - - - -	barrels	810,000
Indian corn - - - -	bushels	1,944,873
Beef - - - -	barrels	134,896
Indian meal - - - -	barrels	111,327
Hams - - - -	pounds	1,904,284
Butter - - - - -	pounds	2,476,550
Cheese - - - -	pounds	1,299,872
Lard - - - - -	pounds	2,565,719
Candles - - - -	pounds	2,239,356
Cotton - - - -	pounds	35,034,175
Tar - - - - -	barrels	58,181
Turpentine - - - -	barrels	77,827
Staves and heading - -	feet	34,614,000
Boards, plank and scantling - -	feet	76,000,000*

These, gentle reader, are the kinds of produce, which the framers of this very profound report were fearful "would not have a market," if "foreign merchandize was excluded." Such are the displays of wisdom and political economy made to the legislature of "the most enlightened nation in the world."

This subject deserves to be further analyzed. To reduce it

* Seybert, 110.

to plain English, it means, that, if the united states laid heavy duties, say 10, 15, 20 or 25 per cent. on silks, sattins, shawls, broadcloths, linens, &c. or prohibited East India cotton goods, the people of the West Indies would refuse to purchase our lumber—the Manchester manufacturers our cotton—and the governments of Spain and Portugal, our flour, Indian meal, &c. &c. Such views of political economy cannot fail to excite a high degree of astonishment at their absurdity.

In the year 1804, the demands of the treasury had greatly increased by an augmentation of expenditure, and by the $15,000,000 of debt funded for the purchase of Louisiana. This required an increase of duties. But the same impolicy and neglect of affording adequate protection to the productive industry of the country that prevailed in the former tariffs, appear in that of this year.

The old system was continued, of raising as large a portion as possible of the impost on articles not interfering with our manufactures, and laying duties comparatively light on manufactures. Accordingly the duties on teas, wines, coffee, sugar, &c. were raised with an intrepidity that bid defiance to the fear of smuggling.

1804.	*Cost.* Cents.	*Duty.* Cents.	Per cent.
Bohea tea, per lb.	14	12	85
Souchong do.	41	18	44
Hyson do.	56	32	57
Hyson skin do.	24	20	83
Imperial do.	75	32	40
Lisbon wine per gallon	80	30	37½
London market Madeira, do.	160	58	36
Coffee, per lb.	15	5	33

While these articles were dutied thus high, cotton and woollen goods, which formed the great mass of the clothing of the country, were subject to only fifteen per cent., which in the improved state of the machinery of Great Britain, and, so far as respects cotton, the low price of labour in the East Indies, was so wholly inadequate for protection, that very few attempts were made to establish them on an extensive scale, and thus the nation was drained of immense sums, for articles of which it could have supplied a superabundance.

It is a remarkable and most extraordinary fact, and scarcely credible, that *woollen goods were never mentioned in the tariff, before* 1816, when th government had been in operation 27 years! They were passed over, and fell within the class of non-enumerated articles. It is impossible to reflect on this fact, without astonishment, and a conviction that there never was adequate attention bestowed on the concoction of the tariff, which, while it was silent respecting those important articles, descended to the enumeration of artificial flowers, cosmetics, bricks and tiles, dentifrice, dates, dolls, essences, fans, fringes, glue, tassels and trimmings, limes and lemons, mittens, gloves, powders, pastes, washes, tinctures, plums, prunes, toys, wafers, &c. &c.

As few persons are aware of the extravagant extent of the importations of clothing, I annex the amount for five years, of articles subject to 15 per cent. duty, of which about nine-tenths were cotton and woollen goods.

1804	$30,285,267
1805	37,137,598
1806	43,115,367
1807	46,031,742
1808	23,780,758
	$180,350,732*

The re-exportation of articles of the same description for these years, was—

1804	$ 000,000	
1805	1,587,801	
1806	2,075,601	
1807	2,197,383	
1808	755,085	
		6,615,870†
Balance		173,737,862
Deduct for sundries, say ten per cent.		17,373,786
Cotton and woollen goods consumed in five years,		$156,364,076

Had the duty been twenty-five per cent., and the imports 100,000,000, the revenue would have gained, and there would have been an immense saving to the nation of above 50,000,000 of dollars in four years! When will statesmen learn the grand secret of "*transforming taxes into useful regulations?*"

* Seybert, 164.

† Idem, page 222.

During these five years, we exported of raw cotton—

1804 - - - - - -	lbs. 35,034,175
1805 - - - - - - -	38,390,087
1806 - - - - - - -	35,657,465
1807 - - - - - - -	63,944,459
1808 - - - - - - -	10,630,445
	lbs. 183,656,631

Although we supplied Great Britain with more than a third of the cotton she used, so little protection was afforded to the manufacture of the article here, that in the year 1805, our consumption was only 1000 bags; whereas, had the fostering care of the government been extended to it, we might have used 100,000. And this all-important manufacture, for which this country is so peculiarly fitted by its capacity of producing the raw material to any extent; its boundless water power; its admirable machinery; and the skill of its citizens, never took root here until the non-intercourse and other restrictive measures, affording our citizens a fair chance in their own market, they were encouraged to turn their attention, and devote their talents and capital to this grand object. In five years, that is, in 1810, merely through this encouragement, the consumption increased tenfold, to 10,000 bales, or 3,000,000 lbs. In five more, in consequence of the war, it rose to 90,000 bales, or 27,000,000 lbs. This affords a clear and decisive proof that nothing but a sound policy was necessary to have brought it early to perfect maturity.

There is not perhaps in history a greater instance of utter impolicy and disregard of the maxims of all profound statesmen, or of the solid and substantial interests of a nation, than this most lamentable fact exhibits. An inexhaustible source of national wealth, power, and resources, and of individual happiness, was bestowed on us by heaven, and prodigally lavished away, in favour of foreign nations, who made use of the wealth thus absurdly bestowed, to jeopardize our independence;—under the absurd idea, that as we had so many millions of acres of back lands uncultivated, we ought not to encourage manufactures!! Ineffable delusion! As if the thousands of men brought up to cotton weaving, who, under proper encouragement, would have migrated to this country, could be immediately transformed into back country farmers, and induced to encounter all the horrors of clearing the wilderness! And as if the vast numbers of old men, of women, and children, who might be most advantageously employed for themselves and for the nation, in this branch, were in any degree calculated for a country life, even under its most inviting form!

CHAPTER V.

Declaration of war. Blankets for Indians. Disgraceful situation of the united states. Governor Gerry. Sufferings of the army. Rapid progress of national industry.

On the 18th of June, 1812, war was declared against Great Britain. This event placed the ruinous and deplorable policy of our government, on the subject of its manufactures, in a glaring point of light. With raw materials in abundance, skill, enterprize, industry, water power, and capital to the utmost extent, to secure a full supply for nearly all our wants, we had, in defiance of the soundest maxims of policy, absurdly *depended on foreign nations for a great variety of necessary articles, and even, Oh, shame! for our clothing, than which the mind of man can hardly conceive of more utter want of policy.*

In consequence of this miserable system, at the commencement of the war, the nation suffered the disgrace of a regular proposition being offered to congress by the secretary at war, *to suspend the non-importation act for the purpose of importing a supply of five or six thousand blankets for the Indians*, for whom the department had not been able to make provision! and who had of course become clamorous at the disappointment! This melancholy tale will hardly find credence. It is, nevertheless, sacredly true; and if dear-bought experience were of any avail in the regulation of the affairs of nations, this simple fact would be an invaluable lesson to our statesmen, to warn them against the rock of depending on foreign nations for supplies of clothing and other necessary articles while they have the raw materials and talents provided at home. But, alas! to the incalculable injury of the nation, this admonitary lesson was wholly disregarded in 1816, as will appear in the sequel.

The good old governor of Massachusetts, Elbridge Gerry, felt deep distress at the bitter draught of the dregs of the chalice of humiliation swallowed at this crisis by the government of the united states, and brought the affair before the legislature of that state.

"It being officially announced, that the Indians complain they "cannot receive the usual supplies of goods, by reason of the "non-importation act, and that they were not to be purchased "within the united states:

"I submit to your consideration, whether it is not incumbent "on this state, to use the means in its power for *enabling the* "*national government to rise superior to such a humiliating cir-* "*cumstance!* In the year 1775, when our war with Great Bri- "tain commenced, and when, immediately preceding it, a non- "importation act had been strictly carried into effect, the state "of Massachusetts apportioned on their towns, respectively, to "be manufactured by them, articles of clothing wanted for their "proportion of the army, which besieged Boston; fixed the pri- "ces and qualities of those articles; and they were duly supplied "within a short period.

"Thus, before we had arrived at the threshold of indepen- "dence, and when we were in an exhausted state, by the antece- "dent, voluntary, and patriotic sacrifice of our commerce, *be-* "*tween thirteen and fourteen thousand cloth coats were manufac-* "*tured, made and delivered into our magazine, within a few* "*months from the date of the resolve which first communicated* "*the requisition.*

"Thirty six years have since elapsed, during twenty-nine of "which we have enjoyed peace and prosperity, and have increas- "ed in numbers, manufactures, wealth and resources, beyond "the most sanguine expectations.

"All branches of this government have declared their opinion, "and I conceive on the most solid principle, that as a nation *we* "*are independent* of any other, for the necessaries, conveniences "and for many of the luxuries of life.

"Let us not, then, at this critical period, admit any obstruc- "tion which we have power to remove, to discourage or re- "tard the national exertions for asserting and maintaining our "rights; and above all, let us convince Great Britain that we "can and will be independent of her for every article of "commerce, whilst she continues to be the ostensible friend, "but the implacable foe of our prosperity, government, union, "and independence."

What a melancholy difference between the two epochs, 1775, and 1812! Strength and vigour in youth—feebleness and decay in manhood! What lamentable havoc of national resources in the interim!

Mr. Gerry says, "*as a nation we are independent of every other.*" This is a most egregious error. "*As a nation,*" extent of resources considered, there was not then, nor is there now, a more dependent people, perhaps, in the world. In our towns and cities, one-half of our population, males and females, are covered with the fabrics and in the fashions of foreign nations. He should have said, "*we may and ought to be independent.*"—Two or three small words make an immense difference.

If any thing could add to the mortification and regret which this circumstance must excite, it is, that the quantity of wool sheared in 1810 was estimated at 13 or 14,000,000 lbs., and in 1812, at 20 or 22,000,000;* and that various promising attempts to establish the woollen manufacture, had been made at different periods, and in various parts of the union, during the preceding years, which, for want of protec- tion, had failed of success.

Next to the waste of the immense advantages we possess for the manufacture of cotton, is to be lamented the impolitic and irreparable destruction of merino sheep, of which we had to the value of about one million of dollars, which government, by an increase of duty on woollens, might have easily preserved. The contrast between our abandonment of them, and the great pains taken, and expense incurred, by different nations to possess themselves of this treasure, is strong and striking.

Hundreds of our ill-fated soldiers, it is said, perished for want of comfortable clothing in the early part of the war, when exposed to the inhospitable climate of Canada.†

The war found us destitute of the means of supplying ourselves, not merely with blankets for our soldiers, but a vast variety of other articles necessary for our ease and comfort, of which the prices were accordingly raised extravagantly by the importers. Our citizens, and among them numbers of our commercial men, entered on the business of manufactures with great energy and enterprize; invested in them many millions of capital; and having, during the thirty months in which the war continued, the domestic market secured to them, they succeeded wonderfully.

Never was there a prouder display of the (I had almost said) omnipotence of industry, than was afforded on this occasion. It furnishes an eternal lesson to statesmen. Our citizens exhibited a spectacle perhaps without precedent. *Unaided by the expenditure of a single dollar by our government*, they attained in two or three years, a degree of maturity in manufactures, which required centuries in England, France, Prussia, &c., and cost their monarchs enormous sums in the shape of bounties, premiums, drawbacks, with the fostering aid of privileges, and immunities bestowed on the undertakers. The supply became commensurate with the demand; and full confidence was entertained that the government and nation, to whose aid they came forward in time of need, would not abandon them to destruction, after the purposes of the moment were answered. Fatal delusion!

* Tench Coxe's Tables, preface, page xiii.

† I have heard a story, which I have reason to believe to be true, but for which however, I do not vouch, that the capture of Amelia Island, by Governor Mitchell, was ordered by government with a view to provide blankets for our suffering soldiers.

Our exports for 1813 and 1814, were only about 31,000,000 of dollars, or 15,500,000 per annum. Hostile fleets and armies desolated those parts of the country to which they had access.—Yet the nation made rapid strides in prosperity by the creative powers of industry. Every man was employed, and every man fully recompensed for his labours. It may, however, be supposed that the farmers suffered heavily by the exclusion of their productions from foreign markets. The fact is otherwise. I state the prices of three articles, flour, beef, and hemp, in the Philadelphia market, in proof of this assertion. Other articles commanded proportionable prices.

	Flour per barrel.	Beef per barrel.	Hemp per ton.
1813. Aug. 23 - - - -	$8 25	$15 50	$210
Nov. 22 - - - -	10 00	15 50	210
1814. Jan. 31 - - - -	8 00	13 50	275
July 4* - - - -	6 86	17 00	250
Dec. 5 - - - -	8 37	19 00	250

What a contrast at present ! We have exported—

In 1816	$64,784,896
1817	68,338,069
1818	73,854,437
	$206,997,402
Average	$68,999,280

That is, above four hundred per cent. more than in 1813 and 1814—and a premature decay has nevertheless been rapidly gaining ground on the nation by the prostration of its industry! What an important volume of political economy! How much more instructive than Condorcet, Smith, Say, Ricardo, and the whole school of economists of this class!

I am aware that from local circumstances, cotton and some other articles were at reduced prices at the places of production during the war, from the difficulty and expense of transportation. The fall of cotton was a natural consequence of the impolicy of the planters in not having previously secured themselves a domestic market.

The following tables exhibit a statement of the great advancement made; and prove that our citizens do not require half the patronage of government, which is afforded by England, France, Austria and Russia, to enable them to enter into competition with the whole world.

* Specie payments were continued till August 1814.

State of the cotton manufacture within thirty miles of Providence, R. I. in 1815, *extracted from a memorial to congress.*

"Cotton manufactories		140
"Containing in actual operation -	spindles	130,000
"Using annually . .	bales of cotton	29,000
"Producing yards of the kinds of cotton goods usually made		27,840,000
"The weaving of which, at eight cents per yard, amounts to		$2,227,200
"Total value of the cloth . . .		$6,000,000
"Persons steadily employed . . .		26,000

State of the cotton manufacture throughout the united states in 1815, *from a report of the Committee of Commerce and Manufactures.*

"Capital	$40,000,000
"Males employed, from the age of seventeen and upwards	10,000
"Women and female children . .	66,000
"Boys, under seventeen years of age . .	24,000
"Wages of one hundred thousand persons, averaging $150 each . . .	$15,000,000
"Cotton wool manufactured, ninety thousand bales, amounting to lbs. . .	27,000,000
"Number of yards of cotton of various kinds,	81,000,000
"Cost, per yard, averaging 30 cents .	$24,300,000

State of the woollen manufacture throughout the united states, in 1815, *from the same.*

"Amount of capital supposed to be invested in buildings, machinery, &c. . .		$12,000,000
"Value of raw material consumed annually	$ 7,000,000	
"Increase of value by manufacturing . . .	12,000,000	
"Value of woollen goods manufactured annually		$19,000,000

"Number of persons employed	constantly .	50,000
	occasionally .	50,000
		100,000

In the city and neighbourhood of Philadelphia, there were employed in 1815—

In the cotton branch - - - - -	2325	persons.
In the woollen - - - - - -	1226	do.
In iron castings - - - - - -	1152	do.
In paper making - - - - - -	950	do.
In smithery - - - - - - -	750	do.

The value of the manufactures of the city of Pittsburg, which in 1815 employed 1960 persons, was 2,617,833 dollars. And every part of the country displayed a similar state of prosperity. How deplorable a contrast our present situation exhibits!

CHAPTER VI.

State of the country at the close of the war. Pernicious consequences to the manufacturers, of the repeal of the double duties, and the enormous influx of foreign merchandize. Mr. Dallas's tariff. Rates reduced ten, twenty, and thirty per cent.

The war was closed under the most favourable auspices. The country was every where prosperous. Inestimable cotton and woollen manufacturing establishments, in which above 50,000,000 of dollars were invested, exclusive of a very great variety of other descriptions, were spread over the face of the land, and were diffusing happiness among thousands of industrious people. No man, woman, or child, able and willing to work, was unemployed. With almost every possible variety of soil and climate—and likewise with the three greatest staples in the world—cotton, wool, and iron—the first to an extent commensurate with our utmost wants, and a capacity to produce the other two to the same extent—a sound policy would have rendered us more independent probably of foreign supplies, for all the comforts of life, than any other nation whatever.

Peace, nevertheless, was fraught with destruction to the hopes and happiness of a considerable portion of the manufacturers. The double duties had been imposed with a limitation to one year after the close of the war. And a tariff as a substitute was prepared by the secretary of the treasury, with duties fixed at the minimum rates which he thought calculated to afford protection to our manufacturing establishments. On many articles these rates were insufficient. Yet had his tariff been adopted, it would probably have saved the country forty or fifty millions of dollars—and prevented a large portion of the deep distress that pervades the land, and which is driving legislative bodies to the desperate measure of suspending the course of justice.* But a deep-rooted jealousy of manufacturers was entertained by many of the members of congress, on the ground of imputed extortion during the war.† The old hacknied themes of "taxing the many for the benefit of the few"—the country not being ripe for manufactures—wages being too high--the immensity of our back lands, &c. &c. &c. were still regarded as unanswerable arguments. In consequence of the combined operation of these causes, the rates proposed by Mr. Dallas, were reduced on most of the leading articles ten, fifteen, and in some cases thirty per cent. Every per cent. reduced was regarded by many of the members as so much clear gain to the country. Some of them appeared to consider manufacturers as a sort of common enemy,‡ with whom no terms ought to be observed; and there was no small number who were disciples of colonel Taylor, of Caroline county, Va.‖ who holds the broad, unqualified doctrine. that every dollar paid as duty or bounty to encourage manufactures, is a dollar "robbed out of the pockets of the "farmers and planters!" Wonderful statesman! Profound policy! How all the Sullys, and Colberts, and Frederics of Europe must "hide their diminished heads" when their practice is put in contrast with this grand system of political economy!

To convey a correct idea of the spirit that prevailed in that congress towards their manufacturing fellow citizens, I annex a

* Measures of this description have been adopted, by five or six states.

† The reader is earnestly requested to peruse the 13th chapter of this small work, for a thorough examination of this senseless and unjust calumny.

‡ Ex-Governor Wright, of Maryland, was among the most violent of the members. His jealousy and hostility were without the least disguise, and were carried to an extent hardly credible. A motion for a reduction of the duty on cottons having failed, he attempted to have it re-considered—on the ground that some of the members who voted in the majority, were concerned in the cotton manufacture!

‖ Colonel Taylor is, I believe, a tobacco planter—and has never, in any of his plausible works, raised his voice against the extravagant duties on snuff and manufactured tobacco On this tender topic he is silent as the grave. Yet a chapter on it would have come from him with great propriety. It is a subject with which he ought to be thoroughly acquainted. I venture to hint, that he might with great advantage read the instructive fable of the lawyer's goring bull, which, with a suitable commentary on snuff and tobacco duties, might be very well prefixed as part of the prolegomena to some of the amusing chapters of his Arator. It may not be amiss, likewise, to whisper gently in his ear, that even tobacco in the leaf is subject to fifteen per cent. which is exactly the same duty as that imposed on silks, linens, clocks, brazing copper, gold leaf, hair powder, printed books, prints, slates, starch, stuff and worsted shoes, sealing wax, thread stockings, &c. &c. Who, then, can reflect without astonishment, that this gentleman and Mr. Garnett take a lead in the opposition to the protection of manufactures, although the rude produce of their own state is protected by the same duty as the above finished manufactures! After this, we may well ask, with amazement, "*what next?*" Be it what it may, it cannot surprise us.

statement of various articles, with the duties as reported by Mr. Dallas, and as finally adopted:—

ARTICLES.	Mr. Dallas's proposed Tariff.	Tariff adopted.
	Per cent.	*Per cent.*
Blank books	35	30
Bridles	35	30
Brass ware	22	20
Brushes	35	30
Cotton manufactures of all sorts	33 1-3	25
(Those below 25 cents per square yard, to be dutied as at 25 cents.)		
Cotton stockings	33 1-3	20
China ware	30	20
Cabinet ware	35	30
Carriages of all descriptions	35	30
Canes	35	30
Clothing, ready made	35	30
Cutlery	22	20
Cannon	22	20
Earthen ware	30	20
Glass ware	30	20
Harness	35	30
Iron ware	22	20
Leather and all manufactures of leather	35	30
Linens	20	15
Manufactures of wood	35	30
Needles	22	20
Porcelain	30	20
Parchment	35	30
Printed books	35	15
Paper hangings	35	30
Paper of every description	35	30
Printing types	35	20
Pins	22	20
Silks	20	15
Silk stockings	20	15
Sattins	20	15
Stone ware	30	20
Saddles	35	30
Thread stockings	20	15
Vellum	35	30
Walking sticks	35	30
Whips	35	30
Woollen stockings	28	20
Woollen manufactures generally	28	25
Boots, per pair	200 cts.	150 cts.
Iron in bars and bolts, per cwt.	75	45
Shoes and slippers of silk, per pair	40	30
Shoes of leather	30	25
Shoes for children	20	15

The various reductions of two and three per cent. evince the huckstering spirit that prevailed, utterly unworthy of the legislature of a great nation. Mr. Dallas made a difference of five and one-third per cent. between the two great articles, cottons and woollens, rating the former at thirty-three and a third, and the latter at twenty-eight, in consequence of our possessing a boundless supply of the raw material of the former, whereas that of the latter was rather limited. After an ardent struggle, the duties were reduced, and both rated alike at twenty-five per cent. All the southern members voted for the reduction, except five, Messrs. Jackson, Marsh, and Newton from Virginia, and Messrs. Calhoun and Mayrant, from South Carolina, who enjoy the melancholy consolation of having endeavoured to stem the storm. The cotton planters who united in the vote for the reduction, have dearly expiated their error, in rendering their fortunes and the prosperity of their country dependent upon the contingencies of foreign markets, instead of securing a large and constantly-increasing market at home. This ought to be resounded in their ears. Rarely has there been much greater impolicy—and rarely has impolicy been more severely and justly punished. They fondly and absurdly thought, that thirty cents per lb. for cotton would last for ever.

The committee of commerce and manufactures; many of the most enlightened members of congress; and the agents of the manufacturers, strongly remonstrated against the reduction of duty; and, with a spirit of prophecy, predicted the fatal consequences, not merely to the manufacturers, but to the nation. But they might as well have attempted to arrest the cataracts of Niagara with a mound of sand. Prejudice was deep, inveterate, and unassailable. It has never in times past had eyes or ears; and, notwithstanding the elevation of character, and the superior illumination to which we fondly lay claim, we are not likely to offer to the admiring world an exception to the general rule. Of this unpalatable position our brief history, alas! affords too many irrefragable proofs.

CHAPTER VII.

Ruin of the manufacturers and decay of their establishments. Pathetic and eloquent appeals to congress. Their contumelious and unfeeling neglect. Memorials neither read nor reported on. Revolting contrast between the fostering care bestowed by Russia on its manufacturers, and the unheeded sufferings of that class of citizens in the united states.

From year to year since that time, ruin spread among the manufacturers. A large portion of them have been reduced to bankruptcy from ease and affluence. Many are now on the brink of it. Most of them had entered into the business during the war, under an impression, as I have already stated, that there was a sort of implied engagement on the part of the government, that, having been found so useful in time of need, they would not afterwards be allowed to be crushed. To what extent there was any foundation for this idea, I am unable to decide. Suffice it to say, that all the calculations predicated on it were wholly and lamentably disappointed. The strong arm of government, which alone could save them from the overwhelming influx of foreign manufactures, by which they were destroyed, was not interposed in their behalf. Noble establishments, the pride and ornament of the country, which might have been rendered sources of incalculable public and private wealth, and which Edward III. Henry IV. Frederick the Great, and Catharine II. would have saved at the expense of millions, if necessary, are mouldering to ruins. And, to crown the whole, millions of capital which had every claim to the protection of government, has become a dead and heavy loss to the proprietors.

At every stage of this lamentable progress, the devoted sufferers not only appealed to the justice, but threw themselves on the mercy of their representatives. The utmost powers of eloquence were exhausted in those appeals, some of which may be ranked among the proudest monuments of human talents.

In the second session of the fourteenth congress, 1816–17, there were above forty memorials presented to the house of representatives from manufacturers in different parts of the united states, and some of them, particularly that from Pittsburg, fraught with tales of ruin and destruction, that would have softened the heart of a Herod. *Not one of them was ever read in the house!* The Pittsburg memorial was, it is true, printed for the use of the members. But this measure produced no effect.

The following is a list of the applications—

No.			*Memorials.*	*Subjects.*
1	1816. Dec.	16	From New York	Iron manufactures.
2		16	New Jersey	do.
3		20	New York	Umbrellas
4		27	Massachusetts	do.
5		30	New Jersey	Iron manufactures.
6	1817, Jan.	6	New Jersey	do.
7		8	New York	do.
8		9	Philadelphia	do.
9		10	Connecticut	Iron manufactures.
10		10	New Jersey	do.
11		13	Pennsylvania	do.
12		13	New Jersey	do.
13		14	Boston	do.
14		16	Kentucky	Bar iron.

No.	1818.		*Memorials.*	*Subject.*
15	Jan.	20	Pennsylvania	Bar iron.
16		22	Pennsylvania	Iron manufactures.
17		27	New Jersey	Bar iron
18		28	Pennsylvania	Iron manufactures.
19		29	Berkshire,	Manufactures generally.
20		29	New York	do.
21		30	New Jersey	Iron manufactures.
22		30	New York	Manufactures generally.
23		30	Oneida county	do.
24		31	New York	do.
25	Feb.	1	Pennsylvania	Iron manufactures.
26		3	New York	do.
27		4	Pennsylvania	do
28		4	New York,	Manufactures generally.
29		4	New York	do.
30		6	Connecticut	Iron manufactures.
31		6	New York and Vermont,	do.
32		8	Pennsylvania	do.
33		11	New Jersey,	Manufactures generally.
34		11	New York	Iron manufactures.
35		13	Rhode Island	Cotton and woollen.
36		13	Connecticut	do.
37		17	Pittsburg,	Manufactures generally.
38		20	Illinois	Lead.
39		24	Baltimore,	Manufactures generally.
40		26	Philadelphia,	do.
41		28	Oneida	do.
42		28	Berkshire	do.

No description could do justice to the force of some of these memorials. I shall therefore present a few short specimens of the facts and reasonings they placed before the eyes of congress, to enable the reader to form a correct estimate of the extremely culpable neglect of the voice of their constituents, displayed by that body. The applications were as ineffectual as those of the congress of 1774, to the ministers of George III, and were treated with as little ceremony.

From a Philadelphia Memorial.

" *We regard with the most serious concern the critical ana dan-*
" *gerous situation in which our manufactures are placed by*
" *the recent and extravagant importations of rival articles;* which,
" owing to the great surplus of them, and to the pressure for
" money, are in many cases sold at such reduced prices, as to
" render it impossible for our manufactures to compete with
" them. We believe that with the interests of the manufacturers

"are connected the best interests of the nation—and that if the "manufactures of the country are deprived of that support from "the legislature of the united states, to which we think they are "fairly entitled, *the evil will be felt not by us merely, but by the* "*whole nation; as it will produce the inevitable consequence of an* "*unfavourable balance of trade, whereby our country will be im-* "*poverished,** *and rendered tributary to foreign powers, whose in-* "*terests are in direct hostility with ours.*"

From the Pittsburg and other Memorials.

"The committee have found that *the manufacture of cottons,* "*woollens, flint glass, and the finer articles of iron, has lately* "*suffered the most alarming depression.* Some branches which "had been several years in operation, have been destroyed or "partially suspended; and others, of a more recent growth, an-"nihilated before they were completely in operation.

"*The tide of importation has inundated our country with fo-* "*reign goods. Some of the most valuable and enterprizing citi-* "*zens have been subjected to enormous losses, and others over-* "*whelmed with bankruptcy and ruin. The pressure of war was* "*less fatal to the hopes of enterprize and industry, than a gene-* "*ral peace, with the calamities arising from the present state of* "*our foreign trade.*

"It was confidently believed, that the destinies of the united "states would no longer depend on the jealousy and caprice of "foreign governments, and that our national freedom and wel-"fare were fixed on the solid basis of our intrinsic means and "energies. But these were 'airy dreams.' A peace was con-"cluded with England, and *in a few months we were prostrate* "*at her feet. The manufacturers appealed to the general go-* "*vernment for the adoption of measures that might enable them* "*to resist the torrent that was sweeping away the fruits of their* "*capital and industry.* Their complaints were heard with a "concern which seemed a pledge for the return of better days. "*The tariff of duties, established at the last session of congress,* "*and the history of the present year, will demonstrate the falsi-* "*ty of their expectations.*

"*England never suffered a foreign government, or a combina-* "*tion of foreign capitalists, by glutting her own market, to crush* "*in the cradle, any branch of her domestic industry. She never* "*regarded, with a cold indifference, the ruin of thousands of her* "*industrious people, by the competition of foreigners.* The bare "avowal of such an attempt would have incurred the indignant "resistance of the whole body of the nation, and met the frowns,

* How fatally and literally has this prediction been realized!

"if not the instant vengeance of the government. The consequences of this policy in England are well known; her manufactures have become a source of wealth incalculable; the treasures of Spanish America are poured into her lap; her commerce is spread over every ocean, and, with a population comparatively small, she is the terror and the spoiler of Europe. Take from England her manufactures, and the fountains of her wealth would be broken up; her pre-eminence among nations would be lost forever.

"For a speedy redress of such pressing evils, we look to the government of the union. *Will they uphold the sinking manufactures of the country, or will they not?* Are their late assurances of aid and protection forgotten with the crisis that gave them birth? Let them realize the hopes of the country, and act with decision before it be too late.

"In the united states we have the knowledge of the labour-saving machinery, and the raw material and provisions cheaper than in Britain; but the overgrown capital of the British manufacturer, and the dexterity acquired by long experience, make a considerable time and heavy duties necessary for our protection.—We have beaten England out of our market in hats, shoes, boots, and all manufactures of leather: we are very much her superior in shipbuilding; these are all works of the hands, where labour-saving machinery gives no aid; so that *her superiority over us in manufactures, consists more in the excellence and nicety of the labour-saving machinery, than in the wages of labour.* With all their jealousy and restrictions upon the emigrations of workmen, the distresses and misfortunes of England will, by due encouragement, send much of her skill and knowledge to our shores; let us be ready to take full benefit of such events, as England herself did, when despotic laws in Germany, and other parts of Europe, drove their manufacturers into Britain, which laid the foundation of her present eminence.

"That the cotton trade and manufacture is a concern of vast importance, and even of leading interest to the country, is a truth, your memorialists conceive, too palpable, to be denied or doubted. Were not our own constant observation and daily experience sufficient to establish it, the prodigious exertions of our ever-vigilant and indefatigable rival, directed against this particular interest, would place the matter beyond a question. For where a judicious and enterprizing opponent (as England undoubtedly is in this respect) directs her strongest engine of hostility, we have reason to conclude there lies our vital and most important concern. This consideration is coming home to us with more and more force; and *the cotton planter, as well as the manufacturer, must have, before this time, discovered the* "*alarming fact, that our great rival has become possessed of both our plants and seeds of cotton, which she is employing all her vast means to propagate in the East Indies and other British possessions, with an energy and success which threaten the most alarming consequences.* When your memorialists consider that the article thus jeopardized is the great staple of the country, they cannot but hope the people and their representatives will be generally convinced, that it is not the interest of individuals alone that is at stake, but that of the whole community.

"*An appeal is made to the equity, to the patriotism of the southern statesman: his aid and co-operation are invoked for the relief of the suffering manufacturers of the northern and middle states.*

"*In the interior of the united states, few articles can be raised which will bear a distant transportation; products much more valuable when the grower and consumer are near each other, are therefore excluded from cultivation. A dependence on foreign markets in the most prosperous times necessarily restricts the labours of agriculture to a very few objects; a careless, decrepit, and unprofitable cultivation is the known result.*

"The propriety of these observations may, in some degree, be illustrated by the difference in value between the land in the vicinity of a large town, and at a greater distance from it. The labour which produces the greatest quantity of subsistence is bestowed on the culture of articles too cumbrous for transportation; and in general a farm which will subsist fifty persons in its vicinity, would not subsist the fifth of that number three hundred miles off. *If the value of land be so much enhanced by the proximity of a market, and so rapidly diminished by the distance of transportation, the introduction of manufactories, and the creation of an interior market, ought to be regarded as peculiarly auspicious to the interest of agriculturists.*

"*Confining our views to the western country, we might emphatically ask, with what exportable commodities shall we restore the balance of trade, now fast accumulating against us?* How arrest the incessant drain of our capital? *Our manufactures are perishing around us, and already millions have escaped, never to return.*"

It will remain an eternal blot on the escutcheon of the fourteenth congress, that these pathetic addresses received no more attention than if they had been from a party of field negroes to a marble-hearted overseer.

The Oneida Memorial stated,

"That the above county contains a greater number of manufacturing establishments, of cotton and woollen, than any

" county in the state, there being invested in said establishments " at least 600,000 dollars.

" That although the utmost efforts have been made by the pro-" prietors to sustain those establishments, their efforts have pro-" ved fruitless, and more than three-fourths of the factories re-" main necessarily closed, some of the proprietors being wholly " ruined, and others struggling under the greatest embarrass-" ment.

" In this alarming situation, we beg leave to make a last ap-" peal to the congress of the united states. While we make this " appeal, our present and extensive embarrassments in most of " the great departments of industry, as well as the peculiar dif-" ficulty in affording immediate relief to manufacturers, are ful-" ly seen and appreciated. Yet your petitioners cannot believe " that *the legislature of the union will remain an indifferent spec-" tator of the wide-spread ruin of their fellow citizens, and look " on, and see a great branch of industry, of the utmost impor-" tance in every community, prostrated under circumstances fatal " to all future attempts at revival, without a further effort for re-" lief.* We would not magnify the subject, which we now pre-" sent to congress, beyond its just merits, when we state it to " be one of the utmost importance to the future interests and " welfare of the united states.

" It is objected that the entire industry of the country may " be most profitably exerted in clearing and cultivating our ex-" tended vacant lands. But *what does it avail the farmer, when " neither in the nation from which he purchases his goods, or " elsewhere, can he find a market for his abundant crops?* Be-" sides, the diversion of labour from agriculture to manufac-" tures, is scarcely perceptible. Five or six adults, with the aid " of children, will manage a cotton manufactory of two thousand " spindles."

These memorials were all referred to the committee of commerce and manufactures, which was then, so far as regarded them, a committee of oblivion. After a lapse of two months, that is, about the middle of February, a bill for the relief of the iron masters was reported—read twice—and suffered to die a natural death; having never been called up for a third reading. The other memorials passed wholly unnoticed—and were never, except three or four, even reported on by the committee! What renders this procedure the more revolting, is, that some of them were from large bodies of men of the first respectability. That from New York was signed by the governor of the state, and other eminent characters. And, moreover, many of the petitioners had agents at Washington to advocate their claims.

The senate displayed the same culpable disregard of the applications, the sufferings, and the distresses of their fellow citizens, engaged in manufactures, as the house of representatives. They afforded no relief—nor did they even once consider the applications of the petitioners. But they paid somewhat more regard to decorum. The petitioners and memorialists had in succession *leave granted them to withdraw their papers*, on the motion of a member of the committee of commerce and manufactures ! !

The practice of congress, it appears, is to read the heads of petitions ; and then, without further enquiry, to refer them to the committee to which the business properly appertains. It cannot fail to excite the astonishment of the citizens of the united states to learn, that when they have found it necessary to meet and address their representatives, elected to guard their interests, and paid liberally for their services, those representatives do not condescend even to hear or read what are their grievances, or the mode of redress proposed ! This is really so very indecorous and so shameful as to be absolutely incredible, if the fact were not established on good authority. Many of the most despotic princes of the East usually read the petitions of the meanest of their subjects. But under the free government of the united states, the great cities of New York, Philadelphia, Baltimore, and Boston, may combine together to seek relief from intolerable grievances ; respectfully address their representatives ; and have their prayers not merely rejected, but not even heard ! The annals of legislation may, I am persuaded, be ransacked in vain for a parallel to this outrageous conduct.

When we reflect on the waste of time in frothy speeches on points of little importance—or on points of great importance, after the subject has been completely exhausted—and compare it with that economy which forbids the spending ten or fifteen minutes in reading a petition from a great city, the capital of a state, with a population of above a million of people, we are lost in astonishment at the introduction of a practice which so egregiously violates every rule of duty, decency, and propriety.

In the subsequent session, 1817-18, the same pathetic appeals to the justice, the humanity, the generosity, the public spirit of congress were made, and with little more effect.

Two unimportant acts alone on the subject of manufactures were passed at this session. One increasing the duties on iron, and the other on copper, saddlery, harness, cut glass, tacks, brads, sprigs, and Russia sheetings. But on the great and important articles of cotton and woollen goods there was no increase of duty. The additional duties on iron have been ineffectual—as the manufacture is at present in a most prostrate state.

From a full consideration of the premises, it is due to justice to state, that the manufacturers of the united states, who, with their families and persons of every description depending on them, amount to 1,500,000 souls * with a capital of $ 150,000,000, and producing probably $ 350,000,000 per annum, have not had that attention from the government to which their numbers and their importance give them so fair a claim.

A large portion of mankind, probably, even in this country, three-fourths have no property but in the labour of their hands. To so many of them as are divested of this by an erroneous policy, *one of the grand objects of government is destroyed*—And, therefore, so far as property is concerned, their situation is no better than that of the subjects of despotism.

I go further. *The situation of the manufacturing capitalists of the united states is incomparably worse than that of the manufacturing capitalists and subjects of the monarchs of Europe*, so far as regards the protection of property.

This strong expression will excite the surprize of some superficial readers. But it is a crisis that demands a bold expression of truth. And the assertion need not be retracted or qualified. Here is the proof. Let Mr. Garnett, or Mr. Pegram, or any of the agricultural delegates refute it. Let us suppose a subject of Russia,† to invest a capital of one hundred thousand dollars, for instance, in a manufacture of calicoes. He has no foreign competitor to dread. The fostering care of the government watches over him. He has loans if necessary. Bounties are also occasionally afforded. No combination of foreign rivals can operate his destruction. The domestic market is secured to him, with no other than the fair and legitimate competition of his fellow subjects, which always guards the rest of the nation against imposition. His plans arrive at maturity. He reaps the rich reward of his talents, his time, his industry, his capital. He gives support to hundreds, perhaps thousands, and daily adds to the wealth, power, resources, and independence of the country affording him full protection; and amply repays her kindness.

Let us turn from this delightful picture of fostering care, under a despotism, to the depressed American capitalist, under a government which, in its principles, is really and truly the best that ever existed. He invests one hundred thousand dollars in a similar establishment; engages hundreds of people in a useful

* From what has appeared of the recent census, I am persuaded this number is far too small.

† The reasoning applies equally to France, England, and Austria.

and profitable manufacture; finally conquers all the various difficulties that new undertakings have to encounter; and brings his fabrics to market, in the hope of that reward to which industry, capital, and talent have so fair a claim. Alas! he has to meet not only the competition of his fellow citizens, but of the manufacturing world. While he is excluded absolutely by prohibition, or virtually by prohibitory duties, from nearly all the markets in Europe, and indeed elsewhere, the East Indies, England, France, and Italy divide the home market with him, which is crowded with cargoes of similar articles, by the cupidity or the distresses, but as often by the stratagems, of foreign manufacturers, in order to overwhelm him, and secure the market ultimately to themselves. Their goods are sent to vendue, and sacrificed below prime cost in Europe. His cannot find a market, but at a sacrifice which ruins him. He implores relief from his unfeeling countrymen. But he implores in vain. Their hearts are steeled against his sufferings. They meet all his complaints, all his prayers, with trite common places about "taxing the many for the benefit of the few, free trade," &c. &c.—and he is charged with extortion by men who for thirty successive years received from him and his brethren extravagant prices for all their productions! He becomes bankrupt, and dies of a broken heart. His family, born to high expectations, are reduced to a state of dependence. His workmen are driven to idleness and want, and exposed to the lures of guilt. The state is deprived of a useful citizen, who might have added to her "*wealth, power and resources*." His fate operates as a beacon to others, to beware of his career. And the wealth of the nation is exhausted to pay for foreign articles, substitutes for which he could have furnished of far better quality, and, though nominally dearer, in reality cheaper. This is the policy, and these are its consequences, advocated by the disciples of Adam Smith. And this is the deleterious policy, fraught with destruction to the happiness of a large portion of its citizens, that is pursued by the united states of America.

Hundreds of capitalists throughout this country—thousands of workmen—millions of destroyed capital—and the general impoverishment of the nation, bear testimony to the correctness of this hideous portrait, so discreditable to our country, such a libel on its mistaken policy.

To such a man what does it signify by what name you call the government? It is, you say, a republic. True. But alas! he is ruined by its impolicy. The most despotic government in the world could do no more than ruin him. And some of them, it appears, would have protectedhim. Therefore, I repeat, so far as property is concerned, the difference, as regards this class of citizens, is against the united states. In fact, the better the form of government, the more grievous their distress Under a despotism "to suffer and submit" would be their "charter." But to be mocked and deluded with the promise of equal rights and equal protection under a free government, and unfeelingly consigned to destruction by their own fellow citizens and representatives, by the men whom they have clothed with the power of legislation—barbs the dart with tenfold keenness

Having submitted this portrait to the citizens of the united states, I ask, whether there be a greater contrast between the conduct of a fond mother towards her only and darling child—and that of a rigorous step-mother, towards a step-child which interferes with her views in favour of her own offspring than there is between the treatment of manufacturers in Russia and in the united states?

If these views be unpalatable. the fault is not mine. Let those answer for them, who have rendered their exposure necessary. Their truth can be judicially proved.

The situation of a very considerable portion of our citizens, is far worse than in the colonial state. They had then no competitors in the markets of their country but their fellow subjects of Great Britain. Now they have competitors from almost every part of Europe and from the East Indies. The case of the paper makers affords a striking illustration of this position One half of them in the middle states are ruined—not by the importation of British paper, of which little comes to this market—but by French and Italian, with enormous quantities of which our markets were deluged for two or three years after the war.

CHAPTER VIII.

Dilatory mode of proceeding in congress. Lamentable waste of time. Statement of the progress of bills. Eighty-two signed in one day! and four hundred and twenty in eleven! Unfeeling treatment of Gen. Stark. Culpable attention to punctilio. Rapid movement of compensation bill.

To every man interested in the honour and prosperity of the country, it is a subject of deep regret to reflect on the mode in which the public business is managed in and by congress. It is the chief source of the distress and embarrassment of our affairs. and requires an early and radical remedy. While in session, a considerable proportion of the members are employed in chatting—writing letters to their friends—or reading letters or newspapers. They pay little or no attention to the arguments of the speakers, except to those of a few of distinguished talents. To some of the orators, however, this is no great disappointment; as their speeches are too often made for the newspapers, and to display their talents to their constituents.

But the lamentable waste of time by the spirit of procrastination in the early part of the session, and by never-ending speechifying throughout its continuance, is the greatest evil, and is discreditable to congress and highly pernicious to the public service. There is in almost every session some subject of real or factitious importance, on which every member who believes he is possessed of oratorical talents, regards himself as bound to harangue, and to "keep the floor," for two, three, four, five or six hours. The merits of the speeches are generally measured by the length of time they occupy. They are all, to judge by the puffs in some of the newspapers, elegant, wonderful, powerful, admirable, excellent, inimitable.

In most cases, it will be found, as is perfectly natural, that the early speeches, on each side, particularly if by men of talents, exhaust the subject; and that those which follow them, do little more than retail the arguments previously advanced. It surely requires no small disregard of decorum for a member to occupy the time of a public body, to whose care are entrusted the concerns of a great nation, with such fatiguing repetitions.

The debate on the repeal of the compensation act cost some weeks; that on the Seminole war, fills six hundred pages; which, if divested of the duplications, triplications, and quadruplications, the rhetorical flourishes, and extraneous matter, would be reduced to two hundred—perhaps to one hundred and fifty. The Missouri question would probably fill from eight hundred to one thousand pages. Some of the prologues to these speeches are, as was humourously observed by a member long since, like "sale coats," calculated to suit almost any other subject equally well. And during this miserable waste of time, excitement of angry passions, and seditious threats of separation, there is a total suspension of the business of the nation, whose blood flows at every pore—whose revenues are failing—whose manufactures are paralized—of whose commerce one half is annihilated—whose merchants and manufacturers are daily swallowed up in the vortex of bankruptcy—whose great staples have fallen in price at least thirty per cent.—and which exhibits in every direction most appalling scenes of calamity and distress!

Some idea may be formed of the mode in which the business of this nation is conducted by its legislature, from the following chronological statement of the periods at which the acts of successive sessions were approved by the presidents. Between their passage in the two houses and the date of the presidents' signatures, there may be some few days difference, for which the reader will make allowance. But be that allowance what it may, it cannot remove the accusation of a most ruinous waste of time, and a most culpable and shameful procrastination of public business in congress.

In the first session of the twelfth congress, which commenced on the 4th of November, 1811, and terminated on the 6th of July, 1812, there were one hundred and thirty-eight acts passed which were signed by the president in the following chronological order—

In November - -	2	Over	73
December - -	8	In May - -	21
January - - -	9	June - - -	17
February - -	14	July 1st - -	8
March - - -	14	July 6th - -	29
April - - -	26		148
	73		

Twelfth congress.—Second session. From November 2, 1812, *to March* 3, 1813.—*Sixty-two acts.*

November - -	1	Over .	16
December - - -	4	February - -	23
January - - -	11	March 3d - -	23
	16		62

Thirteenth congress.—First Session.—From May 24, *to Aug.* 2, 1813.—*Fifty-nine acts.*

May - - -	00	Over .	3
June - - - -	3	July - - -	32
		August 2d - -	24
	3		59

The twenty-four acts signed on the 2d of August, contained *forty-six pages of close print.* The act imposing the direct tax, is in the number, and contains *twenty-two pages.*

Thirteenth congress.—Second session.—From December 6, 1813, *to April* 18, 1814.—*Ninety-five acts.*

December - -	2	Over	16
January - - -	7	March - - -	27
February - -	7	April 1st to 16th -	18
		April 18th -	34
	16		
			95

Thirteenth congress.—Third session. From September 19, 1814, *to March* 3, 1815.—*One hundred acts.*

September - -	00	Over .	18
October - - -	1	January - - -	9
November - -	6	February - -	38
December -	11	March 1st - - -	4
		March 3d - -	31
	18		
			100

The thirty-one acts signed on the 3d of March, contain thirty five pages.

This was the ever memorable session of congress, in which the imbecility of the majority and the factious violence of the minority, brought the nation to the jaws of destruction, previous to the close of the war.

Fourteenth congress.—First session. From December 4, 1815, *to April* 30, 1816.---*One hundred and seventy-two acts.*

December - -	2	Over	35
January - - -	4	April 2d to the 24th	39
February - -	15	26th and 27th	59
March - - -	14	29th - -	31
		30th - -	8
	35		
			172

Fourteenth congress.—Second session. From December 2, 1816, *to March* 3, 1817.—*One hundred and fourteen acts.*

In December - -	00	Over .	18
In January - -	8	On Saturday, March 1st	14
In February - -	10	March 3d - -	82
	18		1 4

The acts of this session are comprised in one hundred pages. Those signed in January occupy three pages and a half---those in February four--those on the first of March nine---and those on the third seventy-three!

Fifteenth congress.--- First session. From November 16, 1817, *to April* 20, 1818.---*One hundred and thirty acts.*

November . .	00	Over .	14
December . . .	1	March	10
January . .	7	April 3d to 18th .	54
February . . .	6	Apri 20th . .	52
	14		130

The fifty-two acts signed on the 20th of April, contain of John E. Hall's edition, no less than eighty-seven pages. In this session there were, it appears, one hundred and six acts passed in seventeen days---and only twenty-four in the preceding four months and a half!

The annals of legislation may be challenged for any parallel case.

Fifteenth congress.—Second session. From November 16, 1818, *to March* 3, 1819. *One hundred and seven acts.*

November . .	00	Over .	11
December . . .	7	February	33
January . . .	4	March 2d	8
		March 3d . . .	55
	11		107

This system of procrastination has been coeval with the government. I am informed by a gentleman of veracity, that General Washington, when an extraordinary number of acts were presented to him on the last day of a session, more than he could correctly decide upon, has expressed a strong and most marked disapprobation of so incorrect a procedure.

Analysis.

Sessions of congress - - - - - - - - -	9
Duration - - - - - - - -	months 39½
Acts passed - - - - - - - - -	988
Of which were signed in eleven days - - -	420

Viz.

1812.	July 6th - - - - - - - - -	29
1813.	March 3d - - - - - - - -	23
	August 3d - - - - - - - -	24
1814.	April 18th - - - - - - - -	34
1815.	March 3d - - - - - - - -	31
1816.	April 26th, 27th and 29th - - - - -	90
1817.	March 3d - - - - - - -	82
1818.	April 20th - - - - - - - -	52
1819.	March 3d - - - - - - -	55
		420

Thus it appears that in *three years and three months* there were 568 acts signed—and in *eleven* days, as I have stated, 420 ! ! Wonderful system of legislation !

No small share of the censure due to the procrastination of the public business, so visible in the above proceedings, justly attaches to the speaker for the time being. He ought to keep a docket of the business brought before the house, and urge committees to perform their duty. Certain days should be appointed to make reports, which ought then to be called for. If not ready, others should be fixed. And whenever the public business is unnecessarily or wantonly procrastinated, his duty requires the use of strong animadversion. This arrangement would be productive of the most salutary consequences. But for want of this or some other system, a very large portion of every session is literally thrown away. And so much of the business is crowded together at the close, that it is impossible to concoct it properly. Ever since the organization of the government, three-fourths of all the important acts have been passed within the last week or ten days of the close of each session.

Is it then surprising that the national business is egregiously ill-managed? That the reiterated requests of so large a portion of our citizens, for a bankrupt and other salutary acts, are of no avail?—How is it possible for the members—how is it possible for the president—to discharge their respective duties conscientiously, with such a system? Can any powers short of superhuman enable the latter to decide on the justice, the propriety, the constitutionality of twenty, thirty, forty, fifty, sixty, seventy, or eighty acts in one or two days? Is not this making a mere mockery of legislation?

Two, three, and sometimes four months are drawled away in the early part of the session—with three, four. six, eight, ten or twelve acts—and afterwards all the business is hurried through with indecent haste. In the one portion of the time, the progress resembles that of the snail or sloth—in the other, that of the high mettled racer. In fact and in truth, if congress desired to bring republican government into disgrace, to render it a bye-word and a reproach, it would not be very easy to devise a plan more admirably calculated for the purpose than a considerable part of their proceedings.

One ruinous consequence attending the system pursued, is, that at the close of every session, some of the most important bills are necessarily postponed.

It is frequently said, in justification of the procrastination of congress, and the little business that is executed in the early part of the session, that the committees are employed in digesting and preparing their reports. It is obvious, that this operation must require considerable time. But whoever reflects on the nature of a large portion of the business that is discussed in that body, will be convinced that it might be despatched in a fifth part of the time it occupies.

Among the acts hurried through at the close of the session, there are frequently some, and among them private ones, which have "dragged their slow length along" for months before, and which might as readily be decided on in a week as in six months. I annex the dates of introduction and of signature of a few, to exemplify this.

		Reported.	*Signed.*
Act to divide the state of Pennsylvania into districts - -	1818.	Feb. 4	April 20
Act for publication of laws, - -		Jan. 16	April 20
Act for the relief of B. Birdsall -		Jan. 27	April 20
Act for incorporating Columbian Institute,		Feb. 3	April 20
Act for relief of General Brown, -		Feb. 9	April 18
Act for relief of T. & J. Clifford -		Jan. 20	April 20

The bill for the relief T. & J. Clifford, which was three months on its passage through the houses, contains about twenty lines, and was for the remission of duties paid on articles not subject to duty. Three days would have answered as well for the discussion as seven years. Such is the case with half the bills that are crowded together at the last day of the session.

It may not be uninteresting to make a few further extracts from the journals, shedding additional light on this important subject.

1819. April 18. "Engrossed bills of the following titles " *(nine in number)* were severally read a third time and passed."

April 20. " Bills from the senate of the following titles *(ten " in number)* were severally read a third time and passed."

Eodem Die. " A message from the senate that they have pass- " ed bills of this house of the following titles, to wit—*(eighteen " in number)*"

By a careful search through the journals of different sessions, we might find three or four hundred bills, thus bundled together, and hastily read off, ten or a dozen en suite.

The case of General Stark deserves to be put on record, to corroborate some of the opinions offered in this chapter.

On the 6th of March, 1818, a petition was presented by this meritorious veteran, representing his necessitous circumstances, and praying that the bounty of the national government might be extended to him, in the decline of life, in compensation of his faithful services in defence of his country. It was referred to a committee, who reported a bill on the 9th, which was read the first and second time on that day. *It then lay over untouched for above five weeks, till Saturday the 18th of April,* when it was passed and sent to the senate, where it was read and referred to the committee on pensions, who reported it on that day without amendments. It was read the third time on Monday the 20th, in committee of the whole, and agreed to *with amendments.* It being against a rule of the senate to pass a bill on the same day in which it has undergone amendments, Mr. Fromentin moved that the rule be dispensed with. *But this motion was unfeelingly rejected.* And as the session was closed that day, the bill of course was lost; and the venerable old hero, about ninety years of age, and bending over the grave, was disappointed at that time of receiving the pittance intended for him. The importance of his victory at Bennington, which led to those all-important events, the battle of Saratoga and the capture of General Burgoyne, which stand conspicuous among the proudest triumphs of the revolutionary war, is so deeply impressed on the public mind, that every good man in the nation felt deep regret and indignation at this very ill-timed and ungracious punctilio.

The compensation bill, which was to render *members of congress salary officers, at the rate of 1500 dollars per annum*, passed by a former congress, forms a proper contrast to the bill in favour of general Stark.

It was read the first and second time in the house of representatives	-	March 6th, 1815.
Read a third time, and passed	- - -	9th
Read first time in senate	- - - -	11th
Second time	- - - - -	12th
Third time and passed	- - -	14th
Laid before the president	- - - -	18th

Approved same day.
What wonderful economy of time!

Thus a bill for their own benefit, which introduced a novel principle into the country, in twelve days passed through all its stages from its inception to the presidential approbation!!

What a striking and indelible reproach to congress arises from a contrast of this case with that of the veteran Stark! How wonderfully their personal interest accelerated their movements!

The citizens of the united states, however, are answerable for a large portion of the derelictions of congress. Most of the members are ambitious of popularity; which forms one of the principal inducements to seek a seat in that body. And the utter inattention too generally displayed by the citizens to the conduct of their representatives, induces a degree of indifference towards the interests and wishes of constituents. A more frequent call for the yeas and nays, by those members who are sincerely desirous of discharging their duty, and of having the public business punctually attended to, together with a publication of lists of votes on all important questions, previous to elections, would operate powerfully on the feelings of the members. If every member whose votes militated with the substantial interests of his country, were sure to be discarded, as he ought to be, on the day of election, the proceedings of congress would exhibit a very different appearance from what they do at present.

CHAPTER IX.

Attempts to prove the state of affairs prosperous. Their fallacy established. Destruction of industry in Philadelphia and Pittsburg. Awful situation of Pennsylvania. 14,537 *suits for debt, and* 10,326 *judgments confessed in the year* 1819. *Depreciation of real estate* 115,544,629 *dollars.*

For a considerable time, elaborate efforts were made to prove that the great mass of our citizens were highly prosperous. Even official messages, at no very distant day, announced this idea. But the veil that obscured the appalling vision of public distress is removed, and there is now no diversity of sentiment on the subject. Bankruptcy of banks—individual ruin—and sheriffs' sales to an extent never known before—the idleness of thousands of those who have no property but in the labour of their hands—resolutions of town meetings—memorials and petitions from almost every part of the middle and eastern states—messages of governors—deliberate instructions of the representative bodies in some of the states—*acts of legislatures, suspending the collection of debts*—and, to close the long train of calamity, the emigration of American citizens to a Spanish colony, seeking an asylum from the distress they suffer in their own country—all distinctly proclaim a deplorable state of society, which fully evinces a radical unsoundness in our policy, loudly and imperiously demanding as radical a remedy. No temporizing expedients will suffice. Nothing short of a complete and permanent protection of the national industry, so as to enable us *to reduce our demands from Europe, within our means of payment*, will arrest us in the career of impoverishment—and enable us to regain the ground we have unhappily lost, and take that high and commanding stand among nations, which nature and nature's God, by the transcendent advantages bestowed on us, intended we should enjoy—advantages which for five years we have so prodigally squandered.

Although the prevailing depression and distress are generally well known, yet few are fully acquainted with their extreme intensity. Indeed, it is at all times difficult and scarcely possible to realize, from general description, the extent of suffering which mankind endure—whether by war, famine, pestilence, or want of employment. In the last case, it would be necessary to traverse by-lanes and alleys—to ascend to garrets—or descend to cellars—to behold the afflicted father, after having pawned his clothes and furniture, destitute of money and credit to support his famishing wife and children—his proud spirit struggling between the heart-rending alternatives of allowing them to suffer under hunger and thirst, or else sinking to apply to the overseers of the poor—to ask alms in the street—or to have recourse to soup-houses for relief.* These are afflicting realities, with which, I hope for the honour of human nature. the presidents and delegates of agricultural societies, who enter the list to prevent the relief of their fellow citizens, and perpetuate their sufferings, are wholly unacquainted,

I cannot here enter into particulars of the awful scenes that overspread the face of the land, and shall confine myself to a slight sketch of the lamentable devastation of national prosperity and private happiness, experienced in Philadelphia and Pittsburg, which so many worthy, but mistaken men are labouring to perpetuate.

By an investigation ordered during last autumn by a town meeting of the citizens of Philadelphia. and conducted by gentlemen of respectability, it appears, so great was the decay of manufacturing industry, that in only thirty out of fifty-six branches of business there were actually 7728 persons less employed in 1819 than in 1816, whose wages amounted to $ 2,366.935. No returns were procured from twenty-six branches, viz.

Bookbinders
Brewers
Brickmakers
Carpenters
Coopers
Chocolate makers
Calico printers
Curriers
Chair makers
Dyers
Engravers
Embroiderers
Glovers
Glass manufacturers
Manufacturers of gun-powder
Painters and glaziers
Plumbers
Shoemakers
Shotmakers
Sugar bakers
Snuff and tobacco manufacturers
Stonecutters
Turners
Tanners
Umbrella makers
Wheelwrights, &c. &c.

Assuming only half the number, in these twenty-six, that were in the other thirty, the aggregate would be 11,592—and, were only one woman or child dependent on each person, the

* Some idea may be formed of the state of our cities, from the circumstance, that in Baltimore, there are no less than twelve stations for distributing soup tickets. In Philadelphia, the distribution is very great, at the rate of a pint to each person.

whole, out of a population of about one hundred and twenty thousand,

Would amount to - - -	persons 23,184
Whose wages would be - - -	$3,550,402
And allowing the work when finished, to be worth double the wages, which is a moderate calculation, the value would be - - -	$7,100,804

lost in a single city in one year!

Let us now survey Pittsburg, where we shall behold a similar scene of devastation. This city in 1815, contained about six thousand inhabitants. It then exhibited as exhilirating a scene of industry, prosperity, and happiness, as any place in the world. Its immense local advantages, seated at the confluence of two noble rivers, forming the majestic Ohio; its boundless supplies of coal; and the very laudable enterprise of its inhabitants. had for a long time rendered it the emporium of the western world. But, alas! the immoderate influx of foreign manufactures, poured in there shortly after the peace, produced a most calamitous reverse. The operations of the hammer, the hatchet, the shuttle, the spindle, the loom, ceased in a great degree. Noble establishments, which reflected honour on the nation, were closed; the proprietors ruined; the workmen discharged; a blight and a blast overspread the face of the city; and the circumjacent country, which had shared in its prosperity, now equally partook of its decline.

By a recent and minute investigation, conducted by citizens of high standing, the following appeared to be the—

Actual state of the city of Pittsburg.

Persons deprived of employment, or less employed in 1819 than in 1816	1288
Supposing only one woman or child depending on each of the above	1288
It would amount to	2576
The amount of work done in 1816 was .	$2,617,833
In 1819	832,000
Loss to Pittsburg	1,785.833
Loss to Philadelphia, as before, . .	7,100,804
Annual loss in two cities in one state . .	$8,886,637

When the other cities and towns throughout the union, where similar devastation has occurred, are taken into view, it will not be an unreasonable calculation to presume it six-fold elsewhere; but to avoid cavil, I will only suppose it treble---

Which will amount to	$26,659,911
Philadelphia and Pittsburg	8,886,637
Total loss of industry	$35,546,548

By the wretched policy of fostering foreign manufactures and manufacturers, and foreign governments; buying cheap bargains abroad, and consigning our own citizens to bankruptcy and beggary!

With these overwhelming facts staring us in the face, is it not insanity to be debating about the causes of the existing distress? Who can entertain a doubt as to the grand and primary cause? Is it not as plain as "the hand writing on the wall?"--- Does it not clearly arise from the destruction of so large a portion of the national industry? What! an annual loss in two cities containing about 130,000 inhabitants, of nearly nine millions of dollars, and proportionable losses almost every where else! Such a course, steadily continued, would impoverish China more rapidly than she has accumulated her immense treasures. It is not therefore wonderful that it has, in a few years, impoverished a nation whose sole patrimony was her industry.

Some public documents have recently appeared, which prove the distress of the country far more intense and extensive than had been previously conceived A committee of the senate of Pennsylvania, appointed to enquire into the extent and causes of the general distress, addressed circulars to all the prothonotaries and sheriffs in the state, whence they collected the following awful facts:

The number of actions brought for debt in the year 1819, was	14,537
The number of judgments confessed . . .	10,326
Exclusive of those before justices of the peace, about half the number.	
Imprisonments for debt in the city and county of Philadelphia	1,808
In Lancaster county	221
In Alleghany county	286

A report made to the house of representatives, by a committee appointed for the same purpose as that in the senate, appears to estimate the depreciation of the real estate in Pennsylvania at one-third of the value ascertained by the united states assessment in 1815, which was, $316,633,889---of course the depreciation is $105,544,629.

A memorial referred to in another report, states---

"That embarrassment is universal; that the sordid and avari-
"cious are acquiring the sacrificed property of the liberal and
"industrious; that so much property is exposed to sale under
"execution, that buyers cannot be had to pay more for it than
"the fees of office."

Would to God, that this affecting picture could be placed in large characters in congress hall, in the president's house, and in the offices of the secretaries of state and the treasury, that they might be led to take the necessary measures as early as possible to relieve such sufferings.

This, let it be observed, is far from the whole of the evil. The comparison is only a retrospective one—to shew the precipitous descent we have made from a towering height. Let us now see the point to which we might, and by a proper policy would have arrived. In five years, from 1810 to 1815, as already stated, the manufacture of cotton increased from 10,000 to 90,000 bales, or 270,000,000 lbs. The other manufactures of the country increased very considerably, but not in the same proportion.

By the statements of the marshals, and the calculations of Mr. Coxe, a gentleman perfectly competent to this service, it appears that the manufactures of the united states in 1810, amounted to 172,000,000 dollars.

Let us suppose that instead of a multiplication nine-fold, such as took place in the cotton branch between 1810, and 1815, the general increase was only fifty per cent. it follows, that in 1815, the whole of our manufactures must have amounted to above 250,000,000 dollars.

Inferring from past experience, they would, under an efficient protection by the government, have increased from 1815, to 1820, fifty per cent. and of course would now be above 370,000-000 dollars.

It is impossible to pursue this train of reflexion, and compare what we might be, with what we are, without sensations of the keenest distress, and a clear conviction of the radical unsoundness of a policy, which has in a few years produced so much destruction of happiness and prosperity.

CHAPTER X.

Causes assigned for the existing distress. Extravagant banking. Transition to a state of peace. Fallacy of these reasons. True cause, destruction of industry. Comparison of exports for six years.

SINCE public attention has been drawn to explore the causes of the existing evils, some of our citizens have ascribed them to the abuses of banking, and others to "*the transition from a state of war to a state of peace*"—overlooking the real cause, the prostration of so large a portion of the manufacturing industry of the nation—and likewise overlooking the strong fact, that all nations have fallen to decay, in proportion as they abandoned, and have prospered in proportion as they protected, the industry of their people.

Let us briefly examine both of these alleged causes of distress.

It is impossible to defend the legislative bodies, who incorporated such hosts of banks at once. They are deserving of the most unqualified censure; and it is to be regretted that they cannot be rendered individually responsible for the consequences. But the mischief that has arisen from those banks, has been greatly overrated. I submit a few facts and reflections on the subject.

With the state of Pennsylvania I am more familiar than with any of the others; and shall therefore found my reasoning on the system pursued here. It will apply, *mutatis mutandis*, to all those which have carried banking to excess.

In 1814, the legislature of this state incorporated forty-one banks, of which only thirty-seven went into operation—of these I present a view—

	Capital authorised.	*Capital paid in.*
Thirty-three country banks -	$12,665,000	$5,294,238
Four city banks - -	3,500,000	2,134,000
	$16,165,000	$7,428,238

Two reports, recently made to the legislature of Pennsylvania, convey an idea that the capital of these banks was much greater than it really was.

"The people of Pennsylvania, during an expensive war, and "in the midst of great embarrassments, established forty-one "new banks, *with a capital of* 17,500,000 *dollars*—and authority "to issue bank notes to double that amount."*

"A bill, authorizing the incorporation of forty-one banking "institutions, *with capitals amounting to upwards of* 17,000,000 "*dollars*, was passed by a large majority."†

Several of them had been in operation previous to the act of incorporation—particularly the Commercial Bank in Philadelphia, with a capital of 1,000,000 dollars, and others with probably capitals of $750,000: so that the addition then made to the banking capital of the state was only about 5,700,000 dollars.

* Report to the house of representatives.

† Report to the senate.

It is perfectly obvious, that in calculating the effects produced by these banks, we must have reference not to the capital *authorized*—but to that actually *paid in*.

Had every one of these banks been fraudulently conducted, and become bankrupt, would it account for the excessive distresses of the state? It would be idle to pretend it. The circumstance would have produced great temporary embarrassment—but our citizens would soon have recovered, had their industry been protected.

The population of the state is above 1,000,000. Its manufactures in 1810, as stated by Mr. Coxe, were 32,000,000 of dollars—and had probably risen in 1814, to 45,000,000. Its domestic exports for the last three years, have been above 20,000,000, or nearly 7,000,000 per annum. Now, can it be believed that the specified increase of banking capital in a state with such great resources, could have produced such ruinous consequences? Surely not.

In cases of great calamities, arising from embargoes, blockades, unexpected war, or peace, New York and Philadelphia have each suffered nearly as much loss as the whole capital of all those banks, and speedily revived like the Phœnix from her ashes.

Let it be observed, that after deducting the capitals of—

The Bank of Lancaster*	$600,000
Marietta	239,430
Pittsburg	316,585
Reading	299,440
Easton	211,830
	$1,667,285

The remaining country banks only average about 125,000 dollars each. Some of them operate in a space, of which the diameter is thirty, forty, or fifty miles. Surely the doctor's apprentice, who, finding a saddle under his patient's bed, ascribed his illness to his having devoured a horse, was not much more ludicrously in error, than those who ascribe the whole or even the chief part of the sufferings of the state to this cause.

Let it be distinctly understood, that I freely admit that some of those banks have done very great mischief, and that several have been improperly conducted. But had the industry of the state been protected, and trade flourished, the great mass of them would have gone on prosperously, and the whole would

* Four of these towns are places of importance, and carry on trade very extensively.

not have produced one-tenth part of the injury that has resulted from those that have been ill-managed.

Before I quit this subject. let me observe, that the greater portion by far of these banks have been, I believe, fairly and honourably conducted: and that little inconvenience was felt by or from any of them, from the time of resuming specie payments, till of late when the unceasing drain of specie exhausted them of the pabulum on which banks are supported, and obliged them to diminish their issues, and to press on their debtors, of whom many were ruined, Notwithstanding all their efforts, several of the banks have been obliged to stop payment.

The idea that the public distresses have been a necessary consequence of "*the transition to a state of peace*," is still more extravagant. To Great Britain the transition was truly formidable. She had by her orders in council, blockades, and fleets, engrossed the supply of a large portion of the continent of Europe, which, on the return of peace, relied on itself, and therefore deprived her of various profitable markets. But I ask any man of common sense, how this applies to our case? Were we at the treaty of Ghent, excluded from any foreign markets which we enjoyed during our short war? Surely not. Far from having our markets circumscribed by "*the transition to a state of peace*," they were greatly enlarged. In 1815, our exports were, as appears below, seven hundred per cent. more than in 1814, and in the three entire years subsequent to the peace, threefold what they were in the three preceding years.

Domestic exports from the united states.

1812 -	$30,032,109	1815 -	$45,974,403
1813 - -	25,008,152	1816 - -	64,781,896
1814 -	6,782,272	1817 -	68,313,500
	61,822,533		179,069,799
Average	20,607,511	Average	59,689,933

That the "*transition*" from an average export of $20,000,000 to nearly $60,000,000, can account for the lamentable and precipitous fall we have experienced, no person of candour will pretend. It would be equally wise to assert, that a man was ruined by raising his income from two thousand dollars to six thousand per annum. If, however, he renounced his industry, and, when he only trebled his income, increased his expenses six fold, then his ruin would be as easily accounted for, as the lamentable picture this country exhibits.

I was, however, in error. The "*transition*" did produce the effect. Should it be asked how? I reply—*The war protected the domestic industry of the nation.* It throve and prospered under that safeguard, which the peace tore down *de fonds en comble.* And congress, whose imperious and paramount duty it was to step in, and replace the protection, failed of that duty The consequences were foretold. The industry of the country was laid prostrate—its circulating medium drained away—its resources exhausted—and distress overspread the face of the land. But it is too farcical for argument to assert that a peace which trebled our exports, necessarily brought on a state of distress and impoverishment, which is chargeable wholly to our short-sighted policy.

CHAPTER XI.

The everlasting complaint of " taxing the many for the benefit of the few." *Fallacy and injustice of it. Amount of impost for fourteen years. For the year* 1818. *Impost for the protection of the products of the soil in that year above* 4,500,000 *dollars.*

THE changes have been rung throughout the united states, since the commencement of the government, on the immensity of the favours conferred on the manufacturers, in point of protection—their insatiable temper—the impossibility of satisfying them—and the dreadful injustice of " taxing the many for the benefit of the few," which have been used as a sort of war whoop for exciting all the base passions of avarice and selfishness in battle array against those to whom the tax is supposed to be paid.

It rarely happens, in private life, that vociferous claims for gratitude can stand the test of enquiry. When weighed in the balance of justice and truth, they are uniformly found wanting. And as a public is an aggregation of individuals, actuated by the same views, and liable to the same and greater errors, it would be extraordinary, if similar claims of collections of people were not found to rest on as sandy a foundation.

To investigate the correctness of this everlasting theme has become a duty. To place the subject on its true ground, will dispel a dense mist of error and delusion with which it is enveloped. If the debt can be paid, let it, in the name of heaven, be discharged, and let us commence *de novo*. If it be beyond the power of payment, let the delinquent parties take the benefit of the insolvent act, and exonerate themselves from a load by which they are crushed as between " the upper and the nether mill-stone."

The expenses of our government require revenues, which have risen from 4,000,000 to 27,000,000 dollars per annum. Provision must be made for this sum in one or all of three modes—by excise—direct taxes, or customs. The first is universally abhorred here. The second are almost equally obnoxious. It therefore follows, that the impost is the next and grand resource. The sum required must be raised without regard to manufactures or manufacturers,—and indeed if there were not a manufacturer in the country. It is out of the power of the government to raise the necessary revenue without laying considerable duties on manufactures—as all other articles such as tea, sugar, wines, coffee, are dutied as high as they will bear. Therefore the manufacturers, who, let it be observed, *bear their own share of all these duties, of every description*, are under no obligation of gratitude whatever for them.

But let us examine the subject more closely. Let us suppose that these duties had been laid solely to serve the manufacturers, without any regard to the emergencies of government—and that the proceeds had been reserved in the treasury. Let us see what would be the extent of the mighty boon.

The whole of this enormous and inextinguishable debt is comprised in the duties imposed on such foreign merchandize as rival our own manufactures. The utmost cravings on the score of gratitude will not dare to charge to the account the duties on sugar, coffee, tea, wine, salt, &c.

The entire impost for fourteen years, from 1801 to 1814, inclusive, was . .		$159,762,602*
On Spirits . . .	$25,441,543	
Wines . . .	7,646,476	
Sugar . . .	19,455,110	
Salt	4,057,047	
Teas . . .	8,565.874	
Coffee . . .	8,777,113	
Molasses . . .	4,980,650	
Sundry articles . .	7,470,317†	
		86,394,130†
Leaving a balance of		$73,368,472
†To which add half of the last item of sundries as probably on manufactures . .		3,735,158
Total		$77,103,630

This is the whole amount levied on *manufactures* of every kind, for fourteen years, being about five millions and a half per annum.

* Seybert, 454. † Idem, 398 to 405.

The white population of that period averaged probably about 7,000,000. Of course the duties paid *on manufactures* amounted to about eighty cents per head! And this is the sum and substance of the "*taxes levied on the many by the few*," and the immense favours conferred on "the few" by "the many!" which have furnished matter for so many tedious speeches in congress, tiresome declamations at public meetings, and verbose newspaper essays and paragraphs without end or number; with which "the welkin has rung"—and which, I repeat, have called into activity all the base passions of our nature, and excited a deadly hostility in the minds of one portion of our citizens against another. The clamour would have been contemptible, had the whole sum been granted as an alms, or through generosity. But when it is considered that every dollar of this sum has been raised for the mere purpose of revenue, language cannot do justice to the feelings the affair is calculated to excite.

I shall now consider the subject at a more recent period.

The whole amount of duties ad valorem for 1818, was	$11,947,260
To which add for manufactures of lead, iron, and steel; glass bottles, copperas, allum, and other articles subject to specific duties	694,493
Total on manufactures	12,641,753
A large portion of those duties was levied on silks, high-priced cambrics and muslins, gauzes, linens, lace shawls, lace veils, pearls, embroidery, gold lace, &c. &c. which our citizens do not manufacture. These duties are by no means chargeable to the protection of manufactures—suppose	1,500,000
Balance of impost supposed for protection of manufactures	$11,141,753

Against this we must set off all the duties levied for the protection of the landholders, viz.

On spirits, for the encouragement of the culture of grain, and the protection of the peach brandies, rye whiskey, &c. of the farmers . . .	$2,646,186
Sugar	1,508,892
Cotton	126,542
Hemp	148,873
Indigo	19,049
Amount carried over	4,449,542

Amount brought forward	4,449,542
Coals	46,091
Cheese	16,694
Impost for protection of landholders . .	$4,512,327
Leaving a balance against the manufacturers of	$6,629,426

When we consider how frugal and economical the great body of our farmers are in the eastern, middle, and western states; how few of them, comparatively speaking, purchase imported articles, except groceries; and how expensively the inhabitants of our cities and towns live in general; it will appear more than probable, that of the goods on which the above duties are collected, not nearly one-half are consumed by farmers.

A view of the preceding tables and statements affords the following results—

1. That the whole amount of the duties levied on manufactured articles of every description, for the year 1818, having been only about 12,600,000 dollars, and the population of the united states at present being about 10,000,000, of whom probably 8,500,000 are white, the average is less than one dollar and a half for the white population.

2. That of this amount about one-eighth part is levied on articles not interfering with, and consequently not chargeable to the account of the protection of, manufactures.

3. That there are duties levied in favour of agriculture equal in amount to more than a third part of those levied on manufactures.

4. That when the latter duties are set off against those levied for the protection of manufactures, the remainder is about seventy-five cents for each free person in the united states.

5. That probably more than half of the goods on which those duties are levied, are consumed in towns and cities—and of course that the amount paid by the farmers and planters is not above sixty cents per head, notwithstanding the senseless and illiberal clamour excited on the subject.

6. That were all the duties on manufactured articles removed, the burdens of the community would not be diminished a single dollar; as there is no more revenue raised than the emergencies of the government require, and of course some other taxes or duties must be devised.

CHAPTER XII.

Immense advantages enjoyed by the landholders for nearly thirty years, viz. an exclusive supply of the domestic market—and excellent foreign markets. Exorbitant prices of the necessaries of life. Great extent of the domestic market. Internal trade of the united states.

For nearly thirty years, the landholders of this country enjoyed a high degree of prosperity. They had almost universally excellent foreign markets for all their productions—and, from the commencement of the government, have had what has been so absurdly termed a "monopoly" of the domestic market, having had the exclusive supply of the manufacturers, who have not consumed of foreign vegetables, bread-stuffs, butcher's meat, fowls, fuel or any other of the productions of agriculture, to the amount of one per cent. per annum. It is, nevertheless, a fact, however incredible, that those citizens, enjoying this important exclusive domestic market, and having laid very high duties on all the articles that interfere with their interests, as snuff, tobacco, cotton, hemp, cheese, coals, &c.; accuse their manufacturing fellow citizens as monopolists; who are not only shut out of nearly all the foreign markets in the world by prohibitions and prohibitory duties; but even in their own markets are exposed to, and supplanted by, foreign adventurers of all countries!!! It is difficult to conceive of a more unjust charge, or one that comes with a worse grace from the accusers.

During this long period, the farmers sold in all cases at high, and in many at most exorbitant prices. To instance a few articles, in order to illustrate the remark: we paid them ten and twelve, and thirteen dollars a barrel for flour—twelve to eighteen cents per lb. for beef and pork—twelve to fourteen cents for tobacco—fifteen to thirty cents for cotton; and in the same proportion for all their other productions, though it is well known, they could have afforded them at half those prices, and made handsome profits. In one word, the history of the world affords few, if any instances of such a long-continued series of prosperity as they enjoyed.

The manufacturers cheerfully paid those prices. The cotton-weaver, the smith, the shoemaker, the carpenter, the labourer, who earned six, seven or eight dollars per week, never lisped a word of complaint, when they paid twelve or thirteen dollars per barrel for flour, eight or ten cents per pound for mutton, &c. &c. Would to heaven they had experienced the same degree of liberality from their farming and planting fellow citizens!

It remains to ascertain the effect of this exclusive market which our manufacturers have for thirty years afforded their agricultural fellow citizens without the least murmur.

It is impossible to ascertain with precision the number of our citizens engaged in manufactures, with their families. The census is miserably defective in this respect. It does not furnish the population of the towns and cities, which would afford a tolerable criterion. We are therefore left to mere estimate.

The highest number that I have ever heard surmised, is two millions ; the lowest, one. Truth, as is generally the case, may lie in the medium. I will therefore assume one million and a half.*

As there may be some objections on the subject of the number thus assumed, I annex the ground on which it rests.

I suppose, as I have stated, the white population of the country to be about 8,500,00 and to be proportioned as follows—

Agriculturists - - - - - -	5,000,000
Artists, mechanics, manufacturers, &c. -	1,750,000
Professors of law and physic, gentlemen who live on their income, merchants, traders, seamen, &c. - - - - - - -	1,750,000
	8,500,000

I believe I would not have been wide of the mark, in adding 500,000 to the second item, and deducting 250,000 from each of the others. But I prefer taking ground as little as possible liable to cavil.

Dirom, an eminent statistical writer, estimates the average annual consumption of grain in England, at two quarters, or sixteen bushels, for each person.† Colquhoun, however, estimates it only at ten bushels. I will assume twelve bushels. At this rate the consumption of the manufacturers would be about 21,000,000 of bushels per annum.

The average price of wheat in the united states during the wars of the French revolution, was about one dollar and seventy-five cents per bushel. For the last two years, it has been about one dollar and twenty-five cents. At the latter rate the amount of grain would be 25,250,000 dollars.

* The recent census will very probably prove that the number is 2,000,000.

† "The average prices of all these several kinds of grain being 20*s.* 6*d.*, the "price of two quarters for the maintenance of each person in these years, only "amounts to 14*s.*" *Dirom on the corn laws and corn trade of Great Britain, Appendix, page* 51.

Dirom states the average daily consumption of flesh meat in Paris at about five ounces and three quarters for each person. An average for London he supposes* probably more than double that amount, or eleven and a half, which is about five pounds per week. As our citizens eat meat oftener, and our working people more generally, than those of most other nations, it will be fair to assume six pounds per week for each person, which is equal to about three hundred and twelve pounds and a half per annum. At eight cents per pound, a moderate average till lately, this amounts to twenty-five dollars per annum, or for the whole 43,750,000 dollars.

Allowing for milk, butter, eggs, vegetables, fruit, lard, firewood, coals, home-made spirits, &c. &c. one dollar per week, it amounts to 91,000,000 of dollars.

Summary.

Grain - - - - - -	$25,250,000
Animal food - - - - - -	43,750.000
Milk, butter, fuel, &c. &c. - - -	91,000,000
Consumption of the manufacturers - -	$159,000,000

Now, this is the market, for bare subsistence, which the manufacturers furnish their agricultural fellow citizens, of whom many regard them with jealousy and murmuring—often with decided hostility—and *assume, that duties imperiously required for the purposes of the treasury are favours conferred on manufacturers !*

That this calculation is not materially wrong, will appear from the following view—A quarter dollar per day, or a dollar and three quarters per week, for the maintenance of each individual, which, as our citizens live, is moderate, would amount to ninety-one dollars per annum, or—

For 1,750,000 people - - -	$159,250,000

Let me further observe, that this is a market which might have been immensely increased annually by immigration, had a sound policy held out suitable encouragement to invite the manufacturers of Europe.

It is not easy to calculate the extent of the market for raw materials which the manufacturers afford their agricultural fel-

* The daily consumption of each individual in Paris, is pretty accurately as-“ certained, from the tax on cattle paid at the barriers, to be about five ounces “ and three quarters. In London it is probably more than double.”—*Idem* 248.

low citizens, and which might have been doubled by a correct system. I will state what I suppose it must have been in 1815, previous to the prostration of manufactures.

Cotton - - - - - - -	$9,000.000
Wool* - - - - - - -	10,000,000
Hemp - - - - - - -	2,000,000
Flax, hides, skins, furs, timber, hops, barley, oats, &c. - - - - - -	8,000,000
	29,000,000
Brought forward, for sustenance - -	159,000,000
Total - - - - - -	$188,000,000

As the illiberal prejudices on this topic, excite jealousies and disgusts which may eventually prove dangerous to the harmony of the nation, too much pains cannot be taken to remove them. I shall therefore place the subject before the reader in a new and not less striking point of view.

I have shewn that the market afforded to their agricultural fellow citizens by the manufacturers, amounts per annum to about $188,000,000.

It is proper to examine the extent of the market reciprocated to them.

It may be assumed that each white person in the union consumes in furniture and clothing, at the average rate of about forty dollars per annum.

This, for the whole of the agriculturists, whom I have estimated at 5,000,000, amounts to - -	$ 200,000,000	
And for the slaves, supposed to be 1,500,000, at 15 dollars per head, to	22,500,000	$ 222,500,000
Per contra. - -		
One-half the farmers throughout the union make three-fourths of their own clothing, &c. which is equal to	$ 75,000,000	
The remaining half probably manufacture about one-third of their clothing, equal to - - -	33,000,000	
	108,000,000	

* Mr. Coxe states an opinion in his tables, that the growth of wool in the united states in 1812, was from 20 to 22,000,000 lbs.

	$	$
Brought forward,	108,000,000	222,500,000
The clothing for the slaves is principally of family fabrics. This would warrant the deduction of the whole 22,500,000. But I suppose the planters may purchase to the average amount of five dollars for each slave, that is, in the whole $7.500,000, which leaves of family fabrics	15.000,000	
Total amount of household fabrics produced and consumed by the agriculturists. -		123,000,000
Leaving the amount of clothing and furniture purchased by them - - - -		99,500,000
Of this amount probably 10 per cent. is of foreign manufacture -	9,950,000	
One-half of the manufacturers, say 750,000, live in country towns or in the country, and purchase probably one-half of their clothing from the farmers in the neighbourhood, say	15,000,000	
		24,950,000
Balance, being the whole of the consumption of articles purchased of our manufacturers by agriculturists - - - - - -		$74,550,000

It thus appears, notwithstanding the clamour against the manufacturers, that they purchase above 110,000,000 dollars annually more from, than they sell to, the agriculturists.

A contrast between the domestic exports and the internal trade of the nation, cannot fail to be interesting, as it will enable us to ascertain whether they have borne in the minds of our citizens and statesmen the comparative rank to which they are entitled.

	$
The domestic exports of the united states for thirty years, from 1789, to 1819, inclusive, have been - - - - - -	1,058,800,898
Average - - - - - - - -	$ 35,293,363

I shall proceed on the assumptions on which I have already ventured; that the agriculturists embrace about 5,000,000 of our white population; that all the other classes of whites, who are consumers of the productions of the farmers and planters, are 3,500,000; and that each of the latter classes, consumes to the amount of a quarter dollar per day, or one dollar and seventy-five cents per week in food and drink. Let us see the result—

3,500,000 of people at one dollar and seventy-five cents per week, equal to $6,125,000 per week, or per annum - - - - -	$318,500,000

Once more.

Our present population is about	white -	8,500,000
	black - -	1,500,000
		10,000,000

The average expenditure of forty dollars per annum, already assumed, for the furniture and clothing of 8,500,000 white people,

Amounts to	$340,000,000
1,500,000 slaves, each 15 dollars . -	22,500,000
	365,500,000
Of which we import about - - -	60,000,000
Leaving a balance furnished by our own industry, of - - - - - -	305,500,000
To which add the above sum for food and drink	318,500,000
It gives a total of - - - -	623,000,000
Raw materials as before - - -	29,000,000
Annual internal trade of the united states -	$657,000,000

What exhilarating views! The domestic market for food and drink is nearly seven hundred—and the internal trade above fourteen hundred per cent. more than the average of the whole of our exports during a period when they were generally at exorbitant rates! How infinitely more worthy of the attention of our citizens, and to be protected by our statesmen, than they have appeared! How transcendently superior to that foreign commerce, which has been fostered with so much care; has excited so many collisions with foreign powers; cost us so much for foreign embassies, navy, and war; and entailed on us so heavy a national debt!

Again.

Our farmers will be astonished to learn that the consumption of Philadelphia in food and drink, supposing the population 125,000 persons, is very nearly equal to the amount of all the *eatable* articles furnished by agriculturists, exported from this country to every quarter of the world.

125,000 persons, at a quarter dollar per day, or one dollar and seventy-five cents per week, consume to the amount of 218,500 dollars per week, or per annum . . .	$11,375,000

Total exports from the united states for 1819, *of the following articles.*

			Custom house valuation.
Hams	lbs.	700,369	$105,055
Pork	bbls.	28,173	563,470
Beef	bbls.	34,966	454,558
Cheese	lbs.	1,148,380	114,838
Sheep		8,445	21,113
Hogs		2,324	13,944
Poultry		1,184	3,552
Indian Corn	bushels	1,086,762	815,072
Wheat	do.	82,065	103,581
Rye	do.	67,605	54,084
Barley	do.	3,047	3,047
Oats	do.	23,284	11,642
Beans	do.	21,162	37,034
Peas	do.	48,400	72,600
Potatoes	do.	76,506	38,253
Apples	barrels	8,253	24,759
Flour	do.	750,660	6,500,000
Meal, rye	do.	48,388	241,940
Indian	do.	135,271	608,720
Buckwheat	do.	203	812
Ship stuff	cwt.	828	4,968
Biscuit	bbls.	54,603	273,015
Do.	kegs	44,184	33,138
Rice	tierces	76,523	2,142,644
Butter	lbs.	911,621	182,324
Horned cattle		347	135,369

Total of exported eatable articles furnished by agriculturists	$12,559,532

CHAPTER XIII.

Calumnious clamour against the manufacturers on the ground of extortion. Destitute of the shadow of foundation. Take the beam out of thine own eye. Rise of merino wool 3 or 400 per cent. Great rise of the price of merchandize after the declaration of war.

THE most plausible argument used to defeat the applications of the manufacturers for relief, and to consign those who have hitherto escaped ruin, to the fate that has befallen so many of their brethren, is the "*extortion*" they are said to have practised during the late war, which, if they have an opportunity, they will, it is asserted, repeat. The justice of this accusation is as firmly believed by a large portion of the people of the united states, as if it were supported by "*proofs from holy writ.*" Persons whose interests are subserved by exciting hostility against the manufacturers, employ great zeal and address in disseminating this prejudice. Unfortunately their efforts have been crowned with success. The accusation, it is true, has been refuted times without number; but, regardless of the refutation, it is still advanced with as much confidence as if disproof had never been attempted, and, indeed, as if disproof were impossible.

This reproachful charge has been recently advanced by a respectable body of planters, whose opportunities and situation in life should have shielded them from falling into such an error. The general meeting of delegates of the United Agricultural Societies of Virginia, in a memorial adopted on the 10th of January, 1820, deprecate the idea of being placed

"At the mercy of an association, who, competition being re-"moved, will no longer consider the intrinsic value of an article, "or what price would afford a fair profit to the manufacturer, "but *how much the necessities of the consumer would enable them* "*to extort. Of this spirit we had a sufficient specimen during* "*the late war with Great Britain.*"

This severe accusation is adduced by

Thomas Cocke,	W. J. Cocke,	Roger A. Jones,	Esqrs.
Edmund Ruffin,	Nichclas Fanleon,	Theophilus Field,	
John Edmonds,	Charles H. Graves,	John Jones, and	
George Blow,	Richard Cocke,	Henry Jones,	
W. P. Ruffin,	John Pegram,		

When these gentlemen were thus denouncing "the extortion practised in consequence of the necessities of the consumer" it is wonderful they did not pause a little and reflect on the price of fifteen dollars per cwt. which they received in 1816 for their tobacco, in consequence of "*the necessities*" of the shippers, whereby so large a portion of those shippers were ruined, and so many respectable families reduced from a state of affluence to penury and dependence! They might also turn their attention to the extravagant price of two dollars, and two dollars and a half per bushel for wheat, and eleven, twelve, thirteen, and fourteen dollars per barrel for flour. These reminiscences would have been rather malapropos, and deranged some of the flowery paragraphs of their memorial. Our own offences are easily forgotten. "They are marked in sand"—while those of our neighbours are "engraven on marble."

As the prejudice on this subject has produced the most deleterious consequences, not merely on the happiness and prosperity of the manufacturers generally, but on the power and resources of the nation, I hope for a candid hearing, while I investigate it, and undertake to prove—

1. That the charge is not only not true, but the reverse of truth; that the rise of price was perfectly justifiable; and that the shadow of extortion did not attach to the procedure.

2. That the charge of extortion would apply with infinitely greater force and propriety to the farmers, planters, and merchants, who in this case are the accusers, than it does to the manufacturers.

The accusation has been more frequently predicated on the rise of the price of broad cloths, than of any other article. As it here presents itself in a tangible form, and subject to the talisman of figures, I shall therefore confine myself to this prominent and conspicuous case; observing, *en passant*, that the facts and reasoning apply equally to other branches. They all stand on nearly the same ground. In every case, in which a rise of price took place, it arose from causes similar to that which operated on broad cloth. Therefore if the charge be disproved in this instance, it falls to the ground on the whole; just as when, during the late war, several vessels were captured in circumstances exactly similar, the trial of one decided the fate of the rest.

The facts of the case are as follows:—superfine broad cloth was sold previous to the war at from eight to nine dollars per yard—during the war, it rose to twelve, thirteen, and fourteen.

On this "*extortion*" the changes have been rung from New Hampshire to Georgia—from the Atlantic to the Mississippi. It is considered as a set off against, and justification of, the wide-spread scene of desolation, the sacrifice of capital, to the amount of millions, the ruin of hundreds of capitalists, and the extreme distress of thousands whose sole dependence is on the labour of their hands—on which congress have for years looked with unfeeling indifference, without taking a single effectual step to relieve the sufferers, or to remove their sufferings.

The value of every manufactured article depends on the price of the raw material—the cost of workmanship—and the profit of the capitalist by whom it is produced.

That a rise in the price of either or both of the two first will justify a rise in the price of the article, is too manifest to require proof.

Now to the senseless and calumnious outcry against "*extortion*," on this subject, it would be sufficient to state the simple fact, that the raw material experienced a most extraordinary rise, as will appear from the following statement of the prices at different periods—

Prices of Merino wool.

1812.	May 1.	per lb.	75 cents.
	July 20.		75 to 100*
	Oct. 1.		75 to 150*
1814.	May 1.		300 to 400*
	Aug. 29.		300 to 400*
	Nov. 14.		300 to 400*

This alone would settle the question beyond the power of appeal.

Let it be observed, that it requires two pounds of wool to make a yard of superfine cloth. Therefore the difference in the price of the raw material accounts for, and fully justifies the rise in the price of the cloth. Two pounds of wool in May, 1812, cost one dollar and fifty cents; in May, 1814, they averaged seven dollars. It follows, that the per centage of profit was not so great on the cloth at fourteen dollars as at eight.

I do not know the expense of workmanship; but shall suppose it five dollars per yard.—Any other sum would answer equally well.

1812. May 1.		1814. May 1.	
2 lbs. wool	$1 50	2 lbs. wool	$7
Workmanship	5 00	Workmanship	5†
	6 50		12
Profit	1 50	Profit	2
Price of cloth	$8 00	Price of cloth	$14
Profit about 20 per cent.		Profit $16\frac{2}{3}$ per cent.	

Wages rose considerably; for however extraordinary it may seem to colonel Pegram and his friends, it is nevertheless true,

*Grotjan's Price Current.

†I have assumed the wages the same in 1814 as in 1812; but as stated in the text, they rose considerably in consequence of the great demand for workmen. I waive the advantage this would afford to the argument.

that a workman thinks he has as clear a right to raise his wages in case of an increased demand, as a planter has to raise the price of his tobacco or cotton in similar circumstances.

There is, moreover, another item of considerable importance to be taken into view.

Owing to the utter impolicy of our government on this point, in not affording adequate protection to the woollen manufacture, the business had been conducted on a very narrow scale previous to the war. The establishments were erected after war commenced, at an enormous expense, and under considerable disadvantages. This alone would warrant the whole of the extra price, in the shape of interest, on the capital thus invested.

I now proceed to prove, that had the woollen and other manufacturers raised the prices of their fabrics, without any rise in the raw materials, or wages, or without any extraordinary expense of buildings, neither the farmer nor the merchant could justly censure them, without at the same time pronouncing their own condemnation.

So far as respects the farmer, I might rest the question on the case stated, of the Merino wool. The rise on this article, from seventy-five cents to three and four dollars, in two years, was among the most extravagant advances ever known in the annals of trade. And if the charge of "*extortion*" would ever fairly lie against a rise in price, it would in this case indubitably.—Never was the admonition—

"*First cast the beam out of thine own eye—and then thou shalt see clearly to cast out the mote out of thy brother's eye.*"

more appropriate. Had the pharisee in the gospel reproached the publican with pride, he would not have been more culpable, than the farmer, who raised his wool three or four hundred per cent. and reproaches the manufacturer with "*extortion*" for raising the cloth, made of that wool, fifty per cent. Indeed in all the exuberant stock of human folly, there cannot be found any thing more extraordinary or extravagant.

But the defence does not rest on this ground alone. It is corroborated by almost every article of agricultural produce, which has always risen in consequence of an increased demand. To remove all doubt, if doubt could have existed, I state from the Philadelphia price current the various prices of four articles at different periods, with the very extraordinary advances on them.

Flour.	1809.	Jan. 16.	per bbl.	$5 50
		March 6.		7 50
	1810.	May 1.		8 00
		Aug. 1.		11 00
Tar.	1813.	Jan. 9.		2 10
		May 8.		4 00

Pitch.	1813.	Jan. 9.		2 50
		May 8.		4 50
		Oct. 9.		5 00
Hams.	1813.	Jan. 9.	per lb.	9½
		May 8.		11
		Oct. 9.		14½

So much for the farmers. Let us now examine how far they are kept in countenance by the proceedings of the merchants.

War was declared on the 18th of June, 1812. An immediate rise of price took place in every article in the market which was either scarce or likely to become so. Some were at once raised fifty, sixty, and seventy per cent. as may be seen by an examination of the following table.

	1812. June 9.	1812. July 13
Imperial tea . per lb.	$1 30	$1 87½
Hyson	96	1 35
Coffee	15½	20
White Havanna sugar, per cwt.	14 75	18 50
Brown do. do.	12 75	16 00

All these advances took place in less than five weeks.

	1812. June 9.	1812. Aug. 10.
Russia hemp per ton	$242 50	$300 00
Havanna molasses	56	72½
Souchong tea	50	75

Salt, per bushel	1812.	May 1.	55
		Aug. 1.	85
	1813.	Oct. 1.	1 35
	1814.	Aug. 1.	2 25
		Oct. 1.	3 00
Tin, per box	1812.	May 1.	28 00
		Aug. 1.	32 00
		Oct. 1.	35 00
	1814.	Aug. 1.	50 00
Plaster Paris, per ton	1812.	June 1.	12 37½
		Aug. 31.	14 50
		Oct. 5.	15 50
		Dec. 14.	17 50

This was all regarded as perfectly fair, honest and honourable. There was not the shadow of "*extortion*" supposed to be in it.

The merchant, who raised his souchong tea fifty per cent. was so deeply engaged in clearing the manufacturer's eye of the "*mote*," that he quite forgot to "*take the beam out of his own.*"

Can the citizen, who buys flour at six dollars, and sells it occasionally in the West Indies for twenty, twenty-five, or thirty dollars, without a deep blush reproach the manufacturer with "*extortion*" for raising broad cloth, from eight to fourteen dollars, when the raw material rose so extravagantly? or even had the price of the latter remained stationary?

Rise of price, in consequence of scarcity or increased demand, is, or is not, "*extortion.*" This is a dilemma, on the horns of which the farmers, planters, and merchants are caught. If it be "*extortion,*" they have been and are "*extortioners*" in the fullest sense of the word; as they always have and always do raise the price of their produce or merchandize, in consequence of scarcity or increased demand. Indeed, if this be extortion, all mankind are extortioners—lawyers, doctors, apothecaries, house owners, ship owners, money lenders, planters, and farmers, without distinction; for they all raise their prices in consequence of an increased demand. But if this be not extortion as it certainly is not, then every man, woman, or child in the nation, from the highest, proudest, haughtiest, and wealthiest, down to the lowest scullion, who has advanced the charge of "*extortion*" against the manufacturers, has broken the eighth commandment of the decalogue, and "*borne false witness against his neighbour.*"

I trust, therefore, that there is no man of liberality in the country, who considers the subject with due attention, but will allow that the incessant clamour against the manufacturers for extortion, is illiberal and disgraceful to the age—utterly destitute of foundation—in direct hostility with that brotherly regard which fellow citizens owe each other, and which is the surest foundation of harmony and happiness in a community; and that it produces a system of conduct inconsistent with the soundest principles of political economy—as well as destructive to the permanent wealth, power, and resources of the nation.

CHAPTER XIV.

The agricultural the predominant interest in the united states. Great advantages to agriculture from the vicinity of manufacturing establishments. Case of Aberdeen. Of Harmony. Of Providence. Fall of lands the result of the decay of manufactures.

As the agriculturists are now, and are likely to be for a century at least, the predominating interest in this country, and have a decided influence in its legislation, it is of immense importance that they should form correct views on the system best calculated to promote the general welfare. And it is much to be regretted that the endeavours to persuade them, that there is an hostility between their interests and those of their manufacturing fellow citzens, have been but too successful. Never was there a prejudice much more unfounded, or more pernicious to their prosperity and to that of the nation at large.

It is proved, (page 336) that the annual consumption of the city of Philadelphia in food and drink, amounts to about 11,000,000 dollars, all paid to the farmers, which is more than one-fifth part of all the domestic exports of the united states for the last year; within ten per cent. of the whole of the articles of food exported within that year; and above thirty per cent. of the average domestic exports of the nation for the last thirty years.

To the farmer and planter the home market is incomparably more advantageous than the foreign. Woeful experience proves that the latter is subject to ruinous fluctuations. Whereas the former is permanent and steady, little liable to vicissitude unless as affected by foreign demand. It furnishes a certain sale for the farmer's vegetables, poultry, fruit, fuel, and various other articles, too perishable, or too bulky in proportion to their value, for exportation. The income from all these forms a most important item in the prosperity of the farmer. This is true, even in small countries, as England, Ireland, and Scotland, of which every part is contiguous to, or not far distant from the advantages of navigation. But it has ten-fold weight in a country like the united states, of which a large and important portion is from three to fifteen hundred miles distant from the emporium to which its productions must be transported before they are put on shipboard to be forwarded to a market. The difference, to these portions of this country, between dependence on a precarious foreign and on a certain domestic market, is probably equal to fifty per cent. of the whole profits of farming.

As theories, however plausible, are liable to great errors, unless supported by the bulwark of facts, I presume that it cannot be unacceptable to the reader, to have these important views substantiated by facts of undeniable authenticity. I therefore submit for consideration the case of the neighbourhood of Aberdeen, in Scotland, and that of the settlement of Harmony in the state of Pennsylvania.

" Have we not opportunities of observing every day, that *in* " *the neighbourhood of a ready market, no inducements are neces-* " *sary to excite the common farmer to become industrious, and* " *carry on improvements of every sort with success?* A particu- " lar case occurs to me just now, that is so directly in point, that " I cannot resist the temptation of producing it, *as an example* " *of the rapid progress with which improvements in agriculture* " *are made when circumstances are favourable.*

" The town of Aberdeen HAS MADE GREAT ADVANCES IN TRADE " AND MANUFACTURES WITHIN THESE THIRTY OR FORTY YEARS " PAST. The number of inhabitants has increased greatly with- " in that period. *Money has become more plenty there than for-* " *merly.* Their manner of living is now more elegant and ex- " pensive; articles of luxury have increased. In consequence " of good roads having become more common, horses and wheel- " carriages have also become extremely numerous. On all " which accounts, *the demand for fresh vegetables has greatly in-* " *creased* in that place within the period above mentioned.

" But on account of the particular situation of that town, it " was a matter of some difficulty to augment the produce of the " fields in that neighbourhood, and supply the daily increasing " demand for these. *This city is placed in the midst of a country* " *that is naturally the most sterile that can possibly be imagined.* " For, unless it be a few hundred acres of ground that lie between " the mouths of the rivers Dee and Don, close by the town, *there* " *was not an inch of ground for many miles around it, that could* " *supply the inhabitants with any of the necessaries of life.* On " the east is the German Ocean. On the south the Grampian " mountains come close to the river, terminating in a head-land " on the south side of the harbour, called the *Girdle Ness:* and " on the west and north, it is environed for many miles with an " extended waste, the most dismal that can be conceived, in " which nothing can be discovered but large masses of stone " heaped upon one another, interspersed here and there with a " few bushes of starved heath, or disjoined by uncomfortable " bogs and spouting marshes, the most unpromising to the views " of the farmer that can possibly be imagined.

" But what is it that human industry cannot perform! what " undertaking is too bold for man to attempt, *when he has the* " *prospect of being repaid for his labour!* Even these dismal "wastes it was imagined, might be converted into corn-fields. "The ground was trenched; the stones were blasted by gun- "powder, and removed at an immense expense; manures were "purchased: and *thousands of acres of this sort of ground are "now waving with the most luxuriant harvests, and yield a rent "from five to eight pounds sterling per acre.*

"In any other part of the world that I have seen, it would be "reckoned impossible to convert such soils to any valuable use; "and the most daring improver that I have met with any where "else, would shrink back from attempting to cultivate a field "which an Aberdeensman would consider as a trifling labour. "Long habit has familiarised them to such arduous undertakings "—undertakings which could not be attempted any where else; "as, unless in such a particular situation as I have described, "the improver could never be repaid. For in what other part "of Europe could a man lay out one hundred pounds sterling, or "upwards, on an acre of ground, before it could be put under "crop, with any prospect of being repaid? yet this is no uncom- "mon thing in that neighbourhood.

"Nor is this all: For to such a height is the spirit for improve- "ment risen in that part of the world, that they are not only "eager to cultivate those barren fields, but even purchase these "dreary wastes at a vast expense for that purpose. The last "spot of ground of this sort that was to be disposed of in that "neighbourhood, was feued off by the town of Aberdeen in the "year 1773, for ever, at an annual quit-rent, or, as we call it, "*feu-duty, of thirty-three or thirty-four shillings sterling per "acre, although it was not then, and never could have been worth "six pence per acre, if left in its native state*—nor could be con- "verted into corn-ground but at an expense nearly equal to that "above-mentioned.

"Could I produce a more satisfactory proof, that A GOOD "MARKET WILL ALWAYS PRODUCE A SPIRITED "AGRICULTURE?"*

To this Scotch case, which is nearly as strong and conclusive as the mind can conceive, I shall add a more recent American one, which has a peculiar interest.

The settlement at Harmony, in the state of Pennsylvania, was begun in the fall of 1804, and is probably the only settlement ever made in America, in which from the outset agriculture and manufactures proceeded hand-in-hand together. The progress to wealth and prosperity, therefore, has been far beyond any previous or subsequent example in this country.

"In 1809, they built a fulling mill, which does a great deal of "business for the country, a hemp mill, an oil mill, a grist mill,

* Anderson on the means of exciting a spirit of National Industry, p. 63.

"a brick warehouse, 46 by 36 feet, having a wine cellar com-"pletely arched over; and another brick building of the same "dimensions. A considerable quantity of land was cleared.—"The produce of this year was 6000 bushels of Indian corn; "4500 bushels of wheat; 4500 bushels of rye; 5000 bushels of "oats; 10,000 bushels of potatoes; 4000 lbs. of flax and hemp; "100 bushels of barley brewed into beer; and 50 gallons of "sweet oil, made from the white poppy, and equal to the import-"ed olive oil. Of this produce they sold 3000 bushels of corn, "1000 bushels of potatoes, 1000 bushels of wheat; and they dis-"tilled 1600 bushels of rye.

"In 1810, a wool-carding machine and two spinning jennies "were erected for the fabrication of broad cloth from the wool "of merino sheep. A frame barn was built, 100 feet long, "and a brick house built, to accommodate twenty weavers' "looms."*

"After breakfast, we visited the different branches of manu-"factures. In the wool loft, eight or ten women were employed "in teazing and sorting the wool for the carding machine which "is at a distance on the creek. From thence the roves are "brought to the spinning house in the town, where we found "two roving billies and six spinning jennies at work. They "were principally wrought by young girls, and they appeared "perfectly happy, singing church music most melodiously. In "the weaving house sixteen looms were at work, besides several "warpers and winders."†

"After dinner we visited the soap and candle works; the dye "works; shearing and dressing works; the turners, carpenters, "and machine makers; and, finally, we were conducted through "the warehouses, which we found plentifully stored with com-"modities; among others, we saw 450 *pieces of broad and narrow "cloth, part of it of merino wool, and of as good a fabric as any "that ever was made in England. We were told, that they could "sell the best broadcloth, as fast as made, at ten dollars per "yard.*"‡

"The society now [1811] consists of about 800 persons, and "the operative members are nearly as follow: one hundred far-"mers; three shepherds; ten masons; three stone-cutters; three "brickmakers; ten carpenters; two sawyers; ten smiths; two "wagon makers; three turners; two nailors; seven coopers; "three rope makers; ten shoemakers; two saddlers; three tan-"ners; seven tailors; one soap boiler; one brewer; four distil-"lers; one gardener; two grist millers; two oil millers; one "butcher; six joiners; six dyers, dressers, shearers, &c. one ful-"ler; two hatters; two potters; two warpers; seventeen weav-

* Melish's Travels, ii. 68. † Idem, 70. ‡ Idem, 71.

"ers; two carders; eight spinners; one rover; one minister of "religion; one schoolmaster; one doctor; one storekeeper, with "two assistants; and one tavernkeeper, with one assistant."*

The original stock, in 1804, was 20,000 dollars, which the settlers expended in the purchase of land, and in supporting themselves till they commenced their operations. And, in 1811, their property amounted to the wonderful sum of 220,000 dollars.

"900 acres of land	$90,000
"Stock of provisions	25,000
"Mills, machinery, and public buildings	21,000
"Dwelling houses	18,000
"Horses, cattle, hogs, and poultry	10,000
"1000 sheep, one-third of them merinoes, of which one ram cost 1000 dollars	6,000
"Stock of goods, spirits, manufactures, leather, implements of husbandry, &c. &c.	50,000
	$220,000†

To this delightful picture of the blessed effects of a judicious distribution of industry, the statesman ought to direct his eyes steadily. It holds out a most instructive lesson on the true policy to promote human happiness, and to advance the wealth, power, and resources of nations. The history of the world may be examined in vain for any instance of such rapid strides made by any body of men, wholly unaided by bounties, premiums, loans, or immunities from government. The Harmonists were true practical political economists. They did not, like so large a portion of the rest of the people of the united states, lavish their wealth on the manufactures of a distant hemisphere, nor buy abroad cheap those articles which they could procure at home. In the sound and strong language of Mr. Jefferson, they "placed the manufacturer beside the agriculturist;" and they have reaped the copious harvest which such a policy cannot fail to secure. One such practical example outweighs volumes of the visionary theories of those closet politicians, who are the dupes of their heated imaginations.

Mr. Gallatin's report on manufactures, dated April, 17, 1810, contains an important statement of the situation of a manufactory in Providence, Rhode Island, which sheds great light on this subject, and which is entitled to the most serious attention of the agriculturists, as placing beyond doubt the advantages they derive from the establishment of manufactories in their neighbourhood.

* Melish's Travels, ii. 77.

† Idem, 80.

In this manufactory there were employed, males - -	24
Females - - - - - - - - - - - -	29
And besides the above, there were employed for the establishment, in neighbouring families, males - - -	50
Females - - - - - - - -	75
	178

Thus, out of one hundred and seventy-eight persons, there were one hundred and four females. The report is so far deficient, that it does not detail the respective ages of the work people; but judging from the state of other manufactories, we may assume that at least half of the whole number were children.

If this be admitted, it will follow, that there were men -	37
Women - - - - - - - - - - -	52
Male and female children - - - - - - -	89
	178

To the farmer this statement presents itself in a peculiarly striking point of light. Of the whole number of persons to whom this manufactory afforded employment, more than two-thirds belonged to the circumjacent farm-houses, who were thus enabled to gather up fragments of time, which would otherwise have been inevitably lost. It is probable that the profits of their labour were nearly equal, perhaps superior to the profits of the farming.

I might cite the cases of Brandywine, Wilmington, Pittsburg, Providence, Lancaster, and a hundred other places in the united states, where the establishment of manufactories, by affording an extensive and advantageous market to the farmer, doubled and trebled the price of the lands in their neighbourhood—and increased in an equal degree the comforts and prosperity of the farmers. And on the contrary, numberless instances are to be met with, in which the recent decline of manufactures has reduced the lands to one half, one third, and in some places one fourth, of the previous price. The average reduction of the price of land in the neighbourhood of Pittsburg is above one half of what it was bought and sold for in 1813, 14, and 15.

The farmers of the united states have been induced to oppose protection to their manufacturing fellow citizens, lest they should be obliged to purchase domestic, at a higher rate than imported manufactures. This erroneous policy has carried its own punishment with it. The reduction in the price of the farmer's produce, which can be obviously traced to the prostration of the manufactories, has in many cases been quadruple the saving in the price of the articles he purchased. I take as examples, raw wool and woollen cloth, and suppose that the farmer could buy foreign cloth for six dollars, and would have to pay, in consequence of protecting duties, nine for American—a difference that never existed in regular trade. The prices of goods purchased at auction, cannot with propriety be taken into account. They baffle all calculation.

Merino wool now sells for fifty cents per pound: of course it would require twelve pounds to pay for a yard of British cloth. But had the woollen manufacture been duly protected, wool would be at least one dollar and a quarter. Thus seven pounds of wool would pay nearly for a yard of domestic cloth, at the presumed advance of price.

Let it be added, moreover, that the farmer would probably sheer twice or three times the quantity of wool, were the price one dollar or one dollar and a quarter, that he does at present: for had the woollen manufacture been protected, the merino sheep in which such immense sums were invested, would have been preserved, instead of so large a portion of them being consigned to the slaughter-house.

Believing that the prejudices prevailing on this subject have done more injury to this country, and more retarded its progress than all the wars it ever carried on, from the landing of "the Pilgrims" to the present hour, I make no apology for adding another instructive quotation from the respectable writer who figures so largely at the commencement of it. Would to heaven that those farmers and planters who form the majority of the legislature of the united states, were duly impressed with the soundness of his statements, and predicated the laws of their country on the useful lessons they furnish! The united states would then present a different spectacle from what they do at present to their friends and enemies—a spectacle of gratulation to the former, and of mourning to the latter.

"*Those who wish to make agriculture flourish in any country,* "*can have no hope of succeeding in the attempt but by bringing* "*commerce and manufactures to her aid; which, by taking from* "*the farmer his superfluous produce, gives spirit to his operations,* "*and life and activity to his mind.* Without this stimulus to "activity, in vain do we use arguments to rouse the sluggish in-"habitants. In vain do we discover that the earth is capable of "producing the most luxuriant harvests with little labour. Our "own abundant crops are produced as undeniable proofs of this "in vain. *But place a manufacturer in the neighbourhood, who* "*will buy every little article that the farmer can bring to market,* "*and he will soon become industrious*—the most barren fields will "become covered with some useful produce. Instead of list- "less vagabonds, unfit for any service—the country will abound "with a hardy and robust race of men, fit for every valuable "purpose: and the voice of festivity and joy be heard in every "corner, instead of the groans of misery and the sighs of discon- "tent."*

With one more extract from another work of considerable repute, I conclude this chapter.

"If a line be drawn upon the map of England, across the "country from Sunderland to Bristol, all the counties on the "west of this line, will be found to contain coal. Formerly "these were the least valuable districts, and the parts of the "country which were the most thinly populated. Hence, when "the constitution of the British parliament was established, the "greatest weight of representation was given to the rich coun- "ties on the other side of that line. Whereas, now, *owing to* "*the establishment of manufactures, the coal counties have become* "*the most populous and wealthy*: and the agricultural districts "have either been comparatively deserted, or at least have not "much increased in population.

"This accounts in some measure for the inequality of our re- "presentation, and shows very distinctly the value of our mines "of coal, and that *by the establishment of manufactures, even the* "*most sterile and forbidding district may be rendered populous,* "*flourishing and opulent.*"†

CHAPTER V.

General reflections on commerce. Highly advantageous when conducted on terms of reciprocity. Commerce of the united states carried on upon very unequal terms. Has produced most injurious consequences. Tables of exports. Estimates of the profits of commerce. Pernicious consequences of the competition of our merchants in the domestic and foreign markets. The ruin of so many of them the result of the excess of their numbers.

THE extent and value of the commerce of the united states have long been prolific themes for orators in congress, and writers of newspapers—and it appears generally assumed to be only second to our agriculture, and far beyond manufactures in importance. It has had incomparably more attention bestowed on it by our government, not only than either agriculture or manu-

* Anderson on National Industry, p. 61.

† Parkes' Chemical Essays, Vol. II. p. 361.

factures but more than both united. A candid investigation of those sounding pretensions, whereby, if correct, they may have the seal of certainty imprinted on them, or, if otherwise, may be reduced to their proper standard, cannot fail to be interesting.

That commerce, properly conducted, on fair and reciprocal terms, is highly beneficial, has never been doubted by any sound mind. It tends to civilize, and increase the comforts of the great family of mankind.

But that it may be, and is occasionally, very injurious, is equally clear. When one nation receives only luxuries from another, and pays for them in necessaries of life, or specie, or in raw materials which would find employment for its own people, who are thus divested of employment, it is eminently pernicious.

To make the matter more clear, I will supppose that England were to furnish France with her raw wool, lead, tin, iron, flax and hemp, and to receive in return Merino shawls, silks, satins, pearl necklaces, diamond watches, &c. the most devoted advocate for commerce would allow this species of it to be extremely pernicious.

Again. If England furnished wool, flax, hemp and iron, and received in return even necessary articles, such as broadcloths, linen, duck, hard-ware, &c. it would be highly disadvantageous, as she would give the produce of the labour of five, ten, or twenty persons for that of one.

But such a commerce would be transcendently pernicious, if England had a large portion of her population wholly unemployed, and capable of manufacturing those articles for her own consumption.

If this reasoning be correct, as applicable to Great Britain, it is difficult to prove why the system should not be equally pernicious to the united states. It is as absurd, as impolitic, and as cruel to our citizens, who are suffering for want of employment, and who could manufacture cotton goods for us, to export such quantities of raw cotton, and receive cambrics and muslins in return, as it would be for England to export her wool, and import her woollen manufactures.

" *Strike, but hear,*" said a general of antiquity, about to offer some unpalatable opinions to a friend. As the views I am going to take of the subject of commerce, however true, are likely to be as unpalatable to the merchants as the opinions of the general to his friend, I say to them " strike, but hear."

I shall attempt to prove—

1. That a large proportion of the productive manufacturing industry of this country has been sacrificed to our commerce.

2. That the commerce of the united states has been constructed upon very unequal terms—and that it has produced most injurious results upon the national prosperity.

3. That its extent and advantages have been overrated. And

4. That the numerous bankruptcies among our merchants have chiefly arisen from the want of protection to manufactures.

These views are so repugnant to the feelings and prejudices of a numerous class of citizens, that I can scarcely hope for a fair discussion. More than half my readers will at once pronounce me deranged—and be disposed to throw the book into the fire. Again, therefore, I say, " strike, but hear."

I. Sacrifice of productive industry.

To prove the sacrifice of productive industry, I refer the reader to the tariffs of 1789,* 1791, 1792, and 1804, where he will find that the duties on seven-eighths of the manufactured goods imported into this country were originally at five—then seven and a half—then ten—then twelve and a half—and at length fifteen per cent. the advance not the result of the applications of the manufacturers for protection, but to meet the increasing demands of the treasury. Hence, I repeat, with every possible advantage of water power, raw materials, machinery, talents, enterprize, industry, and capital, until the declaration of war, three-fourths of the clothing of the inhabitants of all our towns and cities were of foreign fabrics—and the wealth of the nation was lavished to support foreign workmen, and foreign governments, while we had hundreds, nay thousands of citizens capable of supplying them, who were driven in many cases to servile and far less profitable labour.

The experience of our late war, and the immense spring it gave to the industry and manufactures of the country, prove that one-half the protection afforded to the merchants in the China trade would have enabled our citizens to establish the cotton and woollen branches on a liberal scale, and saved many millions of dollars to the country annually. This was unhappily sacrificed by the system of low duties, which was advocated by the merchants, and adopted by congress, in order to promote the interests of commerce. The influence of the former has been successfully exerted at all times, to prevent prohibitions and prohibitory duties.

The unsoundness of the policy this country has pursued, by which it has been virtually placed in the situation of a colony to

* See chapters III. and IV.

Great Britain and the other manufacturing nations of Europe, appears palpable from the following considerations:

So far as respects the cotton and woollen branches, on a large scale, we were almost as completely excluded from them by the impolicy of our tariff until 1812, as if a law had been passed to render their establishment penal. This declaration may surprize—but is nevertheless susceptible of proof. The two strong facts already stated—that with all our advantages for the manufacture of cotton we consumed only 300,000 pounds in the year 1805, although we exported about 38,000,000—and that in 1812, we were so dependent on Europe for woollens, that we had not a supply of blankets for our army, nor were our manufactories at that time in a situation to make provision for the emergency—place the matter beyond doubt. He that will not be convinced by these facts, of the ruinous policy we pursued —and the wanton waste of our resources, would not be convinced, "though one were to rise from the dead."

The tariff of 1789, which established the five per cent. duty, might as well have had the following preface, as the one which was prefixed to it:

"Whereas, although this country has become independent of "Europe in its government, and by its arms—it is expedient "that it should still continue in the colonial state, so far as res- "pects its supplies of all the essential articles for comfort and "convenience:

"Therefore be it enacted, &c. that the duties to be levied on "the importation of manufactures of cotton, wool, linen, pottery, "lead, iron, steel, brass, and wood, be no more than five per cent. "ad valorem."

However ludicrous this may appear, it only gives body and substance to the virtual effects of the tariff.

II.

In order to prove my second position, I subjoin a view of our exports and imports, and a statement of the various species of the former for fifteen years.

Our exports have consisted chiefly of four different species of articles—

1. Necessaries of life.

2. Raw materials, which we ourselves could have manufactured, and which constituted one-fourth part of our exports.

3. Naval stores, of indispensable necessity for the nations which purchased them.

4. The luxury of tobacco, which is about one-eighth part of the whole amount.

Our imports consist principally of—

1. Tea, coffee, wines, spices, cocoa, chocolate, almonds, raisins, &c. which we do not raise, and which of course do not affect our national industry.

2. Spirits, sugar, cotton, indigo, hemp, malt, lead, &c. which interfere with the best interests of our farmers and planters.

3. Manufactures of cotton, wool, leather, iron, &c. &c. which interfere with the interests of our manufacturers, and impoverish the nation, and of which we could, by proper protection, supply ourselves with the greater part.

4. Luxuries, which tend to introduce extravagance, and deprave our morals.

Domestic exports for fifteen years, from 1803 *to* 1817, inclusive.*

Cotton	$154,179,117
Vegetable food	192,564,368
Lumber, masts, &c.	52,796,000
Tobacco	74,768,000
Animal food and animals	34,712,560
Dried salt fish	16,915,256
Pickled fish	4,155,419
Whale oil and bones	2,819,528
Spermaceti oil and candles	1,658,320
Ginseng, peltry, &c.	8,130,305
Naval stores	6,579,931
Pearl and potashes	13,990,000
Manufactures	27,270,000
Uncertain	4,836,000
	$595,374,804
Average	$39,691,653

A cursory glance at our exports, and a comparison of them with our imports, will satisfy the reader, that few nations have carried on commerce to more disadvantage, than we have done a large portion of ours. We have exchanged the most valuable productions of nature in the rudest state, with the least possible degree of labour—and received in return every species of merchandize in its most finished form—of which labour constituted two-thirds, three-fourths, four-fifths, and often nine-tenths of the value. This more particularly applies to cotton, which we have shipped at an average of about twenty-five cents per pound, except Sea Island, and received back at an advance of five fold—and, in the case of the fine articles, of ten fold—thus enabling foreign nations to pay for the whole crop with one-fifth part of it—

* Seybert, 146–7.

and wantonly throwing away the remaining four-fifths. Moreover a large portion of the manufacture being performed by machinery, we have given the labour of twenty or thirty persons for one. Never was there a system more admirably calculated to stunt the growth of a nation; to destroy the effect of the advantages bestowed on it by nature; and to render its inhabitants hewers of wood and drawers of water to other nations.

One view of this subject is so appalling, that it will make the heart ache of every man who has any regard for the real interests of this country, or a wish to advance its wealth, power, and resources.

The increase by manufacture of the value of the raw material of cotton, was in 1815, according to Colquhoun, about five-fold.* Let us see the operation of this portion of our commerce tested by that scale.

We exported, it appears, in fifteen years, cotton to the amount of . . .	$154,179,117
This, according to Colquhoun, produced .	$770,895,585
Leaving to foreign nations the enormous profit of	$616,716,468
Or an annual average of . . .	$41,114,431

Two-thirds of which we might by a sound policy have retained among ourselves.

There can be no doubt that Great Britain defrayed the whole expense of the war against us by the profits she derived from this single article, in a few preceding years.

Thus our short-sighted policy tends to aggrandize, at our own expense, foreign nations with which we have had, and may again have, most perilous collisions.

It now remains to give a general but concise view of the injurious effects produced by our commerce. I shall confine myself to facts of such universal notoriety as to preclude controversy.

Commerce has—

1. In return for our great raw material, cotton, to the amount of many millions of dollars annually, it has deluged us with immoderate quantities of cotton and woollen and other manufactures, whereby millions of capital invested in manufacturing establishments have been lost—hundreds of the proprietors ruined—and thousands of workmen reduced to idleness, and exposed to the lures of dissipation and crime.

2. Subjected us to an expense for foreign intercourse and for the Barbary powers to the amount of nearly 12,000,000 of dollars in twenty years.†

* See Colquhoun on the wealth, power, and resources of the British Empire, page 91.

† Seybert, 712, 713.

3. Bankrupted an immoderate proportion of those who pursued it.

4. Caused a war, by which there is entailed on us a heavy debt of nearly 80,000,000 of dollars, and an annual interest of about 4,500,000 dollars.

5. Rendered a navy necessary, which creates an expense of above 3,500,000 dollars for the present year.

6. Given a prodigious spring to luxury and extravagance, by the superfluous articles it has introduced among us.

7. Drained away the circulating medium of the country, whereby every kind of business is paralized, and the nation impoverished.

8. Rendered us dependent on foreign nations for many of the comforts, and even some of the necessaries of life.

That these consequences have resulted from our commerce, I trust will be admitted. They are considerable drawbacks on its advantages, which ought to be immensely great to countervail them.

It behoves us then to examine the extent and value of this commerce, so highly prized and so dearly bought.

III.

I now proceed to my third point, to prove that the extent and advantages of our commerce have been greatly overrated.

As much as possible to simplify a complicated subject, I shall consider the commerce of the united states under five several heads.

1. The exportation of our superfluous productions.
2. The importation of necessary supplies.
3. The carrying trade.
4. The coasting trade.
5. The shipping.

The first is beyond comparison the most important. In it the whole nation is deeply interested. Much of our prosperity depends on procuring suitable markets for our surplus productions. This affords a strong stimulus to industry, which would otherwise pine and languish.

To enable the reader to judge correctly on this subject, I annex a table of our exports from the organization of the government. For the first six years there was no distinction between foreign and domestic. I have assumed that there were two-fifths of the former, and three-fifths of the latter, which is about the average proportion of the whole of the subsequent period.

Exports from the United States from 1790 *to* 1819, *inclusive.**

Year.	Domestic.	Foreign.	Total.
1790	†12,123,094	‡8,082,026	20,205,156
1791	†11,407,225	‡7,604,816	19,012,041
1792	†12,451,860	‡8,301,238	20,753,098
1793	†15,665,744	‡10,443,828	26,109,572
1794	†19,815,741	‡13,210,492	33,026,233
1795	†28,793,684	‡19,195,788	47,989,472
1796	40,764,097	26,300,000	67,064,097
1797	29,850,206	27,000,000	56,850,206
1798	28,527,097	33,000,000	61,527,097
1799	33,142,522	45,523,000	78,665,522
1800	31,840,903	39,130,877	70,971,780
1801	47,473,204	46,642,721	94,115,925
1802	36,708,189	35,774,971	72,483,160
1803	42,205,961	13,594,072	55,800,033
1804	41,467,477	36,231,597	77,699,074
1805	42,387,002	53,179,019	95,566,021
1806	41,253,727	60,283,236	101,536,963
1807	48,699,592	59,643,558	108,343,150
1808	9,433,546	12,997,414	22,430,960
1809	31,405,702	20,797,531	52,203,233
1810	42,366,675	24,391,295	66,757,970
1811	45,294,043	16,022,790	61,316,833
1812	30,032,109	8,495,127	38,527,236
1813	25,008,152	2,847,845	27,855,997
1814	6,782,272	145,169	6,927,441
1815	45,974,403	6,583,350	52,557,753
1816	64,781,896	17,138,556	81,920,452
1817	68,313,500	19,358,069	87,671,569
1818	73,854,437	19,426,696	93,281,133
1819	50,976,838	19,165,683	70,142,521
	$1,058,800,398	$710,519,854	$1,769,311,698
Average	$35,293,363	$23,680,000	$58,977,056

The surplus productions of the united states, the great and legitimate basis of our foreign trade, are, as appears from this table, far below what might have been expected from the population, and the resources of the country. They average, as we see, only about 35,000,000 of dollars, or about 8,500,000 pounds sterling per annum, from the organization of the government to the close of the last year. The average population of that period has been about 6,500,000 souls. It therefore appears that we have exported only about five dollars and a half per head of our whole population. This nearly corresponds with our recent experience.

During the last five years we exported of domestic productions about 305,000,000 dollars—or 61,000,000 per annum. Our population during this period has probably averaged about

* Seybert, 93. † Estimated at three-fifths of the whole.
‡ Estimated at two-fifths.

9,500,000 souls; which gives an export of only six dollars and a half per head.

It is thus indubitable that this department of our commerce, obviously the most important, has been vastly overrated, and sinks into insignificance, on a comparison with our domestic trade, which, as may be seen (page 335) is nearly fifteen hundred per cent. beyond it. The food and drink of Philadelphia, New York, Boston and Baltimore, supposing them to contain 400,000 souls, at a quarter of a dollar per head daily, amount to more than the average of the whole of our domestic exports!

400,000 persons at a quarter of a dollar per day, consume per annum . . .	$36,500,000

Yet there are hundreds and thousands of citizens of the united states unalterably convinced that the united states owe nearly all their prosperity, all their improvements, all their wealth, to commerce!!

I have in vain sought for a general statement of our imports. It is not to be found either in Seybert or Pitkin. The former, however, gives one for seven years, from 1795, to 1801, inclusive, viz.

1795 - - - - -	$69,756,258
1796 - - - - -	81,436,164
1797 - - - - -	75,379,406
1798 - - - - -	68,551,700
1799 - - - - -	79,069,148
1800 - - - - -	91,252,768
1801 - - - - -	111,363,511
	$576,808,935
Average - - - - -	$82,401,276

It is difficult to calculate the amount of foreign goods consumed in this country. The foreign exports for the seven years above stated, amounted to 236,792,386 dollars. Deducted from the above sum of 576,808,935 dollars, there is, for that period, a balance for home consumption of 340,016,549 dollars, being an average of above 48,000,000 dollars annually. But during this time our commerce was far more flourishing than in other years. I shall, therefore, assume an average consumption of foreign merchandize of 40,000,000 per annum, for the 30 years from 1789 to 1819, which will not be regarded as far from the fact.

Dr. Seybert has hazarded a calculation, that the profits of navigation, are at the rate of fifty dollars per ton—and he therefore sets down an average annual profit of 34,459,350 dollars! which would amount to 1,033,780,500 dollars in thirty years!

It is easy to perceive how extravagantly erroneous this calculation must necessarily be. A vessel of three hundred tons would make, by freight alone, a profit to her owner annually of 15,000 dollars. Yet many of our merchants have had two, three, four, five, and six vessels of this size constantly employed for years—have not lived extravagantly—and yet have finally become bankrupts.

Were the doctor's statement correct, the great body of ship-owners would have become as wealthy as the members of the Medici family.

Ten per cent. is regarded as a fair average of the profits of commerce. For freight I shall assume an equal sum.

Hence is deduced the following result—

Average annual domestic exports -	$35,293,363
Foreign goods consumed here, estimated at	40,000,000
	$75,293,363
Ten per cent. profit - - -	7,529,336
Add an equal sum for profit on freight -	7,529,336
Total - - - -	$15,058,672

The carrying trade is far less important. Without much participation in it, the nation might have enjoyed, and may still enjoy, a most enviable state of prosperity. And it will probably appear, in summing up its advantages and disadvantages, during the whole of our career, that the latter at least equipoise the former.

To form a correct decision on this point, it is necessary to ascertain its extent.

It consists of two distinct branches. In the first, the foreign merchandize *in transitu* touches at our ports. In the second, the voyages are made from one foreign port to another.

Of the first branch we have an accurate account. The treasury returns distinguish between the exports of foreign and domestic articles. But of the second we can only form an estimate.

The foreign exports from the united states, as appears by the preceding table, (page 357) have averaged about 23,680,000 dollars per annum for thirty years.

It is probable that the other branch of the carrying trade is about one half this amount. Some intelligent merchants whom I have consulted, estimate it at from 10 to 15,000,000 of dollars annually. But to afford the utmost latitude to the contrary side of the question, I shall suppose it equal to the first branch.

Thus, then, stands the account of the carrying trade for 30 years.

Foreign exports - - -	$23,680,000
Voyages from one foreign port to another, estimated at - - - - -	23,680,000
	$47,360,000
Profit, ten per cent. - - -	$4,736,000
Add an equal profit for freight, - -	4,736,000
Total profit of carrying trade - -	$9,472,000

Summary.

Profits of trade in exports, and in imports for home consumption - - - -	$15,058,672
Of carrying trade - - -	9,472,000
Coasting trade, supposed - -	4,000,000
Average for 30 years,	$28,540,672

These profits are the utmost that can be claimed on the most liberal calculation. But I must observe that it is difficult to conceive that half of them could have ever accrued; as a very large portion of the merchants who are supposed to have acquired them, have been reduced to bankruptcy. This strong fact is utterly incompatible with the idea of such profits, and I am persuaded would warrant a reduction of fifty or sixty per cent. of the amount.

The offsets have been immense. Shipwrecks—falling markets—and depredations to the amount of probably one hundred millions by the belligerents, under the various orders in council, decrees, &c. The aggregate of all these would probably amount to thirty per cent. on the assumed profits.

But even admitting that the whole sum of twenty-eight millions has been gained annually by commerce, it is worth while to consider whether it has not been rather a dear purchase.

It has cost us from 1796 to 1815—

For foreign intercourse - - - -	$ 9,615,140
Naval department - - - - - -	52,065,691
Barbary powers - - - - - -	2,349,568
War debt - - - - - - -	78,579,022
	$ 142,609,421*
Average per annum - - - - - -	$ 7,130,471

*Seybert 713.

The expenses chargeable to this account at present, and likely to continue, are—

Interest on war debt of $ 78,579,022 - -	$4,714,741
Secretary's estimate for the navy, 1820 - -	3,527,600
Per annum	$ 8,242,341

This is above twenty-five per cent. in perpetuity on those profits of commerce, which are *supposed* to have accrued during the whole of the period in which it had every possible advantage that could be desired by its warmest advocates. It is, moreover, above twenty per cent. of the whole average amount of the exports of the country, embracing the period in which our staples commanded exorbitant prices, which we are never again likely to realize.

I therefore confidently rely, that those who have condescended to "*hear*," though they may have "*struck*," will, however reluctantly, acknowledge that at the touch of the talisman of truth, the boasted advantages of commerce have greatly diminished in amount—and that, however valuable it truly is, it has indubitably cost the country more than it was intrinsically worth.

In taking an account of the numerous offsets—the collisions with the belligerents—the chief part of the expense of the navy—our war—the war debt,—and its interest—it would be unfair not to draw a line of distinction between the different branches of commerce. That important one which consists in the exportation of our surplus productions, and procuring necessary supplies in return, ought certainly to be exonerated from any portion of these heavy items. It might be carried on for a century, without producing any of those consequences. They have sprung almost altogether from the extraneous trade in the colonial productions of the belligerents, which arose from the general state of warfare in Europe, and from the cupidity with which commerce was pursued by our merchants. If this point of view be correct, then the account is reduced within a narrow compass.

It may be useful to hazard a calculation on the present and probable future profits of commerce, in order more fully to prove my position, that it has cost too dear.

The domestic exports of 1819, were - -	$ 50,976,838
Foreign exports - - - - - - - -	19,165,683
Foreign goods consumed here, in 1819 suppose -	60,000,000
	$ 130,142,521

As our markets have stood lately, a profit of eight per cent. is a large allowance - - - -	10,411,401
Present profits on freight and carrying trade -	2,000,000
Coasting trade - - - - - - -	3,000,000
	$ 15,411,401

Thus it appears, that for every dollar of the present gain of the merchants by commerce, the nation at large pays above fifty cents of tax entailed on it by that commerce!

I now invite the attention of the reader to my last position, which is—

IV. That the numerous bankruptcies among our merchants have chiefly arisen from the want of protection to manufactures.

That an immoderate number of our merchants has been reduced to bankruptcy, is universally admitted. The exact proportion cannot be ascertained. It has been carried as high as nine-tenths in Philadelphia New York and Baltimore. This I believe extravagant. I assume two-thirds, which is supposed to be a low calculation. It remains to enquire how this calamitous result has taken place, under what is so generally styled a flourishing state of our commerce.

Various causes have conspired to produce this effect.

Commerce in this country has partaken of the nature of a lottery. The prizes were immense, but very rare—the blanks numerous. It has been attended occasionally with immoderate profits, which have been succeeded by great losses. The profits fostered a spirit of extravagance and luxury, which wasted all the previous temporary advantages, and rendered the merchants unable to contend with the storms of adversity.

But the chief source of the misfortunes of our merchants has been the extravagant number of them—which, as I hope to make appear, has proceeded from the ruinous policy of our tariff.

Had the great leading manufactures of cotton, wool, and iron, with some others, which were arrested by foreign importation, been, as sound policy dictated, duly protected, during the thirty years of the existence of our government, thousands of young men in every part of the united states, who have been devoted to the mercantile profession, and immoderately increased its numbers, would have been employed in those branches.

Many parents have destined their children to the pursuit of commerce, without either the requisite capital, talents, credit, or friends, merely for want of other suitable employment. Hence most of our merchants have generally had two or three, and some as many as four apprentices, who, when free, have become supercargoes, or commenced a profession for which they were wholly incompetent, and thus added to the long list of bankrupts.

The effect of this state of things is, that there have been and probably are more shipping and importing merchants in the united states than in the British dominions in Europe. Almost every little port from Passamaquoddy to St. Mary's, has its body of merchants and importers, more or less numerous, who are constantly supplanting each other in the home and foreign markets, to their mutual ruin. The West Indies have thus proved the grave of the fortunes and happiness of half the merchants that have carried on trade with them. The trade to that quarter, as the prices are constantly fluctuating, affords neither certainty nor security. The markets are either overstocked, or visited by a dearth. When the latter takes place, prices rise extravagantly. Intelligence arrives in this country. Our ports are crowded with shippers, who outbid each other, and raise the prices. Vessels full freighted are dispatched from all our ports. The first cargo, perhaps the second, or third, is sold at a great profit. The glut sinks the price, and all the remainder sell at, and often below, cost. The major part of the business is almost wholly a lottery, or species of gambling, which regular commerce altogether disclaims.

The price of flour in the West Indies frequently rises, and as frequently falls, to the amount of three, four, and five dollars per barrel, in the course of two, three, or four weeks. Hence the merchant whose vessel sails at the rate of nine knots an hour, often makes a fortune—while his less fortunate neighbours, whose rate of sailing is only eight knots, are ruined.

The injurious effects of the inordinate competition, which is the natural consequence of the extraordinary number of our merchants, are fourfold:—

1. Our staples are raised too high at home by the extent of this competition.
2. The same competition reduces them in the foreign markets.
3. It raises the return cargoes in those markets—and finally
4. Reduces the prices of those cargoes in our ports.

These are among the most striking causes of, and satisfactorily account for, the ruin of so large a portion of the mercantile class, and have obviously resulted chiefly, if not altogether, from the depression of manufactures.

I offer a calculation on the subject, which, even if somewhat erroneous, may prove useful.

Suppose the whole number of merchants in the united states, since the year 1789, to have averaged constantly 15,000—and that two thirds of them have failed. Had manufacturing establishments been properly patronized, there probably would not have been more than 10,000; to the mass of whom the profession would have afforded a decent subsistence. In this case, it is probable that the bankruptcies would not have exceeded 2,000. Of course, 8000 would have prospered out of 10,000; whereas, only 5000 have succeeded out of 15,000. Whatever deduction from, or addition to, this calculation may be made, the inference cannot fail to be highly favourable to the general scope of my argument, and to pronounce a strong sentence of condemnation on the ruinous policy this nation has pursued.

Another view may be taken of the subject.

It appears that a large portion of our commerce consists in the transportation of the merchandize and manufactures of other nations from the places of production to this country, and hence to those of consumption respectively. But might not our merchants employ themselves as well in lending facilities to the industry of their fellow citizens as to that of foreign nations? Would not broadcloths from Young & Son's, or Dupont's, or Sheppard's manufactories—or shirtings and sheetings from Schenck's, or from Waltham, load a vessel as well, and pay as good a freight, as from Leeds or Manchester? Would it not be at least as profitable to themselves, and as useful to their fellow citizens and to their country, to export cargoes of home-made goods to South America, and import specie, as to deluge their native country with foreign goods, drain it of its specie, and destroy its productive industry?

As the want of correct views on this point has been among the primary causes of the present distresses of the country, I hope to be pardoned for once more presenting it to the reader. The idea that the want of protection to manufactures has proved highly pernicious to the merchants, by an undue increase of their numbers, will appear plain to those who reflect, that, when by the restrictive system, and the war, there was a market open for, and protection afforded to, domestic manufactures, great numbers of respectable merchants, in all our cities, devoted their time, their talents, and their capital to the cotton and woollen branches, very advantageously for themselves and for the country, while this protection continued—but ultimately to the ruin of many of them. It is obvious that the inducements to commence an early career in manufacturing are greater than to quit another business, and enter on this at an advanced period of life. And therefore it irresistibly follows, that the successful opposition to the establishment of manufactures has been the great cause of the superabundance of merchants, and that from this superabundance has flowed the bankruptcy of so large a portion of them.

It is frequently asserted, that though so many of the merchants have been reduced to bankruptcy, the country has gained even by their ruin. This doctrine, which I have tried to develope, I do not understand. Let us investigate it.

Suppose a farmer to sell 5000 bushels of wheat at two dollars per bushel. The miller grinds it—and sells to the flour merchant, who sells to the shipper. The latter becomes bankrupt, and pays two, three, five, or ten shillings in the pound, as the case may be. Of course the flour merchant, or the miller, or the farmer, suffers a heavy loss. • I cannot see how, from a transaction of this kind, which is an epitome of a large proportion of our mercantile business for years past, the country can be said to have gained. Money, it is true, is put into the pocket of one man, but it is withdrawn from the pocket of another. There is no increase of the national wealth.

Having in this chapter taken ground wholly new, with no former lights to illuminate my path, I may have occasionally wandered into error. But I trust the deviation, whatever it may have been, has not led me far astray—and that the positions I have assumed, and the inferences I have deduced, if not wholly right, are not materially wrong.

CHAPTER XVI.

Fostering care of commerce by congress. Monopoly of the coasting and China trade secured to our merchants from the year 1789. *Revolting partiality. Wonderful increase of tonnage. Act on the subject of plaster of Paris. Law levelled against the British navigation act. Rapidity of legislation.*

The records of American legislation bear the most satisfactory testimony of the transcendant influence of the mercantile interest, and of the unceasing exertions made to fence it round with every species of protection the government could bestow. No fond mother ever indulged a beloved child more than congress has indulged commerce—attended to all its complaints—and redressed all its wrongs.

My limits forbid a detail of the great variety of acts passed for the exclusive benefit of commerce, with which the statute book abounds. I shall confine myself to a few of the most prominent and important.

I. The second act passed by the first congress contained clauses which secured to the tonnage of our merchants, a monopoly of the whole of the China trade—and gave them paramount advantages in all the other foreign trade.

The duties on teas were as follow :

	In American vessels.	In foreign vessels.
Bohea teas - - per lb.	Cts. 9	Cts. 15
Souchong & other black teas	10	22
Hyson teas - - -	20	45
All other green teas -	12	27

The annals of legislation furnish no instance of grosser or more revolting partiality than is displayed in this act, which established the first tariff. A pound of hyson tea, which cost fifty-six cents, if imported in a foreign, paid *twenty-five cents more duty than in an American vessel.* Whereas a yard of broad cloth, or two yards of silk, cambric, or muslin, value five dollars, *paid but twenty-five cents*, all together, or five per cent. Thus the foreign ship-owner was at once shut out of our ports, so far as the China trade was concerned, beyond the power of competition, for the benefit of the American merchant ; whereas the foreign manufacturer was invited in by a low duty: and the possibility of competition on the part of the American manufacturer wholly precluded ! Let me not be misunderstood to regard as incorrect the decided preference given to the American merchant. By no means. My object is to point out the immense inequality of the treatment of two great classes of citizens, which, to the great discredit of our legislation, and the incalculable injury of our country, as I hope is proved in the preceding chapter, pervades our statute book. This is a digression, which the occasion called for. I return.

II. The same act gave our merchants an additional decisive advantage, by allowing a discount of ten per cent. on the duties upon goods imported in American vessels.

III. Such was the fostering care bestowed on the mercantile interest, that the third act was directed wholly for their security. By this act the tonnage duty on vessels belonging to American citizens was fixed at six cents per ton ; on American built vessels, owned wholly or in part by foreigners, thirty cents ; and on all other foreign vessels, fifty cents.

IV. In order to exclude foreign vessels from the coasting trade, they were subjected to a tonnage duty of fifty cents per ton for every voyage ; whereas our vessels paid but six cents, and only once a year.

These four features of decisive protection, were enacted in a single session, the first under the new government. They placed the mercantile interest on high ground, and gave it overwhelming advantages over foreign competitors. In fact, they almost altogether destroyed competition. I shall state their effects at the close of this chapter.

It is not difficult to account for this parental care. The mercantile interest was ably represented in the first congress. It made a judicious selection of candidates, and carried the elections pretty generally in the seaport towns. Philadelphia was represented in the senate by Robert Morris, and in the house of representatives by Thomas Fitzsimons and George Clymer, three gentlemen of very considerable talents, and great influence, particularly the first, who then bore a high rank among the most celebrated merchants of the world. The representation in congress was divided almost wholly between farmers, planters, and merchants. The manufacturing interest was, I believe, unrepresented; or if it had a few representatives, they were not distinguished men, and had little or no influence. It shared the melancholy fate of all unrepresented bodies in all ages and in all nations.

The tariff bears the most unequivocal marks of this state of things. Agriculture and commerce engrossed nearly the whole attention of congress. Their interests were well guarded. Manufactures, as may be seen (page 274) were abandoned to an unequal conflict with foreign rivalship, which consigned a large portion of them to ruin.

I have shewn the revolting neglect, so highly discreditable to congress, with which the applications of the manufacturers have been treated. It now remains to contrast this procedure with the kind attention and fostering care bestowed on the merchants, and the rapidity of motion in their concerns.

On the 29th of July, 1816, the governor of Nova Scotia, by proclamation, announced the royal assent to an act of the legislature of that province, whereby the trade in plaster of Paris was intended to be secured to British or colonial vessels.

To counteract this insidious measure, Mr. Rufus King, on the 17th of February, 1817, in the house of representatives of the united states, presented a resolution, which was carried, "that the committee on foreign relations be instructed to report such measures as they may judge necessary to regulate the importation of plaster of Paris, and to countervail the regulations of any other nation, injurious to our own, relating to that trade."

In four days afterwards, viz. on the 21st, Mr. Forsyth, chairman of that committee, reported a bill to regulate the trade in plaster of Paris, which was read the first and second time on that day, and the third on the 3d of March. The yeas and nays were called, and it was passed by a majority of eighty to thirty-nine. *It was then sent to the senate;* there read three times on the same day, and passed with some amendments—then returned to the house of representatives, who concurred in the amendments, and finally passed the bill. Thus it was *actually read four times, amended and passed in one day*—a case probably without example. It was only fourteen days from its inception to its approbation by the president.

Let it be observed further, that the hostile measure which called forth this spirited act, was only about seven months and a half in existence, when it was thus decisively counteracted. What a contrast between this celerity of operation and the lame and sinister policy observed towards manufacturers!

The all-important act prohibiting the entry into our ports of British vessels arriving from places from which American vessels are excluded, was reported and twice read in senate on the 1st of April, 1818. On the 4th it was read the third time, and passed. On the same day it was read twice in the house of representatives. On the 11th it was read a third time, and passed. On the 16th it was presented to the president--and approved by him on the 18th. Thus it became a law in seventeen days from its presentation.

Let any man, however hostile to manufactures or manufacturers, compare the progress of these two bills, involving such important principles, particularly the latter, with the snail's pace of any bill for the relief of manufacturers, and he will be obliged to confess that congress is actuated by a very different spirit towards the two different descriptions of citizens. The first of these acts is manly and dignified, and worthy of the legislature of a great nation, determined to assert a reciprocity of advantage in its intercourse with foreign nations. The policy and prudence of the second are rather questionable. It was not very likely to succeed; as it was a bold attempt to coerce the British nation to rescind one of the most important features of its navigation act, regarded as the basis of its power and greatness. Both their pride and interest revolted at the measure; and having wholly failed of accomplishing the object in view, its operation is highly pernicious to this country. It has in many instances sacrificed the sale of our staples, in the unavailing effort to obtain the freightage of them. At all events, considering its great magnitude, and its important effects on the agricultural interest, there can be no doubt, that it was too precipitately passed. It was only four days on its passage in the senate—and eight in the house of representatives. Be this, however, as it may, my present object is only once more to place in contrast the paternal care of commerce and the frigid and withering indifference, not to say hostility, towards manufactures, displayed in that body, which ought to "look with equal eye" upon, and to dispense equal justice to, all classes of citizens.

And to close the catalogue, a bill for the protection of commerce is now before congress,* and not likely to meet with much

* This bill was passed in a few days after the above was written—and has equally failed in the grand object of forcing Great Britain to open the ports of her colonies to our shipping.

opposition, which cannot fail to affect the agricultural interest severely, by very materially abridging the markets for their productions. It is calculated to effect the object contemplated by the last mentioned act.

More detail is unnecessary. The position is fully established, that commerce has steadily enjoyed all the protection the government could afford. Every hostile movement on the part of foreign nations, to the injury of our merchants, has been decidedly met and counteracted.

The consequence of this system has been to insure our merchants—

I. The whole of the coasting trade, amounting to 400,000 tons per annum.

II. Eighty-six per cent. of the tonnage engaged in the foreign trade, viz.

Total tonnage in the foreign trade for twenty-two years, from 1796 to 1817, - - tons		18,200,541
Of which there was American -	15,741,632	
Foreign - -	2,458,909	
		18,200,541

And III. An increase of tonnage unexampled in the history of navigation:—

*Tonnage of the united states.**

	Tons.		Tons.
In 1789 - -	201,562	In 1806 -	1,208,735
1790 - - -	478,377	1807 - -	1,268,548
1792 - -	564,437	1808 -	1,242,595
1794 - - -	628,816	1809 - -	1,350,281
1796 - -	831,900	1810 -	1,424,783
1798 - -	898,328	1811 - -	1,232,502
1801 - -	1,033,218	1812 -	1,269,997
1802 - -	892,102	1813 - -	1,166,628
1803 - -	949,171	1814 -	1,159,208
1804 -	1,042,402	1815 - -	1,368,127
1805 - -	1,140,368	1816 -	1,372,218

* Seybert.

CHAPTER XVII.

Erroneous views of the tariff. Protection of agriculture in 1789. *Prostrate state of the staples of South Carolina and Georgia. Ninety per cent. on snuff, and one hundred on tobacco. Striking contrast. Abandonment of manufactures.*

NUMBERS of the farmers and planters of the united states are under a strong impression—

I. That the tariff affords a decided protection to the manufacturers.

II. That it operates as a "heavy tax on the many for the benefit of the few."

And III. That there is no reciprocity in the case—as agriculture is not protected.

That the first position is radically erroneous, is self-evident from the lamentable situation of so large a proportion of the manufactures and manufacturers of the united states, on which I have already sufficiently descanted.

The second is disproved in the eleventh chapter.

To the discussion of the third, I devote the present one.

Few of the productions of agriculture require protection. Their bulk, and the consequent expense of freight, afford them in general tolerable security. But such as are imported, or likely to be, have been subject to high duties from the commencement of the government to the present time.

The articles of which the importation materially affects the interests of the landholders do not much extend beyond hemp, cotton, malt, tobacco, cheese, indigo, coals and potatoes, which, by the tariff of 1789, were subject to the following duties.

		Cents.			*Cents.*
Hemp - -	per cwt.	60	Snuff - -	per lb.	10
Malt -	per bushel	10	Indigo - -	do.	16
Coals - -	do.	2	Cotton - -	do.	3
Cheese -	per lb.	4	Potatoes -	per cent.	5
Manufactured tobacco	do.	6			

The duty on cheese was equal *to fifty-seven per cent.;* on
Indigo about *sixteen;* on
Snuff, *ninety;* on
Tobacco, *one hundred;* on
Coals about *fifteen per cent.*

The duty on the raw materials, hemp and cotton, demand particular attention. They were about twelve per cent.—imposed, in compliance with the suggestions of Mr. Burke, to aid the agriculturists of South Carolina and Georgia, "*because they hoped to be able to raise those articles*."

South Carolina and Georgia at that period were at a very low ebb. Their great staples, rice and indigo, had greatly sunk in price—and they had not as yet entered on the culture of cotton.

Ædanus Burke, in a debate on the tariff, on the 16th of April, 1789, to induce the house to lay a considerable duty on hemp and cotton, gave a melancholy picture of the situation of those states—

"The staple products of South Carolina and Georgia," he observed, "were hardly worth cultivation, on account of their "fall in price. The lands were certainly well adapted to the "growth of *hemp*: and he had no doubt but its culture would "be practised with attention. *Cotton was likewise in contempla-* "*tion among them: and if good seed could be procured*, HE HOPED "MIGHT SUCCEED!! But the low strong rice lands would pro- "duce hemp in abundance, many thousand tons even this year, "if it was not so late in the season."*

In a debate on the same subject, Mr. Tucker, another of the representatives from that state, re-echoed the plaintive strains of his colleague:—

"The situation of South Carolina was melancholy. While "the inhabitants were deeply in debt, *the produce of the state* "*was daily falling in price*. Rice and indigo were become so "low, as to be considered by many not objects worthy of culti- "vation. Gentlemen" he added, "will consider that it is not "an easy thing for a planter to change his whole system of hus- "bandry in a moment. But accumulated burdens will drive to "this, and increase their embarrassments."†

The duty on manufactured tobacco was intended to operate as an absolute prohibition—and was liberally proposed with this view by Mr. Sherman, a representative from Connecticut.

"Mr. Sherman moved six cents per pound on manufactured "tobacco; as he thought *the duty ought to amount to a prohibi-* "*tion*."‡

While these high duties were imposed upon such of the productions of the farmer and planter, as were likely to be imported, all the great leading articles of manufactures, as may be seen, (Chapter III.) were subject to only *five per cent.!!!*

A striking contrast in the tariff for 1789.

	Per cent.		*Per cent.*
Snuff - - - -	90	Woollens - - -	5
Tobacco - - -	100	Cottons - - - -	5

* Debates of congress, vol. I. p. 79.
† Idem, 70. ‡ Idem, 93.

	Per cent.		Per cent.
Indigo - - - -	16	Pottery - - - -	5
Coals - - - -	15	Linen - - - -	5
Cotton - - - -	12	Manufactures of iron -	5
Hemp - - - -	12	lead - -	5
		copper -	5

In the last chapter, I gave a sketch of the fostering care of commerce: Here we see, in the very outset of the government, the same care extended to agriculture, and a most culpable neglect of manufactures—the germ of that cruel and withering system, that has, I repeat, placed this country nearly in the state of a colony to the manufacturing nations of Europe—which, without expending a single cent for our protection, have enjoyed more benefits from our commerce than ever were enjoyed by the mother country, during the colonial state of this continent—and more benefits than any nation ever enjoyed from colonies, except Spain. Perhaps even this exception is superfluous.

In 1790, the tariff was altered, when indigo was raised to twenty-five cents per pound, and coals to three cents per bushel.

In 1792, it was again altered, and hemp raised to twenty dollars per ton, and coals to four and a half cents per bushel.

This was about *twenty per cent.* on hemp, and *twenty-five* on coals—whereas the leading manufactures of cotton, wool, leather, steel, brass, iron, and copper, were only raised to *seven and a half per cent.*

Passing over the intermediate alterations of the tariff, which all bear the same stamp of inequality and partiality, I shall notice the protection afforded at present to the class of articles whereby the interests of the owners and cultivators of the soil, are affected, in contra-distinction to the description of citizens properly styled manufacturers.

1820.	*Prices.**	*Rate of duty.*	*Duty Per cent.*
Hemp, per ton - - - - - - -	$114.00	$ 0.0	26
Cotton, per lb. - - - - - - -	.10	.3	30
Cheese in Holland - - - - -	.10	.9	90
Coals, per bushel - - - - - -	.13	.5	38½
Snuff, average per lb. - - - -	.16	.12	75
Manufactured tobacco† - - -	.10	.10	100
Segars per M† - - - - - - -	5.00	2.50	50
Geneva, per gallon - - - - -	.42	.42	100
Jamaica rum do. - - - - - -	.70	.48	68
Brown sugar, per lb. - - - - -	.6	.3	50

* At the places of exportation respectively.

† See page 374 for the reason why these two articles are placed in this class.

All the other articles, of this class, are subject to fifteen per cent. duty; which, be it observed, is the same as the duty on more than half the manufactures imported into this country.

We find cotton, the staple article of South Carolina, Georgia, Alabama, &c. of which the freight is about thirty per cent. secured by thirty per cent. duty—the staple of Virginia by seventy-five, and one hundred—and the peach brandy and whiskey, of the farmers generally, by sixty-eight and one hundred, while the cotton and woollen branches are exposed to great depression and have been paralized, for want of a duty of thirty-three per cent.!!!

To display the monstrous partiality of this procedure—I shall contrast the duty and freight of a few articles of both descriptions—

	Duty Per ct.	*Freight* Per ct.	*Total.*		*Duty* Per ct	*Freight* Per ct.	*Total.*
Hemp - -	26	24	50	Cotton stockings	25	2	28
Cotton - -	30	30	60	Cambrics - -	25	2	27
Cheese - -	90	10	105	Woollen cloths	25	2	27
Geneva - -	100	15	110	Silks - - -	15	1	16
Rum - - -	68	10	78	Woollen stockings	20	2	22
Snuff - - -	75	5	80	Thread stockings	15	2	17
Tobacco -	100	5	105	Gold leaf - -	15	1	16
Coals - - -	38½	12	½	Linens - - -	15	2	17
Sugar - -	37½	6	43½				

It is scarcely possible to conceive of a more revolting arrangement—or one that more completely violates the holy, the golden rule—

"All things whatsoever ye would that men should do to you, "do you even so to them."

Now in the face of this nation, I venture to ask, is there a respectable man in society, who considers the above items, and will not allow that the protection of agriculture is incomparably more complete than that of manufactures?

And yet, wonderful to tell, the extravagant protection bestowed on the manufacturers, and the want of protection to agriculturists—the insatiable appetite of the former, and the liberality and disinterestedness of the latter, are preached in long-winded speeches in, and memorials to, congress, and as long-winded newspaper essays, and are received as undeniable truths!

Another contrast.

	Present Duty. Per cent.		Present Duty. Per cent.
Potatoes	15	Watches	7½
Butter	15	Jewelry . . .	7½
Flour	15	Inkpowder . .	15
Malt	15	Printed books . .	15
Onions	15	Worsted shoes . .	15
Tobacco in the leaf . .	15	Linens and silks - -	15

Potatoes, onions, and tobacco—linens, silks, and printed books—subject to the same duty! What wonderful talents this tariff displays! How admirably it corroborates the fond "day dreams" in which we indulge ourselves, of our immense superiority over the benighted Europeans, who, *mirabile dictu*, according to judge Story, are studying lessons of political economy under congress—

"The statesmen of the old world, *in admiration of the success* "*of our policy*, are relaxing the rigour of their own systems!!"

So says the celebrated Salem memorial, edited, according to public fame, by this most learned judge.

Objections have been made to the classification of manufactured tobacco and snuff among the articles dutied for the benefit of agriculture; as they fall under the denomination of manufactures. They are, it is true, manufactures. But that they are so extravagantly taxed, is not from any partiality towards the manufacturers of them—but to protect the planters. It requires no moderate share of modesty to assert, and of credulity to believe, that regard for the manufacturers leads to lay a duty of one hundred per cent. on manufactured tobacco, when for five years the manufacturers of woollens and cottons have in vain implored to have the duty on superfine cloth, muslins, and cambrics, raised beyond twenty-five per cent. Even the Jew Apella, capacious as was his gullet, would not be able to swallow this fiction.

I wish it distinctly understood, that as the prices of hemp, Geneva, rum, coals, &c. are subject to frequent fluctuations in foreign markets, I do not pretend to vouch for the critical exactness at the present time, of the preceding quotations. I have collected my information from merchants of character, on whom reliance may be placed, and have every reason to believe that it is substantially correct.

CHAPTER XVIII.

An awful contrast. Distress in Great Britain, because she cannot engross the supply of the world. Distress in the united states, because the home market is inundated with rival manufactures.

THIS shall be a short chapter. But I hope it will make a deep and lasting impression. The subject is of vital importance.

I have drawn several contrasts between our policy and that of foreign nations, to evince the unsoundness and pernicious consequences of the former. To one more contrast I request attention.

Great distress pervades the manufacturing districts of Great Britain, in which commerce largely partakes. And whence does it arise? Because her merchants and manufacturers cannot engross the supply of the world; for their capacity of producing every article made by machinery is commensurate with the wants of the whole human race; and, could they find a passage to the moon, and open a market there, they would be able to inundate it with their fabrics.

Their government, with a fostering and paternal care, which by the contrast reflects discredit on ours, secures them the *unlimited range of the domestic market;* and loses no opportunity, by bounties, drawbacks, and every other means which can be devised, to aid them in their efforts to engross our and all other markets. But the wisdom of the other nations of Europe, guarding the industry of their subjects, excludes them from various markets which they were wont to supply—and baffles their skill and sagacity. The great mass of their surplus productions, is, therefore, disgorged on us, to the destruction of our manufacturers and the impoverishment of the nation.

What a lamentable contrast we exhibit! Our manufacturers suffer equally. Their capital is mouldering away—their establishments falling to ruins—themselves threatened with bankruptcy, and their wives and children with dependence—their workmen dispersed and driven to servile labour and mendicity—and why? Not because they are excluded from foreign markets. They aspire to none. Their distress arises from being debarred of so large a portion of their home market, to which our mistaken policy invites all the manufacturers of the earth!

Thus, while the British government uses all its energies to enable the manufacturers of that nation to monopolize the markets of the united states, our government looks on with perfect indifference, while the ill-fated, depressed, and vilified American, defeated in the unequal struggle with powerful rivals and an energetic government, is bankrupted or beggared—or in danger of bankruptcy or beggary—and in vain invokes its protection! In a word the representatives of the freest people on the globe, have less regard for, and pay less attention to the happiness of, their fellow citizens, than the monarchs of the old world to their subjects.

This is a strong declaration. But it is delivered with great deliberation, and with the most undaunted confidence of its correctness. The shameful and contumelious neglect of the memorials of the manufacturers at each successive session of congress, from 1816, down to the present time, cannot, I am persuaded, be paralleled in the history of England or France. Let it be observed, I except the dependencies of both nations. If the smallest body of manufacturers in England finds itself aggrieved, and applies to the British parliament for redress, a committee is appointed to examine into the case, and to devise a remedy. If such remedy is practicable, it is applied. But we have seen that the petitions and memorials from the great cities of New-York, Philadelphia, Boston, and Baltimore, were not only not complied with, but not even read or reported on, to the indelible discredit of the fourteenth congress.

Our citizens merely seek a portion of that protection which the most despotic monarchs in Europe afford their subjects. But they seek in vain. Pharaoh did not turn a more deaf ear to the applications of the Israelites, than congress have, for five years, to those of their fellow citizens who have contributed to elevate them to the honourable stations they occupy—and who pay their proportions for services from the benefit of which they are in a great measure precluded.

What a hideous, what a deplorable contrast! What a libel on republican government! What a triumph for the friends of monarchy—for those who hold the appalling heresy, to which our career affords some countenance, that man was not made for self-government!

This is so shocking a state of things that with all the evidence of the facts before my eyes, I can scarcely allow myself to credit it! Would to God, it were not true—but alas! it is a most afflicting reality.

CHAPTER XIX.

Encouragement and patronage of immigrants, by England and France. Advantages of the united states. Great numbers of immigrants. Their sufferings. Return of many of them. Interesting table.

Some political economists have asserted that the strength of a nation consists in the number of its inhabitants. This, without qualification, is manifestly erroneous. A numerous population, in a state of wretchedness, is rather a symptom of debility than of strength. Such a population is ripe for treason and spoil. But a dense population, usefully and profitably employed, and in a state of comfort and prosperity, constitutes the pride and glory of a statesman, and is the basis of the power and security of nations. Hence there is scarcely any object which the most profound statesmen and monarchs of Europe, have for ages more uniformly pursued than the encouragement of immigrants possessed of useful talents.

Under all the governments of Europe, therefore, even the most despotic, inducements have been frequently held out to invite a tide of population of this description. And the wealth, power, and prosperity of some of the first rate nations, date their commencement from migrations thus promoted and encouraged. The decay and decrepitude of the nations from which the immigrants have removed, have been coeval and proceeded pari passu with the prosperity of those to which they have migrated.

The woollen manufacture, the main source of the wealth and prosperity of England, dates its great extension and the commencement of its prosperity from the wise policy of Edward III. who invited over Flemish workmen, and accorded them most important privileges.

The horrible persecutions of D'Alva in the Netherlands, and the repeal of the edict of Nantz, in France, at a more recent period, drove thousands of artists of every kind, possessed of great wealth, and inestimable talents, to England, whence she derived incalculable advantages.

Spain, whose policy we despise, repeatedly encouraged settlements of immigrants to establish useful manufactures, which had a temporary success. But the radical unsoundness of her system, and her spirit of persecution, blasted all these promising attempts.

France, under Louis XIV. pursued this system to a greater extent than any other nation. That king gave titles of nobility and pensions and immunities, to various artists and manufacturers, who introduced new branches of industry into his dominions: and a great porton of the wealth which he squandered on the splendor of his court, and on the ambitious projects of his reign, arose from his protection of those immigrants, and the manufactures they introduced.

If this policy were wise, and had the sanction of the statesmen of nations of which the population was comparatively dense, how much more forcibly does it apply to the united states, of which the population bears so small a proportion to the territory!

No country affords more room for immigrants—none would derive more benefit from them—none could hold out so many solid and substantial inducements—and there is none to which the eyes and longings of that active and energetic class of men who are disposed to seek foreign climes for the purpose of improving their condition, are more steadily directed. We have the most valuable staples—the greatest variety of soil, climate, and productions—an almost unlimited extent of territory—and the most slender population in proportion to that territory, of any nation in the world, except the Indians, and perhaps the wandering Tartars. And had manufactures, particularly the cotton, woollen and iron, instead of the paltry duty of five per cent. been early and decisively taken under the protection of the government, at its first organization, in 1789, after the example of other nations, there is no doubt we should have had a tide of immigration beyond any the world has ever witnessed.

From the oppression and misery prevalent in various parts of Europe—from the high idea entertained of the advantages of our government—and from a variety of other circumstances, it is fair to presume, that had immigrants been able at once to find employment at the occupations to which they were brought up, we might have had an annual accession of 30 or 40,000 beyond the numbers that have settled among us. But I shall only suppose 20,000.

To evince what might have been, from what has taken place, I annex the only two tables of immigration I have been able to find. And let it be observed that the first is necessarily very imperfect; as there was no governmental regulation to enforce the collection of accurate statements.

In 1817, 22,240 immigrants arrived in ten ports:—

			18,114
In Boston	2,200	In Baltimore	1,817
New York	7,634	Norfolk	520
Perth Amboy	637	Charleston	747
Philadelphia	7,085	Savannah	163
Wilmington, D.	558	New Orleans	879
	18,114		22,240*

In New York, from March 2, 1818, to Dec. 11, 1819, the numbers reported at the mayor's office, were 18,929.†

			18,532
English	7,539	Portuguese	54
Irish	6,062	Africans	5
French	922	Prussians	48
Welsh	590	Sardinians	3
Scotch	1,942	Danes	97
Germans	499	Russians	13
Spaniards	217	Austrians	8
Hollanders	255	Turk	1
Swiss	372	Polander	1
Italians	103	Sandwich Islanders	2
Norwegians	3	Europeans not described	52
Swedes	28	Passengers do. do.	113
	18,532		18,929

* Seybert, 29.

† Report of the society for the prevention of pauperism, p. 67.

The mayor of New York* has given a calculation, that these were but two thirds of the whole number that arrived. Admitting this estimate, the whole number in twenty-one months was about 28,000, or 16,000 per annum.

Twenty thousand, which I have assumed, as what might have been annually added to our population by a sound policy on the subject of manufactures, will be regarded as probable on a consideration of the preceding statements—particularly the table of the enormous arrivals in New York, notwithstanding a variety of discouraging circumstances, of which the tendency was to repress or even to destroy the spirit of immigration.

Among these, the principal one has been the calamities and wretchedness endured by most of those immigrants, whose fond hopes and expectations were wholly blasted on their arrival here. Thousands and tens of thousands of artists, mechanics, and manufacturers, with talents beyond price, and many of them with handsome capitals, escaped from misery and oppression in Europe, and fled to our shores as to a land of promise, where they expected to find room for the exercise of their industry and talents. But the fond delusion was soon dispelled. As soon as they arrived, they sought employment at their usual occupations. None was to be found. Those whose whole fortune was their industry, wandered through our streets, in search even of menial employments, to support a wretched existence. And numerous instances have occurred, of cotton weavers and clothiers, as well as persons of other useful branches, who have sawed and piled wood in our cities—and some of whom have broken stones on our turnpikes, for little more than a bare subsistence. Many hundreds have returned home, heart-broken, and lamenting their folly, after having exhausted all their funds in the double voyage and inevitable expenses. Their misfortunes operate as a beacon to their countrymen, to shun the rocks on which they have been shipwrecked.

It is easy to estimate the effects that must have been produced by the dismal tales in the letters written by those who remained, and by the verbal accounts of those who returned. It is not extravagant to suppose, that every returned emigrant prevented the emigration of twenty persons, disposed to seek an asylum here. And the melancholy letters, transmitted by those who had no means of returning, must have had nearly equal influence.

Many of those who were unable to return, rendered desperate by distress and misery, have proved injurious to the coun-

* "The chief magistrate of this city has calculated that this number does not "include more than two thirds of the real number." a

a Idem, p. 20.

try, which from their labour might have secured the most eminent advantages.

I hazard an estimate of the gain that might have been made by a sound policy, which would have encouraged manufacturing industry, and promoted immigration, to the extent I have assumed, viz. 20,000 additional per annum, since the commencement of our present form of government.

I will suppose the value of the productive labour of each individual to be only a quarter dollar per day beyond his subsistence, which, for 20,000, would have amounted to $ 1,500,000 per annum. The whole number that would have arrived in the thirty years, would have been 600,000. The annexed table exhibits a result, which petrifies with astonishment, and sheds a new and strong stream of light on the impolicy of our system.

	No. of immigrants.	*Value of labour.*		*No. of immigrants.*	*Value of labour.*
					180,000,000
1789	20,000	$ 1,500,000	1804	320,000	24,000,000
1790	40,000	3,000,000	1805	340,000	25,500,000
1791	60,000	4,500,000	1806	360,000	27,000,000
1792	80,000	6,000,000	1807	380,000	28,500,000
1793	100,000	7,500,000	1808	400,000	30,000,000
1794	120,000	9,000,000	1809	420,000	31,500,000
1795	140,000	10,500,000	1810	440,000	33,000,000
1796	160,000	12,000,000	1811	460,000	34,500,000
1797	180,000	13,500,000	1812	480,000	36,000,000
1798	200,000	15,000,000	1813	500,000	37,500,000
1799	220,000	16,500,000	1814	520,000	39,000,000
1800	240,000	18,000,000	9815	540,000	40,500,000
1801	260,000	19,500,000	1816	560,000	42,000,000
1802	180,800	21,000,000	1817	580,000	43,500,000
1803	300,000	22,500,000	1818	600,000	45,000,000
		$ 180,000,000			*$ 697,500,000

The natural increase of the immigrants by generation, at five per cent. per annum, would make the number amount to above 1,000,000. Of the addition I take no account. I barely mention, that an immigration of 10,000 annually, would, according to this increase, have produced nearly the same result as the assumed number 20,000.

Let us then state the results of different numbers :—

* This table, although tolerably plain and simple, may require some explanation. It is assumed, that 20,000 immigrants would have arrived yearly ; of course, in 1789, there would have been in this country 20,000—in 1790, 40,000—in 1791, 60 000, and so throughout the whole series of years. There is no account taken of the increase of the immigrants by generation.

10,000 immigrants, with the natural increase of five per cent. per annum, at a quarter of a dollar per day, would produce in 30 years about $650,000,000

That of 5,000 with the same increase . . $325,000,000

It is fair to suppose that the articles produced by them would be worth double the labour, or, in the first case, ... $1,300,000,000

In the second $650,000,000

These immense advantages we blindly threw away, while we were scuffling through the world at every point of the compass, and "in every bay, cove, creek, and inlet," to which we had access, for a precarious commerce, which ruined the great mass of the merchants who pursued it---exposed our hardy seamen to stripes and bondage—involved us in unnecessary collisions with the belligerent powers, and finally in war,—and entailed on us a host of foreign ministers—a wasting navy that will cost above 3,500,000 dollars this year—and a debt of nearly 80,000,000 of dollars!

Other views of the subject present themselves.

Although a large proportion of the immigrants who arrive in this and other countries, are dependent on their labour for support, yet many capitalists immigrate; and there would be double, treble, perhaps quadruple, the number of this class, could they employ their capitals advantageously. I will assume an average of one hundred and fifty dollars for each immigrant, in money and property. This would amount to 3,000,000 dollars per annum, or in the whole 30 years to 90,000,000 of dollars.

The consumption of the productions of agriculture by those immigrants, according to the calculation in page 332, at the rate of a quarter dollar per day, would be at present per annum 54,000,000 of dollars, and their clothing and furniture at 40 dollars per annum, 24,000,000.

Calculations have been made of the value to a state of an active efficient individual. In England it was formerly, I believe, supposed to be about 100*l.* sterling. I will suppose each immigrant to be worth three hundred dollars—this would make the amount of the 600,000 immigrants assumed, $180,000,000.

These calculations are all necessarily crude—and admit of considerable drawbacks. But whatever may be the drawbacks, sufficient will remain to prove to the world, that there probably never was a nation which had so many advantages within its grasp—and never a nation that so wantonly threw its advantages away.

Summary.

Suppose 10,000 immigrants annually, with the natural increase of five per cent.	
Amount of labour in thirty years .	$650,000,000
Value of their productions . .	$1,300,000,000
Amount of property imported . .	$90,000,000
Present annual consumption for food, clothes, and furniture, ...	$78,000,000

As this chapter drew to a close, I met with a report made to the house of representatives of the united states, on the subject of immigrants, which deserves some notice.

An application has been recently made to congress by a body of Swiss, for a quantity of land, on more advantageous terms than those on which it is sold by law. The committee, after stating the necessity of lessening the existing indulgences in the sale of the public lands, adds—

"If the public interests should ever justify a relaxation from "them, it would be in favour of American citizens:"

And recommends to the house the following resolution—

"*Resolved*, that the prayer of the petitioners ought not to be "granted."

So far there are reason and propriety in the report. The terms on which lands are sold by the united states are sufficiently favourable for foreigners as well as natives. But when the committee notices the depressed situation of American manufactures, and assigns it as a reason against encouraging the immigration of such a useful body of men, possessed of invaluable talents, it is a full proof that the members did not study the subject profoundly.

"In answer to that part of the petition which declares that one "of the principal objects is 'the domestic manufacture of cot- "ton, wool, flax, and silk;' the committee will only say, that it "may be well considered, *how far it would comport with sound* "*policy to give a premium for the introduction of manufacturers,* "*at a moment when, by the almost unanimous declaration of our* "*manufacturers, it is said they cannot live without further pro-* "*tection.*"

A more obvious idea would have been, to suggest such encouragement of manufactures, as would have relieved our citizens actually engaged in those branches, and held out due inducements for accessions to our population of the sterling character of the applicants in question.

FINIS.

ADDRESS TO CONGRESS:

BEING

A VIEW

OF

THE RUINOUS CONSEQUENCES

OF A

DEPENDENCE ON FOREIGN MARKETS

FOR THE SALE OF THE

GREAT STAPLES OF THIS NATION,

FLOUR, COTTON, AND TOBACCO.

Read before, and ordered to be printed by, the Board of Manufactures of the Pennsylvania Society for the promotion of American Manufactures.

SECOND EDITION.

FIRST PUBLISHED, MAY 10, 1820.

" Our fast-sailing ships which traverse the ocean; our steam-boats which as-
" cend our magnificent and rapid rivers; our improved roads and canals of inte-
" rior communication—all of which were devised for our peculiar benefit—are
" *at present employed principally to aid our rivals,* and to transport commodities
" into the central regions of this great continent, which *check every effort of pro-*
" *fitable industry, and blast every germ of patriotic enterprise.*"—Governor Wolcott.

" *Quicquid delirant reges, plectuntur Achivi.*"—Horat.

ADVERTISEMENT.

THE object of this pamphlet is plain and simple. It is, to prove the ruinous consequences which have attended the dependence on foreign markets for the sale of our staples; the very precarious tenure by which those markets are held; and the superiority, to the agriculturist, of a certain domestic, to a precarious foreign market.

In this address, as in all he has written hitherto on collateral subjects, the writer has depended more on strong and decisive facts, than on abstruse reasonings. The former are almost universally safe guides—the latter mere *ignes fatui*, which too generally lead astray.

The facts respecting the loss of the indigo market, are peculiarly interesting to the cotton and tobacco planters. There is a perfect analogy between the dangers that threaten the trade in their two important staples, and those which formerly threatened and finally supplanted the indigo trade of South Carolina.

Of a rise in the price of either cotton, tobacco, or flour, there is no prospect.

The importation of cotton into Great Britain in 1819 was one-sixth less than in 1818; and yet, notwithstanding this important circumstance, and all the predictions hazarded, and the hopes entertained, of an advance of price, it was by the latest accounts declining.

The prospects for tobacco are still more discouraging. The continental markets are greatly circumscribed by the extension of the culture in that quarter.

The fact of flour being advantageously shipped from France to the West Indies; and the amount of the export of wheat from Odessa, exclude all hopes of advantageous foreign markets for our bread stuffs.

The necessity, therefore, of increasing the domestic market for our cotton and flour, and of limiting the culture of tobacco, appears as plain as the noon-day sun. This can be done effectually, only by the encouragement of our own manufactures, whereby some of the thousands of our citizens whom the depression of manufactures has compelled to become agriculturists, may be induced to return to their former pursuits. The conviction of this truth is rapidly spreading—and cannot fail finally to become general. It is not, however, within human foresight, to divine how long and how severe a course of suffering we must go through, before our councils are influenced by the salutary conviction.

Those merchants, farmers, and planters, who have opposed the protection of manufactures, ought to study the fable of the belly and the members. It is fraught with instruction. Their jealousy of, and refusal of protection to, the manufacturers, form a complete exemplification of that fable, and have led to nine-tenths of the distress and impoverishment of the nation, which have fallen heavily on themselves. For let theorists say what they will, misery and wretchedness must as certainly attend nations, which expend more than their income, as individuals: and had manufactures been properly protected, our imports would have necessarily been limited within narrower bounds, and kept on a level with our exports, so as to prevent that ruinous drain of specie which has paralized every species of industry.

The destruction of so many manufactories throughout the union has deprived the neighbouring farmers of a market for their wool, their garden stuffs, their grain, and a variety of other articles. To this likewise is due the destruction of the merino sheep. The loss of the fleeces of those valuable animals is incomparably more than the farmers gain by buying foreign goods cheap, whereby they consign their brethren to bankruptcy, the nation to impoverishment, and our working people to idleness and want.

The merchant suffers still more severely. If he looks abroad for a profitable market for our staples, disappointment awaits him. For return cargoes, he experiences equal straits. A large portion of his customers are bankrupt, and others on the verge of bankruptcy. Can commerce fail to be ruinous under those circumstances? Was the trade of an embarrassed nation ever advantageous to those who pursued it? Is it wonderful, therefore, that bankruptcy has spread among the merchants in as great a degree as among the manufacturers? It is impossible that so important an interest as that of the manufacturing class, can experience the destruction which has for years befallen it, without the two other classes partaking largely of the misfortune. Our history and that of Spain and Portugal are pregnant proofs of this theory.

As well might we expect to amputate the legs or arms of a human being, without affecting the head or the heart, as that so large a portion of the manufacturers could be consigned to bankruptcy—their capitals to ruin—and the productive industry of probably 60 to 80,000 people be destroyed, without producing deleterious consequences on the whole nation. It will be a subject of astonishment to our posterity how our statesmen could shut their eyes to such an important and obvious truth. They have disregarded the lessons afforded by the history of mankind in every age in which a fatal policy has led governments to neglect the protection of national industry.

The views of the author have been unjustly regarded as hostile to farmers and merchants. Never was there a more unfounded idea. He is a warm friend to both. He has been pleading in their behalf full as much as in that of the manufacturers. There is an identity of interests between them: and until this great truth is fully understood and duly appreciated, this country can never extricate itself from a situation, which has been thus justly characterised by the secretary of the treasury: "*Few examples have occurred, of a distress so general, and so severe, as that which has been exhibited in the united states.*"

In truth, however extraordinary it may appear, the policy he has advocated would be advantageous to the merchants of Great Britain, who, by their cupidity and the inundation of their merchandize, have destroyed their best market, and bankrupted their most valuable customers. Had we gold and silver mines, like Spain and Portugal, to enable us to pay for the extravagant amount of our imports, foreign nations would benefit by the suppression of our industry. But as we depend wholly on the proceeds of that industry, to discharge our engagements, it is their interest to cherish it, and to promote our prosperity. To the mere wily foreign politician, who dreads us as a rising rival, and desires to stunt our growth and enfeeble us, the case is far different. To him no sacrifice can be too great for the accomplishment of this grand object. The important question for us to decide, is, how far we ought to lend ourselves to, and facilitate the accomplishment of, such a sinister and mischievous policy.

Among the considerations which have influenced the writer to pursue these subjects to the extent he has done, one remains to be stated, which is of immense importance.

This is a government of opinion. It is not, it cannot be, supported by physical force against that public opinion. It therefore behoves our rulers to cherish the good will of the citizens, which is the bulwark of our peace and happiness.—But it is fatally true, that a conviction is generally spreading,—that the sufferings of our manufacturers—who constitute one-fifth of the white population of the country—how great and oppressive soever they may be, excite no sympathy in, and look in vain for alleviation from, the congress of the united states—and that the manufacturing subjects of some of the most high-handed despotisms of Europe are treated with infinitely more attention and fostering care by their monarchs, than that useful body of citizens experience from the men whom they aid to clothe with power. The fact is of public notoriety, that for five successive years they have besought their fellow-citizens in vain for relief from most intolerable evils; *that few or none of their memorials have ever been read; and that many of them have not even been reported on.* And, from the ruinous policy we pursue, whereby bankruptcy and distress are spreading through the union, and so many of the working part of our citizens are devoted to idleness; the attachment to the government is naturally impaired. These are weighty considerations, which cannot be disregarded with impunity.

A parent who kept his own children in idleness and want, and fostered and nourished strangers, would be deserving of unqualified censure. Is not this equally true with respect to nations? Have we not thousands of citizens unemployed and in distress, while we lavish our wealth to support and foster the industry of foreigners?

One consideration pleads loudly for a radical change. Our present system has hurled us precipitously from a towering state of prosperity into an abyss of embarrassment, distress, bankruptcy, idleness, failure of revenue, and destruction of credit. May we not solemnly ask our rulers, can any change be for the worse?

POSTSCRIPT.

This pamphlet was written in the hope of its arriving in season at Washington, previous to the fatal vote which rejected the new tariff, and of its evincing to the farmers and planters in that body, the utter impolicy of the system they have pursued, merely as respects their own interests, abstracted from all regard for the sufferings of their fellow citizens, or for the general welfare, topics already copiously discussed. It unfortunately is too late for that purpose—but is nevertheless offered to the public, in order to bring this important subject under discussion during the recess.

The result of this vote is to the last degree appalling to the manufacturers. At least *thirty thousand* of them, in every part of the middle and eastern states, writhing in distress, many of them in positive misery, have respectfully memorialized congress for relief from their intolerable evils. But all their memorials have been in vain. During a tedious session of five months not one of their grievances has been redressed—not one of their sufferings relieved!

This affords an awful view of our situation—of our future prospects. The mind revolts at the consideration.

I believe it may be asserted with safety, that, under circumstances in the least degree similar, such a total disregard of the voice of the people—such a total want of sympathy for their sufferings, has never been exhibited.

Philadelphia, May 10, 1820.

ADDRESS TO CONGRESS.

FELLOW CITIZENS,

You have now to decide on a modification of the tariff, intended to afford protection to that portion of the national industry, devoted to manufactures—as important a question, probably, as any ever submitted to congress, since the organization of the government. Indeed, to those of our citizens engaged in that useful department, the subject is as important as the declaration of independence itself. Should it be decided in the negative, bankruptcy and ruin will be the fate of vast numbers of them, which will render the benefits of independence to them very problematical. I am as ardent a friend of liberty as any man. But liberty is only valuable as it affords security to person and property. And to those who have been, or may be, ruined for want of protection, it is idle to declaim on the advantages of liberty, when property, which gives value to life and liberty, is destroyed—and when distress and dependence are to be their portion. Few will hesitate to subscribe to the strong sentiment of Postlethwaite, "*that men will sooner live prosperously under the worst government, than be ruined under the best.*"

So much has been written on the distresses and bankruptcy of the manufacturers—the ruin of their establishments—the poverty of those who are deprived of employment, and whose only property is in the labour of their hands—that the topic is almost exhausted, and I shall not therefore touch it. Nothing I could state would enhance the affecting portraits, which have been offered to public inspection.

Another fertile topic is the effect the proposed measure would produce on the national prosperity. This has been copiously discussed, as well by those opposed to, as those who advocate, a change of system. I shall therefore waive it, and for the present merely request your attention to considerations of a totally different character, bearing upon your own personal interests; to facts and arguments, which I have subjected to strict scrutiny, and which, I trust, will stand the test of the most rigorous investigation.

Abstracted from the influence of national considerations, your grand object, as members of this community, is to secure good markets and fair prices for your staples. This is not only natural and allowable, but laudable. It is as perfectly right, and as obviously a duty, for planters and farmers to guard their interests, as for merchants and manufacturers to pursue the same system.

I shall treat separately of our three great staples, cotton, flour, and tobacco. And first of

COTTON.

In the opposition the cotton planters have hitherto made to affording full and complete protection to the cotton manufacturers, I presume they supposed they were promoting not only their own interests, but those of the country at large. They were, probably, apprehensive that it would be highly injurious to throw any difficulty in the way of the commerce in a staple which, for four successive years, formed nearly two fifths of the domestic exports of the nation.

	Total exports.	*Cotton.*	*Value.*
1815	$45,974,000	*lbs.* 82,998,747*	$17,529,000†
1816	64,782,000	81,947,086	24,106,000
1817	68,313,500	85,649,328	22,627,614
1818	73,854,437	92,471,178	31,434,258
	$252,923,937		$95,696,872

It is not necessary to criticise this policy severely. The greatest statesmen that ever lived, have erred. And it is not therefore wonderful that our career should be occasionally marked with error.

But I may be permitted to observe, that had the subject received that deep and profound consideration which its importance required, it would have been seen, that the extreme depression of the domestic market, and limiting the nation chiefly to a few foreign ones, could scarcely fail to be pernicious, under any circumstances.

I presume it is scarcely necessary for me to prove, as it is notorious, that the prices of our cotton have been subject to frequent and ruinous fluctuations—and that those fluctuations have arisen from our dependence for the sale of the chief part of our crops, on foreign markets, wherein we meet with formidable competitors.

Great Britain has been for years, and is, the principal market for the cotton of the united states. She receives about three-fourths of this staple exported from this country. The prices here have been uniformly regulated by those in Liverpool, since we commenced the culture of cotton. And the for-

* Seybert, 152. † Idem, 147.

tunes of our planters and merchants have at all times hung in suspense on the news from that port. Hundreds of the latter, who in the morning regarded themselves, and were regarded by others, as men of affluence, have gone to bed in crippled circumstances, or ruined, by the news of a great and unexpected reduction of the price of cotton in Liverpool.

There are now before me two tables of the variations of the prices of cotton in that port, one from 1801 to 1811, and the other for 1813, 1814, 1815, from which I annex abstracts, which afford matter for deep and serious reflection to every person interested in the sale or purchase of this grand staple.

Monthly average prices of upland cotton in Liverpool from 1801 *to* 1811.

		Pence.			Pence.			Pence.
1801.	July	26	1805.	July	20	1808.	Sept.	34
	Sept.	23		Dec.	23		Oct.	37
	Dec.	21	1806.	Jan.	20		Dec.	35
1802.	Jan.	22		March	17½	1809.	Jan.	32
	Feb.	21		June	19		March	29
	March	20		Sept.	23		April	21
	April	19		Nov.	20		May	18
	May	18		Dec.	19		July	16
	June	16	1807.	Jan.	18½		Aug.	20
	July	17		March	20		Dec.	22
	Sept.	18		Oct.	17½	1810.	Feb.	21
1803.	Feb.	16½	1808.	Jan.	17		April	18
	April	15½		Feb.	18		Nov.	16
	June	16½		March	19	1811.	Feb.	15
	Oct.	16		April	21		June	13½
1804.	Oct.	19		June	24		Sept.	12½
	Dec.	21		July	30			

Monthly average prices of upland cotton in Liverpool, for three years.

	1813. Pence.	1814. Pence.	1815. Pence.
January	21¾	35¼	20½
February	23¾	32¼	20¼
March	23¼	31⅛	20¾
April	21½	29	22¼
May	23	25	19¾
June	20½	24½	17½
July	21¾	26½	18¼
August	21¼	31	22¼

	1813. Pence.	1814. Pence.	1815. Pence.
September	22¼	31¼	23½
October	23	30¼	21
November	23½	28¼	18¾
December	24¼	22½	16¾

These tables alone would afford a solution of the problem of the failure of so large a portion of our exporting merchants, for past years.

Great must have been the ruin produced by some of those heavy reductions, of four, five, and six pence per pound in a single month, sometimes in a few days.

The most ruinous consequences attended the reductions of price last year; which arose from the extraordinary increase of the importation into Great Britain of Brazil and East India cotton in 1818:—

Of the former, the importation in	1817 was *bales*,	114,816
	1818	180,077
Or almost sixty per cent. increase		65,261

Of the East India the importations were—

In 1816	bales 30,670
1817	117,454
1818	247,604
	395,728

Thus our cotton planters are at the mercy of the seasons and industry of Brazil and Hindostan. If the seasons be very favourable, and the people very industrious in those countries, an American planter's income may sink down to one or two thousand dollars. But in the contrary case, it may rise to five! What a subject for serious reflection!

East India cotton had been little used in Great Britain before the year 1817. The extreme carelessness in the preparation and cleansing of it, had in a great measure excluded it. But in 1816, on the opening of the trade to the East Indies, the British merchants, induced by the very high price of American and Brazil cotton, turned their attention to the East Indies, where they sent large orders for the ensuing year.

Intelligence of this operation, so very important to the vital interests of this country, was received about the close of the year 1816; and, in the following February, published in detail, with suitable comments* calculated to excite alarm, and produce such precautionary measures as might avert the impending consequences. But the admonitions were wholly disregarded. Not a single measure was predicated on them.

The importation in 1817 of East India cotton into Great Britain was, as already stated, fourfold that of the preceding year. We still reposed in full security, all sails set, gliding before the wind. Not a speck of the approaching storm could be discovered by our statesmen.

In 1818, a new scene opened. The great abundance and the low price of the East India cotton induced the British manufacturers to erect new and alter the old machinery, for the purpose of working up the short staple. Of this important circumstance intelligence was received in all our seaports from the British merchants, who deserve great credit for their candour on the subject. Their letters warned our merchants and planters of the impending danger.

Unfortunately all these symptoms and admonitions were wholly disregarded, like those which had preceded them. Yet there was ample time to have guarded against the fatal result, by reviving the expiring domestic market. An act of twenty lines, subjecting all cottons, *below fifty cents* per yard, to duty as at fifty, on the principle that prevails with respect to those below *twenty-five cents*—and an increase of the duty on higher-priced goods to thirty-three or thirty-seven and a half per cent. would have applied a remedy to the existing, and a preventive to the threatened evils. It would have secured a domestic consumption for such a proportion of the crop, as would have reduced the quantity of our cotton in the British market, and prevented the reduction that took place, with all its ruinous consequences. This measure, the obvious dictate of policy and prudence, was neglected, and dearly have the planters and the nation paid the forfeit.

The British markets were in the summer and fall of 1818 crowded with Brazil and East India cotton. As the importation of ours had not increased, the market was not much overstocked with it.—It is a melancholy fact, nevertheless, that it felt the consequences of the glut and consequent depression of the other species.

On the 28th of Nov. 1818, New Orleans cotton in Liverpool was at an average of *twenty pence half penny*. From that period it began to decline—and continued falling gradually till the 12th of May, when it sunk to *twelve pence three farthings*. For

* Memoir on the culture and manufacture of cotton, by Tench Coxe, Esq. passim.

some time it remained stationary, when it began to rise slowly, and on September 30th was *fifteen pence half penny.*

It is worthy of observation, that the depression here is generally much greater than in the Liverpool market. The above reduction from November 1818, to May 1819, was only *forty per cent.* Whereas, the reduction in the Philadelphia market, in the corresponding period from January to June 1819, was from thirty-three cents to sixteen and a half, or *fifty per cent.*

During the course of last fall and winter, the cotton planters were assured with great confidence, that the East India cotton was found so worthless as to be unfit for use; that the machinery employed to manufacture it was altering for the purpose of being employed on the long staple; and that therefore the prices of united states cotton would rise perhaps to the former grade. "What we wish to be true, we are fond to believe." Implicit credit was given to the information. But it was "hoping against hope; for the predictions have been wholly belied by the fact, as may be seen by the following table.

Prices of Cotton in Liverpool, extracted from the prices current of respectable merchants there.

	1818 Nov. 28.*	1819. May 12.†	1819. Sept. 25.‡	1820. Jan. 20.§	1820. March 1.‖
	d.	*d.*	*d.*	*d.*	*d.*
New Orleans	18 to 23	11 to 14½	13½ to 17	13 to 16½	11½ to 15½
Bowed Georgia	17 to 20	11 to 13	12½ to 1[illegible]	12 to 13	11 to 12¼
Surat - -	10 to 16	7 to 10½	8 to 1[illegible]	7½ to 10½	7 to 10
Bengal -	7 to 12	5¾ to 8	7¾ to [illegible]	[illegible]¼ to 8¾	6½ to 8¼

Average.

	1818. Nov. 28.	1819. May 12.	1819. Sept. 25.	1820. Jan. 20.	1820. Mar. 1.
New Orleans -	20½	12¾	15¼	14¾	13½
Bowed Georgia or Upland -	13½	12	13⅜	12½	11⅝
Surat - -	13	8¾	10½	9	8½
Bengal - -	9½	6⅞	8⅞	8	7⅜

"There have been several fluctuations during this month in "the state of the demand for cotton; but although it has been "generally good, and was at one period very brisk, *yet a decline* "*has taken place in the prices of almost every description:* in sea "island, chiefly of the middle qualities, of 1*d.* to 3*d.*—New Or- "leans, also in the middle qualities, and which does not there- "fore so much affect the extreme quotations, ¾ to 1*d.;* upland

* Bagot & Parr's Price Current.
† Rathbone, Hodgson & Co.
‡ William & James Brown & Co.
§ Morrall and Watson.
‖ Rathbone, Hodgson & Co.

"½*d.;* Brazil ¾ to 1*d.;* and in East India ¼ to ½*d.* per lb." *Rathbone and Hodgson's Price current, Liverpool, March* 1, 1820.

It is hence perfectly obvious, that there is no rational prospect of any favourable change in the price of this important article. On the contrary, *it has been falling from the commencement of the year :* and on the first of March, it appears that New Orleans and uplands were eight or ten per cent. lower than on the 20th of January ; and this, let it be observed, after the predictions so explicitly and confidently hazarded, of a great rise of price!

Notwithstanding the unfavourable character given of the East India cotton, the reduction on it has been rather less than on that of the united states. Since January, Surat cotton, as appears above, has fallen only eight, and Bengal only six per cent.

What renders the recent reduction of our cotton more extraordinary, is that the total importations of 1819 have been very considerably below those of 1818.

Importations of 1818	- - - -	*bales*, 665,300*
1819	- - - - - -	547,247
Decrease	- - - - - - -	118,053

It cannot fail to be useful to examine into the extent of the British market for our cotton, the preservation of which excites so deep a solicitude. I therefore annex—

A table of the importation of united states cotton into Great Britain for five years.

In 1815	- - - - - -	*bales*, 103,037‖
1816	- - - - - - -	166,077‖
1817	- - - - - - - -	198,917†
1818	- - - - - - -	205,881†
1819	- - - - - - - -	206,000‡
		879,912
Average	- - - - - - - -	175,982

According to the celebrated report of the committee of commerce and manufactures of the house of representatives, in 1816, the consumption of cotton in the united states in 1815, was 90,000 bales—or above half the average exportation to Great

* Barber & Co's. price current, Liverpool, January 17, 1820.

‖ Seybert, 92. † Journal of Trade and Commerce, vol. II. p. 113. ‡ Barber & Co's. price current, January 17, 1820.

Britian! What an important fact! This invaluable market, which, by excluding foreign raw cotton, might have been rendered secure from any sensible fluctuation, and which would have been annually increasing, has been nearly destroyed for the sake of securing a foreign market *of not double the extent, subject to abrupt, daily, and most pernicious depressions!*—depressions which have involved in ruin, or at least severely crippled, one-half the merchants engaged in the commerce of this staple!

And it is worthy of the most serious consideration, that although the consumption of cotton in the united states in 1810, was only 10,000 bags, it rose, as before stated, in 1815, to 90,000; of course it had increased nine-fold in five years, merely by the restrictions on British goods previous to, and their exclusion during, the war. It is therefore easy to conceive what progress it would have made since the war, had adequate protection been afforded, and what effect that progress would have had on the prices in foreign markets. Probably half or two-thirds of the quantity exported in 1818 would have been consumed at home.

The effects of a glutted market in the reduction, and of a scarce one in the rise, of prices, are well known. And therefore it is perfectly clear, that so much of our cotton as is consumed at home, operates at all times to prevent a reduction, and frequently to produce a rise, in the foreign markets. This places in a strong light the utter impolicy of the course we have pursued.

A single fact will exemplify this position more completely than a long train of arguments. The total importation into Great Britain in 1819, was, as we have seen, 547,000 bales—and the consumption 420,000. Yet the arrival of so small a quantity as 8000 bales, in the month of January last, produced a reduction of price, of almost ten per cent. on the quantity then in the market:—

" Since the arrival of eight thousand bags of the new crop of " upland cotton, the prices have fallen from thirteen pence and " three quarters to twelve and a half; and *heavy at the latter* " *rate.* Sea Islands *two pence to two pence half penny lower—* " *and the general opinion is in favour of a further reduction.* The " prices are thirty per cent. lower in united states cotton, as " well as in many other articles of American produce, than this " time last year."*

Now if eight thousand bales reduced the price nearly ten per cent. at once, it is easy to conceive the effect of the increased quantity in the market, arising from the destruction of so great a portion of our manufactories as fell sacrifices in 1817 and 1818. It can scarcely be doubted that this cause alone would be suf-

* Barber & Co's. Price Current, Liverpool, Jan. 17, 1820.

ficient to account for the ruinous reduction that took place between November 1818 and May 1819.

Our policy is very different from that of the Dutch, respecting their spices in former times. When their crops were so abundant as to exceed the usual or probable demand, they destroyed the surplus quantity, in order to prevent the article from becoming a drug. We, on the contrary, by fatally allowing the chief part of the domestic market to be destroyed, so far increased the quantity in the British market, that the price was, as we have seen, reduced forty per cent.

A due consideration of the foregoing facts and reasoning will render it probable that the cotton planters would have benefited even by the destruction, on the Dutch plan, of thirty or forty thousand bales of cotton in the summer of 1818; as they might have received more for the remainder than they did for the whole crop; and of course that the loss of the domestic market, which would have consumed far more than that quantity, has been signally injurious to the planters, and probably almost as much as to the manufacturers.

I have not touched on the formidable rivalry in the cotton market, which may be confidently looked for from the new states in South America. In those countries, I am informed, the cotton is produced by a perennial tree, which requires little or no care in the culture. When rivals from this quarter are added to those we have to encounter at present, deep will be the distress and suffering of the cotton planters, through the want of a domestic market, when the capital, to the amount of perhaps 30 or 40,000,000 of dollars invested in the cotton manufacture, is wasted away. Happy will it be for them, if even at this late period, they take proper measures to guard against the evil.

WHEAT AND FLOUR.

The reduction in the price of wheat and flour, the staples on which Pennsylvania, and a large portion of the other middle states rely, is generally supposed to have arisen wholly from the transition of Europe from a state of general war to universal peace. This is an egregious error; which a consideration of the following facts will evince.

War in Europe ceased in 1814. It was partially and for a short time resumed in 1815. The price of flour, nevertheless, underwent little reduction till 1819 and 1820, when it sunk gradually to a rate, which affords the cultivator, whose farm is remote from a seaport, but a sorry remuneration for his toils.—Thus for three or four years the price was not affected by the peace: and surely it cannot be supposed that it required that space of time to convert swords into ploughshares.

I shall endeavour to trace the depression to a very different and remote source—to a rival likely to become every day more and more formidable : but I shall first submit to inspection a

Table of the prices of flour in Philadelphia, Baltimore, New York, and Boston, from the prices current of those places respectively.

	Philad.	Baltimore.	New York		Boston.	
	$	$	$	$	$	$
1817. Oct. 6.	9.50	9.50	10	to 10.12	10.	
1818. Jan. 1.	9.50	9.25	9.37	to 9.50	10.	to 10.25
Ap. 4.	10.	9.25	9.50	to 9.62	10.25	to 10.75
July 2.	10.	10.75	8.37	to 8.62	10.25	to 10.50
Oct. 4.	9.75	9.25	8.62	to 9.25	10.25	to 10.50
1819. May 3.	6.50	6.50	6.87		7.25	
July 12.	6.75	6.50	6.25		7.25	
Dec. 6.	6.12	5.62	6.		6.75	
1820. Ap. 24.	4.75	4.75	4.50		5.25	

Export of wheat and flour from the united states for seventeen years.

	Bushels of Wheat.	Barrels of Flour.
1803 - -	686,451	- - - 1,311,853
1804 - -	127,024	- - - 810,008
1805 - -	18,041	- - - 775,513
1806 - -	86,784	- - - 782,724
1807 - -	1,173,114	- - - 1,249,819
1808 - -	87,330	- - - 263,013
1809 - -	393,899	- - - 847,247
1810 - -	1,752	- - - 778,431
1811 - -	216,833	- - - 1,445,012
1812 - -	53,833	- - - 1,443,493
1813 - -	288,535	- - - 1,260,942
1814 - -		- - - 193,274
1815 - -	17,634	- - - 862,739
1816 - -	52,321	- - - 729,053
1817 - -	96,407	- - - 1,479,198
1818 - -	196,808	- - - 1,157,697
1819 - -	82,065	- - - 758,660
	3,578,831*	16,148,676†
Average	210,519	949,451

* Seybert, 158. † Idem, 152.

Allowing five bushels of wheat to a barrel of flour, 949,451 barrels of the latter would be equivalent to . . .	bushels of wheat	4,747,225
Brought forward - - - -		210,519
Average of fifteen years, equal to .	bushels	4,957,744

This is the average amount of the surplus of this important staple for seventeen consecutive years, of a great nation, with a population from six to ten millions of souls—enjoying natural, moral, and political advantages of the highest order—and for a large portion of the time in full possession of the benefits of a neutral situation, while more than half the civilized world were arrayed in arms for mutual destruction.

It cannot fail to excite astonishment, that the single port of Odessa, which in 1803, contained but 8000 souls, and of which the circumjacent country was then a mere wilderness, in 1815, twelve years afterwards, exported 6,000,000 bushels of wheat. This export was twenty per cent. more than our annual average!

Odessa, through the policy of Alexander, the wisest monarch in Europe, perhaps in the world, has risen to eminence, to extensive commerce, and to a high degree of prosperity, with more rapidity than any other spot on the globe. To judge by its past progress, it is not improbable that its present exportation of wheat equals that of the united states.

The empress Catharine had formed some magnificent projects for the improvement of this town, which were defeated by her death, and the eccentric and extravagant views of her immediate successor. But Alexander early resolved to make sacrifices for the advancement of the place, proportioned to its immense importance.

"In 1803, Odessa contained only eight thousand souls: and "the surrounding country, for many leagues, was *an uncultivated* "*desert*. No sound of rural labour broke upon the ear; not a "house or tree; not a spot of artificial verdure; no trace of "agriculture arrested the eye in wandering over those extensive "wastes, which for centuries had not been furrowed by the plough. "To render this melancholy prospect more striking, dreary, and "fearful, an ancient tumulus, piled for ages over the sepulchre of "some distinguished Scythian chieftain, or the ascending smoke "from the carbine of a wandering Tartar, occasionally appeared "in the barren distance."*

To accomplish the emperor's grand views, no expense nor effort was spared.

* Dearborn's Commerce of the Black Sea, i. p. 236.

" *Emigrants were invited from Bulgaria, Poland, Hungary,* " *Sclavonia, Germany, and other neighbouring countries. Houses* " *were built for the accommodation of the mechanics within the city;* " cattle and agricultural implements furnished to such adven- " turers as came to establish themselves in the environs, who " were divided into villages, and every facility afforded, which " might tend to stimulate them to exertion."*

" Such were the liberal encouragements of the emperor, and " the zealous efforts of the governor, that the population of the " city, in 1811, amounted to twenty-five thousand souls; and " the environs, within a radius of eighty miles, were covered with " thirty thousand inhabitants, and contained forty flourishing " villages. Numerous highly cultivated gardens, and planta- " tions well stocked with herds of cattle, not only supplied the " market with provisions, fruits and vegetables; but furnished " large quantities of wheat, merino wool, butter, tallow, honey, " wax, potatoes, beans, peas and other legumes for exportation. " Plantations of mulberry trees have been commenced for rear- " ing silk worms: and thus lands, which before had no value, " have not only become a source of individual wealth, but inte- " rested the proprietors in the prosperity of the city and whole " territory."†

" Such was the rapid increase of the commerce of Odessa, " that in 1805, six hundred and forty-five sail of vessels arrived, " which exported *wheat alone to the amount of* 5,772,000 rubles: " and in 1815, one thousand five hundred vessels arrived, and " were laden with 6,000,000 *bushels of wheat*, and the various " products of Russia. The exports for 1816 amounted to up- " wards of 60,000,000 of rubles. During the year 1817, " 3,000,000 *bushels of wheat were shipped to the single port of* " *Leghorn, the freight of which amounted to* 1,350,000 *dollars;* " three hundred sail of vessels, averaging 10,000 bushels each, " were employed in this trade: and a third of that number " transported *one million of bushels to Naples, Genoa, and Mar-* " *seilles.* The present population of the city exceeds 40,000, " while that of the surrounding country has increased in an equal " ratio. There are various manufacturing establishments, a " number of corn mills, distilleries and breweries."‡

Among the causes which have operated to reduce the prices of our wheat and flour so low, the success of Odessa holds a conspicuous rank. Many of those markets, which heretofore received our flour at ten, twelve and fourteen dollars per barrel, are supplied from thence at half or two-thirds of the price. And even European wars, on which so large a portion of our policy

* Dearborn's Commerce of the Black Sea, i. p. 236.
† Idem, 237. ‡ Idem, 240.

has heretofore been unfortunately predicated, will in future afford us far more limited markets than formerly. For the capacity of the countries which discharge their produce through that grand emporium, is almost boundless, and the increase of demand to any extent whatever, will produce a commensurate supply. It is therefore beyond doubt, that our range of markets will at all future times be greatly circumscribed by this formidable rival.

Various accounts are given of the price of wheat at Odessa. The highest is fifty cents per bushel. I have heard forty cents stated. But having no means of ascertaining, I do not pretend to vouch for either.

A few observations are called for on the subject of the markets for our flour in Great Britain. Whenever a failure of crops in that country raises the price of wheat to eighty shillings sterling per quarter, the ports, in order to prevent the dangers arising from starving multitudes, are opened to foreign wheat and flour; to ours of course. But if the average be one penny per quarter less, they are closed, except that those articles may be stored for exportation.

In November 1817, when the average of the English wheat markets, for the preceding six weeks, was struck, it proved to be 79*s.* 7*d.* per quarter; consequently the ports were shut to our bread stuffs. Previous appearances had warranted the idea, that they would continue open, and, in consequence, large shipments of flour had been made from this country. *Five pence per quarter more would have prevented their being closed; made an immense difference to our merchants; and saved many of them from the bankruptcy consequent on the reduction of price!* On such trifles depend the fortunes of the American merchants! So critically nice are the calculations made by the British government! so watchful is it of the resources of the nation! what an example does it set in this important respect for other governments! In this country, which has had the experience and the wisdom of all nations to profit by, if the capacity of supply be ten-fold the demand, as is the case with some articles, *there never has been a single prohibition*, of any kind of provisions or merchandize whatever.

During the whole of our progress as a nation, any decisive protection of manufactures has been held to be impolitic and injurious, as interfering with the culture of our lands, an object of incomparably higher importance in the opinion of our statesmen. The errors of this policy are now made manifest to the world. We have an over proportion of agriculturists, for whose produce profitable markets are sought in vain. Our vessels, loaded with flour, sail from island to island in the West Indies, and from port to port in Europe, and generally find it impossible to sell to advantage even at the reduced prices at which the cargoes are now purchased in our markets.

It is scarcely possible to conceive of a more wayward system than we pursue. We employ manufacturers in Europe to clothe us—and we raise here the raw materials to employ, and the necessaries of life to feed them! The world may be challenged for a parallel to this policy! Those necessaries are frequently excluded either by restrictionsor by the abundant crops of the nations which furnish the manufactures:—and at present, wherever received, they are, I repeat, generally either sold at a loss, or at best without profit. Yet we still continue to receive the manufactures, while our citizens, who could furnish them, are idle, and our means of payment daily diminishing by the reduction of the value of our produce: and while the nation is writhing and decaying under this ruinous policy, we fondly flatter ourselves that we are the most enlightened people in the world. How much sounder policy would it be, in the words of Mr. Jefferson, "*to place the manufacturer beside the agriculturist!*" Then the mass of our produce would be subject to no restrictions, nor limitations, nor competition.

In various parts of the union wheat is now sold at twenty-five, thirty, and thirty-seven and a half cents per bushel, and dull even at those prices. Flour in remote situations is at 300, 350, and 375 cents per barrel. It is obvious that at those prices the farmer has a very slender remuneration for his labour, and the employment of his capital. Even in Philadelphia and Baltimore, flour has been sold at 425 cents. Now if some fifty thousand of those manufacturers, whom want of protection has successively for years past forced "*to go back and cultivate the soil,*" in Kentucky, Tennessee, &c. according to the favourite phrase, were employed at their former occupations, providing clothing and other articles for the neighbouring farmers, it would produce a two-fold beneficial effect. It would diminish the number of producers, and of course the surplus of agricultural productions, with most of which foreign markets are overstocked. And it would moreover furnish the farmers with a certain domestic market instead of a precarious foreign one.

I will venture to state the effect in a loose calculation, which, even if incorrect, will enable the reader, after proper drawbacks, to form a tolerably accurate estimate on the subject:—

Suppose each person of the assumed 50,000 manufacturers now employed in agriculture, to raise a surplus of sixty bushels of grain annually, it amounts to - - - - - - - -	*bushels* 3,000,000

	bushels 3,000,000
But if withdrawn from agriculture and employed in manufactures, each would consume of his neighbours' grain annually ten bushels, equal to -	500,000
	3,500,000

The assumption might be extended throughout the union to 100,000 people. The effect would be to diminish the quantity in foreign markets to the above extent—and, of course, prevent the gluts in those markets, which produce the pernicious reductions of price, so severely felt by our farmers and merchants. And further, instead of exhausting the country by the purchase of goods manufactured in Hindostan, England and France, the farmers would procure supplies at their doors, for which they would pay in their own productions. It is unnecessary to enter into detail to prove, as it is easy to conceive, what an immense advantage this would produce, on a large scale, individually and nationally.

TOBACCO.

The reduction of the price of tobacco in the European markets in the course of last summer, spread distress and desolation in the state of Virginia. A general paralysis of enterprize and industry took place in that quarter. Many of the first families were precipitated from a towering state of affluence by this disastrous event It is not improbable that the losses which arose from it, directly and indirectly, were above fifty per cent. of the amount of the whole crop. Many men were in consequence ruined at that period, by indorsation and suretiship, who never owned a hogshead of tobacco.

The result would furnish matter for an ample chapter on the subject of dependence on foreign markets. But I shall be very brief.

The observations made respecting the glut of foreign markets as respects the cotton of the united states, apply to tobacco, and with rather more force ; as the practicability of extending the consumption of the former is far greater than of the latter, with which, of course, the market is more easily and perniciously overstocked. But so far as regards the domestic market, there is a total difference between the two articles. This market is fully secured to the manufacturers of tobacco. The importations have been at all times unimportant, as will appear from the following—

Table of imports of manufactured tobacco, snuff, and segars, for four years.

	Tobacco.	Snuff.	Segars.
	lb.	*lb.*	*M.*
1815	705	1,180	7,657
1816	2,924	395	12,206
1817	3,059	10,925	12,500
1818	103	000	15,723
	6,791	12,500	*M.* 48,086

The duties on manufactured tobacco and snuff are prohibitory —and were so intended from the origin of the government; on a reference to the debates of the first congress, vol. I. page 93, it will appear that Mr. R. Sherman, who moved the duty of six cents per pound on tobacco, distinctly proposed it with this view.

The culture of tobacco in Europe was very inconsiderable formerly. But during the derangements of our commerce by the lawless outrages of the belligerents, and the restrictive systems which grew out of them, and more particularly during our short war with Great Britain, the scantiness of the supply in Europe, with the high prices, the necessary consequence, induced different nations to enter extensively on the culture, so that at present there is probably nearly fifty per cent. more tobacco raised in those countries, than in the united states.

" *The notion that Europe requires eighty or eighty-four thou-*
" *sand hogsheads from America, is without foundation.* The
" mean quantity annually exported from the united states, to all
" parts from 1800 to 1807, was 80,183 hogsheads. But during
" the non-intercourse and the war, *several nations of Europe en-*
" *tered very extensively upon the cultivation of tobacco; and*
" *continue to do so to this day; so that what was formerly requir-*
" *ed is no criterion at all of what is wanted now.* It is stated
" that Holland, the Ukraine, France, Bohemia, and Turkey
" grow 150,000 hogsheads a year; but this opinion cannot be
" founded on any accurate data, and must be considered as
" vague."*

The scarcity of united states tobacco in Europe, at the close of the war, prevented any depreciation of price, although the export in 1815, was 85,189 *hhds.* which included a portion of the old stock. The price was maintained in the two following years, by a reduction of the quantity exported:—

Being in	1816	*hhds.* 69,721
	1817	64,891

* Hughes, Duncan & Co. Liverpool, Nov. 10, 1818.

But these high prices encouraging an increase of cultivation, particularly in Kentucky, the exportation was increased almost 30 per cent. in 1818, and amounted to 84,337 *hhds.*

The exports from New Orleans were about 80 per cent more in 1818 than in 1817; being in the former year 24,138 *hhds.* and in the latter 14,451.

Nearly all the additional quantity exported in 1818, was consigned to Great Britain, the quantity being more than doubled.

The import in 1817 was about	. .	*hhds.* 14,500
1818	. . . .	31,200

"Any expectation of an advance in Virginia must be founded "on the prospect of an export demand; but *the large shipments* "*this year of* 30,000 *of Kentuckies*, of which all that come to Eu-"rope go to the continent, may be found *a sufficient substitute* "*for Virginias*, except for some particular and limited purpose. "The Dutch and some other continental markets are very dull, "giving no indications of want of tobacco, though the winter "months are close at hand, and will soon exclude any further "supply. There cannot, therefore, be any reasonable grounds "of improvement in prices, in whatever direction we look."—*Hughes, Duncan, & Co. Liverpool, Nov.* 10, 1818.

"*Tobacco still remains dull*, and prices have declined ¼ to ½*d* "per lb. A contract has been made in London for 1500 hogs-"heads for the French market, since which the holders are "more firm; but *the stocks in this country are very heavy.*"—John Richardson, Liverpool, December 25, 1818.

"Tobacco. *The import to this port has been* 11,500 *hogsheads;* "*to London* 17,700—from this port the export has been 3300, "and the home consumption 4500—and from London 2000 and "4500—making a total taken out of both ports of 14,300 hogs-"heads, *and leaving a stock here of* 8600, *and in London* 16,500, "*and in other ports about* 2700, *or a total of* 27,000 *hogsheads*—"this is a great accumulation since last year, and has had the "effect of depressing prices considerably, so that they are "now nearly upon a par with those of last Christmas." *Brown & Co. Liverpool, December* 31, 1818.

The annual average consumption of Great Britain, is about 11,000 hogsheads,* and the export about 5,000. The stock therefore on hand at the close of the year 1818, as stated above, was equal to the usual demand for nineteen months. It is not, therefore, wonderful, that such a rapid decline took place in the price, which began in the autumn of that year, and continued till

* "The mean consumption of 1817 and 1818 is 10,880 hhds. shipments to Ire-"land inclusive: and twenty months export in 1817 and 1818, is 9287 hhds.; so "that our present stock is equal to one year's home use, and shipment to Ireland, "and twenty months' export, upon the scale of the last twenty months." *Hughes, Duncan & Co. Nov.* 10, 1818.

June, 1819, when the reduction averaged about sixty per cent., as may be seen in the following table.

	1818. *Sept.* 2.†	1818. *Dec.* 5.‡	1819 *Mar.* 13§	1819. *June* 2.‖
	d.	*d.*	*d.*	*d.*
York and James river: Low and inferior, sound	8¼ to 8½	6 to 6¼	5 to 6	3½ to 4
York and James river: Ordinary and middling,	9 to 9½	7 to 7¼	6½ to 7	4½ to 5
York and James river: Good and fine, - -	9¾ to 10½	8½ to 10½	7¼ to 9	6 to 8½
York and James river: Stemmed, - -	10½ to 13	8½ to 9½	8 to 9	6 to 8½
Rappahannock, - -	7½ to 9	8½ to 9	4½ to 7	3½ to 5½
Do. stemmed, - - -	9½ to 11½	8 to 10	7 to 8	5½ to 6½
Georgia and Carolina, - -	7 to 8	6 to 8	4½ to 7	3¼ to 5
Kentucky, - - - -	7 to 9	6 to 8	4½ to 7	3¼ to 5½

The complaints of overstocked markets and the interference of European tobacco with the sales of that of the united states, on the continent, are to be found in the various prices current received from Liverpool during the last and present years.

" *Tobacco continued in a very depressed state till near the close* " *of last month*, when some purchases were made for export, of " Virginia and Kentucky, at a reduction in the former of ½*d.* and " in the latter ¾*d.* to 1*d.* per lb. from last quotations. *The mar-* " *ket is again very dull, and the stock still heavy, amounting to* " 7100 *hogsheads. A small parcel of five bales has been received* " *from the East Indies.*" Rathbone, Hodgson, & Co. Liverpool, May 12, 1819.

" The stocks of Virginia on the continent are light; *but Ken-* " *tucky heavy.* As, however, of this latter description there is " very little in this kingdom but what is held here, we may ex- " pect to reap the benefit of any orders that may arrive for Ken- " tucky for export. It is stated that *the consumption, on the con-* " *tinent, of American, is materially lessened by the use of tobacco of* " *native growth.*" Brown & Co. Liverpool, 31st Dec. 1819.

" *The stocks of Kentucky on the continent of Europe are heavy,* " other sorts are light; *but the consumption of American there is* " *said to be much lessened by the use of their native growth.*" William Barber & Co. Liverpool, Jan. 17, 1820.

Independent of the rivals in Europe, as above stated, another is coming into the field, which bids fair to become more formidable than any of them, and ultimately perhaps as formidable as the whole. I mean the East Indies.

The importation of tobacco from that quarter is increasing gradually, in the same manner as that of indigo and cotton has done. Want of skill in the packing, it appears, together with

† Yates, Brothers, & Co.

‡ Myers's Mercantile Advertiser.

§ Morrall & Watson.

‖ Yates, Brothers, & Co.

the length of the voyage, operates injuriously on the quality, and of course on the price. It is not difficult to estimate how slender a protection this affords our planters—how easily skill in the packing is to be acquired—and the inconvenience of the long voyage to be guarded against. On the 13th of March, 1819, East India tobacco sold at four pence to five pence halfpenny per pound in Liverpool. At that date, Rappahannock, Kentucky, and Georgia sold at four and a half to seven pence.

"*Good East India leaf would sell well;* but owing to the long "voyage, and want of skill in the packing, generally arrives in a "heated and damaged state. *Good qualities sell generally at four* "*to five and a half pence per pound;* but if heated or damaged, "little or no demand."*

In the Price Current of Rathbone, Hodgson & Co. of March 1, 1820, it is stated, "*From the East Indies we have received an import of* 532 *bales of tobacco.*"

To superficial readers this rivalship will appear unimportant. But such persons are recommended to consider the rapid progress of the importation of East India cotton into Great Britain.

A very slight reflection on this subject, will be ill calculated to soothe their minds. To enable them to form a correct view of the real extent of the danger, I state the import of this article.

Total import of East India cotton into Great Britain for seven years.

1812,	2,607
1813,	1,429
1814,	13,048
1815,	23,357
1816,	30,679
1817,	117,454
1818,	247,604

This table evinces the wonderful capacity of production in that country, which is commensurate with any possible demand, and applies with as much propriety and force to tobacco as to cotton.

The observations made respecting the glut of cotton, are equally applicable to tobacco. Had 20,000 *hhds.* of the latter article been destroyed in 1818, it is not improbable that the residue of the crop would have undergone no material depreciation, and produced far more than the whole.

The git of these remarks on tobacco has no reference to any protection of the domestic market; which, as I have already stated, is completely secured by high duties. My object is to prove,

* Morrall & Watson, Liverpool, March 13, 1819.

that by our dependence on foreign markets for the sale of the other great staples, our bread stuffs—as well as by the precariousness of their prices, particularly at New Orleanst—he farmers of the western country were tempted to go extensively into the culture of tobacco, which produced the extraordinary quantity shipped in 1818, whereby, as we have seen, the British markets were so much overstocked, as to cause the ruinous reduction which took place in that and the following year.

INDIGO.

While our cotton and tobacco planters are indulging the fond hopes of the permanence of the foreign markets, on which they place their chief reliance, for their prosperity and that of their country, it may not be improper to show the uncertainty of the tenure, by the strong case of the indigo market, which is perfectly analagous. It fully evinces the slipperiness of foreign markets, and the impolicy and danger of trusting to them.

Indigo was formerly the chief production of South Carolina, and constituted probably one-third of her exports. At that period there was far less danger of being outdone in that article by a rival in a distant hemisphere, than there is at present of our cotton and tobacco being supplanted in foreign markets. Yet in a few years this rival not only secured those markets, by an improvement of the quality, and a reduction of the price, so low that the article became scarcely worth cultivation in South Carolina, but nearly beat our planters out of their own market.

" The situation of South Carolina," says Mr. Tucker, in a de bate in the house of representatives, in April, 1789, " is melan- " choly. While the inhabitants are deeply in debt, the produce " of the state is daily falling in price. *Rice and indigo have be- " come so low, as to be considered by many not objects worthy of " cultivation.*"*

In the East Indies various unsuccessful attempts had been made at the cultivation of indigo, which had been abandoned. In 1779, it was again undertaken with more spirit, with a liberality worthy of imitation, and finally crowned with complete success.

" *Great advances were made to the cultivators, to the extent of " nearly one million sterling on the security of the produce;* inso- " much that it ultimately became one of the most valuable arti- " cles of exportation from India. Its superior quality recom- " mended it to purchasers both at home and abroad, until the " sales, (which, in 1786, amounted to 245,011 *lbs.* producing

* Debates of Congress, vol. I. p. 70.

" 61,533*l*.) in 1810, advanced gradually to 5,570,024 *lbs*., pro-
" ducing at the sales 1,942,328*l*."*

Thus far Colquhoun. By a more recent publication, it appears that the sales

		lbs.		
In 1815	were	6,738,462	value	$9,798,730
1816		6,978,939		8,571,625

These facts afford important admonitions. By the loan of one million of pounds sterling, a culture was fostered into maturity, which now annually produces to the country an income of nearly double the amount. How wise the appropriation! How worthy imitation! It cannot be doubted that had the whole sum been, not lent, but absolutely bestowed, the disposition would have been eminently advantageous.

Can it be possible that this warning example will be wholly lost on those gentlemen who represent Virginia, South Carolina, and Georgia in congress? Is there any reason to believe that the same degree of perseverance and industry which overcame the difficulties in the culture of indigo, will not overcome those which at present prevent complete success in the production of cotton and tobacco equal to ours? They are both in a more promising state than the culture of Indigo was in 1779. The East Indies possess population, industry, and suitable soil to supply the whole world with those three articles at lower rates than we can possibly do. When we seriously reflect on the exertions they are now making, it would be insanity to place any dependence on their failure. The existing state of affairs, therefore, pronounces in loud tones a warning, which cannot be disregarded without the most serious and permanent injury to the planters as well as the country at large.

* Colquhoun on the wealth, power, and resources of the British empire. Appendix, page 23.

ADDRESS

TO THE

FARMERS OF THE UNITED STATES,

ON THE

RUINOUS CONSEQUENCES TO THEIR VITAL INTERESTS,

OF THE EXISTING

POLICY OF THIS COUNTRY.

SECOND EDITION.

" *Quidquid delirant reges, plectuntur Achivi.*"

When we see a suffering people, " with depressed minds and indolent habits, " we do not ascribe their poverty to the men who govern them: but no one who " sees a mangy, half-starved flock of sheep, ever doubts that it is the fault of the " farmer to whom it belongs."—*Maurice and Berghetta.*

" At the end of thirty years of its operation, this government finds its debt in- " creased $20,000,000 and its revenue inadequate to its expenditure; the national " domain impaired, and $20,000,000 of its proceeds expended; $35,000,000 drawn " from the people by internal taxation; $341,000,000, by impost; yet the public " treasury dependent on loans. In profound peace, and without any national ca- " lamity, the country embarrassed with debts; and real estate under rapid depre- " ciation; the markets of agriculture, the pursuits of manufactures, diminished " and declining; commerce struggling, not to retain the carrying the produce of " other countries, but our own. There is no national interest which is in a health- " ful, thriving condition; the nation at large is not so; the operations of the go- " vernment and individuals alike labour under difficulties, which are felt by all, " and for which some remedy must be discovered. It is not a common occur- " rence in the history of nations, that *in peace the people shall call on the govern-* " *ment to relieve their distresses; the government reciprocate the call, by asking the peo-* " *ple to relieve theirs;* the resources of both exhausted; both marching to poverty " or wealth, (as opinions may vary,) in the same road, on the same principles; " their expenses exceeding their receipts."—*Report of the Committee on Manufactures, Jan.* 15, 1821.

FIRST PUBLISHED FEB. 11, 1821.

PREFACE.

To originality this pamphlet makes scarcely any pretension. The writer has already presented the subject to his fellow citizens, under most of the aspects, and in some cases in the same words, in which it is placed here ; and numbers of gentlemen, of superior talents, have likewise engaged zealously and profoundly in the discussion. A subject so much investigated obviously affords but an exhausted field for cultivation.

It may be asked, why, then, attempt to draw public attention to topics hacknied as these have been? Why not let the subject rest on its merits, as already detailed? The reason is obvious. Those who take the opposite side of the question reiterate arguments and objections fully disproved and obviated from year to year, for thirty years past. And as they retrace the same ground, with the expectation of influencing the opinions and public councils of the nation, it is necessary to follow the example, or submit to the imputation that the cause is incapable of defence. An argument refuted, or a fact disproved, one or five hundred years ago, if advanced anew at present, must be refuted or disproved by nearly the same reasons as formerly.

Some of the topics, however, are new. Others are placed in new points of view, particularly the pernicious effects of the prevailing system on the interests of the farmers. This is a topic of the deepest interest to that class of citizens, and to the nation at large. If the view here taken of it be correct, or not radically erroneous, the agriculturists of this country are as deeply interested in a total change of policy, as the manufacturers. With the latter the suffering began, but the former at present feel it with equal severity.

Manufactures and manufacturers have been sacrificed to revenue, for which our chief dependence has been placed on the impost, which, from 13,000,000 dollars in 1811, was by the war reduced to 5,998,000 dollars in 1814 : and should war be lighted up in Europe, and the flames envelope us, which would not be so extraordinary a circumstance as hundreds that have occurred within the last thirty years, will it not experience the same reduction? In such case, how can revenue be derived from a people, impoverished and embarrassed as so large a portion of our citizens are? The committee of ways and means on the 6th inst. declared, that "*the imposition of an excise* AT THIS "TIME OF EXTREME DISTRESS, *would be unwise, and is not* "*demanded by the state of the treasury; that,* IF IMPOSED, IT "WOULD BE DIFFICULT TO COLLECT; *and,* IF COLLECTED, *it* "*would in some parts of the union be* IN PAPER LITTLE AVAIL-"ABLE."

Can any man of public spirit, interested in the welfare of the nation, without shuddering, read such a lamentable official picture of its situation, after six years of profound peace! Comment is wholly unnecessary. It proclaims in a voice of thunder, that a policy which has precipitated us into such a state, from the high ground we occupied at the close of the war, must be transcendently pernicious—cannot be too soon changed—and that human ingenuity could scarcely devise a change which would not be an improvement. We may truly say with the great lord Chatham, "*If any thing can prevent the consummation of* "*public ruin, it can only be new councils—a sincere change, from* "*a sincere conviction of past errors.*"

A large portion of our citizens suffer intensely. The means of relief are solely within the power of congress. To that body they have applied from year to year in vain. Their petitions have been treated in many instances with such extreme neglect as not to be read or reported on. There has not been the slightest attempt to apply a remedy to any of the evils under which at least a third part of the nation is writhing. This is not the mode in which the attachment of our citizens is to be conciliated. I forbear to prosecute the train of serious and distressing ideas such a view is calculated to excite.

Philadelphia, Feb. 11, 1821.

ADDRESS

TO THE

FARMERS OF THE UNITED STATES.

CHAPTER I.

Object of this address. Immense advantages enjoyed by the united states. Results naturally to have been expected. Cruel disappointment. Lamentable picture of the distressing situation of Pennsylvania. Sketch of the sufferings of the western part of the state of New-York. Delusive idea of prosperity from the cheapness of provisions. A heavy direct tax would scarcely be felt, were industry protected.

FRIENDS AND FELLOW CITIZENS,

I earnestly entreat your serious attention to the discussion of the most important subjects that can occupy your minds—the causes and remedies of your present sufferings. I shall endeavour to point out both, to your conviction. Should I succeed, there is almost a certainty, that these sufferings will be removed, as you have in a great measure the legislation of the nation in your own hands.

Subject my facts, and the deductions from them, to the most severe scrutiny. Give credit to nothing which will not stand that ordeal. For the correctness of my intentions I appeal to that awful tribunal, before which a very few years must necessarily place me. But correctness of intention, as every day evinces, is no security against error. With all the care I have employed to arrive at correct results, a strong degree of excitement—incapacity—or rooted prejudice,—may lead me a devious course, as they have done thousands of men, infinitely my superiors. Therefore, I repeat, investigate for yourselves.

Impressed with a deep conviction that there is an identity of interest between the farmers and manufacturers of this and every country—that one class cannot suffer severely without the other partaking of the calamity—and that the distress and embarrassments under which the farmers, particularly those in the interior of the middle, and nearly throughout the whole of the western states, are at present writhing, are the result of an erroneous policy, predicated on the idea of a supposed hostility of interests between the cultivators of the soil and the manufacturers; I shall endeavour to prove the utter fallacy of the idea of this hostility, and that there is nothing wanting to render our farmers the most prosperous class in the world, but a liberal protection of their fellow-citizens engaged in manufactures.

As a preliminary, I shall take a brief view of the manifold blessings, natural, political, and moral, which this nation enjoys —blessings, never exceeded, and rarely, if ever, equalled.

1. We have almost every possible variety of soil, climate, and natural productions.

2. Our country is intersected by navigable waters to an extent not exceeded by any commercial country in the world. The large rivers on the continent of Europe in general pass through different nations, which in most cases impose restrictions and levy duties, whence arise burdensome obstructions to trade and commerce. Our rivers, great and small, on the contrary, are free as air.

3. Our government is the most free of any that ever existed.

4. Our citizens are industrious, enterprizing, ingenious, and intelligent.

5. We enjoy the blessings of water power for machinery to an extent commensurate with the wants of the whole world.

6. Our farmers are almost universally possessed of the fee simple of the lands they cultivate.

7. Fertile lands can be had in fee simple, and be cleared, for less money than the rent of lands in some parts of Europe.

8. We have no monarchy—no nobility—no established hierarchy.

9. We pay no tithes. The support of the clergy is wholly voluntary.

10. We have no exclusive privileges. Every man can follow whatever trade, profession, or calling, he chooses.

11. Our national debt is very light, not more than ten dollars per head for our white population.

12. Our government is unexpensive. Our contributions to its support are only about three dollars and a half annually per head for the free population, and in the least oppressive form, that of duties on imports.

It can scarcely admit of a doubt, that no nation, ancient or modern, ever possessed more solid advantages than are here enumerated. And it would be natural to presume, that this nation must necessarily enjoy a higher degree of prosperity and happiness, than ever fell to the lot of any other. It is perfectly obvious that nothing but a most erroneous and ruinous policy could possibly prevent that result. Indeed it would be difficult to conceive, if the fact did not stare us in the face, how any policy could possibly be devised, which could strugle with and defeat such a splendid constellation of the choicest blessings, natural, moral, and political, and produce such suffering as pervades a large portion of this nation.

From what might be our situation, let us turn our eyes to what it is. In this view, I shall, as I hinted above, chiefly confine myself to the farmers of those portions of the country specified.

1. Agricultural produce has fallen, in the interior, so low as not to afford an indemnification for the labour and capital it requires; nor will its price bear carriage 150 miles.

2. The farmers in those parts of the country are almost wholly destitute of a circulating medium, and obliged to transact their business by barter.

3. They are harassed with suits, executions, and sacrifices of property at one-half, one-third, and one-quarter of its real value.

4. Besides private debts to a most oppressive amount, a considerable portion of the farmers in the western states, and in the interior of New York, are indebted for instalments on their lands, which they are destitute of the means of paying, and which they have no hopes of ever being able to pay, without a total change of system.

5. One, two, and three instalments are paid for lands, which, by the present reduction of the price of produce, are not worth the balance remaining unpaid.

6. Many farmers cultivate lands, which cost twenty, thirty, and even fifty dollars per acre, of which they sell the produce, at twenty-five cents per bushel for wheat, twelve to fourteen cents for oats—and all other articles in the same proportion.

To this brief statement, let me add a picture of the situation of the great state of Pennsylvania, with a population, at present, probably of about 1,000,000 souls. It is entitled to full credit, as it bears the stamp of a public document. It will apply with sufficient accuracy to all the western states.

During the session of the legislature of Pennsylvania, 1819–20, a committee of the senate was appointed,

"To inquire into the extent and causes of the present general distress, and to recommend to the consideration of the legislature such measures as in their opinion may be calculated to alleviate the public sufferings, and to prevent the recurrence of a similar state of things."

This committee consisted of seven members, Messrs. Raguet, Hurst, Eichelberger, Markley, M'Meens, Rogers, and Breck, who drew a most distressing picture of the state of affairs, under the following heads:—

1. " *Ruinous sacrifices of landed property at sheriffs' sales*, " whereby in many cases, lands and houses have been sold at " *less than a half, a third, or a fourth of their former value, there-* " *by depriving of their homes and of the fruits of laborious years,* " *a vast number of our industrious farmers, some of whom have* " *been driven to seek, in the uncultivated forests of the west, that* " *shelter of which they have been deprived in their native state.*

2. " *Forced sales of merchandize, household goods, farming* " *stock and utensils*, at prices far below the cost of production, " by which numerous families have been *deprived of the com-* " *mon necessaries of life*, and of the implements of their trade.

3. " *Numerous bankruptcies*, and pecuniary embarrassments of " every description, as well among the agricultural and manu- " facturing as the mercantile classes.

4. " *A general scarcity of money* throughout the country, which " renders it almost impossible for the husbandman or other " owner of real estate to borrow even at a usurious interest, and " where landed security of the most indubitable character is of- " fered as a pledge. A similar difficulty of procuring on loan " had existed in the metropolis previous to October last, but has " since then been partially removed.

5. " *A general suspension of labour, the only legitimate source* " *of wealth, in our cities and towns*, by which thousands of our " most useful citizens are rendered destitute of the means of " support, and are reduced to the *extremity of poverty and* " *despair.*

6. " *An almost entire cessation of the usual circulation of com-* " *modities, and a consequent stagnation of business, which is limi-* " *ted to the mere purchase and sale of the necessaries of life*, and " of such articles of consumption as are absolutely required by " the season.

7. " *An universal suspension of all large manufacturing opera-* " *tions*, by which, in addition to the dismissal of the numerous " productive labourers, heretofore engaged therein, *who can find* " *no other employment*, the public loses the revenue of the capital " invested in machinery and buildings.

8. " *Usurious extortions*, whereby corporations instituted for " banking, insurance, and other purposes, in violation of law, " possess themselves of the products of industry without grant- " ing an equivalent.

9. " *The overflowing of our prisons with insolvent debtors*, " most of whom are confined for trifling sums, whereby *the com-* " *munity loses a portion of its effective labour*, and is compelled " to support families by charity, who have thus been deprived of " their protectors.

10. " *Numerous law suits upon the dockets of our courts*, and " of our justices of the peace, which lead to extravagant costs, " and the loss of a great portion of valuable time.

11. " Vexatious losses arising from the depreciation and fluc- " tuation in the value of bank notes, the impositions of brokers, " and the frauds of counterfeiters.

12. " *A general inability in the community to meet with punc- " tuality, the payment of their debts even for family expenses*, " which is experienced as well by those who are wealthy in pro- " perty, as by those who have hitherto relied upon their current " receipts to discharge their current engagements."*

Two reports made by committees of the house of representatives, confirm the above statements, by the following details :—

One committee states, that " that portion of the industry of " our citizens, devoted to manufactures, *is too generally parali- " zed;* that great numbers of extensive manufacturing establish- " ments, in which *immense sums have been invested*, and which " might be *multiplying the wealth and happiness of our citizens*, " and the resources of the state, *are lying idle and falling to " decay;* that a considerable proportion of their proprietors are " reduced to bankruptcy ; that thousands of the workmen, whose

* It is a lamentable fact, scarcely credible, that although this dreadful and affecting picture of general distress, which embraces above a third part of the population of the united states, was either presented to the view, or within the knowledge of congress, at the session of 1819-20, that body adopted no measure whatever towards its alleviation. It may be questioned whether a more complete or unfeeling disregard of such complicated suffering was ever before exhibited by any government whatever.

The words " one-third of the population," embrace the interior of Pennsylvania and New York---and the states of Ohio, Kentucky, Tennessee, and Indiana, of which the population by the late census, is 4,137,952.

Indiana - - - - - -	147,178
New York - - - - - -	1,372,812
Pennsylvania - - - -	1,049,398
Ohio - - - - - -	581,434
Kentucky - - - - - -	564,317
Tennessee - - -	422,813
	4,137,952
Deduct for persons probably not affected by the general distress - - - -	837,952
Remains - - - - -	3,300,000

The total population of the united states, in 1820, was 9,625,734.

Thus it appears that the intense distress and sufferings of above three millions of free citizens, were as wholly disregarded by congress, as the sufferings of so many Helots, by their lords and masters, the Spartans.

"sole dependence is on the labour of their hands, are *destitute* "*of employment*, and thus unable to support themselves and "their families, who are *reduced to want, and exposed to the se*"*ductions of vice and guilt;* in a word, that manufacturers and "manufactures are every where in a state of such extensive de"pression as *to require whatever aid and support the state and* "*general government can afford*, to restore them to that life and "vigour which they enjoyed during the late war."

The other report corroborates this statement by the following extracts from memorials to the legislature:—

"From the fall of every kind of produce, the scarcity of the "circulating medium, and other causes, the general distress of "this part of the state hath become so great and alarming, as to "call for the exercise of the attention and wisdom of the legis"lature: our most industrious citizens are no longer able to "meet their engagements: but their hard-earned property is "daily sacrificed at a nominal value, and falling into the hands "of a few monied speculators.

"That the mass of the people are utterly unable to pay their "debts: that their property is selling at such a rate, that even the "fees of law officers are not realized: that the industrious are "impoverished, whilst the speculating part of the community "are growing daily more wealthy: that the evil is only begin"ning, and demands legislative interposition."

To this picture of the situation of Pennsylvania, I shall add a recent one, of the western section of New York, which is its exact counterpart. It equally and irresistibly evinces how deep-rooted is the evil, how pernicious has been our policy, how intense the degree of suffering, and how imperiously a remedy is required.

Extract from an Address delivered before the Genesee Agricultural Society, at their Cattle-show and Fair, held at Batavia, on the 18th of October, 1820. *By Samuel M. Hopkins, Esq. President.*

"It is now rendered certain, that the conjecture which I of"fered last year, as to the amount of our land debt, was much "below the truth; so that we have probably 4 or 500,000 dol"lars of annual interest accumulating against us—exclusive of "the commercial debt. *So totally has money disappeared, that it* "*may be doubted whether there is in this district enough to pay*

" *interest on the amount of interest.* The country is so newly " settled, that the inhabitants have not in general had time to " raise from the soil, those supplies which an American farm, " under good improvement, is capable of producing. We may " be said to have but three articles of any moment for exporta- " tion, namely, flour, cattle, and potashes; and as far as I know, " *the depression in the prices of these is without a parallel.* Last " year we talked of the difficulties of paying for our lands; this " year the question is, how to exist. The struggle is not now for " property; from this time onwards we shall have to contend for " clothing, and a few other necessaries, without which we must " become a miserable, and, I fear, a barbarous people.*

" On this subject I confess that I am an alarmist. My first " wish would be, if it were possible, to speak in a tone that " should rouse the tenants of every log-house in these counties, " and make them *stand aghast at the prospect of families naked " —children freezing in the winter's storm—and the fathers with- " out coats or shoes to enable them to perform the necessary la- " bours of the inclement season.*

" If I am to be told that my apprehensions are extreme, then " I desire to be informed from whence the supply is to come.— " Can the merchant import clothing, and can we pay for it?— " Will labour or produce exchange for imported goods as it " used to do? Are there sheep enough in the counties to give " wool for half a suit of clothes to every person? Is enough flax " raised to make one shirt a piece?

" But supposing these few pressing wants to be supplied in " time, the general prospect of our affairs is still very gloomy. " *There can be no industry without a motive: and it appears to " me there is great danger that our people will soon limit their " exertions to the raising of food for their families.* It is very appar- " ent that much less ground is sown and planted the present fall " than in late years. A people without income, and without indus- " try will soon neglect those institutions which tend to humanize, " civilize, and improve mankind; there cannot be much ambition " or hope; education will decay, and the decencies of social life " be neglected: Such is the stupid and barbarous condition of " every people in the world who are not spurred on to industry " by a just reward for labour.

" This picture of evils, in all its colouring, is a faithful repre- " sentation of those parts of the country only, which are *new*— " where the lands are *unpaid for*—and which are *remote from " market.* But, *with mitigated shades, it is the picture of the*

* " A quantity of good wheat stored at the mills, has been sold at 37½ cents, at " a voluntary sale. A quantity of excellent flour sent to New York, and sold in " the most economical manner, was found, on an accurate statement, to net 17*s.* " 6*d.* per barrel, ($2 19.)"

"*whole northern half of the united states. As a people we are*
"*growing poor. Those who have capital can find no safe and*
"*productive employment for it. Commerce and navigation lan-*
"*guish; agriculture will not pay expenses.* We need to import
"immensely more than we have means to pay for. The cities
"are eating up their capital; the country is wearing out clothes
"without sufficient means to get new ones, either by manufac-
"ture or purchase. *Meantime our importations of goods go on;*
"*specie is plenty in a few hands—but the country at large, though*
"*overflowing with abundance of its products, has nothing with*
"*which to buy money; and all the ordinary pursuits of life are*
"*palsied for want of a medium of exchange.*"

These statements are given at full length, because there are many citizens, in and out of congress, whose circumstances secure them from a participation in the general distress, and therefore cannot believe in its existence. They decry those who, by pointing out the evil, in its fullest extent, evince the necessity of applying a speedy and radical remedy. This is an extremely erroneous procedure. The unvarnished truth in public and private affairs, is incomparably more safe and more politic, than deception or concealment, with whatever view they may be employed. It is as unwise and pernicious to disguise and palliate the evils of the state, when it is writhing in distress, as for a patient in a dangerous malady to conceal the extent of his disease.

A writer, in a very respectable gazette, lately scouted the idea of distress, when five pounds of flour could be purchased for 12 cents! A most admirable illustration of political economy!—What avails it to the labouring man, who seeks in vain for employment, that flour can be procured at this low rate, and other articles in the same proportion, when he has not wherewith to purchase? His labour is his only fund. The prevailing system annihilates that fund, while the resources of the nation are devoted to support foreign labourers. Better far it were, that he had to pay fourteen dollars per barrel for flour, as he did some years past, and earned five or six dollars per week, than that flour should be, I will not say at three or four dollars, but even at half a dollar per barrel, while he is unable to procure that employment, the want of which disables him from purchasing at any price.

On the situation of the western states, I cannot give any information, of equal authenticity; that is, in the documental form.—

But numberless private letters, from respectable citizens, furnish similar statements, and prove the existence of an equal degree of distress.

Just as this page was going to press, I was furnished with a recent New Orleans price current, in which fresh flour is quoted at three dollars to three dollars and a half—and sour at one dollar and a quarter. The quantity of sour flour is very great; as the glut in the market occasions it to be long on hand—and finally renders no small portion of it unfit for use.

A letter, just received from one of the most respectable merchants in Philadelphia, engaged in the New Orleans trade, states, as follows:—

"Wheat without price or sale; and flour scarcely saleable even at three dollars and a half for the best. *Neither of these articles will pay from the western country this year.*"

From the preceding view it is manifest that the best form of government affords no security for prosperity. The pinching distress under such a form of government, may, by impolicy, be as great and even greater, than under despotisms and wasteful governments. What, in a word, can be more hideous, so far as property is concerned, (and what avails a free government, if it does not afford protection to property, or security for its acquisition?) than—"*a general scarcity of money*"—as "*general a suspension of labour*"—"*ruinous sacrifices of landed property at sheriffs' sales, whereby lands and houses have been sold at less than a half, a third, or a fourth of their former value*"—"*forced sales of merchandize, household goods, farming stock and utensils, at prices far below the cost of production*"—"*an almost entire cessation of the usual circulation of commodities*—"*an universal suspension of all large manufacturing operations—the overflowing of our prisons with insolvent debtors*"—"*property selling at such a rate that even the fees of office are not realized,*"* &c.&c.

* Some gentlemen severely censured me last year for the strong pictures I drew of the calamitous state of affairs, and for "the misery," which I asserted spread over a large portion of the land. They even went so far as to assert that those writings were likely to be highly pernicious to the country, by their effects in Europe, as they might prevent emigration from that quarter. They denied the existence of "*misery*" in any shape or form. With those doctrines I cannot accord. The best mode of inducing our rulers to apply remedies to the public distress, is to depict that distress in its proper colours. To decide on the subject of "*misery,*" it is necessary to ascertain what "*misery*" is. Walker explains it —"wretchedness—unhappiness—calamity—misfortune." I respectfully ask those fastidious gentlemen, whether "*numerous families being deprived of the common necessaries of life*"—the "*prisons overflowing with insolvent debtors*"—and "*vast numbers of industrious farmers being driven from their homes, and forced to seek in the uncultivated forests of the west, that shelter of which they have been deprived in their native state,*" be not as complete proofs of misery as can be exhibited?

However extraordinary or unpalatable it may be, I will risk the consequences of stating a bold truth, that more distress than is here displayed might be sought for in vain, under some of the worst governments in Europe. And further, that this country would be incomparably more prosperous, if we paid direct taxes to the amount of ten, fifteen, or twenty millions of dollars per annum, provided the productive industry of our citizens were adequately protected. While those who depend on their labour, are steadily employed—and those who carry on business have a ready market for the proceeds of their industry, high taxes are never oppressive.

To illustrate this position, I will take the case of a farmer with only one hundred acres of land, and a family of ten persons. I will suppose his land to produce only fifteen bushels per acre; and his surplus, beyond what he consumes, and what he sells, in order to procure such necessaries as he is obliged to purchase, to be only six bushels per acre, or six hundred bushels in the aggregate. Assuming, as I hope will be admitted, that the gain by having a market at his door, instead of sending his produce to a distance of two, three or four hundred miles, as is the case with so many of our farmers, would be at least a quarter dollar per bushel; the establishment of manufactures in his neighbourhood, which would furnish such a market, would secure a clear gain of one hundred and fifty dollars per annum; whereas his share of a direct tax of twenty millions of dollars per annum, could not be ten dollars. I might have assumed an increase of price of three quarters of a dollar per bushel, which would make the gain four hundred and fifty dollars.

The above reasoning applies equally even to journeymen, whose wages I will estimate at only five dollars per week, of whom a large proportion have for a considerable time been unemployed a quarter or half their time.

One quarter of his time, lost to a journeyman, working at five dollars per week, would be per ann. -	$65
Deduct amount of tax on a family of six persons - -	6*
Saving - - - - - - - - - -	59

* This is an extravagant assumption for a person in this sphere of life—and the more completely proves the theory.

CHAPTER II.

Alleged causes of the general distress. Transition from a state of war to peace. Great increase of banks, and their mismanagement. Fallacy of these allegations. Exports during and since the war compared. Real amount of the increase of banking capital far below what is generally believed. List of country banks in Pennsylvania paying specie. Vessels employed in the India trade. Enormous export of specie.

The preceding chapter contains a view of the immense advantages this nation enjoys, and of the lamentable situation in which a large and interesting portion of its citizens are plunged, a situation so little corresponding with those advantages. I shall now endeavour to unfold the causes which have produced so total a failure of the expectations which might have been rationally formed of the state of this country.

Various opinions have prevailed on this subject—and three principal sources of our calamities have been stated.

1. The transition from a state of war to a state of peace, with the general change in the state of affairs in Europe.

2. The undue extension of banks, and their mal-administration.

3. The paralysis of so large a portion of the manufacturing industry of the country by extravagant importations.

Transition to a state of peace.

It requires but a very cursory examination to see, that the operation of this cause, if not wholly ideal, is at least prodigiously overrated. In fact, it would appear more rational to suppose that this "transition" would be salutary than otherwise. Much of the prosperity of all nations depends on having good markets for their surplus produce. The want of them produces stagnation, distress and embarrassment. And as the late war in a great measure deprived us of those markets, and "the transition to peace" restored them to us, it is not easy to comprehend how it can be fairly charged with producing such baleful consequences.

During the war, our exports were reduced within very narrow bounds. Hostilities commenced in June 1812, and peace was signed on the 28th of December, 1814. The war of course continued but about two years and a half. The exports of 1812, were $30,032,100. It is impossible to ascertain what proportion of that amount was shipped before the declaration of war. I shall therefore omit that year, and compare the exports of 1813 and 1814, with those of the subsequent years, in order to decide this important question, and to evince the very unstable foundation on which rests the opinion I have undertaken to combat.

The domestic exports of

1813 were - - - - - - -	$25,008,152
1814 - - - - - - - -	6,782,272
	$31,790,424

being an average of less than sixteen millions per annum.

The domestic exports since the war, have been

1815 - - - - -	$45,974,403
1816 - - - - -	64,781,896
1817 - - - -	68,313,500
1818 - - - - -	73,854,437
1819 - - - - -	50,976,838
1820 - - - - - -	51,683,640
	$355,584,714

being an average of nearly sixty millions per annum, or almost four times as much as the average of the exportation during the war.

In one sense the "transition" may be said to have produced our calamities. It took away the bar that previously existed against the deluge of foreign merchandize by which so large a portion of our manufacturing establishments were subsequently prostrated, and their owners ruined. More of this anon.

That so great an increase in the exports of a country could have any other than a beneficial effect, will not be asserted by any man of candour: and therefore the idea that this produced the general distress is swept away by the force of fact and fair induction, as completely as the mists and fogs which overspread the horizon are swept away by the radiant beams of the sun in his meridian splendor.

It can scarcely be necessary to add any thing further on this subject. But there is another fact which so strongly corroborates the conclusion here drawn, that it would be injustice to the cause, to omit it. War ceased every where early in 1815; and had "*the transition from a state of war to a state of peace*," produced the ruinous situation of affairs which exists at present, its most oppressive effects would have been felt immediately. Distress and calamity would at once have overspread the face of the land, and the country would have been gradually restored in the following years, to that state of prosperity, to which its various blessings afford it a fair claim. But what is the fact? with the exception of some of the manufacturing districts, where industry was paralized early after the war, by a most immoderate influx of foreign merchandise, as, for instance, more particularly Pittsburg, Wilmington, &c. &c. the country in general was prosperous, or at least the range of distress was limited in 1815, 1816, and part of 1817. It was only in 1818 that stagnation and embarrassment began to spread generally, and, in fact, large portions of the country did not feel them even till 1819.

It is to be presumed that these facts are completely conclusive, and finally settle this important question for ever.

Operations of the Banks.

The first alleged source of the prevailing distress being set aside, it is necessary to examine the second, that is, the extravagant extension and mismanagement of banks and banking capital.

That the chapter of banks is a deep stain on the annals of this country, cannot be denied. In various quarters, it has exhibited a high degree of turpitude. In some places, where banks were wholly unnecessary, they were established, for their own particular advantage, by a few individuals, who engrossed a large portion of the stock for the purposes of speculation, and as soon as it was raised to 20 or 30 per cent. above par, they sold out, having cleared hundreds and thousands of dollars; and, in many instances, without the advance of a single dollar. In some quarters, likewise, banks have been grossly mismanaged, through the sinister views, and as often through the inexperience of the directors. But that a large portion of them have been conducted fairly and honourably—and that the evils the others have produced, have been extravagantly over-rated, is more than probable, as may, in some degree, be inferred from the following facts, respecting these institutions in Pennsylvania, in which state the outcry against extravagant banking has been as loud as in any other part of the union. The great "*litter of banks*" of 1814, has been a fertile topic of invective in and out of the state.

Pennsylvania at present, as I have already stated, contains about 1,000,000, souls—46,000 square miles—in 1810, it carried on manufactures to the amount of 44,194,740 dollars—and its domestic exports in 1816, were 7,196,246 dollars. And is it possible, that the extra bank capital, created in this state in 1814, which, beyond the limits of Philadelphia, was only about 5,000,000 of dollars, could account for distress and embarrassments, which were not universally felt for years after, and which increase in pressure, in proportion to our distance from, that year? Had this whole sum, or twice as much, been most egregiously misemployed, or even wholly squandered away, although it would have ruined many, it would not have been felt by the state at large, provided we had a market for our productions, or had our exports borne a proper proportion to our imports.

But the subject may be presented in another point of view. The country banks, which went into operation under the act of 1814, were thirty-three in number. Of these the notes of no less than nine are at present at par in the city of Philadelphia—and those of eight others are only at one, one and a half, two, and three per cent. discount, notwithstanding the pressure and embarrassment of the times.

It will not admit of a doubt that these banks must have been not only ably, but in general correctly managed, to maintain specie payments from the year 1817, when those payments were resumed, to the present time.

It is, however, beyond a doubt, that much mischief has arisen from the banks—and that many useful and worthy men have been ruined by their operations. But, as I observed on a former occasion, they have, in many cases, been far "more sinned against than sinning." The extravagant drain of specie for the China trade, exhausted them of the basis on which the credit and security of banking operations rest, and left them no alternative but to press on their customers, or to stop the payment of specie. They began with the former measure, which produced great distress and embarrassment—but many of them, after all their efforts, found it impossible to continue specie payments.

I annex a list of those seventeen banks, alluded to above, with the state of their notes in the city of Philadelphia, and the amount of their capitals.

		Capital.
Farmers' Bank of Lancaster,	Par	$ 600,000
Easton,	do.	214,770
Germantown,	do.	152,000
Northampton,	do.	125,000
Montgomery County,	do.	76,286
Farmers' Bank of Bucks County,	do.	60,090
Harrisburg,	do.	168,036
Delaware County,	do.	77,380
Chester,	do.	90,000
Farmers' Bank of Reading discount per cent.	3	300,350
Lancaster Bank,	1	159,710
York Bank,	1½	192,940
Chambersburg,	1½	266,765
Gettysburg,	1½	154,553
Carlisle Bank,	1½	162,950
Bank of Swatara,	1½	75,075
Pittsburg,	2	341,035
		$3,216,940
Net capital of the thirty-three banks		$5,000,000

Thus, the capitals of those banks, chartered in 1814, which, by mismanagement or the drain of specie, or both, have been unable to support their credit, by the continuance of specie payments, are about 1,800,000 dollars. To ascribe the mass of suffering, under which this mighty state is agonized, to the operations of these, and indeed of all its banks united, would be as absurd, as to ascribe the death of a man who had been for years taking slow poison, to a slight fever or cholic, which immediately preceded his dissolution.

To enable the reader to form an idea of the excessive extent of the drain of specie for the India trade, I annex a list of the vessels, which, on the 3d of February, 1818, were either absent from the port of Philadelphia, on, or preparing for, voyages to India, China, and other places beyond the Cape of Good Hope, with which our commerce is carried on almost altogether with specie.

Ships.	*Commanders.*	*Destination.*	*Tons.*
Thomas Scattergood,	Warrington,	Canton, via Liverpool, - -	399
Phœnix,	M'Kibbon,	Canton, via Liverpool, - -	404
Clothier,	Phillips,	Canton, via Liverpool, - -	285
Hope,	Moore,	Canton, - - - - -	256
Columbia,	Laler,	Isle of France and Batavia, -	263
George and Albert,	Donaldson,	Canton, - - - - - -	349
Cruttenden,	Turner,	Calcutta, - - - - -	315
London Trader,	Harrison,	Canton, - - - - - -	377
Augustus,	Oliver,	N. W. Coast and Canton, -	279
Natchez,	Warnock,	Batavia, - - - - -	296
Bengal,	Ansley,	N. W. Coast and Canton, -	329
Eliza	Cornish,	Cape of Good Hope & East Indies,	406
Margaret,	Benners,	Batavia, - - - - -	292
Pacific,	Sharp,	Canton, - - - - -	332
Atlas,	Gordon,	Sumatra, - - - - - -	416
Neptune,	Fisher,	Canton, - - - - - - -	292
Governor Hawkins,	Coffin,	Pacific Ocean, - - -	219
Dorothea,	Harman,	Calcutta, via Marseilles, - -	453
Delaware,	M'Pherson,	Calcutta, - - - - -	338
Coromandel,	Day,	India, via Antwerp, - -	340
Bainbridge,	Tomlinson,	Calcutta, - - - - - -	368
Caledonia,	Hill,	Calcutta, - - - - -	445
America	Eldridge,	Batavia, - - - - -	297
Sachem,	Fennel,	Cape of Good Hope, &c. via Brazils,	215
Benjamin Rush,	Wiltberger,	Canton, via Liverpool, - -	385
Helvetius,	Gallegar,	Batavia, - - - - -	330
Rousseau,	M'Levan,	Batavia, - - - - -	306
North America,	Erwin,	Batavia, - - - - - -	388
Bingham,	Wilson,	Batavia, - - - - -	375
Archimedes,	Neal,	Pacific Ocean, - - - - -	354
Brigs.			
Levant,	Skinner,	China, via Leghorn and Smyrna,	210
Saunders,	Clunie.	Manilla, - - - - -	196
		Carried forward	10,509

			Brought forward	10,509
Ship China Packet,	Hewit,	Canton,	fitting out at Philada.	357
Sailed from N. York on Philada. account,				
Ship Rosalie,	Merry,	Canton,		
Ship Athens,	Burdham,	Calcutta,		
Fitting out at N. York on Philada. account,			Amount of tonnage about -	1,500
Ship Solon,	———,	Batavia,		
Ship Edward,	———,	Calcutta,		
Total,	42 vessels	- - -	tonnage	12,366

Estimating the specie of each vessel at $100,000, which I presume to be a low calculation, it would amount to above 4,000,000 of dollars from one port alone, and in one season! How immense must have been the sum exported from all our ports! Is it then wonderful, that the currency of the country has been so prodigiously reduced as is declared by the secretary of the treasury:—

"In 1815, the whole circulation was estimated to have arisen "to 110,000,000 of dollars; and this amount was *probably aug-* "*mented in* 1816. At the close of 1819, it has been estimated, "upon data, believed to be substantially correct, at 45,000,000 "of dollars. According to these estimates, *the currency of the* "*united states has, in the space of three years, been reduced from* "*one hundred and ten millions to forty-five millions of dollars.*

"This reduction exceeds *fifty-nine per cent. of the whole cir-* "*culation of* 1815. The fact that the currency in 1815 and 1816 "was depreciated, has not sensibly diminished the effect upon "the community, of this great and sudden reduction. What- "ever was the degree of its depreciation, it was still the mea- "sure of value. It determined the price of labour, and of all "the property of the community. A change so violent could "not fail, under the most favourable auspices in other respects, "to produce much distress, to check the ardour of enterprise, "and seriously to affect the productive energies of the nation. "The reduction, was, in fact, commenced under favourable aus- "pices. During the year 1817, and the greater part of 1818, all "the surplus produce of the country commanded in foreign mar- "kets higher prices than ordinary. The rate of foreign ex- "change afforded no inducement for the exportation of specie "for the purpose of discharging debts previously contracted. "*The only drain to which the metallic currency was subject, was* "*the demand for it, for the prosecution of trade to the East Indies* "*and to China. In this trade, specie being the principal commodi-* "*ty, and indispensable to its prosecution, the amount exported* "*during those years was very great, and seriously affected the* "*amount of circulation, by compelling the banks to diminish their* "*discounts.*

"*All intelligent writers upon currency agree that where it is* "*decreasing in amount, poverty and misery must prevail.* The "correctness of the opinion is too manifest to require proof. "The united voice of the nation attests its accuracy.

"*As there is no recorded example in the history of nations, of* "*a reduction of the currency, so rapid, and so extensive, so, but few* "*examples have occurred, of distress so general and so severe, as* "*that which has been exhibited in the united states.*"*

From a calm review of the preceding facts and statements, we shall be led to wonder, not, that so many of the banks stopped the payment of specie, but how it was possible for any of them to stand so severe and oppressive a shock—and we shall likewise equally wonder that our distress, great as it is, has not exceeded what we have experienced.

In the course of 1817–18, the Bank of the united states at the great expense of 525,927 dollars, imported 7,311,750 of dollars in specie; but nearly as fast as it arrived, it was swept off into the unfathomable gulf of this exhausting commerce.

CHAPTER III.

Objections to the protection of manufactures. High price of labour. Want of capital. Their fallacy. Labour cheap, and capital abundant, at present, and manufactures not so prosperous as formerly.

From the organization of the federal government to the present time, whenever memorials or petitions were presented to congress, or any efforts made, to procure such a legislative protection for manufactures, as would shield them from the overwhelming competition of foreigners, who enjoyed the advantages of drawbacks and bounties from their respective governments, an ardent opposition has been excited, and numberless objections raised to defeat the applications: and such has been the industry and influence of those citizens hostile to the measure, that however deficient of foundation the objections were, they almost universally sufficed to defeat the object in view.

Particular emphasis has been laid on three of those objections which require some examination.

1. That we were not ripe for manufactures.

2. That protecting duties would tax the many for the benefit of the few—giving the latter a monopoly at the expense of the former.

* Report of Secretary of the Treasury, on the currency, pp. 8, 9.

3. That protection of manufactures would lead to extortion and imposition, as was said to have taken place during the late war.

Of each in order.

I. *That we were not ripe for manufactures.*

This objection rests on two grounds—the high price of labour here—and the want of sufficient capital.

It was asserted with oracular confidence, that until labour was reduced to a level with its price in Europe, we could not possibly compete with the manufacturers in that quarter. They received only enough for a bare subsistence—and as our journeymen and labourers could not be compelled to work on the same terms, it was asserted that manufactures could not possibly flourish here.*

It was replied—but in vain—that numerous branches of manufactures, in which manual labour alone was employed, had, in consequence of public patronage, arrived at perfection, and prospered for many years—witness the manufacture of hats, shoes, boots, paper, books, &c. of which our citizens supplied more than three-fourths, probably nine-tenths, of the whole consumption.

It was equally in vain, to urge the simple, but decisive arguments, that reasoning grounded on the dearness of labour could not by any possibility apply to manufactures carried on by machinery; that our water power gave us an inestimable advantage over those who were obliged to depend on the more expensive operations of steam; that the manufactures in which we were most completely defeated—the importation of which produced the greatest impoverishment of the country—and which most loudly called for protection—were those executed by machinery and water power, aided by the labour principally of women and children; and finally, that the labour in this case was cheap, and of little account, as the chief part of it would otherwise be lost.

These conclusive arguments ought to have decided the question, as they fully proved that whatever difference there might be in the price of labour, public patronage alone was wanting to

* The wages in many branches of business in England have been at all times as high as in Philadelphia, as may be seen by the following extract:

"The average wages of journeymen artisans and manufacturers in London may "be taken at 30*s*. per week, in other cities and towns at 26*s*. and of labourers in "the field including the addition for harvest work, at 14*s*.

"Boys of ten years of age, can almost maintain themselves; and girls from "twelve to fourteen, healthy and well brought up, may do the same."—*Tract on saving banks, by Horace Twiss. London,* 1816.

enable our artisans and manufacturers fully to compete with their rivals in every branch of business. The difficulty and impracticability of struggling with foreign nations, under the disparity of the price of labour, were nevertheless re-echoed through the nation, in spite of these irrefragable facts and reasonings; found ready belief with a large portion of our influential citizens; and aided to defeat the applications of the manufacturers.

It was further asserted, that sufficient capital could not be spared for the purpose of establishing manufactures; that the attempt would force capital into employments less, from those which were more advantageous; and therefore that even on this ground, were there no other objection, the project was premature—would be injurious—and ought to be discountenanced.

The plain inference from these assertions was, that when labour became cheap, and capital abundant, then manufactures would arise as it were spontaneously, as the country would be "*ripe for them.*"

Time always decides between truth and error—strips the latter of its glare of plausibility—and exposes its intrinsic deformity. Pity, however, that this result most frequently does not take place till error has done immense mischief, as has been the case in this instance. The present state of affairs indubitably proves, that to the success of manufactures in this country neither a reduction of the price of labour nor any additional capital was necessary; and that "the one thing needful," was such governmental support as all the wise nations of Europe afford their manufactures.

The period so long hoped for by our political economists has arrived, when the country is, according to their views of the subject, "*ripe*" for manufactures. Labour is now so low that great numbers of people in various quarters of the union, have, during the last eighteen months, worked for their board alone—and thousands have been unable to obtain work on any terms.—Our cities swarm with men, women and children, who, able and willing to work, but, unable to procure employment, immoderately swell our lists of paupers, are supported by the overseers of the poor and by soup-houses—and a gangrene on that society to whose wealth and prosperity they might daily make additions. A statement was lately published by the society for the prevention of pauperism, that there were thirteen thousand paupers, in the city of New York. I cannot ascertain the number in Philadelphia; but it is oppressively great.

Capital, too, is so abundant, that the owners cannot find adequate employment for it. They dare not invest it in manufacturing establishments themselves, from the awful memento afforded by the fate of so large a portion of the manufacturers who ministered so usefully to the wants of the country during the war, and who were so shamefully and ungratefully sacrificed by the policy pursued soon after its close. Nor can they with safety lend it to manufacturers, whose prospects are so precarious and so gloomy.

This, then, according to those citizens, is precisely the time when, from the cheapness of labour, and abundance of capital, the nation is ripe for manufactures—and when they ought to flourish spontaneously.

But, alas! these "*day dreams*" of our political economists are not only not realized, but are put down forever. Manufacturing establishments, on which millions were expended, and which prospered during the war, when labour was dear, are now closed, and sinking into ruins, when labour can be had on the average for two-thirds of the price it commanded at that period—when the necessaries of life are in almost unexampled abundance, and cheaper than they have been for above thirty years—and when, I repeat, the wealthy part of the community know not how to find employment for their capital.

On the question of "ripeness for manufactures," the following opinions of Gen. Jacob Brown, as enlightened an agriculturist, as he proved himself during the war a brave and skilful commander, are entitled to the most serious attention—ought to settle this question—and produce a totally new system of policy. It is impossible for a mind open to conviction to resist the force of his reasoning.

"Other governments do not leave manufactures to force their "way, without public aid, into our markets. They grant premi-"ums and bounties, for the purpose of enabling their manufac-"turers to undersell their rivals. Besides, *combinations are "formed among foreign manufacturers to beat down a manufacture "that is beginning to show itself in a country, which they have "been in the habit of supplying*—combinations, acting upon the "principle of making a temporary sacrifice to secure a perma-"nent good, and looking, too, to their own government, when the "sacrifice is great, for some sort of remuneration—a remuner-"ation often cheerfully bestowed. Thus our country being ripe "for the introduction of a particular manufacture, some public "spirited citizens embark a large part of their property in the "enterprise. *After they have, by great expense, brought their "schemes to maturity, and begin to be cheered with the prospect "of success, the country is flooded with the article by foreigners, "who sell it at a very low price*, and continue so to act, until the "domestic establishment is ruined, calculating, that the com-"plete failure of the plan, with the ruin of the persons engaged "in it, will prevent all similar attempts in future, and thus se-"cure to them, for a long time, the undivided possession of the "market.

"Here, then, the domestic manufacture fails; not because "the country was not ripe for it: not because, things being left "to their natural course, it could not thrive. It is beat down by "an artificial policy. And we may take it for granted, that the "cupidity of foreigners will postpone the successful prosecution "of manufactures in this country, long beyond the natural peri- "od for their introduction, unless our own government adopt a "strong system of counteraction.

"When we consider how very difficult it is at first to compete "with old establishments, which have attained great skill in the "business, in which they are to be contended with, and have "been long in undivided possession of the market, with the fear "of failure, which always exists in reference to new enterprises; "it will not be thought extravagant to say, that *a country may "remain destitute of many important manufactures for half a cen- "tury after it has really become ripe for them*, unless relieved "from the pressure of the difficulties in question, and encouraged "to look them strongly in the face, by a well-founded reli- "ance on the patronage of the government. In no country have "manufactories, requiring great capital and skill, sprung up, in "the first instance, of their own accord, in consequence of the "ripeness of the country for them. No—they have always been "introduced by efforts of public policy. How emphatically was "this the case with respect to England! If she had acted upon the "principle now contended for, that manufactories will always "grow up as soon as it is the interest of the country that they "should do so, she never would have entered into competition "with Flanders. Instead of rising to her present state of wealth "and resource, she would have sunk into a second or third rate "power—comparatively poor and inefficient. And the instan- "ces are not rare, as if in derision of this principle, in which "countries, low in manufacturing industry, have been raised in "a few years, by a wise, protecting policy, to a very high point "of prosperity and wealth.

"Prussia, under the government of the sagacious Frederick, "furnishes a splendid exemplification of this remark. In his "reign, the population and wealth of Prussia were more than "doubled; to which nothing so much contributed as the policy, "which he so firmly and perseveringly pursued, of introducing "the most valuable branches of manufactures into his dominions. "What would have been the reply of this great man, if he had "been told, that it was unwise in him to force up manufactures? "that they should be left to the natural course of things?— "Things, in this respect, can never take their natural course, "until a wise government, by strong protecting duties, gives an "opportunity for the establishment of manufactures within its "limits, and carrying them through the period of infancy.—

"Things are prevented from taking their natural course, by the "artificial policy of foreign governments, and the avaricious "combinations among foreign manufacturers. The moment we "attempt to get rid of their monopoly, by efforts to supply our-"selves, they defeat those efforts by a temporary departure from "their ordinary conduct—the wounds inflicted being not so "much by blows, given in fair combat, as by those, which, if "continued for any length of time, would destroy equally him "who gives, and him who receives them."*

II. *That protecting duties would tax the many for the benefit of the few—giving the latter a monopoly at the expense of the former.*

This objection enlisted the honest feelings and prejudices of a large portion of the community against their fellow citizens engaged in manufactures. They fondly believed that compliance with their wishes, was little less than a license to depredate on the community.

It would not be easy to point out an error in political economy, which has inflicted so much distress on a nation, as this has done on the united states. More than three fourths of the calamities which we have suffered for years past, have arisen from this source; as it has been the principal means of preventing such a modification of the tariff, as would have averted most of the evils under which this nation is writhing.

It is an egregious error to suppose that high duties or prohibitions afford a "*monopoly*" to those in whose favour they are imposed. In order to clear up this point, it is necessary to ascertain the precise import of "*monopoly*," which the most approved dictionaries explain to mean "*the exclusive privilege of selling any thing*."† Now a moment's consideration will evince that there is no power in this nation which can or dare attempt to confer, "*the exclusive power of selling any thing*," except in the case of inventions or discoveries, which may be patented. But this is a case not contemplated by the objection.

We have imported in a single year, to the injury of the cultivators of the soil, 1,027,951*lbs.* of cheese,‡ notwithstanding it was subject to a heavy duty. Suppose the article had been wholly prohibited. Would there, in that case, be any thing like "*a monopoly?*" Not in the least. The making of cheese would be open to every citizen of the united states—manufacturer or merchant, as well as agriculturist, without a single exception. In like manner, were cottons or woollens wholly prohibited,

* Address of Major-General Jacob Brown, Vice-President of the Agricultura Society of Jefferson county, New-York, to the Society, Sept. 1819.

† See Walker and Johnson. ‡ Seybert, p. 165.

instead of being subject to a duty of thirty-three per cent. as contemplated by the new tariff, there would not be the slightest trace of "*monopoly*;" as every citizen might, and hundreds would, at once commence the manufacture.

The prices at first would probably in both cases rise considerably. But the higher they rose at first, the more certain and the greater would be the reduction afterwards. Allured by the extraordinary profits, so much capital would take that direction, that a glut would be produced—and hence the result would be, what has ever followed a glut, that the article would sink below its value.

On this subject the opinion of Alexander Hamilton has been repeatedly and deservedly quoted. It is conclusive and unanswerable:—

"Though it were true, that the immediate and certain effect "of regulations controlling the competition of foreign, with do-"mestic fabrics, was an increase of prices; it is universally true, "that *the contrary is the ultimate effect with every successful ma-"nufacture*. When a domestic manufacture has attained to "perfection, and has engaged in the prosecution of it a compe-"tent number of persons, *it invariably becomes cheaper*. Being "free from the heavy charges which attend the importation of "foreign commodities, it can be afforded cheaper, and according-"ly seldom or never fails to be sold cheaper, in process of time, "than was the foreign article for which it was a substitute. "The internal competition which takes place, soon does away "every thing like monopoly; and by degrees *reduces the price "of the article to the minimum of a reasonable profit on the capi-"tal employed*. This accords with the reason of the thing, and "with experience."*

This opinion is strongly corroborated by the facts contained in the following letter, from as respectable a citizen as any in Philadelphia:—

SIR, *January* 30*th*, 1820.

"In answer to your note of 24th instant, I reply, that the ar-"ticles in our line of business, which have been selling at reduced "prices since they were manufactured in this country, are win-"dow-glass, white lead, oil of vitriol, Glauber's salt, and nearly "all the chemical articles. Window-glass 8 by 10 formerly "cost the importer from 9 to 9½ dollars per box; the manufac-"turers here now sell at 7 dollars. White lead formerly cost "from 14 to 15 dollars; we are now selling at 12 dollars. Oil "of vitriol formerly cost 11 cents per lb. the manufacturer here "now charges 8 cents, and the imported article has lately sold

* Hamilton's Works, Vol. I. Report on Manufactures.

" in this city at 6 cents. Glauber's salt formerly cost 30*s*. ster-
" ling; but, by the late prices current, 18*s*. sterling; it would
" therefore cost to import it about 6 cents per lb. including the
" duty, which is 2 cents per lb.; it is now selling by the manu-
" facturer at from 2½ to 3 cents per lb. and has not been above
" that price for some years past. With respect to chemicals,
" there is no probability of their being again imported; the com-
" petition here will ever keep down the prices; nor is it proba-
" ble that window-glass will be imported, as the manufactories
" now established can supply more than the demand; the prices
" will therefore be kept down by competition.

" I am very respectfully,

" Yours, &c.

" SAMUEL WETHERILL.

" Mr. Mathew Carey."

To these facts it may be added, that, in almost every case, the establishment of a manufacture in this country has kept down the price of the imported article. One item, of public notoriety, often quoted, but unfortunately not sufficiently attended to, deserves more detail than any other, as affording a most practical illustration of this theory.

Immense quantities of low priced muslins were formerly imported into this country from the East Indies, which were invoiced at 6, 7, and 8 cents per yard, and sold in our markets at 20 and 25 cents. As they did not yield much to the revenue, and interfered with the consumption of our cotton wool, they were subjected to a duty equivalent to a prohibition: that is to say, all imported cotton goods, below 25 cents per square yard, were dutied as if they had cost 25 cents.

For example—

1000 square yards muslin at 8 cents . .	$80 00
Duties on 1000 square yards at 6¼ cents .	62 52

This is about 77 per cent, and has altogether closed our markets against those goods.

In consequence of this duty, so much capital has been employed in that manufacture, that American cotton goods, greatly superior in quality and texture, are now sold throughout the united states at 14 and 15 cents, and afford a fair profit to the manufacturer, and a great saving to the nation, independently of the immense sums they retain in the country.

This was a proper opportunity of testing the soundness of the specious idea of "*taxing the many for the benefit of the few*" by prohibitions or prohibitory duties. It did not stand the test. It was found hollow and fallacious, however plausible in appearance. This fact ought of itself to have finally settled the question beyond appeal.

Steam boats afford another satisfactory test, of which the result is the same. The capital requisite to build them being very great, so as very much to circumscribe competition, and being in some degree patented, it might be expected that high prices would be extorted, and the public be imposed on. But in this, as in all other cases, facts put down the theory completely. The rates of freight and passage in these useful vessels are every where moderate; and in many cases competition has reduced them so low, that the boats are a losing concern.

Thus it happens in a variety of manufactures. As soon as they are completely established, and have the market secured, so many persons engage in them, and so great is the competition, that the prices are frequently reduced below those which afford a fair profit; and many of the competitors, whose means are slender, are actually ruined.

I shall doubtless be pardoned for stating the great effect of competition in a case somewhat analagous, which is calculated to throw important light on this subject. The West Indies, depending in general for their bread stuffs, on the united states, are frequently in a state of dearth, approaching to famine. Prices rise to an exorbitant height, so as to afford an immoderate profit to those who can reach the markets in season. So great is the competition, that, in the course of a few weeks, sometimes a few days, the price is reduced within reasonable bounds, and often so low as to produce actual loss.

A few months since, the price of flour at the Havanna was from twenty-five to thirty dollars per barrel. Two or three cargoes arrived, and were sold at those rates. The intelligence reached this country, and so many vessels were despatched hence, and arrived there, nearly together, that the price was reduced to twelve or fourteen dollars, although the duty is $8\frac{5}{8}$ per barrel, and freight probably half a dollar.

III. *That protection of manufactures would lead to extortion and imposition, as is said to have taken place during the late war.*

This objection has been refuted times without number, and a sense of propriety ought to consign it to oblivion. But having recently been confidently advanced by an agricultural society in Virginia, not only as if it had never been answered, but as if it were unanswerable, it cannot be improper to devote a page to the discussion of the foundation on which it rests.

To this allegation it might be sufficient to reply, that those who raised the price of flour from four dollars to fourteen—of tobacco from ninety-five dollars to one hundred and eighty-five per hhd.—of cotton from twelve to thirty cents—and of wool from seventy-five cents to three and four dollars per pound, ought to be eternally silent on the subject of extortion.

However, I shall not rest the defence on this ground.

The war cut off the supplies of foreign goods of almost every kind. As there was a vast amount of capital unemployed, and a prospect offered of a steady and profitable market, manufacturing establishments arose as it were by magic. Numbers of merchants and farmers embarked in the business.

All novel undertakings, particularly when on an extensive scale, are liable to various obstructions, difficulties, and disadvantages. These establishments had their full share. The owners of sites for mills and machinery, took an ungenerous advantage of the opportunity, and demanded exorbitant prices for them. With these demands the manufacturers were obliged to comply. Skilful mechanists were extremely rare—and of course sold their services at extravagant rates. The number of workmen bore no proportion to the demand for them: and they, like the rest, levied heavy taxes on the manufacturers: and finally, the farmers who had sold their wool at fifty and seventy-five cents per pound before the war, gradually raised it to one, two, three, and even, for a short space of time, to four dollars.*

To supply the deficiency of workmen, numbers of apprentices were taken, who were to be instructed in the business. During this process, the want of skill necessarily produced heavy losses and deterioration of the manufactures.

One other evil attended the manufacturers at this period. Many of them who entered on the business with large capitals, which they believed would have been amply adequate for the purpose of erecting the necessary mills and machinery, found those capitals exhausted before half or two-thirds of the works were completed—and were reduced to the alternative of either borrowing money to carry on the business, or sacrificing all they had expended.

Now, combining all these circumstances together, is there a man with any pretensions to candour, who will not be ashamed to join in the senseless clamour against the extortion of manufacturers during the war, when raw materials, labour and machinery, were raised in price; and when, although the raw material, of the woollen branch in particular, was advanced three

* Grotjan's Price Current, Nov. 14, 1814.

or four hundred per cent. the cloth was only advanced about fifty, sixty, or seventy per cent. on the peace prices of the imported cloth? Let it further never be forgotten, that the domestic manufacture was at all times during the war below the imported article, of which it steadily kept down the price. Broad cloth, notwithstanding the great extent of smuggling, would probably have risen to thirty dollars per yard, but for the domestic manufacture of this article.

Similar justification might be offered for any rise of price in other departments; but I shall only add one. Tin was scarce, and in few hands. The merchants raised the price eighty to one hundred per cent. Were not the manufacturers of tin-ware necessarily obliged to raise that article accordingly?

CHAPTER V.

Ruinous consequences, to the farming interest, of the depression of Manufactures. Conversion of manufacturers into farmers—of customers into rivals.

Having presented a sketch of the distresses of the country—the causes to which they have been ascribed—the grounds on which relief has been refused—and endeavoured to trace those distresses to their real source, I now undertake to prove the immense injury to the farming interest which has been produced by the policy we have hitherto pursued—as well as the benefits which would have necessarily flowed from a contrary policy.

The injurious operation of the prevailing system has displayed itself in a variety of ways: but I shall only particularize four, which have borne oppressively on the farming interest.

1. It has converted a large portion of mechanics, manufacturers, and artisans into cultivators of the soil, and of course into rivals, instead of customers.

2. It has destroyed a most invaluable market for raw materials, and for a great variety of other articles, such as fuel, timber, and various horticultural and culinary productions, for which manufacturing establishments afford a ready market to the farmers in their vicinity, and few of which will bear the expenses of transportation.

3. It has discouraged the immigration of manufacturers, mechanics, and artisans, into this country—and

4. It has deprived the children of the farmers of profitable employment in manufacturing establishments.

Should I establish any one of these points, and still more if I establish the whole, it will appear very evident, that the farmers, who have always had a control over the choice of by far the majority of the members of the general and state legislatures, have not well consulted their individual interests.

That agricultural produce is too abundant in the united states, for the markets at home and abroad, is a fact which cannot be disputed for a moment. And it is as clear as the noon day sun, that this must arise from a supernumerary proportion of agriculturists to the other classes. It irresistibly follows that every measure, public or private, which tends to decrease the numbers of the other classes, and to increase that of the farmers, has an injurious bearing on the latter.

I will assume in round numbers, that each farmer raises produce to the amount of one hundred and sixty dollars per annum —that he consumes about eighty dollars—and that the remaining eighty serve to purchase clothing and other articles, and to pay that profit to which human industry is entitled, and which it cannot fail to receive in a well-ordered state of society. Now it follows that every manufacturer, who becomes a farmer, not only withdraws eighty dollars from the market for agricultural productions, but adds eighty to the quantity for sale. So that the effect is doubly injurious—it diminishes the demand—increases the supply—and, operating like a two-edged sword, cuts both ways.

It is obviously difficult to calculate the quantity raised—the quantity consumed—and the surplus—of farms in general. Precision is, however, neither attainable, nor in this case very necessary. Let any quantity be assumed, whether greater or less than I have stated, the result cannot fail to evince the pernicious consequences of forcing manufacturers to become farmers Let the latter class bear strongly in mind, that the operation constantly *converts customers into rivals*. To this important truth they do not appear to have paid any attention whatever. Ruinous are the results to themselves at present, and such they must continue without a total change of system.

That the effect of the policy pursued by this country, from the commencement of its government to the present time, has been to convert great numbers of the customers of our farmers into rivals, will, I trust, clearly appear in the course of this chapter.

When our manufacturers were suffering penury and distress for want of employment, and their wives and children were supported by overseers of the poor and by soup houses—when the establishments of their employers were crumbling into ruins, and their respectful and reiterated petitions for relief were wholly, not to say contumeliously, unnoticed or rejected, they were constantly consoled with the advice to "*go back*," and cultivate the soil. This had become a bye-word, and gone into general use. Necessity compelled thousands of the sufferers from time to time to comply. It is impossible to ascertain with precision the extent to which this operation was carried; but certainly it was immense. Those who consider the stream of population that has constantly flowed to the western country, for thirty years, will probably agree, that I am very moderate when I assume, that in the western states, and the interior of New York and Pennsylvania, there are probably 150,000 persons, manufacturers and descendants of manufacturers, who are now cultivating the soil, but who, under a proper system, would be engaged in manufactures. They quitted the anvil, the saw, the mallet, the shuttle, and the spindle, to which they had been accustomed, for the plough and the harrow, wholly new occupations—many of them with great reluctance. By increasing the surplus, they lower the price, of the productions of the earth, for which there is no adequate market, and thus add to the distress of the farmer, and of the country at large—which must suffer with the sufferings, and prosper with the prosperity, of any considerable class, but more particularly with the sufferings and prosperity of its most numerous class of citizens.

Were it necessary to add any facts or arguments to prove that this number is not extravagant, it would be sufficient to state, that investigations made by committees appointed for that particular purpose, proved that the number of persons who were thrown out of employment by the depression of manufactures, from 1816 to 1819, was—

In Pittsburg - - - - - - - - - - - - - - - -	1,288
Philadelphia, in thirty branches - - - - - - - -	7,288
	8,576

A large portion of whom, as there was in those places a redundancy in nearly all the other branches, must of necessity have "*gone back*" to the western country. The decay of business, and dismissal of workmen, in other places has been very great; in some more, in others less, than the above proportions. In Rhode Island the number of persons employed in the cotton branch alone was diminished 11,337 from 1816 to 1819.

In the chapter on immigration, I shall state such facts, as, taken in conjunction with the above, will prove that instead of 150,000 manufacturers and descendants of manufacturers, now engaged in agriculture, I might have assumed 250,000.

In order satisfactorily to evince the pernicious tendency of this disjointed state of things, it is necessary to establish the great extent of the market, thus destroyed—a market unaffected by embargoes or non-intercourse—independent upon European wars—and not liable to be disturbed by the sinister policy of foreign nations.

I will assume that the animal and vegetable food of each individual of society, before prices fell so extremely low, cost about one dollar per week.* At this rate, 150,000 persons would afford a market for 7,800,000 dollars per annum, which, as will appear by the following table, is nearly half of the amount of the average of the animals and animal and vegetable food exported to all the world, for the last eighteen years; and three-fourths of the whole of the exports of that description for the year 1820. I regret that I cannot carry the table farther back than the year 1803, at which period it commences in Seybert's statistics.

Table of Exports of animals and animal and vegetable food from 1803 *to* 1820 *inclusive.*†

	Animals and animal food.	Vegetable food.		Animals and animal food.	Vegetable food.
1803	$ 4,135,000	14,080,684		25,978,568	105,837,368
1804	4,284,568	12,080,684	1812	1,657,000	17,797,000
1805	3,385,000	11,752,000	1813	1,101,000	19,375,000
1806	3,274,000	11,050,000	1814	482,000	2,216,000
1807	3,086,000	14,432,000	1815	1,332,000	11,234,000
1808	968,000	2,550,000	1816	2,093,000	13,151,000
1809	1,811,000	8,751,000	1817	2,069,000	22,954,000
1810	2,169,000	10,750,000	1818	1,936,000	19,048,000
1811	2,866,000	20,391,000	1819	2,025,000	10,473,000
			1820	2,447,000	8,401,000
$	25,978,568	[illegible]5,837,368			
			Tota $	41,120,568 $	230,486,368

Animals and animal food - - - - - - - -	$41,120,568
Vegetable food - - - - - - - - - - - - -	230,486,368
Total for 18 years - - - - - - - - - -	$271,606,936
Average	$15,089,274

It is of importance to ascertain what proportion this bears to the total consumption of the country.

* Let it be remembered that this calculation embraces a period during a large portion of which flour was from eight to fourteen dollars per barrel—butchers' meat from six to twelve cents per pound—butter twenty-five to thirty cents—a turkey one dollar—fuel five to eight dollars per cord, &c. &c.

† Seybert, p. 147.

The population according to the census

Of 1800, was - - - - - - - - - - - - - -	5,319,762
1810 - - - - - - - - - - - - - - - - -	7,239,903
1820 - - - - - - - - - - - -	9,625,734
	22,185,399
Average population of the whole period, about	7,400,000

Let us suppose, as before, that the consumption of animal and vegetable food for each person, white and black, has been one dollar per week. The consumption of the united states at that rate would be 348,000,000 dollars per annum.

Synopsis.

Average annual domestic consumption of animal and vegetable food at one dollar per week, for 7,400,000 persons - - - - - - - -	$384,000,000
Average annual exportation, about 4 per cent. of the domestic consumption - - - -	$15,000,000

Yet this trivial exportation raised the price, most exorbitantly, of the immense quantity consumed at home.

In the preceding view of the injury received by the farmers from 150,000 manufacturers and descendants, being occupied in agriculture, I have not stated the extent of the evil. The calculation is made as if these persons were removed out of the states, or had merely ceased to eat and drink. In that case, the farmers would *only lose* so many customers—but alas! they have, as already stated, converted these valuable customers into rivals. It is therefore necessary to calculate what surplus they can bring into market, to compete with that class of society into which they have been with so much impolicy compelled to enter. I presume thirty dollars per head will not be regarded as extravagant, which will amount to four millions five hundred thousand dollars annually added to the quantity in the market.

Synopsis.

Amount of animal and vegetable food that would be required from the farmers by the 150,000 manufacturers, had they not become farmers themselves, at only one dollar per week - -	$7,800,000
Supplies raised by them for sale - - - - - -	4,500,000
Actual annual injury to the farming interest	$12,300,000

Thus, it appears clearly, that the conversion of so many manufacturers into farmers, not only destroys a most invaluable market, one-third of that afforded by the wars and desolations of Europe, and which their cessation has literally annihilated, but adds nearly a third part of the quantity which found a market abroad. Is it then wonderful that throughout a large part of the western country wheat averages a quarter dollar per bushel, and that other articles are at an equally low rate?

How utterly unlike the policy of the Dutch, so often quoted, has been that of our farmers! Whenever the harvest of spices, of which the Dutch had for a long time the monopoly, was too abundant, they destroyed a part proportioned to the extra quantity, in order to prevent their becoming a drug in consequence of the glut. Our farmers on the contrary by their legislation, have uninterruptedly pursued a system of which the direct and necessary effect is to increase the number of their rivals, and the surpluses, and of course to produce a glut. They have most unfortunately for themselves succeeded in this wayward policy.

Those who have studied the state of markets with attention, know the effect of superabundance and scarcity in enhancing and reducing the price of commodities. The scarcity or superabundance bears but a small proportion to the enhancement or reduction.

The Havanna case stated, Chap. v. is sufficient to establish the effect of competition in lowering prices.

I will now present two important instances of the effect of scarcity or increased demand enhancing the price of the necessaries of life to an extraordinary and almost incredible extent.

The year 1799 was very unfavourable for wheat in England. The weather was uncommonly wet, and the average deficiency throughout the kingdom, according to Arthur Young, one of the most accurate writers in Europe, on agricultural affairs, who made the most minute investigation of the subject, was about seven twentieths, or a little above one-third of the usual crop.* Yet the price rose one hundred per cent in about a year—notwithstanding the most extraordinary exertions on the part of the government to prevent it by high bounties on importation, and by regulating the consumption of bread by law, forbidding the use of it until one day old—and notwithstanding, likewise, the substitution of potatoes and various other kinds of vegetable food in place of wheat.

* The question of scarcity plainly stated, and remedies considered. By Arthur Young, Esq. F. R. S. and Secretary to the Board of Agriculture. Page 31.

Average price of Wheat per bushel in England, in 1799, 1800.

		s.	d.			s.	d.
1799	March - - -	6	2	1799	September - - -	9	5
	April - - -	6	8		October - -	10	5
	May - - -	7	7		November -	11	3
	June - - -	7	11		December - -	11	8
	July - - -	8	4	1800	January - -	11	10
	August - - -	9	1		February - -	12	8*

Of the exertions made to prevent famine, some idea may be formed from a statement of the amount of grain imported into England from Sept. 26, 1799, to Sept. 27, 1800.

1,261,932	quarters of wheat and flour, equal to 10,095,456 bushels of - - - - - - - - - - - - -	wheat
67,988	- - - - - - bushels - - - - -	barley
479,320	- - - - - - do. - - - - -	oats
300,693	- - - - - - cwt. - - - - -	rice†

The manufacture of starch and distillation of spirits from grain were moreover prohibited.‡

This is a strong case, and would of itself be sufficient to establish by analogy how very powerful is the effect of superabundance in reducing price, which is exactly equal to the operation of scarcity in its enhancement.

But a much stronger domestic case presents itself, which deserves serious attention. It speaks volumes on this subject.

The price of superfine flour in our seaport towns was about four dollars per barrel at the commencement of the French revolution. It rose during the progress of that memorable era in the history of the world, to 6, 8, 10, 12, and even 14 dollars per barrel, in consequence of the demand for Europe and the West Indies. The average was probably eight.

It might naturally be concluded, that one-half, or at least one-third of our crops of wheat, was exported. It will therefore appear astonishing that the quantity was not one-fifth part of what was consumed at home, as will appear by the following

* Idem, pp. 49 and 61.
† Dodsley's Annual Register, vol. 42, page 104.
‡ Idem, p. 127.

Table of the exports of wheat and flour from the United States from 1791 *to* 1820.*

	Bushels of wheat.	Barrels of flour.		Bushels of wheat.	Barrels of flour.
1791	1,018,339	619,681		5,611,275	12,190,931
1792	853,790	824,464	1806	86,784	782,724
1793	1,450,575	1,074,639	1807	766,814	1,249,819
1794	696,797	846,010	1808	87,330	263,813
1795	141,273	687,369	1809	393,889	846,247
1796	31,226	725,194	1810	325,924	798,431
1797	15,655	515,633	1811	216,833	1,445,012
1798	15,021	567,558	1812	53,832	1,443,492
1799	10,056	519,265	1813	288,535	1,260,943
1800	26,853	653,052	1814		193,274
1801	239,929	1,102,444	1815	17,634	862,739
1802	280,281	1,156,248	1816	62,321	729,053
1803	686,415	1,311,853	1817	96,407	1,479,198
1804	127,024	810,008	1818	196,808	1,157,697
1805	18,041	777,513	1819	82,065	750,660
			1820	22,137	1,177,036
	5,611,275	12,190,931		8,308,588	26,631,069

Export of flour - - - - - - - - - -	barrels	26,631,069
wheat 8,308,588 bushels, equal to barrels of flour - - - - - -		1,661,717
Total for thirty years - - - - - - - - - -		28,292,786
Average - - - - - - - - - - - - - - - -		9,430,92[illegible]

In order to ascertain the consumption, it remains to calculate the average population of that period.

Population in 1790 - - - - - - - - - - - - -	3,929.326
1800 - - - - - - - - - - - - -	5,319,762
1810 - - - - - - - - - - - - -	7,239,903
1820 - - - - - - - - - - - - -	9,625,734
Total - - - - - - - - - - - - - - - - -	26,114,725

Being for the whole period an average of about 6,550,000.

I will assume, that about 3,000,000 of these persons consumed wheaten flour of various kinds; and that their consumption was about one barrel and three quarters per annum, which is the average admitted by some of the best English statistical writers. This will give an annual consumption of 5,250,000 of barrels of flour. It is hence manifest, that the annual export of 960,000

* Pitkin's Tables, p. 111.

barrels raised the price of above 5,250,000 from four dollars to an average of eight.

Supposing that about 2,000,000 of the free citizens of the united states were not farmers; and consumed, as above, one barrel and three quarters each, per annum, equal in the whole to 3,500,000 barrels; it will appear that by this rise they paid their farming fellow citizens 14,000,000 of dollars per annum extra for their flour, in consequence of the war in Europe. This, from the year 1791 to 1815, a period of twenty-five years, would amount to 350,000,000 dollars on that single article—and all other articles rose in nearly the same proportion.

I have just received a Pittsburg price current, which, with "a pencil of light" displays the ruinous effects of our system on the farmers. They hailed the arrival of the day when manufactured articles would be cheap, as a Millennium. The day has arrived. Manufactures are as low as they could desire. What is the consequence? Their best customers are bankrupted. And their own situation is incomparably worse than ever it was. Cheap as manufactures are, it requires far more labour to buy them than was necessary when they were dear.

Pittsburg, Feb. 5, 1821.

Flour - - - - -	per barrel	$1 75	Pork - - - -	per pound *cts.*	3
Whiskey - - - -	per gallon	16	Veal - - - -	do.	3
Wheat - - - -	per bushel	37½	Venison - - -	do.	3
Oats - - - - - -	do.	15	Butter - - - -	do.	12½
Corn - - - - - -	do.	25	Lard - - - -	do.	6
Apples - - - -	do.	25	Bacon - - - -	do.	6
Beef - - - - -	per pound	3			

When superfine broad cloth during the war was fourteen dollars per yard, they could buy a yard for two barrels of flour. The same kind of cloth, imported, can now be had for ten dollars—but requires at Pittsburg nearly six barrels of flour to pay for it. If this monstrous and lamentable fact, does not awaken the farmers out of their lethargy—display their vital interests in their true colours—and lead them to use their efforts to effect a change of system, it will deserve to be ranked among the most inexplicable instances of impolicy to be found on human records.

These facts and suggestions are on a topic of immense importance, not merely to the farmers, but to the entire nation. They are most respectfully submitted to public consideration, with a firm belief that they are radically correct—or at least that any errors—*quos incuria fudit*—will not materially affect the result.

CHAPTER VI.

Advantages of the immigration of the productive classes of Society. Policy of France and England. Ruinous of the former—profoundly wise of the latter. Case of Flanders. Immigration into the united states.

THE second pernicious effect of our present system of policy on the nation at large, but more particularly on the farmers, is, that its obvious tendency has been to discourage immigration of useful members of society belonging to the manufacturing class, who would afford a market for the surplus of the produce of the soil.

It would be superfluous to undertake to prove the advantages of an increase of any of the productive classes of society. It is admitted by all wise statesmen, that the strength of the state, and the pride of its rulers, is a numerous and useful population, steadily employed in adding to the wealth and resources of the country. A numerous population, partly unemployed, or engaged in labour which does not recompense the capital, time, and industry bestowed on it, as has been the case with so large a portion of our citizens, proves a radical unsoundness in its policy.

Immigrations of the productive classes have been encouraged in countries with population tenfold greater than ours, in proportion to their extent, and have been found eminently beneficial. History is replete with monitory examples on this important point.

Flanders for centuries possessed a monopoly of the woollen trade, and derived immense wealth by drawing the raw material from England, and supplying her and other nations with the manufactured article at treble, quadruple, and quintuple the price of the wool. A small number of immigrants, encouraged by Edward III. introduced improvements, and extended the manufacture in England, and laid the foundation of the future greatness of that nation, which was thereby liberated from the tribute she had been accustomed to pay to the talents and skill of the native country of those immigrants.

France had for years a monopoly of some of the most valuable manufactures in the world, which the emigrants whom the repeal of the edict of Nantz drove out of the kingdom, spread throughout Europe. England, by this wicked and impolitic measure, acquired such accessions of talent, skill, and capital, as greatly facilitated her progress to the high standing she has enjoyed among the nations of the earth.

Those who fled to Saxony increased and improved the manufactures of the country, and communicated the art of making that elegant tint, called Saxon blue, which has been a great source of wealth and prosperity to that nation.*

There is not, perhaps there scarcely ever was, a country in the world to which the immigration of productive labourers ought to be more an object of desire than the united states. Our population bears a smaller proportion to our territory, than that of any other nation.

There is no nation, moreover, to which those ardent and active spirits, who, suffering hardships and penury at home, seek to mend their fortunes in foreign climes, look with more eagerness than the united states. The eyes of Europe are directed hither.

The distresses, oppression, and misery, which the labouring classes in Europe have suffered, and still suffer, would have doubled the immigrations, had proper encouragement been afforded. Many of the manufacturing portion of those who arrived, in general found it difficult to locate themselves in our cities, where every place was filled. Some of them "*went back*" to the western states, and devoted themselves to the culture of the soil—others found employment at their proper trades in country towns—but no small portion of them returned to their native countries.

The policy pursued by our government from its commencement, was calculated to crush all attempts at the great manufactures of clothing, on which so large a portion of the national wealth has been expended, to support the manufacturers and governments of Europe.

I do not aver this was the intention: but it was a necessary effect of the system. For some years after the adoption of the federal constitution, the duty on cotton and woollen goods was only five per cent. ad valorem—it then rose, in consequence of the increased wants of the treasury, to seven and a half—and some years afterwards to twelve and a half.

It would be an insult to the common sense of the reader to suppose that any competition could be maintained, under such duties, by our citizens with the manufacturers of England,

* "Those who fled to Saxony were received with that humanity which distress is entitled to, and with a liberality of welcome which might be expected from an enlightened and patriotic sovereign. They contributed to perfect the manufactures of the country, and laid the foundation of that fame which it has since attained on account of the perfection of its colouring. They were the first who introduced among the work people that particular tint which is denominated the Saxon blue. *In every place where the fugitives fixed their subsequent abode, they contributed, by their exertion, their skill, connections, and capital, to the success of the native manufactures, and enabled them with more decided superiority to rival those of France."—Luccock on Wool, page* 60.

possessed of immense capitals—labour-saving machinery—governmental protection in the domestic market—and, in a word, of every advantage which the most enlightened policy could afford. The contest would have been wholly hopeless. It would have been the attack of a sloop of war on a vessel of the line—a dwarf on a Hercules.

The consequence was such as might have been expected. In the year 1800 there were used in manufacturing establishments in the united states only 500 bales of

cotton, or - - - - - - - -	lbs. 150,000*
In the same year we exported - -	lbs. 17,789,263†
And, wonderful fact! we imported, of goods paying 12½ per cent. ad valorem, - -	$ 16,637, 257‡
of which three-fourths were for clothing, or about - - - - - - - -	$ 12,000,000
In 1805, we consumed in manufacturing establishments 1000 bales - - - - -	lbs. 300,000§
In the same year we exported - -	lbs. 29,602,428‖
And imported goods at 15 per cent. ad valorem to the amount of - -	$ 37,137,596¶
of which, as before, about three-fourths were for clothing, - - - - - - -	$ 28,000,000

It would be difficult to find an instance, in the annals of commerce, of such a ruinous traffic—such a prodigal waste of national resources.

On the wretched and depressed state of the woollen manufacture, it is enough to refer to the never-to-be-forgotten fact, that shortly previous to the commencement of the late war, when there was a non-intercourse with England, such was the difficulty of procuring five or six thousand blankets for the Indians, that a formal proposition from the secretary at war was laid before congress, to suspend that act, in order to obtain the supply. A more admonitory example never occurred, of the folly and danger of depending on foreign nations for articles of prime necessity.

The linen, cotton, stocking, pottery, stone, earthen ware, and various other manufactures stood on nearly the same ground of depression. Almost the only establishment for hosiery in the country was at Germantown.

It is therefore obvious that from 1789 till the period of the restrictive system in 1808–9, there was no encouragement for cotton, woollen, linen, or stocking weavers, potters, or persons

* Report of the Committee on Commerce and Manufactures.
† Seybert, 95. ‡ Idem, 163.
§ Report of the Committee on Commerce and Manufactures.
‖ Seybert 112. ¶ Idem 164.

of a variety of other trades and professions; that vast numbers were probably prevented from migrating to this country; and that those who arrived here, and did not return, were obliged to betake themselves to other occupations—among which there can be no doubt thousands devoted themselves to agriculture.

From the preceding statement it is manifest that our policy has discouraged the immigration of manufacturers—has in some measure compelled immigrants of that description to become farmers and of consequence rivals to those to whom they would otherwise have been customers—and that so far as it has operated in this respect, it has been among the sources of the present distress of the respectable class of agriculturists.

The demand for our agricultural productions in Europe and the West Indies, during the continuance of the wars of the French revolution, prevented the development of the ruinous consequences of this policy. They are now visited on us with unmitigated severity.

It remains to ascertain the extent of immigration, notwithstanding all these untoward and inauspicious circumstances.

The want of data prevents me from going farther back than 1817. I shall therefore confine myself to that and the three succeeding years.

According to Dr. Seybert, the immigrations in the year 1817, into ten ports were 22,240.*

Boston - - -	2,200	Baltimore - -	1,817
New York - -	7,634	Norfolk - - -	520
Perth Amboy - -	637	Charleston - -	747
Philadelphia - -	7,085	Savannah - - -	163
Wilmington, D. -	558	New Orleans - -	879
			22,240

The immigrants registered in the port of New York, in the years 1818 and 1819, according to a statement of the mayor of that city were 19,885.

The mayor states that there is one-third of the whole number omitted—this would make the total 28,827.

It is probable that about two-fifths of all the immigrants into this country arrive in New-York.

This would make, in 1818 and 1819, for all the united states, - - - - - - - 70,000

Or, per annum, - - - - - 35,000

* Statistics, p. 29.

But I shall assume that the numbers in the rest of the union are only equal to those who arrived in New York, which, notwithstanding the variety of discouraging circumstances that existed, makes, per annum, about - 28,000

It is difficult to conceive the extent to which immigration would have been carried, had those who arrived, been able to locate themselves comfortably, and to write home such flattering accounts as in that case they would have done, to those who were panting to follow them. It is not improbable that it would have amounted to 50 or 60,000 per annum, who would have added immensely to the wealth, power, and resources of the country.

The secretary of the treasury, in a report on the subject of the tariff in 1820, presents a sound and luminous observation on the subject of manufactures generally, and on the effect which would be produced by an adequate protection.—He says,

" The situation of the countries from which our foreign ma-" nufactures have been principally drawn, authorises the expec-" tation, that in the event of a monopoly of the market being " secured to our manufacturing fellow citizens, *a considerable* " *portion of the manufacturing skill and industry of those coun-* " *tries will be promptly transferred to the united states, and incor-* " *porated with the domestic capital of the union.*"

Here, in a few words, is developed an outline of the true policy of the united states, to which, unfortunately, scarcely any attention has been paid. A monopoly, by which he meant an absolute prohibition, was not necessary: such a degree of protection as would have prevented our citizens from being driven out of their own markets, would have been amply sufficient. But we prefer having our workmen in Europe—raising food and raw materials—and shipping them there to feed and keep them employed. The number of persons thus usually labouring for us in Europe, would, if removed to this country, afford a market for nearly the whole surplus of food we export. And thus, to use, the words of the secretary, it was in our power by proper encouragement, to have "*promptly transferred to the united states a considerable portion of the skill and industry*" of a great part of the nations of Europe.

The distresses and wretchedness suffered by the immigrants, in 1819, were truly lamentable. They wandered about our streets, as I have stated, after having exhausted their resources in search of employment, but in vain. Persons who had been brought up to nice and elegant branches of business, were by necessity compelled to saw and split wood, and perform other laborious and painful offices for a livelihood. Great numbers of those who had the means of returning, availed themselves of the opportunity, and gave as tremendous accounts of the country as

Joshua's messengers gave of Canaan. Numerous applications were made to the British consuls here and elsewhere, by some of the sufferers, who could not find work, and who had no means of returning, to procure them passages home—which in some instances were accorded—in others refused.

The number of persons who have thus returned, has been far more considerable than is supposed. I make no doubt that they amounted to 1200 per annum for the last three years. Sixty have recently sailed in one vessel from New York, according to a statement from the British consul there—and twenty, thirty, forty, and fifty, have from time to time sailed in different vessels from that port and from Philadelphia. Some of them have tried their fortunes in a settlement on the island of Cuba: and some have gone to Canada and the other British settlements on this continent.

It is fair to presume that the terror inspired by every returned emigrant, prevented the emigration of numbers of those who had previously yearned after this country.

In consequence, immigration, in 1820, sunk down to 7001, according to a semi-official statement in the National Calender, for 1821, in which a novel classification is adopted—Useful and productive class; useful unproductive; ornamental and amusing unproductive.

Useful and productive class - - - - -	1,987
Useful unproductive class - - - - - - -	1,730
Ornamental and amusing unproductive class -	148
Persons whose occupations are unknown - -	3,136
	7,001

Of the first class there were,	farmers, - - -	806
	planters, - - -	66
	gardeners, - -	25
		897

The remaining 1090 of the first class comprise persons of the following trades.

Artificer	1	Dyers	3	Rigger	1
Bakers	58	Fishermen	4	Rope makers	5
Basket makers	5	Flaxdresser	1	Rule makers	2
Blacksmiths	35	Goldsmith	1	Saddlers	4
Block makers	7	Gunsmiths	3	Sail makers	2
Boat builders	4	Harness makers	3	Seamstresses	10
Book binder	1	Hatters	5	Ship carpenters	5
Boot makers	3	Iron founder	1	Shoemakers	82
Bricklayers	6	Labourers	289	Silversmiths	2
Brickmaker	1	Leather dresser	1	Slater	1
Brazier	1	Mantua makers	5	Soap boilers	2
Brass founders	2	Manufacturers	7	Stay makers	2
Brewers	6	Masons	12	Stone cutters	8
Butchers	37	Mattrass maker	1	Sup. of glass works	1
Button maker	1	Mechanics	31	Tailors	55
Cabinet makers	22	Milliners	17	Tailor and farmer	1
Carpenters	114	Millers	9	Tanners	5
Chair makers	4	Millwrights	2	Tanner and currier	1
Chandlers	6	Morocco dresser	1	Tinker	1
Cloth dressers	3	Nail maker	1	Tobacconists	6
Clothiers	9	Painters	13	Turner	1
Cloth manufacturer	1	Paper makers	2	Umbrella makers	2
Coopers	33	Pin and needle makers	2	Watch makers	6
Coppersmiths	4	Plasterers	7	Weavers	61
Cotton spinner	1	Plumbers	3	Wheelwrights	4
Curriers	10	Potters	2	White smiths	4
Cutlers	5	Printers	4	Waxmakers	2
Distillers	5	Refiner	1		
					1090
				Brought down	897
				Total	1987

Here a most serious reflection strikes the mind. A nation with a thousand millions of acres uncultivated, and not likely to be fully cultivated for centuries to come—with almost every advantage that heaven ever bestowed on any portion of the globe—a nation, which, under a sound policy, could provide for half the population of Europe—and which, more than any nation in the world, would be benefitted by immigration—receives an accession of 1987 persons of the most useful classes of society—farmers—planters—gardeners—manufacturers—mechanics—artisans—and labourers—of whom a considerable portion have families—and this accession, strange as it may appear, is of very doubtful advantage either to the country or themselves!*

In the present state of things, can the accession of 806 farmers be beneficial? Is not the class of farmers already too numerous, and the produce of agriculture too abundant, and so cheap as not to pay for the labour, time, talent, and capital it requires? Does not every farmer who arrives from abroad increase the surplus, and is not the tendency, of course, to lower the prices, already ruinously depressed? On the other hand, can the arrival of blacksmiths, masons, carpenters, coopers,

* Written in Feb. 1821.

weavers, &c. &c. be advantageous,—as there are so many of them here destitute of employment? Does not every one who arrives, if employed, displace some one of our actual citizens? In the absence of every other proof of the unsoundness of our policy, this would be abundantly sufficient to establish it beyond the power of contradiction.

CHAPTER VII.

Market for raw materials destroyed. Quantity of wool in 1820. *Increase. State of the sheep and the woollen manufacture in England and France.*

DURING the war, the prosperous state of manufactures afforded the farmers an advantageous market for raw materials, as wool, iron, hemp, flax, leather, &c. &c. the want of which that class of citizens feel most oppressively by the depression and downfall of so many large establishments. This circumstance has powerfully co-operated in producing the present stagnation and distress, which they feel so severely. Were this market revived, it would spread prosperity where gloom and dismay prevail.

In this investigation I shall not consider any of the raw materials, except wool. The calculations are more simple, and reducible to a more tangible form. But all the reasoning which applies to wool, so far as regards the farming interest, will apply with equal force to hemp, flax, skins, hides, timber, &c.

It is to be regretted that the statistics of the united states are in a very imperfect state, and do not afford such materials for calculation as would be requisite to arrive at that degree of certainty which the importance of the subject requires. We must avail ourselves of the best which the nature of the case affords.

Of the quantity of our sheep—the amount of their flocks—the value of the wool—and the extent of the woollen manufacture, there is scarcely a trace to be found, previous to the publication of Mr. Coxe's Tables, drawn from the returns of the marshals, in 1810, when the restrictive system had given a considerable spring to manufactures generally.

Mr. Coxe states, that it was believed that the growth of wool in the united states, in 1812, was from 20, to 22,000,000 *lbs.**—but that there were some who made a higher estimate.

* Statement of the arts and manufactures of the united states, for the year 1810, page 13.

The quantity had increased, in two years, several millions of pounds.

It would be waste of time to prove, that such a protection as is afforded to the woollen manufacture in England and France, would have created so great a demand for wool, as would have inclined and justified the farmers in increasing the numbers of their sheep, which would have diminished the number of acres employed in raising grain, and thus lessened that surplus of the latter, which has produced the great reduction of the price of bread stuffs.

It will not be controverted that in the eight years which have elapsed since 1812, the increase would probably have been 50 per cent.—which would give 30, to 32,000,000*lbs.*

The briskness of demand would have secured a good price. I do not calculate on the very extravagant prices which prevailed during the war, two, three, and four dollars per pound for washed merino wool. I will suppose that the price of common wool, now fifty cents per lb. would be steady at seventy-five cents.

It is difficult to ascertain what is the quantity sheared at present. Whether it has increased, decreased, or remained stationary since 1812, we have no means of ascertaining. The lamentable havoc made of the merino sheep would lead to the belief that there was rather a decrease. But I will admit that it has remained stationary. At all events, if it has increased, it does not affect the calculation; as whatever may be the number, at present, adequte protection of the woollen manufacture would, as already stated, have increased it probably 50 per cent.

Suppose it now 22,000,000 lbs. at half a dollar, it amounts to - - - - - -	$11,000,000
But assuming an increase of quantity, not of 50 per cent. but of 30, it would amount to	lbs. 28,600,000
And assuming, that a proper encouragement of manufactures would have raised the price to 75 cents, 28,600,000 lbs. would amount to -	$21,450,000

Here (beyond the power of contradiction) would be a difference in one single article in favour of the farming interest of $ 10,000,000. Had I assumed a twofold increase, of quantity and price, as I believe I might have done, it would have made a difference of above $30,000,000. But it is preferable to be within such boundary lines as even an opponent must admit.

The gain to the farmers by an increased consumption of hemp, flax, leather, &c. would probably equal that on wool. Details are unnecessary—as a very slight consideration is sufficient to evince the great importance of these almost inexhaustible sources of wealth.

A slight sketch of the state of the sheep, the wool, and woollen manufacture in England and France. may throw some light on this subject, and shew what immense advantages they derive, and which we might derive from a due encouragement of this branch of industry.

The sheep and lambs in Great Britain and Ireland, are, according to Colquhoun -		40,000,000
The woollen manufacture in England from		
English wool - -	£20,000,000	
Spanish wool - - -	6,000,000	£
		26,000,000
Cost of the raw material - - - -		8,000,000
National gain - - - - - -		£ 18,000,000*
Equal to - - - - - - -		$ 81,000,000
The average amount of Spanish wool imported into England for six years, from 1807 to 1812 - - - - - - -	lbs.	7,329,795 †
The annual weight of the wool shorn in France is - - -	killogrammes	37,188,910
Of which the value is - - -	Fr.	81,339,317
The whole trade in wool, and fabrics of wool, in France, is - - - - -	Fr.	238,133,932 ‡
Equal to about - - - - -		$ 47,000,000

I shall close this subject with a brief sketch of the state of the sheep and the wool in a single county in England.

Lincolnshire contains 75,000 souls—1,848,000 acres of land—2,400,000 sheep—and of wool, according to Arthur Young, in 1799, it produced 21,600,000 lbs.||

The sheep, however, it is to be observed, are the long fleeced, which yield nearly twice as much wool as the other species. This wool is adapted to coarse goods, as blankets, kerseys, &c.

Luccock, who has written much more recently than Young, viz. in 1809, gives a different account of the state of Lincolnshire, as regards the number of sheep. His statement is as follows—

* Wealth, Power and Resources of Great Britain, p. 91. † Ibid.

‡ Chaptal, De L'Industrie Francoise, vol. ii. pp. 132. 135.

|| General view of the Agriculture of the County of Lincoln, p. 367.

	Sheep.	Weight of fleece.
Lincoln rich land	1,241,625	8 lbs.
Marshes	87,500	9
Miscellaneous land	505,657	8
	1,834,782	

As there are but 87,500 sheep, whose fleeces exceed eight pounds—that weight may be said to be the average of the county. The average of that species throughout England, appears by the same author, about 7½ lbs.

An important fact has recently occurred, which greatly elucidates this subject—

The Oriskany Manufacturing Company have purchased for six thousand dollars, 9000 lbs. of wool, shorn from the flock of Mr. Isaac Smith. This immense amount of a single purchase, abundantly proves the transcendently ruinous effects on the agricultural interest of the destruction of so many manufacturing establishments as have fallen sacrifices to the pernicious policy of the tariff of 1816.

CHAPTER VIII.

The last injurious effect of the prevailing system is, that it deprives the wives and children of the farmers and country labourers of profitable employment in manufacturing establishments.

Among the host of objections which have been arrayed against the encouragement of manufactures, the folly and the evil consequences of withdrawing labourers from the culture of the soil, employment so much more useful, innocent and profitable, held a conspicuous place, and afforded ample scope for declamation. It did not avail, as I have already stated, that few or none of the male sex were wanted for those manufactures which required protection.

The rise of manufacturing establishments throughout the united states, elevated thousands of the young people of both sexes, but principally the females, belonging to the families of the cultivators of the soil in their vicinity, from a state of penury and idleness to competence and industry. Their fall has precipitated large numbers of them to their former state.

On this subject, I shall advance but few facts—but I trust they will be found decisive.

At Waltham factory, near Boston, on which the opposers of the protection of manufactures place so much reliance, there are, as we have seen, but 14 men to 286 women and children. These last are chiefly the daughters of the neighbouring farmers.

There is another extensive factory, situated at Fishkill, on the North River, where there are from 70 to 80 persons employed, of whom five-sixths are girls and young women, some of whom, before the establishment of the factory, were, with their parents, in a state of poverty and idleness, bare-footed, and living in wretched hovels. But since that period, they are comfortably fed and clothed—their habits and manners and dwellings greatly improved—and they have become useful members of society. Their wages vary according to their skill and industry, from one dollar and a quarter per week to three dollars.

Similar cases, to a very great extent, are to be found, throughout the united states, in every place where manufactories are established.

Mr. Gallatin, in conformity with a call from congress, in the year 1810, made an interesting report on the state of the manufactures of the united states, which contains a great body of most useful information. One important fact, bearing upon the present subject, is deserving of the most serious attention of the farmers.

There was then a factory in Rhode Island, which, as he states, empoyed—

In the factory.			In neighbouring families.		
Males,	24		Males,	50	
Females,	29		Females,	75	
	—	53		—	125

Judging from the state of other establishments, it is fair to presume that more than one-half of the whole number were probably young females, who, but for this factory, would have been without employment, and spending their time perniciously—a burden to their parents and society—trained up to vicious courses—but thus happily preserved from idleness and its attendant vices and crimes—and whose wages probably averaged one dollar and a half per week, or 7000 dollars per annum, distributed among fifty or sixty of the adjacent farmers. Those employed "in the neighbouring families," were persons principally devoted to farming, who by these means were enabled to "*gather up the fragments of time*," which would otherwise be wholly "*lost*."

At the date of the recent census, there were of free white females, between 10 and 16 years of age,	604,912
Of 16, and under 26 - - - - - -	780,865
	1,385,477
Supposing the agricultural class to embrace five-eighths of the whole population, then of the above number there are, belonging to that class -	865,920

The services of females of the specified ages, employed in agriculture—for, which, moreover, above one-half of them are too young or too delicate—are very unproductive. At manufactures they are far more valuable, and command higher wages, as I have already stated, from one dollar and a quarter to three dollars per week.

It will not be unfair to assume, that, under a proper order of things, manufactures of various kinds would find employment for - - - 200,000

of them, embracing the chief part of those who are 10, 11, 12, and 13 years of age, whose labour would otherwise be of little value.

As objections may be made to the number of 200,000, exclusive of those now employed in agriculture and manufactures, I state the data on which it is predicated.

The committee of commerce and manufactures, in their report of the year 1816, state, that, of the persons employed in the cotton manufacture, the preceding year, viz. 100,000

There were males below 17 years of age	24,000	
Of 17 and above - - - - -	10,000	
Women and female children - -	66,000	
		100,000

About the same number of persons were employed in the woollen manufacture—but the proportions of the sexes are not stated. They were probably about the same as in the cotton branch.

It is to be presumed, as about 120, or 130,000 females were employed in two branches, which were then only in their infancy, particularly the woollen—that the number I have assumed is very far too low.

Now, supposing the wages to average but two dollars per week, which, in a flourishing state of manufactures, would be moderate, it would amount, for the 200,000, to the enormous sum per annum of - - - - - -	$20,800,000
Supposing the raw materials to be fifty per cent. more than the wages, the manufactured articles would amount to about per annum -	$50,000,000

absolutely saved to the nation.

A large portion of the wages would go to enrich the farmers, and extricate them from their present distress.

But to avoid all cavil, I shall assume the number of females thus employed to be only 120,000, and the wages to average only one dollar and a half, which would amount to, per annum	$9,360,000
And supposing the raw material only equal to the wages, the manufacture would amount to	$18,720,000

These facts and arguments require no comment. They speak to the farming interest in language not to be misunderstood—evince the ruinous consequences of the prevailing system—and point out the imperious necessity of a speedy and effectual change.

CHAPTER IX.

Conclusion. Recapitulation of the disadvantages of the present system. Extent of the advance proposed by the new tariff. Imports, and duties ad valorem, for the year 1820.

We have seen that the prevailing system produces the most serious injury to the farming interest, in four different points:

1. It increases the number of the producers, and the surplus, of bread stuffs, and of course reduces the price.

2. It discourages the immigration of thousands of persons, who would be customers to the farmers.

3. It in many cases impairs—and in a variety wholly destroys the market for raw materials.

4. It deprives the young, particularly the female branches of the families of the farmers, of useful employment, whereby, instead of aiding in the general support, they are rendered rather burdensome.

To compensate for this catalogue of evils, there ought to be some mighty and obvious advantages, which would not only counterbalance, but outweigh them. This requires to be ascertained.

The investigation is of great importance.

The grand object is to procure *goods* from foreign countries, *cheaper* than the same kinds can be procured at home.

I suppress the crowd of reflections which arise in the mind, at the idea of consigning our workmen to pauperism—their employers to bankruptcy—magnificent establishments to decay and ruin, once the scenes of joy and gladness—of industry and happiness—of increase to the wealth and resources of the nation—for any possible gain, even if the amount were twenty fold what is supposed These reflections would lead to uncomfortable feelings, and might excite ill will.

I suppress likewise all considerations of the transcendent impolicy of exhausting the country of its specie—paralizing every species of industry—and supporting foreign manufacturers, while our own are suffering.—I shall confine myself to ascertain the amount of the gain, real or supposed; that is, what advantage is derived from an adherence to the old, and rejection of the proposed tariff.

The whole amount of the importations of 1820, which paid duties ad valorem, was - - $39,885,467

This embraced a great variety of manufactured articles not at all affecting the national industry—and of course not requiring any alteration in the duty, as well as articles not belonging to the class of manufactures. But I will for the sake of argument admit that the whole belonged to that class.

The white population of the united states is presumed to be nearly - - - - - 8,000,000

Of course the ad valorem importations do not average five dollars per head.

Were the duties doubled, and even were there no diminution of imports, the burden would not be felt, provided the country was in a prosperous situation.

But there was no idea of doubling the duties.

It remains to ascertain what was actually contemplated, and what would have been the effect of the proposed alteration of the tariff.

The amount of the ad valorem duties, which embrace very nearly the whole of the manufactured articles, about which alone there is question, was, for the last year, - - - - - $8,076,161

The average of the duties was about 22 per cent.

Merchandise paying duties ad valorem, imported into the united states, A. D. 1820.

1,679,284	dollars, at	7½	per cent.	$125,946 28
13,971,593	do.	15	do.	2,095,738 95
5,979,736	do.	20	do.	1,195,947 23
16,355,698	do.	25	do.	4,088,924 43
11,215	do.	27½	do.	3,084 12
1,882,399	do.	30	do.	564,719 79
5,542	do.	32½	do.	1,801 05
$39,885,467				$8,076,161.85*

* Report of the Secretary of the Treasury.

It was proposed to raise to 33⅓ those which now pay 25, which constitute nearly one-half of the whole, and embrace all the articles of cotton and woollen goods, except a very few of the former, invoiced below 25 cents per yard. The rate proposed is one-third advance on the existing tariff.

Those articles on which the advance is greater, are unimportant. I will, however, suppose, that the advance on the whole would be 37½ per cent.; the addition, then, supposing—which is not likely—the same amount of goods imported, would be - - - - - $ 3,028,560

This is the whole amount of the additional duties proposed to be laid by the new tariff, so far as manufacturers or manufactures are concerned, which have excited so much opposition from one end of the country to the other—an opposition which might lead to the opinion, that the plan was fraught with certain ruin, not only to the whole body of the farmers but to the nation.

The white population, as I have stated, is about 8,000,000

The addition to the tariff is intended to produce about - - - - - - - $ 3,000,000

Or 37½ cents per head, of which the manufacturers themselves would pay their full proportion. And as they and their families amount to about 1,500,000 souls, they would contribute at least 5, or 600,000 dollars.

Should it be asserted that the prices of domestic manufactures would be extravagantly enhanced, in consequence of the new tariff, I refer to Chap. IV. where that objection is fully answered.

The assertion that the manufacturers would pay their full proportion may require some explanation. In this there is no difficulty. The manufacturers of woollens would pay the duty on cottons, linens, silks, iron, &c.—the manufacturers of cotton would pay those on woollens, linens, &c.—and thus of all the other branches.

When we are all laid in our graves—and the passions have subsided, which the struggle, *whether we should work for ourselves, and feed and pay our workmen at home, or have our labour performed in Europe and the East Indies, and feed and pay the workmen there, has excited*—our posterity will mourn for the conduct of their ancestors, that there should be any diversity of sentiment on such a subject—and that so much deadly hostility should prevail against a measure of such obvious utility.

THE

FARMER's & PLANTER's FRIEND.

NO. I.

"The uniform appearance of an abundance of specie, as the concomitant of "a flourishing state of manufactures, and of the reverse, where they do not pre- "vail, afford a strong presumption of their favourable operation on the wealth of "a country."—*A. Hamilton.*

"Those who wish to make agriculture flourish in any country, can have no "hope of succeeding in the attempt but by bringing commerce and manufac- "tures to her aid; which, by taking from the farmer, his superfluous produce, "gives spirit to his operations, and life and activity to his mind."—*Anderson on National Industry.*

To the Farmers and Planters of the united states.

Friends and Fellow Citizens,

I REQUEST a patient and unbiassed consideration of a few brief essays, intended to display the baleful effects on your vital interests, which have flowed and continue to flow from the discouragement and depression manufactures have experienced, and from the numerous disadvantages under which manufacturers have laboured.

I invite a candid discussion of a subject which yields to none in importance—as well as a manly exposure of any errors I may fall into. No man can be more ready to point them out, than I shall be to acknowledge them.

The reasoning I shall employ, shall not be drawn from any consideration of, or regard for, the interests of the manufacturers. Arguments of this description have for years been reiterated in vain, until the subject is entirely exhausted. It would therefore be waste of time to touch on those topics. By arguments of a totally different character, entirely derived from a regard for your own dearest interests, I hope to prove that the embarrassments of our farmers, and the dangers impending over our planters, can be as fairly traced to the depression of manufactures, as any effect whatever can be traced to its exciting cause; that a total change of system may, and that nothing but such a change can, meliorate your situation.

In the present number I shall confine myself to the case of the farmers alone. I shall in future numbers discuss that of the planters.

I venture to assume as undeniable, a few plain propositions, so notoriously true as, I trust, to preclude the possibility of controversy by any fair or candid reader.

I. The present prices of nearly all kinds of the necessaries of life, and of some of the raw materials, produced by the farmers of the united states, are so low, in consequence of their great superabundance, as in most cases not to remunerate, and, in the best situations, to afford but a slender reward for the labour, time, and capital employed, more especially at a distance from the seaboard.

II. Hence a large proportion of our farmers, particularly in the western and in the interior of the middle states, are in a state of suffering and embarrassment.

III. This superabundance, and the consequent suffering of our farmers, must necessarily arise from this class of citizens being too numerous in proportion to the other classes.

IV. Hence every operation, public or private, which has increased, or may increase, the number of farmers, and consequently the surplus produce, without a proportionate increase and still more with a positive decrease, of the other classes, or without opening new markets, of which there is scarcely a prospect, must have tended, and now tends, to aggravate the evil.

These postulata being admitted, it only remains to prove, that the system of our government has had a steady, undeviating tendency to convert manufacturers into farmers, in order to establish the radical unsoundness of that system, so far as respects the farmers, and its pernicious operation on this numerous and respectable class of citizens. This tendency I undertake to demonstrate by the following facts and inductions.

The manufactures that minister to the clothing of mankind, are by far the most important; afford employment to the greatest number of people; and are therefore most particularly entitled to the fostering care of every government. It is therefore an extraordinary and astonishing fact, that until the commencement of the restrictive system, in 1807, the manufacture of cottons, linens, and woollens, except in private families, was almost wholly unknown in this country—although we exported on an average 30,000,000 lbs. of cotton annually; and had the capacity of raising wool and flax to an extent commensurate with our utmost wants. To this hour, manufactories of hosiery, linen, silk, delft, china, and cutlery, with all the other species of fine iron and steel, &c. &c. are nearly strangers in the land. Various other manufactures, for which our country is admirably fitted, exist only to a very limited extent, in consequence of our markets being glutted with rival articles of foreign production.

From the commencement of our government, thousands of persons have arrived in this country, from year to year, who were brought up to the cotton, woollen, linen, silk, hosiery, and other branches, and who, finding no employment in their proper sphere, devoted themselves to agriculture, which, during the wars of the French revolution, was prosperous, and held out strong temptations to allure them to devote themselves to that useful and important branch of industry. So long as the foreign markets afforded a vent for our surplus produce, the operation of this course of things, although it restricted the progress and prosperity of the country, was not injurious to the farmers: but it was not very difficult to anticipate that its pernicious consequences would freely and fully develop themselves in a season of peace, when those markets, which were then open to the products of our agricultural industry, would be closed. These consequences are now deeply and vitally felt by the farmers.

To appreciate the extent of the evil, with any thing like mathematical precision, is obviously impracticable. Data of this character are wholly unattainable. We must be satisfied to approximate as nearly as possible to facts. The calculations must, however, be more or less erroneous. But the errors cannot affect the position, that the effect of the system is highly pernicious to the farmers—and will only, as the case may be, somewhat diminish or increase the quantum of the evil, either below or beyond the reality.

It is difficult to ascertain the extent of immigration into this country, from the want of statistical tables on the subject. The information we have is imperfect. I must avail myself of what I am able to glean up, which do not extend beyond five years.

In 1816, according to various statements in the Weekly Register, there arrived at least Emigrants	20,000
In 1817, according to Dr. Seybert, there arrived in ten ports,	22,240*
In 1818 and 1819. according to the mayor of New York, there arrived in that single port,†	28,000
Supposing that the numbers who arrived in all the other ports in the united states in 1818 and 1819, were only equal to those who landed in New York, it would make the total in these two years, no less than	56,000
or, per annum, - - - - - -	28,000

* Statistics, page 29.

† Reports of Cadwallader D. Colden, late Mayor of New York.

In 1820, according to the National Calendar, the whole that arrived in the united states, were 7,001

Now, from these data, an average of 15,000 annually might be assumed, without any danger of error. But to avoid controversy, I confine myself to 9,000

This would give from 1789 to 1820, a total of 279,000

In 30 years, by natural increase, they would probably amount to above - - - - 480,000

Thus far I trust the calculation will be admitted to be moderate. It now remains to estimate what proportion of this number, originally manufacturers, probably became farmers, in consequence of the want of encouragement in their respective occupations. This estimate must, it is true, be somewhat vague—but there are important data on which to found a calculation.

From the best information I am able to procure, it appears that one half, probably two thirds of the emigrants to this country, are English and Irish. Of the former nation a large portion have been cotton and woollen manufacturers: and of the latter, at least three fourths have come from Ulster, where the linen manufacture prevails almost universally, and of course a large proportion belonged to that branch. There are considerable districts in the state of Pennsylvania which are chiefly, and some almost wholly, inhabited by Ulstermen and their descendants.

When, moreover, we take into consideration, that, from 1789 to 1807, there were, as I have stated, scarcely any of the great manufacturers of woollen, cotton, linen, hosiery, silk, china, glass, delft, pottery, cutlery, and all the fine branches of iron and steel, carried on here—that some of these even now are unknown—and that the others are generally in a languid state, it will not be regarded as extravagant to suppose, that nearly one fourth part of the above number, or 100,000 persons, being about 17,000 families, emigrants or descendants of immigrants, are at present occupied in agriculture, whose proper sphere would be manufactures.

Besides these, there are immense numbers of other citizens, whom the same reasons as have operated on the immigrants, together with the downfal of so many manufacturing establishments since 1816, have forced to become farmers.

On this subject, again, I am straitened for data. There are some, however, very important and semi-official, which afford a good basis whereon to predicate a tolerably correct estimate.

In the year 1819, the distress of the manufacturers throughout the middle and eastern states, produced exertions to ascertain the extent of the decay of manufactures; and investigations took place, which throw a flood of light on this subject.

It appeared, that in Philadelphia and its immediate vicinity, in thirty branches of business, there were 7,288 persons less employed in 1819 than in 1816. There were twenty-six other branches from which no returns could be procured. Estimating these twenty-six at only one half of the other thirty, the total number would be nearly 11,000. Many of them were men with families: and it will not therefore be unfair to add 5,000 for wives and children, making an aggregate of 15,000. Of these no small portion "*went back*" to cultivate the soil.

The number of persons bereft of employment in Pittsburg appeared, by similar investigations, to be 1,288, whose dependents might be about an equal number, forming a total of—2,576.

In Rhode Island similar enquiries took place: and it appeared that in 1819, there were several thousands thrown out of employment in that state, chiefly in the cotton and woollen branches.

The same effects were produced in various other quarters, throughout the middle and eastern states, to a very considerable extent, especially in the state of Yew York; but the details are not sufficiently precise to enable me to enter into particulars.

These data, duly considered, afford reason to believe, that at least 15,000 workmen, with families averaging six persons, have, since 1816, when devested of employment at manufactures, "*gone back*" to cultivate the soil, which, with the immigrants and descendants of immigrants already stated, would make an aggregate of about 190,000 souls.

But I will only suppose 10,000 families, or 60,000 souls, for the second description. This will give an aggregate of 160,000 souls.

I wish it distinctly understood, that I am not tenacious of these numbers. They must, I repeat, be vague, and may be erroneous, either too high or too low, without materially affecting my deductions. It is sufficient for the argument, that no man can deny, that the total absence for a long time of so great a number of the most important manufactures in the world—and the frequent stagnation in others, in consequence of the glut of foreign goods in our markets, must necessarily have driven thousands of persons from manufactures to agriculture. This is the theory on the subject—and it is notorious that the fact corresponds with and corroborates the theory.

In my next number, I shall investigate in detail the operation of this state of things on the interests of the farmers. In the mean time, I recommend to them never for a moment to lose sight of the all-important truth, that every manufacturer, compelled to have recourse to agriculture, is transformed from a customer into a rival.

GUATIMOZIN.

Philadelphia, March 26, 1821.

NO. II.

"The restrictive regulations which in foreign markets *abridge the vent for the increasing surplus of our agricultural products*, serve to beget an earnest desire, that *a more extensive demand for that surplus be created at home*."—Hamilton.

"While the necessities of nations exclusively devoted to agriculture, for the fabrics of manufacturing nations, are constant and regular; *the wants of the latter for the products of the former, are liable to very considerable fluctuations and interruptions*."—Idem.

"If Europe will not take from us the products of our soil, on terms consistent with our interest, *the natural remedy is to contract as fast as possible our wants of her*."—Idem.

THESE three mottoes contain a summary of the imperious duty of this nation to herself. If duly considered and acted on, they would be sufficient to decide the important question, agitated with so much zeal and ardour— What duties or restrictions the united states should impose on the fabrics of foreign nations?

The free people of the united states are at present about 8,000,000. Raising bread-stuffs constitutes the chief dependence of a part—and the sole dependence of the remainder—of the inhabitants of seven states, containing about 4,340,000 of souls.

	Slaves.	Total.
New-York	10,888	1,372,812
New Jersey	7,557	277,575
Pennsylvania	211	1,049,398
Delaware	4,509	72,749
Ohio	000	581,434
Kentucky	126,730	564,317
Tennessee	130,107	422,813
	280,002	4,341,098
Deduct for slaves		280,002
Free population of seven states		4,061,096

In those states, it is true, there are numbers of farmers engaged in other pursuits, besides raising of bread-stuffs—but there is a sufficient number engaged in the culture of grain in Virginia, Maryland, and other states, not included in the above list to counterbalance those. But strking off the 1,061,096, for persons not engaged in this species of agriculture, it will leave 3,000,000 of people being about three-eighths of the white population of the nation, whose main dependence, I repeat, for paying for the productions of Europe, rests on raising and selling of bread-stuffs—and yet they are actually excluded either by prohibitions, or prohibitory duties, from the sale of this species of produce to fifty-seven millions of the inhabitants of that quarter of the globe.

Great Britain and Ireland -	Inhabitants	18,000,000
France - - - - - - -		29,000,000
Spain - - - - - - - -		10,730,000
Portugal - - - - - - - -		2,650,000
		60,380,000

These nations comprise about one-third part of the population of Europe.

By an ordinance of the Cortes of Spain, ratified by the king, on the 6th of September, 1820, the importation of wheat, barley, rye, Indian corn, millet, oats, and other foreign grain, is prohibited, unless the price of the fanega of wheat, (one bushel and five-eighths) which regulates every other species of grain, exceed four dollars—and a quintal, or one hundred pounds of flour, exceed six dollars. That is, unless wheat is at two dollars and a half per bushel, and flour at ten dollars and a half per barrel. This is indubitably equivalent to a prohibition.

American and other foreign wheat and flour cannot be sold for consumption in Great Britain, unless the quarter of wheat, (eight bushels,) exceed 80*s*. sterling. That is, unless wheat be about $2.22 per bushel, which it has not been since the year 1817. Of the exact price at which bread-stuffs may be imported into Portugal, I have not adequate information. Suffice it to say they are at present excluded.

American flour is only admitted in France on bond for exportation to the French colonies, or elsewhere. It is absolutely prohibited for *home consumption*.

Here a solemn pause is necessary. We receive French silks, and British linens, at fifteen; China ware, cotton and woollen stockings, and manufactures of steel, at twenty; and fine muslins, laces, gauzes, woollen goods, &c. at 25 per cent. duty: yet, wonderful to tell, neither France nor Great Britain will receive, on any terms whatever, one barrel of our flour, nor one bushel of our wheat, or Indian corn, for their own consumption, in payment for those articles. If this be reciprocity, and freedom of trade, language has wholly lost its original meaning.

Surely then the time has arrived, when, as "*Europe will not take from us*" so large a portion of "*the products of our soil*," on any "*terms*," we should apply what Alexander Hamilton calls the "*natural remedy;*" that is, "*contract as fast as possible our wants of her:*"—and, for "*the increasing surplus of our agricultural products, create a more extensive demand at home.*"

This, however, is somewhat of a digression. I resume the subject of my first address.

I trust I have therein made it appear that very large numbers of persons, whose proper province was manufactures, have, from want of encouragement in their original occupations, been compelled to betake themselves to agriculture. I ventured an estimate, that about 27,000 families, or 160,000 persons immigrants, descendants of immigrants, and others, were in this predicament.

It now remains to calculate the degree of the evil. For this purpose, it is necessary to ascertain the extent of the market they would afford the farmers, but for their change of profession —as well as that of the surplus beyond their own consumption, which they raise for sale in their present occupation.

In estimating the value of their consumption, I shall not predicate it on the extravagant war prices, nine, ten or twelve dollars per barrel for flour—twelve cents per pound for beef and pork—thirty-seven and a half cents for butter, &c. &c.; nor on the late reduced prices, which are in many cases below those that existed previous to the adoption of our present constitution. I will take it at a medium, say six dollars per barrel for flour, and other articles in proportion.

I presume it will be conceded, that the food and drink of each individual in society is worth about one dollar per week, equal to fifty-two dollars per annum.

At this rate, these 160,000 persons stated above, consume annually to the value of $8,320,000, which they now raise themselves, but which they would be obliged to purchase of their farming fellow citizens, had they remained in their original occupations.

In order to appreciate the importance of this market to the farming interest, let it be considered, that the whole amount of animals and animal and vegetable food exported from the united states from 1803 to 1820, inclusive, averaged only about 15,000,000 of dollars per annum, as will appear from the following.

*Table of Exports from the united states, of animals and animal and vegetable food from 1803 to 1820 inclusive.**

	Animals and animal food.	Vegetable food.
1803	$4,134,000	14,080,784
1804	4,284,568	12,080,684
1805	3,385,000	11,752,000
1806	3,274,000	11,050,000
1807	3,086,000	14,432,000
1808	986,000	2,550,000
1809	1,811,000	8,751,000
1810	2,169,000	10,750,000
1811	2,856,000	20,391,000
1812	1,657,000	17,797,000
1813	1,101,000	19,375,000
1814	481,000	2,216,000
1815	1,332,000	11,234,000
1816	2,093,000	13,151,000
1817	2,069,000	22,954,000
1818	1,936,000	19,048,000
1819	2,025,000	10,473,000
1820	2,447,000	8,401,000
Total	$41,120,568	230,486,368

Animals and animal food - -	$41,120,568
Vegetable food - - - -	230,486,368
Total for 18 years - - -	271,606,936
Average - - - - - -	$15,089,274

Thus it appears, that the favourite doctrine, which has for thirty years been preached to, and forced on, our manufacturers, to "*go back*" to cultivate the soil, has deprived our farmers of a domestic market, independent of the frowns or smiles of foreign nations, as well as of the variety of fluctuations to which foreign markets are liable,—a domestic market, I say, which is equal to above fifty per cent. of the market afforded by all the foreign world, for our animals and animal and vegetable food, even at the very extravagant prices which occasionally prevailed during the wars of the French revolution.

* Seybert's Statistics, page 147

This simple fact holds out to the farming interest an admonitory lesson of the most impressive kind, and evinces that the ruin, which the want of protection has inflicted on so large a portion of the manufacturers, has recoiled with equal pressure and violence on the farmers. This case bears as strong testimony to the sterling wisdom of the fable of the belly and the members, as the world has ever witnessed. May it never in future be forgotten or neglected by American legislators!

GUATIMOZIN.

NO. III.

"In vain do we discover that the earth is capable of producing the most luxu-"riant harvests with very little labour. Our abundant harvests are produced as "undeniable proofs of this in vain: But *place a manufacturer in the neighbourhood, "who will buy every little article that the farmer can bring to market, and he will "soon become industrious. The most barren fields will then become covered with some "useful produce.*"—Anderson on national Industry. Page 62.

"The difference, however, is very great between a market obtained abroad "and one that arises from manufactures being established in the neighbourhood: "*for many articles that the farmer could dispose of with profit, do not admit of being "carried to foreign markets in any case whatever; so that he who has to rely upon "these alone, must be subjected to very great inconveniences. All sorts of green crops "come under this denomination.*" Idem, page 68.

THE amount of the raw materials which the 27,000 families stated in my former address, would consume, had they remained in the class of manufacturers, is of much greater magnitude than the amount of their food and drink and that of their families.

An examination of the census of the united states will evince, that above one-fourth part of our population, is composed of males, of and above 16 years of age.

CENSUS OF 1820.

Free white males below 16, - - - -		1,956,365
— — — of 16 and above, - -		2,015,801
		3,972,166
Free white females below 16, -	1,884,534	
— — — of 16 and above,	1,979,382	
		3,863,916
Total free whites, - - - - - -		7,836,082

In the families of manufacturers, the males of 16 and above, are almost universally employed in the business of manufacturing; as also many of the males below 16, and the females of various ages. Of the 160,000 persons, who, as stated in my former number, depend on farming instead of manufactures, I shall, therefore, according to the above abstract of the census, assume, that one-fourth, or 40,000, being the males of and above 16, would be actually engaged in manufacturing; and endeavour to make an estimate of the raw materials they would consume had they not changed their profession.

In many branches of business, the raw materials very far exceed the wages paid to the workmen—in others they are about equal—and in some few they are below.

It may therefore be assumed, that the raw materials are, on an average, at least equal in amount to the wages of the workmen. an average which, I am persuaded, is very far below the real state of the affair.

Setting aside the present wages, which are greatly reduced, it may be stated, that for thirty years from the organization of our present form of government, the wages of males employed in manufactures have been from four to ten dollars per week. A few species have been at the extremes—but the great mass have been at five, six, and seven dollars. I presume I may venture on an average of five dollars and three quarters throughout all the branches—and that it will be readily admitted that the workmen consume respectively of wool, cotton, hemp, flax, leather, silk, timber, grain for distillation, &c. &c. an equal amount weekly.

Raw materials to the amount of five dollars and three quarters per week, consumed by 40,000 workmen, would amount annually to $11,960,000, the sale of which has been thus lost to the farmers.

But serious as these evils are, they are very far indeed from the whole that they suffer by this deranged state of society, as will soon appear.

These 40,000 farmers raise a surplus of agricultural produce beyond their own consumption, which, of course, comes into the market; presses on that of their brethren; and contributes to reduce its price. Let us try to estimate the amount of this extra surplus, and its probable operation on the farming interest in general.

In the American Farmer of the 16th inst. there is an extraordinary account of the produce of 960 acres of ground, cultivated by ten regular labourers. The proprietor,—a Mr. T. says, that with these labourers, in favourable years, he raises

Of wheat, - - - bushels,	4,500
Indian corn, - - - - -	3,000
Rye, - - - - - -	500
	8,000

and further, that he hires no extra labour.

This is at the rate of 800 bushels per man. But as this is a most extraordinary rate of production, it would be unfair to make a general average from Mr. T's farm. I shall, therefore, as I am sincerely desirous of avoiding controversy, instead of an average produce of 800 bushels assume only 200 bushels per man, beyond their own consumption.

At this rate, the 40,000 males, above the age of 16, whom I suppose capable of field labour, produce, per annum, a surplus of 8,000,000 of bushels of the various kinds of grain,—wheat, maize, rye, barley, oats, &c.

It will, doubtless, astonish the reader to learn, that this is twenty-seven per cent. more than the average exportation from the united states, of wheat, flour, Indian corn, and Indian meal, from the year 1801 to 1816, inclusive, being sixteen of the most favourable years this country has experienced, from the hour when Columbus landed, to the present time. The export of rye, barley, oats, &c. has been quite unimportant, and not worth taking into the account.

Table of the exports of wheat, flour, Indian corn, and Indian meal, from 1801 *to* 1816.*

	Wheat, Bushels.	Flour, Barrels.	Indian Corn, Bushels.	Indian Meal, Bushels.
1801	239,929	1,102,444	1,768,162	919,355
1802	280,281	1,156,248	1,633,283	266,816
1803	686,415	1,311,853	2,079,608	133,606
1804	127,024	810,008	1,944,873	111,327
1805	18,041	777,513	861,501	116,131
1806	86,784	782,724	1,064,263	108,324
1807	766,814	1,249,819	1,018,764	136,460
1808	87,330	263,813	249,533	30,818
1809	393,889	846,247	522,047	57,260
1810	325,924	789,431	1,054,252	86,744
1811	216,833	1,445,012	2,790,850	147,426
1812	53,832	1,443,492	2,039,999	90,810
1813	288,535	1,260,943	1,486,970	58,508
1814	.....	193,274	61,284	26,438
1815	17,634	862,739	830,561	72,364
1816	62,321	729,053	1,077,614	89,119
	3,651,586	15,024,613	20,483,478	2,451,506

* Pitkin's Statistics, pp. 111, 121.

Wheat, bushels	- - - - - - -	3,651,586
Flour, 15,024,513 barrels, equal to bushels of wheat	- - - -	75,123,065
Indian corn, bushels	- - - - -	20,483,478
Indian meal, do.	- - - - - -	2,451,506
Total for 16 years,	- - - bushels	101,709,635
Annual average,	- - - - - -	6,356,852

It is easy to conceive, that the great surplus of 8,000,000 bushels of grain, must have a decided and irresistible influence in depressing the price of our bread-stuffs at home and abroad. The exact extent of the depression is not so easily ascertained. I shall endeavour by analogy to arrive as near the truth as possible.

I shall suppose, by way of illustration, that 150,000 barrels of flour are necessary for the support of a certain district of country for a given time, and that the fair price is ten dollars per barrel. If the supply be limited to 100.000 barrels, the price will probably rise to 20, 25, or perhaps 30 or 35 dollars. If, on the contrary, there arrive 200,000, it will sink down to five or six, or perhaps to four.

Of this reasoning, the West Indies constantly offer examples. New-Orleans likewise exhibits cases of both effects, enhancement and reduction, often alternated monthly. An immoderate quantity of the produce of the western country, particularly flour, is occasionally collected there. The danger of its becoming sour, induces the owners to urge the sale. The price sinks in proportion to the quantity in market, and the eagerness to sell. The low price tempts speculators to purchase largely, and thus the market is cleared of the superabundance. The prices then frequently rise as high beyond the proper level, as they had before been depressed.

The grain crops in England in 1799 fell short one-third, according to the statement of Arthur Young, secretary to the board of agriculture. Prices rose, in consequence, one hundred per cent. in twelve months, notwithstanding every effort of the government to keep them down by bounties on importation—and notwithstanding immense importations—and likewise the substitution of potatoes and various other articles in lieu of grain.

It requires little sagacity to deduce from this statement of cause and effect, which are as constant and uniform as any of the operations of society, the pernicious results of a system which constantly tends to increase the number of producers, and of course the quantity of the fruits of the earth, and to narrow the markets for them. Of this two-edged sword, the farmers at present feel the edge with awful severity.

Let me once more repeat the all-important, but neglected truth, that the conversion of manufacturers into farmers has a four-fold pernicious operation on the latter class—*It increases their surplus—diminishes their market—lessens their customers—and increases their rivals.*

Another evil of serious importance to the farmers, resulting from this state of affairs, remains to be considered. We have seen that at the late census there were in the united states, of free white females of sixteen and upwards, no less than 1,979,382. Three-fourths of our population belong to the class of cultivators of the soil; which, of course, embraces 1,480,000 females of the specified ages. Were manufactures carried on with proper spirit, throughout the nation, a very considerable number of these females, and indeed of those below 16, as well as the male children of farmers, of that age, would find employment in sewing, spinning, carding, weaving, &c. &c. for the manufacturers. I will suppose that 200,000 females would be thus employed, and at the low average wages of one dollar and a half per week. This would amount per annum to $15,600,000.

Should any idea be entertained that the number here assumed is too high, it will be removed by the consideration of a few facts.

The Waltham factory in the neighbourhood of Boston, employs about 260 females, of various ages, principally the daughters of the adjacent farmers.

By the decline of the paper manufacture in 1818 and 1819, there were, within 30 miles of Philadelphia, nearly 800 persons bereft of employment, of whom two-thirds were females, and, like the former, chiefly the daughters of the farmers of the vicinity.

Mr. Gallatin, in his Report on Manufactures, states, that of 178 persons dependent for support on a factory in Rhode Island,

there were in the establishment males - -	24	
Females, - -	29	53
Employed in neighbouring families,		
Males, - -	50	
Females, - -	75	125
		178

The latter 125 principally belonged to farm houses.

A cotton mill was lately burned at Patapsco, in the neighbourhood of Baltimore, whereby about one hundred persons were thrown idle, of whom three-fourths were females of the same description generally as those already stated.

Combining these circumstances with the number of manufactories which have of late years been partially suspended, or wholly shut up—and likewise taking into view the hundreds of those establishments which would be called into existence, by an adequate encouragement of manufactures, it is easy to perceive, that the number of females assumed, far from being too great, must be regarded as very moderate indeed.

One more evil to the farmers remains to be considered.

In calculating the number of our citizens, who depend for a support on raising bread-stuffs. to avoid controversy I assumed only 3,625,734. Our population being at present 9,625,734, it would thence follow that 6,000,000 are purchasers of bread-stuffs from the residue. But I shall only suppose the number of purchasers to be 4,000,000, which includes the clergy, lawyers, merchants, mechanics, manufacturers, tradesmen, seamen, clerks, and those planters, who, employed chiefly in raising cotton, tobacco, and sugar for sale, purchase wheat flour for their own use and that of their families, except their slaves. That is, that nearly one half of our population depend for food on the other.

Now, the annual consumption of grain of each individual, may be fairly estimated at about nine bushels. At this rate the

4,000,000 of persons above stated purchase bushels	36,000,000
The grain distilled last year was about -	10,000,000
And the grain exported averages annually about	6,000,000
Total bushels of grain - - - - -	52,000,000

Assuming what cannot be denied, that the great surplus of 8,000,000 of bushels of grain raised by the 40,000 males of 16 years of age and upwards, whom I have stated as compelled to become farmers by want of encouragement in manufactures, has been a grand and efficient cause of the reduction of the price of the necessaries of life—and assuming, also, that the reduction has been only thirty-three cents and a third per bushel on grain, it amounts, on the above 52,000,000 bushels, to $ 17,333,333.

It now remains to sum up the whole of these various items:

Loss of the sale of provisions for 160,000 persons	$6,240,000
Loss of market for raw materials - -	11,960,000
Loss of labour of women - - - -	15,600,000
Loss on 52,000,000 bushels of grain - -	17,333,333
Total annual loss on the farming interest	$45,133,333

Although I believe these calculations substantially correct, yet I am very far from being tenacious of their critical exactness. As I have struck into a path literally untrodden, it would be very extraordinary, if, considering the meagreness of the data I had, my estimates were absolutely free from error. But whatever may be the drawbacks made upon them, they cannot destroy the important inference, that the policy hitherto pursued in this country, by compelling manufacturers to "*go back*" to cultivate the soil, is fraught with the most pernicious consequences, not merely to the farming interest, but to the nation at large.

GUATIMOZIN.

Philadelphia, *March* 30, 1821.

NO. IV.

" Considering how fast and how much the progress of new settlements in the " united states must increase the surplus produce of the soil, and weighing seri- " ously the tendency of the system, which prevails among most of the commercial " nations of Europe, whatever dependence may be placed on the force of natu- " ral circumstances to counteract the effects of an artificial policy: *there appear " strong reasons to regard the foreign demand for that surplus, as too uncertain a " reliance, and to desire a substitute for it in an extensive domestic market.*

" To secure such a market, *there is no other expedient, than to promote manufac- " turing establishments.* Manufacturers, who constitute the most numerous class, " after the cultivators of the land, are for that reason the principal consumers of " the surplus of their labour.

" This idea of an extensive domestic market for the surplus produce of the " soil, is of the first consequence. *It is, of all things, that which most effectually " conduces to a flourishing state of agriculture.* If the effect of manufactories " should be to detach a portion of the hands, which would otherwise be engaged " in tillage, it might possibly cause a smaller quantity of lands to be under culti- " vation: but by their tendency to procure a more certain demand for the sur- " plus produce of the soil, they would, at the same time, cause the lands, which " were in cultivation, to be better improved and more productive. And while, " by their influence, *the condition of each individual farmer would be meliorated, " the total mass of agricultural productions would probably be increased* For this " *must evidently depend as much, if not more, upon the degree of improvement, than " upon the number of acres under culture.*

" It merits particular observation, that *the multiplication of manufactories not " only furnishes a market for those articles which have been accustomed to be produced " in abundance, in a country; but it likewise creates a demand for such as were either " unknown or produced in inconsiderable quantities.* The bowels as well as the sur- " face of the earth are ransacked for articles which were before neglected. " Animals, plants, and minerals acquire a utility and value, which were before " unexplored.

" The foregoing considerations seem sufficient to establish as general proposi- " tions, that it is the intererest of nations to diversify the industrious pursuits of " the individuals who compose them—that *the establishment of manufactures is " calculated not only to increase the general stock of useful and productive labour, " but even to improve the state of agriculture in particular, certainly to advance the " interests of those who are engaged in it.*"—Alexander Hamilton, vol. 1. p. 182.

I MOST earnestly entreat you, as you value your own happiness and welfare, and the lasting prosperity, wealth, power and resources of your country, to weigh well the preceding quotation. It contains sound lessons of infinite importance to you, whether considered in a national or private point of view. It emanated from a man of a powerful mind, who could not be suspected of any undue bias in favour of manufactures, his connexions and friends being almost universally among the mercantile portion of the community. Thirty years have elapsed since he announced, with a prophetic spirit, what ought to be written in letters of gold, as a perpetual warning to the cultivators of the soil, viz:—" that *there appear strong reasons to regard the foreign demand as too uncertain a reliance for our surplus—and to desire a substitute for it in an extensive domestic market.*" And has not time, which has blighted the prospects and happiness of thousands of our farmers, and is now equally blighting those of the planters, stamped the seal of profound wisdom on the admonition, so fatally slighted—to secure the "substitute" of "*an extensive domestic market,*" for the "*uncertain reliance on a foreign demand for our surplus?*" Had this "*extensive domestic market*" been secured, we should not at present see cotton selling at 10, 12, and 13 cents per lb. Happy will it be, if, even at this late hour, we dispel the delusion excited by a reliance on plausible, but fallacious theories, scouted and rejected by all the wise nations in Europe, of which the ruinous consequences have been unerringly predicted for years in vain.

In my former numbers, I presented a sketch of the pernicious consequences experienced by the farmers from the depression of manufactures; from the steady, consequent conversion of manufacturers into farmers; and from the regular increase of the surplus of agricultural produce, while the market for that surplus has been as regularly diminishing.

To fulfil my purpose, I proceed to investigate the operation of this state of things on the Cotton Planters.

The want of an advantageous market for their productions, which has produced so much ruin among the manufacturers, and converted so many of them into farmers, has also been, as already stated, grievously felt by, and has borne hard on, the latter class, and converted numbers of them into planters.

The culture of grain for a considerable time past, even in those parts of the country possessing great local advantages, has been almost as unprofitable as any of the various manufactures, which have decayed under the withering influence of excessive importations. But in situations remote from the advantages of seaports, it has been absolutely a losing concern. This has been remarkably the case in a large portion of the western, and the interior of the middle states. It is doubtful whether there has not been an avarage loss, in that section of the union, on the two last crops of grain. The evil has been gradually increasing, till at length it has arisen to such a height, that in many places, remote from New Orleans, from which the farmers of Ohio, Kentucky, Tennessee, Alabama, &c. are distant 7 or 800 miles on an average, the prices of the produce of the soil, fertile and luxuriant as that soil is, would not defray the mere expenses of harvesting and carrying it to market. To send a cargo of flour from these remote situations to New Orleans would bring the cultivator in debt.

The price of sweet flour at New Orleans, on the 7th of March was from two dollars and a half to three dollars—and of sour, of which there is usually a large proportion on hand, one dollar and a quarter to one dollar and a half. The freight from Louisville to New Orleans is one dollar. When to this are added commission and other incidental expenses, it is obvious how ruinous a business farming is under these circumstances.

Superfine flour has lately been sold at Pittsburg, at a dollar and a half per barrel—wheat in many parts of the western states is selling at 20 to 37½ cents per bushel, and nearly all other articles, the produce of the soil, in about the same proportion.

Thus unhappily situated, the farmers in that quarter naturally sought for some other mode of employing their industry, time, and capital. They beheld their fellow citizens, the planters, making rapid fortunes, while their own circumstances were daily becoming worse. Cotton and tobacco, the produce of those fellow citizens, moreover, were not liable to serious injury by remaining on hands, waiting for a market. And as their own soil and climate were adapted for the same culture, it is not, therefore, extraordinary that they entered the lists, and that numbers of them converted their farms into cotton and tobacco plantations.

But the conversion of arable lands into plantations, did not produce the whole of the evil. Hundreds of citizens who settled on new lands, and who, in a different order of things, would have devoted their attention to farming, now cultivate cotton and tobacco instead of grain.

In consequence, the crop of cotton—to confine myself for the present to this article—was about forty per cent. greater in 1820, than in 1819: and therefore, although the domestic consumption had very much increased during last year, the exportation was forty-five per cent. more than in 1819, or any former year.

The recent great increase in the domestic consumption has arisen from two causes. The general embarrassment and stagnation of business had very much reduced the importation of cotton and every other kind of goods, and of course extended the market for domestic articles. But a more efficient cause of the increased consumption of cotton wool, was the superior excellence of the coarse domestic cotton goods, with their comparative cheapness, and the very great reputation they had acquired, by which they gained almost universally a decided preference over the imported articles, which created a very extraordinary demand for them, and, of course, what Mr. Hamilton states as a grand desideratum, "*an extensive domestic market*" for raw cotton.

The domestic consumption of cotton in 1819 is estimated to have been about 80,000 bales, at 300 lbs per bale, or - - -	lbs.	24,000,000
The amount exported, was - - - -		87,997,045*
Crop of 1819 - - - - - -	lbs.	111,997,045
Whereas the domestic consumption in 1820, was, from the best information I can obtain, 110,000 bales, or - - - -	lbs.	33,000,000
The amount exported - - - - -		127,860,152*
Crop of 1820 - - - - - -	lbs.	160,860,152

Our export to England in 1819, was	bales 204,831†		
In 1820 - -	301,928†		lbs.
Excess in 1820	97,097	equal to about	29,129,100

To enable the reader to appreciate the effects of this great surplus, I submit to his inspection a comparative statement of our exportation of cotton for the two last years, with the custom house valuation, which, in 1819, was, for Sea Islands, forty-five cents, and for all other kinds, twenty-two cents per pound—and in 1820, thirty-two cents for the former, and sixteen for the latter.

This mode of valuation, it is true, is not, nor can it be, critically exact. But as it has been the same in both years, whatever may be its errors, they cannot affect the inductions which the comparison affords.

*Exports of Cotton from the united states.**

	1819.		
Sea Island - - -	lbs. 7,488,775	valuation	$ 3,369,949
Other kinds - - -	80,508,270		17,711,820
Total -	lbs. 87,997,045		$ 21,081,769

* Reports of the Secretary of the Treasury.
† Rathbone, Hodgson, & Co's Price Current, Liverpool, Jan. 10, 1821.

	1820.		
Sea Island - - - -	lbs. 11,569,015	valuation	$ 3,702,085
Other kinds - - - -	116,291,137		18,606,582
Total -	lbs. 127,860,152		$ 22,308,667

The preceding statements and tables demand the most serious attention. They strikingly corroborate Dean Swift's idea, that in political arithmetic two and two do not always make four.

It appears that in 1820 we exported of Sea Island cotton - - - - - - -	lbs. 4,080,240
Of other kinds - - - - - - -	35,782,867
	lbs. 39,863,107

more than in 1819, whereas we received for the greater quantity exported in 1820, only - $1,227,898 more than for the smaller quantity in the preceding year.

The quantity was increased about forty-five per cent.; but the net proceeds only about six!

The profound system of the Dutch, with respect to their spices, has often been in vain inculcated on our citizens. That sagacious nation guarded against the pernicious consequences of a glutted market, by proportioning the supply to the demand. But, alas! the natural and inevitable consequence of our system is diametrically the reverse. It increases the number of the cultivators of the soil beyond the due and proper proportion to the rest of the community—produces a glut of the fruits of the earth—diminishes the number of purchasers of those fruits—and of course, inflicts distress on the class of agriculturists, by measures intended to aid and protect them. It is impossible to trace the progress of this system with a calm and unbiassed mind, without a conviction that from this source arises the depression of the prices of the products of our soil, and the sufferings which that depression has inflicted or may inflict on the cultivators.

It is well known that the price of cotton in this country is regulated by that of the surplus which we export to great Britain; and every man of candour will admit that the extraordinary exportation of the article to that country in 1820, satisfactorily accounts for the great and oppressive reduction of the price of the whole crop, whereby an increase of nearly 40,000,000 of pounds of cotton exported, produced an increase in value of only 1,227,898 dollars. It is as natural an effect for a very great surplus of any article to reduce its price immoderately, as of fire to produce heat, or frost to produce cold.

Had we, in the last year, either raised 40,000,000 lbs. less of cotton, and 5 or 6,000,000 bushels less of grain; or had we created, as we might easily have done. "a domestic market" for the surplus as a "substitute" for the foreign demand, neither of these important staples would have experienced the extreme and pernicious reduction of price which has taken place. We should probably have received more for the reduced quantity than we have done for the whole.

But we are not left to theory in this case. There are strong facts to corroborate it. The consumption of cotton in Great Britain was considerably greater in 1820 than in 1819.

Taken for home use in 1819 - - -	bales	418,500
in 1820 - - - -		486,750
Increase in 1820 - - - - - -		68,250*

It cannot be doubted, that this great increase of consumption in Great Britain, would have produced a rise in the price of our cottons, had not the increase in their importation been considerably greater than the increase in consumption: and therefore, I repeat, there is every reason to conclude that had we exported to Great Britain only 200,000 bales, we should probably have received as much perhaps for them more than we have done for the 300,000 we did export.

But our increased exportation was much aided in preventing a rise of price, and in producing the injurious depression. The importation of Brazil cotton into England in 1820 was greatly increased—while that of the East Indies, owing to the failure of the crops there, was much diminished—and that from the West Indies and other parts remained nearly stationary. I annex a general statement of the whole importations for the two years.

	1819.		1820.	
United States -	204,831 bales		301,928 bales	
Brazil and Portugal	125,230		179,673	
West Indies, &c. -	30,603		32,221	
		360,664		513,822
East India - - -		185,121		57,909
Total - -		545,785†	Total	571,731†

From this view it appears that the importation of our cottons and those of Brazil and Portugal exceeded, by above

* Bolton and Ogden's Price Current, Liverpool, Jan. 13, 1821.
† Rathbone, Hodgson & Co.'s Price Current, Jan. 10, 1821.

150,000 bales, or about 45,000,000 of pounds, that of the year 1819. Hence arose the reduction of price. The decrease in the importation of East India cotton did not produce any favourable effect on the market; as there is a sufficient quantity on hands of that kind to supply the demand for about three years.

In order to show the rise and fall of the market, I annex the prices of Upland Cotton, in Liverpool, at the commencement of each month for the four last years, and the two first months of the present one.

	1817.* *Pence.*		1818.* *Pence.*		1819.† *Pence.*		1820.† *Pence.*	
January	from 19½	to 21	from 18¼	to 21¼	from 17	to 19½	from 12	to 14
February	19	21	18¾	21½	15	17	11½	12¾
March	20	22	19	21¾	14	16	11¾	12¼
April	19	21½	20½	21¾	12	13½	11	12¼
May	17½	20½	20	21½	11	13	11¼	12½
June	16½	20	19½	21¼	10¾	12¾	11½	13
July	18	20½	19½	21½	10¾	13	11	12¾
August	19½	22	19½	22	12½	14½	11	13
September	19¾	23	19½	21½	13	15	10½	12½
October	19½	23	18	21	12	14	9¼	12
November	18¼	22	17	20	12	13½	9¼	12
December	19	22½	17	19½	12½	14	9	11¼

1821. January 1, from 8*d.* to 10½*d.* February 1, from 7¼*d* to 10*d.*

From the above statement, it appears that the article was reduced from Jan. 1819 to Jan. 1820, about 30 per cent.—and from the latter period to Jan. 1821 about 32.

This reduction is of most serious importance, not only as it regards the interests of the planters, but as it regards those of the nation. Forming, when at its maximum rates, above one-third part of the whole amount of our exports, which at best scarcely sufficed to pay for our enormous importations, its reduction, united with that which has taken place in the prices of our other staples, still further increases the difficulty of paying for those importations.

The stock on hand in Great Britain has been gradually increasing from year to year. At the close of 1820, it was between three and four times as great as at the close of 1817. Yet the importation has not increased by any means in the same proportion. I annex a statement of the importation and consumption for five years—and the stock on hand at the close of each year. No notice is taken of the quantity exported from Great Britain to the continent.

* Lawrence, Willis & Co.'s Price Current, Jan. 1, 1819.

† Rathbone, Hodgson & Co.'s Price Current, Jan. 10, 1821.

	Importation.	*Consumption.*	*Stock on hand at the close of each year.*
In 1816	lbs. 370,000*	lbs. 345,800†	lbs. 76 600‡
1817	477,160	407,000	114,600
1818	665,300	429,729	290,180
1819	545,785	418,500	352,500
1820	571,731	486,750	407,500

The stock on hand at the close of 1819 and 1820, having been nearly seven-eighths of the consumption of these two years, it is not extraordinary that a great reduction has taken place within that period.

We have seen the pernicious effects of our system on the national resources, and on our means of paying for those articles which luxury seduces, or necessity compels, us to purchase in Europe and the East Indies. It will shed a strong glare of light on the subject to exhibit its operation on individual wealth and prosperity. It will then appear in broad day light, that the advantages which have been held out to the farmers and planters, as the necessary result of buying cheap goods from abroad, cannot for a moment come into competition with the injurious consequences which flow from such a system. I will state the case of a planter who raises 30,000 pounds of cotton annually.

The expense of cultivation is variously estimated. I have heard it raised as high as eleven, and reduced as low as seven cents per pound. I will assume nine cents as about a fair average. But whether this be too high or too low cannot materially affect the conclusion.

1819.

30,000 lbs. of cotton at 22 cents	$6,600
Expense of cultivation at 9 cents per lb. . . .	2,700
Net profit, 1819, ...	$3,900

1820.

30,000 lbs. of cotton at 16 cents	$4,800
Expense of cultivation at 9 cents	2,700
Net profit, 1820, ...	$2,100

1821.

30,000 lbs. of cotton estimated at 12 cents . . .	$3,600
Expense of cultivation at 9 cents	2,700
Net profit, 1821, ...	$900

* Bolton, Ogden & Co. January 13, 1821. † Idem. ‡ Idem.

Here is a regular depreciation of property to an extent of which the examples are rare.

A planter's net income sinks in one year from 3,900 dollars to 2,100; and in another year to 900; in one case 46, and in the other 57 per cent. reduction. Whatever may be the size of the planter's possessions, or the amount of his produce, the diminution of income is in the same exact proportion.

These evils might be borne with patience, were there a rational prospect of melioration in the state of affairs--were the planters able to look forward with any well-founded hope, to such a rise of price, not to the old rate, which is utterly beyond the most remote probability, but to such a rate as would afford a reasonable reward for capital, time, and industry, usefully employed. But this is entirely hopeless without a total change of system. The tide of migration to Alabama, Louisiana, Missouri, and Florida, will be immense. A large portion of the lands in that section of the union, are admirably calculated for, and doubtless will be devoted to, the culture of cotton, as farming has become so unprofitable an employment. It is therefore highly probable that the quantity raised will regularly increase in a ratio which not only precludes the hope of a rise in price, but even renders a further reduction absolutely certain.

I have stated twelve cents as the probable average price for 1821; but for a variety of reasons it is manifestly too high. The price was steadily on the decline in Liverpool at the date of the last advices. Considerable sales had been made at very reduced rates, as will appear from the following extract from the price current of Maury and Latham, dated Feb. 22d, 1821.

"Since our respects of the 16th instant, the demand for cotton has been pret-"ty fair, but very heavy as to price. The sales of the 18th, 19th, and 20th, were "2676 bales, including 1430 Uplands, a 7¾ a 8¼ for old—and 8½ a 9½ for new—"100 a 9¾ and 15 a 10d—56 Orleans a 8¼ a 11½—226 Tennessees a 7 a 8½—120 "Sea Islands a 13 a 19½. Yesterday the demand was fair; and one cargo of Up-"lands, of good fair quality, was taken by a speculator, a 8¾, a low price; holders "in general continue to realize; and the average sales of Uplands which a week "ago were at 9d. are now barely 8¾. Except a small cargo from Wilmington, "and another from Charleston, no other vessels with cotton have arrived from "the united states, since the 8th instant, owing to contrary winds: but with a "change, we may expect considerable supplies. The demand for goods and "yarn has been rather better in Manchester, for a few days past."

Even before the receipt of the late discouraging accounts, cotton in the southern markets had greatly fallen in price. There is now before me a Darien price current, dated March 17, 1821, which quotes

Sea Island cotton	- - -	24 to 25 cents.
Upland Cotton	- - -	10 to 11½

Public sales were made at Savannah on the 14th of March, at the following rates:

23 bags a	-	11½ cents.	70 bags a	-	12⅜ cents.
8 a	-	12	50 a	-	12⅞
20 a	-	12¼	25 a	-	13¼

In Charleston, on the 31st ult. upland cotton was from 11 to 14 cents, and of dull sale.

When the commissions and incidental expenses are deducted from the above prices, it is easy to see that the net proceeds will fall very far short of the average price which I have admitted for the present year.

At New Orleans, on the 24th of February, the prices were:

Prime - - - - -	16 to 17 cents.
Second quality - - - -	14 to 15½
Tennessee - - - -	11 to 14

It is obvious that the purchasers at the prices above stated at New Orleans, must suffer heavy loss, probably 15 per cent.

The candour of the Liverpool merchants is entitled to great praise. In their circulars they display extraordinary intelligence, and an honourable disposition to keep their friends in this country well informed not merely of the actual state of affairs, but of the future and even remote prospects, in order to guard against the ruinous consequences which flow from those sudden and extreme fluctuations to which the market is constantly liable. Their views of the subject are remarkably luminous; and it is their unequivocal opinion that there is no prospect of an improvement of prices without a diminution of production.

Bolton, Ogden & Co. in their circular of January 13th, 1821, state—

"As the overwhelming stocks and probable extent of the imports of this year "do not justify any reasonable hope of improvement in the prices, the holders in "general continue to be anxious sellers, apprehending *a still further decline* "*when the new crop of American cotton begins to come freely forward.* Uplands "now sell at 7½ to 10¼; those of the new crop at 8¾ to 10¼; Alabamas and Ten- "nessees at 7½d to 8½; New Orleans 8 to 12d.—and a few extra fine at 12½. "Sea Islands are particularly dull, and sell at 14d. to 21d.

"*The stocks in the hands of the dealers are estimated as being from 15 to 20,000* "*bags more than they were at this period last year.*

"From the moderate prices of cotton, the more general employment of the "working classes of this country, and the fair though not high prices of labour, "with the low rates of provisions, we think there is a just ground to presume up- "on a continuance of the present rate of consumption of cotton manufactures, "and even to presume upon some increase. But *while the imports continue to* "*exceed that consumption, great as it is, the prices must continue to decline; and will* "*no doubt become so low as to cease to remunerate the planter for the expenses of pro-* "*duction, and thereby to diminish the future growth.* The low prices and better "qualities of American and Brazil cotton, it may be noticed, are not unlikely to "have the effect of causing them to be substituted for part of the present con- "sumption of East India cotton. *It ought also to be kept in view, that the state of*

" *the currency in this country, and the diminished amount of capital, are circumstan-* " *ces likely to continue to operate very powerfully in keeping all articles, and particu-* " *larly those of which there is any excess, in the supply,* AT VERY LOW PRICES."

Morrall and Watson, under the same date, corroborate those views :—

" The import this month is expected to be considerable; and seeing the pre- " sent disposition of importers to sell on arrival, there seems little chance of any " early amendment in prices. On the contrary, indeed, *as there appears to be too* " *much cotton grown,* it becomes doubtful if prices will improve, *unless the produce* " *is diminished :* and time alone can show how far the present reduced rates may " have that effect, or tend to keep back supplies."

John M'Adam & Co. on the 20th of same month, state—

" *As each succeeding arrival from this country will furnish worse and worse ac-* " *counts of our markets, it is to be hoped that the prices on your side will decline in* " *the course of the season, so as to render shipments safe and perhaps profitable.*"

Maury & Latham, on the same day, write to the same effect :—

" The increased cultivation in the united states, Brazil, and the East Indies, " must *gain greatly upon the consumption.* With this view of the subject, *it* " *would be hazardous to hold out any expectation of permanent improvement in price,* " *low as it certainly is.*"

Yates, Brothers, & Co. on the 31st of the same month, write :—

" If it be true, as stated in the advices from the united states, that the " crop now coming forward, will be *at least equal to the last,* the stock of Ameri- " can cotton in this country must continue to accumulate still more, even sup " posing there should be some further increase in the home consumption, " which indeed is probable, as the lower qualities of boweds and Orleans are " getting into greater use as substitutes for Surats, the prices of the latter hav- " ing lately experienced little decline in proportion to those of the former.

" *While this excess of supply continues, prices must be very low : and it is natural* " *to expect that a reduction will take place in the united states corresponding with the* " *rates paid in this country.*"

A more recent account from Liverpool, states—

" Our cotton market is in a wretched state—and I declare I can see no pros- " pect of any improvement for some time. Some of our largest importers force " it off as it arrives. Fair uplands are only worth 9*d.* to 9¼*d.* There is not " one bale in a hundred that will bring 10*d.* Sea Islands are very difficult of " sale."

Crowder, Clough & Co. under date, Feb. 10, write :—

" Our market closes this week, *worse, absolutely, than it has ever been yet :* and " we consider the price of uplands to be at ¼ per lb. lower ; for 9*d.* can with " difficulty be had for qualities which commanded 9¼ readily last week."

My next number shall be devoted to a further examination of the causes of the decline of the price of cotton, and of the practicability of applying a remedy to a state of things so injurious to national and individual prosperity.

Philadelphia, April 7, 1821.

GUATIMOZIN.

NO. V.

"No earthly method remains for encouraging agriculture, where it has not "reared up its head, *that can be considered in any way efficacious, but the establish-"ing proper manufactures in those countries you wish to encourage.*" Anderson on Industry, page 70.

"If a manufacture be established in any rich and fertile country, by convening "a number of people into one place, who *must all be fed by the farmer*, without "interfering with any of his necessary operations, *they establish a ready market for "the produce of his farm, and thus throw money into his hands, and give spirit and "energy to his culture.*" Idem, page 37.

"Insurmountable obstacles lie in the way of a farmer in an unimproved coun-"try, who has nothing but commerce alone to depend upon for providing a mar-"ket for the produce of his farm."—*Idem.*

"*The aggregate prosperity of manufactures, and the aggregate prosperity of agri-"culture, are intimately connected.*" A. Hamilton's Report on Manufactures.

"In places where manufacturing institutions prevail, besides the persons regu-"larly engaged in them, they afford occasional and extra employment to indus-"trious individuals and families who are willing to devote the leisure resulting "from the intermissions of their ordinary pursuits, to collateral labours, as a re-"source for multiplying their acquisitions or their enjoyments. *The husbandman "himself experiences a new source of profit and support, from the encreased industry "of his wife and daughters; invited and stimulated by the demands of the neighbour-"ing manufactories.*" *Idem.*

"The exertions of the husbandman will be steady or fluctuating—vigorous or "feeble, *in proportion to the steadiness or fluctuation, adequateness or inadequateness "of the markets on which he must depend for the vent of the surplus, which may be "produced by his labour*; and such surplus, in the course of things, will be greater "or less in the same proportion. For the purpose of this vent, *a domestic market "is greatly to be preferred to a foreign one; because it is, in the nature of things, far "more to be relied on.*" *Idem.*

"*There are natural causes tending to render the external demand for the surplus of "agricultural nations a precarious reliance.* The difference of seasons in the "countries which are the consumers, make immense differences in the produce "of their own soils, in different years, and consequently in the degrees of their "necessity for foreign supply. Plentiful harvests with them, especially if similar "ones occur at the same time in the countries which are the furnishers, occasion, "of course, a glut in the markets of the latter." *Idem.*

"The regulations of the several countries with which we have the most exten-"sive intercourse, throw serious obstructions in the way of the principal staples "of the United States. *In such a position of things, the united states cannot ex-"change with Europe on equal terms; and the want of reciprocity would render them "the victim of a system which should induce them to confine their views to agriculture, "and refrain from manufactures. A constant and encreasing necessity on their part "for the commodities of Europe, and only a partial and occasional demand for their own,* "in return, could not but expose them to a state of impoverishment, compared "with the opulence to which their political and natural advantages authorise them "to aspire." *Idem.*

"*The substitution of foreign for domestic manufactures, is a transfer to foreign "nations of the advantages accruing from the employment of machinery, in the modes "in which it is capable of being employed, with most utility and to the greatest extent.*" *Idem.*

UNLESS I am greatly deceived, my last Number IV. accounted satisfactorily for the recent serious and injurious depression of the price of cotton, the primary staple of this country; and proved that in the present and probable future state of the culture of that article, in the united states and elsewhere, there is no hope of a favourable change—in fact that there is every appearance of a great further depression—unless efficient measures be adopted to extend and secure the domestic market, so as to diminish our exportable surplus. The vital importance of this topic will justify me in devoting the present number to an investigation of the causes that led to the excessive and pernicious reduction of price which took place in this country during the first six months of the year 1819, and produced such a serious diminution of income to the planters, and so much bankruptcy among our exporting merchants. I shall also exhibit a view of the present state of the British market, with respect to East India cotton, in order to remove some errors which prevail with many of our citizens on this topic.

The importation of cotton into Great Britain from this country, the Brazils, Portugal, and the West Indies, in 1811, 12, 13, 14, and 15, was on a limited scale, and scarcely commensurate with the demand, particularly in the last year, when the consumption greatly increased immediately after the pacification of Europe. In consequence prices rose very high, ranging from 1*s*. 6*d*. to 2*s* 6*d* sterling per pound. The average price of our bowed cotton in Liverpool, during the year 1814, was 29*d*. sterling, and in 1815, 20*d*. I am unable to state the average of 1816; but, at the cl se of that year, the price was from 17¾*d*. to 20½*d*.

At the close of the year 1814, the stock on hand in Great Britain was 80,600 bales; of 1815, 79,900; and of 1816, 76,600.* This was not more than was necessary for the consumption of twelve or fourteen weeks.

The increasing demand for this staple, the scantiness of the supply, and the consequent high prices, induced the manufacturers and merchants of Great Britain to direct their attention to the East Indies, the trade to which country had been released from the monopoly of the East India Company; and in 1816 large orders were sent for Bengal and Surat cotton, of which the importation in previous years had been wholly unimportant, even during our war, which had greatly abridged the supplies from the united states.

Importation of East India Cotton into Great Britain, for ten years.

			Bro't over, bales,			153,708
1807,	-	bales, 11,404	1812,	-	-	2,607
1808,	-	- 12,512	1813,	-	-	1,429
1809,	-	- 35,764	1814,	-	-	13,048
1810,	-	- 79,382	1815,	-	-	22,670
1811,	-	- 14,646	1816,	-	-	30,670
		153,708				224,132
					Average,	22,413

* Maury & Latham's Price Current for January 20, 1821.

The importation, in 1817, in consequence of the new speculations, increased to 117,454 bales, being above five times the average of the ten preceding years.

Cotton imported into Great Britain in 1817.

East India,	bales	117,454
United states,		198,917
Brazil, and Portugal,		114,816
West Indies, &c.		47,208
	Total,	478,395

The East India Cotton, it appears, was very nearly one-fourth of the whole quantity.

To this operation, which ought to have excited the most serious alarm, no attention whatever was paid by congress. There was not the slightest effort made to carry into effect the sage recommendation of Alexander Hamilton, to "*secure a domestic market*" as a "*substitute*" for that "*foreign demand*" which was too "*uncertain a reliance*" for "*the surplus*" of this important staple.

A candid development of past errors is always useful, as affording salutary admonitions for future conduct. It is much to be regretted that these admonitions are so generally disregarded.

The striking impolicy of the apathy and neglect on the part of congress, and particularly the cotton planters in that body, will appear palpable by a statement of the average amount of the importation of our cotton into Great Britain for that and three preceding years, and a comparison of that average with the quantity above stated imported in 1817 from the East Indies. The three intervening years of war are omitted.—

Importation of united states cotton into Great Britain.

1811,	bales,	128,200
1815,		201,000
1816,		166,000
1817,		195,560
	Total,	690,760
	Average,	172,690

A very slender consideration of the subject would have naturally excited anticipations of the most unfavourable results, from a formidable rival having entered the lists, possessing a boundless capacity of production, and at once pouring into the market about 68 per cent. of our former supplies. This was ominous of a fearful change in the resources of this country.

In 1818, the importation of East India Cotton greatly increased. It exceeded that from the united states about 20 per cent.—and was actually 37 per cent. of the whole importation of that year.

Cotton imported into Great Britain in 1818.

United states, - - -	bales 206,728
East India, - - - - - -	244,608
Brazil and Portugal, - - - -	160,130
West India, &c. - - - - -	54,877
Total,	666,338*

These rapid strides were regarded by congress, like those of the preceding year, with an apathy and indifference wholly unaccountable. This was a dereliction of duty, which entailed the most serious injury on the planters and exporting merchants.

Should it be asked what remedy could congress have applied to this menacing evil, I reply that I hope to make it appear in the ensuing number, that a simple and efficacious remedy was in their power.

The consumption of Great Britain in 1818, was

United states, - - -	bales, 160,870
East India, - - - - - -	98,700
Brazil and Portugal, - - - -	124,200
West Indies, &c. - - - - -	45,950
Total,	429,720†

The plea of ignorance could not be alleged to justify or extenuate the utter neglect of precautionary measures. The most luminous accounts of the precarious situation of that market, and the formidable rivalry that existed, were, in 1818, as in the preceding year, transmitted to this country by the Liverpool merchants, and disseminated through the union in the newspapers, as may be seen by the following extracts. But menacing as was the danger, and admonitory as were the advices, there was not a single step taken to avert the impending storm.

"The most remarkable increase of imports, has been in East India cotton : and "the stock of this description is considerably heavier than it was. But *the consumption of it is increasing very rapidly ;* being now *very probably not less than* 1,000 "*bales per week more than it was last year.*"‡

* Laurence, Willis & Co's price current, Jan. 1, 1819.

† Duff, Findlay & Co.'s price current, Jan. 6, 1821.

‡ Yates, Brothers, & Co. Liverpool, July 1, 1818.

"Of Tenessees we have a less favourable opinion. *They are more on a level with* "*good Bengals, and middling Surats;* and are likely to accompany them in any "decline. East India cotton, except Surats of a quality that is convertible to the "same purposes as ordinary Boweds and Orleans, must decline; as the very heavy "imports are not likely to be checked till the crop of 1817, and perhaps not till "that of 1818, is shipped. *Surats still leave a profit;* though Bengals lose consi- "derably. But Bengals will probably decline in India, so as to meet the decline "here, and *still continue to be grown and shipped.*"*

"The use both of Bengal and Surat is become very considerable; and while "there continues so great a relative difference in price between them and the "descriptions with which they come more immediately in competition, *there* "*seems good reason to apprehend that their use will continue to extend.*"†

"Our present heavy stock of East India cotton which will continue to increase "for some time yet, and the fact that it is getting more into use by *the spinners* "*altering their machinery for using it,* on account of the very low prices, will pre- "vent any considerable advance on American cotton for the greater part of next "year. *It would, therefore, be very hazardous to ship upland and New Orleans* "*cotton but at a very great reduction of former prices. Yesterday we had two more* "*cargoes of Surat cotton from America,* which, with two cargoes this day from "Bombay direct, must have the effect of depressing this description of cotton "still more."‡

"The demand there now is for good Surat cotton, will very *seriously interfere* "*with American cotton,* particularly uplands of an inferior quality, and will have "the effect of depressing them in price."§

"From a review of the imports and stock at the end of each year, it appears "that there has been *an increase in* 1818 *in the consumption of India of* 26,000 *bags;* "of Brazil also some increase; but *a decrease of American of about* 12,000"¶

"Upland cotton, the leading article of import from the united states, is *likely* "*to be much interfered with by East India cotton, to the spinning of which many of* "*our mills are adapting their machinery, and many new ones are building, solely cal-* "*culated to consume it.* There seem to be no limits to the quantity that can be "produced in that country, and which is materially aided by the low price of la- "bour. *During the first six months of the last year, they exported* 100,000 *bales more* "*than they did the preceding twelve months!* Its extreme low price will force it "into consumption, to the *exclusion of other descriptions.*"**

"The importers of Alabama cotton have endeavoured to establish a distinction "between this description and Tennessee, in favour of the former: but *both kinds* "*are in the highest disrepute, and cannot be valued at more than twelve pence to* "*twelve pence halfpenny per pound. East India cotton is not quoted lower.* But we "think the latest sales, both of Surat and Bengal, have been on a decline of a "farthing per pound.††

The fatal consequences of this competition, and of the neglect to apply a remedy, did not, however, begin to develope themselves in Liverpool till the commencement of 1819. The average price of boweds there on the 1st of January in that year, was $18\frac{3}{4}$ pence; they fell in February to 16—in March to 15—in April to $12\frac{3}{4}$—in May to 12—and in June to $11\frac{3}{4}$.

In Philadelphia, the average price of Louisiana, Tennessee and Georgia Cotton, in December, 1818, and till about the close of

* Yates, Brothers, & Co. Liverpool, Nov. 10, 1818.
† Cropper, Benson, & Co. Liverpool, 11th Month, 30th, 1818.
‡ John Richardson, Liverpool, December 28th, 1818.
§ Idem, January 1, 1819.
¶ Yates, Brothers, & Co. Liverpool, January 2, 1819.
** W. & James Brown, & Co. Liverpool, January 13, 1819.
†† Rathbone, Hodgson, & Co. Liverpool, September 30, 1819.

January 1819, was 33 cents per lb. The advices from Liverpool reduced it, towards the end of the latter month, to 26½ cents, and it continued to decline gradually till the 25th of June, when it arrived at its ultimate price of depression; that is, 16½ cents per lb. being a reduction of fifty per cent in about five months.

It is very desirable, but extremely difficult, to ascertain the precise amount of the loss to the exporting merchants, and the diminution of income to the planters, produced by this depreciation. I will hazard an estimate, which, I trust, will be found not far from the truth.

The crop of this country for the year 1818, may be safely stated at about 130,000,000 of pounds. The amount exported, according to the report of the secretary of the treasury, was above 92,000,000 of pounds. The remainder was consumed in manufactories and in private families. The depression in Liverpool having commenced in January, it must have fallen on a portion of the old crop and nearly the whole of the new, as scarcely any of the latter could, at that time, have been sold in England.

It remains to ascertain the operation of the reduction I have stated. As it was gradual, from 33 cents to 16½, I shall assume, that

lbs.		$
10,000,000	were sold at 33 cents, - -	3,300,000
20,000,000	at 26 1-2 cents, - - - -	5,300,000
20,000,000	*a* 24 cents, - - - - - -	4,800,000
30,000,000	*a* 22 - - - - - - - - -	6,600,000
20,000,000	*a* 20 - - - - - - - - -	4,000,000
20,000,000	*a* 18 - - - - - - - - -	3,600,000
10,000,000	*a* 16 1-2* - - - - - -	1,625,000
lbs. 130,000,000		Dollars, 29,221,000

This forms an average of about 22½ cents, and nearly corresponds with the custom-house valuation, which is 22 cents for the whole year.†

The entire crop, at 33 cents, the price before the reduction began, would have produced $42,900,000, making a difference of 13,675,000 dollars of which probably 5,000,000 were lost by the merchants, who purchased on a market steadily failing—and the remainder a positive diminution of the income of the planters.

I deem it necessary to repeat what I have already stated, that

* There was a gradual, but small rise in the price after June: and therefore I have estimated that 30,000,000 lbs. were sold at 22 cents.

† Report of the Secretary of the Treasury for 1819.

in these calculations I do not pretend to critical correctness, which is in this case absolutely unattainable. But I believe them substantially correct, and approximating as near to the truth as is practicable.

Many of our citizens—planters and merchants—flatter themselves into an opinion, that the competition of the East India cotton with that of the united states, in the markets of Great Britain, is wholly at an end, the former having been found so far inferior, as to be nearly, if not altogether abandoned by the manufacturers of that country. This idea has been industriously propagated, and fondly believed, throughout the united states. That it is a complete "day dream," will satisfactorily appear from an examination of the following facts.

The decrease of the importation of this cotton has arisen from the failure of the crops in the East Indies, which has produced such a scarcity there, and in China, that the East India Company in January last purchased 10,000 bales in London and shipped them for the latter country. And it was expected they would for the same purpose make a further purchase of 18.000 bales.

"The East India Company have purchased 10,000 bags of India cotton for "shipment to China: and it is expected that they will take a further quantity, "by some persons stated at 18,000 bags, for the same purpose."*

While our cotton, however, continues at or near its present depressed price, the consumption of that of the East Indies will be very considerably limited in Great Britain. At those prices, united states cotton is more advantageous to the manufacturer than either Bengal or Surat, at their respective rates, the difference in the price not being equal to the difference in the staple. But those kinds will unfortunately always serve as a check to prevent the rise of ours.

Notwithstanding the low rates of our cotton, and its superiority over that of the East Indies, the consumption of the latter is considerable, and increased last year about fifty per cent. beyond that of 1819.

Consumption of Cotton in Great Britain in 1819 *and* 1820.

		1819.	1820.
United States, - - - -	bales	209,000	246,900
East India. - - - - -		49,600	74,400
Brazil and Portugal, - - -		126,400	135,100
West India and other kinds - -		33,500	30,350
	Total,	418,500	486,750†

* Rathbone, Hodgson & Co's price current, June 20, 1821.
† Maury & Latham's price current, Jan. 20, 1821.

It thus appears, that the consumption of East India cotton last year, was about fifteen per cent. of the whole quantity used in Great Britain; one half as much as that of Brazil, and nearly one third as much as that of the united states.

It is an extraordinary and unaccountable fact, that notwithstanding the great importation of East India cotton in 1817 and 1818, the price of that species has by no means experienced such an oppresssive reduction as that of the united states, Brazil, Portugal, &c. as will appear from the following

Table of the Prices of Cotton in Liverpool, at the close of the last three years.

	Boweds.	Bengals.	Surats.	Maranhams.	Pernams.
	d. *d.*	*d.* *d.*	*d.* *d.*	*d.* *d.*	*d.* *d.*
1818.	17 to 20	7 1-2 to 10 1-2	8 to 14 1-2	20 to 21	22 1-2 to 24
1819.	13 1-2 to 14	7 to 8 3-4	7 1-2 to 10 1-2	15 1-2 to 16	17 to 18
1820.	8 1-4 to 10 3-4	6 to 7 3-4	7 1-4 to 9	11 to 12	11 3-4 to 13*

It thus appears, that the price of our cotton has experienced a reduction of nearly 50 per cent. from the 31st of December 1818 to the 31st of the same month, 1820; Maranham and Pernambuco, 45; but Surat only 27 per cent., and Bengal only 25.

It was my intention to have undertaken to establish the position that Congress had a preventative in its power for a portion of the injurious effects of the reduction of price of 1819, and 1820. But it would have extended this essay to an unreasonable length, and therefore I postpone it till my next number.

GUATIMOZIN.

April 15, 1821.

P. S. The following extracts of letters from Liverpool, under date of the 10th of February, afford complete additional corroboration of the views held out in No. IV.

"Our market is in a very depressed state; indeed it is impossible to say how "much lower it will go. We should think, however, it has nearly seen its low- "est for uplands. *It is difficult to effect sales of the short staple cotton of Carolina "and Georgia at 9d per lb. to any extent*, unless the quality is very good. We have "sold, it is true, 100 bales prime old New Orleans at 10*d.* which were bought early "in the season at high rates on speculation, and have been held until the present "period. *As to sea island, we cannot give you a better idea of them than to inform "you that our broker bought this morning forty bags branded* "Belfair," *at* 16*d.* "These cottons, we conceive, are so well known in your market, that you will "by them be able to fix a standard for all others."

"*The losses on this article will, I fear, ruin many of the importers: and few will "be able to stand so great a reduction of property.* The last accounts from your "side of the water quote cotton at 15 a 16 cents, and from New Orleans 15 1-2 a "17 cents. *This is very little less than what cotton sells for here, say nothing of "charges;* and this has been the case for the last nine months. What the result "will be no one can tell; but I fear dreadful."

* Duff, Findlay & Co's price current, Jan 6, 1821.

NO. VI.

"If the system of perfect liberty to industry and commerce, were the pre-
" vailing system of nations, the arguments which dissuade a country in the pre-
" dicament of the united states, from a zealous pursuit of manufactures, would
" doubtless, have great force."*** " But this system is far from characterising
" the general policy of nations. The prevalent one has been regulated by an
" opposite spirit. The consequence of it is, that the united states are, to a cer-
" tain extent, in the situation of a country precluded from foreign commerce.
" They, can, indeed, without *difficulty, obtain from abroad the manufactured sup-*
" *plies of which they are in want. But they experience numerous and very injurious*
" *impediments to the emission and vent of their commodities.* Nor is this the case in
" reference to a single foreign nation only. *The regulations of several countries*
" *with which we have the most extensive intercourse, throw serious obstructions in the*
" *way of the principal staples of the united states.*"—Alexander Hamilton's report on manufactures.

Friends and Fellow Citizens,

MANY of our citizens, among whom are classed no small number who rank high in station and talents, ascribe the decline of the national prosperity chiefly to the transition from a state of war to a state of peace; and are firmly persuaded that nothing but a renewal of war in Europe, which would afford us a market for the superabundant produce of our soil, can completely restore us, and place us on the high ground we formerly occupied.

This is a view of our affairs, as gloomy and disheartening as it is erroneous. It is predicated on the idea, that the prosperity or misery of nations depends on circumstances over which they have no control; that they are not moulded and fashioned by their own policy; and that a nation, super-eminently blessed as we are, with every advantage. natural, moral, and political, is doomed to suffer distress and embarrassment, unless other nations are ravaged and desolated by wars and famines!

This idea can never be admitted for a moment. It is belied by the history of every nation, wise or unwise, ancient or modern; by which it is proved, that nations, like individuals, make their own fortunes; that wise systems of policy will produce prosperity, and unwise ones distress; that the degree of prosperity or distress will always be in due proportion to the degree of the wisdom or folly of their policy; that when a nation is in a state of suffering and distress, unless produced by some very extraordinary and inevitable calamity, as earthquakes, famines, invasions, &c. it affords conclusive evidence against its policy; that no natural or other advantages, how transcendantly great soever, will insure prosperity to a nation, under an unsound policy; that the contrary policy will successfully struggle against and overcome the greatest natural disadvantages ; and finally, that when nations are not ground down by wasteful and profligate governments, and grievous and grinding taxes, a sound system will insure their prosperity, whether universal peace prevail, or the whole world be engaged in warfare. A corollary from all this is, that as our government is neither wasteful nor profligate, nor our taxes oppressive, our present distresses can be charged only to our wayward policy.

Spain, Ireland, France, and the united states, most forcibly illustrate this theory. Spain enjoys a fertile soil and mild climate, and has derived immense wealth from her colonies ; and yet she has for centuries been miserable and wretched, through the insane policy she pursued, whereby her wealth was lavished on strangers, while her own people were pining in idleness and want. Should she escape, as heaven send she may, the fangs of the Holy Alliance, and persevere in the sound system of policy she has recently adopted, she will, within a few years, attain that grade in the scale of nations, to which she is eminently entitled by her local situation and immense advantages.

Ireland is blessed with natural advantages at least equal to those of England—and yet has at all times exhibited a most lamentable picture of poverty and wretchedness, while England, until of late, has enjoyed a high degree of prosperity. This arose principally from the circumstance, that the middle and higher orders in the dependent kingdom were clothed by the manufactures of the dominant one, and the wealth of Ireland was lavished to support the industry of England.

France exhibits a strong case on the opposite side of the question. She was wasted by a tedious and bloody war, of above twenty years duration ; suffered for three or four years the havoc and ravage of numerous hosts of licentious soldiers ; and was laid under a heavy contribution of about 100,000,000 dollars.* From all these enormous evils she has recovered in a few years, by the system of protecting her domestic industry, and not lavishing her wealth on strangers. She now enjoys, in consequence of this system, a state of higher and more substantial prosperity than she has known for a century : her political state I forbear to discuss, as unconnected with the present question.

The situation of the united states, alas ! affords a complete contrast to that of France, and a most irrefragable illustration of this theory. For nearly twenty years, while millions of armed men were devastating large portions of Europe, we enjoyed the benefits of neutral commerce, to an extent scarcely

* The contribution was fixed at 700,000,000 livres, equal to about 130,000,000 of dollars—but a part of it, I believe, was remitted.

ever, perhaps never enjoyed by any other nation. This was succeeded by a short war, of two years and a half, in which to use the words of Mr. Wyndham, "*we were hardly scratched*," —and which, in fact, rather advanced than retrograded our prosperity. It was closed under the most favourable auspices, and every man, woman, and child, able and willing to work, was usefully employed for individual advantage, and steadily adding to the wealth and resources of the nation. The voice of peace, and happiness, and joy, was heard throughout the land. But soon the glorious prospect was changed. The country was deluged with *cheap goods* from abroad—great numbers of our citizens were devoted to idleness and penury—establishments, on which millions had been expended—which gave employment to thousands, and wrought up, during the war, more than two-thirds of the average annual export of cotton wool from the united states to all Europe, from the year 1800 to 1814*—were closed, and their proprietors consigned to bankruptcy—a large portion of the energy and enterprize of the nation was paralized—gloom and distress pervaded the land—the circulating medium vanished to pay for luxuries we did not want, and for necessaries which we might have produced at home. For a time the farmers escaped the pernicious consequences of the system—the planters still longer. But it has at length reached both classes—and a painful state of things has been produced thus justly depicted by the secretary of the treasury, and by a committee of the house of representatives of the united states:—The former declares,

* As this assertion will excite surprise, I annex a statement of our exports of cotton, with the custom house valuation, from 1800 to 1814, from Pitkin's Statistical View, page 133.

1800	lbs. 17,789,803	$3,556,000
1	20,911,201	4,182,000
2	27,501,075	5,250,000
3	42,105,623	7,920,000
4	38,118,041	7,650,000
5	38,370,000	9,445,000
6	35,657,465	8,332,000
7	63,944,459	14,232,000
8	10,630,000	2,221,000
9	50,980,255	8,515,000
10	93,261,462	15,508,000
11	62,058,236	9,652,000
12	28,887,377	3,080,000
13	19,110,016	2,324,000
14	17,729,007	2,683,000
	567,054,020	104,550,000
Average	lbs. 37,803,601	$6,970,333

The quantity consumed in the united states in 1815, was, 27,000,000 lbs.; of course above two-thirds of this average.

that "*few instances have occurred, of a distress so severe as that* "*which has been exhibited in the united states*"—and the latter, that "*the imposition of an excise* AT THIS TIME OF EXTREME "DISTRESS, *would be unwise, and is not demanded by the state* "*of the public treasury. If imposed, it would be difficult to col-* "*lect; and, if collected, it would, in some parts of the union, be* "*in paper little available.*"*

These statements are recent. The first was made in February, 1820; and the second, a short time previous to the close of the last session of congress.

These strong facts can never be set aside by abstract theories, however plausible, and however supported by names of great celebrity. As truth requires no adventitious support, to establish its authority: so error cannot be converted into truth, nor folly into wisdom, by the glare of exalted names.

Having in my former numbers discussed the question of the causes of the present situation of the planters, I now, according to my promise, shall attempt to prove that it was in the power of Congress to apply a preventive to the depression of the prices of Cotton, in 1819, and a palliative in 1820; and, after its occurrence, to alleviate the evils it produced.

To prove what might have been done in 1818, or what may be done now, it is necessary to display what has been done already: and fortunately such progress was made in the manufacture of cotton goods, during the two years and a half of war, the only period since the commencement of our government in which it had a fair chance of supplying the domestic market, as to leave no doubt of the capacity of the country to consume so much of the raw material as would prevent that glut in Europe, which produced depression and all its ruinous consequences.

The duty imposed on cotton and woollen goods, in 1789, was only five per cent. It was raised afterwards to 7½, to 10, to 12½ and at a late period to 15, which was the rate at the commencement of the war, when it was raised to 25.

The great advantages the British manufacturers possessed, of immense capitals, machinery of the most perfect kind, the entire supply of the home market, the profits of which enabled them to make sacrifices on the goods they sent abroad, discouraged our citizens generally from any serious effort at the establishment of the cotton manufacture in the united states, on a large or extensive scale, for the first twenty years of the operations of our government. The few that were made, proved ruinous for the undertakers, and prevented others from engag-

* As numbers of our citizens deny the existence of distress at present, I quote the precise words of two public documents, of respectable authority, on the subject. Were it necessary, others of equal weight might be added, from messages of governors, and reports of state legislatures.

ing in the same speculations; for truly did Alexander Hamilton pronounce, that "the undertakers of new manufactures have to "contend, not only with the natural disadvantages of new un-"dertakings, but with the gratuities and remunerations which "other governments bestow. *To be enabled to contend with "success, it is evident that the interference and aid of their go-"vernment are indispensible.*"

Therefore, notwithstanding the immense exportation of the raw material, amounting in 12 years, from 1800 to 1811 inclusive to 500,228,152 lbs.* of which we received back a great portion, manufactured, at nearly fivefold its original value,† the consumption of that raw material in manufacturing establishments in the united states was

In 1800,	only	500 bales	or	150,000 lbs.‡	of cotton.
1805,		1000		300,000	

The restrictive system, called into existence by the depredations of the belligerents, gave a considerable spring to the manufacture, so that in 1810 the consumption was extended to 10,000 bales, or 3,000,000 lbs.§

From this time till the declaration of war in June, 1812, it made considerable progress—but there are no means of ascertaining its extent. The war, in a great measure, cut off our foreign supplies of cotton and other goods, which of course produced such a scarcity and rise of their price, as held out very great inducements to our enterprizing citizens, to vest in manufactories the immense superfluous capital then divested by the war of employment in commerce. The progress in the cotton branch, was such as might have been expected from the boundless supply of the raw material. Great numbers of extensive establishments rapidly arose in every quarter of the middle and eastern states, which supplied the great mass of the consumption of the country. By a statement presented to Congress by a respectable body of cotton manufacturers, and incorporated into the celebrated Report of the commitee on commerce and manufactures already quoted, it appears that in 1815, the following was the state of the cotton manufacture throughout the united states.

* Pitkin, page 133.

† This is the increase the raw material receives by manufacture. Colquhoun, in his View of the wealth, power and resources of Great Britain, page 91, gives this statement of the cotton manufacture of that country.

Export and consumption,	*l.* 29,000,000
Raw material,	6,000,000
Sterling	*l.* 23,000,000

A clear advantage to that nation of above $100,000,000.

‡ Report of the Committee of Congress, on commerce and manufactures, 1816.

§ Idem.

Capital invested,		$40,000,000
Males employed from 17 upwards,	10,000	
Below seventeen,	24,000	
Women and female children,	66,000	
		100,000
Cotton wool manufactured,		bales 90,000
Equal to,		lbs. 27,000,000
Number of yards of cotton,		81,000,000
Cost [supposed to be the current price] per yard, 30 cents,		$24,300,000

Of this statement, I believe, the accuracy was never questioned until last fall, when a writer in the National Gazette, under the signature of SAY, declared it incorrect, without adducing any proof and resting his dictum altogether on what he pronounces as the utter improbability of the statement.

Not knowing on what data the estimate of the consumption was predicated, I am unable to substantiate it by reference to authorities. But I hope to adduce such a number of collateral and cogent facts, as will satisfy every man who bestows that degree of consideration on them, which the importance of the question requires, that SAY did not sufficiently investigate the evidence, of which the case was susceptible, previous to his unqualified rejection of the statement.

A comparison of the quantity of cotton exported, and of cotton manufactures imported, previous to and during the war, will shed considerable light upon the subject.

The export of cotton in	1809, was	lbs. 50,980,255
	1810,	93,261,462
	1811,	62,058,236
		206,299,953*
Export in	1812,	lbs. 28,887,377
	1813,	19,110,016
	1814,	17,729,007
		lbs. 65,726,400†

The difference between the two periods is above 140,000,000 of pounds, which, at the first blush, might appear to be the quantity manufactured in the country during the war. But there are two important deductions to be made from this balance; first, the diminution of cultivation during that period, in consequence of the want of opportunity of transporting the article to

* Pitkin, 133.

† Ibid.

market from New Orleans and other southern ports—and secondly, the quantity stored there till the war was over. I will allow for diminution of culture, lbs. 35,000,000

allow for diminution of culture,	lbs. 35,000,000
Quantity stored, - - - -	30,000,000
	65,000,000
This, deducted from the above amount of	140,000,000
Leaves a balance of	75,000,000

or 25,000,000 lbs. per annum, for the domestic consumption during the war. To this let us add the previous domestic consumption, which, by the statement of the committee of commerce and manufactures, appears, as we have seen, to have been, in 1810, about 3,000,000 of pounds. The aggregate exceeds the statement in the report of the committee.

That I have made a greater allowance for stored cotton than was necessary, is obvious from the export of the three years subsequent to the war, in the first of which all the old stock must have been cleared out.

1815,	lbs. 82,998,747
1816,	81,947,116
1817,	85,649,328
	lbs. 250,595,191†

This exceeds the export of the three years previous to the war, only 44,000,000 lbs.—although the cultivation must have been very considerably extended during the three years, 1815, 16 and 17; of course the admission of 30,000,000 of pounds remaining of the crops of 1812–13–14, I repeat, is too great.

I trust that SAY himself will have the candor to admit that these tables are abundantly sufficient to decide the question. But its magnitude induces me "to make assurance doubly sure," and adduce other corroborations of the correctness of the statement of the committee.

For this purpose I proceed to a comparison of the amount of cotton goods imported previous to, and during the war, which will throw considerable additional light on the subject.

The importation of articles subject to 15 per cent. duty, which embraced cotton and woollen goods, and a very few others, in 1804, 5, and 6, was as follows:—

† Pitkin, 133.

	In American vessels.	In Foreign vessels.
1804,	$ 30,285,267	$ 1,615,861
1805,	37,137,598	2,046,451
1806,	43,115,367	1,434,756
	110,538,232	5,097,068
		110,538,232
		*115,635,300
Deduct for re-exportation - - - - -		3,663,402
		111,971,898
Deduct also 10 per cent. for other articles subject to the same duty - - -		11,197,189
Net		100,774,709
It may be assumed that one half was cotton goods equal to - - - - - -		50,387,354
Average		16,795,778
Our population increased from 1806 to 1814,† about 40 per cent, and of course our consumption increased in the same ratio, equal to - - - - - - -		6,718,311
		23,514,089
The prices of goods, moreover, were at least, one third higher in 1814 than in 1806. Therefore I add - - - - - - -		7,838,029
This makes a total of		31,352,118

This, I presume, will be freely admitted as the probable value of the cotton goods consumed in 1814 in the united states at the then prices. Deducting $1,421,629, being one half of the whole amount of the goods imported that year subject to 25 per cent. duty (which embraced cottons and woollens) it leaves nearly $30,000,000, or less than four dollars per head, for the whole population, to be supplied by the domestic cotton manufacture, which considerably exceeds the amount stated in the report of the committee of commerce and manufactures.

* Seybert, 164.

† I prefer predicating the calculation on the year 1814, to 1815, as the importation of the former year was of little importance, and left all the void to be filled by the domestic manufacture: whereas the importations of the last six months of 1815, were immense. There was, however, little diminution in the manufacture in 1815: the shock it received began early in 1816.

But this is by no means the whole of the evidence. An important document exists, of no ordinary character and authority, of which I submit an abstract:---

In 1819, in consequence of the depression of the cotton manufacture in Rhode Island, an investigation was instituted into its situation in 1815, in order to ascertain by comparison the extent of the declension, by which it appeared that there had been in the latter year, within 30 miles of Providence,

Cotton manufactories,		140
Containing, in actual operation,	spindles,	130,000
Using annually,	bales of cotton,	29,000
	Equal to lbs.	8,700,000
Producing yards of cotton goods,		27,840,000
The weaving of which, at 8 cents per yard, cost,		$2,227,200
Total value of the cloth,		6,000,000
Persons steadily employed,		26,000

The sphere of inquiry embraced in the statement presented to congress, was so wide, and the difficulty of procuring information from such various quarters, so great, that however upright, intelligent, and industrious, the inquirers were, the result of the investigation might be considerably erroneous. But in the case of Rhode Island, if the details be incorrect, it must have arisen from downright fraud and imposture. The sphere of inquiry was so limited---the facts of such public notoriety—and misstatements so open to immediate detection, as would deter the parties from imposition, even if uninfluenced by honour and principle. The investigation was, moreover, conducted under the inspection of the late Mr. Burral, a respectable member of the Senate of the U. S. and other gentlemen, whose characters and standing in society, afforded full guarantee for the fairness and candour of their statement, which is, therefore, as well entitled to credit as any other public document whatever. If it is to be rejected without conclusive and overwhelming evidence, and even without a plausible appearance of error, to what document shall we give credence?

This being premised, let us see how it bears on this important topic. SAY asserts, that there were not 60,000 persons employed in these manufactures,* that is, I presume, those of cotton; whereas we find 26,000 employed in a small corner of

* I have had considerable difficulty to ascertain the precise meaning of *Say*, and whether he did not extend his denial to both woollen and cotton manufactures; as he had been previously discussing the subject of both. His words are—"*I do not believe the persons employed in these manufactures amounted to 60,000.*" But the construction of the different sentences appears to warrant the limitation to the cotton branch. If otherwise, it appears most extravagantly erroneous.

the country. He scouts the idea of 90,000, bales of cotton being consumed in the whole of the united states, whereas there were 29,000 bales consumed in that limited space. Surely, then, he must be in error—surely he did not duly consider the subject—and as surely there cannot be the shadow of a doubt that the manufacturers in the rest of the union, consumed the remaining 61,000 bales—or that the number of persons stated to have been employed is within due bounds.

I might here close the subject. But at the hazard of being prolix, I subjoin a few strong facts.

The cotton factories in the single county of Oneida, N. Y. consumed in 1815, no less than 400,000 lbs. of cotton, equal to about 1300 bales.*

Those in Connecticut, contain 50,000 spindles, and are capable, if all were employed, as by due encouragement they might be, of manufacturing 9,960,000 yards of cloth annually, and employing 10,000 persons, exclusive of weavers.†

The Eagle factory in Trenton wove in 1815, 10,000 yards per week, equal to 520,000 per annum.‡

The Waltham factory consumed in 1819, about 1400 bales of cotton—produced 1,250,000 yards of cloth—and employed about 300 persons. It was in operation in 1815, but on what scale I cannot ascertain; probably however, not near so great.

In Philadelphia and its vicinity, in 1815, there were 2325 persons employed in the manufacture of cotton. Supposing 900 to have been weavers, and to have produced 10 yards per day, it amounted to 2,673,000 yards per annum—and, at three yards to the pound, was equal to 2,408 bales.

When these facts are duly considered—and further, that a large portion of the paper mills throughout the middle states were at that period converted to the purpose of making cotton cloth—that establishments of this kind were, as I have said, spread over the middle and eastern states, in every direction, and even in some of the southern states, as far as North Carolina, no doubt can be entertained of the correctness of the statement of the committee of commerce and manufactures.

The manufacture did not, as I have already observed, receive any material check in 1815, notwithstanding the flood of goods poured into the country during the last half of that year. These were generally sold very high, owing to the existence of the double duties, and the general rage for opening stores and purchasing goods. The repeal of the double duties in June, 1816, and the daily increasing supplies from Europe, arrested the sales of the domestic goods in that year, and produced that scene of distress of which I have given a slight sketch at the commencement of this essay.

* Address of the National Institution of New York.

† Idem.

‡ Idem.

Among the pernicious consequences of this state of things, was a diminution of the domestic consumption of cotton, probably to the amount of half—at least two-fifths—of the quantity used before. This diminution continued for the two succeeding years, and was probably at least 10,000,000 pounds per annum; whereas, had the manufacture been duly fostered, it would certainly have increased 5,000,000. This will be admitted by those who consider that the business was in its infancy—had grown in five years from a consumption of 10,000 bales to 90,000—that it had as yet been chiefly confined to coarse goods—and that even of those various kinds were not as yet manufactured, but would have been produced in great abundance with proper encouragement.

In order to ascertain the effect the abstraction of 15,000,000 pounds of our cotton from the British market would have produced, in 1818, it is necessary to take into view the amount of this cotton imported into Great Britain, and consumed, in that year.

Imported,	bales, 219,950
Consumed,	160,870
Surplus,	bales, 59,080
Equal to	lbs. 17,724,000*

It is therefore, I think, a rational conclusion, that had our manufactures been in the prosperous condition in which a due degree of patronage would have placed them, such an extra portion of the raw material would have been consumed at home in 1818, as would have reduced the exportation to Great Britain to a level with the consumption in that country, and prevented the depression of price which produced so much ruin to the merchants, and diminution of income to the planters.

It may be asked what would be a "*due degree of patronage?*" I will for a moment suppose that the duty on cotton goods had been raised in 1818, to 33 per cent, (the duty proposed in 1816, by Mr. Dallas)—and that all goods below 30 cents per yard, were subject to duty as if they cost 30. Were this the case, the domestic consumption would doubtless not only be raised to what it was in 1815, viz. 90,000 bales—but would be increased so far beyond that quantity as to consume the whole extra portion exported that year to Great Britain.

I now proceed to consider the case of last year, in order to ascertain whether the reduction which then took place, might not have been wholly or at least partly obviated.

* Maury & Latham's Price Current, Liverpool, January 20, 1821.

The importation of united states cotton into Great Britain in 1820, was greatly increased beyond any former year, being

		bales, 301,928
Whereas in 1819, it was only		204,631
An increase of		97,297*
However the consumption had also greatly increased, being in 1820,	246,900	
Whereas it was in 1819, only	209,000	
Increase		37,900*
Thus the difference of increase between the importation and consumption was only,		bales 59,397
	Equal to	17,819,100 lbs.

I have already stated that a variety of circumstances combined to increase the domestic consumption last year, among which the most powerful were a deficiency of important manufactures, owing to the general pressure of the times, with the embarrassments of the importers—and the superiority and cheapness of the domestic articles. Still the manufacture was not carried even last year to any thing like the extent of which it is susceptible. Had it been in this situation, it would have probably consumed the surplus of our exportation, as it might have done in 1818, and thus prevented this recent depreciation.

It would, however, be idle to suppose that any encouragement that can be given to the domestic cotton manufacture would keep pace with such a rapid increase of the raw materials, as 39,000,000 lbs. per annum, in this country,† and such an increase as is likely to take place in South America. In this state of things, the only radical remedy is such a general encouragement of domestic manufactures, as will restore the deranged equilibrium of the different pursuits of society, and not only prevent the manufacturing class from crowding on the agriculturists, who are already too numerous in proportion to our population, but induce some of the former who have been driven to enter the lists with the latter, to return to their old ranks, and thus (to confine myself for the present,

* Maury & Latham's Liverpool Price Current, January 20, 1821.

† The export of 1819, was 87,997,045 lbs.; whereas it was in 1820, no less than 127,860,152 lbs. See Reports of the Secretary of the Treasury.

to the culture of cotton,) diminish the production and increase the domestic consumption of that most important raw material. The same reasoning will apply to flax, hemp, leather, timber, and the other numerous articles for which the manufacturers would by due encouragement furnish a most valuable market to their agricultural fellow citizens.

GUATIMOZIN.

April 24, 1821.

P. S. The duties mentioned in this essay are those stated in the tariff—to which, in every case, ten per cent. must be added.

Strictures on Mr. Cambreleng's Work, entitled, "An examination of the New Tariff."

NO. I.

About the close of the last session of Congress, Mr. Cambreleng, a respectable citizen of New York, who has been since elected a member of that honourable body, published "*An Examination of the New Tariff*," of which the object is to display, in the most formidable and terrific colours, the oppressive and ruinous consequences of the adoption of that important measure. According to this gentleman, it would infallibly destroy the commerce of the country—degrade, debase, and plunder the agriculturists--erect the manufacturers into a lordly aristocracy, to the utter prostration of the democracy of the nation—and visit us with all the miseries suffered by the English nation—miseries which, according to Mr. C. arise from what he stigmatizes as the odious system of "restriction;" of which system, it is to be observed, the grand and paramount object is to foster domestic industry, by preventing the interference of foreign manufactures and foreign grain, with those of that nation!!! In one word, all the most tremendous evils that ever issued from Pandora's Box, are to be disgorged on the land, should this deleterious tariff be adopted.

Mr. Cambreleng's work has shared the fate of a thousand others, which, in different nations and at different periods, have been written on topics of deep interest: such topics universally excite diversity of sentiment, and strong party feeling. Its defects have been overlooked by the opposers of the legislative protection of domestic manufactures, and its merits by those of opposite sentiments. By the former it has been and is extravagantly eulogised. They regard it as the Alpha and Omega of political economy—as forever settling this important question, without appeal—and as overwhelming, not only the report of Mr. Baldwin, and the addresses of the Society for the promotion of National Industry, but even the celebrated report of Alexander Hamilton. This great statesman, according to Mr. Cambreleng, must have been a very shallow political economist; as Mr. C. confidently believes be has triumphantly established the futility of almost every part of the elaborate and profound system advocated my Mr. H. with all the powers of mind he was, by friends and enemies, allowed to possess.—There is scarcely a point in his report unassailed by Mr. C.

I shall remark on a variety of his criticisms in the course of these strictures; but, for the present, shall confine myself to a single one. The culture of cotton had just commenced in the united states, and the result of the experiment being then in a great degree uncertain, Mr. Hamilton expressed an opinion, that "the extensive culture of cotton could perhaps hardly be expected, but from the previous establishment of the domestic manufacture of the article." On this very natural position, Mr. C. triumphantly asks, "when a man of acknowledged abilities speculates on our industry with so little success, *what confidence can we repose in the system by which his measures were regulated?*"* This sweeping denunciatory query is, however, kindly softened down by an apology for the Secretary's ignorance. "Mr. Hamilton wanted that familiar and minute knowledge of the operations of money, credit and trade, which no man can have without much practical experience, or a long life devoted to this particular study."†

On the other hand, the friends of protecting duties almost universally regard "*the Examination*" as an inferior and flimsy performance. They assert that its postulata are unsound—that in most instances it begs the question—that it ascribes effects to causes with which they have no connection—that a large portion of its reasoning is founded on a most extravagant error, which vitiates and overturns the most vital part of the work---that in the attempt to account for the distresses of England, it wholly overlooks her wild and wasteful wars, on which have been prodigally lavished, within the last half century, at least $8,000,000,000---her oppressive taxes, the result of that enormous expenditure---her grinding tythes, whereby the tenth part of the produce of the soil is devoted to the support of a lordly hierarchy---in a word, overlooking all the variety of powerful causes of her distresses, it ascribes them wholly to that system whereby she has been enabled to lay the whole world

* Examination of the Tariff. † Idem p. 24.

under contribution by the products of her industry, to subsidize half the monarchs of Europe, and to decide the destinies of that quarter of the globe.

Submitted as " the Examination" has been to the public, it has become a fair subject of discussion, which, if it be sound and correct, cannot fail to enhance its usefulness, by the diffusion of its doctrines more fully: but if fallacious and pernicious, its errors ought to be clearly pointed out and exposed, in order to guard against the ruinous consequences which never fail to result from errors on the important subject Mr. Cambreleng has undertaken to investigate.

Persuaded that it contains a variety of positions and assumptions destitute of foundation, and leading to very pernicious results, I solicit the public attention to an examination of them. It is not, however, my intention to enter into a regular review of its contents. This would require more time than I can spare, and more attention than the public would bestow on the subject—and also a volume as large as Mr. C.'s book. I shall confine myself to a few leading points, passing over those of minor importance. NECKER.

July 10, 1821.

NO. II.

AS facts are the basis on which all reasonings on political economy ought to be predicated, I shall only undertake the examination of some of the leading ones adduced by Mr. Cambreleng, passing by most of his abstract reasonings under the idea that if the basis can be fairly undermined, the superstructure of argument will of course crumble into ruins.

I do not, however, intend to travel with him into the interior of Russia, to ascertain the cost of a Berkovitz of hemp at Toola, Calooga, or Oral to the south of Moscow—nor to the mountains of Bohemia, to investigate the cost of the manufacture of common glass—because I have no means—nor is there one person in 10,000 in this country who has—to test these statements.

I shall confine myself in a great measure to investigate assumed facts on this side of the Atlantic, which may be at once submitted to the talisman of truth ; as, the criteria being within our grasp, if correct, they may be fully verified—or if otherwise, easily disproved.

Mr. Cambreleng, in the threshold of his work, passes an encomium on the Congress of 1790, for their fairness and impartiality—for the " equal protection" which they afforded to manufactures, in common with every other "branch of industry"—

"Circumstances have conspired to augment our duties on im-
"portations higher than ever was contemplated by the Congress
"of 1790, the members of which had all laboured to bestow on
"this nation the best of governments—and *who equally protect-*
"*ed every branch of industry.*"*

It is difficult to conceive of a greater error than is conveyed in the last sentence of this paragraph. I hope to make it appear that it is destitute of even the shadow of foundation.

I am rejoiced that Mr. Cambreleng hazarded this most extraordinary assertion—as it affords a legitimate opportunity of developing the withering system pursued towards manufactures at the commencement of our government—and the very partial and inequitable scale on which "protection" was dealt out to the different "branches of industry."

There are three great interests in the united states, the agricultural, manufacturing, and commercial—the two first occupied in producing food, clothing, and other necessaries, as well as conveniences and luxuries—the third, in conveyance of productions to consumers.

It may—indeed it must—be assumed, that when Mr. Cambreling clearly and explicitly declares, that "*the congress of* 1790, *equally protected every branch of industry*," he means that they guarded them by duties from the interference of foreign rivalship. This was the only protection that body could afford—and this is the only meaning of the words. Any other construction would be nonsense, and is therefore inadmissible. Let us examine how far he is borne out in his assertion by the fact.

It is necessary, however, in order to a correct decision upon the subject, to offer a few prefatory observations explanatory of the nature of "protection of every branch of industry." No subject can be fairly discussed, without a correct understanding of the meaning of its terms.

To the merest novice in trade, commerce, and political economy, it must be perfectly obvious, that articles of great bulk, and little value, may, when imported, be subject to such a heavy per centage of freight, as as to afford adequate protection to the domestic manufacture without any duty. It may be sufficient to cite the case of common chairs, tables, and other articles of furniture, the freight of which from Europe would probably be 50 per cent. This view may be extended even to articles of superior value, but of great bulk, of which the freight would be 10, 20, or 30 per cent—as cheap pleasure carriages and various other articles.

* Examination, page 12.

On the other hand, articles of small bulk and great value, pay a very light per centage of freight, which affords little or no protection to the domestic manufacturer. For instance, silks, gauzes, chintzes, watches, jewelry, &c.

To exemplify this doctrine. It will, I trust, be admitted, that the manufacturer of pleasure carriages, which would pay a freight suppose of 20 per cent, would be better "protected" by a duty of two per cent, making an aggregate burden on the foreign article of 22, than the manufacturer of chintzes, which pay but one or two per cent. freight, would be by a duty of 12 per cent. which would be an aggregate burden of only 14.

Again. Articles of limited production do not require an equal degree of protection with those of which the production is in some measure boundless.

From these simple and clear premises, it follows that agricultural articles, as hemp, flax, cotton, tobacco, potatoes, &c. being bulky in proportion to their value, as well as of limited production, require, to afford them adequate protection, far less duty than articles produced by machinery; as, for instance, cotton goods, of which the manufacture may be carried to almost any extent. Great Britain, with two or three years of preparation to provide an adequate increase of the raw material, might supply half the globe with this article. Whereas no country could ever export, nor did any country, even in time of famine, ever import one fifth part of the productions of the earth necessary for its consumption.

The year 1799, was a year of great scarcity of grain in Great Britain, approaching to famine, which was warded off solely by the extraordinary vigilance and exertions of the government. The importation of bread stuffs was accordingly unprecedentedly large. Yet it was not one tenth part of the consumption—and would not suffice to support the population for five weeks. The average of the animal and vegetable food, exported from the united states, for eighteen years, from 1803 to 1820 inclusive,* was only 15,000,000 of dollars—but the consumption, at one dollar per week, for each person, was $364,000,000, estimating the average population for the whole period at 7,000,000: Thus the export was little more than four per cent. of the consumption of the nation.

If, therefore, the duties laid on agricultural articles, by "the Congress of 1790," which, according to Mr. Cambreleng, "*equally protected every branch of industry*," were merely as high as those on manufactured articles produced by machinery, even then Mr. Cambreleng's position is incorrect; as in that case "every branch of industry" would not be "equally protected." But should it appear, as I trust it will, that the per centage of

* Seybert's Statistics, page 147.

the duties on all such agricultural articles as are usually imported, was double, treble, or quadruple that of those imposed on manufactured ones, then his position is the reverse of truth; and it will follow that the Congress, which he has so highly eulogized, manifested gross partiality in their own favour—and disregard of the interests and equal claims of their manufacturing fellow-citizens.

In truth, that Congress had the candour, at an early period, to abandon the idea of protecting manufactures, as will appear from the following facts, for which I am indebted to Mr. Cambreleng.

The preamble to the first tariff, enacted July 20, 1789, ran—"Whereas it is necessary for the support of government, for "the discharge of the debts of the united states, and *the encou-"ragement and protection of manufactures*, that duties be laid on "goods, wares, and merchandize imported." The preamble of the second tariff, enacted Aug. 10, 1790—after recapitulating the former one, as is usual in such cases—concludes thus—"*And whereas the support of government and the discharge of "said debts*, render it necessary to increase the said duties." For this procedure Mr. Cambreleng accounts thus: "From the "omission to mention manufactures in this law repealing that "of 1789, it is evident that *the Congress of* 1790, *intended when "these duties should be no longer required for the debt or expen-"ses of government, that the manufacturers should not have a "right to insist on their being continued.*"* It is for Mr. Cambreleng to reconcile this fact, with the "equal protection," for which he has given that Congress such large credit, and with the impartiality which ought to characterise the legislature of a free people. NECKER.

NO. III.

HOPING the reader will bear steadily in mind the postulata in my last number, respecting the very great difference of protection, in regard to freight, between articles of which the bulk is great in proportion to their value, as hemp, coals, potatoes, &c. —and those which embrace great value in small compass, as silks, gauzes, jewelry, &c. I proceed to develop the system pursued in the two tariffs enacted by the congress of 1789–90, which, according to Mr. Cambreleng, afforded "*equal protection to every branch of industry.*"

* Examination, page 31.

The duty imposed in 1789 on the important manufactures of *flax*, *cotton*, *hemp*, *iron*, *steel*, *brass*, *lead*, *copper*, *china*, *delft*, *pottery*, *and wood*, was only five per cent.!! There were a few articles subject to 7½, to 10, to 12½, and pleasure carriages to 15. But on the great mass of manufactures, embracing nearly fifteen sixteenths of the whole, there was imposed the minimum of duty, 5 per cent.

To exhibit the proportion which the articles paying the various rates of duty bore to each other, I annex a statement of the amount of the merchandize subject to ad valorem duties, imported in 1789, and 1790.

	1789	1790
At 5 per cent.	$7,136,578	$14,605,713
7½	520,182	1,067,143
10	305,248	699,149
12½	5	
15	2,700	4,876
	$7,964,713	$16,376,881*

Thus the manufacturers of the united states, who had borne their full share of the "heat and burden" of the revolutionary war, and almost universally advocated with zeal and ardour, the adoption of the Federal Constitution, received, at the outset of the government, from their fellow citizens in congress, the "*equal protection*," forsooth, of a paltry duty of *five per cent.* to guard them against the overwhelming competition of foreign rivals, who possessed immense capitals, improved machinery, and skill of the first order; at home enjoyed exclusively the domestic market; had our market for their surplusses; and were moreover shielded by the powerful protection of their respective governments! Never was there a more unequal conflict.

No man of candour can or will pretend that these duties could operate as "protection." To suppose that cotton or woollen manufacturers in the united states, without machinery and with slender capital, skill, and experience, with Mr. Cambrelings "*equal protection*" of five per cent. duty, and one or two per cent. freight, could enter into successful competition with the manufacturers of Europe, would be as absurd as to suppose that an immature stripling could enter the lists with, and overcome, a full-grown man in possession of all his physical powers.

The consequences of this miserable system were such as might have been expected. Various attempts were made at dif-

* Seybert's Statistics, page 158.

ferent times, at Patterson and elsewhere, to establish the woollen and cotton manufactures by native citizens, and by emigrants possessed of the necessary skill and moderate capitals. They almost universally failed. Of this there needs no further proof, so far as respects the woollen manufacture, than the well-known lamentable and disgraceful fact, that previous to the commencement of the late war, that "*branch of industry*" was in so abject a state, that our government found it scarcely possible to furnish a quantity of blankets to the Indians, to the amount of a few thousand dollars; so that the Secretary at war thought it necessary to apply to congress to repeal the non intercourse act, in order to admit a supply from Great Britain! No language could do justice to the censure due to the mistaken policy which produced such a deplorable state of things, after the operation of the most perfect form of government the world ever saw, for twenty-three years, during which time we lavished probably 8 or 10,000,000 of dollars annually for woollen goods, two-thirds of which we could ourselves have furnished.

The situation of the cotton branch was nearly as prostrate. The whole amount of cotton used in manufacturing establishments in 1805, after the government had been 16 years in operation, was only 1000 bales,* or 300,000 lbs. although we exported, in that and the five preceding years, above 180,000,000 of lbs.

Cotton exported from the united states from 1800 *to* 1805, *inclusively.*

1800	lbs. 17,789,803
1801	20,911,201
1802	27,501,075
1803	41,105,623
1804	38,118,041
1805	38,390,087
Total in 6 years,	lbs. 183,815,830
Average,	30,635,971†

For every dollar we received for this raw material, we paid on the average nearly five, for such part as we received back in a manufactured state.‡

* Report of the Committee of Congress on Commerce and Manufactures, 1816

† Pitkin's Tables, pages 132, 133.

‡ This is the proportion between the raw material and the manufactured article, stated by Colquhoun in his "Wealth, Power and Resources of Great Britain," page 91. "The export and consumption of this article may amount to 29,000,000*l.* from which is to be deducted 6,000,000*l.* for the raw material, leaving 23,000,000*l.*"

It is very true, Mr. Cambreleng indulges in glowing descriptions of the wonderful prosperity of this manufacture, "*under our old and moderate duties, long before the war*"* In due season I hope that "*a plain tale will put down*" this most extraordinary assumption, and prove that it is "like the baseless fabric of a vision," which "leaves not a trace behind." I request the indulgence and patience of the reader till the appearance of my fifth number, which shall be devoted to the discussion of this particular point.

Having displayed the "*protection*," which, according to Mr. C. was afforded to manufactures by what he styles "*the venerable system of* 1790,"† it remains now to investigate what "*protection*" the agriculturists, who were a decisive majority in Congress, probably nine-tenths, afforded themselves.

The only articles of which the importation affected the interests of the agriculturists, and which were subject to specific duties, by the tariffs of 1789 and 1790, were cotton—hemp—tobacco—snuff—cheese—indigo—malt—sugar—and spirits. All the other articles, not being enumerated, were subject to five per cent. duty. Thus *cambrics, broadcloths, linens, silks, &c. paid only the same duty as potatoes, or onions!!*

On the above articles, the following duties were imposed in 1789.

Hemp per cwt.	cents 60	equal to	12 per cent.
Cotton per lb.	3		11
Indigo per lb.	16		14
Cheese per lb.	4		57
Manufactured tobacco per lb.	6		66
Snuff per lb.	10		40
Malt per bushel	10		17
Muscovado sugar per lb.	1		20
Distilled spirits other than Jamaica proof, per gallon	8		20
Total for the nine articles			257‡
Average			28½

Thus the average of the duties imposed for the protection of agriculture, was nearly 29 per cent: that is, 500 per cent.

* Examination.

† Idem, page 116.

‡ Let it be noticed, that I do not pretend that these duties are all exact to a cent. I have made every exertion, but found it very difficult, to ascertain the prices of these several articles in the year 1789: some errors may therefore have crept in. But they are inconsiderable, and cannot possibly affect the general result materially. The per centage of cotton, indigo, cheese, manufactured tobacco, sugar, and distilled spirits, is, I believe, literally correct.

more than was imposed on the great mass of manufactured articles, by that "*venerable system*," which is the object of Mr. Cambreleng's admiration. And yet there was then, as now, a constant clamour against "manufacturing monopolies," "undue protection" and "*taxing the many for the benefit of the few!*"

The protection of indigo, by a duty of 14 per cent. was not deemed sufficient. In 1790, it was raised to 25 cents per lb. which was about 22 per cent. Hemp, however, was in the same year reduced to 54 cents per cwt. which was nearly 11 per cent.

Some very witty gentlemen have made themselves very merry at the "*bull*," as they call it, of charging the duties on manufactured tobacco and on snuff to the account of the agriculturists; there being, forsooth, no snuff raised by the farmers, and both articles being manufactures!! This is most pitiful sophistry. These extravagant duties were not imposed for the protection of the manufacturers of those articles, but to secure to the planters the exclusive market for their tobacco, by altogether shutting out supplies from abroad. Let it be distinctly observed, that this view of the case was clearly expressed in Congress. Mr. Sherman, a member from Connecticut, in a spirit of kindness and liberality towards the tobacco planters, moved for six cents per lb. on manufactured tobacco, "*as he thought the duty ought to amount to a prohibition.*"* Can there be the shadow of any other reason assigned, why the "manufacturers" of tobacco should be protected by a duty of sixty-six per cent. when the manufacturers of cottons and woollens could not procure any higher duty than 5 per cent? It would be waste of words and mockery of the reader, to use any arguments to enforce so plain a proposition.

In this view of the subject, it does not appear surprising that this Congress, at its second session, felt ashamed of the words in the preamble of the old tariff, which assigned among the reasons for its enaction "the encouragement and protection of manufactures," and accordingly struck them out of the new one. To continue them would have been a mere delusion.

The decisive protection of tobacco produced the effect which adequate protection has always done in all similar cases. It nearly expelled the foreign rivals from our market, as will appear from the following statement of the

* Debates of Congress, Vol. I. p. 93.

Imports of manufactured tobacco into the united states, from 1805 *to* 1819 *inclusive.**

1805,	lbs. 4,093	Brought forward	lbs. 50,405
1806,	9,840	1813,	7,762
1807,	10,261	1814,	2,161
1808,	4,233	1815,	705
1809,	636	1816,	2,924
1810,	900	1817,	3,924
1811,	18,114	1818,	103
1812,	2,328	1819,	3,297,
	50,405		lbs. 71,281

Thus for fifteen years the whole amount of manufactured tobacco imported into the united states, was only 71,281 lbs. or an average of 4700 lbs. per annum, while we exported about 70,000 hhds. annually, amounting, at 1300 lbs. to the hogshead, to 91,000,000 lbs.

To the candid, honourable planters of tobacco, "protected," from the outset of the government, by a duty of 66 per cent.—to the cotton planters and growers of hemp, protected by a duty, the one of eleven, the other of twelve, and freight of six per cent.—I make a solemn appeal. Can you, gentlemen, lay your hands on your hearts, and aver, that, while the domestic market was thus secured to the American agriculturists, it was fair—or right—or just—or impartial—or consistent with the divine rule—"Do as you would be done by," that your fellow citizens, the manufacturers, should be overwhelmed by foreign rivals, under a duty of five per cent. imposed merely for the purpose of revenue?

I might here close the discussion, having, I trust, fully established the position with which I commenced, viz. that Mr. Cambreleng's assertion that "*the venerable system*" of the Congress of 1790, "*afforded equal protection to every branch of industry*," is wholly destitute of foundation. But there are other views to be taken of the subject, which place it on much stronger ground, than I have yet assumed, as will appear from a comparison of the aggregate protection, arising from freight and duty, of four agricultural and four manufacturing articles.

COTTON.	1790.	*COTTON GOODS.*	
	per cent.		per cent.
Duty,	11	Duty,	5
Freight,	6	Freight,	1
Total,	17	Total,	6

* Seybert, page 165.

HEMP.

Duty,	12
Freight,	6
Total,	18

CHEESE.

Duty,	57
Freight,	2
Total,	59

INDIGO.

Duty, in 1790,	22
Freight,	1
Total,	23

WOOLLEN GOODS.

Duty,	5
Freight,	1
Total,	6

IRON WARES.

Duty,	5
Freight,	3
Total,	8

LINEN.

Duty,	5
Freight,	1
Total,	6

One more view must appal every man who feels for the honor of the country, at the partial and miserable policy of this "*venerable system.*"

STRIKING CONTRASTS.

	Duty.
6 *lbs. of cheese, value* 42 *cents, paid*	24 *cents.*
But 10 *yards of linen, value* $5, *paid only*	25 *cents.*
8 *lbs. of cotton, value* 220 *cents, paid*	24 *cents.*
But 10 *yards of cotton goods, value* $5, *paid only*	25 *cents.*
4 *lbs. of manufactured tobacco, value* 36 *cents, paid*	24 *cents.*
A yard of broadcloth, value $5, *paid but*	25 *cents.*

The "equal protection" afforded to commerce, the third "*branch of industry,*" claims a separate discussion, and is therefore reserved for my next number.

NECKER.

July 21, 1821.

NO. IV.

TO redeem my pledge, I proceed to investigate the extent of the "*protection*" afforded to commerce, the third "*branch of industry,*" by the "venerable system" of 1789–90, in order to ascertain, whether it was "*equal,*" according to Mr. Cambreling, or superior, or inferior, to that bestowed on manufactures.

At the commencement of the government, in 1789, the commerce of the united states was at a low ebb. Our tonnage, according to Dr. Seybert, was inadequate to the transportation of our produce. One third of what was employed for this purpose belonged to foreigners.*

Congress laudably and promptly adopted the most vigorous, salutary and efficient measures to extend it, as I shall make appear. Had they afforded manufactures half the aid and protection commerce received from them, the advances of the country to wealth, power and prosperity, would have been far more rapid than they have been. Two hundred millions of money would probably have been saved, and tens of thousands of valuable immigrants been added to our population.

The third act passed by the first congress, decided the contest between American and foreign shipping; gave the form a most decided ascendency; and laid the foundation of its wonderful increase; so that in 1809, it was equal to that possessed by Great Britain in 1789.†

By this act, foreign vessels, engaged in the coasting trade, were subject to a tonnage duty of fifty cents for every entry. Whereas American vessels paid only six cents per ton, and but once a year.

Let us see the operation of this truly national act—

A foreign vessel of 100 tons, engaged in the coasting trade, and making suppose twelve to sixteen entries in the year, would pay 6 or 800 dollars per annum—but an American of the same dimensions, would pay but six dollars. This was a virtual prohibition, and nearly expelled foreign vessels from this trade. Yet effectual as was this protection, it was not deemed sufficient. Some years afterwards, foreign vessels were prohibited from engaging in the coasting trade on any terms.

The discrimination in the foreign trade made by this act was somewhat varied. American vessels engaged in this trade, paid six cents tonnage for every entry—foreign vessels fifty as before. In addition to this advantage, there was a discount allowed, of 10 per cent. on the duties upon goods imported in American vessels. Thus a foreign vessel of 500 tons, engaged in the foreign trade, and making two entries per annum, would pay 500 dollars; whereas an American vessel of similar dimensions, would pay only 60—independent of the important advantage of the discount on the duties upon the cargo. The following tables will evince the salutary effects of this wise law, and the unprecedented increase of shipping it produced.

* Seybert's Statistics, page 292. † Idem, 294.

Statement of the tonnage employed in the foreign trade of the united states from the year 1789 *to* 1804,*

	American.	Foreign.	Total.
1789,	tons. 127,980	tons. 106,654	tons. 234,634
1790,	355.079	251,058	606,137
1791,	363.852	240,740	604.592
1792,	414,679	244,278	658.957
1793,	448,864	164,676	613.540
1794,	527,196	84,521	611,717
1795,	585,994	62,549	648.543
1796,	678,160	49,960	728,120
1797,	612,014	76,693	688,707
1798,	523,051	88,568	611,617
1799,	628,511	109.599	738,110
1800,	686,104	122,403	808,507
1801,	851,709	157,270	1,008,979
1802,	796,619	145,519	942,138
1803,	787,600	163,714	951,489
1804,	822,026	122,141	944,166

Rapid progress of American tonnage from 1789 *to* 1805.†

1789,	tons. 201,562	1798	tons 898,328
1790,	478.377	1799	946,408
1791,	502,146	1800	972,492
1792,	564.437	1801	1,033,218
1793,	491,780	1802	892,101
1794,	628,816	1803	949,147
1795,	747,963	1804	1,042,403
1796,	831,900	1805	1,140,368
1797,	876,912		

But the advantages in favour of the American merchants engaged in the China trade, were incomparably greater than in the other branches. The discrimination in the duties on teas was enormous---and, like the tonnage in the coasting trade, amounted to a virtual prohibition of foreign vessels.

Schedule of the duties on teas, by the act of 1789.

	In American vessels.	In foreign vessels.
Bohea tea, per lb.	6 cents	15 cents.
Souchong and other black teas,	10	22
Hyson tea,	20	45
Other green teas,	12	27
	48	109
Average,	12	27¼

* Seybert, p. 318.

† Idem, 317.

In order to evince the great extent of the protection thus afforded to commerce, I shall not—as Mr. Cambreleng says—have recourse to " vague declamations about these matters, which would not satisfy sensible men." I shall, " therefore explain my calculations by figures," and state the case of a cargo of 30,000 lbs bohea—20,000 lbs. souchong—and 30,000 lbs. hyson tea.

	Duty in an American vessel.	Duty in a foreign vessel.
30,000 lbs. bohea	$ 1,800	$ 4,500
20,000 lbs. souchong	2,000	4,400
30,000 lbs. hyson	6,000	13,500
	$ 9,800	$ 22,400

Whoever compares this admirable regulation, in favour of commerce, founded on the experience of the most trading nations of the globe, with the paltry duty of five per cent. on the manufactures of cotton, wool, iron, steel, brass, &c. will be struck with amazement at the shocking contrast it exhibits—at the fostering care bestowed on one "*branch of industry*"—and the almost total disregard of another branch, of at least equal utility and of equal claims and rights. Let it be distinctly observed, that all idea is disclaimed in the most unequivocal manner, of censuring the protection of commerce.—This part of the system is entitled to the most unqualified approbation. To the inequality of the protection afforded manufactures alone, I wish to turn the reader's attention.

A brief analysis of Mr. Cambreleng's " venerable system."

We have seen,

I. That the " protection" afforded to the great mass of manufactures was 5 per cent.

II. But that those articles usually imported, which affected the agricultural interest, were subject to duties, varying from 12 to 66 per cent, and averaging 29 per cent.

III. And that the merchants were effectually secured in the exclusive possession of the coasting and China trade, and had such advantages in every other species of trade, that their shipping was more than doubled in one year—trebled in six—and quadrupled in eight.

CONTRAST.

	Duty.
50,000 dollars worth of manufactures of cotton, wool, iron, brass, steel, &c. paid	$ 2,500
62,500 lbs. of cheese, value $4375, paid	2,500

12,500 lbs. of hyson tea, value $7500, when imported in an American vessel, paid	2,500
But 5600 lbs. of the same tea, value $3600, if imported in a foreign vessel, paid	2,520

ONE MORE CONTRAST.

A yard of broadcloth, value $5, paid	25 cents.
A pound of hyson tea, value 60 cents, imported in a foreign vessel, paid	45 cents.
Being an addition to the duty when imported in an American vessel, of	25 cents.

Notwithstanding the immense difference in the protection afforded by government to the several "branches of industry," the agriculturists and merchants have been constantly complaining of the "monopolies" of the manufacturers—and of their "taxing the many for the benefit of the few." This is precisely analogous to the case of the monk and lay-brother in the School for Scandal. The former, rioting on all the good things that smiling Plenty could spread before him, from her cornucopia, reproaches the latter, who is the very picture of Famine, with gormandizing, because he has picked up some of the crumbs that fell from a cake which the monk is greedily devouring.

I will propose two queries to Mr. Cambreleng, on which to exercise his talents, and to prove how well founded is his admiration of this "venerable system."

Can any satisfactory reason be assigned why the raw materials, cotton and hemp, paid a duty of twelve—cheese of 57—and manufactured tobacco of 66 per cent. while manufactures of flax, cotton, wool, iron, steel, &c. paid but 5?

Can there be any adequate reason, why the American merchant, in his conflict with a foreigner, should have had a discrimination in the duty on teas to the amount of 125 per cent. while the American manufacturer, in his conflict with his foreign rival, had only five per cent. protection? When these questions are answered, more shall succeed them.

On a fair view of the subject, it may be pronounced, that a more partial or unequal scheme of policy has rarely been seen, in any age or nation, pretending to equal rights, than Mr. Cambreleng's "*venerable system*" of 1789—90; that it as scrupulously guarded the interests of two "branches of industry," as it neglected those of the third; that it partook largely of the spirit which breathes in the legislation of "*mother countries*," as they are absurdly called, for their colonies; and that it adds one to the thousand previous instances, to prove, that where the legislation of a nation is confined to one or two descriptions of citizens, the others rarely experience equal justice.

These are bold averments. But they are not lightly hazarded. They are matured and deliberate convictions, the result of a sober and serious reflection as I have ever bestowed on any subject. They are true or false. If true, they ought, however unpalatable -- and greatly unpalatable they must be to some of our citizens—to be loudly proclaimed, and have been too long suppressed. For their truth, I make myself responsible. If, however, they are false, let their errors be pointed out, and they shall be acknowledged and retracted by

NECKER.

July 30, 1821.

NO V.

Mr. Cambreleng's views of the early prosperity of the cotton "*branch of industry*" come next under discussion. In various parts of his work he most unequivocally asserts that this branch was in a most flourishing state, "*under the old and moderate duties*" previous to the war.

"From the advantages naturally possessed by the united "states, in the production of the raw material; from the en- "couragement afforded by the emigration of English manufac- "turers, and the substitution of machinery for manual labour, "it was evident that manufactures of this raw material would "be *among the first objects of attention in this country*. We "accordingly find that in 1790, a factory existed with a capital "of $500,000.* And the cotton manufactories, as we shall "see, with the aid of these powerful causes, *continued to flour-* "*ish*."†

"Our present duties are high enough for revenue. *Our cot-* "*ton factories never flourished more than they did under our old* "*and moderate duties, long before the war*—and certainly they "do not stand in need of high duties now."‡

This splendid detail is a mere "*beau ideal*"—or "fancy sketch" Closing the historic page, and unmindful of the facts of the case, it draws largely on imagination.

The "society" referred to by Mr. Cambreleng, was established at Patterson in New Jersey, and, under a more auspicious regime, could not have failed of signal success. The place possesses every possible advantage for manufactures on a large and magnificent scale. Suitable sites were purchased—and machinery and workmen provided. Nothing was wanting but the

* For this fact Mr. Cambreleng refers to Mr. Hamilton's Report.
† Examination, page 37. ‡ Idem.

favour and protection of government. A duty equal to that imposed on hemp or cotton, or a third part of that on tobacco, or cheese, would have rendered Patterson a mine of individual and national wealth and prosperity. All applications for the purpose were wholly in vain. The congress of that day regarded with the same withering indifference, the decline of the establishment as their successors have in 1816, 17, 18, 19 and 20, regarded the calamitous scenes exhibited in Pittsburg at Brandywine, in Philadelphia, and elsewhere.* The danger of smuggling—the high rate of wages—the injustice of "*taxing the many for the benefit of the few*"—our want of ripeness for manufactures—the enormous extent of our back lands—the purity of a country life, with the immorality of manufacturing establishments—and the great variety of other reasons, if reasons they can be called, which have been so constantly used ever since, were then adduced with success, to defeat the applications of the manufacturers, and prevent a compliance with their petitions. The protection of government, which, to the success of this important undertaking, so worthy of national support, was as necessary as the alternation of heat and rain, to secure a plentiful harvest, was withheld. The duty remained at five per cent. while, as we have seen, cheese was protected by a duty of fifty-seven, and manufactured tobacco by 66 per cent. The consequences were fatal, as was foreseen and predicted. The establishment went to ruins—the undertakers were bankrupted—the capital invested was wholly sacrificed—the workmen were dispersed, and generally "went back" to cultivate the soil—and the undertaking served as "*an awful beacon*" to warn our citizens of the folly of engaging in manufacturing establishments on a large scale, under a government which left them to struggle against the overwhelming superiority of for-

* It ought to be borne in remembrance, that above forty petitions and memorials, with thousands of signatures, were presented in 1816—17, to the fourteenth Congress at its second session, by the suffering manufacturers in Boston, Providence, Newhaven, Hartford, New York, Philadelphia, Baltimore, Pittsburg, Berkshire, in Massachusetts, Oneida county in New York—and from various other towns and places in Massachusetts, Connecticut, Rhode Island, New York, New Jersey, Pennsylvania, Kentucky, and Illinois; praying for protection against the overwhelming competition of foreign nations, with whose merchandize, to an enormous amount, the country was deluged, whereby their capitals, to the amount of millions, were nearly destroyed, and their hopes of prosperity in the pursuit of their lawful avocations blasted; that *not one of them was ever read in the house; that they were not even reported on, except those that respected the iron business;* and that not one single measure was adopted to afford relief to the applicants. Such flagrant and unfeeling disregard of public distress, such gross neglect of the voice of constituents, was probably never displayed by any other legislature in any age or nation. This was the memorable Congress, which passed the act to render themselves salary officers, with 1500 dollars per annum. This act went through the houses almost without debate, and, in twelve days from its inception, became a law!

eign rivals, with a "*protecting duty*" of 5, 7½, or 12½ per cent!! The admonition was not lost, as will appear in the sequel.

Yet this is the case on which Mr. Cambreleng, unhappily for his cause, relies, to establish the prosperity of the cotton "branch of industry." If it proves nothing else, it most satisfactorily proves how careless he must have been in his investigations—and how cautiously he is to be received as authority.

Cotemporaneously with the establishment at Patterson, a respectable society was formed in Philadelphia, which embraced a considerable portion of our citizens. A cotton factory on an extensive scale was established, and struggled with foreign rivals for some time. But the struggle was equally unavailing with that at Patterson. The undertaking shared the same fate; looked in vain to the government for protection; went to decay; and was finally "blotted from the map" by a conflagration, the work of a wretched incendiary.

Having now dismissed these two establishments, I proceed to detail the real state of the cotton manufactory under "the old and moderate duties" of "*the venerable system*" of the Congress of 1790, which "*equally protected every branch of industry.*"

With all the immense advantages for the cotton manufacture possessed by this country—boundless water power—raw material to an unlimited extent—hundreds of immigrants brought up to the manufacture—and citizens of the utmost energy and enterprize—it made so little progress from 1789 till the close of the year 1807, that there were at the latter period but 8000 spindles in operation in manufacturing establishments, in Massachusetts, Connecticut and Rhode Island---that is, at the expiration of the eighteenth year of the operation of a government, which, we are gravely assured, "afforded equal protection to every branch of industry."

This is a strong assertion, and demands irrefragable proof, which shall be given.

Mr. Gallatin was instructed, by a resolution of the house of representatives of the united states, to institute an inquiry into the state of the manufactures of this country. With this order he complied, with his usual indefatigable industry, and accordingly made report on the 17th of April, 1810. His statements are in the most direct hostility with the captivating descriptions of Mr. Cambreleng.

"The first cotton mill was erected in the state of Rhode-"Island, in the year 1791; another in the same state in the "year 1795; and two more in the state of Massachusetts, in "the years 1803 and 4."*

* Gallatin's report on manufactures.

This was the wonderful state of prosperity of the cotton manufacture, in 1804, after a lapse of fifteen years from the date of the "*venerable system of* 1789."

"During the three succeeding years, ten more were erected, "or commenced in Rhode Island, and one in Connecticut, mak-"ing altogether fifteen mills erected *before the year* 1808, work-"ing at that time about 8000 spindles, and producing about "300,000 lbs. of yarn a year."*

What a prodigious contrast between this plain statement, and the view presented in the "*Examination* of the tariff!" The one offers the dreary and desolate face of winter—the other all the loveliness and bloom of spring.

For some of the numerous errors of Mr. Cambreleng's book, apology can readily be made. Its publication was, according to his own statement, "of necessity hastened, that it might anticipate the vote on the tariff," and defeat the views of the manufacturers. On some points it was difficult to procure documents under such circumstances of haste. But when he could not procure them, he ought not to have used such strong and positive assertions and assumptions, so very wide of the real state of the case.

An egregious error of Mr. C. respecting the cotton "branch of industry" is an idea clearly held out, that it was injured by the embargo and other restrictive measures.

"We have," says Mr. C. "in the preceding chapter, traced "the history of our cotton factories to the present time; and "have also noticed that "*their natural vigour was such, that* "*though distracted by embargoes, restrictions and war, they still* "*increased.*"†

I trust I have satisfactorily proved, that there was no such "natural vigour" in the cotton factories as is here asserted; and that the whole number of spindles employed *before the year* 1808, was only 8000. Now it remains to prove, that so far from being "distracted," their progress was prodigiously accelerated, by "embargoes, restrictions and war."

We have seen how slender was their progress till the close of 1807. The embargo took place about that time. As to the subsequent progress, I refer Mr. C. and his friends to Mr. Gallatin, who says—"Returns have been received of 87 mills "which were erected at the end of the year 1809—Sixty-two of "which, (48 mules and 14 horse mills) were in operation, and "worked at that time 31,000 spindles. The other 25 will be in "operation in the course of this year [1810,] and, together with "the former ones (almost all of which are increasing their ma-

* Gallatin's report on manufactures.

† Examination of the tariff.

"chinery,) *will, by the estimates received, work more than* 80,000 "*spindles at the commencement of the year* 1811."*

So much for the "*distractions of the embargo and restrictions.*" Now for the effect of the war. In 1815, the capital invested in this branch was $40,000,000—the cotton consumed 90,000 bales—the number of people employed 100,000—the wages paid annually $15,000,000—and the value of the cotton produced, $24,300,000.‡

Would it not be a work of extreme supererogation, to add a fact or an argument, to prove how radically Mr. Cambreleng's statement on this subject is wrong in all its points?

NECKER.

NO. VI.

To the Friends of Natural Rights, alias, the Cambrelengian Philosophers.

Gentlemen,

It is, you will suppose, with the utmost fear and trembling, that I venture to enter the lists against so formidable a phalanx, armed with the tremendous weapons you employ with such prodigious skill and facility. Those weapons are as truly formidable as langrage, Congreve rockets, red hot balls, fire ships, and infernal machines in warfare. The oratory of Æschines, Demosthenes, or Cicero—the logic of Aristotle, Locke, Watts, or Blair—and the political economy of Colbert, Sully, Elizabeth, Frederick, or Hamilton—could no more withstand you than a sloop of war could withstand a well-directed broadside from a seventy-four. What chance, then, can the poor "Careyan Philosophers," as you judiciously, and humourously, and wittily style your antagonists, have in the conflict with you? None. We must beat a retreat—burn our books and papers, including "the library of old Statisticus"—succumb to your irresistible lucubrations—and, if pursued, surrender at discretion.

To prove that my terrors, however extreme, are not irrational, and that I do not overrate the destructive nature of the logical weapons you employ, it will be proper to describe them, which I shall do in brief. They are—a most outrageous misrepresentation and caricature, not to say falsification of the positions and statements of your antagonists—intrepid assertions, not only without the shadow of proof, but without an attempt at proof—puerile personalities—a quibbling evasion of facts which

* Mr. Gallatin's report.

† Report of the committee of commerce and manufactures, 1816.

cannot be disproved—an unceasing attempt at humour, wholly out of time and place—in a word, the reverse of every thing like fair or dignified argument.

Those who carry on a polemical campaign with such weapons, have an immeasurable advantage over their antagonists: for without one fair or candid quotation from their writings—without a single relevant fact—without the slightest study or examination of the subject—without disproving a fact or refuting an argument—they can silence and bear down all opposition, and, carrying on "a windy war of words," throw dust in the eyes of their opponents and those of the public.

But, gentlemen, powerful as is this system of warfare, and great as is your ability in carrying it on, I cannot flatter you in the opinion that you are the inventors of it. No. It has existed from the earliest periods of human controversy to the present time, and been invariably called in to aid a feeble cause: a sound one scorns such an auxiliary. But though I cannot admit your claim to the invention, I freely allow that you have great merit in its improvement. You far excel your predecessors in the various manœuvres and stratagems of which the system is susceptible.

Mr. Cambreleng wrote a book against the tariff, containing a number of vital errors calculated to mislead the public mind on this important subject. I regarded it not merely as a right, but a duty to point out those errors. I have done it, I trust, in a manner becoming a gentleman, without an offensive or illiberal line or word. If I have succeeded in establishing those errors, the course for Mr. Cambreleng or his friends to pursue, is to retract them—not, as you have done, to involve the subject in mists and confusion, in order to prevent a correct public decision. But if I have failed, let the failure be proved, and I shall acknowledge my mistake.

You have, *ad captandum*, accused me of an "*unnatural hostility to farmers*." You are called upon either to produce a sentence which warrants this accusation; to admit that you have been guilty of calumny; or else to let the matter pass *sub silentio*, and acquiesce in the public decision on the case.

Your reflections on my age—my "*patriarchate*," &c. &c. I will not say, I despise. That would be a very harsh word. But this I *will* say, in perfect soberness, that I regard them with the most sovereign indifference, and as a proof either of the acknowledged weakness of your cause, or the want of judgment of its advocates. On these topics you may freely ring the changes to the utmost extent of the powers of your prolific pens.

Of your evasion of facts, incapable of disproof, I will furnish but one instance:—

Mr. Cambreleng asserted that "the Congress of 1790, equally protected every branch of industry;" and on the basis of this assertion, erected a splendid fabric of eulogium on that Congress, and held out their example to be followed at present.

This dictum I fully disproved, by reference to documents, and shewed that while the great mass of manufactures were left to struggle under "*a protection*," as it is incorrectly called, of five per cent. commerce experienced the most ample, liberal, and complete protection:—

I. By a discrimination in the duty on the tonnage engaged in the foreign trade, equal to 700 per cent. on every voyage: for American vessels paid but six cents per ton, while foreign paid 50. Laws of Congress, Vol. II. page 6.

II. By a discrimination in the duty on the tonnage engaged in the coasting trade, equal to above 4000 per cent. per annum, in the case of only six entries in the year.

For American vessels engaged in the coasting trade, paid but six cents tonnage duty per annum; while foreign paid 50 cents on every entry.

III. By a discrimination in the duties on teas imported in foreign and American vessels, equal to 125 per cent. whereby the China trade was secured to the American merchants:

	In American vessels.	In Foreign vessels.
Duty on Bohea tea per lb.*	6 cents.	15 cents.
Souchong and other black teas,	10	22
Hyson,	20	45
Other green teas,	12	27
	48 cts.	109 cts.
Average,	12	27¼

IV. By an addition of 10 per cent. to the duties on goods imported in foreign vessels.

To which I now add:

V. By a bounty, in 1790, of ten cents per quintal on dried fish, and ten cents per barrel on salted fish and provisions.

Now this is a plain case, in which there is no room for subterfuge or evasion. It is a mere question, whether five per cent. is equal to 125, or to 700. If not, Mr. C's assertion is wholly destitute of foundation.

* These duties were imposed in 1789—but were modified in 1790, when the duties on teas imported in American vessels were considerably raised. The discrimination was thus reduced to about 50 per cent. on an average, which was, as every person must allow, as total and complete a prohibition of the trade to foreigners, as the duties of 1789.

And what are the arguments you advance to support Mr. Cambreleng, or to overturn my statements? With the following four lines, you suppose you have gained a complete triumph over these important facts:

"Then comes No. IV, with its attendant tables, to show us "how sumptuously the merchants fared at this bounty board— "*Will Monsieur Necker tell us the merchants were very formidable in the Congress of* 1790?"

Now, Messieurs "Friends of Natural Rights," I ask what bearing has this query on the subject? The only points at issue in this case, are not, whether "the merchants were very formidable in the Congress of 1790"—but whether their interests were fully and completely protected—and whether equal protection was extended to "every other branch of industry," as Mr. Cambreleng has erroneously asserted? I trust I have fully proved the affirmative of the one, and the negative of the other question. That the merchants must have had great influence, the result makes manifest. They were most ably represented. From these points you display your address in withdrawing the public attention.

Of the "*outrageous misrepresentation*," of the positions of your antagonists, I shall furnish a few out of the numerous instances wherewith your three numbers abound:—

"These disinterested and self-styled patriots, approaching "us with the tones of sweet persuasion, and expressing the tenderest solicitude for our welfare, tell us that *we never can* "*be rich and happy until we bind our wants, our rights, and* "*inclinations, with irritating and unnatural restrictions; until* "*we clothe one branch of industry with a general monopoly;* and "impose on the mass of the community *the bonds* of colonial "vassalage.

"*Agriculture and commerce ruin a nation;* labour can never "be productive but in manufactures.

"When some branches of industry languish, all the atten- "tion of government should be bestowed on that branch "which remains profitable; for it is a settled maxim in political "economy, that *a bounty should never be granted, until he who* "*is to receive it is able to do without it.*

"The proper way to enlarge the demand for surplus grain or "other productions, is to confine the sale to the domestic mar- "ket.

"Government was never instituted to secure personal rights, "or to preserve the morals or happiness of the people; but "only to superintend the wealth of the nation: for, it is a set- "tled maxim, that *no nation can be enriched without an entire* "*sacrifice of morals, rights, and happiness.*

"It is a vulgar notion, that the property which a citizen pos-
"sesses, actually belongs to him: for *he is a mere tenant, labor-*
"*er or agent of the government*, to whom all the property in the
"nation legitimately belongs.

"The government may, therefore, manage this property ac-
"cording to its own fancy, and shift capitalists and labourers
"from one employment to another.

"Should a citizen be thus transferred from trade to trade,
"and thereby lose that which he *supposed* to be his own pro-
"perty, and find his family in want, *he could have no right to*
"*complain: the government would have only used its own pro-*
"*perty in experiments to increase its capital.*"—Friends of Natu-
"ral Rights, No. III.

In what page of the writings of the friends of the protection of manufactures, have you found these sentiments? Where can you produce any thing that looks even like the shadow of them? And if you cannot, how can you justify such a monstrous perversion of their views—such a wanton departure from fact?

The history of controversies, religious and political, affords hundreds of instances of books being condemned, and many of them burned, through the artifice of making partial, insulated extracts from the matter which they contained, whereby their authors were made to speak a language wholly foreign from their hearts. Your procedure is still more extraordinary. You make no extracts, partial or impartial—but absolutely fabricate for your antagonists a system utterly abhorrent from their views. Your sketch is as foreign from theirs as light from darkness—virtue from vice. This is the true plan of the inquisition, whereby the destined victim, previous to immolation, is clothed in a San Benito dress, ornamented with devils and "*goblins damned*" in torments, to excite the horror of the spectators. I appeal to the good sense of the readers of the Intelligencer, whether a more outrageous violation of fact can be found, than the preceding extracts exhibit. If the system of the "Careyan Philosophers," be dangerous and destructive, there can be no need of such unprecedented fabrication.

I will not ask whether this procedure is honourable, or generous, or liberal—but merely whether it is honest? Whether it is not unworthy of gentlemen—discreditable to the cause you advocate—and an insult to an enlightened public?

The cause at issue is one of immense importance. Let it be fairly argued. Let that side whose arguments are most cogent, triumph. But let not means be resorted to, which would answer equally well for the worst, and against the best, cause that ever existed.

NECKER.

Philadelphia, Sept. 1, 1821.

NO. VII.

I PROCEED to notice a few more of the very numerous errors in Mr. Cambreleng's book. These are, it is true, far inferior in importance to those I have already developed—and are adduced principally to afford further corroboration of the extreme carelessness, in point of fact, displayed in the Examination, which, in a work of this kind, is a radical and vital defect.

"It may be fairly presumed, that a day labourer in a facto-"ry, will remain and die in that condition; and probably all "that he can leave his family will be that state of dependence "in which he has lived. The very house which his family oc-"cupies, belongs to the proprietor of the factory. Such is too "generally the produce of the labour of that man who depends "on a factory for employ. He may add to the population of "the nation, which he would do in any case. *But he adds no-"thing to the wealth of the nation by accumulating property for him-"self*—the best possible wealth for a free government."—Examination, page 7.

This statement is intended to excite, and has excited jealousy against the manufacturers, and hostility against any modification of the tariff, as if the benefits to arise from protecting duties, would have no operation in favour of the large class of working people, but centre wholly in the hands of capitalists. Were this objection really well founded, it would afford an argument of no small force against the proposed system. But it is so wholly the reverse, that in many of the trades carried on in this country, there is not the least difficulty for a journeyman to commence operations on his own account. It is much more practicable than for a country labourer. I will exemplify this argument by the cotton branch—but the reasoning will apply with nearly equal force to a great proportion of the other branches.

A cotton weaver earns here five or six dollars per week. A sober, industrious, frugal man can support an average family of four persons on four dollars. A loom costs about twelve. With the savings of a very few weeks, therefore, a workman can purchase a loom; commence business; and, Mr. Cambreleng's assertion to the contrary notwithstanding, may "*add to the wealth of the nation, by accumulating property for himself—the best possible wealth for a free government.*"

This, let it be added, is not a "day dream"—a "fancy sketch," calculated to dazzle or amuse. It is a sober reality. There are hundreds of persons in this single branch, of this precise description, in Pennsylvania, New York, Massachusetts, Connecticut, and Rhode Island, who are now working on their own account, after having been, at no very distant period—many of them within the last four, five, or six months—employed as journeymen. In the city of Philadelphia alone, the number is so great as to be scarcely credible. At a late public sale of looms belonging to a factory, the buyers of this class were so numerous, that the looms sold very nearly as high as they originally cost.

This state of things is by no means confined to this single branch. It extends, I repeat, to a very large proportion of the others. And it would not be extravagant to assert, that far more than half of the master manufacturers throughout the united states, even of those who conduct business on a large and extensive scale, were originally journeymen.

There are, it is true, some branches, which require very large capitals, and which cannot, of course, be commenced so soon, nor on such easy terms. But there are scarcely any, which frugality and industry will not enable a journeyman to commence in process of time.

In various parts, indeed throughout Mr. Cambreleng's work, he has fallen into an egregious error on the subject of Mr. Hamilton's Report, which he gives as the foundation of the tariff of 1790.

" The report was acted on by the Congress of 1790, so far " as it related to the revenue; but that Congress cautiously " omitted adopting the language of the report, as far as it re- " lated to the encouragement of manufactures."—Examination, p. 26.

" In consequence of Mr. Hamilton's report, and the neces- " sities of the government, a new revenue law was enacted on " the 16th of August, 1790."—Idem, p. 30.

This " revenue law" was enacted at the date stated by Mr. Cambreleng. But Mr. Hamilton's profound and celebrated report was dated December 5, 1791. It could not, of course, have been the basis of the " new revenue law." To all its wise suggestions and admonitions, Congress never paid the least attention. They were to that body a complete dead letter, to the manifest injury of the nation.

" If the British system be adopted, *it must gradually transfer " the legislative power in this country, from the farmers to the ma- " nufacturers;* this being the inevitable effect of taxing the one " class to enrich the other; thereby impoverishing the class tax- " ed, and diminishing their numbers."—Idem, p. 9.

This assertion is truly ludicrous. The idea that the increase of the duties on cottons, woollens, iron, &c. &c. eight, ten, or twelve per cent. or even fifteen or twenty, had it been contemplated to raise them so high, would, "*transfer the legislative power from the farmers to the manufacturers*," betrays a wonderful degree of credulity; for I will not allow myself to believe that Mr. C. holds out this phantom to terrify the farmers, without being himself affected with the hideous spectre.

"Mr. Hamilton's great object, in his report on manufactures, "was to establish a system of revenue to meet the expenses of "the government, and pay the interest of the public debt."—Examination, page 25.

Some of Mr. Cambreleng's errors, as I have already observed, are entitled to apology, from his "publication," according to his own account, being "of necessity hastened that it might anticipate the vote on the new tariff." But for the present error there is no apology whatever. Mr. Hamilton's Report was to be had without any difficulty; and it is to be presumed Mr. C. must have had it in his possession—otherwise it would have been highly improper to refer to, and comment on it as he has done. Now, it requires but a very cursory examination, to see that the alpha and omega of this report were the protection and encouragement of manufactures. These form the object and end of all his reasonings—all his facts. Never was a subject more elaborately and convincingly discussed—and never was a system more ably and unanswerably supported. It is impossible to read the report with due attention, and with a mind open to conviction, without being a convert to its doctrines. Revenue is but rarely mentioned, and never otherwise than incidentally. Mr. H. successfully combats all the objections to his system on the ground of its pretended tendency to impair the revenue, by the following, among other irrefragable reasons.

"The possibility of a diminution of the revenue may present "itself," says Mr. Hamilton, "as an objection to the arrange- "ments which have been submitted.

"But there is no truth which may be more firmly relied on, "than that *the interests of the revenue are promoted by whatever* "*promotes an increase of national industry and wealth.*

"In proportion to the degree of these, is the capacity of every "country to contribute to the public treasury: and where the "capacity to pay is increased, or even is not decreased, the only "consequence of measures which diminish any particular re- "source, is a change of the object.

"The measures, however, which have been submitted, taken "aggregately, *will, for a long time to come, rather augment than* "*decrease the public revenue.*"—Hamilton's Works, Vol. I. page 275.

This, I presume, proves that Mr. Hamilton's "great object" was not "to establish a sytem of revenue"—but to promote the industry, whereby the capacity to raise a revenue would be greatly enhanced.

I return again to the Examination:—

"If the citizens of the united states," says Mr. Cambreleng, "want to see *a democratic tariff, let them look at that of* 1790.— "The men who framed it knew what equal rights were, because "they had fought bravely for them. In that tariff they will "not find the poor paying a higher duty than the rich for the "same article. *Each man was then taxed according to his ability: "and luxuries paid the highest rate of duty.*"—Examination, page 94,

I shall make a very fair comparison of the duties on different articles in this "*venerable*," this "*democratic tariff*," in order clearly to establish how inexcusably wide of the mark Mr. Cambreleng has diverged in this statement. I will take on the one side articles used exclusively by the rich—and on the other, articles in daily use by the poor, and I trust the reader will be lost in astonishment at the utter inequality and injustice of this tariff, although, as we are exultingly told, "the men who framed "it, knew what equal rights were, because they had fought "bravely for them." Strong positive facts are not to be set aside or refuted by a few sounding phrases, however plausibly or dogmatically delivered.

I confine myself on the one side, to silks, sattins, superfine broadcloths, gauzes, rich chintzes, gold watches, pearls, diamonds, paste work, embroidery, jewelry, and laces—and on the other to bohea tea, brown sugar, coffee, salt, cheese, and molasses—and by these articles shall bring to the test the accuracy of Mr. Cambreleng's encomiums on this "*democratic tariff.*"

The articles in the first class are easily dispatched, They were all subject to one simple duty, which was no more than *five per cent.*

The other articles require more detail. They were subject to specific duties, as it would have been too revolting to have fixed ad valorem duties so extravagantly and iniquitously high as the amount they really paid.

Bohea tea and brown sugar are exclusively used by the poor. The former cost at that period, 15 cents per lb. and paid a duty of ten cents, equal to *sixty-six per cent.*

Brown sugar cost about six cents, and paid a duty of one and a half, which is *twenty-five per cent.*

Salt cost about 15 cents per bushel, and paid 12, which is *eighty per cent.*

Cheese cost about 8 cents per lb. and paid 4 cents duty, equal to *fifty per cent.*

Molasses cost 24 cents per gallon, and paid 3 cents duty, equal to *twelve per cent.*
Coffee cost 12 cents, and paid 4 cents only, equal to *thirty-three per cent.*

Now, courteous reader, are you not lost in admiration of the "*democratic principles*" of this "*venerable tariff!*" and of the profound regard for "*equal rights*," of "the men who framed it," and "who bravely fought for them?"

Let us calmly examine the operation of this very "venerable tariff," in order that "he who runs may read" its *democracy.*

A poor man with a family of four persons will consume about one third of a pound of tea, and three pounds and a half of sugar in the week, equal per annum to 17 lbs. of the former and 180 lbs. of the latter.

17 lbs. bohea tea,	cost $2 55	and paid duty	$1 70
180 lbs. of brown sugar	cost 10 80	and paid duty	2 70
First cost,	$13 33	Duty,	$4 40

I will suppose a rich man to consume for himself and family in the year, 12 yards of superfine broad cloth, at four dollars, and 80 yards of silks, sattins, gauzes, chintzes, &c. at half a dollar.

12 yards broad cloth	$48	paid duty	$2 40
80 yards silks, &c.	40	paid duty	2 00
First cost,	$88	Duty,	$4 40

Note. These prices and duties refer to the year 1790.

Thus the poor man paid on less than 14 dollars, in necessaries, as much duty as the rich man on 88, partly luxuries! So much for Mr. Cambreleng's "*democratic tariff*"—and so much too for the impartiality of the first Congress, who "knew what equal rights were"—as "they had bravely fought for them." The reader must, therefore, clearly agree with Mr. Cambreleng, that "*each man was taxed according to his ability!!!*" and that "*luxuries paid the highest rate of duty!!!*"

Much comment on this cannot be necessary. It requires but a single glance to perceive, that a more unjust, partial, unequal or impolitic system can scarcely be conceived. It taxed necessaries high, and luxuries low, and thus bore hard on the poor—and lightly on the rich. It taxed most exorbitantly all the articles which we could not or did not produce, and admitted at the minimum rate of duty all the important articles, of which the manufacture was or could be established in the country.—It was admirably calculated—I do not pretend (as I only discuss its actual operation) to say intended—it was, I repeat, admirably calculated to promote the manufactures of Europe, and to depress those of this country.*

A recent writer has triumphantly asked, what connexion has this tariff with the present policy of this country? Let him make this enquiry of Mr. Cambreleng. It was he, not I, who introduced it on the tapis.

NECKER.

Philadelphia, *Sept.* 17, 1821.

NO. VIII.

I HAD determined to discontinue these strictures—but on casting my eye again over Mr. Cambreleng's work, I find so many important mistakes remaining unnoticed, that I have judged it necessary to resume the subject.

Among the multifarious errors in the writings of the opposers of a modification of the tariff, the most serious and pernicious is, the assumption of consequences from the measure, of which it is not, and cannot be susceptible. They conjure up a hideous monster, with a Gorgon's head, the creature of a wild imagination. Of this monster they display the terrible features, to affright and terrify the public. They give him battle with great zeal and ardour, and obtain an easy triumph—which they magnify into a victory over the projected measure. This is a revival of the heroic achievements of Don Quixote, and a speedy conversion of windmills into giants—of flocks of sheep into legions of armed men. On such terms literary and polemical honours are of easy attainment.

* This is a very strong assertion, but has been coolly and deliberately weighed, and is fearlessly advanced. It challenges Mr. Cambreleng and all his friends for a refutation. The reputation, talents, public spirit, or integrity of the first Congress, which have been pressed into the service, by a recent writer, have nothing to do with the question, and are introduced merely to throw dust in the eyes of the public, and withdraw attention from the real merits of the case. Had that Congress been composed wholly of Washingtons, Franklins, Jeffersons, Hancocks, Adamses, Rutledges, Randolphs, Jays and Clintons, this circumstance would not convert their errors into wisdom, nor their aristocratic tariff into a "democratic" one. And I trust there cannot be found in the wide compass of the united states, a single man who has any reputation to lose, who will dare to assert, that it was wise, just, fair, equitable, or consistent with sound policy, to tax bohea tea at 66 per cent; coffee at 33; salt at 80; molasses at 12; brown sugar at 25, and cheese at 50, while silks, sattins, embroidery, watches, gauzes, chintzes and pearls were subject to only five per cent; and the great leading manufactures of cotton, wool, hemp, flax, &c. to the same low duty. Never in the whole history of trade, commerce, or political economy, has there been a similar case exhibited.

I will not assert that this system proceeds from a deliberate intention to lead the reader astray—or to deceive the nation. The course I have pursued with Mr. Cambreleng forbids this assumption. Knowing the powerful influence of prejudice, I am willing to suppose that the errors here complained of, result from any other source than wilful misstatement.

Among the cases of this kind, is to be enumerated Mr. Cambreleng's anticipation of the "*prohibition of the exportation of cotton*," as the result of the new tariff! This tremendous result is to be produced not by a direct or positive act for the purpose ---but is to be indirectly accomplished in a "*smoother way*," of which Mr. Cambreleng himself shall furnish an explanation, whereby the reader will be able to judge of the fallacy or the soundness of his views.

"The policy of the government ought to keep in view the "market for our surplus cotton. *If we adopt the wild scheme "of coercing Great Britain, and ruining her factories, by prohi-"biting the exportation of our cotton to England!!!* it will ter-"minate like our former experiments. It will not answer to tell "us, there is no intention of prohibiting the exportation of our "surplus cotton; a system which virtually effects it, is only a "*smoother way* of doing the same thing: the difference is in "form, not in motive or result."—*Examination, page* 43.

Now, courteous reader, what is the very "*smooth way*" in which this terrific consequence is to be produced--this "*wild scheme of coercing Great Btitain*," whereby "*the exportation of our surplus cotton*" is to be "*prohibited*," and the "*factories of England to be ruined?*" You will probably suppose it is by a prohibition, or something approaching to a prohibition, of the importation from Great Rritain, of cotton manufactures of every description---as scarcely any thing short of this "*wild measure*" could produce such an awful result.

In these suppositions, you would be egregiously in error.--- I will state exactly what is the change the proposed tariff would make in the existing duties on manufactured cotton. At present cotton goods below 25 cents per square yard, are dutied as if they cost 25 cents; and all above that price pay 27½ per cent. on the invoice.

By Mr. Baldwin's tariff, all European cotton goods above 25 cents per square yard, would pay 33 per cent.; those below that price, 33 per cent. on 25 cents; and those from beyond the Cape of Good Hope, 40 per cent.

Thus it appears that this desperate confederacy for the purpose of "*coercing Great Britain*," and "*ruining her factories*," "by *prohibiting the exportation of our surplus cotton*," resolves itself into a simple addition of 8 per cent, to the existing duties on cotton goods. That is, that such goods as now pay 25 per cent. shall in future pay 33.

It is difficult to treat such monstrous errors on so important a subject with good humour. Waving all idea of sinister motives, they betray such a carelessness of investigation—such an intrepid assumption of positions diametrically opposite to the real state of the case—and such an extravagant delusion, as excite astonishment, and justly merit severe censure. They forbid reliance on the dicta of writers who are led so far astray by their passions or prejudices.

Let it be observed that Mr. Cambreleng has asserted unequivocally, not only that the present high duty on cotton goods below 25 cents per square yard, is equivalent to a prohibition, (see Examination, page 45,) but that our cotton goods had for ten previous years superseded the use of the coarse East India cottons. Therefore, as the low-priced goods, according to his view of the subject, are, even at present, effectually excluded, the question of "*ruining the British manufactories*" turns merely on the 8 per cent. which, as I have stated, is to be added to the duties on those above 25 cents per square yard. It is scarcely necessary to add, that the 40 per cent. on East India cottons could not "ruin the British factories;" on the contrary, by excluding many of the articles now imported from beyond the Cape, they would afford a vacuum to be filled with British goods.

Once more. "If our laws *prohibit importations*," [what an important little word is *if!* We might simply reply—*but if they do not*, what then?] "the farmer must necessarily carry his "produce where he can exchange it for the articles he wants, "to the domestic manufacturer, or his agent, the merchant.--- "It is idle to think that we can long find a market abroad for "the produce of our farms, *if we take nothing but money in ex-* "*change.*"

What a mighty fabric is here erected—no less than the prohibition of importations—and the receipt of "*nothing but money*" for our productions! What an extraordinary and pernicious change in our affairs! But never was there a fabric erected on a more tottering and unstable foundation. The whole rests on two *ifs*. It requires but slender powers of logic to see how ill able they are to support this mighty burden. It is to be regretted that Mr. Cambreleng did not preface his hypothesis with another *if*, and make a trio of them. For instance —*If* we cease to use tea, coffee, W. I. rum, sugar and brandy, wines, pepper, salt, cashmere shawls, Leghorn hats, superfine cloths, &c. in such a case what will become of our commerce— and our merchants—and where shall we find a market for our surplus productions?

In order to tranquillize Mr. Cambreleng's fears, and to prove that our dangers are not quite so formidable as he appears to suppose—let it be observed that the duties on teas, coffee, sugar, molasses, salt, wines and spirits, amounted in 1819, to $9,631,738—and rating them at 40 per cent. of the cost, which is about a fair average, the value of the imports was above 24,000,000 of dollars. Adding to this sum three or four millions for raw materials, and 10 or 12 millions for broad cloths, fine muslins, gauzes, Leghorn bonnets, Cashmere shawls, gold and silver plate, jewelry, watches, millinery, embroidery, and an immense variety of other articles, which we shall continue to import, let the tariff be regulated as it may, the whole will amount to a sum, perhaps equal to our exports at the present or any probable future prices. I hope this statement will remove Mr. Cambreleng's apprehensions, and those of his numerous friends and well wishers.

"England," says Mr. Cambreleng, "which has now the "largest portion of manufaturing population, with all her pro- "hibitions, bounties and monopolies, *did not increase her ma- "nufactures in one hundred years, as much as we have done in "thirty.*"

For the manufactures of the united states, I shall go back to 1790 and extend no farther than 1820, which will embrace Mr. Cambreleng's "thirty years."

In the former year the population of this country was about 4,000,000. Estimating the consumption of the nation, of manufactured articles, at the low average of 20 dollars per head,

the total would be,	$80,000,000
Deduct imported manufactures,	16,372,000*
Consumption of domestic fabrics,	$63,628,000

In 1810, according to the returns of the marshal's, the manu-

factures of the united states were,	$172,761,977
Allowing 50 per cent. increase from that period, equal to	86,380,988
They were in 1820, about	$259,142,965
Deduct amount in 1790,	63,628,000
Leaves a total increase in "30 *years*" of	$195,514,965

According to Mr. Cambreleng, this exceeds the increase of English manufactures in "*one hundred years.*"

Mr. C. will be petrified with astonishment to find that the

* Seybert's Statistics, page 158. I here take into view all the articles subject to ad valorem duties, which include nearly all the manufactures imported.

increase of *a single manufacture*, not in "one hundred years," but in about *forty*, has been nearly, if not fully equal to the above.

The cotton manufacture in England, in the year 1783, amounted to sterling 960,000*l*.*

Whereas in 1812, it was 29,000,000*l*.†

I have no exact statement of its extent in 1820, and must therefore have recourse to an estimate. Of the data on which it is grounded, the reader must judge.

The cotton *imported* into England in 1811, was, 326,141 bales‡

and the *consumption* in 1820, was 470,000§

I have no means of ascertaining how much was exported in the former year, but presume at least 26,000 bales. This would leave for the *consumption* about 300,000. The weight is, I have reason to believe, considerably heavier than formerly; it is therefore probable that the consumption in 1820 was 66 2-3d per cent. more than in 1812. But only supposing the manufacture to have increased one half, which must be considerably below the real fact, it amounted in 1820, to

	Sterling *l*.43,500,000
Deduct, in 1783,	960,000
Leaves an increase in 37 years,	*l*.42,600,000
Equal to about	$186,000,000

Several years after the commencement of the reign of George III. it amounted only to 200,000*l*.‖

Thus it appears that this manufacture increased in Great Britain between 1763 and 1783, from 200,000*l*. to 960,000*l*.—between 1783 and 1812, from 960,000*l*. to 29,000,000*l*.—and between 1812 and 1820, to 43,000,000*l*.; that is to say, about five fold in 20 years—and about 40 fold in 37. Whereas all our manufactures united increased in Mr. Cambreleng's "30 years" only three fold. So much for his accuracy and the dependence to be placed on his vaunted work. Let it be noted, moreover, that our population has increased from 1790 to 1820, about 140 per cent; that is, from 4 to about 19,600,000. Whereas the increase in Great Britain from 1790 to 1812, was only about 20 per cent. In the former year it was 10,242,000; in the latter 12,353,000.**

* Macpherson's Annals of Commerce, Vol. 4. page 16.
† Colquhoun on the wealth, power and resources of Great Britain, page 91.
‡ Seybert's Statistics, page 91.
§ Price Current of Bolton, Ogden and Co. Liverpool, Jan. 13, 1821.
‖ Macpherson, vol. iv. page 132.
** Colquhoun, page 10.

It may be supposed that the increase of the cotton branch has impaired that of the woollen. The reverse is the fact. The woollen manufacture in 1783, was 16,800,000*l.**
Whereas in 1812 it was 26,000,000*l.*†

NECKER.

Philadelphia, Nov. 21, 1821.

* Macpherson, vol. iv. page 15.
† Colquhoun, page 91.

FINIS.

INDEX.

Extract from the American Farmer.

"Had we anticipated the masterly and patriotic addresses of the Philadelphia Society for the promotion of National Industry, before the publication of our first number, we should gladly have remained silent. We should have blushed to speak on subjects to be simultaneously discussed in a manner far transcending our ability. And now, could we know that all the readers of the American Farmer would peruse the numbers of those excellent addresses, no more of our comparatively trifling essays would appear. But our belief to the contrary, and the expectation which may have been justly excited, must be our apology for continuing our numbers. We are happy to find in what we have seen of that grand production, some notions which we had conceived, fully confirmed; and we hope not a little praise may be rendered to its author, if some of the bright rays which have been shed on ourselves, should be occasionally, but faintly, reflected upon our readers."

Extract of a letter from John Adams, Esq. ex-president, to the Editors of the Manufacturers and Farmer's Journal.

"The gentlemen of Philadelphia have published a very important volume upon the subject, which I recommend to your careful perusal."

Extract of an Address from Benjamin Austin, Esq.

"This subject has produced researches, which demonstrate the abundant resources of our country, and the practicability of accomplishing those important objects, (the establishment of national manufactures) with the aid of government. Among the foremost, the Philadelphia Society for the promotion of National Industry, is entitled to our thanks for their perseverance in this national and laudable pursuit."

Extract of a letter from General Harrison to one of the members of the Philadelphia Society for the promotion of American Manufactures.

"I should be wanting in candour not to acknowledge, that I have been converted to my present principles in favour of manufactures, by the luminous views upon the subject which have been published by your society."

Yours, &c.

W. H. HARRISON.

Extract of a letter from the Hon. Oliver Wolcott, Esq. Governor of the State of Connecticut, dated Litchfield, June 13, 1821, *to the author.*

"I have received your pamphlet addressed to the farmers and planters of the United States. My opinions on the interesting subjects, which you have undertaken to discuss, are coincident with yours —and I do all in my power to recommend them to the public. I believe that the people in this part of the country, have settled down in a firm conviction, that we must protect our internal industry. *Your writings have done much to produce this conviction*—and I consider you as a distinguished benefactor of our country."

Extract of a letter from the Hon. James Madison, ex-president of the United States, dated Montpelier, May 26, 1821, *to the same.*

"I have received your pamphlet, [The Address to the Farmers and Planters of the United States,] of which I cannot say less, than that it *exhibits the same extent of statistic research—the same condensation of ideas—and the same tone of disinterested patriotism,* which have been remarked in other publications from the same pen."

Extract of a letter from Governor Clinton to Joseph Coppinger.

"Mr. Carey's indefatigable and enlightened efforts in favour of this great department of human industry, [domestic manufactures,] entitle him to the thanks and encouragement of every friend of America."

National progress to prosperity or to decay.

Dedicated to the Legislature and Executive of the United States.

" CHOOSE YE."

NATIONAL INDUSTRY

" In all its shapes and forms,"

PROTECTED.*	UNPROTECTED.†
1. Prohibitions of what can be advantageously made at home.	1. Heavy duties on teas, wines, coffee, spirits, salt, pepper, &c.
2. Protecting duties.	2. Light duties on manufactures.
3. Moderate importations.	3. Immense importations.
4. Industry fostered and prosperous.	4. Great bargains of cheap foreign goods.
5. Every person able and willing to work employed.	5. Drain of specie.
6. Early and numerous marriages.	6. Remittances of government and bank stock.
7. Population rapidly increasing.	7. Decay of national industry.
8. Poor rates diminishing.	8. Workmen discharged.
9. Bankruptcies rare.	9. Poor rates augmented.
10. Great accession of immigrants and capital.	10. Increase of idleness, pauperism, and guilt.
11. Numerous houses building.	11. Soup houses.
12. Credit preserved at home and abroad.	12. Manufacturing establishments in ruins.
13. Revenue increasing.	13. Manufacturers bankrupt.
14. Capital, talent, and industry, sure of success.	14. Merchants and traders following in their train.
15. Debts easily collected.	15. Marriages rare.
16. Property rising in value.	16. Population sluggish.
17. General prosperity.	17. Immigration discountenanced.
18. New towns springing up.	18. Emigrations in quest of an asylum abroad.
19. Cordial attachment to government.	19. Capital, talents and industry, wanting employment.
	20. Staples sinking in price.
	21. Distress and ruin of agriculturists.
	22. Credit impaired at home and abroad.
	23. Banks stopping payment.
	24. Sheriffs' sales.
	25. Houses falling to decay.
	26. General embarrassment.
	27. Monied men engrossing the estates of the distressed.
	28. Failure of revenue.
	29. Legal suspension of the collection of debts.
	30. Applications for relief wholly disregarded, or unfeelingly rejected.
	31. Alienation from a government regardless of the sufferings of its citizens.

* With some very slight variations, this sketch applies to the state of France, since the downfall of Bonaparte. It is a fair picture of every country in which industry is protected.

† This is a striking likeness of the situation of a very large portion of the United States in the calamitous and never-to-be-forgotten years 1816, 1817, 1818 and 1819; and partly of Holland, since the year 1816.

Dedicated to the Legislature and Executive of the United States.

AN EXEMPLAR OF FREE, EQUAL, AND RIGHTEOUS GOVERNMENT.

" *All men have equal rights.*"—" *Allegiance is due only to protection.*"—Bishop of Derry.

AGRICULTURE.

Our farmers and planters have, from the organization of the government, enjoyed $\frac{99}{100}$ths of the domestic market; and, until lately, have had excellent foreign markets.

Protecting duties.

	Per cent.
Muscovado Sugar	100
Cheese	40 to 90
Spirits	70 to 140
Manufactured tobacco,	60 to 80
Snuff	80 to 90
Cotton	33 to 40
Hemp	26
Tobacco in the leaf	15
Potatoes	15
Rice	15
Wheat	15
Beans	15
Oats	15
Pitch	15
Tar	15
Turpentine	15
Beef	15
Pork	15
Hams	15

MANUFACTURES.

Our manufacturers are supplanted in the domestic market by France, England, Ireland, Scotland, Italy, Russia, Sweden, the East Indies, &c.

And are almost altogether shut out of all the foreign markets.

Protecting duties.

	Per cent.
Watches	7½
Silks	15
Clocks	15
Linens	15
Worsted shoes	15
Woollens	25
Cambrics	
Manufactures of leather	30

Expenses for the protection of Manufactures.

Bounties	$0000
Premiums	0000
Loans	0000
Immunities	0000
Total expense for protecting manufactures for 33 years	$0000

COMMERCE.

Our merchants have enjoyed the whole of the coasting trade for 33 years.

Their shipping has carried on 86 per cent. of the foreign trade for the same space of time.

Past expenses for the protection of Commerce.

Foreign intercourse for 20 years, from 1796 to 1815	$9,615,140
Naval department	52,065,691
Barbary Powers	2,349,568
War debt	78,579,022
Total for 20 years	$142,609,421
Average per ann. from 1796 to 1815	$7,130,471

Present expenses for Commerce.

Interest on $78,579,022, debt contracted during the last war	$4,714,741
Secretary's estimate for navy, 1821	3,302,592
Actual annual disbursement for commerce	8,018,333
Average annual domestic exports, from 1790 to 1821	$36,067,388

Thus the actual disbursements are 22 per cent. on the average of the domestic exports for 33 years!!